ACCA

PAPER P1

GOVERNANCE, RISK AND ETHICS

S T U D Y T E X T

BPP Learning Media is an **ACCA Approved Content Provider**. This means we work closely with ACCA to ensure this Study Text contains the information you need to pass your exam.

In this Study Text, which has been reviewed by the **ACCA examination team**, we:

- Highlight the most important elements in the syllabus and the key skills you need

- Signpost how each chapter links to the syllabus and the study guide

- Provide lots of exam focus points demonstrating what is expected of you in the exam

- Emphasise key points in regular fast forward summaries

- Test your knowledge in quick quizzes

- Examine your understanding in our practice question bank

- Reference all the important topics in our full index

BPP's **Practice & Revision Kit** products also support this paper.

FOR EXAMS IN SEPTEMBER 2016, DECEMBER 2016, MARCH 2017 AND JUNE 2017

BPP
LEARNING MEDIA

First edition 2007
Ninth edition February 2016

ISBN 9781 4727 4427 2
(Previous ISBN 9781 4727 2679 7)

e-ISBN 9781 4727 4669 6

British Library Cataloguing-in-Publication Data

A catalogue record for this book
is available from the British Library

Published by

BPP Learning Media Ltd
BPP House, Aldine Place
London W12 8AA

www.bpp.com/learningmedia

Printed in the United Kingdom by

Polestar Wheatons
Hennock Road
Marsh Barton
Exeter
EX2 8RP

Your learning materials, published by BPP Learning Media Ltd,
are printed on paper obtained from traceable sustainable sources.

We are grateful to the Association of Chartered Certified Accountants
for permission to reproduce past examination questions. The
suggested solutions in the practice answer bank have been prepared
by BPP Learning Media Ltd, unless otherwise stated.

Contents

Helping you to pass

BPP Learning Media – ACCA Approved Content Provider

As ACCA's **Approved Content Provider**, BPP Learning Media gives you the **opportunity** to use study materials reviewed by the ACCA examination team. By incorporating the examination team's comments and suggestions regarding the depth and breadth of syllabus coverage, the BPP Learning Media Study Text provides excellent, **ACCA-approved** support for your studies.

The PER alert

Before you can qualify as an ACCA member, you not only have to pass all your exams but also fulfil a three year **practical experience requirement** (PER). To help you to recognise areas of the syllabus that you might be able to apply in the workplace to achieve different performance objectives, we have introduced the 'PER alert' feature. You will find this feature throughout the Study Text to remind you that what you are **learning to pass** your ACCA exams is **equally useful to the fulfilment of the PER requirement**.

Your achievement of the PER should now be recorded in your online *My Experience* record.

Tackling studying

Studying can be a daunting prospect, particularly when you have lots of other commitments. The **different features** of the Study Text, the **purposes** of which are explained fully on the **Chapter features** page, will help you while studying and improve your chances of **exam success**.

Developing exam awareness

Our Study Texts are completely **focused** on helping you pass your exam.

Our advice on **Studying P1** outlines the **content** of the paper, the **necessary skills** you are expected to be able to demonstrate and any **brought forward knowledge** you are expected to have.

Exam focus points are included within the chapters to highlight when and how specific topics were examined, or how they might be examined in the future.

Using the syllabus and study guide

You can find the syllabus and study guide on pages xvii-xxx of this Study Text.

Testing what you can do

Testing yourself helps you develop the skills you need to pass the exam and also confirms that you can recall what you have learnt.

We include **Questions** – lots of them – both within chapters and in the **Practice Question Bank**, as well as **Quick Quizzes** at the end of each chapter to test your knowledge of the chapter content.

Chapter features

Each chapter contains a number of helpful features to guide you through each topic.

Topic list

Topic list	Syllabus reference

What you will be studying in this chapter and the relevant section numbers, together with ACCA syllabus references.

Introduction

Puts the chapter content in the context of the syllabus as a whole.

Study Guide

Links the chapter content with ACCA guidance.

Exam Guide

Highlights how examinable the chapter content is likely to be and the ways in which it could be examined.

> Knowledge brought forward from earlier studies

What you are assumed to know from previous studies/exams.

> FAST FORWARD

Summarises the content of main chapter headings, allowing you to preview and review each section easily.

Examples

Demonstrate how to apply key knowledge and techniques.

Key terms

Definitions of important concepts that can often earn you easy marks in exams.

Exam focus points

When and how specific topics were examined, or how they may be examined in the future.

Formula to learn

Formulae that are not given in the exam but which have to be learnt.

Gives you a useful indication of syllabus areas that closely relate to performance objectives in your Practical Experience Requirement (PER).

 Question

Gives you essential practice of techniques covered in the chapter.

Case Study

Real world examples of theories and techniques.

Chapter Roundup

A full list of the Fast Forwards included in the chapter, providing an easy source of review.

Quick Quiz

A quick test of your knowledge of the main topics in the chapter.

Practice Question Bank

Found at the back of the Study Text with more comprehensive chapter questions. Cross referenced for easy navigation.

Studying P1

The **P1 Governance, Risk and Ethics** syllabus has been written with a different focus from the exams that you have sat so far. The exam is not about learning law, accounting standards or complicated calculation techniques. Instead it seeks to promote the underlying themes of **professionalism and accountability**. You cannot be professional in one area and unprofessional in another.

1 What P1 is about

1.1 Underlying themes

The syllabus shows how accounting is **underpinned by governance and ethics**, and the need for accountants to **repay the trust** that society puts in them. A key element of governance is the concept of **accountability**, particularly of directors and auditors. There is an emphasis on the **agency relationship** between stakeholders and business managers, including directors and accountants. Governance is itself supported by **sound internal control systems**, **internal audit** and **rigorous risk management**. **Judgement**, underpinned by professional competence and ethics, is also a key theme. Lastly, students are expected to consider carefully the concept of **professionalism**, and to discuss how the accountant should contribute to society.

The paper's main themes should be seen as interconnected: 'Every right implies a responsibility; for each opportunity there is an obligation and all rewards carry related risks.'

1.2 Governance and responsibility

Chapter 1 demonstrates the importance of the underlying themes of the syllabus. Corporate governance is a central part of the syllabus. Instead of going straight into the detailed requirements of the corporate governance reports, it discusses in detail the **concepts** that underpin good corporate governance, the agency relationship, the **constituencies** (shareholders and other stakeholders) that corporate governance is designed to serve and the **extent of responsibilities** towards different stakeholders.

Chapter 2 deals with the basis of corporate governance legislation and codes, whether they are based on **principles or a detailed rulebook** and how governance codes incorporate wider ideas of social responsibility. **Chapter 3** covers governance best practice, drawing on examples from different codes from all over the world.

1.3 Internal control and risk

We consider Sections B to D of the syllabus together in Section B of this book. The syllabus highlights the following issues, as they have proved to be problematic in recent corporate failures.

- **Internal control**
- **The identification and assessment of risk**
- **Controlling and mitigating risk**

These issues also play a crucial part in an accountant's responsibility to act in the public interest and the interests of shareholders.

'Sound systems of internal analysis, control and audit underpin all effective corporate governance systems. Effective management at the strategic level rests on the assumption that internal control activities can be controlled, verified and reported on internally. If management loses control of internal systems and procedures, any claim of sound governance is lost ... The same is true of risk. Being aware of all possible risks, understanding their potential impact, as well as the probability of occurrence, are important safeguards for investors and other shareholders.'

In **Chapter 4** therefore we examine the objectives of control and risk management systems. We also look at systems that have been developed internationally, including the COSO enterprise risk management model.

Chapters 5 to 8 are organised around the stages identified in the COSO enterprise risk management model. Chapter 5 deals with the underlying factors that affect how a business is controlled and how risk is managed. These include how much **appetite** the business has for risk, and how **environmental factors** within the business affect control and risk management. We also look at the importance of **setting business objectives** that are consistent with the risk that directors, shareholders and other stakeholders wish the business to bear.

Chapters 6 and 7 deal with the various stages of **risk assessment and management**, including internal control procedures that act to reduce risk.

Chapter 8 brings out two other elements that are vital in control systems. These are a two-way flow of **appropriate information** between the board and managers and staff. This should enable the board and managers to carry out effective **monitoring** of operations, and provide feedback so that systems and controls can be improved. The results of business monitoring will also form the basis for external reporting about the company's systems.

1.4 Professional values and ethics

This section of the syllabus requires you to think carefully about the ethical assumptions that guide individual behaviour and underpin the role of accountants. **Chapter 9** is a very important chapter in this text, dealing with the **ethical stances** of individuals and also the **factors** that determine the ethical decisions individuals take. In the exam you may have to argue from a specific ethical position, even if you don't agree with the position.

In **Chapter 10** you need to **look critically** at the ethical codes accountants follow as well as the codes that businesses operate. It is true that you need to have a good knowledge of what the accountancy profession's codes say on **ethical threats and conflicts** and to be able to use that knowledge in recommending solutions to ethical dilemmas. However, you are also expected to question how much help the codes actually are in resolving dilemmas and whether the ethical frameworks are in the best interests of society and the accountancy profession. The exam may ask you to **question the role of the accountant** in protecting shareholder wealth and focusing on the performance of capital investment. Does this mean that accountancy is a servant of capital and makes the implicit assumptions about morality that capitalism does?

Chapter 11 looks at **corporate social responsibility**, concentrating on what organisations have done to address issues such as **sustainability** and the implications for accounting, disclosure, control systems and audit.

2 Skills you have to demonstrate

2.1 Knowledge and application

Even with exams you've previously taken, you'll remember that passing didn't just mean reproducing knowledge. You also had to **apply** what you knew. At Professional level, the balance is tilted much more towards application. You will need a sound basis of technical knowledge. The exams will detect whether you have the necessary knowledge. However, you won't pass if you just spend your time acquiring knowledge. Developing application skills is vital.

2.2 Application skills

What application skills do you need? Many P1 questions will include detail in a scenario about a specific organisation. The following skills are particularly important when you're dealing with question scenarios.

(a) **Identifying the most important features** of the organisation and the organisation's environment. Clues to these will be scattered throughout the scenario. The technical knowledge that you have should help you do this, but you will also need business awareness and imagination. There will be a main theme running through most scenarios that you'll need to identify.

(b) **Using analysis techniques** will give you more insight into the data that you're given.

(c) **Selecting real-life examples** that are relevant to the scenario. You should look at contemporary business stories and try to identify P1 issues, for example directors' remuneration.

(d) **Making informed judgements** that follow from your analysis about what the organisation is doing and should be doing.

(e) **Communicating clearly and concisely** your analysis and recommendations. Perhaps you will be reporting to a specific individual. If so, you should take into account the needs of this individual.

3 How to pass

3.1 Study the whole syllabus

You need to be comfortable with **all areas of the syllabus**. Compulsory Question 1 will always span a number of syllabus areas and other questions may do so as well. In particular, you must have a very good knowledge and awareness of the themes in the ethical section of the syllabus, as compulsory Question 1 will always include an element on ethics.

The examination team has also stressed that study and revision should cover the entire syllabus in detail. Students should not question-spot or prioritise one area of the syllabus over another. The examination team has identified in its examination team's reports those topics which students who question-spotted clearly believed would not be examined, but unfortunately were.

3.2 Focus on themes, not lists

There are quite a number of lists in the texts. This is inevitable because corporate governance guidance quoted as best practice is often in list form. Lists are also sometimes the clearest way of presenting information. However, the examination team has stressed that passing the exam is not a matter of learning and reproducing lists. Good answers will have to **focus on the details in the scenario** and **bring out the underlying themes** that relate to the scenario. The points in them will have more depth than a series of single-line bullet points.

3.3 Read around

Wider reading will help you understand the main issues businesses face. Reading the business pages of newspapers will highlight key business risks organisations face and topical corporate governance issues. General news pages may cover significant ethical and corporate responsibility issues. You should also refer to websites of organisations promoting social responsibility, such as CERES.

3.4 Lots of question practice

You can **develop application skills** by attempting questions in the Practice Question Bank and later on in the BPP Learning Media Practice & Revision Kit.

4 Answering questions

4.1 Analysing question requirements

It's particularly important to **consider the question requirements carefully** to make sure you understand exactly what the question is asking, and whether each question part has to be answered in the **context of the scenario** or is more general. You also need to be sure that you understand all the **tasks** that the question is asking you to perform.

Remember that every word will be important. If for example you are asked to 'Explain the importance of identifying all risks that Company X is facing', then you would explain that:

- Taking risks is bound up with strategic decision-making
- Some risks may have serious consequences
- Identifying all risks means they can be prioritised and managed efficiently and effectively

You would **not** identify all the risks that Company X would be facing.

4.2 Understanding the question verbs

Important!

> In the report for the first P1 exam, the examination team highlighted lack of understanding of the requirements of question verbs as the most serious weakness in many candidates' scripts. The examination team will use question verbs very deliberately to signal what is required.

Verbs that are likely to be frequently used in this exam are listed below, together with their intellectual levels and guidance on their meaning.

Intellectual level		
1	Define	Give the meaning of
1	Explain	Make clear
1	Identify	Recognise or select
1	Describe	Give the key features
2	Distinguish	Define two different terms, viewpoints or concepts on the basis of the differences between them
2	Compare and contrast	Explain the similarities and differences between two different terms, viewpoints or concepts
2	Contrast	Explain the differences between two different terms, viewpoints or concepts
2	Analyse	Give reasons for the current situation or what has happened
3	Assess	Determine the strengths/weaknesses/importance/significance/ability to contribute
3	Examine	Critically review in detail
3	Discuss	Examine by using arguments for and against
3	Explore	Examine or discuss in a wide-ranging manner
3	Criticise	Present the weaknesses of/problems with the actions taken or viewpoint expressed, supported by evidence
3	Evaluate/critically evaluate	Determine the value of in the light of the arguments for and against (critically evaluate means weighting the answer towards criticisms/arguments against)
3	Construct the case	Present the arguments in favour or against, supported by evidence
3	Recommend	Advise the appropriate actions to pursue in terms the recipient will understand

A lower-level verb such as define will require a more **descriptive answer**. A higher-level verb such as evaluate will require a more **applied, critical answer**. The examination team has stressed that **higher-level requirements and verbs** will be most significant in this paper; for example, critically evaluating a statement and arguing for or against a given idea or position. The examination team aims to set questions that provide evidence of student understanding.

Certain verbs have given students particular problems.

(a)   **Identify and explain**

Although these verbs are both Level 1, the examination team sees them as requiring different things. You have to go into more depth if you are asked to **explain** than if you are asked to **identify**. An explanation means giving more detail about the problem or factor identified, normally meaning that you have to indicate **why** it's significant. If you were asked to:

(i)   **Identify the main problem with the same person acting as chief executive and chairman** – you would briefly say excessive power is exercised by one person.

(ii) **Explain the main problem with the same person acting as chief executive and chairman** – you would say excessive power is exercised by one person and then go on to say it would mean that the same person was running the board and the company. As the board is meant to monitor the chief executive, it can't do this effectively if the chief executive is running the board. You may also be asked to explain or describe something complex, abstract or philosophical in nature.

(b) **Evaluate**

Evaluate is a verb that the examination team uses frequently. Its meaning may be different from the way that you have seen it used in other exams. The examination team expects to see arguments for **and** against, or pros **and** cons for what you are asked to evaluate.

Thus for example if a question asked you to: 'Evaluate the contribution made by non-executive directors to good corporate governance in companies', you would not only have to write about the factors that help non-executive directors make a worthwhile contribution (independent viewpoint, experience of other industries) but you would also have to discuss the factors that limit or undermine the contribution non-executive directors make (lack of time, putting pressure on board unity).

If the examination team asks you to critically evaluate, you will have to consider both viewpoints. However, you will concentrate on the view that you are asked to critically evaluate, as the mark scheme will be weighted towards that view.

4.3 Analysing question scenarios

When reading through the scenario you need to think widely about how the scenario relates to the underlying themes of the syllabus, and also important content from whatever areas of the syllabus the question covers:

(a) **Corporate governance**

In questions on **corporate governance**, you are likely to be looking out for **weaknesses** in the current arrangements and trying to **recommend improvements** that are line with governance best practice.

(b) **Control systems**

With **control systems** questions, you are most likely to be interested in the **design and appropriateness of the control systems**, whether there are **obvious shortcomings** with them, and also **details of the control environment**.

(c) **Culture**

If you are asked about the organisation's **culture and ethos**, you should be looking for evidence of directors' views and actions and for signs of how the tone is being set at the top of the organisation. You should also look for evidence of how the ethos is being established further down the organisation, in particular how the organisation's **culture, systems, procedures, reward mechanisms, human resource policies and training** are used to embed the tone of the organisation.

(d) **Risks**

With **risks** you are looking for the **most significant ones**. If these are not highlighted, you should look for the risks that are **connected with the organisation's strategy** or which **relate to significant changes** that the organisation and its business environment are going through, or are about to go though. You should also try to determine the extent to which **risk awareness is embedded** in the **organisation's culture**.

(e)   **Risk management**

If you are asked how organisations should **respond to particular risks**, you'll need to use the scenario detail to determine how serious these risks are, and suggest **responses** that are **relevant** to **counter the risks** and **appropriate for the organisation**. It's no use, for example, suggesting that the organisation sets up a large risk management function if it is not big enough to warrant one.

(f)   **Ethics**

With **ethical issues** you are not just looking to determine the **ethical issues at stake**. You also need to consider the **ethical position of the organisation** and individuals and the **factors that determine the ethical position**. These will be significant when you think about solutions to the ethical problems.

(g)   **Framework**

Look out in any question scenarios or frameworks for hints that you may have to provide a critique of the **overall framework or model** that is being operated. If you're basing your answer on content from corporate governance or ethical codes, will you have to criticise the principles or rules on which they are founded. If you have to make recommendations that benefit shareholders, consider whether the shareholders' viewpoint is the most valid or if other stakeholders' interests should be taken into account.

4.4 Consider the moral and ethical frameworks

The examination team has stressed that these will affect the judgements you make when answering questions as they do in real life. In particular, the stakeholders **affected** by **business and strategic decisions** and whether some stakeholders are being favoured over others need to be considered.

Remember, the exam is designed to make you take a questioning approach to wide issues, and this may mean having to argue in favour of a viewpoint with which you don't agree.

4.5 Content of answers

Well-judged, clear recommendations grounded in the scenario will always score well as markers for this paper have a wide remit to reward good answers. You need to be **selective**. As we've said, lists of points memorised from texts and reproduced without any thought won't score well.

Important!

> The examination team identified lack of application skills as a serious weakness in many student answers. What constitutes good application will vary question by question but is likely to include:
>
> - Only including technical knowledge that is **relevant** to the scenario; for example, although the SPAMSOAP mnemonic can be a useful memory aid, you shouldn't quote it in full just because the question requirements contain the word 'control'
> - Only including scenario details that **support the points** you are making, for example quoting from the scenario to explain why you're making a particular recommendation
> - **Tackling the problems** highlighted in the scenario and the question requirements
> - Explaining **why** the factors you're discussing are significant
> - Taking a **top-down strategic approach** – remember that at Professional level you're meant to be adopting the viewpoint of a partner or finance director and that excessive detail about operations is not important

5 Gaining professional marks

As P1 is a Professional level paper, four or five **professional level marks** will be awarded in the compulsory question. The examination team has stated that some marks may be available for presenting your answer in the form of a letter, presentation, memo, report, briefing notes, management reporting, narrative or press statement. You may also be able to obtain marks for the layout, logical flow and presentation of your answer. You should also make sure that you provide the points required by the question.

Whatever the form of communication requested, you will **not** gain professional marks if you fail to follow the basics of good communication. Keep an eye on your **spelling and grammar**. Also think carefully, am I saying things that are **appropriate in a business communication**?

6 Brought forward knowledge

You will have covered some of the corporate governance, company law and ethics contents of P1 in law and auditing papers that you have previously sat.

However, because the students studying this paper will have sat different variants of the law and auditing exams, this text includes full coverage of the knowledge you need for this exam even though some of it has been covered in other exams.

Knowledge brought forward from F9 on ways of quantifying risks and uncertainty and expected results may also be helpful. You may also have to use the techniques for interpreting financial information that you covered in F7.

7 ACCA ethics module

We would **strongly recommend** that you sit the module before taking P1. The module will give you insights to a range of ethical perspectives that will be valuable in your professional career, and will also assist you in tackling the ethics content of the P1 syllabus and indeed the syllabuses of other Professional level exams.

The exam paper

Format of the paper

The time allowed is 3 hours and 15 minutes. The paper consists of two sections.

		Number of marks
Section A:	1 compulsory case study	50
Section B:	Choice of 2 from 3 questions (25 marks each)	50
		100

Section A will be a compulsory case study question with typically four or five sub-requirements relating to the same scenario information. The question will usually assess and link a range of subject areas across the syllabus. It will require students to demonstrate high-level capabilities to understand the complexities of the case and evaluate, relate and apply the information in the case study to the requirements.

The case study will be between 400 and 700 words long. The examination team has stressed the importance of reading the case in detail, taking notes as appropriate and getting a feel for what the issues are. Scenarios may be drawn from any situation involving aspects of governance. This is likely to be, but need not be, in an organisational setting.

Professional marks will be available in Section A for presentation, logical flow of argument and quality of argument.

Section B questions are more likely to assess a range of discrete subject areas from the main syllabus section headings. They may require evaluation and synthesis of information contained within short scenarios and application of this information to the question requirements.

Although one subject area is likely to be emphasised in each Section B question, students should not assume that questions will be solely about content from that area. Each question will be based on a shorter case scenario to contextualise the question.

The paper will have a global focus.

The exam may include some simple arithmetic calculations. Students should not expect complicated calculations but should be prepared to manipulate numerical data, and accordingly a calculator may be helpful.

Analysis of past papers

The table below provides details of when each element of the syllabus has been examined in exams since June 2009 and the question number and section in which each element appeared. Further details can be found in the Exam Focus Points in the relevant chapters.

Covered in Text chapter		D15	J15	D14	J14	D13	J13	D12	J12	D11	J11	D10	J10	D09	J09
	GOVERNANCE AND RESPONSIBILITY														
1	Scope of governance	1a	2c	1a	1a 1c		1d	2a, c 4b, c	1d, 2a		3a, b	1a, c	1b, 4a	3a	
1	Agency	1a	2a	1d		2b	3b		1d				1c		1c
3	Board of directors		1b 1d	2b 3a 3b 4c		3b, 4a	4c		3c, 4b, c	2b	1d, 4c	3b		1c, 2a, b, c	1e, 3a, d
3,5,8	Board committees		3a 3b 3c				3a	2b		2b		3c			
3	Directors' remuneration	1b					1c	4b, c			3a		2a, b		3c
2	Different approaches to governance		1a	2b 2c		2a, c	4a	2b	4a	2a					
2,11	Corporate social responsibility	1c, 2a	2b			3c							1a		1d
3	Reporting and disclosure				2c 4c					1b,2 c3c	1c	3c			3b
2	Public sector governance			2a 2b											
	INTERNAL CONTROL AND REVIEW														
4,5,7,8	Management control systems			4b			1c	1d	1c				3a, b		
4,7,8,10	Internal control, audit and compliance	1d		4a		1d	2a	3a, b		1c	1a		3c	1b	1b
7,8	Internal control and reporting	1d				2b	2c						1c		
8	Management information								3c					1d	
	IDENTIFYING AND ASSESSING RISK														
5,7	Risk and the risk management process	3a	1d		2a				1a		2a				
6	Risk categories		1c	1c	2b		3c		1d	1c, 3b			2c, 4a		
5,7,8	Risk identification, measurement and assessment				1d	4b	1a, 3a			1c	2c		1d		4b

Covered in Text chapter		D15	J15	D14	J14	D13	J13	D12	J12	D11	J11	D10	J10	D09	J09
	CONTROLLING AND MANAGING RISK														
5,8	Risk targeting and monitoring	3b, 3c							2b, c					4c	4a
5,7,8	Risk reduction and control		4c			1b	3c	1b	2c		2d	4b, c		4a, b	
5,7	Risk, avoidance, retention and modelling					1b						2b			4c
	PROFESSIONAL VALUES, ETHICS AND SOCIAL RESPONSIBILITY														
9	Ethical theories	4a, 4b	4a		4a		1d	4a	1b		1b	1b		1a	1a
9,11	Different approaches to ethics and social responsibility	2b	2b	1d	4b					4a, b, c	1d	4d			2c
10	Professions and the public interest				3c						4b				2a
10	Professional practice and codes of ethics	1c			1b	4c			3b	1a					
10	Conflicts of interest and consequences of unethical behaviour	4b		1b 3c	3a			1c	3a		4a	3a	4c	3b,c	2b
9,10	Ethical characteristics of professionalism					4c							2c, 4b	3b	
11	Integrated reporting and sustainability	2b, 2c	4b	1d	3b	1a	1b	1a				2a, b	1d		

BPP
LEARNING MEDIA

Syllabus and study guide

The P1 syllabus and study guide can be found below.

Governance, Risk and Ethics (P1) September 2016 to June 2017

This syllabus and study guide is designed to help with planning study and to provide detailed information on what could be assessed in any examination session.

THE STRUCTURE OF THE SYLLABUS AND STUDY GUIDE

Relational diagram of paper with other papers

This diagram shows direct and indirect links between this paper and other papers preceding or following it. Some papers are directly underpinned by other papers such as Advanced Performance Management by Performance Management. These links are shown as solid line arrows. Other papers only have indirect relationships with each other such as links existing between the accounting and auditing papers. The links between these are shown as dotted line arrows. This diagram indicates where you are expected to have underpinning knowledge and where it would be useful to review previous learning before undertaking study.

Overall aim of the syllabus

This explains briefly the overall objective of the paper and indicates in the broadest sense the capabilities to be developed within the paper.

Main capabilities

This paper's aim is broken down into several main capabilities which divide the syllabus and study guide into discrete sections.

Relational diagram of the main capabilities

This diagram illustrates the flows and links between the main capabilities (sections) of the syllabus and should be used as an aid to planning teaching and learning in a structured way.

Syllabus rationale

This is a narrative explaining how the syllabus is structured and how the main capabilities are linked. The rationale also explains in further detail what the examination intends to assess and why.

Detailed syllabus

This shows the breakdown of the main capabilities (sections) of the syllabus into subject areas. This is the blueprint for the detailed study guide.

Approach to examining the syllabus

This section briefly explains the structure of the examination and how it is assessed.

Study Guide

This is the main document that students, learning and content providers should use as the basis of their studies, instruction and materials. Examinations will be based on the detail of the study guide which comprehensively identifies what could be assessed in any examination session. The study guide is a precise reflection and breakdown of the syllabus. It is divided into sections based on the main capabilities identified in the syllabus. These sections are divided into subject areas which relate to the sub-capabilities included in the detailed syllabus. Subject areas are broken down into sub-headings which describe the detailed outcomes that could be assessed in examinations. These outcomes are described using verbs indicating what exams may require students to demonstrate, and the broad intellectual level at which these may need to be demonstrated (*see intellectual levels below).

Learning Materials

ACCA's Approved Content Programme is the programme through which ACCA approves learning materials from high quality content providers designed to support study towards ACCA's qualifications.

ACCA has three Approved Content Providers, Becker Professional Education, BPP Learning Media and Kaplan Publishing.

For information about ACCA's Approved Content Providers please go to ACCA's Content Provider Directory.

The Directory also lists materials by other publishers, these materials have not been quality assured by ACCA but may be helpful if used in conjunction with approved learning materials or for variant exams where no approved content is available. You will also find details of Additional Reading suggested by the examining teams and this may be a useful supplement to approved learning materials.

ACCA's Content Provider Directory can be found here –
> http://www.accaglobal.com/uk/en/student/acca-qual-student-journey/study-revision/learning-providers/alp-content.html

Relevant articles are also published in Student Accountant and available on the ACCA website.

INTELLECTUAL LEVELS

The syllabus is designed to progressively broaden and deepen the knowledge, skills and professional values demonstrated by the student on their way through the qualification.

The specific capabilities within the detailed syllabuses and study guides are assessed at one of three intellectual or cognitive levels:

Level 1: Knowledge and comprehension
Level 2: Application and analysis
Level 3: Synthesis and evaluation

Very broadly, these intellectual levels relate to the three cognitive levels at which the Knowledge module, the Skills module and the Professional level are assessed.

Each subject area in the detailed study guide included in this document is given a 1, 2, or 3 superscript, denoting intellectual level, marked at the end of each relevant line. This gives an indication of the intellectual depth at which an area could be assessed within the examination. However, while level 1 broadly equates with the Knowledge module, level 2 equates to the Skills module and level 3 to the Professional level, some lower level skills can continue to be assessed as the student progresses through each module and level. This reflects that at each stage of study there will be a requirement to broaden, as well as deepen capabilities. It is also possible that occasionally some higher level capabilities may be assessed at lower levels.

LEARNING HOURS AND EDUCATION RECOGNITION

The ACCA qualification does not prescribe or recommend any particular number of learning hours for examinations because study and learning patterns and styles vary greatly between people and organisations. This also recognises the wide diversity of personal, professional and educational circumstances in which ACCA students find themselves.

As a member of the International Federation of Accountants, ACCA seeks to enhance the education recognition of its qualification on both national and international education frameworks, and with educational authorities and partners globally. In doing so, ACCA aims to ensure that its qualifications are recognized and valued by governments, regulatory authorities and employers across all sectors. To this end, ACCA qualifications are currently recognized on the education frameworks in several countries. Please refer to your national education framework regulator for further information.

Each syllabus contains between 23 and 35 main subject area headings depending on the nature of the subject and how these areas have been broken down.

GUIDE TO EXAM STRUCTURE

The structure of examinations varies within and between modules and levels.

The Fundamentals level examinations contain 100% compulsory questions to encourage candidates to study across the breadth of each syllabus.

The Knowledge module is assessed by equivalent two-hour paper based and computer based examinations.

The Skills module examinations F5-F9 are paper

based exams containing a mix of objective and longer type questions with a duration of three hours 15 minutes. From September 2016 these exams will also be available as computer-based exams. Further information will be released on these in April 2016. The *Corporate and Business Law* (F4) paper is a two- hour objective test examination which is also available as a computer based exams for English and Global variants, as well as paper based for all variants.

The Professional level papers are all of three hours 15 minutes duration and, all contain two sections. Section A is compulsory, but there will be some choice offered in Section B.

ACCA has removed the restriction relating to reading and planning time, so that while the time considered necessary to complete these exams remains at 3 hours, candidates may use the additional 15 minutes as they choose. ACCA encourages students to take time to read questions carefully and to plan answers but once the exam time has started, there are no additional restrictions as to when candidates may start writing in their answer books.

Time should be taken to ensure that all the information and exam requirements are properly read and understood.

The Essentials module papers all have a Section A containing a major case study question with all requirements totalling 50 marks relating to this case. Section B gives students a choice of two from three 25 mark questions.

Section A of both the P4 and P5 Options papers contain one 50 mark compulsory question, and Section B will offer a choice of two from three questions each worth 25 marks each.

Section A of each of the P6 and P7 Options papers contains 60 compulsory marks from two questions; question 1 attracting 35 marks, and question 2 attracting 25 marks. Section B of both these Options papers will offer a choice of two from three questions, with each question attracting 20 marks.

All Professional level exams contain four professional marks.

The pass mark for all ACCA Qualification examination papers is 50%.

GUIDE TO EXAMINATION ASSESSMENT

ACCA reserves the right to examine anything contained within the study guide at any examination session. This includes knowledge, techniques, principles, theories, and concepts as specified.

For the financial accounting, audit and assurance, law and tax papers except where indicated otherwise, ACCA will publish *examinable documents* once a year to indicate exactly what regulations and legislation could potentially be assessed within identified examination sessions..

For paper based examinations regulation *issued* or legislation *passed* on or before 31st August annually, will be examinable from 1st September of the following year to 31st August ^{t} of the year after that. Please refer to the examinable documents for the paper (where relevant) for further information.

Regulation issued or legislation passed in accordance with the above dates may be examinable even if the *effective* date is in the future.

The term issued or passed relates to when regulation or legislation has been formally approved.

The term effective relates to when regulation or legislation must be applied to an entity transactions and business practices.

The study guide offers more detailed guidance on the depth and level at which the examinable documents will be examined. The study guide should therefore be read in conjunction with the examinable documents list.

Syllabus

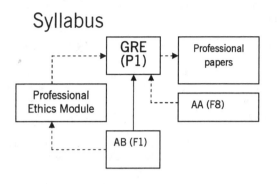

AIM

To apply relevant knowledge, skills and exercise professional judgement in carrying out the role of the accountant relating to governance, internal control, compliance and the management of risk within an organisation, in the context of an overall ethical framework.

MAIN CAPABILITIES

On successful completion of this paper, candidates should be able to:

A   Define governance and explain its function in the effective management and control of organisations and of the resources for which they are accountable

B   Evaluate the Professional Accountant's role in internal control, review and compliance

C   Explain the role of the accountant in identifying and assessing risk

D   Explain and evaluate the role of the accountant in controlling and mitigating risk

E   Demonstrate the application of professional values and judgement through an ethical framework that is in the best interests of society and the profession, in compliance with relevant professional codes, laws and regulations.

RELATIONAL DIAGRAM OF MAIN CAPABILITIES

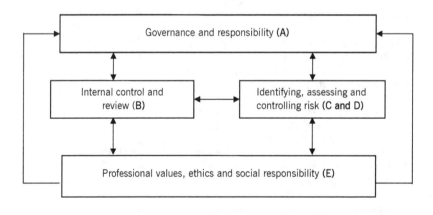

RATIONALE

The syllabus for Paper P1, *Governance, Risk and Ethics*, acts as the gateway syllabus into the professional level. It sets the other Essentials and Options papers into a wider professional, organisational, and societal context.

The syllabus assumes essential technical skills and knowledge acquired at the Fundamentals level where the core technical capabilities will have been acquired, and where ethics, corporate governance, internal audit, control, and risk will have been introduced in a subject-specific context.

The GRE syllabus begins by examining the whole area of governance within organisations in the broad context of the agency relationship. This aspect of the syllabus focuses on the respective roles and responsibilities of directors and officers to organisational stakeholders and of accounting and auditing as support and control functions.

The syllabus then explores internal review, control, and feedback to implement and support effective governance, including compliance issues related to decision-making and decision-support functions. The syllabus also examines the whole area of identifying, assessing, and controlling risk as a key aspect of responsible management.

Finally, the syllabus covers personal and professional ethics, ethical frameworks – and professional values – as applied in the context of the accountant's duties and as a guide to appropriate professional behaviour and conduct in a variety of situations.

DETAILED SYLLABUS

A   Governance and responsibility

1.   The scope of governance

2.   Agency relationships and theories

3.   The board of directors

4.   Board committees

5.   Directors' remuneration

6.   Different approaches to corporate governance

7.   Corporate governance and corporate social responsibility

8.   Governance: reporting and disclosure

9.   Public sector governance

B   Internal control and review

1.   Management control systems in corporate governance

2.   Internal control, audit and compliance in corporate governance

3.   Internal control and reporting

4.   Management information in audit and internal control

C   Identifying and assessing risk

1.   Risk and the risk management process

2.   Categories of risk

3.   Identification, assessment and measurement of risk

D   Controlling risk

1.   Targeting and monitoring risk

2.   Methods of controlling and reducing risk

3.   Risk avoidance, retention and modelling

E   Professional values, ethics and social responsibility

1.   Ethical theories

2.   Different approaches to ethics and social responsibility

3.   Professions and the public interest

4.   Professional practice and codes of ethics

5.   Conflicts of interest and the consequences of unethical behaviour

6.   Ethical characteristics of professionalism

7.   Social and environmental issues in the conduct of business and of ethical behaviour

APPROACH TO EXAMINING THE SYLLABUS

The syllabus is assessed by a three-hour 15 minutes paper-based examination.
The examination paper will be structured in two sections. Section A will be based on a case study style question comprising a compulsory 50 mark question, with requirements based on several parts with all parts relating to the same case information. The case study will usually assess a range of subject areas across the syllabus and will require the candidate to demonstrate high level capabilities to evaluate, relate and apply the information in the case study to several of the requirements.

Section B comprises three questions of 25 marks each, of which candidates must answer two. These questions will be more likely to assess a range of discrete subject areas from the main syllabus section headings, but may require application, evaluation and the synthesis of information contained within short scenarios in which some requirements may need to be contextualised.

Study Guide

A GOVERNANCE AND RESPONSIBILITY

1. The scope of governance

a) Define and explain the meaning of corporate governance.[2]

b) Explain, and analyse the issues raised by the development of the joint stock company as the dominant form of business organisation and the separation of ownership and control over business activity.[3]

c) Analyse the purposes and objectives of corporate governance in the public and private sectors.[2]

d) Explain, and apply in context of corporate governance, the key underpinning concepts of: [3]
   i) fairness
   ii) openness/transparency
   iii) innovation
   iv) scepticism
   iii) independence
   iv) probity/honesty
   v) responsibility
   vi) accountability
   vii) reputation
   viii) judgment
   ix) integrity

e) Explain and assess the major areas of organisational life affected by issues in corporate governance.[3]
   i) duties of directors and functions of the board (including setting a responsible 'tone' from the top and being accountable for the performance and impacts of the organisation)
   ii) the composition and balance of the board (and board committees)
   iii) relevance and reliabilityof corporate reporting and external auditing
   iv) directors' remuneration and rewards
   v) responsibility of the board for risk management systems and internal control
   vi) the rights and responsibilities of shareholders, including institutional investors

vii) corporate social responsibility and business ethics.

f) Compare, and distinguish between public, private and non-governmental organisations (NGO) sectors with regard to the issues raised by, and scope of, governance.[3]

g) Explain and evaluate the roles, interests and claims of, the internal parties involved in corporate governance.[3]
   i) Directors
   ii) Company secretaries
   iii) Sub-board management
   iv) Employee representatives (e.g. trade unions)

h) Explain and evaluate the roles, interests and claims of, the external parties involved in corporate governance.[3]
   i) Shareholders (including shareholders' rights and responsibilities)
   ii) Auditors
   iii) Regulators
   iv) Government
   v) Stock exchanges
   vi) Small investors (and minority rights)
   vii) Institutional investors (see also next point)

i) Analyse and discuss the role and influence of institutional investors in corporate governance systems and structures, for example the roles and influences of pension funds, insurance companies and mutual funds.[2]

2. Agency relationships and theories

a) Define and explore agency theory.[2]

b) Define and explain the key concepts in agency theory.[2]
   i) Agents
   ii) Principals
   iii) Agency
   iv) Agency costs
   v) Accountability
   vi) Fiduciary responsibilities
   vii) Stakeholders

c) Explain and explore the nature of the principal-agent relationship in the context of corporate governance.[3]

d) Analyse and critically evaluate the nature of agency accountability in agency relationships.[3]

e) Explain and analyse the following other theories used to explain aspects of the agency relationship.[2]
   i) Transaction costs theory
   ii) Stakeholder theory

3. The board of directors

a) Explain and evaluate the roles and responsibilities of boards of directors.[3]

b) Describe, distinguish between and evaluate the cases for and against, unitary and two-tier board structures.[3]

c) Describe the characteristics, board composition and types of, directors (including defining executive and non-executive directors (NED).[2]

d) Describe and assess the purposes, roles and responsibilities of NEDs.[3]

e) Describe and analyse the general principles of legal and regulatory frameworks within which directors operate on corporate boards:[2]
   i) legal rights and responsibilities,
   ii) time-limited appointments
   iii) retirement by rotation,
   iv) service contracts,
   v) removal,
   vi) disqualification
   vii) conflict and disclosure of interests
   viii) insider dealing/trading

f) Define, explore and compare the roles of the chief executive officer and company chairman.[3]

g) Describe and assess the importance and execution of, induction and continuing professional development of directors on boards of directors.[3]

h) Explain and analyse the frameworks for assessing the performance of boards and individual directors (including NEDs) on boards.[2]

i) Explain the meanings of 'diversity' and critically evaluate issues of diversity on boards

of directors.[3]

4. Board committees

a) Explain and assess the importance, roles and accountabilities of, board committees in corporate governance.[3]

b) Explain and evaluate the role and purpose of the following committees in effective corporate governance:[3]
   i) Remuneration committees
   ii) Nominations committees
   iii) Risk committees.
   iv) Audit committees

5. Directors' remuneration

a) Describe and assess the general principles of remuneration.[3]
   i) purposes
   ii) components
   iii) links to strategy
   iv) links to labour market conditions.

b) Explain and assess the effect of various components of remuneration packages on directors' behaviour.[3]
   i) basic salary
   ii) performance related
   iii) shares and share options
   iv) loyalty bonuses
   v) benefits in kind
   vi) pension benefits

c) Explain and analyse the legal, ethical, competitive and regulatory issues associated with directors' remuneration.[3]

6. Different approaches to corporate governance

a) Describe and compare the essentials of 'rules' and 'principles' based approaches to corporate governance. Includes discussion of 'comply or explain'.[3]

b) Describe and analyse the different models of business ownership that influence different governance regimes (e.g. family firms versus joint stock company-based models).[2]

c) Describe and critically evaluate the reasons behind the development and use of codes of practice in corporate governance (acknowledging national differences and convergence).[3]

d) Explain and briefly explore the development of corporate governance codes in principles-based jurisdictions.[2]
   i) impetus and background
   ii) major corporate governance codes
   iii) effects of

e) Explain and explore the Sarbanes-Oxley Act (2002) as an example of a rules-based approach to corporate governance.[2]
   i) impetus and background
   ii) main provisions/contents
   iii) effects of

f) Describe and explore the objectives, content and limitations of, corporate governance codes intended to apply to multiple national jurisdictions.[2]
   i) Organisation for economic cooperation and development (OECD) Report (2004)
   ii) International corporate governance network (ICGN) Report (2005)

7. **Corporate governance and corporate social responsibility**

a) Explain and explore social responsibility in the context of corporate governance.[2]

b) Discuss and critically assess the concept of stakeholder power and interest using the Mendelow model and how this can affect strategy and corporate governance.[3]

c) Analyse and evaluate issues of 'ownership,' 'property' and the responsibilities of ownership in the context of shareholding.[3]

d) Explain the concept of the organisation as a corporate citizen of society with rights and responsibilities.[3]

8. **Governance: reporting and disclosure**

a) Explain and assess the general principles of disclosure and communication with shareholders.[3]

b) Explain and analyse 'best practice' corporate governance disclosure requirements.[2]

c) Define and distinguish between mandatory and voluntary disclosure of corporate information in the normal reporting cycle.[2]

d) Explain and explore the nature of, and reasons and motivations for, voluntary disclosure in a principles-based reporting environment (compared to, for example, the reporting regime in the USA).[3]

e) Explain and analyse the purposes of the annual general meeting and extraordinary general meetings for information exchange between board and shareholders.[2]

f) Describe and assess the role of proxy voting in corporate governance.[3].

9. **Public sector governance**

a) Describe, compare and contrast public sector, private sector, charitable status and non-governmental (NGO and quasi-NGOs) forms of organisation, including purposes and objectives, performance, ownership and stakeholders (including lobby groups)[2]

b) Describe, compare and contrast the different types of public sector organisations at subnational, national and supranational level[2]

c) Assess and evaluate the strategic objectives, leadership and governance arrangements specific to public sector organisations as contrasted with private sector[3].

d) Discuss and assess the nature of democratic control, political influence and policy implementation in public sector organisations including the contestable nature of public sector policy[3].

e) Discuss obligations of the public sector organisations to meet the economy, effectiveness, efficiency (3 E's) criteria and promote public value[3].

B INTERNAL CONTROL AND REVIEW

1. Management control systems in corporate governance

a) Define and explain internal management control.[2]

b) Explain and explore the importance of internal control and risk management in corporate governance.[3]

c) Describe the objectives of internal control systems and how they can help prevent fraud and error.[2]

d) Identify, explain and evaluate the corporate governance and executive management roles in risk management (in particular the separation between responsibility for ensuring that adequate risk management systems are in place and the application of risk management systems and practices in the organisation).[3]

e) Identify and assess the importance of the elements or components of internal control systems.[3]

2. Internal control, audit and compliance in corporate governance

a) Describe the function and importance of internal audit.[1]

b) Explain, and discuss the importance of, auditor independence in all client-auditor situations (including internal audit).[3]

c) Explain, and assess the nature and sources of risks to, auditor independence. Assess the hazard of auditor capture.[3]

d) Explain and evaluate the importance of compliance and the role of the internal audit function in internal control.[3]

e) Explore and evaluate the effectiveness of internal control systems.[3]

f) Describe and analyse the work of the internal audit committee in overseeing the internal audit function.[2]

g) Explain and explore the importance and characteristics of, the audit committee's relationship with external auditors.[2]

3. Internal control and reporting

a) Describe and assess the need to report on internal controls to shareholders.[3]

b) Describe the content of a report on internal control and audit.[2]

c) Explain and assess how internal controls underpin and provide information for accurate financial reporting.[3]

4. Management information in audit and internal control

a) Explain and assess the need for adequate information flows to management for the purposes of the management of internal control and risk.[3]

b) Evaluate the qualities and characteristics of information required in internal control and risk management and monitoring.[3]

C IDENTIFYING AND ASSESSING RISK

1. Risk and the risk management process

a) Define and explain risk in the context of corporate governance.[2]

b) Define and describe management responsibilities in risk management.[2]

c) Explain the dynamic nature of risk assessment.[2]

d) Explain the importance and nature of management responses to changing risk assessments.[2]

e) Explain risk appetite and how this affects risk policy.[2]

2. Categories of risk

a) Define and compare (distinguish between) strategic and operational risks.[2]

b) Define and explain the sources and impacts of common business risks.[2]
   i) market
   ii) credit
   iii) liquidity
   iv) technological
   v) legal
   vi) health, safety and environmental
   vii) reputation
   viii) business probity
   ix) derivatives

c) Describe and evaluate the nature and importance of business and financial risks.[3]

d) Recognise and analyse the sector or industry specific nature of many business risks.[2]

3. Identification, assessment and measurement of risk

a) Identify, and assess the impact upon, the stakeholders involved in business risk.[3]

b) Explain and analyse the concepts of assessing the severity and probability of risk events.[2]

c) Describe and evaluate a framework for board level consideration of risk.[3]

d) Describe the process of and importance of, externally reporting on internal control and risk.[2]

e) Explain the sources, and assess the importance of, accurate information for risk management.[3]

f) Explain and assess the ALARP (as low as reasonably practicable) principle in risk assessment and how this relates to severity and probability.[3]

g) Evaluate the difficulties of risk perception including the concepts of objective and subjective risk perception.[3]

h) Explain and evaluate the concepts of related and correlated risk factors.[3]

D CONTROLLING AND MANAGING RISK

1. Targeting and monitoring of risk

a) Explain and assess the role of a risk manager in identifying and monitoring risk.[3]

b) Explain and evaluate the role of the risk committee in identifying and monitoring risk.[3]

c) Describe and assess the role of internal or external risk auditing in monitoring risk.[3]

2. Methods of controlling and reducing risk

a) Explain the importance of risk awareness at all levels in an organisation.[2]

b) Describe and analyse the concept of embedding risk in an organisation's systems and procedures.[3]

c) Describe and evaluate the concept of embedding risk in an organisation's culture and values.[3]

d) Explain and analyse the concepts of spreading and diversifying risk and when this would be appropriate.[2]

e) Identify and assess how business organisations use policies and techniques to mitigate various types of business and financial risks.[3]

3. Risk avoidance, retention and modelling

a) Explain, and assess the importance of, risk transference, avoidance, reduction and acceptance.[3]

b) Explain and evaluate the different attitudes to risk and how these can affect strategy.[3]

c) Explain and assess the necessity of incurring risk as part of competitively managing a business organisation.[3]

d) Explain and assess attitudes towards risk and the ways in which risk varies in relation to the size, structure and development of an organisation [3]

E PROFESSIONAL VALUES, ETHICS AND SOCIAL RESPONSIBILITY

1. Ethical theories

a) Explain and distinguish between the ethical theories of relativism and absolutism.[2]

b) Explain, in an accounting and governance context, Kohlberg's stages of human moral development.[3]

c) Describe and distinguish between deontological and teleological/consequentialist approaches to ethics.[2]

d) Apply commonly used ethical decision-making models in accounting and professional contexts [2]
    i)   American Accounting Association model
    ii) Tucker's 5-question model

2. Different approaches to ethics and social responsibility.

a) Describe and evaluate Gray, Owen & Adams (1996) seven positions on social responsibility.[2]

b) Describe and evaluate other constructions of corporate and personal ethical stance:[2]
    i)   short-term shareholder interests
    ii)   long-term shareholder interests
    iii) multiple stakeholder obligations
    iv)   shaper of society

c) Describe and analyse the variables determining the cultural context of ethics and corporate social responsibility (CSR).[2]

d) Explain and evaluate the concepts of 'CSR strategy' and 'strategic CSR' [2].

3. Professions and the public interest

a) Explain and explore the nature of a 'profession' and 'professionalism'.[2]

b) Describe and assess what is meant by 'the public interest'.[2]

c) Describe the role of, and assess the widespread influence of, accounting as a profession in the organisational context.[3]

d) Analyse the role of accounting as a profession in society.[2]

e) Recognise accounting's role as a value-laden profession capable of influencing the distribution of power and wealth in society.[3]

f) Describe and critically evaluate issues surrounding accounting and acting against the public interest.[3]

4. Professional practice and codes of ethics

a) Describe and explore the areas of behaviour covered by *corporate* codes of ethics.[3]

b) Describe and assess the content of, and principles behind, *professional* codes of ethics.[3]

c) Describe and assess the codes of ethics relevant to accounting professionals such as the IESBA (IFAC) or professional body codes.[3]

5. Conflicts of interest and the consequences of unethical behaviour

a) Describe and evaluate issues associated with conflicts of interest and ethical conflict resolution.[3]

b) Explain and evaluate the nature and impacts of ethical threats and safeguards.[3]

c) Explain and explore how threats to independence can affect ethical behaviour.[3]

d) Explain and explore 'bribery' and 'corruption' in the context of corporate governance, and assess how these can undermine confidence and trust. [3]

e) Describe and assess best practice measures for reducing and combating bribery and corruption, and the barriers to implementing such measures.[3]

6. Ethical characteristics of professionalism

a) Explain and analyse the content and nature of ethical decision-making using content from Kohlberg's framework as appropriate.[2]

b) Explain and analyse issues related to the application of ethical behaviour in a professional context.[2]

c) Describe and discuss 'rules based' and 'principles based' approaches to resolving ethical dilemmas encountered in professional accounting.[2]

7. Integrated reporting and sustainability issues in the conduct of business

a) Explain and assess the concept of integrated reporting and evaluate the issues concerning accounting for sustainability (including the alternative definitions of capital:.[3]
   (i)   Financial
   (ii)   Manufactured
   (iii)   Intellectual
   (iv)   Human
   (v)   Social and relationship
   (vi)   Natural

b) Describe and assess the social and environmental impacts that economic activity can have (in terms of social and environmental 'footprints' and environmental reporting)).[3]

c) Describe the main features of internal management systems for underpinning environmental and sustainability accounting such as EMAS and ISO 14000.[1]

d) Explain and assess the typical content elements and guiding principles of an integrated report, and discuss the usefulness of this information to stakeholders.[3]

e) Explain the nature of social and environmental audit and evaluate the contribution it can make to the assurance of integrated reports.[3]

SUMMARY OF CHANGES TO P1

ACCA annually reviews its qualification so that they fully meet the needs of stakeholders including employers, students, regulatory and advisory bodies and learning providers.

There are no syllabus changes effective from September 2016 and the next update will be September 2017.

Governance and responsibility

Scope of corporate governance

Topic list	Syllabus reference
1 Definitions of corporate governance	A1
2 Corporate governance and agency theory	A2
3 Types of stakeholders	A1, A7
4 Roles of stakeholders	A1
5 Major issues in corporate governance	A1

Introduction

We start this Text by discussing corporate governance, a fundamental topic in this paper. You have encountered corporate governance already in your law and auditing studies, but this syllabus requires a deeper understanding of what has driven the development of corporate governance codes over the last 15 years.

We start by looking at the principles that underpin corporate governance codes. Some will be familiar from what you have learnt about ethics in auditing. We shall examine ethics in detail in Part C of this Text, but you'll find that certain ethical themes recur throughout this book.

In Section 2 we show how corporate governance has partly developed in response to the problem of agency – the difficulty of ensuring that shareholders are able to exercise sufficient control over directors and managers, their agents. In Section 3 we consider the interests of other stakeholders in corporate governance. As we shall see in later chapters, a key issue in the development of corporate governance is how much, if at all, directors/managers have a responsibility to consider the interests of stakeholders other than shareholders. The examiner has stressed the need for understanding that business decisions are affected by, and can affect, many people inside and outside the business.

In the last section we introduce other major corporate governance issues. We shall see how corporate governance guidelines address these in the next two chapters.

Study guide

		Intellectual level
A1	**The scope of governance**	
(a)	Define and explain the meaning of corporate governance.	2
(b)	Explain and analyse the issues raised by the development of the joint stock company as the dominant form of business organisation and the separation of ownership and control over business activity.	3
(c)	Analyse the purpose and objectives of corporate governance in the public and private sectors.	2
(d)	Explain and apply in the context of corporate governance the key underpinning concepts.	3
(e)	Explain and assess the major areas of organisational life affected by issues in corporate governance.	3
(f)	Compare and distinguish between public, private and non-governmental organisations (NGOs) with regard to the issues raised by, and the scope of, governance.	3
(g)	Explain and evaluate the roles, interests and claims of the internal parties involved in corporate governance.	3
(h)	Explain and evaluate the roles, interests and claims of the external parties involved in corporate governance.	3
(i)	Analyse and discuss the role and influence of institutional investors in corporate governance systems and structures, for example the roles and influences of pension funds, insurance companies and mutual funds.	2
A2	**Agency relationships and theories**	
(a)	Define and explore agency theory.	2
(b)	Define and explain the key concepts in agency theory.	2
(c)	Explain and explore the nature of the principal-agent relationship in the context of corporate governance.	3
(d)	Analyse and critically evaluate the nature of agency accountability in agency relationships.	3
(e)	Explain and analyse the following other theories used to explain aspects of the agency relationship: Transactions cost theory and Stakeholder theory.	2
A7	**Corporate governance and corporate social responsibility**	
(b)	Discuss and critically assess the concept of stakeholder power and interest using the Mendelow model and how this can affect strategy and corporate governance.	3

Exam guide

You may be asked about the significance of the underlying concepts in Section 1, or to analyse a corporate governance scenario in terms of the agency responsibilities directors or auditors have towards various stakeholders, given the claims the stakeholders have on the organisation. Questions may also examine the roles of other participants in corporate governance. Questions will not always be about listed companies. They will also cover public sector organisations and charities. The issues highlighted in the last section could well be important problems in a scenario question. To quote the examiner: 'Most questions will involve some focus on, or connection with, the stakeholders and how their agents act on their behalf. Students will have to identify the relevant stakeholders primarily by assessing their power and interest.'

1 Definitions of corporate governance

FAST FORWARD

Corporate governance, the system by which organisations are directed and controlled, is based on a number of concepts, including transparency, independence, accountability and integrity.

1.1 What is corporate governance?

Key term

Corporate governance is the **system** by which organisations are directed and controlled. *(Cadbury report)*

Corporate governance is a **set of relationships** between a company's directors, its shareholders and other stakeholders. It also provides the structure through which the objectives of the company are set, and the means of achieving those objectives and monitoring performance, are determined. (OECD)

Exam focus point

An exam question on corporate governance might start by asking you to define what corporate governance is.

A number of comments can be made about these definitions of corporate governance.

(a) The **management, awareness, evaluation and mitigation of risk** are fundamental in all definitions of good governance. This includes the operation of an **adequate and appropriate system of control**.

(b) The notion that **overall performance is enhanced** by **good supervision** and **management** within **set best practice guidelines** underpins most definitions.

(c) Good governance provides a **framework** for an organisation to pursue its strategy in an **ethical and effective** way and **offers safeguards against misuse of resources**, human, financial, physical or intellectual.

(d) Good governance is not just about externally established codes; it also requires a willingness to **apply the spirit** as well as the letter of the law.

(e) Good corporate governance can **attract new investment** into companies, particularly in developing nations. It should mean that shareholders can **trust** those responsible for running and monitoring the company.

(f) **Accountability** is generally a major theme in all governance frameworks, including accountability not just to shareholders but also to other **stakeholders**, and accountability not just by directors but by auditors as well.

(g) Corporate governance **underpins capital market confidence in companies** and in the government/regulators/tax authorities that administer them. It helps **protect the value of shareholders' investment**.

1.1.1 History of governance

Governance focuses on ownership because ownership, and therefore financing, results in businesses being formed and expanded. Different systems of governance are seen as best practice in different countries, as we shall see later in this text. However, much of the governance debate has been seen in the context of the so-called Anglo-Saxon model where ownership and management are separate, and companies can obtain a listing on a stock exchange where their shares are bought and sold.

1.1.2 Governance in companies and non-governmental organisations

Although mostly discussed in relation to large quoted companies, governance is an issue for all corporate bodies, commercial and not for profit, including public sector and non-governmental organisations. There are certain ways in which companies might differ from other types of organisation, such as their ownership (principals), their mission and the legal/regulatory environment within which they operate.

Public sector organisations are organisations that are **controlled by one or more parts of the state**. Their functions are often to **implement government policy** in secretarial or administration areas. Some are supervised by government departments (for example hospitals or schools). Others are devolved bodies, such as local authorities, nationalised companies (majority or all of the shares owned by the Government), supranational bodies or non-governmental organisations.

These organisations are in the public sector because the control over a particular public service, utility or public good is seen as so important that it cannot be left to the profit-motivated sector, which may for example seek to close socially vital loss-making services, such as bus routes.

Objectives will be determined by the political leaders in line with government policy. They are likely to focus on **value for money and service delivery objectives**, possibly underpinned by legislation. The level of control may be high, leading to accusations of excess bureaucracy and cost.

In many countries there are thousands of charities and voluntary organisations that exist to fulfil a particular purpose, maybe social, environmental, religious or humanitarian. Funds are raised to support that purpose. Charities are not owned as such, but will be primarily responsible to the **donors** of funds and the **beneficiaries** (those who receive money or other aid) out of the charities' resources. Charities will be subject to their own legal regime that grants privileges (for example tax concessions) but imposes requirements on how funds can be spent and the charities' assets managed.

As well as being crucial to passing P1, you also need to be able to demonstrate your contribution to effective and appropriate governance in your area of responsibility in order to fulfil performance objective 4 of your PER.

1.2 Corporate governance concepts

One view of governance is that it is based on a series of underlying concepts.

1.2.1 Fairness

The directors' deliberations and also the systems and values that underlie the company must be **balanced** by taking into account everyone who has a legitimate interest in the company, and respecting their rights and views. In many jurisdictions, corporate governance guidelines reinforce legal protection for certain groups, for example minority shareholders. It should mean the company deals **even-handedly** with others.

1.2.2 Transparency   12/07, 12/08, 6/11, 6/13, 6/14

Key term

> **Transparency** means **open and clear disclosure** of relevant information to shareholders and other stakeholders, as well as not concealing information when it may affect decisions. It means open discussions and a default position of information provision rather than concealment.

Disclosure in this context obviously includes **information in the financial statements**, not just the numbers and notes to the accounts but also narrative statements such as the directors' report and the operating and financial or business review. It also includes all **voluntary disclosure**; that is, disclosure above the minimum required by law or regulation. Voluntary corporate communications include management forecasts, analysts' presentations, press releases, information placed on websites and other reports such as standalone environmental or social reports.

The main reason why transparency is so important relates to the **agency problem** that we shall discuss in Section 2, the potential conflict between owners and managers. Without effective disclosure the position could be unfairly weighted towards managers, since they have far more knowledge of the company's activities and financial situation than the owner/investors. Avoidance of this **information asymmetry** requires not only effective disclosure rules but also strong internal controls that ensure the information that is disclosed is **reliable**. Information also needs to be published in sufficient detail to meet the needs of shareholders/owners. Publication of abbreviated information may be counter-productive and may give the impression of concealment rather than openness.

Linked with the agency issue, publication of relevant and reliable information **reassures investors and underpins stock market confidence** in how companies are being governed and thus **significantly**

influences market prices. International accounting standards and stock market regulations based on corporate governance codes require information published to be **true and fair**. Information can only fulfil this requirement if adequate disclosure is made of uncertainties and adverse events. It is therefore clear that financial data will be insufficient without supporting explanation.

Circumstances where concealment may be justified include discussions about **future strategy** (knowledge of which would benefit competitors), **confidential** issues relating to individuals and discussions leading to an agreed position that is then made public.

Case Study

Ethics guru Chris Macdonald has raised a number of issues with the concept of transparency.

1. The requirement of transparency to check how directors (agents) are doing indicates a big problem with governance. If shareholders had complete confidence in directors, there would be no concern about transparency.

2. Transparency assumes that those who receive information are well informed but problems may arise through misinterpretation. The example quoted was a hospital executive being criticised for having the perk of expensive membership of an exclusive private club. However, if the executive was responsible for fundraising, the club would provide networking opportunities with members who could make large donations to the hospital.

3. In the context of directors' remuneration (discussed in Chapter 3) evidence suggests that full transparency can ratchet up average reward. A chief executive, seeing how much other chief executives in their sector are earning, may want their rewards to match theirs. A remuneration committee may regard the fact that its chief executive is earning below average remuneration as poor publicity for the chief executive and the company.

4. Full transparency of rewards of one type may lead to those in positions of trust to seek less visible, and perhaps more costly, rewards. For example, the 2009 scandal about excessive expenses being claimed by UK Members of Parliament was linked to the political unacceptability of increasing MPs' salaries significantly. To head off a revolt by members, the Conservative Government in the 1980s introduced a big increase in members' expense allowances, with the minister responsible allegedly telling MPs 'go out boys and spend it.'

Exam focus point

> Weighing up transparency against confidentiality may be difficult and hence the examiner tests it regularly. Remember that sometimes there may be valid commercial reasons for keeping information away from those who may use it against the company. On the other hand, greater transparency and providing a full explanation for controversial actions can be an effective means of responding to critics.

1.2.3 Innovation

The concept of innovation in the approach to corporate governance recognises the fact that the needs of businesses and stakeholders can change over time. It also has an impact on how organisations respond to meeting the 'comply or explain' requirement contained in various codes of corporate governance that are currently in effect.

1.2.4 Scepticism

The UK Corporate Governance Code, under the heading of 'Leadership', encourages non-executive directors (NEDs) to adopt an air of scepticism so that they can effectively challenge management decisions in their role of scrutiny. Applying professional scepticism is also an important part of the role of auditors and audit committees. ISA 200 defines professional scepticism as: 'An attitude that includes a questioning mind, being alert to conditions which may indicate possible misstatement due to error or fraud, and a critical assessment of audit evidence.' This does not mean that all management decisions and evidence have to be approached with suspicion or mistrust; but rather that an open and enquiring mind

must always be employed. A healthy corporate culture and environment is one that encourages and enables such scepticism to thrive.

1.2.5 Independence

Key term

> **Independence** is the avoidance of being unduly influenced by vested interests and free from any constraints that would prevent a correct course of action being taken. It is an ability to stand apart from inappropriate influences and be free of managerial capture, to be able to make the correct and uncontaminated decision on a given issue.
>
> Independence is a quality that can be possessed by individuals and is an essential component of professionalism and professional behaviour.

An important distinction generally with independence is **independence of mind and independence of appearance**.

- **Independence of mind** means providing an opinion without being affected by influences compromising judgement.
- **Independence of appearance** means avoiding situations where an informed third party could reasonably conclude that an individual's judgement would have been compromised.

Independence is an important concept in relation to directors; in particular, **freedom from conflicts of interest**. Corporate governance reports have increasingly stressed the importance of **independent non-executive directors**, directors who are not primarily employed by the company and who have very strictly controlled other links with it. They should be in a better position to **promote the interests of shareholders and other stakeholders**. Freed from pressures that could influence their activities, independent non-executive directors should be able to carry out **effective monitoring** of the company and its management in conjunction with equally independent external auditors on behalf of shareholders.

Non-executive directors' lack of links and limits on the time that they serve as non-executive directors should promote **avoidance of managerial capture** – accepting executive managers' views on trust without analysing and questioning them.

As you will remember from Paper F8, the **independence of external auditors** from their clients is also important in corporate governance (covered further in Chapter 10). As the auditor is acting on behalf of the shareholders and **not** the client, close friendship with the client may influence the external auditor's judgement, and mean that the external auditor is not effectively representing the shareholders' interests. Internal auditors also need to be **independent** of the colleagues whom they are auditing (discussed in Chapter 8).

A complication when considering independence is that there are varying degrees of independence, lying between **total independence** (no knowledge/connection with the other party) and **zero independence** (inability to take a decision without considering the effect on the other party). In real-life situations the two extremes are unlikely, but in most situations independence should be as near to total independence as possible.

Question   External auditor independence

Why is the independence of external auditors so important?

Answer

(a)   Shareholders and other stakeholders need a trustworthy record of directors' stewardship to be able to take decisions about the company. Assurance provided by independent auditors is a key quality control on reliability.

(b)   An unqualified report by independent external auditors on the accounts should give them more credibility, enhancing the appeal of the company to investors.

(c)   A lack of independence may mean that an effective audit is not done. Thus the shareholders are not receiving value for the costs of the audit.

(d)   A lack of independence may lead to a failure to fulfil professional requirements. Failure to do this undermines the credibility of the accountancy profession and the standards it enforces.

1.2.6 Probity/honesty

Hopefully this should be the most self-evident of the principles. It relates to not only telling the truth but also not misleading shareholders and other stakeholders. Lack of probity includes not only obvious examples of dishonesty, such as taking bribes, but also reporting information in a slanted way that is designed to give an unfair impression.

Guidance in the UK charitable sector has defined probity in terms of receipt of gifts or hospitality by trustees. The Code stresses that all gifts should be clearly recorded, and trustees should not accept gifts with a significant monetary value or lavish hospitality. They should certainly not accept gifts or hospitality which may seem likely to influence their decisions.

1.2.7 Responsibility

Responsibility means management accepting the credit or blame for governance decisions. It implies clear definition of the roles and responsibilities of the roles of senior management.

The South African King report stresses that, for management to be held properly responsible, there must be a system in place that allows for **corrective action and penalising mismanagement**. Responsible management should do, when necessary, whatever it takes to set the company on the right path.

King states that the board of directors must act responsively to, and with responsibility towards, all stakeholders of the company. However, the responsibility of directors to other stakeholders, both in terms of to **whom** they are responsible and the **extent** of their responsibility, remains a key point of contention in corporate governance debates. We shall discuss the importance of stakeholders later in this chapter.

The limits of responsibility and how responsibility is enforced will be a recurring theme throughout this text, developed further in:

- Chapters 2-3, on corporate governance
- Chapters 4-8, covering directors' responsibilities in respect of risk management and internal control
- Chapters 9-10, covering accountants' responsibilities to clients and society
- Chapter 11, covering corporate social responsibility

1.2.8 Accountability   12/12

> Corporate **accountability** refers to whether an organisation (and its directors) is **answerable** in some way for the consequences of its actions.

Directors being answerable to shareholders have always been an important part of company law, well before the development of the corporate governance codes. For example, companies in many regimes have been required to provide **financial information** to shareholders on an **annual basis** and hold **annual general meetings**. However, particularly because of the corporate governance scandals of the last 30 years, investors have demanded greater assurance that directors are acting in their interests. This has led to the development of corporate governance codes, which we shall consider in the next chapter.

Making accountability work is the responsibility of **both** parties. Directors, as we have seen, do so through the quality of information that they provide whereas shareholders do so through their willingness to **exercise their responsibility as owners**, which means using the available mechanisms to query and assess the actions of the board.

Public sector accountability

The accountability relationship will be different for bodies owned or run by national or central government. The nature of the relationship may be clear – that government determines objectives. How accountability is demonstrated and enforced may depend though on how coherent the objectives are. The main problem will often be where the body's main objectives are non-economic, but the Government also wishes to limit the amount it spends on the body.

As with responsibility, one of the biggest debates in corporate governance is the extent of management's **accountability** towards **other stakeholders**, such as the community in which the organisation operates. This has led on to a debate that we shall discuss in Chapter 10 about the contents of accounts themselves.

In the context of public service, the UK Nolan Committee on Standards in Public Life commented that **holders of public office** are **accountable** for their decisions and actions to **the public**, and must submit themselves to whatever scrutiny is appropriate for their office.

A wider issue with the extent of accountability in the public sector is the **extent of accountability towards different groups in society**. For example, politicians can be seen as being accountable to the body of taxpayers as a whole – it is their interests that parliamentary bodies have been established to represent. However, politicians are also accountable to a group within the category of taxpayers – the voters who voted for them. This raises the issue of what happens if the actions politicians take advantage their voters, but disadvantage other taxpayers. More controversially, there is the issue of the extent to which politicians should be accountable to donors who pay significant sums to finance their political activities.

Exam focus point

> The examiner has commented:
>
> 'When I say accountability, I mean companies to investors, professionals to their values, business systems to their stakeholders and so forth.'
>
> These comments emphasise that accountability, like responsibility, is a topic that underpins much of the rest of this text and will be a key feature in many exam questions. The comments indicate that it is possible to be accountable to an abstract set of values. However, much of the discussion about accountability focuses on the extent of accountability to stakeholders, particularly when stakeholder interests differ.

1.2.9 Reputation   6/14

Reputation is determined by how others view a person, organisation or profession. Reputation includes a reputation for **competence**, supplying good quality goods and services in a timely fashion, and also being managed in an orderly way. However, a **poor ethical reputation** can be as serious for an organisation as a poor reputation for competence.

The consequences of a poor reputation for an organisation can include:

- Suppliers' and customers' unwillingness to deal with the organisation for fear of being victims of sharp practice
- Inability to recruit high-quality staff
- Fall in demand because of consumer boycotts
- Increased public relations costs because of adverse stories in the media
- Increased compliance costs because of close attention from regulatory bodies or external auditors
- Loss of market value because of a fall in investor confidence

Case Study

Over the past few years the American retail giant Wal-Mart has made efforts to improve its reputation in various ways. These have included improving its labour and healthcare records, donating to not for profit organisations and promoting the case that it helps economic growth and provides healthy groceries. This has partly been for strategic purposes, as the company has sought to open stores in cities in face of local hostility, due to the adverse effect on other local retailers.

Unfortunately Wal-Mart's attempts to portray itself as more ethical have been undermined by a recent bribery scandal, as we shall see in Chapter 10.

We shall see later on in this Text how risks to an organisation's reputation depend on how likely other risks are to crystallise.

In the context of governance, reputation also means **personal and professional reputation**, and the **moral reputation of the accountancy profession** as a whole. All are influenced by the extent to which individuals or members of the profession demonstrate the other underlying concepts we have discussed.

1.2.10 Judgement
6/14

Judgement means the board **making decisions that enhance the prosperity** of the organisation. This means that board members must acquire a broad enough knowledge of the business and its environment to be able to provide meaningful direction to it. This has implications not only for the attention directors have to give to the organisation's affairs, but also on the way the directors are recruited and trained.

As you will see when you come to study Paper P3, the complexities of senior management mean that the directors have to bring **multiple conceptual skills** to management that aim to maximise long-term returns. This means that corporate governance can involve balancing many competing people and resource claims against each other. Although, as we shall see, risk management is an integral part of corporate governance, corporate governance isn't just about risk management.

1.2.11 Integrity
6/10, 06/13

Key term

> 'Integrity means straightforward dealing and completeness. What is required of financial reporting is that it should be honest and that it should present a balanced picture of the state of the company's affairs. The integrity of reports depends on the integrity of those who prepare and present them.'   (*Cadbury report*)
>
> **Integrity** (means that) holders of public office should not place themselves under any financial or other obligation to outside individuals or organisations that might influence them in the performance of their official duties.   *UK Nolan Committee Standards on Public Life*

Integrity can be taken as meaning someone of **high moral character**, who sticks to strict moral or ethical principles no matter the pressure to do otherwise. In working life this means adhering to the highest standards of professionalism and probity. **Straightforwardness, fair dealing and honesty in relationships** with the different people and constituencies whom you meet are particularly important. Trust is vital in relationships and belief in the integrity of those with whom you are dealing underpins this.

Integrity is an underlying principle of corporate governance. All those in agency relationships should possess and exercise absolute integrity. To fail to do so breaches the relationship of trust. The Cadbury report definition highlights the need for **personal honesty and integrity** of preparers of accounts. This implies qualities beyond a mechanical adherence to accounting or ethical regulations or guidelines. At times accountants will have to use judgement or face financial situations which aren't covered by regulations or guidance, and on these occasions integrity is particularly important.

Integrity is an essential principle of the **corporate governance relationship**, particularly in relationship to representing shareholder interests and exercising agency (discussed in Section 2). Monitoring and hence agency costs can be reduced if there is trust in the integrity of the agents. In addition, we have seen that a key aim of corporate governance is to inspire confidence in participants in the market and this significantly depends on a **public perception of competence and integrity**.

Integrity is also one of the fundamental principles discussed in the IESBA code of ethics (see Chapter 10). It provides assurance to those with whom the accountant deals of good intentions and truthfulness.

Exam focus point

> The Pilot Paper asks for an explanation of what integrity is, and its importance in corporate governance. The December 2007 exam asked about the significance of transparency. The June 2013 exam had a question about the importance of integrity and transparency. You may be asked similar questions about other principles.

2 Corporate governance and agency theory 6/08, 6/09, 6/10

FAST FORWARD

Agency is extremely important in corporate governance, as the directors/managers are often acting as agents for the owners. Corporate governance frameworks aim to ensure directors/managers **fulfil their responsibilities** as agents by requiring disclosure and suggesting they be rewarded on the basis of performance.

2.1 Nature of agency   12/14, 6/15

Key term

> **Agency relationship** is a contract under which one or more persons (the principals) engage another person (the agent) to perform some service on their behalf that involves delegating some decision-making authority to the agent.
> (Jensen and Meckling)

You will have encountered agency in your earlier studies, but a brief revision will be helpful. There are a number of specific types of agent. These have either evolved in particular trades or developed in response to specific commercial needs. Examples include factors, brokers, estate agents, bankers and auctioneers.

Agency in the context of director-shareholder relationships is discussed below. However, there are many other types of agency relationships. Corporate governance guidance is concerned with the shareholder-auditor agency relationship as well as the shareholder-manager relationship. The auditors act as the shareholders' agents when carrying out an audit, and thus the shareholders wish them to maintain their independence of the management of the company being audited. The problems auditors have when attempting to maintain their independence is dealt with in governance guidance.

Exam focus point

> Question 1 in June 2009 asked about the agency relationship between a bank and the trustees of a pension fund that invested in the bank. However, not all organisations have private shareholders/investors. June 2010 Question 1 examined the agency situation in a nationalised company wholly owned by the home country government. Not only the Government but also the taxpayers are principals there. Managers running a charity will be acting as agents for the trustees who represent the principals (donors and recipients of aid). In December 2013 there was a question requiring a definition of agency in the context of corporate governance.

2.2 Accountability and fiduciary responsibilities

2.2.1 Accountability

Key term

> In the context of agency, **accountability** means that the agent is **answerable under the contract** to their principal and must account for the resources of their principal and the money they have gained working on their principal's behalf.

Two problems potentially arise with this.

- How does the principal **enforce this accountability** (the agency problem, see below)? As we shall see, the corporate governance systems developed to monitor the behaviour of directors have been designed to address this issue.
- What if the agent is **accountable to parties other than their principal** – how do they reconcile possibly conflicting duties (for the stakeholder view see Section 3)?

Key term

> **Fiduciary duty** is a duty of care and trust which one person or entity owes to another. It can be a legal or ethical obligation.
>
> In law it is a duty imposed on certain persons because of the position of trust and confidence in which they stand in relation to another. The duty is more onerous than generally arises under a contractual or tort relationship. It requires full disclosure of information held by the fiduciary, a strict duty to account for any profits received as a result of the relationship, and a duty to avoid conflicts of interest.

Under English law company directors owe a fiduciary duty to the company to exercise their powers *bona fide* in what they **honestly consider to be the interests** of the company. This duty is **owed to the company** and not generally to individual shareholders. In exercising the powers given to them by the constitution the directors have a fiduciary duty not only to act *bona fide* but also only to use their powers **for a proper purpose**. The powers are restricted to the purposes for which they were given.

Clearly the concepts of fiduciary duty and accountability are very similar though not identical. Where certain wider responsibilities are enshrined in law, do directors have a duty to go beyond the law, or can they regard the law as defining what society as a whole requires of them?

2.2.3 Fiduciary relationship with stakeholders   12/07

Evan and Freeman have argued that **management bears a fiduciary relationship to stakeholders** and to the corporation as an abstract entity. It must act in the interests of the **stakeholders as their agent**, and it must act in the interests of the **corporation to ensure the survival** of the firm, safeguarding the long-term stakes of each group. Adoption of these principles would require significant changes to the way corporations are run. Evan and Freeman propose a **'stakeholder board of directors'**, with one representative for each of the stakeholder groups and one for the company itself. Each stakeholder representative would be elected by a stakeholder assembly. Company law would have to develop to protect the interests of stakeholders.

Exam focus point

> Question 4 in December 2007 asked students not only to explain what fiduciary responsibility was but also to argue the case in favour of extending it. This illustrates that the examiner does not regard fiduciary duty as a legal concept set in stone, but one that can be used flexibly. A question in June 2013 asked for a description of fiduciary duty in the context of the case presented in the question.

2.2.4 Performance

The agent who agrees to act as agent for reward has a **contractual obligation** to perform their agreed task. An unpaid agent is not bound to carry out their agreed duties. Any agent may refuse to perform an illegal act.

2.2.5 Obedience

The agent must act strictly in **accordance with their principal's instructions** provided that these are lawful and reasonable. Even if they believe disobedience to be in their principal's best interests, they may not disobey instructions. Only if they are asked to commit an illegal act may they do so.

2.2.6 Skill

A paid agent undertakes to maintain the standard of **skill and care** to be expected of a person in their profession.

2.2.7 Personal performance

The agent is presumably selected because of their personal qualities and owes a duty to **perform their task themselves** and not to delegate it to another. But they may delegate in a few special circumstances, if delegation is necessary, such as a solicitor acting for a client would be obliged to instruct a stockbroker to buy or sell listed securities on a stock exchange.

2.2.8 No conflict of interest

The agent owes to their principal a duty not to put themselves in a situation where their **own interests conflict** with those of the principal. For example, they must not sell their own property to the principal (even if the sale is at a fair price).

2.2.9 Confidence

The agent must keep in **confidence** what they know of their principal's affairs even after the agency relationship has ceased.

2.2.10 Any benefit

Any benefit must be handed over to the principal unless they **agree** that the agent may **retain it**. Although an agent is entitled to their agreed remuneration, they must account to the principal for any other **benefits**. If they accept from the other party any **commission or reward** as an inducement to make the contract with him, it is considered to be a bribe and the contract is fraudulent.

2.3 Agency in the context of the director-shareholder relationship   6/08

Agency is a significant issue in corporate governance because of the **dominance of the joint-stock company**, the company limited by shares as a form of business organisation. For larger companies this has led to the **separation of ownership of the company** from its **management**. The owners (the shareholders) can be seen as the **principal**, the management of the company as the **agents**.

Although ordinary shareholders (equity shareholders) are the owners of the company to whom the board of directors is accountable, the actual powers of shareholders tend to be restricted. They normally have no right to inspect the books of account, and their forecasts of future prospects are gleaned from the annual report and accounts, stockbrokers, journals and daily newspapers.

The day-to-day running of a company is the responsibility of the directors and other managers to whom the directors delegate, not the shareholders. For these reasons, therefore, there is the potential for **conflicts of interest** between management and shareholders.

Exam focus point

December 2013 Question 2 asked students to explain agency in the context of corporate governance.

2.4 The agency problem

The agency problem in joint stock companies derives from the principals (owners) not being able to run the business themselves and therefore having to rely on agents (directors) to do so for them. This **separation of ownership from management** can cause issues if there is a breach of trust by directors by intentional action, omission, neglect or incompetence. This breach may arise because the directors are **pursuing their own interests** rather than the shareholders' or because they have **different attitudes to risk taking** to the shareholders.

For example, if managers hold none or very few of the equity shares of the company they work for, what is to stop them from working inefficiently, concentrating too much on achieving short-term profits and hence maximising their own bonuses, not bothering to look for profitable new investment opportunities, or giving themselves high salaries and perks?

One power that shareholders possess is the right to **remove the directors** from office. But shareholders have to take the initiative to do this and, in many companies, the shareholders lack the energy and organisation to take such a step. Ultimately they can vote in favour of a takeover or removal of individual directors or entire boards, but this may be undesirable for other reasons.

2.5 Agency costs

To alleviate the agency problem, shareholders have to take steps to exercise control, such as attending AGMs or ultimately becoming directors themselves. However, agency theory assumes that it will be **expensive and difficult to**:

- Verify what the agent is doing, partly because the agent has available more information about his activities than the principal does

- Introduce mechanisms to control the activities of the agent

The principals therefore incur agency costs, which are the costs of the **monitoring** that is required because of the **separation of ownership and management**.

Common agency costs include:

- Costs of studying company data and results
- Purchase of expert analysis
- External auditors' fees
- Costs of devising and enforcing directors' contracts
- Time spent attending company meetings
- Costs of direct intervention in the company's affairs
- Transaction costs of shareholding

To fulfil the requirements imposed on them (and to obtain the rewards of fulfilment) managers will spend time and resources proving that they are maximising shareholder value by, for example, providing increased disclosure or meeting with major shareholders.

Agency costs can be expensive for shareholders only holding shares in a few companies. For larger-scale investors, holding a portfolio containing the shares of many different companies, agency costs can be prohibitive. This illustrates the importance of minimising agency costs by aligning the interests of shareholders and directors.

Exam focus point

Your syllabus stresses the significance of agency problems in public listed companies.

2.6 Resolving the agency problem: alignment of interests

Agency theory sees employees of businesses, including managers, as individuals, each with their own objectives. Within a department of a business, there are departmental objectives. If achieving these various objectives leads also to the achievement of the objectives of the organisation as a whole, there is said to be alignment of interests.

Key term

Alignment of interests is accordance between the objectives of agents acting within an organisation and the objectives of the organisation as a whole. Alignment of interests is sometimes referred to as goal congruence, although goal congruence is used in other ways, as you will see in your P3 studies.

Alignment of interests may be better achieved and the 'agency problem' better dealt with by giving managers some profit-related pay, or by providing incentives that are related to profits or share price. Examples of such remuneration incentives are:

(a)   **Profit-related/economic value-added pay**

Pay or bonuses related to the size of profits or economic value-added.

(b) **Rewarding managers with shares**

This might be done when a private company 'goes public' and managers are invited to subscribe for shares in the company at an attractive offer price. In a management buy-out or buy-in (the latter involving purchase of the business by new managers, the former by existing managers), managers become joint owner-managers.

(c) **Executive share option plans (ESOPs)**

In a share option scheme, selected employees are given a number of share options, each of which gives the holder the right after a certain date to subscribe for shares in the company at a fixed price. The value of an option will increase if the company is successful and its share price goes up, therefore giving managers an incentive to take decisions to increase the value of the company, actions congruent with wider shareholder interests.

Such measures might merely encourage management to adopt **'creative accounting'** methods which will distort the reported performance of the company in the service of the managers' own ends.

An alternative approach is to attempt to **monitor managers' behaviour**; for example, by establishing **'management audit'** procedures, to introduce **additional reporting requirements**, or to seek **assurances** from managers that shareholders' interests will be foremost in their priorities. The most significant problem with monitoring is likely to be the **agency costs** involved, as they may imply **significant shareholder engagement** with the company.

2.7 Other agency relationships

2.7.1 Shareholder-auditor relationship

The shareholder-auditor relationship is another agency relationship on which corporate governance guidance has focused. The shareholders are the principals, the auditors are the agents and the audit report the key method of communication.

2.7.2 Shareholder-auditor relationship in public companies

An agency problem with auditors is that auditors may not be independent of the management of the companies that they audit. They become too close to management or are afraid that management will not give them non-audit work.

Corporate governance codes have sought to address this problem. However, the shareholder-auditor relationship in public companies imposes its own complexities. The auditors are acting as shareholders' agents in **monitoring the stewardship of directors.** However, as we shall see in Chapter 8, the (non-executive) directors, who are on the audit committee, effectively also act as shareholders' agents in **monitoring the auditors**. They are responsible for recommending the appointment and removal of the external auditors, fixing their remuneration, considering independence issues and discussing the scope of the audit.

The implication perhaps in most governance guidance is that the external auditors and non-executive directors are 'on the same side', with conflicts most likely to arise in tensions with executive directors (hence the possibility being raised in governance guidance of the external auditors and audit committee meeting without executive management being present). The situation breaks down if there is conflict between auditors and non-executive directors. Auditors then have the right to qualify their audit reports and make statements if they resign, but this is clearly a sign of problems that may require stakeholder intervention, time and cost.

2.7.3 Agency costs of external audit

Direct costs are obviously the audit fee. In addition, there will be the time spent by management and employees dealing with the information and preparing information for the auditors.

The amount of audit costs is not solely determined by the shareholders, but also influenced by the **professional institutes** to which the auditors belong and **national and international government bodies**. These institutions can influence audit fees directly, for example through rules on low-balling (fees that are too low). They can also impose requirements that indirectly add to the costs of audit. For example, **institutes and standard-setting bodies** lay down requirements that auditors must fulfil, impacting on the quality of work and the costs to be recovered. Governments, too, can take measures that will affect costs. For example, recent EU proposals (discussed further in Chapter 10) would require compulsory rotation of auditors every few years. This would most probably increase audit costs over time because new auditors would incur set-up costs when they started acting for a new client.

This in turn raises the issue of the extent to which influences other than shareholder opinions should determine audit work and audit costs. One argument might be that the audit fee is effectively a cost of risk management which reduces the earnings available to shareholders. If the shareholders are happy with the audit fee being low and hence the audit work carried out being limited, this implies that they are happy to accept increased risk in return for lower audit costs and higher earnings – it is fundamentally a risk-return decision. Well-informed potential investors and markets will take a similar view.

Critics of this view would argue that the impact of a company that has been inadequately audited falling into difficulties is potentially severe and goes well beyond the loss of shareholders' investment. Employees, customers and suppliers can all be adversely affected and the wider economy may also be damaged if the company is large enough.

2.7.4 Other relationships

Other significant agency relationships include directors themselves acting as principals to managers/employees as agents. It is of course a significant responsibility of directors to make sure that this agency relationship works by establishing **appropriate systems of performance measurement and monitoring** (discussed in Chapter 8). In turn managers will act as principals to employees. There is also the relation between directors/managers and creditors, where creditors are seeking the payment of invoices on a timely basis.

Question
Agency costs of shareholding

What factors might increase the agency costs incurred by a shareholder in a public company?

Answer

Concerns over strategies and risks

A major concern in practice is likely to be if the shareholder is concerned about the strategies being adopted or the level of risks being taken, either too high or low. Arguably, if the shareholder is dissatisfied it can sell its shares and invest in companies whose strategies it trusts and whose risk appetites it shares. However in practice transaction costs plus the risk of not realising the full potential value from a sale may mean the shareholder is reluctant to sell.

Lack of communication by company

If the company does not, or is unwilling to, communicate proactively what shareholders wish to know, shareholders will need to find other means of obtaining information or make efforts to express their dissatisfaction. One thing acknowledged by the boards of companies that have been recently involved in controversy over executive pay (discussed further in Chapter 3) has been the need to communicate better with shareholders about directors' remuneration.

Inadequacy of governance arrangements

The shareholder may need to spend more effort monitoring what the company is doing if it feels the corporate governance arrangements are inadequate. Particular concerns might be a very powerful chief executive and a lack of a strong non-executive director presence on the board.

Conflicts with other shareholders

The shareholder may have to incur costs and time if other, more powerful shareholders do not appear to share the shareholder's concerns about the company in which they have invested. A common criticism in recent years is that institutional shareholders have given boards an easy ride, and failed to use the power their large shareholdings gives them to press the concerns of small shareholders without much influence.

2.8 Agency and public sector organisations

Public sector organisations also incorporate an agency relationship between the principals (the political leaders and ultimately the taxpayers/electors) and agents (the elected and executive officers and departmental managers). Because the taxpayers and electors have differing interests and objectives, establishing and monitoring the achievement of strategic objectives, and interpreting what is best for the principals, can be very difficult.

The agency problem in public services is also enhanced by limitations on the audit of public service organisations. In many jurisdictions the audit only covers the integrity and transparency of financial transactions and does not include an audit of performance or fitness for purpose.

2.9 Agency and charities

The agents in a charity are those responsible for spending donations and grants given. They include the directors and managers of the charitable services. Controls are needed to ensure that the interests of the principals (donors and recipients of charitable services) are maintained, and that funds are **used for the intended purpose and not embezzled or used for self-enrichment**.

Charities ensure that the agency problem is reduced and the goodwill of donors maintained by having a board of directors to run the charity, but also **trustees** to ensure that the board is **delivering value to donors** and to ensure that the **charity's aims are fulfilled**. The trustees generally share the values of the charity and act like non-executive directors of public companies (discussed in Chapter 3). The trustees are likely to have the power to recruit and dismiss directors.

Agency problems in charities may not just arise from managers' activities. An ambiguous relationship between the aims of the charity and commercial requirements may cause difficulty. Trustee prejudices may also hinder the relationship, particularly if they are trying to represent donors and beneficiaries who are largely silent. A lack of commercial knowledge and an unwillingness to change attitudes by the trustees may make the relationship problematic.

Publication of information about the contribution that the charity makes can help resolve the agency problem in charities. An annual report that clearly states how the charity is run and how it has delivered against its stated terms of reference and objectives can increase the confidence of donors, beneficiaries and regulators. A comprehensive audit of this information will reinforce its usefulness.

2.10 Transaction costs theory

Transactions cost theory is based on the work of Cyert and March and broadly states that the way the company is **organised** or **governed** determines its control over transactions. Companies will try to keep as many transactions as possible in-house in order to **reduce uncertainties** about dealing with suppliers, and about purchase prices and quality. To do this, companies will seek **vertical integration** (that is, they will purchase suppliers or producers later in the production process).

Transaction cost theory also states that managers are also **opportunistic** ie organise their transactions to pursue their own convenience. They will also be influenced by the **amounts** that they **personally will gain**, the probability of **bad behaviour** being **discovered** and the extent to which their actions are **tolerated** or even encouraged in corporate culture.

A further aspect of the theory is that managers will behave rationally up to a point, but this will be **limited by the understanding of alternatives that they have**.

The implications of transaction cost theory are that management may well **play safe**, and concentrate on easily understood markets and individual transactions they can easily control. This may mean that the company runs efficiently and, in its way, effectively. However, a focus on low-risk activities may discourage potential investors who are looking for a large return. Alternatively, shareholders dissatisfied with low profits may seek greater involvement in governance.

Internally senior managers will need to assess the impact of opportunistic issues, since this should determine the degree of monitoring that is needed over the activities of operational managers.

Thus despite differences of emphasis, transaction cost theory and agency theory are largely attempting to tackle the same problem, namely to ensure that managers effectively pursue shareholders' best interests.

3 Types of stakeholders   12/07, 6/08, 12/08, 6/10

FAST FORWARD

> Directors and managers need to be aware of the **interests of stakeholders** in governance; however, their responsibility towards them is judged.

3.1 Stakeholders

Key term

> **Stakeholders** are any entity (person, group or possibly non-human entity) that can **affect** or **be affected by** the achievements of an organisation's objectives. It is a **bi-directional** relationship. Each stakeholder group has different **expectations** about what it wants and different **claims** on the organisation.

3.1.1 Stakeholder claims   12/12

The definition above highlights the important point for both business ethics and strategy, that stakeholders do not only just exist but also have claims on an organisation. Some stakeholders want to influence what the organisation does. Others are mainly concerned with how the organisation affects them and may want to increase or decrease this effect. However, there is the problem that some stakeholders do not know that they have a claim against the organisation, or know that they have a claim but do not know what it is.

A useful distinction is between direct and indirect stakeholder claims.

(a) Stakeholders who make **direct claims** do so with their own voice and generally do so clearly. Normally stakeholders with direct claims themselves communicate with the company.

(b) Stakeholders who have **indirect claims** are generally unable to make the claims themselves because they are for some reason inarticulate or voiceless. Although they cannot express their claim directly to the organisation, this does not necessarily invalidate their claim. Stakeholders may lack power because they have no significance for the organisation, have no physical voice (animals and plants), are remote from the organisation (suppliers based in other countries) or are future generations.

We shall discuss further the legitimacy of stakeholder claims and direct and indirect stakeholders later in this section.

Exam focus point

> If you are asked to describe and assess a claim in the exam, remember that the fact that some stakeholders have no voice does not invalidate their claims. Sometimes their claims may be the most powerful of all.

3.1.2 Importance of recognition of stakeholder claims   12/12

Knowledge of who stakeholders are and what claims they make is a vital part of an organisation's **risk assessment**, since the **claims** made by the stakeholder can affect the achievement of objectives. Stakeholders also have **influences** over the organisation. It is important to identify what these are and how significant they are, since it may determine the organisation's decision if it has to decide between competing stakeholder claims. We discuss the assessment of the influence of stakeholders in terms of their power and interest below. An organisation also needs to know where likely **areas of conflict and tension between stakeholders** may arise.

3.1.3 Misinterpretation of stakeholder claims

As we shall see later in this chapter, **assessment of stakeholder claims** is potentially a difficult, subjective process. Organisations may also **misinterpret** the claims that stakeholders have or are making. This can mean that organisations take wrong or unnecessary actions, or fail to take the right actions, to deal with stakeholder concerns. It also may distort organisational priorities. There is possibly also an increased chance of **conflict** between the organisation and some stakeholders, as stakeholders who have strong grounds for feeling that their concerns are not being addressed properly take action.

Exam focus point

December 2012 Question 4 required students to identify and describe stakeholders and stakeholder claims in a scenario.

3.2 Stockholder theory (shareholder theory)   12/08

The theory that focuses on the interests of shareholders is known as stockholder theory, since it is mostly discussed in American literature.

Stockholder theory states that shareholders alone have a legitimate claim to influence over the company. It uses agency theory to argue that shareholders (as principals) own the company. Hence directors as agents have a moral and legal duty only to take account of shareholders' interests. As it is assumed that shareholders wish to maximise their returns, then directors' sole duty is to pursue profit maximisation.

This is the view of the pristine capitalist category defined by Gray, Owen and Adams that we shall consider further in Chapter 11.

3.3 Problems with stockholder view

Modern corporations have been seen as **so powerful, socially, economically and politically**, that **unrestrained use of their power** will inevitably **damage other people's rights**. For example, they may blight an entire community by closing a major factory, inflicting long-term unemployment on a large proportion of the local workforce. They may use their purchasing power or market share to impose unequal contracts on suppliers and customers alike. They may exercise undesirable influence over government through their investment decisions. There is also the argument that corporations exist within society and are **dependent on it for the resources** they use. Some of these resources are obtained by direct contracts with suppliers but others are not, being provided by government expenditure.

Exam focus point

Remember in the exam that the stockholder view isn't just an economic argument. Behind it is an ethical argument of fairly rewarding those who supply the company with its capital.

3.4 Stakeholder theory   12/08, 6/09

Stakeholder theory proposes **corporate accountability** to a broad range of stakeholders. It is based on companies being so large, and their impact on society being so significant, that they cannot just be responsible to their shareholders. There is a moral case for a business knowing how its decisions affect people both inside and outside the organisation. Stakeholders should also be seen not as just existing, but as **making legitimate demands** on an organisation. The relationship should be seen as a **two-way** relationship. There is much debate about which demands are legitimate, as we shall discuss below.

What stakeholders want from an organisation will vary. Some will actively seek to influence what the organisation does and others may be concerned with limiting the effects of the organisation's activities on themselves.

Relations with stakeholders can also vary. Possible relationships can include conflict, support, regular dialogue or joint enterprise.

Exam focus point

If you're asked to argue in favour of the stakeholder perspective in the exam, you're likely to have to consider a number of different groups of stakeholders. December 2008 Question 1 required students to assess an ethical decision from the wider stakeholder perspective.

To what extent do you believe that animals should be considered as stakeholders? This is more than just a hypothetical question.

- Vegetarians do not eat meat because they believe that eating meat is wrong. Animals are ends in themselves, and do not exist just for our pleasure.

- Some anti-vivisection campaigners, such as The Body Shop, a cosmetics retailer, state they are against 'animal testing'.

- Even if animals are to be eaten, some cultures require them to be treated well, according to humane standards, as animals are capable of suffering.

- The moral status of particular species of animals varies from **culture** to **culture**. Pigs are 'unclean' in Judaism and Islam. Beef is forbidden to Hindus. British people do not eat 'horse', although horses are eaten in other European countries. Similarly, eating dogs is perfectly acceptable in some cultures, but is totally unacceptable elsewhere. Guinea pigs are a food staple in the Andean countries, but are school pets in Britain. In some cultures, insects are eaten, in others, not.

- How would your views differ if you believed, as is the case in some religions, that animals contain the reincarnated souls of dead people?

- How would your view change if you believed that, like humans, some animal species are able to 'learn', exhibit altruistic behaviour, and that our sense of right and wrong results from evolutionary adaptation of the social behaviour patterns of our primate ancestors? (De Waal, 2001)

3.5 Instrumental and normative view of stakeholders

Donaldson and Preston suggested that there are two motivations for organisations responding to stakeholder concerns.

3.5.1 Instrumental view of stakeholders

This reflects the view that organisations have **mainly economic responsibilities** (plus the legal responsibilities that they have to fulfil in order to keep trading). In this viewpoint fulfilment of responsibilities towards stakeholders is desirable because it contributes to companies maximising their profits or fulfilling other objectives, such as gaining market share and meeting legal or stock exchange requirements. Therefore a business does not have any moral standpoint of its own. It merely reflects whatever the concerns are of the stakeholders it cannot afford to upset, such as customers looking for green companies or talented employees looking for pleasant working environments. The organisation is using shareholders **instrumentally** to pursue other objectives.

3.5.2 Normative view of stakeholders

This is based on the idea that organisations have moral duties towards stakeholders. Thus accommodating stakeholder concerns is an end in itself. This suggests the existence of **ethical and philanthropic responsibilities** as well as economic and legal responsibilities and organisations focusing on being **altruistic**.

The normative view is based on the ideas of the German philosopher Immanuel Kant. We shall discuss these in detail in Chapter 9. For now, Kant argued for the existence of **civil duties** that are important in maintaining and increasing the net good in society. Duties include the **moral duty to take account of the concerns and opinions** of others. Not to do so will result in breakdown of social cohesion leading to everyone being morally worse off, and possibly economically worse off as well.

Exam focus point

A question issued by the examiner required students to apply these two views of stakeholders to viewpoints expressed by directors.

3.6 Classifications of stakeholders

Stakeholders can be classified by their proximity to the organisation.

Stakeholder group	Members
Internal stakeholders	Employees, management
Connected stakeholders	Shareholders, customers, suppliers, lenders, trade unions, competitors
External stakeholders	The Government, local government, the public, pressure groups, opinion leaders

There are other ways of classifying stakeholders.

3.6.1 Legitimate and illegitimate stakeholders

Stakeholder group	Members
Legitimate stakeholders	Those who have valid claims on the organisation
Illegitimate stakeholders	Those whose claims on the organisation are not valid

This is possibly the most subjective distinction of all, depending as it does on views of which stakeholders should have a claim against the organisation. However, it is also the **most important**. A number of bases have been suggested for determining legitimacy.

- A contractual or exchange basis

- Different types of claim including legal, ownership or the firm being responsible for their welfare

- Stakeholders having something at risk as a result of investment in the firm or being affected by the firm's activities

- Moral grounds; that the stakeholders benefit from or are harmed by the firm, or that their rights are being violated or not respected by the firm

Ultimately how the **legitimacy of each stakeholder's claim** is viewed may well depend on the ethical and political perspective of the person judging it. The stockholder view for example would make the distinction solely on whether the stakeholder has an active economic relationship with the organisation. Stakeholders who might be difficult to categorise in this way include pressure groups and charities. However, others would argue for a wider definition, maybe including distant communities, other species, or future generations.

The problem of perception can result in **conflict** between stakeholders and the organisation. Stakeholder may claim legitimacy wrongly or management views of legitimacy may not be the same as stakeholders' own perceptions.

3.6.2 Direct and indirect stakeholders

Stakeholder group	Members
Direct stakeholders	Those who know they can affect or are affected by the organisation's activities – employees, major customers and suppliers
Indirect stakeholders	Those who are unaware of the claims they have on the organisation or who cannot express their claim directly – wildlife, individual customers or suppliers of a large organisation, future generations

This classification links to the discussion above about direct and indirect claims. It demonstrates a potential problem; that stakeholders who have the largest claim on an organisation may not be aware of its activities and its impact on them. A further issue is that indirect stakeholders' claims have to be interpreted by someone else in order to be directly expressed. How can we tell what future generations would say? Do environmental pressure groups fairly interpret the needs of the natural environment?

3.6.3 Recognised and unrecognised stakeholders

Stakeholder group	Members
Recognised stakeholders	Those whose interests and views managers consider when deciding on strategy
Unrecognised stakeholders	Those whose claims aren't taken into account in the organisation's decision-making – likely to be very much the same as illegitimate stakeholders

3.6.4 Narrow and wide stakeholders   6/09

Stakeholder group	Members
Narrow stakeholders	Those most affected by the organisation's strategy – shareholders, managers, employees, suppliers, dependent customers
Wide stakeholders	Those less affected by the organisation's strategy – government, less dependent customers, the wider community

One implication of this classification might appear to be that organisations should pay most attention to narrow stakeholders, less to wider stakeholders.

Exam focus point

Question 1 in June 2009 asked students to identify three narrow stakeholders and assess the impact of the events described in the scenario on them.

3.6.5 Primary and secondary stakeholders

Stakeholder group	Members
Primary stakeholders	Those without whose participation the organisation will have difficulty continuing as a going concern, such as shareholders, customers, suppliers and government (tax and legislation)
Secondary stakeholders	Those whose loss of participation won't affect the company's continued existence, such as broad communities (and perhaps management)

Clearly an organisation **must** keep its primary stakeholders happy. The distinction between this classification and the narrow-wide classification is that the narrow-wide classification is based on how much the **organisation affects** the stakeholder. The primary-secondary classification is based on how much the **stakeholders affect the organisation**.

3.6.6 Active and passive stakeholders

Stakeholder group	Members
Active stakeholders	Those who seek to participate in the organisation's activities. Active stakeholders include managers, employees and institutional shareholders, but may also include other groups that are not part of the organisation's structure, such as regulators or pressure groups
Passive stakeholders	Those who do not seek to participate in policy making, such as most shareholders, local communities and government

Passive stakeholders may nevertheless still be interested and powerful. If corporate governance arrangements are to develop, there may be a need for powerful passive shareholders to take a more active role. Hence, as we shall see below, there has been emphasis on institutional shareholders who own a large part of listed companies' shares actively using their power as major shareholders to promote better corporate governance.

3.6.7 Voluntary and involuntary stakeholders

Stakeholder group	Members
Voluntary stakeholders	Those who engage with the organisation of their own free will and choice, and who can detach themselves from the relationship – management, employees, customers, suppliers, shareholders and pressure groups
Involuntary stakeholders	Those whose involvement with the organisation is imposed and who cannot themselves choose to withdraw from the relationship – regulators, government, local communities, neighbours, the natural world, future generations

3.6.8 Known and unknown stakeholders

Stakeholder group	Members
Known stakeholders	Those whose existence is known to the organisation
Unknown stakeholders	Those whose existence is unknown to the organisation (undiscovered species, communities in proximity to overseas suppliers)

This distinction is important if you argue that an organisation should seek out all possible stakeholders before a decision is taken. The implication of this view is that the organisation should aim for its policies to have **minimum impact**.

Exam focus point

The examiner may ask you in your exam to identify the stakeholders mentioned in a case scenario, using stockholder and stakeholder perspectives.

3.7 Assessing the relative importance of stakeholder interests

Apart from the problem of taking different stakeholder interests into account, an organisation also faces the problem of **weighing shareholder interests** when considering future strategy. How, for example, do you compare the interest of a major shareholder with the interest of a local resident coping with the noise and smell from the company's factory?

3.8 Power and interest

One way of weighing stakeholder interests is to look at the **power** they exert and the **level of interest** they have about its activities.

Mendelow classifies stakeholders on a matrix whose axes are **power** held and likelihood of showing an **interest** in the organisation's activities. These factors will help define the type of relationship the organisation should seek with its stakeholders and how it should view their concerns. Mendelow's matrix represents a continuum, a map for plotting the relative influence of stakeholders. Stakeholders in the bottom right of the continuum are more significant because they combine the highest power and influence.

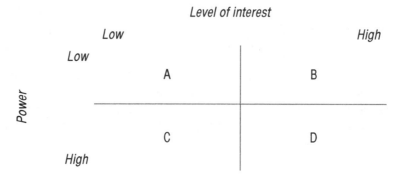

(a)   **Key players** are found in Segment D. The organisation's strategy must be **acceptable** to them, at least. An example would be a major customer.

(b)   Stakeholders in Segment C must be treated with care. They are capable of moving to Segment D. They should therefore be **kept satisfied**. Large institutional shareholders might fall into Segment C.

(c)   Stakeholders in Segment B do not have great ability to influence strategy, but their views can be important in influencing more powerful stakeholders, perhaps by lobbying. They should therefore be **kept informed**. Community representatives and charities might fall into Segment B.

(d)   Minimal effort is expended on Segment A.

Stakeholder mapping is used to assess the significance of stakeholders. This in turn has implications for the organisation.

(a)   The framework of corporate governance and the direction and control of the business should recognise **stakeholders' levels** of **interest** and **power**.

(b)   Companies may try to **reposition** certain stakeholders and discourage others from repositioning themselves, depending on their attitudes.

(c)   Key **blockers** and **facilitators** of change must be identified.

(d)   Stakeholder mapping can also be used to establish **future priorities**.

3.8.1 Using Mendelow's approach to analyse stakeholders

Power means who can exercise **most influence** over a particular decision (though the power may not be used). These include those who **actively participate** in decision-making (normally directors, senior managers) or those whose views are **regularly consulted** on important decisions (major shareholders). It can also in a negative sense mean those who have the right of veto over major decisions (creditors with a charge on major business assets can prevent those assets being sold to raise money). Stakeholders may be more influential if their power is combined with:

- **Legitimacy**: the company perceives the stakeholders' claims to be valid
- **Urgency**: whether the stakeholder claim requires immediate action

Level of interest reflects the **effort** stakeholders put in to attempting to participate in the organisation's activities, whether they succeed or not. It also reflects the amount of knowledge stakeholders have about what the organisation is doing.

Question	Mendelow's matrix

Goaway Hotels is a chain of hotels based in one country. Ninety per cent of its shares are held by members of the family of the founder of the Goaway group. None of the family members is a director of the company. Over the last few years, the family has been quite happy with the steady level of dividends that their investment has generated. Directors are encouraged to achieve high profits by means of a remuneration package with potentially very large profit-related bonuses.

The directors of Goaway Hotels currently wish to take significant steps to increase profits. The area they are focusing on at present is labour costs. Over the last couple of years, many of the workers they have recruited have been economic migrants from another country, the East Asian People's Republic (EAPR). The EAPR workers are paid around 30% of the salary of indigenous workers, and receive fewer benefits. However, these employment terms are considerably better than those that the workers would receive in the EAPR. Goaway Hotels has been able to fill its vacancies easily from this source, and the workers from the EAPR that Goaway has recruited have mostly stayed with the company. The board has been considering imposing tougher employment contracts on home country workers, perhaps letting the number of dismissals and staff turnover of home country workers increase significantly.

In Goaway Hotels' home country, there has been a long period of rule by a government that wished to boost business and thus relaxed labour laws to encourage more flexible working. However, a year ago the opposition party finally won power, having pledged in their manifesto to tighten labour laws to give more rights to home country employees. Since their election the new Government has brought in the promised labour legislation, and there have already been successful injunctions obtained, preventing companies from imposing less favourable employment terms on their employees.

An international chain of hotels has recently approached various members of the founding family with an offer for their shares. The international chain is well known for its aggressive approach to employee relations and the high demands it makes on its managers. Local employment laws allow some renegotiation of employment terms if companies are taken over.

Required

Using Mendelow's matrix, analyse the importance of the following stakeholders to the decision to change the employment terms of home country's workers in Goaway Hotels.

(a)   The board of directors
(b)   The founding family shareholders
(c)   The trade unions to which the home country workers belong
(d)   Migrant workers

Answer

Remember that we are talking about one specific decision so we need to focus on that decision.

The board of directors

Power: Low, surprisingly perhaps. However, the new employment legislation appears to limit significantly directors' freedom to reduce labour costs by changing contractual terms. The directors also have little say over the decision of shareholders to sell shares. (This demonstrates that you cannot take anyone's role for granted.)

Level of interest: High, as this is a major decision, integral to the directors' plans for the future of the Goaway hotel chain. It may also have a significant effect on their remuneration.

Shareholders

Power: High, because the shareholders are currently in a position to sell their shares if they feel that they have received a good offer. If they do, unions and employees may find that the international company is able to take a much tougher approach.

Level of interest: Low, as none of them participate actively in Goaway's decision-making. Their main concern is whether to continue to take dividends or realise a capital gain from their investment.

Trade unions

Power: High. This is because they have the economic power to take legal action to prevent Goaway from changing their members' employment terms.

Level of interest: High. This is because they wish to protect their members.

Migrant workers

Power: Low. This is because replacement workers can be recruited easily from the home country.

Level of interest: Low. The migrant workers seem quite happy with their current employment terms, even though these are not as favourable as the home country's workers.

3.8.2 Problems with stakeholder mapping

There are however a number of issues with Mendelow's approach:

(a)   It can be **very difficult to measure each stakeholder's power and influence**.

(b)   The map is **not static**. Changing circumstances may mean stakeholders' positions move around the map. For example, stakeholders with a lot of interest but not much power may improve their position by combining with other stakeholders with similar views.

(c)   The map is based on the idea that **strategic positioning**, rather than moral or ethical concerns, should govern an organisation's attitude to its stakeholders.

(d)   If there are a number of key players, and their views are in conflict, it can be very difficult to resolve the situation, hence there may be **uncertainties** over the organisation's future direction.

(e)   Mendelow's matrix considers power and influence but fails to take **legitimacy** into account. Legitimacy is a distinct concept from power. For example, minority shareholders in a company controlled by a strong majority may not have much power, but law in most countries recognises that they have legitimate rights which the company must respect. Mitchell, Agle and Wood argue that legitimacy is a desirable social goal, dependent on more than the perception of individual stakeholders.

Exam focus point

Please remember that Mendelow's grid is a tool to be applied to help you understand the importance of different stakeholders. It is not something to be discussed every time you see the word stakeholder.

The examiner's report for the December 2007 exam complained that, when the question asked students to explain the importance of identifying stakeholders, this did **not** mean, as many students thought it did, describing the Mendelow matrix or each stakeholder's position on the Mendelow matrix.

3.9 Reconciling viewpoints of different stakeholders

Jensen argued that **enlightened long-term value maximisation** offers the best and fairest method of reconciling the competing interests of stakeholders. Enlightened long-term value maximisation means pursuing profit maximisation, but with regard to **business ethics** and the **social consequences of the organisation's actions**. It is like the expedient stance identified by Gray, Owen and Adams, which we shall cover in Chapter 11. Jensen argued that the problem with traditional stakeholder theory is that it gave no indication of how to trade off competing interests. Lacking measurable targets, managers are therefore left unaccountable for their actions.

4 Roles of stakeholders

FAST FORWARD

Governance reports have emphasised the role of **institutional investors** (insurance companies, pension funds, investment houses) in directing companies towards good corporate governance.

4.1 Roles of stakeholders in corporate governance

Corporate governance reports worldwide have concentrated significantly on the roles, interests and claims of the internal and external stakeholders involved.

4.2 Directors

The powers of directors to run the company are set out in the company's **constitution or articles**.

Under corporate governance best practice there is a distinction between the role of **executive directors**, who are involved **full time in managing the company**, and the **non-executive directors**, who primarily focus on **monitoring**. However, under company law in most jurisdictions the legal duties of directors and responsibility for performance, controls, compliance and behaviour apply to both executive and non-executive directors.

The role of directors in corporate governance is obviously central. In future chapters we shall examine what happens when directors fail to exercise proper supervision.

4.3 Company secretary

Company legislation in many countries requires companies to appoint a company secretary as a condition of registration. The secretary is seen as an important figure in ensuring compliance with legal and other regulatory frameworks. Legislation makes reference to certain specific duties of the company secretary but does not provide a general definition of what the company secretary should do. The secretary's precise duties will vary according to the size of company. The most important duties, however, will be in the following areas.

(a) **Arranging meetings of shareholders and the board of directors**

Duties include giving notice of the meeting, issuing the agenda in advance, attending the meeting and ensuring that proper procedures are followed, drafting and circulating the minutes. Importantly the secretary may be responsible for **communicating** the **decisions** to the **staff** of the company or to outsiders. The secretary may also advise the board about their regulatory and legal responsibilities and duties.

(b) **Signing, authentication and maintenance of documents and registers**

The secretary will normally be responsible for completing and signing the annual return of the company and delivering various other statutory documents, including the annual accounts, to the authorities. The secretary is also responsible for maintaining the statutory registers.

(c) **General administrative duties**

The secretary may act as the general administrator and head office manager. Tasks include ensuring compliance with the company's constitution and other statutory and regulatory requirements, such as the Listing Rules. The secretary may also be responsible for **maintaining the accounting records** required by law, **corresponding with legal advisers**, tax authorities, trade associations, etc and **administering the office**.

4.3.1 Independence and competence of the secretary

Whatever the duties of the secretary, their **ultimate loyalty** must be to the company. This may mean the secretary coming into conflict with, for example, a director or even the chief executive. If one of the directors has a clear **conflict of interest** between their duties to the company and their personal interests, the company secretary should ensure that the board minutes reflect the conflict. If the conflict prevents a director from voting and being counted in the quorum at the board meeting, the proper procedure should be followed.

Because of the legal knowledge that the secretary needs to have, in many countries the secretary of a listed or public company is required to be a member of an accountancy or company secretarial body.

4.3.2 Statement of best practice

ICSA, the Institute of Chartered Secretaries and Administrators, has published a Statement of Best Practice on reporting lines for the company secretary.

(a) The company secretary is **responsible** to the **board**, and should be **accountable** to the board through the chairman on all matters relating to their duties as an officer of the company (the core duties).

(b) If the company secretary has other executive or administrative duties beyond the core duties, they should **report** to the **chief executive** or such other director to whom responsibility for the matter has been delegated.

(c) The company secretary's **salary**, share options and benefits should be **settled** by the **board** or remuneration committee on the recommendation of the chairman or chief executive.

ICSA has argued strongly in favour of the importance of the role its members undertake. ICSA has campaigned, unsuccessfully, against the removal of the requirement in UK law for a private company to be required to appoint a company secretary. Public companies in the UK are still required to appoint a secretary.

ICSA has highlighted the following contributions that a secretary can make.

(a) **Probity of the company**

A company secretary is responsible for **protecting** the **probity** of a company. They are a guard against the directors acting in their own interests rather than those of the company. An important aspect of the role is to remind directors of their responsibilities. The secretary also acts to **protect the interests of third-party shareholders and other stakeholders**, and is also responsible for interpreting the decisions of the board and ensuring they are implemented throughout the company.

(b) **Legal compliance**

Under companies' legislation, the secretary (as an officer of the company) is held responsible for numerous **breaches** of law. Directors' **priorities and areas of expertise** may not be in the areas of governance and compliance.

(c) **Governance**

ICSA argues that, if a secretary is appointed when a company is formed, this should mean that the principles of compliance and good governance are **embedded** in the company's procedures from the start. These aspects will be of critical importance as the company grows towards listing.

4.4 Sub-board management

Their interests are similar to the directors in many respects, and they may be concerned with corporate governance from the viewpoint of being potential main board directors. They will also be interested in how corporate governance decisions **impact on their current position** (how much decision-making will be delegated to them and in what areas? What parameters will they be obliged to follow?). As employees, managers will also have **interests in pay and working conditions** as described below.

Although sub-board management does not have ultimate responsibility for decision-making within a company, its role in corporate governance is vital. In order to function effectively the board needs to be supported by a strong senior management team, responsible for implementing strategy and controlling and co-ordinating activities. The management team will be responsible for:

- Helping to set the tone of the company (we discuss this in Chapter 5)
- Supervising the implementation of control and risk management procedures (discussed in Chapter 7)
- Providing information that directors need to make decisions about strategy, risk management and control (discussed in Chapter 8)

Shortcomings in any of these areas could seriously undermine the effectiveness of governance.

4.5 Employees

Employees of course play a vital role in the **implementation of strategy**. They need to **comply with the corporate governance systems** in place and **adopt appropriate culture**. Their commitment to the job may be considerable, involving changes when taking the job (moving house), dependency if in the job for a long time (not just financial but in utilising skills that may not be portable elsewhere) and fulfilment as a human being (developing a career, entering relationships).

Employees will focus on how the company is **performing**, and how the company's performance will impact on their **pay and working conditions**. UK company law has required the directors to have regard to the interests of the company's employees in general as well as the interests of its members. Other European jurisdictions have gone further in terms of employee participation.

Employees also have information requirements. Surveys suggest that the most interesting information for employees is information **concerned with the immediate work environment** and which is **future-orientated**. There are a number of ways in which this information can be provided.

- An organisation-wide employee report
- Organisation-wide information on financial results, information on personnel or sales at a unit level
- Statements by managers on their individual activities
- Separate inserts about each division

Employees' contribution to corporate governance is to implement the risk management and control procedures. As we shall see in Chapter 5, the company's culture will impact significantly on this, so that if enforcement measures are lax or employees do not have the skills or knowledge necessary to implement procedures, governance will be undermined.

Employees also have a role in giving regular feedback to management and of whistleblowing serious concerns. Again, poor communication, perhaps because employees are scared to raise issues or management won't listen, will impact adversely on governance.

Exam focus point

The role of employees as informants was tested in the Pilot Paper Question 4. Staff demonstrating a lack of awareness of risk was an issue in December 2007 Question 2.

4.6 Trade unions   6/10

Trade unions exist to protect employee interests, so will be interested in the pay, prospects and working conditions of their members. They may be concerned about aspects of poor corporate governance; for example, failure by directors to **communicate** with employees or failure to protect whistleblowers. Trade unions will also be concerned about a **lax control and risk environment**, which may jeopardise health and safety or which permits bullying or discrimination by managers or other employees. However, they may also be concerned with an environment that is excessively controlling and which **curtails their members' privacy at work**. Their influence will depend on the percentage of employees that are members. Trade unions can distribute **information to employees** or **ascertain their views**.

A good relationship with trade unions can have many benefits for a company. Union members will often have similar objectives for the organisation to senior management and **share management's values**. The trade unions can harness this and help ensure that the workforce is committed to implementing strategy. Unity between management and unions will appeal to those who do business with the company. A good relationship can help **maximise productivity** by a contented workforce.

Trade union influence can also act as a balancing factor in corporate governance, highlighting abuses by management which would also concern shareholders.

Trade unions are also exercising their influence through **pension funds**, pressing for change by use of voting rights. The strength of trade unions varies from country to country. In France, where union rights are extended to all employees, unionisation has a greater impact on corporate decision-making than it can do in the UK where only union members benefit from collective bargaining agreements.

In some jurisdictions trade unions will have a formal role in governance, possibly on a two-tier board which we shall look at later on. Trade unions may play a role that is supportive of governance or hostile to it. For example, management attempts to encourage whistleblowing of other employees' poor practice may meet with resistance.

4.7 Suppliers

Major suppliers will often be key stakeholders, particularly in businesses where **material costs and quality** are significant. Supplier co-operation is also important if organisations are trying to improve their management of assets by keeping inventory levels to a minimum. They will need to rely on suppliers for reliability of delivery. If the **relationship with suppliers deteriorates** because of a poor payment record, suppliers can limit or withdraw credit and charge higher rates of interest. They can also reduce their level of service, or even switch to supplying competitors.

4.8 Customers

Customers have increasingly high **expectations of the goods and services** they buy, both from the private and public sectors. These include not just low costs, but value for money, quality and service support.

In theory, if consumers are not happy with their purchases, they will take their business elsewhere next time. With increasingly competitive markets, consumers are able to exercise increasing levels of power over companies.

More sophisticated analysis of consumer behaviour has also enhanced the importance of consumers. Dissatisfied customers are **more likely to make their views known** than satisfied customers. Moreover, businesses now believe that normally the costs of retaining existing customers are significantly less than those of obtaining new customers.

Consumers are increasingly evaluating goods and services not just on the basis of how they will satisfy their immediate material needs but also on how they will satisfy their **deeper moral needs**. For example, a shopper may prefer one brand of baked beans not for its taste but because the manufacturer supports a good cause of which the consumer approves.

4.8.1 Public sector requirements

Public sector governance requirements stress the need for assessing the effectiveness of policy and arrangements for dialogue with users of services. The UK *Good Governance Standard for Public Services* points out that organisations can use a range of methods to find out the views, and promote the involvement of service users, including citizens' juries and community time banks (mutual volunteering by members of the public working alongside service providers to support their neighbours).

4.9 External auditors

The external audit is one of the most important corporate governance procedures. It enables investors to have much greater **confidence** in the information that their agents, the directors/managers, are supplying. The main focus of the external audit is on giving assurance that the accounts give a true and fair view but external auditors can provide other audit services such as social and environmental audits (discussed in Chapter 11). They can also highlight governance and reporting issues of concern to investors. External auditors are employed to scrutinise the activities of the managers, who are the shareholders' agents. Their audit fees can be seen as an agency cost. As discussed above, this means that external auditors are also the shareholders' agents. Auditors are also acting on behalf of regulators and the government, and perhaps other stakeholders.

Because of the significance of the external audit, the external auditors must be **independent**.

A balance is required between working constructively with company management and at the same time serving the interests of shareholders. The balance can be attained by companies **establishing audit committees** and the accounting profession **developing effective accounting standards**.

4.10 Regulators

Key term

> **Regulation** can be defined as any form of interference with the operation of the free market. This could involve regulating demand, supply, price, profit, quantity, quality, entry, exit, information, technology, or any other aspect of production and consumption in the market.

This category includes government bodies, such as health and safety executives, and regulators, such as the financial services authorities, utility regulators and charity commissioners, among many others relevant to specific types of industry. Regulator approval will be required before the organisation is allowed to operate and receive the benefits of action; for example, favourable tax status for charities or being able to offer financial advice for financial services institutions.

4.10.1 Methods of regulation

Legislators and regulators affect organisations' governance and risk management. They establish **rules and standards** that provide the impetus for management to ensure that risk management and control systems meet minimum requirements. They also conduct inspections and audits that provide useful information and recommendations regarding possible improvements. Regulators will be particularly interested in **maintaining shareholder-stakeholder confidence** in the information with which they are being provided.

In specific situations regulators may have other actions available.

Competition authorities are responsible for ensuring diversity wherever possible, but sometimes the industry is a natural monopoly.

The two main methods used to regulate monopoly industries are as follows.

(a)   **Price control**

The regulator agreeing the output prices with the industry. Typically, the price is progressively reduced in real terms each year by setting price increases at a rate below that of inflation. This has been used with success by regulators in the UK but can be confrontational.

(b)   **Profit control**

The regulator agreeing the maximum profit that the industry can make. A typical method is to fix maximum profit at x% of capital employed. However, this does not provide any incentive to make more efficient use of assets. The higher the capital employed, the higher the profit will be.

In addition, the regulator will be concerned with:

(a)   Actively **promoting competition** by encouraging new firms in the industry and preventing unreasonable barriers to entry

(b)   Addressing **quality** and **safety** issues and considering the **social implications** of service provision and pricing

4.10.2 Costs of regulation

The potential costs of regulation include the following.

(a)   **Enforcement costs**

Regulation can only be effective if it is properly monitored and enforced. **Direct costs** of enforcement include the setting up and running of the regulatory agencies – employing specialist staff, monitoring behaviour, prosecuting offenders (or otherwise ensuring actions are modified in line with regulations). **Indirect costs** are those incurred by the regulated (eg the firms in the industry) in conforming to the restrictions.

(b)   **Regulatory capture**

This refers to the process by which the regulator becomes **dominated and controlled by the regulated firms**, such that it acts increasingly in the firm's interests, rather than those of consumers. This is a phenomenon that has been observed in the US (where economic regulation has always been more widespread).

(c)   **Unintended consequences of regulation**

An example is the so-called 'Aversch-Johnson effect'. This refers to the tendency of rate of return (profit) regulation to encourage firms to become too capital intensive and therefore minimise their return on capital. Companies try to **maximise their asset base** so that their return on capital employed is low. It appears to be a concern in the telecommunications industry. In other words, firms regulated in this way have an incentive to choose a method of production that is not least-cost, because it involves too high a ratio of capital to labour.

4.10.3 Regulation and stakeholders

Where privatisation has perpetuated monopolies over natural resources, industry regulatory authorities have the role of ensuring that **consumers' interests** are not subordinated to those of other stakeholders, such as employees, shareholders and tax authorities. The regulator's role may be 'advisory' rather than statutory. It may extend only to a part of a company's business, necessitating a fair allocation of costs across different activities of the company.

Case Study

Benston (2000) provides six reasons for the regulation imposed to protect consumers of banking, securities and insurance. Regulations are imposed to:

- Maintain consumer confidence in the financial system
- Ensure that a supplier on whom consumers (eg of a major utility) rely does not fail
- Ensure that consumers receive sufficient information to make 'good' decisions and are dealt with fairly
- Ensure fair pricing of financial services
- Protect consumers from fraud and misrepresentation
- Prevent invidious discrimination against individuals

4.10.4 Regulators and corporate governance

Regulators will also be concerned with how corporate governance guidance affects the way organisations deal with changing circumstances.

 Case Study

A good example of a major change requiring a different approach to regulation has been the liberalisation of the activities by financial institutions in many countries. The traditional separation of financial institutions into banks, insurance companies, brokers and investment companies has been abolished and financial institutions engage in all these activities. The risks to which a multiproduct financial institution is exposed can be significantly different to the risks that each of the individual component parts eg the banking division are exposed.

In practice, the task of keeping regulation up to date and relevant is made more challenging by the pace of innovation in financial products and the development of financial markets and institutions and by globalisation.

The question that arises is: How much regulation should there be? And is there perhaps an optimal level of regulation?

According to McMenamin in *Financial Management – An Introduction*, 'regulation is essentially a question of balance ... too little or ineffective regulation leaves the markets open to abuse, too much regulation makes markets rigid, costly to operate and uncompetitive'.

As a result of the problems in the banking sector over the last few years, the distinction between regulation of banks' retail activities (operations concerned with customer deposits, business lending and the transmission of money) and investment activities has been much debated.

In June 2010 the Independent Commission on Banking in the UK (the Vickers Commission, chaired by economist Sir John Vickers) was set up by the incoming Coalition Government. It produced its final report in September 2011. The report recommended that UK banks' domestic retail operations (operations concerned with customer deposits, business lending and the transmission of money) should be ring-fenced from their wholesale and investment operations. Retail banking activities should be carried out by separate subsidiaries within banking groups, with the ringfenced part of the bank having its own board and being legally and operationally separate from the parent bank. Retail banks should have equity capital of 10% of risk-weighted assets and UK banking groups should have primary loss-making capacity of at least 17-20% – equity, bonds and cocos (contingent convertible notes) – to act as a safety buffer.

Non-retail parts of banking groups should be allowed to fail. The report anticipated that this would mean that their cost of capital went up. However, the lack of guaranteed government support for investment activities should mean that banks were less likely to take excessive risks in this area.

Banks were given until 2019 to implement these requirements fully, a period felt by some commentators to be very lengthy. The time period was set to coincide with the international capital requirements changes being introduced by the Basel regulators.

In May 2012 the UK Government set out details of a banking reform bill, giving the UK Treasury the power to ringfence the retail operations of large banks from their investment divisions, and to ensure that depositors recover their money before unsecured creditors if a bank becomes insolvent.

4.10.5 Regulators and charities

As previously mentioned, charities receive favourable regulatory treatment but in return they must demonstrate their benevolent purposes and apply for recognition by the country's charity commission or equivalent.

4.11 Government

Most governments do not have a direct economic/financial interest in companies (except for those in which they hold shares). However, governments often have a strong indirect interest in companies' affairs, hence the way they are run and the information that is provided about them.

(a)   Governments raise **taxes** on sales and profits and on shareholders' dividends. They also expect companies to act as tax collectors for income tax and sales tax. The tax structure might influence investors' preferences for either dividends or capital growth. Economic policies such as deregulation may be influenced by the desire for economic growth and increased efficiency.

(b)   Governments pass and enforce laws, and also establish and determine the **overall regulatory and control climate** in a country. This involves exertion of fiscal pressure, and other methods of state intervention. Governments also determine whether the regulatory framework is **principles or rules based** (discussed later in the text).

(c)   Governments may **provide funds** towards the cost of some investment projects. They may also encourage private investment by offering tax incentives.

(d)   In the UK, the Government has made some attempts to encourage more private individuals to become company shareholders, by means of:

   (i)   Attractive **privatisation** issues (such as in the electricity, gas and telecommunications industries)

   (ii)   **Tax incentives**, such as ISAs (Individual Savings Accounts), to encourage individuals to invest in shares

(e)   Governments also influence companies, and the relationships between companies, their directors, shareholders and other stakeholders.

4.11.1 Objectives of public sector organisations

One problem, which we discussed in the context of agency, is that objectives of public sector organisations have to be established in the light of political pressures, caused by varying taxpayer demands. Some taxpayers may want a public sector organisation to do much more, others may want it to do less or cease to exist with a resultant tax saving. Control mechanisms such as audit can test the **integrity and transparency of transactions, but may not cover performance or fitness for purpose**.

4.11.2 Privatisation

Key term

> **Privatisation** means that the Government attempts to establish an accurate market value for a state-owned enterprise and then sell shares in that enterprise on the country's stock exchange.

Privatisation has been an instrument of policy used by a number of governments over recent years in industries such as energy, water, transport and minerals. The privatised organisation is no longer controlled by the state. Instead it is subject to company law and listing rules. The company may be exposed to a competitive market for the first time, requiring a different skill set from its directors and a large internal culture change.

4.11.3 Nationalisation

Key term

Nationalisation involves the Government taking a business from its shareholders into public ownership.

During the second half of the 20th century the governments of many developed countries moved away from nationalisation, taking many companies out of public ownership and into the private sector. Nationalised industries have been more important in developing countries.

However, recent developments in the financial sector, such as the UK Government nationalising the Northern Rock bank, have focused attention on nationalisation and its implications, including implications for governance and stakeholders.

Key issues here are the **reasons for** nationalisation and the **length of time** for which businesses will be nationalised. The UK Government stated when Northern Rock was nationalised that nationalisation would be a temporary measure. The precedent may have been the purchase of the Johnson Matthey bank by the Bank of England under a short-term rescue package in the 1980s, with Johnson Matthey subsequently trading profitably.

However, the purchase of Northern Rock and intervention in other banks could be seen as helping to guarantee the country's **financial infrastructure**. This might otherwise be undermined by a lack of confidence and result in economic recession or collapse. Other infrastructure investments (for example Network Rail in the UK) have tended to be for the longer term.

Northern Rock's nationalisation must also be seen in the context of other UK Government measures to boost the economy, including encouragement of bank lending. This raises the issue of how far the Government should intervene in the operations of the bank, so that the bank's lending decisions clearly reflect government objectives.

This uncertainty of motivation means that there is also a lack of clarity over the significance of different stakeholders in the bank's operations.

(a)   The Government presented the nationalisation in terms of it acting as agents for the **taxpayers**, who were effectively the new shareholders. The decision to nationalise was portrayed as the best economic decision in the circumstances. The Government rejected two rescue bids by Virgin and the bank's management on economic grounds.

(b)   However, government intervention has also served the interests of the **depositors** in the banks, who would otherwise have risked losing some of their savings.

(c)   The position with regard to **borrowers** is complex. If the bank is to be sold on as a going concern, over-generous packages to borrowers will not increase its attractiveness to potential purchasers.

Traditionally, however, ideas of equity and fairness have been applied in public sector organisations – how do they relate to borrowers here?

Exam focus
point

As nationalisation is currently a topical issue, the issues raised by having government and taxpayers as principals rather than shareholders will be examinable.

4.12 Stock exchanges

Stock exchanges provide a means for companies to **raise money** and investors to **transfer their shares** easily. They also provide information about company value, derived from the supply of, and demand for, the shares that they trade. Stock exchanges list companies whose shares can be held by the general public (called public companies in many jurisdictions). Many such companies have a clear separation between ownership and management.

Stock exchanges are important because they provide **regulatory frameworks** in principle-based jurisdictions. In most countries, listing rules apply to companies whose shares are listed on the stock exchange. Stock exchange regulation can therefore have a significant impact on the way corporate governance is implemented and companies report. The UK is a good example of this, with the comply or explain approach being consistent with the approach of self-regulation of London institutions. In America, by contrast, a more legalistic and rules-based approach has been adopted, in line with the regulatory approach that is already in place.

4.13 Institutional investors 12/10, 6/14

Key term

> **Institutional investors** have large amounts of money to invest. They are covered by fewer protective regulations, on the grounds that they are knowledgeable and able to protect themselves. They include investors managing funds invested by individuals. The term also includes agents employed on the investors' behalf.

Institutional investors are now the biggest investors in many stock markets but they might also invest venture capital, or lend directly to companies. UK trends show that institutional investors can wield great powers over the companies in which they invest.

| Question | Institutional investors |

Before looking at the following paragraph, see if you can list the major types of institutional investor in the UK.

The major institutional investors in the UK are:

- **Pension funds**
- **Insurance companies**
- **Investment and unit trusts** (set up to invest in portfolios of shares)
- **Venture capital organisations** (investors particularly interested in companies that are seeking to expand)

Their funds will be managed by a fund manager who aims to benefit investors in the funds or pension or policy holders. Although fund managers will use lots of different sources of information, their agency costs will be high in total because they have to track the performance of all the investments that the fund makes.

4.13.1 Advantages and disadvantages of institutional investment

In some respects the **institutional investor** fulfils a desirable role. People should ideally be in pensionable employment or have personal pension plans, and the funds from which their pensions will be payable should be held separately from the companies by whom they are employed. Similarly, investors should have the opportunity to invest through the medium of insurance companies, unit trusts and investment trusts.

However, the dominance of the equity markets by institutional investors has possibly undesirable consequences as well.

(a) **Excessive market influence**

For capital markets to be truly competitive there should be no **investors** who are of **such size** that they **can influence prices**. In the UK, transactions by the largest institutions are now on such a massive scale that considerable price movements can result.

(b)   **Playing safe**

Many institutions tend to **avoid shares** which are seen as **speculative** as they feel that they have a duty to their 'customers' to invest only in 'blue chip' shares (ie those of leading commercially sound companies). As a result, the shares of such companies tend to be relatively expensive.

(c)   **Short-term speculation**

Fund managers are sometimes accused of **'short-termism'** in that they will tend to seek short-term speculative gains or simply sell their shares and invest elsewhere if they feel that there are management shortcomings. Pension fund trustees are also accused of being over-influenced by short-term results because of the lack of time they have to go into the company's performance in detail. However, arguably, institutional investors have become so influential that they are less able to divest from companies without suffering a substantial loss in order to liquidate their holdings. They have therefore been forced to adopt a more long-term outlook.

(d)   **Lack of power of investors**

Investors in investment and pension funds **cannot directly influence the policy** of the companies in which their funds invest, since they do not hold shares themselves and cannot hold the company accountable at general meetings.

4.13.2 Role of institutional investors

UK guidance has placed significant emphasis on the role of institutional investors in promoting good corporate governance. The UK Corporate Governance Code states that shareholders should enter into a dialogue with companies based on the **mutual understanding of objectives**, taking into account the size and complexity of the companies and the risks they face. Their representatives should attend company annual general meetings and make considered use of their votes.

UK guidance stresses that institutional investors should consider, in particular, companies' governance arrangements that relate to **board structure and composition**. They should enter a dialogue about departures from the Code if they do not accept the companies' position.

4.13.3 Statement of best practice

The UK Corporate Governance Code refers to guidance in the UK Stewardship Code, published in July 2010 and revised in September 2012. The Stewardship Code states that institutional investors should:

(a)   Disclose how they will **discharge their responsibilities**

(b)   **Operate a clearly disclosed policy** for managing conflicts of interest

(c)   **Monitor performance of investee companies** to gain assurance on the operation of the board and its committees by attending meetings of the board and the AGM and should be particularly concerned with departures from the UK Corporate Governance Code, and also seek to identify threats to shareholder value at an early stage

(d)   **Establish clear guidelines** on when they will actively intervene, when they are concerned about strategy and performance, governance or approach to risk

(e)   Be willing to act **collectively with other investors**, particularly at times of significant stress or when the company's existence appears to be threatened

(f)   Operate a clear policy on **voting and disclosure of voting activity**; they should not necessarily support the board

(g)   **Report** to their clients on their stewardship and voting activities; they should consider obtaining an independent audit opinion on their engagement and voting processes.

As well as this guidance, the Myners report on proxy votes and the role of owners in administering them is also relevant to the role of institutional investors and their fund managers (see Chapter 3).

4.13.4 Means of exercising institutional investors' influence

A number of different methods may be effective.

(a) **One to one meetings**

These discuss strategy, whether objectives are being achieved, how the company is achieving its objectives and the quality of management. However, new information cannot be divulged to any single analyst or investor in these meetings, as it would give that investor an information advantage over others.

(b) **Voting**

Generally institutional investors would prefer to work behind the scenes and to avoid voting against the board if possible. If they were intending to oppose a resolution, they should normally state their intention in advance. Most corporate governance reports emphasise the importance of institutional investors exercising their votes regularly and responsibly.

(c) **Focus list**

This means putting companies' names on a list of underperforming companies. Such companies' boards may face challenges.

(d) **Contributing to corporate governance rating systems**

These measure key corporate governance performance indicators such as the number of non-executive directors, the role of the board and the transparency of the company.

4.13.5 Intervention by institutional shareholders

In extreme circumstances the institutional shareholders may intervene more actively, by for example calling a company meeting in an attempt to unseat the board. The UK Institutional Shareholders' Committee has identified a number of reasons why institutional investors might intervene.

- Fundamental concerns about the **strategy** being pursued in terms of products, markets and investments
- **Poor operational performance**, particularly if one or more key segments has persistently underperformed
- Management being dominated by a small group of executive directors, with the **non-executive directors failing to hold management to account**
- **Major failures in internal controls**, particularly in sensitive areas such as health and safety, pollution and quality
- **Failure to comply with laws and regulations or governance codes**
- **Excessive levels of directors' remuneration**
- **Poor attitudes towards corporate social responsibility**

Case Study

The response by institutional investors in the UK to the Vickers report on the banking sector discussed above raised questions about their attitudes towards wider stakeholder concerns. *The Telegraph* in the UK reported in September 2011 that a 'secret' meeting between the leading investors and members of the Treasury Select Committee had taken place. At this meeting investors had apparently demanded that the provisions of the Vickers report should be watered down, stating that they would prevent the market value and return on equity of banks improving from unacceptably low levels. Investors alleged that the proposals would put UK banks at a significant disadvantage compared with competitors in America and Europe.

Concerns were also expressed by those working within the banking sector. On the morning of 14 September 2011 Carsten Kengeter, the head of UBS's investment bank, voiced concerns about the costs of ringfencing retail banking operations from investment banking activities. Hours later he was being briefed on a very large alleged rogue trading scandal at UBS (discussed further in Chapter 6), a scandal which some commentators suggested vindicated proposals for separating different banking functions.

The publication of guidance recently has made intervention by institutional shareholders a topical area. Question 1 in December 2010 asked students to consider what might prompt intervention and at what point it should happen.

4.14 Small investors

The Organisation for Economic Co-operation and Development suggested that a key principle of corporate governance is that all shareholders should be treated **equally**. However, if institutional investors become more influential, they may be treated better by company managers.

Small investors include shareholders who hold small numbers of shares in companies, trusts and funds. They may not have the same ease of access to information that institutional investors possess, or the level of understanding of experts employed by institutional investors. Their portfolios are likely to be narrower and they may be less able to diversify risk away. These problems can handicap their position.

4.15 Stakeholders in the not for profit sector

In many countries there are thousands of charities and voluntary organisations that exist to fulfil a particular purpose, maybe social, environmental, religious or humanitarian. In most countries they are allowed tax privileges and reduced legal requirements. Charities will be accountable to those who supply them with donations. **Transparency**, particularly as regards who receives aid and the reasons for expenditure for non-charitable purposes, will be significant.

4.15.1 Primary stakeholders

Primary stakeholders of charities include not only donors and regulators but also grant providers, service users and the general public.

4.15.2 Representing stakeholder interests

As previously discussed, some stakeholders may not have their own voice (for example animals benefiting from the work of animal charities) and it will be up to trustees to represent their interests as best they can.

A number of issues will influence trustees' decisions.

(a) **Prioritisation of resources**

Depending on how widely the charity's purposes are defined, there is likely to be a variety of uses to which the charity's resources can be put. These will have varying impacts, **direct and indirect, short and long term**. Animal charities spending considerable sums of money on **publicity campaigns** may help educate the public and, over the longer term improve the treatment of animals and change society's basic values. However, they will have no direct impact on animals that are currently suffering.

(b) **Taking over government roles**

There may be some tasks in society that charities take over because government is **not providing a particular service or not providing it very well**. For example in some countries animal charities have taken over stray control services, carrying out a range of humane actions rather than the brutal, undiscriminating, catch and kill activities of public sector animal catchers.

Charity trustees may have to answer criticism from donors and other stakeholders if they do this. Some supporters may argue that the task has to be done and it is in line with the charity's purposes. Others may argue that the charity should not be supplying services that governments should provide, and it takes resources away from other, important, charitable activities. There may also be a conflict between a desire to co-operate with government when providing a service and a campaigning desire to expose government shortcomings.

(c)   **Best interests**

Trustees may face conflicting opinions about what the **best interests of animals** are. One distinction in the context of animal charities is the difference between animal welfare and animal liberation. **Animal welfare** is often defined as the desire to prevent unnecessary suffering and ensure a good quality of life and humane death, while not being opposed in principle to the use of animals. By contrast most **animal liberationists** are fundamentally opposed to the use or ownership of animals by humans. Liberationists would claim that many of the situations accepted by animal welfarists would inevitably compromise the wellbeing of the animal and its ability to live in accordance with its natural needs.

4.15.3 Conflicts between stakeholders

There may be a conflict between the objectives of different stakeholders, arising partly from a **lack of clarity** on how far commercial objectives can be pursued without compromising a charity's mission. Some stakeholders have demanded that charities should be run on more commercial lines, attempting to make the most of resources and with chief executives drawn from the private sector. Other stakeholders (volunteers, some donors) have objected that this has meant charities moving too far away from their charitable objectives. Trustees have often struggled to resolve these conflicts and change historical ways of operation, particularly if they themselves **lack commercial skills or understanding**.

4.15.4 Disclosure by charities

In some jurisdictions charities face a light disclosure regime which allows them to provide **minimal financial detail**. Charities have been criticised for this and some have responded by making fuller disclosures than required by law.

The strategy for dealing with stakeholders set out in *Good Governance: A Code for the Voluntary and Community Sector* is that trustees should ensure that they identify those with a legitimate interest in their work. They need to ensure there is a strategy for regular and effective communication with them about the organisation's achievements and work, including the board's role and the organisation's objectives and values.

The Code sees openness and accountability as follows.

- It means ensuring stakeholders have the knowledge and opportunity to hold trustees to account.
- It means demonstrating that the charity learns from mistakes and errors, for example by having clear and effective complaints procedures and using the feedback to learn and improve performance.
- It means ensuring the principles of equality and diversity are applied, and that information and meetings are accessible to all sectors of the community.
- It means keeping membership records up to date, seeking members' views and encouraging members to participate in governance.
- It means acting on broader responsibilities towards communities, wider society and the environment. Some charities demonstrate that they are delivering value to donors and users of the service by measuring and publishing the **contribution they make**. Some use a social or environmental reporting framework (discussed further in Chapter 11). This includes details of how the charity is run and how it delivers against its terms of reference and its objectives. This can demonstrate accountability and transparency and increase the confidence of primary stakeholders.

4.16 Stakeholder and agency theory

Quinn and Jones argued that agency theory does not allow managers to **avoid their normal moral obligations**, particularly avoiding harm to others, respecting the autonomy of others, telling the truth and honouring agreements. Only after fulfilling these can they maximise shareholder wealth. The agency-principal relationship can only be meaningful if managers attend to the moral principles.

The opposite view was forcefully argued by Milton Friedman. Friedman claimed that managers are responsible to owners who generally are aiming to make as much money as possible. If managers are argued to have social responsibilities, then they have to act in some ways that are not in the interest of the owners, **their principals**, and they will be spending money for purposes other than those authorised. They are not therefore acting properly as agents. Instead they are in effect raising taxes and deciding how these taxes should be spent, which is the proper function of government, not agents.

4.17 Stakeholder theory and company law

Although company law reforms in various countries have attempted to place some emphasis on ethical and social responsibility, a key foundation of company law in most jurisdictions remains the **fiduciary and legal obligations** that managers have to **maximise shareholder wealth**. Therefore under law, if managers are to fulfil responsibilities to a wider stakeholder base, there must, according to capitalist thinking, be a business profit case for doing so (Freidman's argument above).

Some commentators have tried to reconcile stakeholder and agency theory by arguing that managers are stakeholders, responsible as **agents to all other stakeholders**. Although stakeholders have divergent interests that may be difficult to reconcile, that does not absolve management from at least trying to reconcile their interests. Managers are, after all, certainly responsible to all shareholders and different shareholders have divergent interests.

Exam focus point

> The examiner has commented that the issue of stakeholders lies at the heart of most discussions of ethics. Being able to identify the stakeholders mentioned in a case scenario and describing their claims on the organisation is an important skill for P1 candidates to develop.

5 Major issues in corporate governance

FAST FORWARD

> Key issues in corporate governance reports have included the **role of the board**, the **quality of financial reporting and auditing**, **directors' remuneration**, **risk management** and **corporate social responsibility**.

We shall expand on these issues in the next two chapters, but for now let's examine the major areas that have been affected by corporate governance.

5.1 Duties of directors

The corporate governance reports have aimed to build on directors' duties as defined in statute and case law. These include the **fiduciary duties** to act in the **best interests of the company**, use their powers for a **proper purpose**, **avoid conflicts of interest** and exercise a **duty of care**.

5.2 Composition and balance of the board

A feature of many corporate governance scandals has been boards dominated by a **single senior executive** or 'small kitchen cabinet' with other board members merely acting as a rubber stamp. Sometimes the single individual may bypass the board to action their own interests. The report on the UK Guinness case suggested that the Chief Executive, Ernest Saunders, paid himself a £3 million reward without consulting the other directors.

Even if an organisation is not dominated by a single individual, there may be other weaknesses in board composition. The organisation may be run by a small group centred round the chief executive and chief financial officer, and appointments may be made by personal recommendation rather than a formal, objective process.

As we shall see, the board must also be **balanced** in terms of skills and talents from several **specialisms** relevant to the organisation's situation and also in terms of **age** (to ensure senior directors are bringing on newer ones to help succession planning).

5.3 Reliability of financial reporting and external auditors

Issues concerning **financial reporting and auditing** are seen by many investors as crucial because of their central importance in ensuring management accountability. They have been the focus of much debate and litigation. While focusing the corporate governance debate solely on accounting and reporting issues is inadequate, the greater regulation of practices such as off-balance sheet financing has led to **greater transparency** and a **reduction in risks** faced by investors.

External auditors may not carry out the necessary questioning of senior management because of fears of **losing the audit**, and internal auditors do not ask awkward questions because the chief financial officer **determines their employment prospects**. Often corporate collapses are followed by criticisms of external auditors, such as the Barlow Clowes affair where poorly planned and focused audit work failed to identify illegal use of client monies.

5.4 Directors' remuneration and rewards

Directors being paid excessive salaries and bonuses has been seen as one of the major corporate abuses for a large number of years. It is inevitable that the corporate governance codes have targeted this issue.

5.5 Responsibility of the board for risk management and internal control systems

Boards that meet irregularly or fail to consider systematically the organisation's activities and risks are clearly not fulfilling their responsibilities. Sometimes the failure to carry out proper oversight is due to a **lack of information** being provided, which in turn may be due to inadequate systems being in place for the **measurement** and **reporting of risk**.

5.6 Rights and responsibilities of shareholders

We saw in Section 3 how shareholders' rights and the role of shareholders, particularly institutional shareholders, has been the subject of much debate. Shareholders should have the right to receive all **material information** that may affect the value of their investment and to **vote** on measures affecting the organisation's **governance**.

5.7 Corporate social responsibility and business ethics

The lack of consensus about the issues for which businesses are responsible and the stakeholders to whom they are responsible has inevitably made corporate social responsibility and business ethics an important part of the corporate governance debate.

5.8 Public and non-governmental bodies corporate governance   6/11

Many of the principles that apply to company corporate governance also apply to government bodies or other major entities such as charities. Boards will be required to act with **integrity**, to **supervise the body's activities properly** and to **ensure appropriate control and risk management and reporting systems** are being maintained. However, governance arrangements will also reflect the strategic purpose of the organisation. Governance should always ensure that income is being used to **optimal effect** and that operations are being **run efficiently**.

5.8.1 Composition of boards

This may be determined by regulation or may be tailored by the body's constitution. There may be more than one board. There could be an **executive board** for overseeing operations, and a **supervisory board** of **trustees**. For charities, **trustees** should ensure that the **objectives and policies reflect its fiduciary purposes**. The supervisory board may also include representatives of all major stakeholder groups, to ensure stakeholder interests are being represented.

The supervisory board will also need to consider the composition of the executive board and whether to recruit directors from the private sector to run the organisation.

5.8.2 Conduct of directors

Directors may be subject to **organisation or sector-specific** controls to ensure that they act in the public interest. In charities trustees may be particularly concerned that the salaries and benefits that the directors receive are reasonable given the purposes of the charity and also the need to reward the directors fairly for the responsibilities that they undertake.

5.8.3 Compulsory regulations vs voluntary best practice

Certain guidelines that are voluntary best practice in the corporate sector may be compulsory for some other sorts of organisation, for example maintenance of an internal audit department.

 Case Study

The UK *Good Governance; A Code for the Voluntary and Community Sector* illustrates the variety of obligations that charities have to regulators. The Code requires trustees to ensure compliance with:

- The governing document
- Regulators' requirements, particularly as regards submission of information
- Maintenance of records and production of accounts

Areas of legislation with which some or all charities may have to comply include:

- Charity

- Company

- Trust

- Industrial and provident society

- Employment

- Health and safety

- Data protection

- Equality

- Other relevant legislation, including fundraising, protection of children and vulnerable adults, provision of health or care services, provision of financial advice, housing and tenancy law

The guidance states that the board must also act prudently to protect the reputation, assets and property of the organisation, and to ensure that assets and property are only used to deliver stated aims.

5.8.4 Disclosure of internal control

Central government bodies in the UK are an example of bodies that are required to make disclosures about specific controls, such as risk registers, training, key performance indicators and reporting systems.

 Question   Concepts

We end each chapter by including questions that require you to think widely about what you've just covered. Sometimes they'll involve comparisons between material in different parts of this chapter.

For this chapter, consider the concepts discussed in Section 1. Which of them do you think corporate governance guidance may address most effectively? Which of them do you think that governance codes do not cover very well?

Answer

With these questions, there is no right answer, and often we shall do no more than give our own opinions.

Certainly most governance guidance covers **transparency** quite thoroughly and is reinforced by the requirements of financial reporting standards. However, this has been because lack of transparency has been a major issue of concern in various governance scandals, notably in Enron. Is guidance on transparency essentially reactive?

You may feel, having read Section 3, that directors might have most difficulty applying the concept of **fairness**. Most governance guidance has done no more than address this topic in general terms, leaving directors to decide how to give shareholders' interests appropriate priority, and decide between the competing interests of other stakeholders. Probably the South African King report goes furthest in addressing this issue.

'Stakeholders such as the community in which the company operates, its customers, its employees and its suppliers need to be considered when developing the strategy of a company.'

However, the King report does not accept the full concept of accountability to all legitimate stakeholders.

'The stakeholder concept of being accountable to all legitimate stakeholders must be rejected for the simple reason that to ask boards to be accountable to everyone would result in their being accountable to no one. The modern approach is for a board to identify the company's stakeholders, including its shareowners, and to agree policies as to how the relationship with those stakeholders should be advanced and managed in the interests of the company.'

Chapter Roundup

- **Corporate governance**, the system by which organisations are directed and controlled, is based on a number of concepts including transparency, independence, accountability and integrity.

- **Agency** is extremely important in corporate governance, as often the directors/managers are acting as agents for the owners. Corporate governance frameworks aim to ensure directors/managers **fulfil their responsibilities** as agents by requiring disclosure and suggesting they be rewarded on the basis of performance.

- Directors and managers need to be aware of the **interests of stakeholders** in governance; however, their responsibility towards them is judged.

- Governance reports have emphasised the role of **institutional investors** (insurance companies, pension funds, investment houses) in directing companies towards good corporate governance.

- Key issues in corporate governance reports have included the **role of the board**, the **quality of financial reporting and auditing**, **directors' remuneration**, **risk management** and **corporate social responsibility**.

Quick Quiz

1   Corporate governance focuses on companies' relationships with all stakeholders, not just shareholders.

   True   ☐

   False   ☐

2   Name five concepts that underlie corporate governance.

3   Fill in the blank:

     .... means straightforward dealing and completeness.

4   Why is agency a significant issue in corporate governance?

5   Fill in the blank:

     .... means that persons owe a duty to others because of the position of trust and confidence they hold in relation to those others.

6   Name three methods of rewarding management that can help to ensure alignment of interests.

7   Which of the following is not generally classified as an institutional shareholder?

   A   Pension funds   C   Central government
   B   Investment trusts   D   Venture capitalists

8   What are the main fiduciary duties of directors?

Answers to Quick Quiz

1   True

2   Any five of:

     Fairness, Openness/Transparency, Independence, Probity/Honesty, Responsibility, Accountability, Reputation, Judgement and Integrity

3   Integrity

4   Because of the separation of ownership (principal) from management (agent)

5   Fiduciary

6   Profit-related/economic value-added pay, shares, executive share option plans

7   C   Central government

8   Acting in the best interests of the company, using their powers for a proper purpose, avoiding conflicts of interest, the duty of care

Now try the question below from the Practice Question Bank.

Number	Level	Marks	Time
Q1	Examination	25	49 mins

BPP
LEARNING MEDIA

Approaches to corporate governance

Topic list	Syllabus reference
1 Basis of corporate governance guidance	A6
2 Corporate governance codes	A6
3 Sarbanes-Oxley	A6
4 Corporate social responsibility	A7
5 Public sector governance	A9

Introduction

Having described the underlying principles and issues behind the development of corporate governance in Chapter 1, in this chapter we discuss how corporate governance codes have developed. In Section 1 we see the development of many codes in the context of a desire to develop principles-based guidance and also as a function of the share ownership patterns of the economies to which the codes relate. In Section 2 we discuss briefly the main codes that have been developed worldwide, both in individual countries and for a number of jurisdictions (the OECD and ICGN reports).

Because of its differing approach to regulation generally, and also specifically because of the fallout from the collapse of Enron, America has developed a more prescriptive approach to corporate governance, the Sarbanes-Oxley Act. We cover this legislation in Section 3. We give more detail about it than other regulations/guidance, since the examiner has emphasised its importance as the most influential corporate governance instrument of recent times, influencing practice globally because of the international significance of American business.

In Section 4 we discuss the very important topic of corporate social responsibility, the concepts that lie behind it and how it has influenced the development of corporate governance. Corporate social responsibility ideas are significant in Part E of the syllabus, which we shall cover in Chapters 9 to 11.

Finally in Section 5 we look at the public sector and the specific governance issues that affect different types of public sector organisations.

Study guide

		Intellectual level
A6	**Different approaches to corporate governance**	
(a)	Describe and compare the essentials of rules- and principles-based approaches to corporate governance, including discussion of comply or explain.	3
(b)	Describe and analyse the different models of business ownership that influence different governance regimes (eg family firms vs joint stock company-based models).	2
(c)	Describe and critically evaluate the reasons behind the development and use of codes of practice in corporate governance (acknowledging national differences and convergence).	3
(d)	Explain and briefly explore the development of corporate governance codes in principles-based jurisdictions (impetus and background, major corporate governance codes, effects of).	2
(e)	Explain and explore the Sarbanes-Oxley Act as an example of a rules-based approach to corporate governance (impetus and background, main provisions/contents, effects of).	2
(f)	Describe and explore the objectives, content and limitations of corporate governance codes intended to apply to multiple national jurisdictions (OECD, ICGN).	2
A7	**Corporate governance and corporate social responsibility**	
(a)	Explain and explore social responsibility in the context of corporate governance.	2
(b)	Discuss and critically assess the concept of stakeholder power and interest using the Mendelow model and how this can affect strategy and corporate governance.	3
(c)	Analyse and evaluate issues of ownership, property and the responsibilities of ownership in the context of shareholding.	3
A9	**Public sector governance**	
(a)	Describe, compare and contrast public sector, private sector, charitable status and non-governmental (NGO and quasi-NGO) forms of organisation, including purposes and objectives, performance, ownership and stakeholders (including lobby groups).	2
(b)	Describe, compare and contrast the different types of public sector organisations at subnational, national and supranational level.	2
(c)	Assess and evaluate the strategic objectives, leadership and governance arrangements specific to public sector organisations as contrasted with private sector.	3
(d)	Discuss and assess the nature of democratic control, political influence and policy implementation in public sector organisations including the contestable nature of public sector policy.	3
(e)	Discuss the obligations of public sector organisations to meet the economy, effectiveness, efficiency (3 Es) criteria and promote public value.	3

Exam guide

You may well have to discuss the implications of basing governance guidance on principles. The examination team has stated that knowledge of the main features and advantages and disadvantages of codes in general is important, but line by line knowledge isn't required.

As regards specific codes, the main themes of Sarbanes-Oxley may be tested. The examination team has stressed that, although the UK Corporate Governance Code sets out good practice (and students from anywhere in the world would do well to have some knowledge of UK practice), answers based on the students' local codes of practice would be equally acceptable. Students in countries without detailed codes could use UK or international codes to underpin their answers.

The existence of wider social responsibilities is likely to be a theme in many questions.

1 Basis of corporate governance guidance   12/14, 6/15

FAST FORWARD

Globalisation, the **treatment of investors** and **major corporate scandals** have been major driving forces behind corporate governance developments.

Many governance codes have adopted a **principles-based approach** allowing companies flexibility in interpreting the codes' requirements and to explain if they have departed from the provisions of the code.

Insider systems are where listed companies are owned by a small number of major shareholders.

Outsider systems are where shareholdings are more widely dispersed, and the management-ownership split is more of an issue.

1.1 The driving forces of governance code development

Corporate governance issues came to prominence in the US during the 1970s and in the UK and Europe from the late 1980s. The main, but not the only, drivers associated with the increasing demand for the development of governance were:

(a) **Increasing internationalisation and globalisation**

This has meant that investors, and institutional investors in particular, began to invest outside their home countries. The King report in South Africa highlights the role of the free movement of capital, commenting that investors are promoting governance in their own self-interest.

(b) **Investor concerns**

The **differential treatment of domestic and foreign investors**, both in terms of reporting and associated rights/dividends, and the excessive influence of majority shareholders in insider jurisdictions caused many investors to call for parity of treatment.

(c) **Quality of accounts**

Issues concerning **financial reporting** were raised by many investors and were the focus of much debate and litigation. Shareholder confidence in what was being reported in many instances was eroded. While corporate governance development isn't just about better financial reporting requirements, the regulation of practices such as off-balance sheet financing has led to greater transparency and a reduction in risks faced by investors.

(d) **National differences**

The characteristics of individual countries may have a **significant influence** in the way corporate governance has developed. The King report emphasises the importance of qualities that are fundamental to the South African culture, such as collectiveness, consensus, helpfulness, fairness, consultation and religious faith in the development of best practice.

(e) **Scandals**

An increasing number of **high profile corporate scandals** and collapses including Polly Peck International, BCCI and Maxwell Communications Corporation prompted the development of governance codes in the early 1990s. However, other scandals since then have raised questions about further measures that may be necessary.

1.2 Development of corporate governance codes

To combat these problems, codes of best practice were developed in many jurisdictions. Some of the main provisions of codes have been clear attempts to deal with difficult situations. The problem of an overbearing individual dominating a company has been countered by recommendations in many codes that different directors occupy the positions of a company of chief executive officer and chairman at the head of a company.

The development of codes has also been prompted by the need to clarify ambiguities in the law, or require a higher standard of behaviour than local legislation requires. Codes have also been developed to ensure local companies comply with international best practice.

1.3 Principles of governance

Whether or not the detailed guidance is mostly in the form of principles or rules, there are a number of underlying principles that underpin most codes worldwide, based on what the codes are meant to achieve. This list is based on a number of reports:

(a) **Ensure adherence** to and **satisfaction** of the **strategic objectives** of the organisation, thus aiding effective management

(b) **Convey and reinforce the requirements relating to governance** in local statutes and listing rules

(c) Assist companies in **minimising risk**, especially financial, legal and reputational risks, by ensuring appropriate systems of financial control for monitoring risk and ensuring compliance with the law are in place

(d) **Promote ethical behaviour** with **integrity**, meaning that straightforward dealing and completeness are particularly important

(e) **Underpin investor confidence**, partly in response to the driving forces behind governance discussed above

(f) **Fulfil responsibilities to all stakeholders** and to **minimise potential conflicts of interest** between owners, managers and the wider stakeholder community

(g) **Establish clear accountability** at senior levels within an organisation; however, one danger may be that boards become **too closely involved with day-to-day issues** and do not delegate responsibility to management

(h) **Maintain the independence** of those who scrutinise the behaviour of the organisation and its senior executive managers; independence is particularly important for **non-executive directors** and **internal and external auditors**

(i) **Provide accurate and timely reporting of trustworthy/independent financial and operational data** to both the management and owners/members of the organisation, to give them a true and balanced picture of what is happening in the organisation

(j) **Encourage more proactive involvement** of owners/members in the effective management of the organisation through recognising their responsibilities of oversight and input to decision-making processes via voting or other mechanisms

(k) **Use direct behaviour**, as the importance of ensuring that boards take specific actions will influence the amount of detailed requirements within codes

1.4 Principles or rules? 6/08, 12/11, 12/12, 12/13

A continuing debate on corporate governance is whether the guidance should predominantly be in the form of principles, or whether there is a need for detailed laws or regulations.

UK guidance has generally suggested that a voluntary code coupled with disclosure would prove more effective than a statutory code in promoting the key principles of **openness, integrity and accountability**.

Nevertheless the UK guidance has also gone beyond broad principles and provided some specific guidelines. These have aimed to promote an **understanding of directors' responsibilities** and **openness about the ways they have been discharged**. Specific guidelines also help in **raising standards of financial reporting** and **business conduct**, aiming to remove the need for statutory regulation.

Case Study

A principles-based approach to regulating the behaviour of motorists might say that motorists should drive safely having regard to traffic and road conditions whereas a rules-based approach might specify that motorists should not drive at speeds in excess of 100 km/h.

This example of motoring regulation indicates a basic weakness with both types of regime. Using a principles-based approach, what criteria can be used to determine when a motorist is not driving safely? The motorist being involved in an accident perhaps, but the accident may have been due to other factors. One problem with a rules-based approach is that attention is focused on whether the rules have been broken, and not perhaps on more relevant factors. For example, a motorist driving on a motorway at 100 km/h on a day where the motorway was seriously affected by snow might be obeying the law, but would clearly be driving at an undesirably fast speed.

1.5 Characteristics of a principles-based approach 12/11

(a) **Focus on aims**

The approach focuses on **objectives** (for example the objective that shareholders holding a minority of shares in a company should be treated fairly) rather than the **mechanisms** by which these objectives will be achieved. Possibly therefore principles are easier to integrate into strategic planning.

(b) **Flexibility**

A principles-based approach can lay stress on those elements of corporate governance to which rules **cannot easily be applied**. These include overall areas, such as the requirement to maintain sound systems of internal control, and 'softer' areas, such as organisational culture and maintaining good relationships with shareholders and other stakeholders.

(c) **Breadth of application**

Principles-based approaches can be applied across **different legal jurisdictions** rather than being founded on the legal regulations of one country. The OECD guidelines, which we shall cover later in this chapter, are a good example of guidance that is applied internationally.

(d) **Comply or explain**

Where principles-based approaches have been established in the form of corporate governance codes, the specific recommendations that the codes make have been enforced on a **comply or explain basis**.

(e) **Role of capital markets**

Principles-based approaches have often been adopted in jurisdictions where the governing bodies of **stock markets** have had the prime role in setting standards for companies to follow.

Listing rules include a requirement to comply with codes but, because the guidance is in the form of a code, companies have more flexibility than they would if the code was underpinned by legal requirements.

In 2010, when the Combined Code was amended and renamed the UK Corporate Governance Code, there appeared to be increased emphasis on the spirit of the Code and the principles, encouraging boards to think about how to apply the principles. The comply or explain approach was covered in a separate section, which emphasised that non-compliance may be justified so long as the code principles were followed and the justification for non-compliance explained in the annual report. This was in response to criticisms that were raised during the consultation on the amendments, that many investors appeared to want to just see compliance (tick-box) and would not take into account whether the reasons for non-compliance were acceptable.

A new version of the UK Code published in September 2012 gave more guidance on the explanations required. A company should demonstrate that what it was doing was **consistent with the underlying governance principles**, **contributed to good governance** and **promoted delivery of business objectives**. It should set out the **background**, provide a clear **rationale** for the action it was taking, and **describe actions** taken to address any additional risks and maintain conformity with the relevant principle. The explanation should indicate whether the deviation from the Code's detailed provisions was **limited in time** and, if so, when the company intended to **return to conformity** with the Code's provisions.

Other codes have moved away from talking in terms of comply or explain. The United Nations Code has used an adopt or explain approach. The Netherlands code and the South African King report have used an apply or explain approach. King comments that directors may conclude that following a recommendation may not be in the best interests of the company. The board could decide to apply the recommendation differently, or apply another practice and still achieve the most important principles of governance. Explaining how the principles and recommendations were applied, or the reasons for non-application, results in compliance.

1.6 Characteristics of a rules-based approach

(a) **Emphasis on achievements**

Rules-based systems place **more emphasis** on definite **achievements** rather than underlying factors and control systems. The EMAS environmental management system (discussed further in Chapter 11) is a good example of a system based on rules, with requirements for **targets to be set** and disclosure requirements of whether or not targets have been achieved. However, there may be little incentive to **achieve more** than is required by the rules.

(b) **Compulsory compliance**

Rules-based approaches allow no leeway. The key issue is whether or not you have **complied with the rules**. There is no flexibility for different circumstances, for organisations of varying size or in different stages of development.

(c) **Visibility of compliance**

It should in theory be **easy to see** whether there has been compliance with the rules. Comparison between companies should be straightforward. However, that depends on whether the rules are **unambiguous**, and the **clarity of evidence** of compliance or non-compliance).

(d) **Limitations of rules**

Enforcers of a rules-based approach (regulators, auditors) may find it difficult to deal with **questionable situations** that are not covered sufficiently in the rulebook. This was a problem with Enron. The company kept a number of its financial arrangements off its balance sheet. Although this approach can be seen as not true and fair, Enron could use it because it did not breach the accounting rules then in existence in America. Keeping legislation up to date to keep loopholes closed is a reactive and probably costly process.

(e)   **Criminal sanctions**

Rules-based approaches to corporate governance tend to be found in legal jurisdictions and culture that lay great emphasis on **obeying the letter of the law** rather than the spirit. Serious breaches will be penalised by criminal sanctions. They often take the form of legislation themselves, notably the Sarbanes-Oxley Act which we shall discuss later in this chapter as the most relevant example of a rules-based approach. The amount of legislation for businesses in these jurisdictions may give rise to **significant compliance costs**.

1.7 Advantages of a principles-based approach

Possible advantages of basing corporate governance codes on a series of principles are as follows.

(a)   **Avoids legislation**

It avoids the need for **inflexible legislation** that companies have to comply with even though the legislation is not appropriate.

(b)   **Less costly**

It is less burdensome in **terms of time and expenditure**. Although governments have not been directly involved in many of the bodies that have established corporate governance practice, they clearly have a major interest and have made their views known. In many countries there are continual pressures from businesses for governments to 'reduce the burden of red-tape.' A principles-based approach can avoid the need for excessive information provision, management and reporting costs, and complex monitoring and support structures.

(c)   **Appropriate for company**

A **principles-based approach** allows companies to **develop their own approach** to corporate governance that is appropriate for their circumstances within the limits laid down by stock exchanges. For example, it may be excessive to impose on companies in lower risk industries the same mandatory reporting requirements that companies in higher risk industries face. It should suffice that shareholders are happy with the extent of reporting in lower risk industries.

(d)   **Flexibility**

A principles-based approach can allow for **transitional arrangements and unusual circumstances**. If one of the directors leaves the board suddenly, there may be a period of technical non-compliance until the director is replaced. However, most shareholders should generally be satisfied, provided the non-compliance is explained.

(e)   **Emphasis on explanations**

Enforcement on a **comply or explain basis** means that businesses can explain why they have departed from the specific provisions if they feel it is appropriate. In many instances now, the departures from best practice described in reports are of a minor or temporary nature. Explanations of breaches have generally included details of how and when non-compliance will be remedied.

(f)   **Emphasis on investor decisions**

A principles-based approach accompanied by disclosure requirements puts the **emphasis on investors** making up their own minds about what businesses are doing (and whether they agree departures from the codes are appropriate).

1.8 Principles-based approach in action: The Hampel report

Of the major corporate governance reports, the Hampel report (1998) in the UK came out the strongest in favour of a principles-based approach. The committee preferred relaxing the regulatory burden on companies and was against treating the corporate governance codes as sets of rules, judging companies by whether they have complied ('box-ticking'). The report states that there may be **guidelines** which will

normally be appropriate but the differing circumstances of companies mean that sometimes there are valid reasons for exceptions.

'Good corporate governance is not just a matter of prescribing particular corporate structures and complying with a number of hard and fast rules. There is a need for broad principles. All companies should then apply these flexibly and with common sense to the varying circumstances of individual companies. Companies' experience of the codes has been rather different. Too often they believe that the codes have been treated as sets of prescriptive rules. The shareholders or their advisers would only be interested only in whether the letter of the rule has been complied with.'

The issue of box-ticking was still being raised when the UK Code was being reviewed in 2009. The UK Financial Reporting Council highlighted **disclosure** as a particular issue, seeing a need for rationalisation of disclosures and development of disclosures that investors found informative, rather than companies being forced to comply with requirements that were not necessary for their circumstances.

1.9 Criticisms of a principles-based approach

There are a number of problems with a principles-based approach that were highlighted when the Hampel report was debated and have been raised since.

(a) **Broadness of principles**

Principles may be **so broad** that they are of very little use as a guide to best corporate governance practice. For example, the suggestion that non-executive directors from a wide variety of backgrounds can make a contribution is seen as not strong enough to encourage companies away from recruiting directors by means of the 'old boy network' (relying on their current business and social contacts).

(b) **Misrepresents company attitudes**

Comments about **box-ticking** are incorrect for two reasons. Firstly, shareholders do not apply that approach when assessing accounts. Secondly, it is far less likely that disasters will strike companies with a 100% compliance record since they are unlikely to be content with token compliance, but will have set up procedures that contribute significantly to their being governed well.

(c) **Consistency between companies**

Investors cannot be confident of **consistency of approach**. Clear rules mean that the same standards apply to all directors. A principles-based approach **promotes a 'level playing field'**, preventing individual companies gaining competitive or cost advantages with lower levels of compliance.

(d) **Confusion over rules**

There may be **confusion over what is compulsory and what isn't**. Although codes may state that they are not prescriptive, their adoption by the local stock exchange means that specific recommendations in the codes effectively become rules, which companies have to **obey in order to retain their listing**.

(e) **Inadequate explanation**

Some companies may perceive a principles-based approach as **non-binding** and fail to comply without giving an adequate or perhaps any explanation. Not only does this demonstrate a failure to understand the **purpose of principles-based codes** but it also casts aspersions on the integrity of the companies' decision-makers. A rules-based approach, particularly if backed by criminal sanctions, may give shareholders more confidence that the company and its directors are complying.

(f) **Investor misunderstanding**

A principles-based approach depends on markets understanding the **seriousness of non-compliance and revaluing shares appropriately**. However, non-specialist shareholders may not interpret the significance of disclosures correctly.

(g) **Shareholder rights**

It's been suggested that a principles-based approach requires a regime where shareholders have **meaningful rights in law**, such as being able to vote individual directors off the board.

Exam focus point

June 2008 Question 4 asked whether a rules-based approach or principles-based approach should be applied in a developing country. In December 2012 and December 2013 there was a question on the difference between rules-based and principles-based approaches to corporate governance.

1.10 Application of principles-based approaches by investors

In practice comply or explain has not led to lots of companies treating compliance as voluntary. Analysts and investors have taken breaches, particularly by larger listed companies, very seriously. The reputation of companies has been adversely affected if they have tried to justify non-compliance on the grounds of excessive trouble or cost. However, the value of smaller or recently quoted companies has been less affected by non-compliance. Stock markets have effectively allowed these companies more latitude even though they have breached the governance codes.

1.11 Influence of ownership

A key distinction that has been drawn between the corporate governance systems worldwide in different regimes has been between the insider and outsider models of ownership, although in practice most regimes fall somewhere in between the two.

1.12 Insider systems (family companies)   6/10

Insider or relationship-based systems are where most companies listed on the local stock exchange are owned and controlled by a **small number of major shareholders**. The shareholders may be members of the company's founding families, banks, other companies or the Government.

The reason for the concentration of share ownership is the legal system. There tends to be more diverse shareholder ownership in jurisdictions such as the UK that have **strong protection** for minority shareholders.

Family companies are perhaps the best example of insider structures. Agency is not really an issue with families because of their direct involvement in management. Individual behaviour may be influenced not only by corporate ethical codes but also by the **family's ethical beliefs**. Family companies may wish to invest for the long term. However, their longevity depends on the willingness of family members to continue to be actively involved. Family companies also depend on the maintenance of **family unity**. If this breaks down, governance may become very difficult.

Exam focus point

The scenario in June 2008 Question 3 concerned a family-dominated company with various governance issues.

1.12.1 Advantages of insider systems

(a)   It is easier to establish ties between **owners and managers**. In particular controlling families often participate in the management of companies.

(b)   The agency problem and costs of monitoring are reduced if the owners are also involved in **management**.

(c)   Even if the owners are not involved in management, it should be easier to **influence company management** through **ownership and dialogue**.

(d)   A smaller base of shareholders may be more flexible about **when** profits are made and hence more able to take a **long-term view**. Accessing longer-term capital may be easier.

1.12.2 Disadvantages of insider systems

(a) There may be **discrimination against minority shareholders** as regards, for example, availability of information and ultimately expropriation of the wealth of minorities.

(b) Evidence suggests that controlling families tend **not to be monitored effectively** by banks or by other large shareholders.

(c) Insider systems often do not develop **more formal governance structures** until they need to, for example as a forum for resolving family disagreements or dealing with controversial issues such as succession planning. If they do not develop, then arguments between the controlling directors can undermine personal and professional relationships and company performance.

(d) Insider firms, particularly family firms, may be reluctant to employ outsiders in influential positions and may be **unwilling to recruit independent non-executive directors**.

(e) Evidence suggests that **insider systems are more prone to opaque financial transactions** and misuse of funds.

(f) For capital markets to be truly competitive there should be **no investors** who are on **their own** of **such size** that they **can influence prices**. As we have already seen in many capital markets, transactions by the largest shareholders are now on such a massive scale that considerable price movements can result.

(g) As previously discussed, many large shareholders (particularly financial institutions) tend to **avoid shares** that are seen as **speculative** and invest only in 'blue chip' shares (ie those of leading commercially sound companies). As a result, the shares of such companies tend to be relatively expensive.

(h) **Succession issues** may be a major problem. A vigorous company founder may be succeeded by other family members who are less competent or dynamic.

<table>
<tr><td>**Exam focus
point**</td><td>June 2010 Question 4 looked at a scenario where one family member appeared to be defrauding others.</td></tr>
</table>

Case Study

Sir Adrian Cadbury, chairman of the committee that produced the seminal Cadbury report in the UK, was also responsible for a report in 2000: *Family Firms and their Governance: Creating Tomorrow's Company from Today's*. In the report Cadbury discussed the stages of establishing corporate governance structures in a family firm, from a family assembly through to a board of directors including members from outside the family. Cadbury commented that establishing a formal board was the key stage of progressing from an organisation based on family relationships to an organisation based on business relationships, and that the establishment of a board provided necessary clarification of responsibilities and the process for taking decisions.

Cadbury commented that in order to manage growth successfully family firms had to:

- Be able to recruit and retain the very best people for the business
- Develop a culture of trust and transparency
- Define logical and efficient organisational structures

1.13 Outsider systems

Outsider systems are ones where shareholding is more widely dispersed, and there is the **manager-ownership separation**. These are sometimes referred to as Anglo-American or Anglo-Saxon regimes.

1.13.1 Advantages of outsider systems

(a)   The separation of ownership and management has provided an impetus for the development of **more robust legal and governance regimes** to **protect shareholders**.

(b)   Shareholders have voting rights that they can use to **exercise control**.

(c)   Hostile takeovers are far more frequent, and the threat of these acts as a **disciplining mechanism** on company management.

1.13.2 Disadvantages of outsider systems

(a)   Companies are more likely to have an **agency problem** and **significant costs of agency**.

(b)   The larger shareholders in these regimes have often had **short-term priorities** and have preferred to sell their shares rather than pressurise the directors to change strategies.

Exam focus point

> Although the British and American systems can both be classified as outsider systems, don't necessarily assume that exam scenarios will always be about such systems. Some questions may well be set on insider systems, and focus on the implications for corporate governance of operating within insider systems.

2 Corporate governance codes   6/13

FAST FORWARD

> Major governance guidance includes the **UK Corporate Governance Code**, the **South African King report** and the **Singapore Code of Corporate Governance**. International guidance includes the **OECD principles** and the **ICGN report**.

2.1 Major governance codes – UK

2.1.1 The Cadbury report

The Cadbury committee in the UK was set up because of the lack of confidence perceived in financial reporting and in the ability of auditors to provide the assurances required by the users of financial statements. The main difficulties were considered to be in the relationship between **auditors and boards of directors**. In particular, the commercial pressures on both directors and auditors caused pressure to be brought to bear on auditors by the board and the auditors often capitulated. Problems were also perceived in the ability of the board of directors to control their organisations.

(a)   **Corporate governance responsibilities**

   The roles of those concerned with the financial statements are described in the Cadbury report, published in 1992.

   (i)   The **directors** are responsible for the corporate governance of the company.

   (ii)   The **shareholders** are linked to the directors via the financial reporting system.

   (iii) The **auditors** provide the shareholders with an external objective check on the directors' financial statements.

   (iv)   Other concerned **users**, particularly employees (to whom the directors owe some responsibility) are indirectly addressed by the financial statements.

(b)   **Code of Best Practice**

   The **Code of Best Practice** included in the Cadbury report and subsequently amended by later reports was aimed at the directors of all UK public companies, but the directors of all companies were encouraged to use the Code.

2.1.2 The Greenbury code

In 1995, the **Greenbury committee** published a code which established principles for the determination of **directors' pay** and detailing disclosures to be given in the annual reports and accounts.

2.1.3 The Hampel report

In 1998, the **Hampel committee** followed up matters raised in the Cadbury and Greenbury reports, aiming to restrict the regulatory burden on companies and substituting principles for detail whenever possible. Under Hampel:

(a)   The accounts should contain a **statement** of how the company applies the corporate governance principles

(b)   The accounts should **explain their policies**, including any circumstances justifying departure from best practice

2.1.4 Combined Code and UK Corporate Governance Code

The London Stock Exchange subsequently issued a combined corporate governance code in 1998, which was derived from the recommendations of the Cadbury, Greenbury and Hampel reports.

Since the publication of the Combined Code a number of reports in the UK have been published about specific aspects of corporate governance.

- The **Turnbull report** (1999, revised 2005) focused on risk management and internal control.
- The **Smith report** (2003) discussed the role of audit committees.
- The **Higgs report** (2003) focused on the role of the non-executive director.

We shall discuss some of the detailed provisions of these codes later in this Text.

The Combined Code was revised a number of times after its original publication in 1998. The May 2010 revision changed the name of the code to the **UK Corporate Governance Code**. The latest Code (September 2012) is summarised in an Appendix to Chapter 3 of this Text.

Exam focus point

> Although you can quote from local or international codes when answering questions, the examiner has recommended that all P1 students read the UK Corporate Governance Code.

2.2 Major governance codes – South Africa

South Africa's major contribution to the corporate governance debate has been the **King report**, first published in 1994 and updated in 2002 and 2009 to take account of developments in South Africa and elsewhere in the world.

The King report differs in emphasis from other guidance by advocating an integrated approach to corporate governance in the interest of a wide range of stakeholders – embracing the social, environmental and economic aspects of a company's activities. The report encourages active engagement by companies, shareholders, business and the financial press and relies heavily on disclosure as a regulatory measure.

2.3 Singapore Code of Corporate Governance

The Singapore Code (published 2001, revised 2005, with consultations on further revisions in 2011) of Corporate Governance takes a similar approach to the UK Corporate Governance Code with the emphasis being on companies giving a detailed description of their governance practices and explaining any deviation from the Code. Some guidelines, particularly on directors' remuneration, go beyond that of the UK. Revisions to the Code in 2005 reflected recent concerns. They included expanding the role of the audit committee, requiring companies to have procedures in place for whistleblowing and the separation of substantive motions in general meetings.

2.4 Effects of corporate governance reports

The OECD report (see below) emphasises that codes may leave shareholders and other stakeholders with uncertainty concerning their **status**. Market credibility therefore requires that their status in terms of **coverage**, **implementation**, **compliance** and **sanctions** should be clearly specified.

As far as the UK Codes are concerned, a survey of institutional investors carried out in 2000, two years after the Combined Code was first issued, suggested that provisions of the Codes had had varying impacts. There had been effective implementation of proposals relating to **board structure**, **non-executive directors** and **board committees**. However, the reports had only had a limited effect on **director remuneration levels**, though there had been greater compliance with guidance relating to **length of directors' service contracts** and **severance arrangements**.

2.5 Convergence of international guidance

Because of increasing international trade and cross-border links, there is significant pressure for the development of internationally comparable practices and standards. Accounting and financial reporting is one area in which this has occurred. Increasing international investment and integration of international capital markets has also led to pressure for standardisation of governance guidelines, as international investors seek **reassurance about the way their investments are being managed** and the **risks** involved.

Unsurprisingly the convergence models that have been developed lie between the **insider/outsider** models and between **profit-orientated and ethical stakeholder approaches**.

2.6 OECD guidance

The Organisation for Economic Co-operation and Development (OECD) has carried out an extensive consultation with member countries, and developed a **set of principles of corporate governance** that countries and companies should work towards achieving. The OECD has stated that its interest in corporate governance arises from its concern for **global investment**. Corporate governance arrangements should be credible and understood across national borders. Having a common set of accepted principles is a step towards achieving this aim.

The OECD developed its Principles of Corporate Governance in 1998 and issued a revised version in April 2004. They are non-binding principles, intended to assist governments in their efforts to evaluate and improve the legal, institutional and regulatory framework for corporate governance in their countries.

They are also intended to provide guidance for stock exchanges, investors and companies. The focus is on stock exchange listed companies, but many of the principles can also apply to private companies and state-owned organisations.

The OECD principles deal mainly with governance problems that result from the **separation of ownership and management** of a company. Issues of ethical concern and environmental issues are also relevant, although not central to the problems of governance.

2.6.1 The OECD principles

The OECD principles are grouped into five broad areas.

(a)   **The rights of shareholders**

Shareholders should have the right to **participate and vote in general meetings** of the company, **elect** and **remove members of the board** and **obtain relevant and material information** on a timely basis. Capital markets for corporate control should function in an **efficient and timely manner**.

(b)   **The equitable treatment of shareholders**

All shareholders of the same class of shares should be treated equally, including **minority shareholders** and **overseas shareholders**. **Impediments** to **cross-border shareholdings** should be **eliminated**.

(c) **The role of stakeholders**

Rights of stakeholders should be **protected**. All stakeholders should have **access to relevant information** on a regular and timely basis. **Performance-enhancing mechanisms** for employee participation should be **permitted to develop**. Stakeholders, including employees, should be able to **freely communicate their concerns** about illegal or unethical relationships to the board.

(d) **Disclosure and transparency**

Timely and accurate disclosure must be made of all material matters regarding the company, including the financial situation, foreseeable risk factors, issues regarding employees and other stakeholders and governance structures and policies. The company's approach to disclosure should promote the provision of analysis or advice that is relevant to decisions by investors.

(e) **The responsibilities of the board**

The board is responsible for the **strategic guidance** of the company and for the **effective monitoring** of management. Board members should act on a fully informed basis, in good faith, with due diligence and care and in the **best interests of the company and its shareholders**. They should treat **all shareholders fairly**. The board should be able to exercise **independent judgement**. This includes assigning independent non-executive directors to appropriate tasks.

<table>
<tr><td>Exam focus point</td><td>This summary is worth remembering for the exam because it incorporates many key ideas from corporate governance codes around the world.</td></tr>
</table>

2.7 ICGN report

The International Corporate Governance Network (ICGN) issued a report (published in 2005, revised in 2009) aiming to enhance the guidance produced by the OECD. The purpose is to provide **practical guidance** for boards to meet expectations so that they can **operate efficiently** and **compete for scarce capital effectively**. The ICGN believes that companies will only achieve value in the longer term if they manage effectively their **relationships with stakeholders** such as employees, customers, local communities and the environment as a whole.

The ICGN guidance emphasises the following points in particular.

2.7.1 Sustainable value

The objectives of companies should be to **generate sustainable shareholder value over the long term**. This means that companies have to manage effectively the governance, social and environmental aspects of the activities as well as the financial.

2.7.2 Board

(a) The **structure of boards** will depend on **national models**. Boards should be responsible for guiding corporate strategy, monitoring performance and the effectiveness of corporate governance arrangements, dealing with succession issues, aligning remuneration with the company's interests, ensuring the integrity of systems and overseeing disclosure. Boards need to generate effective debate and discussion about current operations, potential risks and proposed developments.

(b) Directors should have appropriate **skills, competence, knowledge and experience**, and a diversity of perspectives. They should **demonstrate independent judgement** and **fulfil their fiduciary duties to** shareholders and the company. All directors need to **allocate sufficient time** to the company. They should have **appropriate knowledge of the company** and **access to its operations and staff**.

(c) Directors should be **re-elected at least once every three years**.

(d) The board's chair should not be the current or former Chief Executive Officer. Corporations should establish **audit, compensation and nomination/governance committees**.

(e) There should be a formal process for **evaluating the work of the board** and **individual directors**.

2.7.3 Corporate culture

(a)   The board should promote an ethical corporate culture, with a focus on **integrity**.

(b)   Companies should take steps to ensure that ethical standards are adhered to, including developing an **organisation-wide code of ethics**.

(c)   Areas codes should cover include **bribery and corruption, employee share dealing and compliance with laws**.

(d)   Companies should have **whistleblowing** channels in place for employees, suppliers or stakeholders to raise issues of non-compliance.

2.7.4 Risk management

(a)   Companies need to **take risks** but should also have proper risk management procedures in place.

(b)   The board must ensure that effective and dynamic processes are in place for **analysing and managing risks**. It should ensure that the company's risk-bearing capacity and the tolerance levels for key risks mean that the company does not exceed an **appropriate risk appetite**. Boards should disclose sufficient information about risk management to reassure shareholders.

2.7.5 Remuneration

(a)   Senior managers' remuneration should be **aligned with value-creation drivers** over an appropriate time period. Pay structures should **align manager and shareholder interests, reinforce corporate culture** and **not reward the taking of inappropriate risks**.

(b)   Companies should clearly disclose **remuneration policies and structures, particularly performance metrics**. Disclosure should also include justification of annual awards in the context of annual performance. Shareholders should be able to vote annually on remuneration packages and policies.

2.7.6 Audit

(a)   A robust and independent annual audit is an essential part of a company's checks and balances. Its scope should be prescribed by law, but the audit committee should also ensure that it is **sufficient** for the company's purposes. Shareholders should have the **right to expand the scope of the audit**.

(b)   Companies should establish an **effective internal audit function** or explain why they have not done so. The audit committee should **oversee the company's relationship with the external auditor**.

2.7.7 Disclosure and transparency

(a)   Companies should **openly communicate** their aims, challenges, achievements and failures on a timely basis, affirming annually the accuracy of financial accounts. Reporting of **relevant and material non-financial information** is an essential part of disclosure.

(b)   Companies should also disclose appropriate data about major shareholders and relationships within the corporate group.

2.7.8 Shareholders

(a)   Companies should **act to protect shareholders' rights** to vote. Divergence from shareholders having one vote for each share they own should be justified. Shareholders should be able to vote on removing individual directors and auditors.

(b)   Major changes affecting the **equity, economic interests** or **share ownership rights** of existing shareholders should not be made without prior shareholder approval.

(c)   Institutional shareholders should be able to **discharge their fiduciary duties** to vote. They should be able to consult with management.

(d)   Shareholders should be able to take **action against inequitable treatment**.

2.7.9 Shareholder responsibilities

(a) Shareholders should act in a responsible way that is **aligned with the objective of long-term value creation**. Institutional shareholders should **recognise their responsibilities** to beneficiaries, savers and pensioners. They should take account of governance risk factors and the riskiness of a company's business model.

(b) Shareholders should actively vote in a **considered manner** at general meetings. Institutional shareholders should publicly disclose their **voting policies and practices**.

2.8 Significance of international codes

Codes such as the OECD code have been developed from best practice in a number of jurisdictions. As such, they can be seen as **representing an international consensus**. They stress global issues that are important to companies operating in a number of jurisdictions. The OECD code for example emphasises the importance of **eliminating impediments to cross-border shareholdings** and **treating overseas shareholders fairly**.

Although the OECD code is **non-binding**, its principles have been incorporated into national guidance by a number of countries including Greece and China. The OECD principles have also been used by such organisations as the World Bank as a basis for assessing the corporate governance frameworks and practices in individual countries. These assessments are used to determine the level of policy dialogue with, and technical assistance given to, these countries.

The fact that the local codes of different countries are based on the same international code means that **compliance costs for companies** who are **operating in many jurisdictions** will be reduced. It also gives investors **some confidence** about the application of governance rules.

The development of international codes should also be seen in the context of the **development of robust financial reporting rules**, since investors' concerns with unreliable accounting information has meant that they have questioned corporate governance arrangements. Developments in international accounting standards aim to **promote greater international harmony in accounting practice**, and international convergence on governance is consistent with this.

2.9 Limitations of international codes

A number of problems have been identified with international codes.

(a) International principles represent a **lowest common denominator** of general, fairly bland, principles.

(b) Any attempt to strengthen the principles will be extremely difficult because of **global differences** in legal structures, financial systems, structures of corporate ownership, culture and economic factors.

(c) As international guidance has to be based on **best practice** in a number of regimes, development will always lag behind changes in the most advanced regimes.

(d) The codes have **no legislative power**.

(e) The costs of following a very structured international regime (such as one based on **Sarbanes-Oxley**) may be **very burdensome** for **companies based in less developed countries**, who are not operating worldwide.

2.10 Contribution of corporate governance codes

However the individual provisions of the codes are viewed, they have undoubtedly made a number of contributions to the corporate environment.

(a) The reports have **highlighted the contributions good corporate governance** can make to companies.

(b) The codes have **emphasised certain dangers** that have contributed to corporate governance failure, for example individuals having too great an influence.

(c)   The provisions have **provided benchmarks** that can be used to judge the effectiveness of internal controls and risk management systems.

(d)   The guidelines have **promoted specific good practice** in a number of areas, for example non-executive directors, performance-related pay and disclosure.

(e)   The recommendations have highlighted the importance of basic concepts and highlighted how these can be put into practice, for example **accountability** through recommendations about organisation-stakeholder relationships and **transparency** by specifying disclosure requirements.

2.11 Impact of corporate governance codes

A survey by McKinsey in 2002 suggested that investors were **prepared to pay a premium** to invest in a company with good corporate governance. Important signs of good corporate governance for investors included boards with a majority of independent non-executive directors, significant director share ownership and share-based compensation, formal director evaluation and good responsiveness to shareholder requests for information.

As far as company performance is concerned, surveys suggest that firms with strong shareholder rights had higher firm value, higher profits, higher sales growth and also lower capital expenditure and fewer acquisitions. The reason may be that active shareholders give managers less scope to take risks or be negligent about internal control systems. On the other hand, there appears to be little evidence that **leadership structure and board composition** have much impact on corporate performance.

Question   UK Corporate Governance Code

The UK Corporate Governance Code is a London Stock Exchange requirement for listed companies. It is recommended for other companies. Some argue that the code should be mandatory for all companies.

Required

(a)   Discuss the benefits of the UK Corporate Governance Code to shareholders and other users of financial statements.

(b)   Discuss the merits and drawbacks of having such provisions in the form of a voluntary code.

Answer

(a)   **Benefits of the UK Corporate Governance Code**

Shareholders

Of key importance to the shareholders are the suggestions that the UK Corporate Governance Code makes in respect of the **annual general meeting**. In the past, particularly for large listed companies, AGMs have sometimes been forbidding and unhelpful to shareholders. The result has been poor attendance and low voting on resolutions.

The UK Code requires that separate **resolutions** are made for identifiably different items which should assist shareholders in understanding the proposals laid before the meeting.

It also requires that **director** members of various important board committees (such as the remuneration committee) be **available** at AGMs to answer shareholders' questions.

Internal controls

Another important area for shareholders is the emphasis placed on directors' monitoring and assessing **internal controls** in the business on a regular basis. While it is a statutory requirement that directors safeguard the investment of the shareholders by instituting internal controls, this additional emphasis on quality should increase shareholders' confidence in the business.

Directors' re-election

The requirements of the code also make the **directors more accessible** to the shareholders. They are asked to submit to re-election every three years. They are also asked to make disclosure in the financial statements about their responsibilities in relation to preparing financial statements and going concern.

Audit committee

Lastly, some people would argue that the existence of an **audit committee** will lead to shareholders having greater confidence in the reporting process of an entity.

Other users

The key advantage to other users is likely to lie in the increased emphasis on internal controls as this will assist the company in operating smoothly and increasing viability of operations, which will be of benefit to customers, suppliers and employees.

(b) **Voluntary code**

Adherence to the UK Corporate Governance Code is not a statutory necessity, although it is possible that in the future such a code might become part of company law.

Advantages

The key merit of the code being voluntary for most companies is that it is **flexible**. Companies can review the code and make use of any aspects which would benefit their business.

If they adopt aspects of the code, they can disclose to shareholders what is being done to ensure **good corporate governance**, and which aspects of the code are not being followed, with reasons.

This flexibility is important, for there will be a **cost of implementing** such a code, and this cost might outweigh the benefit for small or owner-managed businesses.

Disadvantages

Critics would argue that a voluntary code allows companies that should comply with the code to **get away with non-compliance** unchallenged.

They would also argue that the **type of disclosure** made to shareholders about degrees of compliance could be **confusing and misleading** to shareholders and exacerbate the problems that the code is trying to guard against.

3 Sarbanes-Oxley

FAST FORWARD

The **Sarbanes-Oxley legislation** requires directors to **report on the effectiveness of the controls over financial reporting, limits the services auditors can provide** and requires listed companies to establish an **audit committee**. It adopts a **rules-based** approach to governance.

3.1 The Enron scandal

The most significant scandal in America in recent years has been the Enron scandal, when one of the country's biggest companies filed for bankruptcy. The scandal also resulted in the disappearance of Arthur Andersen, one of the Big Five accountancy firms, who had audited Enron's accounts. The main reasons why Enron collapsed were overexpansion in energy markets, too much reliance on derivatives' trading which eventually went wrong, breaches of federal law, and misleading and dishonest behaviour. However, enquiries into the scandal exposed a number of weaknesses in the company's governance.

3.1.1 Lack of transparency in the accounts

This particularly related to certain investment vehicles that were kept off balance sheet. Various other methods of inflating revenues, offloading debt, massaging quarterly figures and avoiding taxes were employed.

3.1.2 Ineffective corporate governance arrangements

The company's management team was criticised for being arrogant and overambitious. *The Economist* suggested that Enron's Chief Executive Officer, Kenneth Lay, was like a cult leader with his staff and employees fawning over his every word and following him slavishly. The non-executive directors were weak, and there were conflicts of interest. The chair of the audit committee was Wendy Gramm. Her husband, Senator Phil Gramm, received substantial political donations from Enron.

3.1.3 Inadequate scrutiny by the external auditors

Arthur Andersen failed to spot or question dubious accounting treatments. Since Andersen's consultancy arm did a lot of work for Enron, there were allegations of conflicts of interest.

3.1.4 Information asymmetry

Information asymmetry is the agency problem of the directors/managers knowing more than the investors. The investors included Enron's employees. Many had their personal wealth tied up in Enron shares, which ended up being worthless. They were actively discouraged from selling them. Many of Enron's directors, however, sold the shares when they began to fall, potentially profiting from them. It is alleged that the Chief Financial Officer, Andrew Fastow, concealed the gains he made from his involvement with affiliated companies.

3.1.5 Executive compensation methods

These were meant to align the interests of shareholders and directors, but seemed to encourage the overstatement of short-term profits. Particularly in the US, where the tenure of chief executive officers is fairly short, the temptation is to inflate profits in the hope that share options will have been cashed in by the time the problems are discovered.

3.2 The Sarbanes-Oxley Act 2002

In the US the response to the breakdown of stock market trust caused by perceived inadequacies in corporate government arrangements and the Enron scandal was the **Sarbanes-Oxley Act 2002**. The Act applies to all companies that are required to file periodic reports with the Securities and Exchange Commission (SEC). The Act was the most far-reaching US legislation dealing with securities in many years and has major implications for public companies. Rule-making authority was delegated to the SEC on many provisions.

Sarbanes-Oxley shifts responsibility for financial probity and accuracy to the board's **audit committee**, which typically comprises three independent directors, one of whom has to meet certain financial literacy requirements (equivalent to non-executive directors in other jurisdictions).

Along with rules from the Securities and Exchange Commission, Sarbanes-Oxley requires companies to increase their financial statement **disclosures**, to have an internal **code of ethics** and to impose **restrictions on share trading** by, and **loans to**, corporate officers.

3.3 Detailed provisions of the Sarbanes-Oxley Act

3.3.1 Oversight Board

The Act set up a new regulator, **The Public Company Accounting Oversight Board (PCAOB)**, to oversee the audit of public companies that are subject to the securities laws.

The Board has powers to set **auditing, quality control, independence and ethical standards** for registered public accounting firms to use in the preparation and issue of audit reports on the financial statements of listed companies. In particular the board is required to set standards for registered public accounting firms' reports on listed company statements on their internal control over financial reporting. The board also has **inspection and disciplinary powers** over firms.

3.3.2 Auditing standards

Audit firms should **retain working papers** for at least seven years and have **quality control standards** in place, such as second partner review. As part of the audit they should review internal control systems to ensure that they **reflect the transactions** of the client and provide **reasonable assurance** that the transactions are recorded in a manner that will **permit preparation** of the **financial statements** in accordance with **generally accepted accounting principles**. They should also review records to check whether **receipts** and **payments** are being made **only in accordance with management's authorisation**.

3.3.3 Non-audit services

Auditors are expressly prohibited from carrying out a number of services including internal audit, bookkeeping, systems design and implementation, appraisal or valuation services, actuarial services, management functions and human resources, investment management, legal and expert services. **Provision of other non-audit services** is only allowed with the **prior approval** of the **audit committee**.

3.3.4 Quality control procedures

There should be **rotation** of lead or reviewing audit partners every five years and other procedures such as independence requirements, consultation, supervision, professional development, internal quality review and engagement acceptance and continuation.

3.3.5 Auditors and audit committee

Auditors should discuss **critical accounting policies**, **possible alternative treatments**, the management letter and unadjusted differences with the audit committee.

3.3.6 Audit committees

Audit committees should be established by all listed companies.

All members of audit committees should be **independent** and should therefore not accept any **consulting** or **advisory fee** from the company or be affiliated to it. At least one member should be a financial expert. Audit committees should be responsible for the **appointment, compensation** and **oversight** of auditors. Audit committees should establish mechanisms for dealing with complaints about accounting, internal controls and audit.

3.3.7 Corporate responsibility

The **chief executive officer** and **chief finance officer** should **certify the appropriateness of the financial statements** and that those **financial statements fairly present the operations and financial condition** of the issuer. If the company has to prepare a restatement of accounts due to material non-compliance with standards, the **chief finance officer and chief executive officer** should **forfeit their bonuses**.

3.3.8 Off-balance sheet transactions

There should be **appropriate disclosure of material off-balance sheet transactions** and other relationships (transactions that are not included in the accounts but that impact on financial conditions, results, liquidity or capital resources).

3.3.9 Internal control reporting (the Section 404 requirement)

S 404 of the Act states that annual reports should contain **internal control reports** that state the responsibility of management for establishing and maintaining **adequate internal control over financial reporting**. Annual reports should contain an **assessment** of the **effectiveness** of the **internal control over financial reporting**, and a statement identifying the framework used by management to evaluate the effectiveness of the company's internal control over financial reporting.

External auditors should report on this assessment, having carried out independent testing of the control system.

To carry out their review effectively, management is likely to have to rely on internal audit work on the control systems. Internal auditors' work would include:

- Identifying controls at an entity and operational level
- Reviewing the completeness of documentation
- Testing controls
- Advising on the contents of the statement of effectiveness of the internal control system and the disclosure of material weaknesses

Companies should also report whether they have adopted a **code of conduct** for senior financial officers and the content of that code.

3.3.10 Whistleblowing provisions

Employees of **listed companies** and **auditors** will be granted whistleblower protection against their employers if they **disclose private employer information** to parties involved in a fraud claim.

3.4 Impact of Sarbanes-Oxley in America

The biggest expense involving compliance that companies are incurring is fulfilling the requirement to ensure their **internal controls** are properly documented and tested, and there is better communication about controls to shareholders. US companies had to have efficient controls in the past, but they now have to document them more comprehensively than before, and then have the external auditors report on what they have done. This has arguably resulted in greater market confidence in American companies.

The Act also formally stripped accountancy firms of almost all non-audit revenue streams that they used to derive from their audit clients, for fear of conflicts of interest. The Act makes clear that there needs to be distance between companies and external auditors. External auditors' position has also been strengthened by the requirement for listed companies to operate effective audit committees.

For lawyers, the Act strengthens requirements on them to whistleblow internally on any wrongdoing they uncover at client companies, right up to board level.

3.5 International impact of Sarbanes-Oxley

The Act also has a significant **international dimension**. About 1,500 non-US companies, including many of the world's largest, list their shares in the US and are covered by Sarbanes-Oxley. There were complaints that the new legislation conflicted with local corporate governance customs and, following an intense round of lobbying from outside the US, changes to the rules were secured. For example, German employee representatives who are non-management can sit on audit committees, and audit committees do not have to have board directors if the local law says otherwise, as it does in Japan and Italy.

In addition, as America is such a significant influence worldwide, arguably Sarbanes-Oxley may influence certain jurisdictions to adopt a more rules-based approach.

3.6 Criticisms of Sarbanes-Oxley

Monks and Minnow have criticised Sarbanes-Oxley for **not being strong enough** on some issues, for example the selection of external auditors by the audit committee, and at the same time being over-rigid on others. Directors may be less likely to consult lawyers in the first place if they believe that legislation could override lawyer-client privilege.

In addition, Monks and Minnow allege that a Sarbanes-Oxley compliance industry has sprung up focusing companies' attention on complying with all aspects of the legislation, significant or much less important. This has **distracted companies from improving information flows** to the market and then allowing the market to make well-informed decisions. The Act has also done little to address the temptation provided by generous stock options to inflate profits, other than requiring possible forfeiture if accounts are subsequently restated.

Most significantly perhaps there is recent evidence of companies turning away from the US stock markets and towards other markets, such as London. The number of initial public listings fell in New York after the introduction of Sarbanes-Oxley and rose in stock exchanges allowing a more flexible, principles-based approach. An article in the *Financial Times* suggested that this was partly due to companies tiring of the **increased compliance costs** associated with Sarbanes-Oxley implementation and allegedly reduced flexibility and corporate risk-taking.

In particular, directors of smaller listed companies have been unhappy with the requirement for companies to report on the effectiveness of their internal control structure and procedures for financial reporting. They have argued that gathering sufficient evidence for auditors on the internal controls over financial reporting is expensive and less important for small companies than for large ones. In addition, the nature of the **regulatory regime** may be an increasingly significant factor in listing decisions. A rules-based approach means compliance must be absolute. The comply or explain choice is not available.

Case Study

The following summary compares the main points of UK and US guidance.

	UK guidance	US guidance
Scope	All types of internal control including financial, operational and compliance	Internal control over financial reporting
Audit committee	Smith report states this should consist of independent non-executive directors, at least one having relevant and recent financial experience	Should consist of independent directors, one of whom should be a financial expert
Audit rotation	Ethical guidance states lead audit partner should be rotated at least every five years, other key audit partners at least every seven years	Rotation of lead partner required every five years
Non-audit services	Audit committee should review non-audit services provided by auditor to ensure auditor objectivity and independence is safeguarded. Accountancy bodies state that executing transactions or acting in management is not compatible with being an objective auditor. Other services cast doubts on objectivity	Auditors forbidden by law from carrying out a number of non-audit services including internal audit, bookkeeping, systems design/implementation, valuation, actuarial, management, expert services
Reports on internal control	Accounts to include statement of responsibility of management for internal controls. Also disclosure that there is a process for identifying, evaluating and managing risks and how board has reviewed this	Accounts should include statement of responsibility of management for internal controls and financial reporting and accounts should also include audited assessment of financial reporting controls
Code of ethics	No equivalent guidance	Companies should adopt a code of ethics for senior financial officers
Certification by directors	Under UK legislation directors are required to state in directors' report that there is no relevant audit information that they know and that auditors are unaware	Certification of appropriateness and fair presentation of accounts by chief executive and chief finance officer

Exam focus point

In his 2008 article on corporate governance, the examiner emphasised the importance of students understanding that the form and enforcement of corporate governance guidelines is an important part of corporate activity, as these systems underpin investor confidence. Students need to realise that Sarbanes-Oxley has been, and continues to be, an important influence on international corporate governance.

Debates on organisations' **social responsibilities** focus on what these responsibilities are, how organisations should deal with stakeholders and what aspects of an organisation's environment, policies and governance are affected.

4.1 Pressures on organisations

12/10

Organisations face a number of pressures from different directions to be socially responsible.

4.1.1 Governance requirements

The 2009 update of the South African King report emphasised the importance of **sustainability**, linking it with the value of ethics and improved ethical standards. The King report stresses that sustainability is a business opportunity to eliminate or minimise adverse consequences for the company, on the community and on the environment and to improve the impact of the company's operations on the economic life of the community. The triple bottom line (economic, social and environmental responsibilities) enables a company to be relevant to society and the natural environment.

4.1.2 Stakeholder expectations

Pressures on organisations to widen the scope of their corporate public accountability come from **increasing expectations of stakeholders** and **knowledge** about the **consequences of ignoring such pressures**. The King report stresses the importance of engagement with external stakeholders, and individual workers and stakeholders being able to communicate openly.

Stakeholders include communities (particularly where operations are based), customers (product safety issues), suppliers, supply chain participants and competitors. Issues such as plant closures, pollution, job creation and sourcing can have powerful **social effects** on these stakeholders.

4.1.3 Reputation risk

We shall discuss the importance of **loss of corporate reputation** in later chapters. Increasingly a business must have the reputation of being a **responsible business** that enhances long-term shareholder value by addressing the needs of its **stakeholders**.

4.2 Significance of corporate social responsibility

Businesses, particularly large ones, are subject to increasing expectations that they will exercise corporate social responsibility. Carroll's model of social responsibility suggests there are four levels of social responsibility.

4.2.1 Economic responsibilities

Companies have economic responsibilities to shareholders demanding a good return, to employees wanting fair employment conditions and customers who are seeking good-quality products at a fair price. Businesses are set up to be properly functioning economic units and so this responsibility forms the basis of all others.

4.2.2 Legal responsibilities

Since laws **codify society's moral views**, obeying those laws must be the foundation of compliance with social responsibilities. Although in all societies corporations will have a minimum of legal responsibilities, there is perhaps more emphasis on them in continental Europe than in the Anglo-American economies where the focus of discussion has been on whether many legal responsibilities constitute excessive red tape.

4.2.3 Ethical responsibilities

These are responsibilities that require corporations to act in a **fair and just way** even if the law does not compel them to do so.

4.2.4 Philanthropic responsibilities

According to Carroll, these are **desired** rather than being required of companies. They include charitable donations, contributions to local communities and providing employees with the chance to improve their own lives.

4.3 Corporate social responsibility and stakeholders

Inevitably discussion on corporate social responsibilities has been tied in with the stakeholder view of corporate activity, the view that as businesses benefit from the goodwill and other tangible aspects of society, that they owe it **certain duties** in return, particularly towards those affected by its activities.

As discussed in Chapter 1 organisations need to identify and classify stakeholders systematically and decide on how they will respond to stakeholder claims. The Mendelow model is one method of assessing the power and interest of stakeholders.

4.3.1 Problems of dealing with stakeholders

Whatever the organisation's view of its stakeholders, certain problems in dealing with them on corporate social responsibility may have to be addressed.

(a)   Collaborating with stakeholders may be **time consuming** and **expensive**.

(b)   There may be **culture clashes** between the company and certain groups of stakeholders, or between the values of different groups of stakeholders with companies caught in the middle.

(c)   There may be **conflict between the company and stakeholders** on certain issues when they are trying to collaborate on other issues.

(d)   **Consensus** between different groups of stakeholders may be difficult or impossible to achieve, and the solution may not be economically or strategically desirable.

(e)   Influential stakeholders' **independence** (and hence ability to provide necessary criticism) may be compromised if they become too closely involved with companies.

(f)   Dealing with certain stakeholders (eg public sector organisations) may be complicated by their being **accountable in turn to the wider public**.

4.4 Impact of corporate social responsibility on strategy and corporate governance

Social responsibilities can impact on what companies do in a number of ways.

4.4.1 Objectives and mission statements

If the organisation publishes a mission statement to inform stakeholders of strategic objectives, **mention of social objectives** is a sign that the board believes that they have a significant impact on strategy.

4.4.2 Ethical codes of conduct

As part of their guidance to promote **good corporate behaviour** among their employees, some organisations publish a **business code of ethics**. We shall look at these in Chapter 10.

4.4.3 Corporate social reporting and social accounts

We shall see in Chapter 11 how organisations, as part of their reporting on operational and financial matters, report on **ethical or social conduct**. Some go further, **producing social accounts** showing quantified impacts on each of the organisation's stakeholder constituencies.

4.4.4 Corporate governance

Impacts on corporate governance could include representatives from key stakeholder groups on the board, or perhaps even a **stakeholder board of directors**. It also implies the need for a binding corporate governance code that regulates the rights of stakeholder groups.

4.5 Ownership and corporate social responsibility

Having talked about the social responsibilities of companies, we also need to consider the responsibilities of shareholders in companies. This is complicated by the nature of ownership of shares. Shareholders are not buying something tangible that they can use as they please and regulate how others use it. Instead shareholders are buying a **right to participate in risks and rewards** from a separate legal entity.

One view is that shareholders have **responsibilities arising directly out of their rights**, particularly the rights to vote in an annual general meeting. The argument is that they should use the voice they have at the annual general meeting. If they own a large block of shares, they should make the most of the influence this gives them to ensure good corporate governance and accountability for decisions made.

A wider view is that shareholders, by buying shares in the hope of an opportunity of greater returns than they could achieve from a safe investment, also have a responsibility to society in the same way as they would be responsible for controlling tangible property that they owned. They should be insisting that those managing the company carry out a policy that is consistent with the **public welfare**. Institutional investors can help achieve this by having publicly-stated policies that they will only invest in companies that demonstrate corporate social responsibility.

One of the main problems with this view in relation to large corporations is the **wide dispersion of shareholders**. This means that shareholders with small percentage holdings have negligible influence on managers. In addition the ease with which shareholders can **dispose of shares** on the stock markets arguably loosens their feeling of obligation in relation to their property. This then raises the question of why the speculative (and possibly short-term) interests of shareholders should prevail over the longer-term interests of other stakeholders.

In corporate governance discussions, the idea of ownership responsibilities has had a significant influence because of the importance of **institutional shareholders**. Not only do they have the level of shareholdings that can be used as a lever to pressure managers, but they themselves have **fiduciary responsibilities** as trustees on behalf of their investors.

Exam focus point

> In the exam you may have to bring these ideas in when discussing the role of institutional shareholders.

Question

Writing a code

If you were writing a corporate governance code, would you employ a principles-based or rules-based approach?

Answer

In the end it would depend on the society in which you lived and what you were trying to achieve in the code.

A society with an emphasis on obeying a **strict legal code** would probably be most comfortable with a governance framework that reflected this and was very much **rules-based**. Similarly a society with an active legal profession in pursuit of any loopholes they can find probably needs some watertight rules. You would also probably prefer a governance framework that was rules-based if your objectives were **fairly**

narrow, if you were concerned with specific abuses rather than all-round corporate governance. In effect you would be developing a framework similar to many accounting standards, which in recent years have aimed to narrow (or eliminate) choices in accounting practice.

A society where the emphasis was on being a 'sound' corporate citizen (a good member of the Stock Exchange club perhaps) and which focused on following best practice with limited law or regulations in support would probably be most happy with a **principles-based approach**. You would also have to use that approach if your code covered governance best practice over a wide spectrum, since many aspects of governance cannot be easily defined in terms of following simple rules.

You may have taken the compromise position, that the code should be a combination of general principles with some specific provisions, for example requiring all listed companies to have an audit committee. The risk with doing this may be that companies focus on complying with the specific provisions, and neglect the governance areas covered by the vaguer, more general principles. However, research suggests that companies that happily comply with specific provisions in codes also have a good compliance record with the more general recommendations.

5 Public sector governance   12/14

FAST FORWARD

The **public sector** is different from the private sector in a number of ways but in general the main differences are in the aims and purposes of the public sector, its sources of funding and accountability.

5.1 Forms of organisations

5.1.1 Public sector

In a mixed economy the public sector delivers those goods and services that cannot or should not be provided by private sector companies or the business sector. The public sector provides services for the population either free of charge or for a cost. The services provided may be on a national level, such as a national health service, or on a local level, such as libraries. The public sector may be funded from local taxation, from central government grants, or from a combination of the two.

Public services are funded by taxpayers and are administered by elected officials at national level (Members of Parliament) or at local level (local councils or municipalities). See also Chapter 1, Section 2.8 for a discussion of agency arrangements in the public sector.

5.1.2 Private sector

This comprises a large variety of organisations with the principal aim of, in simple terms, making a profit for the benefit of individual owners or shareholders who provide the capital or funding for commercial activity.

5.1.3 Charities

These are organisations set up for not for profit purposes, funded from donations.

5.1.4 Non-governmental organisations (NGOs) and quasi-autonomous non-governmental organisations (QUANGOs)

QUANGOs are bodies set up by central government to carry out functions similar to government but with non-elected executive members. The UK Cabinet Office's definition of a QUANGO is:

> '... a body which has a role in the processes of national government, but is not a government department, or part of one, and which accordingly operates to a greater or lesser extent at arm's length from Ministers.'

The following table shows the main characteristics of these types of organisation.

	Public sector	Private sector	Charitable status	NGOs/quasi NGOs
Purposes and objectives	Public service	Profit	Relief of poverty, research, etc	As defined by owners
Performance	Central regulation	Financial reporting standards	SORP	Set outcomes
Ownership	Government	Partners/shareholders	Donors	Government
Stakeholders (including lobby groups)	The public, central government, service users	Shareholders, regulators, taxation authorities	Service users	Government, lobbying groups

Lobbying groups are those that come together with a common interest, with a view to influencing government policy. They may come under criticism if they are seen to have sufficient power to influence policy in their favour.

5.2 Levels of public sector organisations

- **Subnational**
  A division of government below central level, for example a state, county or province

- **National**
  Central government, normally based in the capital city of a country

- **Supranational**
  Above individual national governments, for example the European Union

5.3 Public and private sector arrangements

- Strategic objectives

  Private sector companies' reasons for existing are set out in the Memorandum and Articles of Association or similar document. Strategic objectives are set by the board of directors and are monitored against specific targets, such as increase in profit or market share.

  In the public sector objectives are determined by the funding body in the first instance although institutions may have a level of autonomy in how they operate and may be able to set local targets to meet specific needs.

- Leadership

  In the private sector leadership is provided by the board of directors and decisions are in some cases (eg appointing the external auditor) ratified by a majority of shareholders. Leadership in the public sector is founded on high standards of behaviour and leading by example.

  In the UK, leadership is one of the seven principles of public life as determined by the Nolan committee in 1995, the other six being selflessness, integrity, objectivity, accountability, openness and honesty.

- Governance arrangements

  Public sector organisations must have arrangements in place to demonstrate that public money is being used appropriately and that specified objectives are being met in the provision of public services. Audit or inspection regimes may be in place to report on success in achieving objectives.

5.4 Characteristics of public sector governance

- Nature of the state

  The characteristics of a state vary considerably depending on whether it is a democracy, whether it has a formal constitution and so on. The UK, for example, is a constitutional monarchy where the monarch is the head of state (a largely ceremonial role) and the Prime Minister is the head of the Government. Most states require the following four 'organs of state' in order to function.

  (a) Legislature – makes the laws
  (b) Judiciary – interprets the law
  (c) Executive – government departments headed by cabinet ministers
  (d) Secretariat – the administration or 'civil service'

- Nature of democratic control

  In a democracy the Government is answerable ultimately to the electorate. This may be at national or local level.

- Policy implementation

  At central government level policy implementation is the responsibility of the Ministers in charge of government departments. In local government the Council conducts its affairs through officers who head the various service departments in the local authority.

- Accountability and reporting

  Public entities generally need to demonstrate that they have used public money for the purposes intended and have obtained value for that money. One way of measuring this is to evaluate performance against the three 'Es':

  Economy – obtaining inputs of the appropriate quality at the lowest price available

  Efficiency – delivering the service to the appropriate standard at minimum cost, time and effort

  Effectiveness – achieving the desired objectives as stated in the entity's performance plan

Exam focus point

This is a new topic in the P1 syllabus, examinable from December 2014. You are strongly advised to read the two articles on this area written by the P1 examining team; these articles are called 'Public Sector Governance – Part 1' and 'Public Sector Governance – Part 2' and can be accessed via the ACCA website.

Chapter Roundup

- **Globalisation**, the **treatment of investors** and **major corporate scandals** have been major driving forces behind corporate governance developments.

  Many governance codes have adopted a **principles-based approach** allowing companies flexibility in interpreting the codes' requirements and to explain if they have departed from the provisions of the code.

  Insider systems are where listed companies are owned by a small number of major shareholders.

  Outsider systems are where shareholdings are more widely dispersed, and the management-ownership split is more of an issue.

- Major governance guidance includes the **UK Corporate Governance Code**, the **South African King report** and the **Singapore Code of Corporate Governance**. International guidance includes the **OECD principles** and the **ICGN report**.

- The **Sarbanes-Oxley legislation** requires directors to **report on the effectiveness of the controls over financial reporting, limits the services auditors can provide** and requires listed companies to establish an **audit committee**. It adopts a **rules-based** approach to governance.

- Debates on organisations' **social responsibilities** focus on what these responsibilities are, how organisations should deal with stakeholders and what aspects of an organisation's environment, policies and governance are affected.

- The **public sector** is different from the private sector in a number of ways, but in general the main differences are in the aims and purposes of the public sector, its sources of funding and accountability.

Quick Quiz

1 Box-ticking is a major criticism of a principles-based approach to corporate governance.

   True ☐

   False ☐

2 Fill in the blank:

   Countries where most listed companies are owned and controlled by a small number of major shareholders are known as .... systems.

3 Which UK report concentrated on establishing principles for the determination of directors' pay and disclosures about directors' remuneration in the accounts?

   A   The Cadbury report   C   The Hampel report
   B   The Greenbury report   D   The Turnbull report

4 What are the five major areas covered by the OECD principles?

5 Which major corporate scandal primarily prompted the development of the Sarbanes-Oxley rules?

6 Which of the following types of work are external auditors allowed to carry out for audit clients under the Sarbanes-Oxley rules?

   A   Internal audit   C   Taxation advice
   B   Systems design and implementation   D   Investment management

7 Sarbanes-Oxley requires accounts to include an assessment of the effectiveness of the internal control structure and the procedures for financial reporting.

   True ☐

   False ☐

8 What were the four levels of corporate social responsibility suggested by Carroll?

1   False. Box-ticking is a major criticism of a rules-based approach.

2   Insider systems

3   B   The Greenbury report

4   Rights of shareholders, equitable treatment of shareholders, role of stakeholders, disclosure and transparency, responsibilities of the board

5   Enron

6   C   Taxation advice (although the approval of the client's audit committee is required)

7   True

8   • Economic   • Ethical
    • Legal   • Philanthropic

Now try the question below from the Practice Question Bank.

Number	Level	Marks	Time
Q2	Examination	25	49 mins

Corporate governance practice and reporting

3

Topic list	Syllabus reference
1 Role of the board	A3, A4
2 Board membership and roles	A3
3 Directors' remuneration	A5
4 Relationships with shareholders and stakeholders	A8
5 Reporting on corporate governance	A8

Introduction

In this chapter we see in more detail how corporate governance reports have tried to address the issues we've discussed in the first two chapters, particularly the last section of Chapter 1. A quick glance at the contents of this chapter reveals that a properly functioning board is central to good corporate governance, hence we spend a lot of time discussing who should be on the board and what they should be doing. Section 3 deals with the perennially controversial area of directors' remuneration.

In the last two sections we deal with the areas of relationships with shareholders and stakeholders. Section 4 focuses on methods of communication, particularly general meetings. Section 5 deals with what is reported to shareholders. Remember that one aspect of the principal-agent problem is information asymmetry, agents (directors/managers) being in possession of more information than principals (shareholders). The disclosure provisions in legislation and corporate governance reports aim to address this issue.

In this chapter we have tried to mix and match codes with issues, mentioning specific codes such as the UK Corporate Governance Code that contain particularly important governance provisions. However, the examiner has stressed that worldwide convergence has meant that similar codes operate in many jurisdictions, and that it will be acceptable to refer to **relevant** provisions of your local code or international codes when answering questions.

Study guide

		Intellectual level
A3	**The board of directors**	
(a)	Explain and evaluate the roles and responsibilities of boards of directors.	3
(b)	Describe, distinguish between and evaluate the cases for and against unitary and two-tier structures.	3
(c)	Describe the characteristics, board composition and types of directors (including defining executive and non-executive directors).	2
(d)	Describe and assess the purposes, roles and responsibilities of non-executive directors.	3
(e)	Describe and analyse the general principles of the legal and regulatory frameworks within which directors operate on corporate boards.	2
(f)	Define, explore and compare the roles of the chief executive and company chairman.	3
(g)	Describe and assess the importance, and execution, of induction and continuing professional development of directors on boards of directors.	3
(h)	Explain and analyse the frameworks for assessing the performance of boards and individual directors (including NEDs) on boards.	2
(i)	Explain the meanings of diversity and critically evaluate issues of diversity on boards of directors.	3
A4	**Board committees**	
(a)	Explain and assess the importance, roles and accountabilities of board committees in corporate governance.	3
(b)	Explain and evaluate the role and purpose of the following committees in effective corporate governance: remuneration committee, nominations committee, risk committee, audit committee.	3
A5	**Directors' remuneration**	
(a)	Describe and assess the general principles of remuneration.	3
(b)	Explain and assess the effect of various components of remuneration packages on directors' behaviour.	3
(c)	Explain and analyse the legal, ethical, competitive and regulatory issues associated with directors' remuneration.	3
A8	**Governance: reporting and disclosure**	
(a)	Explain and assess the general principles of disclosure and communication with shareholders.	3
(b)	Explain and analyse best practice corporate governance disclosure requirements.	2
(c)	Define and distinguish between mandatory and voluntary disclosure of corporate information in the normal reporting cycle.	2
(d)	Explain and explore the nature of, and reasons and motivations for, voluntary disclosure in a principles-based reporting environment (compared with, for example, the reporting regime in the USA).	3
(e)	Explain and analyse the purposes of the annual general meeting and extraordinary general meetings for information exchange between the board and shareholders.	2
(f)	Describe and assess the role of proxy voting in corporate governance.	3

Exam guide

The exam is likely to include many questions like Question 1 in the Pilot Paper, requiring assessment of the strength of corporate governance arrangements in a particular organisation. This chapter provides the benchmarks against which arrangements can be assessed. You may also see quite specific part questions on aspects of corporate governance, such as the role of non-executive directors.

1 Role of the board

> **FAST FORWARD**
>
> The board should be responsible for taking major **policy** and **strategic** decisions.
>
> Directors should have a **mix of skills** and their **performance** should be assessed regularly.
>
> Appointments should be conducted by formal procedures administered by a **nomination committee**.

1.1 Definition of board's role

If the board is to act effectively, its role must be defined carefully.

Case Study

The South African King report provides a good summary of the role of the board.

> 'To define the purpose of the company and the values by which the company will perform its daily existence and to identify the stakeholders relevant to the business of the company. The board must then develop a strategy combining all three factors and ensure management implements that strategy.'

The King report stresses that the board is responsible for assets and for ensuring the company follows its strategic plan. For management to be held properly responsible, there must be a system in place that allows for **corrective action** and **penalising mismanagement**. Responsible management should do, when necessary, whatever it takes to set the company on the right path.

The UK Corporate Governance Code provides an alternative definition.

> 'The board is collectively responsible for promoting the success of the company by directing and supervising the company's affairs.
>
> The board's role is to provide entrepreneurial leadership of the company, within a framework of prudent and effective controls which enable risk to be assessed and managed.
>
> The board should set the company's strategic aims, ensure that the necessary financial and human resources are in place for the company to meet its objectives and review management performance.
>
> The board should set the company's values and standards and ensure that its obligations to its stakeholders and others are understood and met.'

For governmental organisations, the UK's *Good Governance Standard for Public Services* defines the primary functions of the governing body as:

- Establishing the organisation's strategic direction and aims, in conjunction with the executive
- Ensuring accountability to the public for the organisation's performance
- Ensuring that the organisation is managed with probity and integrity

This involves:

- Constructively challenging and scrutinising the executive
- Ensuring that the public voice is heard in decision-making
- Forging strategic partnerships with other organisations

1.2 Scope of role

To be effective, boards must **meet frequently**. The Singapore Code of Corporate Governance emphasises the need for boards to meet regularly and as warranted by circumstances. Companies should amend their constitutions to provide for telephonic and videoconference meetings. The ICGN guidelines emphasise the importance of the non-executive directors meeting in the absence of the executive directors as often as required and on a regular basis.

Directors should have **sufficient time** to fulfil their responsibilities. The UK Corporate Governance Code states that the boards should not agree to a full-time executive director taking on more than one non-executive directorship in a FTSE 100 company nor the chairmanship of such a company. The time commitment for non-executive directors should be set out when they are appointed, and they should undertake to have sufficient time to discharge their role.

1.2.1 Matters for board decision

The board should have a **formal schedule of matters** specifically reserved to it for decision at board meetings. Some would be decisions such as **mergers and takeovers** that are **fundamental** to the business and therefore should not be taken solely by executive managers. Other decisions would include **acquisitions and disposals of assets of the company** or its subsidiaries that are material to the company, **investments, capital projects, bank borrowing** facilities, **loans** and foreign currency transactions, all **above a set size** (to be determined by the board).

1.2.2 Other tasks

- Monitoring the chief executive officer
- Overseeing strategy
- Monitoring risks, control systems and governance
- Monitoring the human capital aspects of the company eg succession, morale, training, remuneration, etc
- Managing potential conflicts of interest
- Ensuring that there is effective communication of its strategic plans, both internally and externally

Case Study

For the voluntary sector, the UK's *Good Governance: A Code for the Voluntary and Community Sector* lays much the same requirements on trustees that governance codes lay on boards of directors. Even though trustees are acting in an unpaid capacity, they are still accountable for their organisation performing well and upholding its values. The code stresses the importance of the board being well organised and the board, subcommittees and offices having clear responsibilities. The code also contains various ethical requirements, including integrity, avoidance of conflicts of interest, responsiveness and accountability. The Code stresses the board of trustees' role in ensuring compliance with the objects, purposes and values of the organisation and with its governing document.

The Code also lays more stress than the governance codes targeted at listed companies on trustees focusing on the strategic direction of their organisation and not becoming involved in day-to-day activities. The chief executive officer should provide the link between the board and the staff team, and the means by which board members hold staff to account.

Other areas in the Code which go beyond the requirements for companies are for trustees to uphold and apply the principles of **equality and diversity**, and for the organisation to be fair and open to all sections of the community in all its activities.

For the public sector, the *Good Governance Standard for Public Services* stresses the need to focus on the organisation's purpose and on outcomes for service users and the rest of the community when making decisions. These decisions should be informed and transparent.

1.3 Attributes of directors

In order to carry out effective scrutiny, directors need to have **relevant expertise** in industry, company and functional area and governance. The board as a whole needs to contain a **mix of expertise** and show a **balance** between **executive management** and **independent non-executive directors**. The South African King report, reporting within a racially mixed region, stresses the importance of also having a good **demographic balance**.

1.3.1 Moral attributes

The King report lists five moral attributes that individual directors should have:

- **Conscience** – acting with intellectual honesty and independence of mind in the best interests of the company and its stakeholders, avoiding conflicts of interest

- **Inclusivity** – taking into account the legitimate interests and expectations of stakeholders

- **Competence** – having the knowledge and skills required to govern a company effectively

- **Commitment** – diligently performing duties and devoting enough time to company affairs

- **Courage** – having the courage to take the necessary risks and to act with integrity

1.3.2 Possession of necessary information

As we have seen in the last chapter, in many corporate scandals, the board was not given full information. The UK's Higgs report stresses that it is the responsibility both of the chairman to decide what information should be made available and of directors to satisfy themselves that they have **appropriate information** of **sufficient quality** to make sound judgements. The South African King report highlights the importance of the board receiving **relevant non-financial information**, going beyond assessing the financial and qualitative performance of the company and looking at **qualitative measures** that involve **broader stakeholder interests**.

Case Study

Corporate governance expert Professor Richard Leblanc commented that good boards 'are independent, competent, transparent, constructively challenge management and set the ethical tone and culture for the entire organisation.' In organisations where there were corporate misdeeds or ethical failures, there were generally also board problems. Common defects included 'undue influence, bullying, poor design, lack of industry knowledge and directors who are not engaged.'

1.4 Diversity   12/13

Key term

> **Diversity** is the variation of social and cultural identities among people existing together in a defined employment or market setting.   (Cox)
>
> Primary categories of diversity include age, race, ethnicity and gender while secondary categories of diversity include education, experience, marital status, beliefs and background.

The UK Corporate Governance Code states that, when directors are appointed, the board should have due regard for the benefits of diversity on the board, including gender diversity. In its 2011 green paper the European Commission stated that a diversity of expertise and backgrounds is essential if the board is to function efficiently. The Commission highlighted a variety of professional backgrounds, national or regional backgrounds and gender diversity as the most significant considerations when assessing diversity.

An earlier UK report, the 2003 Tyson report on the recruitment and development of non-executive directors, highlighted the benefits that diversity can bring:

(a) **Talent**

A company committed to diversity has the best chance of **finding and employing the best available talent** rather than artificially limiting itself.

(b) **Broad range of knowledge**

No one individual director can be **knowledgeable and informed about all aspects of business** given the information and expertise necessary for boards to govern listed companies effectively.

Management literature suggests that groups make better decisions if the available information is more diverse, provided the group understands who knows what and takes advantage of the knowledge. One example is having foreign nationals on the board, which should enhance knowledge of the global environment within which most listed companies operate. Diverse boards should avoid the 'group-think' that can occur when boards have similar backgrounds.

(c) **Greater range of constituencies**

Diverse boards can **reach out more effectively to a broader range of constituencies** to help them deal with problems. They can also send **positive signals** to different stakeholder groups and contribute to a better understanding of the stakeholder groups that underpin commercial success.

(d) **Independence and judgement**

A board with a broad range of experience is more likely to develop **independence of mind** and a probing attitude. It can also enhance corporate decision-making by having sensitivity to a wider range of risks to its reputation.

(e) **Corporate citizen**

Greater diversity can **enhance a company's reputation as a corporate citizen** that understands its community. Following from that, a company can have the objective of its board reflecting the make-up of the society within which it operates, in order to maximise its **strategic fit** with the community. Fairly reflecting the community can also be seen as **strengthening the social contract** between a company and its stakeholders.

However, some studies have found that diversity can result in lower cohesion and trust unless members are trained to work together and boards are effectively led.

1.4.1 Gender diversity

Much of the debate about diversity has focused on the issue of the proportion of women on boards.

The Davies report on women on boards in the UK in 2011 highlighted the following arguments in favour of greater female representation.

(a) **Improving performance**

Studies suggest that female non-executive directors **contribute more effectively** than male non-executives, preparing more conscientiously for board meetings and being more prepared to ask awkward questions and to challenge strategy. Studies also suggest that a gender-balanced board is more likely to pay attention to managing and controlling risk.

(b) **Accessing the widest talent pool**

In Europe and the US women account for approximately six out of ten university graduates and in the UK women make up almost half the labour force. Businesses will not perform to their maximum capability if they do **not utilise this pool of talent effectively**.

(c) **Being more responsive to the market**

Surveys suggest that in the UK women **hold almost half the wealth** and are responsible for about 70% of household **purchasing decisions**. As women are often the customers of the company's products, having more women directors can **improve understanding of customer needs**. Large companies in consumer-facing industries have a higher proportion of women on their boards than big companies in other sectors.

(d) **Achieving better corporate governance**

Studies have shown that boards with a significant number of women on them demonstrated better governance behaviour in a number of ways. A Canadian study provided evidence that gender-balanced boards were more likely to **measure and monitor strategy**, **adhere to ethical guidelines** and **ensure better communication** with a focus on non-financial performance measures such as employee and customer satisfaction, diversity and corporate social responsibility. There is evidence from the UK that balanced boards are better at focusing on **succession planning** and **new director training and induction**. UK evidence suggests that balanced boards are also more likely to carry out **effective reviews** of the whole board's skills, knowledge and experience, and of board performance.

The Davies report made a number of recommendations which, it was hoped, would promote an increase in the number of female directors:

- FTSE 350 companies setting out the **percentage of women** they aimed to have on their boards, with larger companies aiming for a minimum 25%

- Quoted companies being required to **disclose the proportion of women** on their boards, in senior executive positions and female employees in the whole organisation

- Listed companies establishing a **policy concerning boardroom diversity**, including measurable objectives for implementing the policy

- Disclosures in the corporate governance report about **progress in achieving diversity** and also the work of the nomination committee in promoting diversity; investors should pay close attention to what boards are doing

- Other recommendations included **advertising non-executive positions** and search firms **drawing up a code of conduct**; recruitment should utilise not only executives within the corporate sector but also women from **outside the corporate mainstream**, including entrepreneurs, academics, civil servants and women with professional service backgrounds, with training opportunities being provided as required

Elsewhere some countries have introduced quotas backed by legislation or regulation. In Norway legislation required all private listed companies to raise the proportion of women on their boards to 40% by 2008. Other countries include promotion of gender diversity as part of the comply or explain requirements. However, in some leading countries, for example Japan and Brazil, the proportion of women on boards has remained low and static.

The year after the Davies report was published saw the biggest ever increase in the UK in the percentage of women on boards, compared with numbers plateauing in the three years before the report's publication. At a similar rate of increase, FTSE 100 boards should achieve the target of having a minimum of 25% women directors by 2015. However, the number of female non-executive directors was increasing at a much faster rate than executive directors, indicating that companies were not appointing many of their female executives as directors.

1.4.2 Quotas

An issue currently under discussion at national and EU level is whether diversity, particularly gender diversity, should be imposed by mandatory quotas.

Arguments in favour of quotas include the following.

(a) **Effectiveness**

Quotas backed by legal sanctions can **achieve results quicker** than voluntary action. Norway achieved full compliance when it imposed a gender quota, whereas other European countries have seen much slower progress.

(b) **Disappearance of barriers**

Quotas force firms to **deal with issues** holding underrepresented groups back.

However, a number of arguments have been raised against quotas.

(a) **Excessive regulation**

A number of business leaders have argued that it is **not up to governments** to lay down regulations on the composition of boards. Composition needs to be determined by companies recruiting on merit according to their needs.

(b) **Tokenism**

If a candidate was believed to be appointed primarily because they belonged to the right underrepresented group, their contribution **might not be taken seriously**. Critics of this argument however claim that if candidates are appointed purely on a token basis, this is due to poor work by the nomination committee.

(c) **Need to address other issues first**

The Davies report suggested that a key barrier to more diverse recruitment was a lack of flexibility in work-life balance. Writing in the *Financial Director,* Shima Barakat suggested that a lack of **family-friendliness in work policies** was a significant issue for both sexes. Other issues that companies needed to address to improve the pool of future candidates were tailored development programmes, increasing the visibility of high-performer role models and external recruitment.

(d) **Multiple directorships**

If the recruitment pool from the underrepresented group is small, the same people may end up holding multiple directorships, **limiting their contribution to individual companies**. Critics have highlighted a group of around 70 women in Norway who hold a number of directorships each.

(e) **Other methods**

The response to the UK Davies report suggests that **other methods** to encourage companies can achieve some improvements.

 Case Study

An article in *The Wall Street Journal* in January 2010 highlighted the potential problems with diversity, and possible solutions to these issues.

Problems

Initial stereotyping

Existing directors may scrutinise new board members carefully and may easily stereotype them quickly as, for example, 'Activist' or 'Typical accountant'. This risk is greater if, at the first board meetings the newcomer attends, the new director asks basic questions or takes a different perspective from the rest of the board. The newcomer may be dismissed as clueless.

Lasting impressions

Having created a (misleading) impression in their own minds about the new director, long-serving directors may use subsequent evidence about the newcomer to reinforce their initial views, remembering anything that gives further support to the stereotype they have formed and blocking information that doesn't fit.

Culture

If a new director comes from a business or organisational environment with a different culture, the existing directors may react adversely if the newcomer behaves in a way that would be accepted in their normal environment, but is not accepted in their company. The newcomer may come from a background where interruptions are encouraged, but this may not be the way the board that the new director has joined is used to operating.

Confirmation from others

Like-minded board members may compare notes on a new colleague and support each other's impressions.

Reinforcing behaviour

If existing directors take an adverse view of newcomers, they may start reacting to them in an unfriendly manner and exclude them from informal discussions. This may result in the newcomer becoming defensive or oversensitive. Current directors may combine against the newcomer or the board may split into factions.

Solutions

Recruitment

When recruiting new members, nomination committees should consider personalities of candidates carefully. In particular they should assess whether potential directors realise how they come across to others and their ability to disagree constructively. A newcomer's lack of basic knowledge may result in the newcomer asking questions that the existing directors should still be asking, but have not done for a long time.

Assist newcomers

The chairman should ensure that newcomers are welcomed and have a chance to make a favourable first impression. Particularly at their first few board meetings, the chairman should aim to draw out the contribution of newcomers.

Be prepared for dissension

Boards should be able to cope with constructive and civil discussion. If board members feel inhibited from expressing their views because of fears of conflicts, or dissenting views are not reconciled, the board will not be effective. The chairman must encourage directors to express vague concerns. It is also useful for boards to have a devil's advocate figure, but this role should be filled by different directors at different times. Having the same director act the role the whole time, particularly if the director is perceived as representing a minority viewpoint, may lead to the director being stereotyped as a cynic and the director's views ignored.

1.5 Role and function of nomination committee 6/08, 12/13

In order to ensure that balance of the board is maintained, corporate governance codes recommend that the board sets up a **nomination committee,** made up wholly or mainly of independent non-executive directors, to oversee the process for board appointments and make recommendations to the board. The nomination committee needs to consider:

- The **balance** between executives and independent non-executives
- The **skills**, **knowledge** and **experience** possessed by the current board
- The **need for continuity** and succession planning
- The desirable **size** of the board
- The need to attract board members from a **diversity** of backgrounds

The nomination committee should ensure that appointments to the board are made using **objective criteria**. However, the criteria should not be so restrictive that it limits too greatly the number of candidates.

Case Study

It is also very important for charities to ensure that trustees have a suitable range of skills. The *Good Governance: A Code for the Voluntary and Community Sector* stresses the importance of trustees having the diverse range of skills, experience and knowledge necessary to run the organisation effectively.

The collective experience of trustees should ideally cover the following areas.

- Providing effective strategic leadership and working as a team
- Direct knowledge of the organisation's beneficiaries and users, and of their needs and aspirations
- Governance, general finance, business and management
- Human resources and diversity
- The operating environment and the risks that exist for the organisation
- Other specific knowledge such as fundraising, health, social services, property or legal

Codes stress that, as well as considering these issues when appointments are made, the nomination committee should regularly review the **structure, size** and **composition** of the board, and keep under review the **leadership needs** of the company.

It should also consider whether non-executive directors are spending **enough time** on their duties and other issues relating to re-election and reappointment of directors and membership of board committees.

Case Study

One area of concern is whether individual directors are exercising disproportionate influence on the company. For example, Boots prohibited the chairman of the remuneration committee from serving on the audit committee and vice versa.

The UK Corporate Governance Code emphasises that the procedures for recruiting directors must be formal, rigorous and transparent. To help ensure this a majority of committee members should be **independent non-executive directors**. The UK Code recommends that an **external search consultancy** and **open advertising** should be used, particularly when appointing a non-executive director or chairman.

The UK Higgs report made a number of suggestions about possible sources of non-executive directors.

- Companies operating in international markets could benefit from having at least one non-executive director with international experience.
- Lawyers, accountants and consultants can bring skills that are useful to the board.
- Listed companies should consider appointing directors of private companies as non-executive directors.
- Including individuals with charitable or public sector experience but strong commercial awareness can increase the breadth of diversity and experience on the board.

1.6 Induction of new directors   12/09

The UK Higgs report provides detailed guidance on the development of an induction programme tailored to the needs of the company and individual directors.

Build an understanding of the nature of the company, its business and its markets	<ul><li>The company's culture and values</li><li>The company's products or services</li><li>Group structure/subsidiaries/joint ventures</li><li>The company's constitution, board procedures and matters reserved for the board</li><li>The company's principal assets, liabilities, significant contracts and major competitors</li><li>Major risks and risk management strategy</li><li>Key performance indicators</li><li>Regulatory constraints</li></ul>
Build a link with the company's people	<ul><li>Meetings with senior management</li><li>Visits to company sites other than headquarters, to learn about production and services, meet employees and build profile</li><li>Participating in board's strategy development</li><li>Briefing on internal procedures</li></ul>
Build an understanding of the company's main relationships including meetings with auditors	<ul><li>Major customers</li><li>Major suppliers</li><li>Major shareholders and customer relations policy</li></ul>

1.7 Continuing professional development of board

The Higgs report points out that to remain effective, directors should **extend their knowledge and skills** continuously. The report suggests that professional development of potential directors ought to concentrate on the **role of the board**, **obligations** and **entitlements** of existing directors and the **behaviour** needed for effective board performance.

For existing directors, significant issues that professional development should cover on a regular basis include:

- Strategy

- Management of human and financial resources

- Audit and remuneration issues

- Legal and regulatory issues

- Risk management

- The effective behaviour of a board director such as influencing skills, conflict resolution, chairing skills and board dynamics

- The technical background of the company's activities so that directors can properly appreciate the strategic considerations (for example in fast-evolving fields such as financial services or technology)

The Higgs report suggests that a variety of approaches to training may be appropriate, including lectures, case studies and networking groups.

1.8 Performance of board

Appraisal of the board's performance is an important control over it, aimed at **improving board effectiveness, maximising strengths and tackling weaknesses**. It should be seen as an essential part of the **feedback** process within the company and may prompt the board to change its **methods** and/or **objectives**. The UK Corporate Governance Code recommends that **performance of the board, its committees and individual directors** should be formally **assessed once a year**. Ideally the assessment should be by an external third party who can bring **objectivity** to the process.

In order to be conducted effectively, the appraisal of the whole board will need to include:

- A review of the board's systems (conduct of meetings, work of committees, quality of written documentation)

- Performance measurement in terms of the standards it has established, financial criteria, and non-financial criteria relating to individual directors

- Assessment of the board's role in the organisation (dealing with problems, communicating with stakeholders)

If the review is carried out internally, board members may be asked to assess performance using a questionnaire based on the best practice of an effective board. The questionnaire may be supplemented by interviews.

The Higgs report provides a list of the criteria that could be used.

- Performance against objectives
- Contribution to testing and development of strategy and setting of priorities
- Contribution to robust and effective risk management
- Contribution to development of corporate philosophy (values, ethics, social responsibilities)
- Appropriate composition of board and committees
- Responses to problems or crises
- Are matters reserved for the board the right ones?
- Are decisions delegated to managers the right ones?
- Internal and external communication
- Board fully informed of latest developments
- Effectiveness of board committees
- Quality of information
- Quality of feedback provided to management
- Adequacy of board meetings and decision-making
- Fulfilling legal requirements

Parker suggests that a key aspect of board appraisal is whether the board focuses on long-term issues and vision, or spends too much time on day-to-day management matters.

Case Study

Corporate Governance: A Practical Guide published by the London Stock Exchange and the accountants RSM Robson Rhodes suggests that board evaluation needs to be in terms of clear objectives. Boards ought to be learning lessons from specific decisions they have taken. (Did they receive adequate information? Did they address the main issues well?)

Considering how the board is working as a team is also important. This includes such issues as encouragement of criticism, existence of factions and whether dominant players are restricting the contribution of others. The guidance suggests involving an external facilitator to help discover key issues.

The guide also compares the working of an effective board with other types of board and suggests that boards should consider which unsuccessful elements they demonstrate.

Type of board	Strengths	Weaknesses
Effective board	• Clear strategy aligned to capabilities • Vigorous implementation of strategy • Key performance drivers monitored • Effective risk management • Focus on views of City and other stakeholders • Regular evaluation of board performance	
The rubber stamp	• Makes clear decisions • Listens to in-house expertise • Ensures decisions are implemented	• Fails to consider alternatives • Dominated by executives • Relies on fed information • Focuses on supporting evidence • Does not listen to criticism • Role of non-executives limited

Type of board	Strengths	Weaknesses
The talking shop	• All opinions given equal weight • All options considered	• No effective decision-making process • Lack of direction from chairman • Failure to focus on critical issues • No evaluation of previous decisions
The number crunchers	• Short-term needs of investors considered • Prudent decision-making	• Excessive focus on financial impact • Lack of long-term, wider awareness • Lack of diversity of board members • Impact of social and environmental issues ignored • Risk averse
The dreamers	• Strong long-term focus • Long-term strategies • Consider social and environmental implications	• Insufficient current focus • Fail to identify or manage key risks • Excessively optimistic
The adrenaline junkies	• Clear decisions • Decisions implemented	• Lurch from crisis to crisis • Excessive focus on short term • Lack of strategic direction • Internal focus • Tendency to micro-manage
The semi-detached	• Strong focus on external environment • Intellectually challenging	• Out of touch with the company • Little attempt to implement decisions • Poor monitoring of decision-making

1.9 Performance of individual directors

Separate appraisal of the performance of the chairman and the CEO should be carried out by the non-executive directors, but **all** directors should have some form of individual appraisal. Criteria that could be applied include the following.

- **Independence** – free thinking, avoids conflicts of interest
- **Preparedness** – knows key staff, organisation and industry, aware of statutory and fiduciary duties
- **Practice** – participates actively, questioning, insists on obtaining information, undertakes professional education
- **Committee work** – understands process of committee work, exhibits ideas and enthusiasm
- **Development of the organisation** – makes suggestions on innovation, strategic direction and planning, helps win the support of outside stakeholders

1.10 Legal and regulatory frameworks

When defining the scope of their role, boards must comply with the **legal and regulatory framework** of the jurisdiction(s) within which they operate. These affect not just the scope of the board's role, but also the appointment and removal of directors. You will have covered key aspects of the framework in your company law studies, but we include a brief reminder of the main elements of the law in most

jurisdictions. The directors must also comply with the company's constitution (articles in the UK); we discuss below some common provisions in these internal regulations.

1.10.1 Legal rights

Directors are entitled to **fees and expenses** as directors according to the company's constitution, and emoluments and compensation for loss of office in line with their service contracts (discussed below).

1.10.2 Legal responsibilities

Directors have a **duty of care** to show **reasonable competence** and may have to **indemnify the company** against loss caused by their negligence. Directors are also said to be in a **fiduciary position** in relation to the company. They must act honestly in what they consider to be the best interest of the company and in good faith.

The UK Companies Act 2006 sets out seven statutory duties of directors.

- Act within their powers
- Promote the success of the company
- Exercise independent judgement
- Exercise reasonable skill, care and diligence
- Avoid conflicts of interest
- Do not accept benefits from third parties
- Declare an interest in a proposed transaction or arrangement

1.10.3 Duty to act within powers

The directors owe a duty to **act in accordance with the company's constitution**, and only to exercise powers for the purposes for what they were conferred. They have a **fiduciary duty** to the company to exercise their powers *bona fide* in what they honestly consider to be the interests of the company.

In exercising the powers given to them by the articles the directors have a fiduciary duty not only to act *bona fide* but also only to use their powers for a proper purpose. The powers are restricted to the **purposes** for **which they were given**. They should also act in accordance with decisions reached at board and company meetings and in compliance with the law.

1.10.4 Duty to promote the success of the company

An overriding theme of the Companies Act 2006 is the principle that the **purpose of the legal framework** surrounding companies should be **to help companies do business**. Their main purpose is to create wealth for the shareholders.

In essence, this principle means that the law should encourage a **long-term outlook** and **regard for all stakeholders** by directors and that **stakeholder interests** should be **pursued** in an **enlightened** and **inclusive** way.

The requirements of this duty are difficult to define and possibly problematic to apply, so the Act provides directors with a **list** of issues to keep in mind. When exercising this duty directors should consider:

- The **consequences of decisions** in the long term
- The **interests** of their **employees**
- The need to **develop good relationships** with **customers** and **suppliers**
- The **impact of the company** on the **local community** and the **environment**
- The desirability **of maintaining high standards of business conduct** and a **good reputation**
- The need to **act fairly as between all members** of the company

This list identifies areas of **particular importance** and **modern day expectations** of **responsible business behaviour**; for example, the interests of the company's employees and the impact of the company's operations on the community and the environment.

The **Act does not define** what should be regarded as the **success of a company**. This is down to a director's judgement in good faith. This is important, as it ensures that business decisions are for the directors rather than the courts. No guidance is given for what the **correct course of action** would be where the various **duties are in conflict**.

1.10.5 Duty to exercise independent judgement

Directors should **not delegate** their powers of decision-making or be **swayed by the influence of others**. Directors may delegate their functions to others, but they must continue to make independent decisions.

1.10.6 Duty to exercise reasonable skill, care and diligence

Directors have a **duty of care** to show **reasonable skill, care and diligence**.

Section 174 provides that a director owes a duty to their company to exercise the same standard of 'care, skill and diligence that would be exercised by a reasonably diligent person with:

(a)   The general knowledge, skill and experience that may reasonably be expected of a person carrying out the functions carried out by the director in relation to the company; and

(b)   The general knowledge, skill and experience that the director has.'

There is therefore a **reasonableness test** consisting of two parts.

(a)   Did the director act in a manner reasonably expected of a person performing the same role?

A director, when carrying out their functions, must show such **care** as could **reasonably** be expected from a **competent person** in that role. If a 'reasonable' director could be expected to act in a certain way, it is no defence for a director to claim, for example, lack of expertise.

(b)   Did the director act in accordance with the skill, knowledge and experience that the director actually has?

The duty to be competent extends to **non-executive directors**, who may be liable if they fail in their duty.

1.10.7 Duty to avoid conflict of interest   12/10

A conflict of interest in the context of directors' duties most often means a situation where directors face influences that tempt them not to act in the best interests of the company.

As **agents**, directors have a **general duty to try to avoid a conflict of interest**. In particular:

(a)   The directors must **retain their freedom of action** and **not fetter their discretion** by agreeing to vote as some other person may direct.

(b)   The directors owe a fiduciary duty to **avoid a conflict of duty and personal interest**.

(c)   The directors **must not obtain any personal advantage** from their position as directors **without the consent of the company** for whatever gain or profit they have obtained.

Any **action** against a director in connection with a conflict of interest will normally be **taken by the company**. The type of remedy will vary with the breach of duty.

(a)   The director may have to **account for a personal gain**.

(b)   If they contract with the company in a conflict of interest the **contract may be rescinded by the company**. However, the company cannot both affirm the contract and recover the director's profit.

(c)   The court may declare that a transaction is *ultra vires* or **unlawful**.

The company's constitution may not allow directors to have any contracts with the company. If it allows contracts, then directors are likely to have to disclose their interest to the rest of the board. Legal provisions may reinforce or be stricter than the constitution, prohibiting certain transactions (for example loans to directors) and only allowing some transactions if they are ratified by a shareholder vote (transactions above a certain size). Directors of listed companies may face stricter legal requirements.

Conflicts of interest are discussed further in Chapter 10.

1.10.8 Duty not to accept benefits from third parties

This duty **prohibits the acceptance of benefits** (including bribes) from third parties conferred by reason of them being a director, or doing (or omitting to do) something as a director.

1.10.9 Duty to declare interest in proposed transaction or arrangement

Directors are required to disclose to the other directors the nature and extent of any interest, direct or indirect, that they have in relation to a **proposed transaction** or **arrangement** with the **company**.

1.10.10 Insider dealing/trading   6/11

In most regimes it is a criminal offence for directors and others to use inside information that they have to gain from buying or selling shares in a stock market. **Inside information** has been defined as information that is specific and precise, has not yet been made public, and if made public would have a significant effect on the share price (it is **price-sensitive information**).

For directors, an obvious example would be using the advance knowledge they have of the company's results to make gains before the information is released to the market. Rules in many countries therefore include prohibition in directors dealing in shares during a **close period**, defined as a specific period (60 days for example) before the publication of annual or period results.

As well as being a criminal offence, it is also an abuse of **directors' roles as agents**, a clear instance of directors using the superior information they have for their benefit, rather than putting shareholders' interests first. It also undermines the capital markets by deterring investors who do not have access to privileged information and therefore feel that market distortions will result in insufficient returns for the risks that they face.

 Case Study

Company directors are not the only persons who may be accused of insider trading. In 2012 Cheng Yi Liang, a long-serving employee of the US Food and Drug Administration (FDA), was found guilty of misusing confidential information and sentenced to five years in prison. The FDA is responsible for drug approval in the US. Not only does it receive confidential information about companies, but the status of an application is itself highly price-sensitive information, since the public announcement of approval of a drug can have a huge impact on share price.

Ethics guru Chris Macdonald highlighted that Cheng Yi Liang did not breach ethical obligations to corporate shareholders – he had none. Instead he undermined the principles of exchange of information on which a free market is based.

1.11 Leaving office   12/13

1.11.1 Departure from office   6/09

A director may leave office in the following ways.

- **Resignation** (written notice may be required)
- Not **offering themselves for re-election** when their term of office ends
- **Failing to be re-elected**
- **Death**
- **Dissolution of the company**
- Being **removed** from office
- **Prolonged absence** meaning that director cannot fulfil duties (may be provided in law or by company constitution)
- Being **disqualified** (by virtue of the constitution or by the court)
- **Agreed departure**, possibly with compensation for loss of office

1.11.2 Time-limited appointments

Under the company's constitution or the director's service contract, some roles, particularly those of chief executive or chairman, may be for a fixed period. Ordinary directors may have to retire from the board on reaching a **retirement age** and may or may not be able to seek re-election.

In addition, some corporate governance guidelines suggest that non-executive directors should hold their post for a limited length of time. The UK Corporate Governance Code suggests that a non-executive director should normally serve for six years. Value may be added in exceptional circumstances by a non-executive director serving for longer, but the reasons need to be explained to shareholders. Higgs suggests that after nine years on the board non-executive directors should face annual re-election.

1.11.3 Retirement by rotation   6/08

Directors are often required to retire from the board and seek re-election. In many jurisdictions it is once every three years, although UK guidance has reduced the period to one year for large listed companies (discussed below). Managing directors may be exempt from the provisions about re-election of directors. The provisions may be enshrined in law, but in most jurisdictions, the company's **constitution or articles** prescribe the rules on rotation. Directors will generally be entitled to seek re-election if they have retired by rotation and the provisions may assume that the retiring directors are deemed to be reappointed. However, retirement by rotation provisions allow shareholders a regular opportunity to vote directors out of office.

Retirement by rotation has the following benefits for companies.

(a)   **Shareholder rights**

Retirement gives shareholders their main chance to judge the contribution of individual directors and **deny them re-election** if they have performed inadequately. It is an important mechanism to **ensure director accountability**.

(b)   **Evolution of the board**

Compulsory retirement of directors forces directors and shareholders to consider the need for the board **to change over time**. The fact that only some directors retire each year means that, if board changes are felt to be necessary, they can happen gradually enough to ensure some **stability**.

(c)   **Costs of contract termination**

By limiting the length of service period, **the compensation paid to directors for loss of office** under their service contracts will also be limited. Contracts may well expire at the time the director is required to retire and if then the director is not re-elected, no compensation will be payable.

Exam focus point

In June 2008 students came up with a number of incorrect definitions of retirement by rotation.
- Doing different jobs in the same company
- Finding a successor to replace you as a director
- Having to wait to leave the board, if too many directors want to leave at the same time

1.11.4 Re-election of directors

In May 2010 the UK Corporate Governance Code introduced the requirement for directors of FTSE 350 companies (the biggest listed companies) to face re-election every year. Directors of smaller listed companies should face re-election every three years.

Reaction to this new provision has been mixed. Sir David Walker, author of the Walker Review into banking governance, welcomed the new provision because it would introduce more discipline into boardrooms.

'Provision for annual election of the chairman and other board members should introduce welcome additional encouragement and discipline to both shareholders and board members in seeking to promote the best possible long-term performance in the intensely competitive environment in which so many UK companies now operate.'

However, Richard Lambert, director-general of the Confederation of British Industry (CBI), took the opposite view.

'It could promote a focus on short-term results, make boards less stable and discourage robust challenges in the boardroom.'

In July 2010 representatives of three institutional shareholders wrote to the *Financial Times* stating their opposition to the new provisions. They did not believe that the new provisions would increase accountability. Instead they claimed the provisions would result in a short-term culture, with boards being distracted by short-term voting outcomes. They felt the requirement was detrimental to building long-term relationships with boards, and ran counter to the Stewardship Code for Institutional Investors (covered in Chapter 1). The investors said they would support boards who gave valid and reasonable explanations for continuing to re-elect directors every three years.

1.11.5 Removal from office

The company's constitution may allow for a director's removal from office for a variety of reasons. These could include absence from board meetings for a long time, mental health problems or bankruptcy. The constitution or the directors' service contract may allow for removal for disciplinary reasons or on grounds of incompetence, although incompetence may be difficult to prove.

Local law or the company's constitution may also allow removal of directors by board vote, or by a shareholder vote, perhaps in a company meeting convened for that purpose.

1.11.6 Disqualification

Directors may be legally disqualified by the **court or government action**. Depending on the regime, possible grounds for disqualification may include failing to keep proper accounting records, not filing accounts, returns or other statutory documents and trading when their company is insolvent.

Disqualification is likely to mean that a person cannot be a director of any company and that the person cannot act as if they are a director or influence a board in other ways.

Case Study

UK law provides that a director may be removed from office by an ordinary resolution (75% vote in favour) passed in general meeting. Company articles may contain additional provisions, such as allowing removal by a resolution of the board of directors. These provisions permit a company to dismiss a director without observing the formalities of the statutory procedures. However, if the director also has a service agreement, they may still be entitled to compensation for its breach by their dismissal.

In addition to any provisions of the articles for removal of directors, a director may be removed from office under statute by ordinary resolution (50+% vote in favour) of which special notice (28 days) to the company has been given by the person proposing it.

This statutory power of removal overrides the articles and any service agreement (but the director may claim damages for breach of the agreement). The power is, however, limited in its effect:

(a) A member who gives special notice to remove a director cannot insist on the inclusion of their resolution in the notice of a meeting unless they qualify by representing sufficient members.

(b) A director may be irremovable if they have 'weighted' voting rights and can prevent the resolution from being passed.

In reality the combination of the company law requirements and the provisions of a director's service contract may make it difficult to remove a director until their term of office is complete.

1.11.7 Service contracts

Service contracts set out terms and conditions of directors' appointment, including duties, remuneration, constraints on activities while acting as a director, the duration of the appointment (fixed-term contract) or the required minimum period of notice (a rolling contract). There may be other provisions connected with departure, including termination without notice, payment in lieu of notice, whether the director can be placed on gardening leave and restrictions on subsequent employment (for example joining competitors).

Legal provisions in many regimes have tended to focus on requirements for companies to **keep contracts** and make them **available for shareholder inspection**. In many countries, it has been corporate governance codes that have dealt with the most controversial issues, including remuneration, the term of the contract and payments on termination of contract.

Some governance guidance states that the notice period on the contracts should be one year or less. If the director has to be given a longer period at first in order to secure agreement to join, the initial period should subsequently be reduced.

2 Board membership and roles

FAST FORWARD

Division of responsibilities at the head of an organisation is most simply achieved by separating the roles of chairman and chief executive.

Independent non-executive directors have a key role in governance. Their number and status should mean that their views carry significant weight.

2.1 Board membership

Key issues for consideration are:

- **Size** – with greater size can come greater opportunities for representation of varied views. However, this can be at the expense of ease of operation and coherence of decision-making.

- **Inside/outside mix** – what proportion should be executive decision-makers whose main employment is by the company and what proportion should be outsiders?

- **Diversity** – the issues here include male/female mix, representation from ethnic minorities and representatives from professions other than business (for example academia).

2.2 Chairman and CEO

Ultimate leadership of the organisation consists of a number of strands, most importantly:

- Leading the board of directors – the **chairman**
- Leading the management team at and below board level – the **chief executive officer or CEO**

2.2.1 Role of chairman   12/07, 6/09, 12/09

The UK Higgs report provides a thorough analysis of the role of the chairman. Higgs comments that the chairman is 'pivotal in creating the conditions for overall board and individual director effectiveness, both inside and outside the boardroom'. The chairman is responsible for:

(a) **Running the board and setting its agenda**

The chairman should ensure the board focuses on **strategic matters** and takes account of the key issues and the concerns of all board members. He should ensure the contributions of executives and non-executives are co-ordinated and good relationships are maintained.

(b) **Ensuring the board receives accurate and timely information**

We shall discuss this further later in the Text, but good information will enable the board to take sound decisions and monitor the company effectively.

(c) **Ensuring effective communication with shareholders**

The chairman should take the lead in ensuring that the board develops an understanding of the views of major investors. The chairman is often the **public face** of the company as far as investors are concerned.

(d) **Ensuring that sufficient time is allowed for discussion of controversial issues**

All members should have enough time to **consider critical issues** and not be faced with unrealistic deadlines or decision-making.

(e) **Taking the lead in board development**

The chairman is responsible for **addressing the development needs** of the board as a whole and enhancing the effectiveness of the whole team, also **meeting the development needs of individual directors**. The chairman should ensure that the induction programme for new directors is **comprehensive, formal and tailored**.

(f) **Facilitating board appraisal**

The chairman should ensure the performance of the whole board, board committees and individuals is evaluated at least once a year.

(g) **Encouraging active engagement by all the members of the board**

The chairman should promote a culture of **openness and debate**, by, in particular, ensuring that non-executive directors make an **effective contribution** to discussions.

(h) **Reporting in and signing off accounts**

Financial statements in many jurisdictions include a **chairman's statement** that must be compatible with other information in the financial statements. The statement provides an opportunity for the chairman to demonstrate that they are acting in the shareholders' best interests, and to provide an independent view of the company's affairs. The statement can also explain how the chairman is exercising their role and highlight other aspects of corporate governance that might be of concern to the shareholders.

The chairman may also be responsible for signing off the financial statements.

Higgs goes on to provide a description of an effective chairman, who:

- Upholds the highest standards of integrity and probity

- Leads board discussions to promote effective decision-making and constructive debate

- Promotes effective relationships and open communication between executive and non-executive directors

- Builds an effective and complementary board, initiating change and planning succession

- Promotes the highest standards of corporate governance

- Ensures a clear structure for, and the effective running of, board committees

- Establishes a close relationship of trust with the CEO, providing support and advice while respecting executive responsibility

- Provides coherent leadership of the company

Exam focus point

As you can see above, the examiner emphasised the importance of the role of the chairman by examining it in both the 2009 papers.

2.2.2 Role of CEO   6/09, 6/11

The CEO is responsible for **running the organisation's business** and for **proposing and developing the group's strategy** and overall commercial objectives in consultation with the directors and the board. The CEO is also responsible for **implementing the decisions of the board** and its committees, **developing the main policy statements** and **reviewing** the business's **organisational structure and operational performance**.

The CEO is the senior executive in charge of the management team and is answerable to the board for its performance. They will have to formalise the roles and responsibilities of the management team, including determining the degree of delegation.

A guidance note that used to supplement the UK Combined Code suggests that the major responsibilities of the CEO will be as follows.

(a) **Business strategy and management**

The CEO will take the lead in **developing objectives and strategy** having regard to the organisation's stakeholders, and will be responsible to the board for ensuring that the organisation achieves its objectives, optimising the use of resources.

(b) **Investment and financing**

The CEO will **examine major investments**, capital expenditure, acquisitions and disposals and be responsible for identifying new initiatives.

(c) **Risk management**

The CEO will be responsible for **managing the risk profile** in line with the risk appetite accepted by the board. They will also be responsible for ensuring that appropriate planning, operational and control systems and internal controls are in place and operate effectively. The CEO has ultimate ownership of the control systems and should take the lead in establishing the control environment and culture.

(d) **Establishing the company's management**

The CEO will provide the nomination committee with their view on the **future roles and capabilities** required of directors, and make recommendations about the recruitment of individual directors. They will also be responsible for recruiting and overseeing the management team below board level.

(e) **Board committees**

The CEO will make **recommendations** to be discussed by the board committees on **remuneration policy**, **executive remuneration** and **terms of employment**.

(f) **Liaison with stakeholders**

Like the chairman, part of the CEO's role will be to deal with those interested in the company. The chairman's focus, however, will often be on dealing with shareholder concerns, whereas the CEO will also be **concerned with other major stakeholders** who impact on the company's operations, for example its most important customers.

2.3 Division of responsibilities 12/07, 12/11

All governance reports acknowledge the importance of having a division of responsibilities at the head of an organisation to avoid the situation where one individual has **unfettered control** of the decision-making process.

The simplest way to do this is to require the roles of **chairman** and **CEO** to be held by two different people, for the following reasons.

(a) **Demands of roles**

It reflects the reality that both jobs are **demanding roles** and ultimately the idea that no one person would be able to do both jobs well. The CEO can then run the company. The chairman can run the board and take the lead in liaising with shareholders.

(b) **Authority**

There is an important difference between the authority of the chairman and the authority of the chief executive, which having the roles taken by different people will clarify. The chairman **carries the authority of the board** whereas the chief executive has the authority that is **delegated by the**

board. Separating the roles emphasises that the chairman is acting on behalf of the board, whereas the chief executive has the authority given in their **terms of appointment**. Having the same person in both roles means that **unfettered power** is concentrated into one pair of hands. The board may be ineffective in controlling the chief executive if it is led by the chief executive.

(c) **Conflicts of interest**

The separation of roles avoids the risk of **conflicts of interest**. The chairman can concentrate on representing the interests of shareholders.

(d) **Accountability**

The board cannot make the CEO **truly accountable** for management if it is led by the CEO.

(e) **Board opinions**

Separation of the roles means that the board is more able to **express its concerns effectively** by providing a point of reporting (the chairman) for the non-executive directors.

(f) **Control over information**

The chairman is responsible for obtaining the information that other directors require to **exercise proper oversight and monitor the organisation effectively**. If the chairman is also chief executive, then directors may not be sure that the information they are getting is sufficient and objective enough to support their work. The chairman should ensure that the board is receiving sufficient information to make **informed decisions**, and should put pressure on the chief executive if the chairman believes that the chief executive is not providing adequate information.

(g) **Compliance**

Separation enables compliance with governance best practice and hence reassures shareholders.

That said, there are arguments in favour of the two roles being held by the same person.

(a) **Creation of unity**

Having a single leader **creates unity** within the company. Having two leaders that disagree can create deadlock.

(b) **Acquisition of knowledge**

The holders of both posts need **considerable knowledge** of the company. A non-executive chairman may struggle to acquire this knowledge due to constraints on his time.

The UK Corporate Governance Code also suggests that the CEO should not go on to become chairman of the same company. If a CEO did become chairman, the main risk is that they will interfere in matters that are the responsibility of the new CEO and thus exercise undue influence over them.

Case Study

The issue of separation of duties was highlighted by the testimony of Paul Moore, former head of the group regulatory risk at HBOS, to the UK House of Commons' Treasury Select Committee. Moore's evidence to the Treasury Select Committee on HBOS (and other banks) stated:

'There has been a completely inadequate "separation" and "balance of powers" between the executive and all those accountable for overseeing their actions and "reining them in" ie internal control functions such as finance, risk, compliance and internal audit, non-executive Chairmen and Directors, external auditors, the FSA, shareholders and politicians.'

We shall return to Paul Moore's evidence later in this text.

Case Study

In July 2011 the international media conglomerate, News Corporation, faced a scandal arising from allegations of phone hacking at the UK paper, the *News of the World*. A public inquiry headed by judge Sir Brian Leveson and police investigations sought to establish what had happened and who may have been responsible for any dubious conduct.

The scandal also, however, pointed a spotlight on other aspects of News Corporation's affairs, including its corporate governance arrangements. Rupert Murdoch was both Chief Executive Officer and Chairman of the Board at News Corporation, as well as being its most significant shareholder. This meant that he was able to run board meetings and control the information flow. How independent the independent non-executive directors were and how much ability they had to debate what was going on was considered questionable.

This was not the first time that concerns had been raised about the corporate governance of companies controlled by Rupert Murdoch. Rupert Murdoch bought *The Times* and *The Sunday Times* in the UK in the early 1980s. The board of Times Newspapers also included National Directors, independent national figures of stature whose role it was to protect the editorial independence of the newspapers from interference by the owner. One of Rupert Murdoch's first actions was to appoint two new National Directors, without first seeking the approval of the existing National Directors. Agendas were not circulated to directors ahead of board meetings, and board meeting dates were often changed at short notice, meaning some directors could not attend. In 1985 Murdoch informed the National Directors by fax of his intentions to appoint Charles Wilson as editor of *The Times* without consulting them in advance.

Eventually Rupert Murdoch asked the National Director who had been most critical, the historian Hugh Trevor-Roper, to leave the board. Trevor-Roper agreed but commented: 'For an "independent" director to be asked by the chairman to resign with only a weekend's notice, and without time to consult those whom he ought to consult, does look rather peremptory.'

2.3.1 Alternative arrangements

UK guidance recommends that if the posts were held by the same individual, there should be a **strong independent element** on the board with a recognised senior member. A **senior independent non-executive director** should be appointed who would be available to shareholders who have concerns that have not been resolved through the normal channels.

 Case Study

A good illustration of how sensitive an issue the same person acting as chief executive and chairman can be was the experience of Marks & Spencer in the UK in 2008. Sir Stuart Rose had been group chief executive for a number of years, and was considered generally to have been successful in this role. In March 2008 the group proposed that Sir Stuart take on the role of executive chairman as well as being chief executive. This clearly breached the guidance in the Combined Code that the same person should not be both chief executive and chairman, and that the chief executive should not go on to become chairman. Marks & Spencer's justification for non-compliance with the Combined Code was that it would allow the company extra time to find a new chief executive within the company.

However a number of institutional investors objected to this arrangement. In spite of meeting with Marks and Spencer board representatives, Legal & General maintained its objections, stating that it did not support the dilution of corporate governance standards, particularly in leading UK companies. Peter Chambers, Chief Executive of Legal & General Investment Management, commented: 'We believe we have a moral responsibility to uphold corporate ethics in the UK and believe bellwether companies in the UK share this responsibility . . . We don't think they [M&S] should be explaining why they are not complying – they should be complying.' Richard Buxton of Schroders, another investor in Marks & Spencer, commented: 'For such a household name to do this sets an appalling precedent.'

Marks & Spencer proposed a number of concessions to alleviate investor concerns. These included:

- Sir Stuart standing for re-election every year at the company's annual general meeting, starting in July 2008
- His pay remaining unchanged
- Two new non-executive directors being appointed
- M&S reverting to having a separate chairman and chief executive once Sir Stuart's tenure as executive chairman ended

In early 2010, Marc Bolland took over from Stuart Rose as chief executive, but Stuart Rose continued as non-executive chairman until the end of 2010.

Exam focus point

Be careful, if you're asked about the role of the chief executive or chairman, to see whether you are supposed to cover specific aspects of the role. For example, if you were asked about the chief executive's role in internal control, you should not write about their role in developing strategy.

2.4 Board committees   6/15

Many companies operate a series of board sub-committees responsible for supervising specific aspects of governance. Operation of a committee system does not absolve the main board of its responsibilities for the areas covered by the board committees.

However, good use of committees seems to have had a positive effect on the governance of many companies. Higgs found evidence that committees had given assurance that important board duties were being discharged rigorously.

The main board committees are:

- **Audit committee** – arguably the most important committee, responsible for liaising with external audit, supervising internal audit and reviewing the annual accounts and internal controls. The audit committee's work is discussed further in Chapter 8.
- **Nomination committee** – responsible for recommending the appointments of new directors to the board. We have discussed their work above.
- **Remuneration committee** – responsible for advising on executive director remuneration policy and the specific package for each director (discussed in Section 3).
- **Risk committee** – responsible for overseeing the organisation's risk response and management strategies (discussed in Chapter 5).

Corporate governance guidance has concentrated on the work of the audit, remuneration and nomination committees. The Higgs report recommends that no one individual should serve on all committees. Most reports recommend that the committees should be staffed by non-executive directors and preferably **independent non-executive directors**. We shall now consider the role of non-executive directors to see why their role is deemed to be so significant.

2.5 Non-executive directors   12/08, 12/09, 06/13

Key term

Non-executive directors have no executive (managerial) responsibilities.

Non-executive directors should provide a **balancing influence**, and play a key role in **reducing conflicts of interest** between management (including executive directors) and shareholders. They should provide **reassurance** to shareholders, particularly institutional shareholders, that management is acting in the interests of the organisation.

Exam focus point

The P1 exams so far have demonstrated the importance of non-executive directors as central figures in corporate governance. You need a good understanding of who non-executive directors are, what they do, why they are of benefit to the organisation, and the problems that exist in relation to them.

2.6 Role of non-executive directors

The UK's Higgs report provides a useful summary of the role of non-executive directors.

(a)   **Strategy**

Non-executive directors should contribute to, and challenge the direction of, strategy. They should use their own business experience to reinforce their contribution. The Walker review on corporate governance in UK banks and other financial institutions highlighted the challenge stage as an essential part of board discussions: 'The most critical need is for an environment in which effective challenge of the executive is expected and achieved in the boardroom before decisions are taken on major risk and strategic issues.'

(b)   **Scrutiny**

Non-executive directors should scrutinise the performance of executive management in meeting goals and objectives and monitor the reporting of performance. They should represent the shareholders' interests to ensure agency issues don't arise to reduce shareholder value.

(c)   **Risk**

Non-executive directors should satisfy themselves that financial information is accurate and that financial controls and systems of risk management are robust. (These may include industry-specific systems, such as in the chemical industry.)

(d)   **People**

Non-executive directors are responsible for determining appropriate levels of remuneration for executives and are key figures in the appointment and removal of senior managers and in succession planning.

The UK Higgs report suggests that non-executive directors have 'an important and inescapable relationship with shareholders'. Higgs recommends that one or more non-executive directors should take direct responsibility for shareholder concerns, and should attend regular meetings with shareholders. One method of enhancing the contribution of non-executive directors is to appoint one of the **independent non-executive directors** as **senior independent director** to provide a sounding board for the chairman and to serve as an **intermediary** for the other directors and shareholders if they have concerns they cannot resolve through other channels.

Exam focus point	The examiner sees the contribution of non-executive directors as centred on these four elements. Question 1 in December 2007 not only required discussion of these four roles, but discussion of the tensions between them.

For the public sector, the *Good Governance Standard for Public Services* defines the role of non-executive directors as:

- Contributing to strategy by bringing a range of perspectives to strategic development and decision-making

- Making sure that effective management arrangements and an effective team are in place at the top level of the organisation

- Delegating decisions not reserved for the governing body

- Holding executives to account through purposeful challenge and scrutiny

- Being extremely careful about getting involved in operational detail for which responsibility is delegated to the executive

2.6.1 Advantages of non-executive directors

Non-executive directors can bring a number of advantages to a board of directors.

(a) **Experience and knowledge**

They may have **external experience and knowledge which executive directors do not possess**. The experience they bring can be in many different fields. They may be executive directors of other companies, and have experience of different ways of approaching corporate governance, internal controls or performance assessment. They can also bring knowledge of markets within which the company operates.

(b) **Perspective**

Non-executive directors can provide a **wider perspective** than executive directors who may be more involved in detailed operations.

(c) **Reassurance**

Good non-executive directors are often a **comfort factor** for third parties such as investors or creditors.

(d) **Contribution**

The English businessman Sir John Harvey-Jones pointed out that there are **certain roles** non-executive directors are well suited to play. These include 'father-confessor' (being a confidant for the chairman and other directors), 'oil-can' (intervening to make the board run more effectively) and acting as 'high sheriff' (if necessary taking steps to remove the chairman or chief executive).

(e) **Dual roles**

The most important advantage perhaps lies in the dual nature of the non-executive director's role. Non-executive directors are **full board members** who are expected to have the level of knowledge that full board membership implies.

At the same time, they are meant to provide the so-called **strong, independent element** on the board. This should imply that they have the knowledge and detachment to be able to **monitor the company's strategy and affairs effectively**. In particular they should be able to assess fairly the remuneration of executive directors when serving on the remuneration committee, be able to discuss knowledgeably with auditors the affairs of the company on the audit committee and be able to **scrutinise strategies for excessive risks**.

In addition, of course, appointing non-executive directors ensures compliance with corporate governance regulations or codes.

2.6.2 Problems with non-executive directors

Nevertheless there are a number of difficulties connected with the role of non-executive director.

(a) **Lack of independence**

In many organisations, non-executive directors may **lack independence**. There are in practice a number of ways in which non-executive directors can be linked to a company, as suppliers or customers for example. Even if there is no direct connection, potential non-executive directors are more likely to agree to serve if they admire the company's chairman or its way of operating.

(b) **Prejudice**

There may be a **prejudice in certain companies** against widening the recruitment of non-executive directors to include people proposed other than by the board or to include stakeholder representatives.

(c) **Preferences of best directors**

High-calibre non-executive directors may gravitate towards the **best-run companies**, rather than companies which are more in need of input from good non-executives.

(d) **Enforcing views**

Non-executive directors may have **difficulty imposing** their views on the board. It may be easy to dismiss the views of non-executive directors as irrelevant to the company's needs. This may imply that non-executive directors need good persuasive skills to influence other directors. Moreover, if executive directors are determined to push through a controversial policy, it may prove difficult for the more disparate group of non-executive directors to oppose them effectively.

(e) **Prevention of problems**

Sir John Harvey-Jones has suggested that not enough emphasis is given to the role of non-executive directors in **preventing trouble**, in warning early on of potential problems. Conversely, when trouble does arise, non-executive directors may be expected to play a major role in rescuing the situation, which they may not be able to do.

(f) **Time available**

Perhaps the biggest problem which non-executive directors face is the **limited time** they can devote to the role. If they have valuable experience, they are also likely to have time-consuming other commitments. In the time they have available to act as non-executive directors, they must contribute as knowledgeable members of the full board and fulfil their legal responsibilities as directors. They must also serve on board committees. Their responsibilities mean that their time must be managed effectively, and they must be able to focus on areas where the value they add is greatest. However, expectations of non-executive directors are increasing. The 2009 Walker review of UK financial institutions recommended that a minimum expected annual time commitment of 30 to 36 days to a major board should be clearly indicated in letters of appointment.

(g) **Weakening board unity**

Some commentators have suggested that non-executive directors can **damage company performance** by **weakening board unity** and **stifling entrepreneurship**. Agrawal and Knoeber suggested that boards are often expanded for political reasons, to include stakeholder representatives with concerns other than maximisation of financial performance.

2.7 Number of non-executive directors

Most corporate governance reports acknowledge the importance of having a significant presence of non-executive directors on the board. The question has been whether organisations should follow the broad principles expressed in the Cadbury report:

> 'The board should include non-executive directors of sufficient character and number for their views to carry significant weight.',

or whether they should follow prescriptive guidelines. New York Stock Exchange rules now require listed companies to have a majority of non-executive directors (ie more than half the board). Other codes, such as the Singapore code, suggest at least a third of the board should be independent (non-executive) directors.

2.8 Independence of non-executive directors   12/10

Although non-executive directors can fulfil the roles described above even if they are not independent, the presumption in governance reports is that non-executive directors' contribution is enhanced if they are independent. Various safeguards can be put in place to ensure that non-executive directors remain independent. Those suggested by the corporate governance reports include:

(a) **Connections**

Non-executive directors should have **no business**, **financial** or other **connection** with the company. Recent reports have widened the scope of business connections to include anyone who has been an employee or auditor, or had a material business relationship (such as being a supplier or significant customer) over the last few years, or served on the board for more than nine years.

(b) **Cross-directorships**

This is where an executive director of Company A is a non-executive director of Company B, and an executive director of Company B is a non-executive director of Company A. These are a particular threat to independence, often increased by **cross-shareholdings**. The problem is that non-executive directors will sit in judgement on executive directors when, for example, they consider their remuneration. Having one director sit in judgement on another who in turn is sitting in judgement on them is an obvious conflict of interest, with directors being concerned with their own interests rather than shareholders'.

(c) **Share options**

They should **not take part in share option schemes** and their service should not be pensionable, to maintain their independent status. This is intended to help ensure non-executive directors' detachment from executive directors, and means that they can offer advice and scrutiny that is not influenced by an interest in the company's share price in the short term.

(d) **Appointment terms**

Appointments should be for a **specified term** (often three years) and reappointment should not be automatic. The board as a whole should decide on their nomination and selection.

(e) **Advice**

Procedures should exist whereby non-executive directors may take **independent advice**, at the company's expense if necessary. This helps the non-executive directors gain outside, objective advice on areas of concern.

However, the requirements do vary jurisdiction by jurisdiction, reflecting different approaches to the drafting of codes of governance. In some jurisdictions factors that impair independence are stressed; others emphasise positive qualities that promote independence. Ultimately, as the ICGN guidelines point out, all definitions come down to non-executive directors being **independent-minded**, which means exercising objective judgement in the best interests of the corporation whatever the consequences for the director personally.

2.8.1 Maintaining independence of non-executive directors

One way of increasing independence of the non-executive directors as a whole is to **recruit non-executive directors from outside the industry in which the company operates**. Networks threatening independence can build up within industries as staff move between companies and collaborate on industry bodies. Non-executive directors from within the industry may also be influenced by the assumptions and prejudices of the industry.

However, the disadvantage of recruiting non-executive directors from outside the industry is that they may lack strategic awareness of industry issues, technical knowledge and a network of contacts. In practice the effectiveness of many boards is probably maximised by including a mixture of non-executives from within the industry with technical expertise, and industry outsiders with wider regulatory, political or social insight.

Exam focus point

> Whenever a question scenario features non-executive directors, watch out for threats to, or questions over, their independence. These could include personal or business relationships. The examiner highlighted the independence of non-executive directors in an article about independence published in August 2011, so it is very likely to be examined in future.

2.9 Characteristics of non-executive directors

The UK Higgs report summed up the characteristics of the effective non-executive director.

- Upholds the highest ethical standards of integrity and probity
- Supports executives in their leadership of the business while monitoring their conduct

- Questions intelligently, debates constructively, challenges rigorously and decides dispassionately
- Listens sensitively to the views of others inside and outside the board
- Gains the trust and respect of other board members
- Promotes the highest standards of corporate governance and seeks compliance with the provisions of the Code wherever possible

Higgs suggests that the following issues should be considered when appraising the performance of non-executive directors.

- Preparation for meetings
- Attendance level
- Willingness to devote time and effort to understand the company and its business
- Quality and value of contributions to board meetings
- Contribution to development of strategy and risk management
- Demonstration of independence by probing, maintaining own views and resisting pressure from others
- Relationships with fellow board members and senior management
- Up to date awareness of technical and industry matters
- Communication with other directors and shareholders

2.10 Multi-tier boards   12/09

Some jurisdictions take the split between executive and other directors to its furthest extent.

2.10.1 Corporate governance arrangements in Germany

Institutional arrangements in German companies are based on a **dual board**.

(a)   **Supervisory board**

A **supervisory board** has workers' representatives and stakeholders' management representatives including banks' representatives. The board has no executive function, although it does review the company's direction and strategy and is responsible for **safeguarding stakeholders' interests**. It must receive formal reports of the state of the company's affairs and finance. It approves the accounts and may appoint committees and undertake investigations. The board should be composed of members who, as a whole, have the required **knowledge, abilities and expert experience** to complete their tasks properly and are sufficiently independent.

(b)   **Management board**

A **management or executive board**, composed entirely of managers, will be responsible for the day-to-day **running** of the business. The supervisory board appoints the management board. Membership of the two boards is entirely separate.

2.10.2 Corporate governance arrangements in Japan

In Japan there are three different types of board of director.

- **Policy boards** – concerned with long-term strategic issues
- **Functional boards** – made up of the main senior executives with a functional role
- **Monocratic boards** – with few responsibilities and having a more symbolic role

Perhaps unsurprisingly, one of the main features of this structure is that decision-making is **generally thorough** but slow. This has been considered acceptable in a culture where the stress is on long-term decisions. Directors are supposed to continue to promote the interests of employees once they join the board, in line with corporate culture. Entry of executives onto the board is **controlled** by the chairman, who may seek the advice of others (frequently bankers).

2.11 Unitary boards vs multi-tier boards

2.11.1 Advantages of unitary boards

(a) **Common legal responsibility**

All participants in the single board have equal legal responsibility for management of the company and strategic performance. This implies a **more active approach** by those directors who are not executive directors and therefore act in an independent and 'supervisory' capacity.

(b) **Inclusion in decision-making**

If all the directors attend the same meetings, the **independent directors** are **less likely** to be **excluded from decision-making and given restricted access to information**. Boards that take all views into account in decision-making may end up making better decisions.

(c) **Questioning**

The **presence of non-executive directors** with different viewpoints to question the actions and decisions of executive directors as they are taking place **should lead to better decisions being made**.

(d) **Maintenance of better relationships**

The **relationship** between **different types of directors** may be **better** as a single board promotes easier co-operation.

2.11.2 Disadvantages of unitary boards

(a) **Objectivity of monitoring**

Non-executive directors' primary role is to monitor decision-making by executive directors. They may find it very difficult to monitor objectively if they are also **significantly involved in decision-making** themselves.

(b) **Time requirements**

The time requirements on non-executive directors may be **onerous**, both in terms of the time spent in board meetings and the commitment required to **obtain sufficient knowledge** about the company to properly fulfil their monitoring role.

(c) **Entrenchment of divisions with employees**

In some jurisdictions, for example the UK, the unitary board can be seen as emphasising a division between directors and employees who are not represented on the board.

(d) **Relationships with shareholders**

Similarly the unitary board also **emphasises the divide between the shareholders and the directors**. Shareholder representatives cannot be included on the board other than as directors. However, if shareholder representatives are appointed as directors, it means that they may face a conflict between promoting the interests of the shareholder group they represent, and acting in the interests of the company as a whole. If shareholder representatives are not on the board, then **the general meeting** may be the only time that shareholder grievances or concerns can be raised effectively.

2.11.3 Advantages of multi-tier boards

(a) **Separation of duties**

The main argument in favour of multi-tier boards is the **clear and formal separation** between the monitors and the executive directors being monitored.

(b) **Guarding role**

The supervisory/policy board has the **capacity** to be an **effective guard** against management inefficiency or worse. Indeed its very existence may be a **deterrent** to fraud or irregularity in a similar way to the independent audit.

(c) **Interests of stakeholders**

The supervisory/policy board should **take account of the needs of stakeholders** other than shareholders, specifically **employees**, who are clearly important stakeholders in practice. The system actively **encourages transparency within the company**, between the boards and, through the supervisory board, to the employees and the shareholders. It also **involves the shareholders and employees** in the supervision and appointment of directors.

(d) **Role of strategic board**

If the split of the board is on strategic/operational lines, a small strategic board may be able to act more **quickly and decisively** than a larger board that includes everyone with operational responsibilities.

2.11.4 Disadvantages of multi-tier boards

(a) **Lack of clarity**

Confusion over authority and therefore a **lack of accountability** can arise with multi-tier boards. This criticism has been particularly levelled at Japanese companies where the consequence is allegedly often over-secretive procedures.

(b) **Ineffectiveness of supervisory board**

In practice, the supervisory/policy board may not be as effective as it seems in theory. The **executive management board may restrict the information passed on** to the supervisory board and the boards may only liaise infrequently.

(c) **Lack of independence**

The supervisory board may not be as **independent** as would be wished, depending on how rigorous the appointment procedures are. In addition, members of the supervisory board can be and indeed are likely to be shareholder representatives. This could detract from legal requirements that shareholders don't instruct executive directors how to manage if the supervisory board was particularly strong.

(d) **Limitations of strategic board**

Exclusion of board members, particularly those with operational responsibilities from important strategic discussions, may result in decisions that do not take full account of all the important factors. Directors who are not consulted may not support the decisions, particularly if they regard them as **unworkable**.

Exam focus point

Question 1 of the Pilot Paper included a good illustration of the sort of requirement you might face. It asked for students to construct a case for (argue in favour of) the company in the scenario adopting a unitary board structure. This meant that students had to use their knowledge of the features of different board structures **and** appreciate why the company in the scenario should adopt a unitary structure.

2.11.5 The future global position

Proposals to introduce two (or more) tier boards have been particularly criticised in the UK and US. Critics claim that moves to increase the involvement of non-executive directors (influenced ironically by Sarbanes-Oxley) are a step on the slippery slope towards two-tier boards. The German and Japanese models also appear to be coming under pressure to change as a result of globalisation of capital markets and cross-border mergers and acquisitions.

3 Directors' remuneration

FAST FORWARD

Directors' remuneration should be set by a **remuneration committee** consisting of independent non-executive directors.

Remuneration should be dependent on **organisation** and **individual performance**.

Accounts should disclose **remuneration policy** and (in detail) the **packages of individual directors**.

3.1 Purposes of directors' remuneration

Clearly adequate remuneration has to be paid to directors in order to attract and retain individuals of **sufficient calibre**. Remuneration packages should be structured to ensure that individuals are **motivated to achieve performance levels** that are in the company and shareholders' best interests as well as their own personal interests.

Case Study

In November 2008 Peter Wuffli, former chief executive of the Swiss bank UBS, revealed that he had handed back SFr 12 million (£6.7 million) in bonus entitlements in sympathy with its plight. The decision contributed to pressure on other UBS directors and directors of other banks to renounce incentive payments gained through past performance.

3.1.1 Need for guidance

However, directors being paid excessive salaries and bonuses has been seen as one of the major corporate abuses for a large number of years. It is inevitable that the corporate governance provisions have targeted it. However, this is not necessarily to the disadvantage of the high-performing director, since guidance issued has been underpinned by a distinction between reasonable rewards that are justified by performance, and high rewards that are not justified and are seen as unethical.

The **Greenbury committee** in the UK set out principles which are a good summary of what remuneration policy should involve.

- Directors' remuneration should be set by **independent members** of the board.
- Any form of bonus should be related to **measurable performance** or enhanced shareholder value.
- There should be **full transparency of directors' remuneration**, including pension rights, in the annual accounts.

3.2 Role and function of remuneration committee   6/10

The remuneration committee plays the key role in establishing remuneration arrangements. In order to be effective, the committee needs to **determine** both the organisation's **general policy** on the **remuneration of executive directors** and **specific remuneration packages** for each director.

The UK Corporate Governance Code suggests measures to ensure that the committee is **independent**, including requiring the committee to be staffed by **independent non-executive directors,** ensuring that executive directors do not set their own remuneration levels. Measures to ensure independence include stating that the committee should have **no personal interests** other than as shareholders, no conflicts of interest and no day-to-day involvement in running the business.

Guidance from the Association of British Insurers stresses the importance of remuneration committees bringing **independent thought and scrutiny** to the development and review process, together with an understanding of the drivers of the business that contribute to shareholder value. The Financial Stability Forum emphasises the importance of committee members having sufficient **risk measurement expertise**.

They must also have the ability to make fair decisions about how remuneration should vary during periods of loss.

3.3 Remuneration policy

Issues connected with remuneration policy may include the following.

- The **pay scales** applied to each director's package
- The **proportion** of the **different types of reward** within each package
- The **period** within which performance related elements become payable
- What proportion of rewards should be related to **measurable performance** or enhanced shareholder value, and the balance between **short- and long-term performance elements**
- **Transparency of directors' remuneration**, including pension rights, in the annual accounts

3.3.1 Positioning of company

When establishing remuneration policy, the remuneration committee has to take into account the position of its **company relative to other companies**. The UK Greenbury report highlighted a number of factors which the remuneration committee should consider.

- Recruitment and retention difficulties
- The behaviour of others in the sector
- Level of competition
- Risks, challenges, complexity, diversity and international spread of the business
- Special expertise and understanding required

Use of an external consultant can help the committee objectively determine the other companies that should be used as benchmarks and avoid using a skewed sample for comparison. However, the UK Corporate Governance Code points out the need for directors to treat such comparisons with caution, in view of the risk of an upward ratchet in remuneration levels with no corresponding improvement in performance. Guidance from the Association of British Insurers suggests that companies need to provide justification for paying directors salaries above median levels and points out that paying salaries below median levels gives more scope for performance-related incentives. The emphasis needs to be on remuneration committees asking searching questions about the data they are given.

- How appropriate are the comparator companies and should a broader cross-section be used?

- How widely dispersed are remuneration levels within the comparator group of companies and would removing one or two companies significantly affect the mean or range?

- How reliable and up to date is the data?

A further question is how big a part comparisons should play, in particular in determining salary levels, and how much should remuneration also be influenced by individual responsibilities, internal relativities and job security.

Case Study

The German Corporate Governance Code suggests that criteria for determining the appropriateness of remuneration of individual directors include tasks the directors do, personal performance, the economic situation, the performance and outlook of the enterprise and internal and external comparisons of common levels of remuneration. Monetary remuneration should include fixed and variable elements, with variable elements based on a multi-year assessment. Remuneration arrangements should not encourage the directors to take unnecessary risks.

3.3.2 Performance measures

A key issue in determining remuneration policy is over which performance measures are used to determine the remuneration of directors. There are a number of potential problems with this decision.

- Simply, the **choice of the wrong measure**, achieving performance that does not benefit the company significantly and does not enhance shareholder value
- Excessive focus on short-term results, particularly **annual financial performance** (which can also be manipulated)
- Remuneration operating with a **time delay**, being based on what happened some time ago rather than current performance

Other issues the remuneration committee have to consider include:

- The potentially complex relationships with a variety of **strategic goals and targets** (including cost of capital, return on equity, economic value added, market share, revenue and profit growth, cost containment, cash management, compliance goals, revenue and environment goals)
- The **differentials at management/director level** (difficult with many layers of management)
- The **ability of managers to leave**, taking clients and knowledge to a competitor or their own new business
- **Individual performance** and additional work/effort

UK guidance also suggests that remuneration should be assessed by **non-financial metrics** and designed to allow voluntary elements to be **reclaimed** in the event of misstatement or misconduct.

3.4 Elements of remuneration packages   12/07, 6/09, 6/10, 12/11, 06/13

Packages will need to **attract, retain and motivate directors** of sufficient quality, while at the same time taking shareholders' interests into account as well.

However, assessing what the levels of executive remuneration should be in an imperfect market for executive skills may prove problematic. The remuneration committee needs to be mindful of the **implications** of **all aspects** of the package as well as the individual contributions and additional work effort made by each director. Important factors to take into account include:

- The **market rate** – the transfer value if a director was to move to a comparable position in another company
- **Legal, fiscal or regulatory constraints** such as a compulsory multiple between the highest and lowest paid in an organisation
- **Previous performance in the job** and the **outcome of performance reviews**
- **Stakeholder opinion and ethical considerations**

3.4.1 Basic salary

Basic salary will be in accordance with the terms of the directors' **contract of employment**, and is not related to the performance of the company or the director. Instead it is determined by the **experience, performance and responsibilities** of the director, and also what other companies might be prepared to pay (the **market rate**).

3.4.2 Performance-related bonuses

Directors may be paid a cash bonus for good (generally accounting) performance. To guard against excessive payouts, some companies impose limits on bonus plans as a fixed percentage of salary or pay.

Transaction bonuses tend to be much more controversial. Some chief executives get bonuses for acquisitions, regardless of subsequent performance, possibly indeed further bonuses for spinning off acquisitions that have not worked out.

Alternatively **loyalty bonuses** can be awarded merely to reward directors or employees for remaining with the company. Loyalty bonuses have been criticised for not being linked to performance. Sometimes they are granted for past loyalty without the director guaranteeing that they will remain with the company. There have been examples of directors leaving their company a short time after receiving a loyalty bonus.

The link between remuneration and company performance is particularly important. Recent UK guidance has stressed the need for the performance-related elements of executive directors' remuneration to be **stretching** and **designed to align their interests with those of shareholders** and **promote the long-term success of the company**. Remuneration incentives should be **compatible with risk policies and systems**.

Governance guidance has also suggested that short-term bonuses should be partially deferred, providing scope for companies to reclaim variable bonuses if subsequent results are disappointing.

Case Study

Writing in the UK *Guardian* newspaper in 2012, distinguished commentator Sir Simon Jenkins argued that bonuses for directors should be banned. Sir Simon argued that many directors were already exceptionally well paid. Bonuses were an unjustified appropriation of profits that rightly belonged to those who owned the company, the risk-bearing shareholders. Any monies that shareholders wanted distributed within the company should be shared equally between directors and staff. Bonuses had nothing to do with incentive and instead were regarded as an entitlement. The same often applied to the public sector where the criteria on whether a senior employee would receive a bonus would be subjective and overwhelmingly influenced by the individual concerned. Jenkins summed up:

'I cannot see what is so special in the psychology of a senior executive that makes him respond to a financial incentive, when the same mechanism apparently has no effect on lesser mortals.'

3.4.3 Shares

Directors may be awarded shares in the company with limits (a few years) on when they can be sold in return for good performance.

3.4.4 Share options

Share options give directors the right to purchase shares at a specified exercise price over a specified time period in the future. If the price of the shares rises so that it exceeds the exercise price by the time the options can be exercised, the directors will be able to purchase shares at lower than their market value.

Share options can be used to **align management and shareholder interests**, particularly options held for a long time when value is dependent on long-term performance. The UK Corporate Governance Code states that shares granted or other forms of remuneration should not vest or be exercisable in **less than three years**. Directors should be encouraged to hold their shares for a further period after vesting or exercise. Grants should be phased rather than being in one block.

The performance criteria used for share options are a matter of particular debate. Possible criteria include the company's performance relative to a group of **comparable companies**.

There are various tricks that can be used to reduce or eliminate the risk to directors of not getting a reward through stock options. Possibilities include grants that **fail to discount for overall market gains**, or are cushioned against loss of value through **compensatory bonuses** or **repricing**.

The UK Corporate Governance Code states that non-executive directors should not normally be offered share options, as options may impact on their independence.

3.4.5 Benefits in kind

Benefits in kind could include transport (eg a car), health provisions, life assurance, holidays, expenses and loans. The remuneration committee should consider the benefit to the director and the cost to the company of the complete package. The committee should also consider how the directors' package relates

to the package for employees. Ideally perhaps the package offered to the directors should be an extension of the package applied to the employees.

Loans may be particularly problematic. Recent corporate scandals have included a number of instances of abuses of loans, including a $408 million loan to WorldCom Chief Executive Officer Bernie Ebbers. Using corporate assets to make loans when directors can obtain loans from commercial organisations seems very doubtful, and a number of jurisdictions prohibit loans to directors of listed companies.

3.4.6 Pensions

Many companies may pay pension contributions for directors and staff. In some cases, however, there may be separate schemes available for directors at higher rates than for employees. The UK Corporate Governance Code states that as a general rule only **basic salary** should be **pensionable**. The Code emphasises that the remuneration committee should consider the pension consequences and associated costs to the company of basic salary increases and any other changes in pensionable remuneration, especially for directors close to retirement.

The Walker report on UK financial institutions responded to concerns raised about aspects of pension arrangements. It recommended that no executive board member or senior executive who leaves early should be given an automatic right to retire on a full pension – that is, through enhancement of the value of their pension fund.

3.5 Remuneration packages

As well as considering the magnitude of different elements, remuneration committees need to view the overall remuneration package for each director, and assess whether the relative weightings of each element are appropriate, particularly the balance between **basic rewards** and **incentive**. A well-balanced package should aim to **reduce agency costs** by ensuring that directors' (agents') interests are aligned with those of shareholders (principals). This means the package should reward directors who meet targets that further the interests of shareholders. The committee will need to take into account the following factors when deciding what weightings are appropriate.

3.5.1 Strategic objectives

Remuneration packages need to be **consistent** with the business's strategies. Guidance from CIMA in a 2010 discussion paper stresses the need for executive pay policies to be aligned with a clear link to business strategy, with proportionate bonuses linked to performance and risk. This implies the need for clear determination of business objectives (discussed further in Chapter 5) and careful design of packages. There should be a match between long-term business objectives and remuneration methods, such as share incentive plans, and short-term objectives and remuneration, particularly bonuses.

Of course one strategic objective may be maintaining reputation as a good corporate citizen. This may lead companies to be cautious about the maximum levels of remuneration directors are given, or be particularly concerned about headline-grabbing elements of directors' packages, for example bonuses.

Case Study

According to BP's remuneration report, bonuses were determined not only by operating cash flows and level of total shareholder return compared with other major oil companies, but also other strategic imperatives including reserve replacement, process safety and rebuilding trust.

3.5.2 Risk

The Financial Stability Forum stresses the importance of packages reflecting the risks companies face. The Forum suggests that compensation must be symmetric with risk outcomes, meaning that the bonus component should be as variable downwards in response to poor performance as it is upwards in response to good performance. It must reflect risk time horizons, with payments not being made in the short term when risks are realised over the longer term. The Forum suggests that the mix of different elements within the package must be consistent with risk alignment and will vary by director and employee.

The remuneration committee's influence can be particularly important here. The committee should be able to review what directors are **doing to achieve the targets** they have been set, and be able to penalise directors if it has evidence that they are taking excessive risks to achieve their targets.

3.5.3 Balancing of different elements

In order to achieve a fairly balanced package, the remuneration committee needs to consider how the package is balanced in different ways.

(a) **Fixed and variable elements**

A pay package that is designed to **retain directors**, for example when there is a very active market for executives, is likely to include a high fixed element. As discussed above, however, most governance reports stress the importance of reward depending to a significant degree on corporate and individual performance. That said, too high a weighting towards variable, performance-related elements, particularly if the targets set are tough, may disincentivise directors.

(b) **Immediate and deferred elements**

Most governance guidance stresses that a part of remuneration ought to be **deferred** in order to ensure that directors are not rewarded excessively for gains in performance that turn out to be temporary. The remuneration committee will need to consider the period for deferment of bonuses, the minimum vesting period for stock options and shares and whether some or all shares granted should be retained until the end of employment.

(c) **Long-term and short-term elements**

The UK Corporate Governance Code stresses the need for reward packages to be designed to promote the success of companies over time, with a **bias towards longer-term elements**. However, remuneration committees cannot completely ignore the views of influential shareholders who strongly desire short-term success.

(d) **Cash and non-cash elements**

This can include balancing salaries and bonuses with benefits and pensions, depending on the requirements and needs (for example tax efficiency) of individual directors. Most governance codes here concentrate on the balance between **cash and share-balanced rewards**, which also links into the immediate/deferred and short-term/long-term considerations described above.

Exam focus point

> The Pilot Paper asked how the different elements of packages can be used as a control mechanism to align directors and shareholders' interests, and help resolve the agency problem. December 2007 Question 2 asked about the role of performance-role pay and for an assessment of a director's remuneration package. June 2009 Question 3 asked students to criticise an unsatisfactory package. June 2010 Question 2 required discussion of another controversial package and also inadequate scrutiny by the remuneration committee. Undoubtedly future exams will also contain scenarios where directors' remuneration is an important issue, since controversies about excessive remuneration are regularly reported.

3.6 Service contracts and termination payments

Length of service contracts can be a particular problem. If service contracts are too long, and then have to be terminated prematurely, the perception often arises that the amounts paying off directors for the remainder of the contract are essentially rewards for failure. Most corporate governance guidance suggests that service contracts greater than 12 months need to be carefully considered and should ideally be avoided. A few are stricter. Singapore's code suggests that notice periods should be six months or less.

Some companies have cut the notice period for dismissing directors who fail to meet performance targets from one year to six months. Other solutions include continuing to pay a director to the end of their contract, but ceasing payment if the director finds **fresh employment**, or paying the director for **loss of office** in the form of **shares**.

3.7 Remuneration of non-executive directors

The International Corporate Governance Network (ICGN) issued guidance on the remuneration of non-executive directors in 2010 and produced further draft guidance in 2012.

The ICGN focuses on recommending methods that preserve the independence of non-executive directors. It suggests that an **annual fee or retainer** should be the preferred method of cash remuneration. Fees can vary according to the responsibilities that non-executive directors have and the demands made on their time. Non-executive directors who are members of board committees could be reasonably paid higher fees, with chairs of board committees being given additional amounts.

Alternatively the ICGN allows non-executive directors to be paid in shares that **vest in them immediately**. These shares should come with requirements about long-term ownership and holding attached, with directors holding the shares for a specified period after they retire from the board.

The ICGN believes that all non-executive directors should hold an amount of equity in the company that is **significant** to them. This should help ensure that their interests are aligned with shareholders. It would be best if these holdings were bought by the directors out of their own pockets, but giving shares to them as part of their remuneration is an acceptable alternative. The guidance prohibits transactions or arrangements that reduce the risks of share ownership for non-executive directors.

The guidance states, however, that non-executive directors should **not receive shares on a deferred basis**, **share options or performance-based remuneration**, as these might compromise their independence. Non-executive directors should also not receive:

- **Attendance fees** in addition to their basic fees – attendance at meetings is a primary duty of non-executive directors
- **Severance fees**
- **Rights to participate in defined benefit retirement schemes,** since non-executive directors are elected representatives of shareholders and not employees

3.7.1 Determining remuneration of non-executive directors

To avoid the situation where the remuneration committee is solely responsible for determining its own remuneration, the UK Corporate Governance Code states that the board or the shareholders should determine the remuneration of non-executive directors within the limits prescribed by the company's constitution.

3.8 Remuneration disclosures

In order for readers of the accounts to achieve a fair picture of remuneration arrangements, the annual report would need to disclose:

- Remuneration policy
- Arrangements for individual directors

UK regulations emphasise the importance of detailed disclosure of **performance conditions** attached to remuneration packages, such as the reasons for choosing those conditions and the methods used to determine whether the conditions have been met. A key comparison required by regulations is a line graph showing the total shareholder return on the company's shares over a five year period and the total shareholder return on a holding of a portfolio of shares over the same period representing a named broad equity market index.

Other disclosures that may be required by law or considered as good practice include the **duration of contracts with directors**, and **notice periods and termination payments** under such contracts. Details of

external remuneration consultants employed by the remuneration committee to advise on determining remuneration should be provided.

 Case Study

Good examples of where specific country disclosure requirements have gone further are the provisions in the Singapore Code of Corporate Governance which also prescribes disclosure of:

- The remuneration packages of the top five **key executives** who are not directors
- Details of the remuneration of employees who are **immediate family members** of the directors

3.9 Voting on remuneration

Along with disclosure, the directors also need to consider whether members need to signify their approval of remuneration policy by voting on the **remuneration statement** and elements of the remuneration packages, for example long-term incentive schemes. Any vote could be binding on the company or advisory. The legal impediment to voting on the overall remuneration of individual directors is the employment **contract** between the company and its directors. The shareholders cannot force the company to commit a breach of contract.

 Case Study

Votes on remuneration and their consequences were very frequently in the news in the UK and other countries in Spring 2012.

Citigroup	Shareholders rejected the chief executive's £9.4 million pay package for a year in which its shares fell by 44%. This was the first vote against a pay package in America since the say on pay legislation was introduced. Citigroup responded by saying it would look at a more formula-based method for setting pay.
Central Rand Gold	75% of shareholders voted against the remuneration report. The chief executive subsequently resigned.
Capital Shopping Centres	Almost 30% of shareholders voted against pay policies. In response the chairman of the remuneration committee promised to carry out a review of remuneration policy, focusing on areas including 'providing value for shareholders by rewarding executives primarily for results and aligning [rewards] with best practice'.
AstraZeneca	The chief executive and chairman resigned ahead of the annual general meeting after pressure from shareholders and non-executive directors.
Barclays	Nearly a third of voting shareholders failed to back remuneration policies, including the chief executive's £17 million pay package. This vote came after concessions from the chief executive and finance director about performance conditions attached to bonuses. Revelations later in 2012 about alleged fixing of the LIBOR rate resulted in the departure of the chairman and chief executive of Barclays, and Alison Carnwath, chair of the remuneration committee, also resigned.
Man Group	33% of the shareholders failed to support Alison Carnwath's re-election as director, apparently because of her failure to take a strong enough line on executive pay in her role as chair of the remuneration committee of Barclays.

Trinity Mirror	The chief executive resigned after leading shareholders, who disliked her £1.7 million pay package, put pressure on the rest of the board, threatening to vote against their re-election. During her ten years as chief executive, the publisher's market capitalisation fell from more than £1bn to £80m, and its share price fell by over 90% to 30p. During that period, her total remuneration was more than £14 million.
	Following her decision to resign, almost 50% of shareholders failed to back the remuneration report at the company's annual general meeting.
Aviva	The chief executive resigned after shareholders rejected the remuneration report. However, although the company's share price fell by 60% during his tenure, it was reported that he would leave the company with a £1.75 million pay-off.
William Hill	Almost half the shareholders opposed the chief's new pay package, including a £1.2 million retention bonus.

There are a number of issues arising from these examples of shareholder activism.

(a) The greater willingness of shareholders to intervene came after the UK Government announced proposals in January 2012 for a shareholder vote on the remuneration report to be binding.

(b) There was also systematic pressure on representatives of institutional investors, particularly from pension funds and shareholder advisory bodies such as PIRC and ISS.

(c) Communication by shareholders with the board before the annual general meeting proved to be very influential means of putting pressure on directors. For example, the chief executive of Trinity Mirror resigned before the AGM after shareholder criticism. Boards have acknowledged that more communication with shareholders is needed and remuneration committees need to be more proactive in explaining to shareholders what is happening on executive pay and why.

(d) Shareholders seemed to prefer to vote against the remuneration report rather than against the re-election of directors. However, the proportion of shareholders voting against reappointment has increased, particularly against chairs of remuneration committees who have failed to curb executive pay.

(e) There were a number of instances where directors who had left boards prematurely received settlements under their service contracts that were criticised for being excessive. This is an aspect of director reward that may receive greater attention from shareholders in future when the terms are granted, rather than when the director leaves the company.

4 Relationships with shareholders and stakeholders

FAST FORWARD

The board should maintain a **regular dialogue with shareholders**, particularly **institutional shareholders**. **The annual general meeting** is the most significant forum for communication.

How much organisations consider the interests of other stakeholders will depend on their **legal responsibilities** and the extent to which they view **stakeholders as partners**.

4.1 Rights of shareholders

The OECD guidelines stress the importance of the **basic rights of shareholders**. These include the right to secure methods of ownership registration, convey or transfer shares, obtain relevant and material information, participate and vote in general meetings and share in the profits of the company. Under the OECD guidelines shareholders should also have the right to participate in, and be sufficiently informed on, decisions concerning fundamental changes such as amendments to the company's constitution.

The guidelines also stress the importance of treating all shareholders of the same class equally, particularly protecting minority shareholders against poor treatment by controlling shareholders.

4.2 Relationships with shareholders

A key aspect of the relationship is the accountability of directors to shareholders. This can ultimately be ensured by requiring all directors to submit themselves for **regular re-election** (the corporate governance reports suggest once every three years is reasonable).

The need for regular communication with shareholders is emphasised in most reports. Particularly important is communication with **institutional shareholders**, such as pension funds who may hold a significant proportion of shares. The UK Corporate Governance Code states that non-executive directors, in particular the senior independent director, should maintain regular contact with shareholders. The board as a whole should use a variety of means for ascertaining major shareholders' opinions, for example face to face contact, analysts or brokers' briefings and surveys of shareholders' opinions.

4.3 General meetings

4.3.1 Annual general meetings

The annual general meeting is a statutorily protected opportunity for members to have a regular discussion about their company and its management. It allows the board to discuss the results of the company and explain the future outlook. Shareholders vote on the appointment of directors and auditors and the level of dividends to be paid.

The annual general meeting is the most important formal means of communication with shareholders. Governance guidance suggests that boards should **actively encourage** shareholders to attend annual general meetings. UK guidance has included some useful recommendations on how the annual general meeting could be used to **enhance communication** with shareholders, by giving shareholders an opportunity to ask questions and use their votes.

(a)   Notice of the AGM and related papers should be **sent** to shareholders **at least 20 working days** before the meeting.

(b)   Companies should consider providing a **business presentation** at the **AGM**, with a question and answer session.

(c)   The **chairs of the key sub-committees** (audit, remuneration) should be **available to answer questions**.

(d)   Shareholders should be able to **vote separately** on each substantially separate issue. The practice of 'bundling' unrelated proposals in a single resolution should cease.

(e)   Companies should propose a resolution at the AGM relating to the **report and accounts**.

(f)   The UK Stewardship Code 2012 **emphasises the importance of institutional shareholders** attending annual general meetings and **using their votes**, to translate their intentions into practice. Institutional shareholders should provide their clients with details of how they've voted.

(g)   Codes with international jurisdiction, such as the OECD principles, emphasise the importance of **eliminating impediments to cross-border voting**.

The most important document for communication with shareholders is the annual report and accounts, covered in Section 5 below.

4.3.2 Other general meetings

General meetings may also be convened to discuss issues that cannot wait until the next annual general meeting. In some jurisdictions company meetings that are not annual general meetings are called **extraordinary general meetings**, although this term is no longer used in English law.

Local legislation will impose conditions on the power to call other general meetings. Directors may be given power under the articles to call a meeting at any time they see fit. Under English law for public companies, members requisitioning a general meeting must hold at least 10% of the paid up share capital holding voting rights.

Often other general meetings are called to authorise a major strategic move, such as a large acquisition or to respond to a significant strategic threat. Shareholders may requisition a general meeting if they have urgent concerns about how the company is being run. In Chapter 1 we discussed circumstances in which institutional shareholders may intervene in a company, such as major failings in internal control. Ultimately institutional shareholders may intervene by requisitioning a general meeting.

General meetings can help reassure shareholders by allowing a two-way discussion between themselves and directors. On the other hand, they can be a means of holding directors to account and ultimately passing a vote of no confidence.

4.4 Proxy votes   12/11

Key term

> A **proxy** is a person appointed by a shareholder to vote on behalf of that shareholder at company meetings.

Under most regimes a member of a company, who is entitled to attend and vote at a meeting of the company, has a statutory right to appoint an agent, called a 'proxy', to attend and vote for them. There may be rules governing how many proxies a member can appoint, whether the proxy has to be a member, whether the proxy has a right to speak and when the proxy can vote.

Proxy forms can allow the shareholder either to **instruct the proxy** how to vote on some or all motions, or nominate someone attending the meeting (often a director) to exercise the shareholders' vote at their discretion. This is particularly relevant when the board's view is carried by proxy votes (including proxies which the board has the discretion to exercise), despite the feeling of the meeting being against the board on the motion.

Also, unless a standard proxy card is very elaborately worded, it cannot anticipate all the possible amendments to the resolution(s) set out in the notice of the meeting. If a substantial amendment is carried, the proxy's authority to vote is unaffected – but they no longer have instructions as to how they should vote. They should exercise their discretion in whatever fashion they honestly believe is likely to reflect the wishes of the shareholder.

4.4.1 Advantages of proxy voting

(a)   **Attendance**

Institutional shareholders often hold shares in hundreds of companies. It is impractical to expect their representatives to attend every annual general meeting. Even if they could, the **associated agency costs** would be considerable and the usefulness of being present would be limited if all the votes were routine. Using a proxy means that **their votes can be exercised**, in accordance with best practice. It also gives smaller shareholders who cannot attend meetings in person the chance to have some influence over the company's strategies and policies.

(b)   **Representative of shareholders' views**

If only those who attend the annual general meeting are allowed to vote and only a small number of shareholders attend, the votes taken may **not be representative** of the views of the shareholder body as a whole. Proxies mean that the views of those not attending the annual general meeting are reflected in the general meeting votes and the votes should thus be more representative of shareholder opinion.

4.4.2 The Myners report

The Myners report in the UK *Review of the Impediments to Voting UK Shares* (2004) aimed to address concerns about problems in administering proxy votes and the beneficial owners not taking sufficient interest in the votes. The report makes a number of recommendations.

(a)   **Beneficial owners**

Beneficial share owners should ensure that their agreements with investment managers and custodians who are accountable to them should include **voting standards**, **establish a chain of responsibility** and an **information flow** on voting and **require reports** by investment managers on how they have **discharged their responsibilities**. Investment managers should decide a voting policy and stick to it.

(b) **Electronic voting**

The report recommends the adoption of **electronic voting** to enhance the efficiency of the voting process and to reduce the loss of proxy votes.

(c) **Stock lending**

Stock lending is a temporary transfer of shares or other securities, from a borrower to a lender, with agreement by the borrower to return the securities to the lender at a prearranged time. The report comes down against **stock lending** on the grounds that voting rights are effectively transferred, and lending sometimes takes place specifically to transfer voting rights. Myners recommends that stock should be recalled if there are votes on contentious issues.

(d) **Investment managers**

Investment managers should **report to their clients** how they have exercised their voting responsibilities.

(e) **Procedures at meetings**

Myners addresses the situation where votes at company meetings are decided on a show of hands, with one vote per member present, unless a poll is called. Myners suggests that a **poll** should be called on **all resolutions**. The report also recommends that proxy forms should include a **vote withheld box**, to identify the extent to which shareholders are consciously abstaining. The report also recommends giving the right to speak and the right to vote on a show of hands to anyone who has been appointed to act as a proxy by a member (an alternative to filling in a proxy form).

4.5 Relationships with stakeholders

How much the board is responsible for the interests of stakeholders other than shareholders is a matter of debate. The Hampel committee claimed that, although relationships with other stakeholders were important, making the directors responsible to other stakeholders would mean there was **no clear yardstick** for judging directors' performance.

However, the OECD guidelines see a rather wider importance for stakeholders in corporate governance, concentrating on employees, creditors and the Government. Companies should behave ethically and have regard for the environment and society as a whole.

The OECD guidelines stress that the corporate governance framework should therefore ensure that respect is given to the **rights of stakeholders** that are protected by law. These rights include rights under labour law, business law, contract law and insolvency law.

The OECD guidelines also state that corporate governance frameworks should permit **'performance-enhancing mechanisms** for stakeholder participation'. Examples of this are employee representation on the board of directors, employee share ownership, profit-sharing arrangements and the right of creditors to be involved in any insolvency proceedings.

The UK Hermes Principles emphasise that companies should support **voluntary and statutory** measures that **minimise the externalisation of costs** to the detriment of society at large.

5 Reporting on corporate governance

FAST FORWARD

> Annual reports must **convey** a **fair and balanced view** of the organisation. They should state whether the organisation has complied with governance regulations and codes. It is considered best practice to give specific disclosures about the board, internal control reviews, going concern status and relations with stakeholders.

5.1 Importance of reporting

The Singapore Code of Corporate Governance summed up the importance of reporting and communication rules:

> 'Companies should engage in regular, effective and fair communication with shareholders ... In disclosing information, companies should be as descriptive, detailed and forthcoming as possible, and avoid boilerplate disclosures.'

Good disclosure helps reduce the gap between the information available to directors and the information available to shareholders, and addresses one of the key difficulties of the agency relationship between directors and shareholders.

5.2 Principles vs compulsory

The emphasis in principles-based corporate governance regimes is on **complying or explaining**. Companies either act in accordance with the principles and guidelines laid down in the code or explain why and specifically how or in what regard they have not done so.

The London Stock Exchange requires the following general disclosures.

(a)   A **narrative statement** of how companies have **applied the principles** set out in the UK Corporate Governance Code, providing explanations which enable their shareholders to assess how the principles have been applied.

(b)   A **statement** as to whether or not they **complied** throughout the accounting period with the **provisions** set out in the UK Corporate Governance Code. Listed companies that did not comply throughout the accounting period with all the provisions must specify the provisions with which they did not comply, and give reasons for non-compliance.

Case Study

The Catlin Group disclosed examples of non-compliance in a couple of areas.

The Company complies with the UK Corporate Governance Code other than in respect of the following.

- Until 30 June, one member of the Compensation Committee (Michael Eisenson) was not 'independent' due to his affiliation with a shareholder. Since 30 June, all members of the Compensation Committee are independent, so membership is now compliant with the Code.

- Certain directors' appointment letters, originally issued some years ago, do not specify a minimum time commitment. The affected individuals have been directors for at least five years, and over that time each has demonstrably devoted sufficient time and attention to their responsibilities.

Beyond these basic requirements disclosure guidelines in principles-based regimes tend to be based on the ideas of **providing balanced and detailed information** that enables shareholders to assess the company's potential. They acknowledge that **judgement** is important in deciding what to disclose.

5.3 Reporting requirements   12/08, 6/14

The corporate governance reports suggest that the directors should **explain** their **responsibility for preparing accounts**. They should **report that the business is a going concern**, with supporting assumptions and qualifications as necessary.

In addition, further statements may be required depending on the jurisdiction, such as:

(a)   Information about the **board of directors**: the composition of the board in the year, information about the independence of the non-executives, frequency of, and attendance at, board meetings, how the board's performance has been evaluated; the South African King report suggests a charter of responsibilities should be disclosed

(b)   Brief reports on the **remuneration, audit, risk and nomination committees** covering terms of reference, composition and frequency of meetings

(c)   An explanation of directors' and auditors' **responsibilities** in relation to the accounts and any significant issues connected with the preparation of accounts, for example changes in accounting standards having a major impact on the accounts

(d)   Information about **relations with auditors**, including reasons for change and steps taken to ensure auditor objectivity and independence when non-audit services have been provided

(e)   An explanation of the basis on which the company **generates or preserves value** and the **strategy** for delivering the objectives of the company

(f)   A statement that the directors have reviewed the **effectiveness** of **internal controls**, including risk management

(g)   A statement on relations and **dialogue with shareholders**

(h)   A statement that the company is a **going concern**

(i)   **Sustainability reporting**, defined by the King report as including the nature and extent of social, transformation, ethical, safety, health and environmental management policies and practices

(j)   A **business review** or **operating and financial review (OFR)**

Furthermore, the information organisations provide cannot just be backward-looking. The King report points out that investors want a forward-looking approach and to be able to assess companies against a **balanced scorecard**. Companies will need to weigh the need to keep commercially sensitive information private with the expectations that investors will receive full and frank disclosures. They should also consider the need of other stakeholders.

5.3.1 The Operating and Financial Review/Management commentary

The UK's Accounting Standards Board summarised the purpose of such a review:

> 'The Operating and Financial Review (OFR) should set out the directors' analysis of the business, in order to provide to investors a historical and prospective analysis of the reporting entity "through the eyes of management".'

In the UK guidance about the OFR was first published in 1993. The implementation of the 2006 Companies Act meant that the OFR was abolished in 2008, but most of the content originally recommended by the Accounting Standards Board should be now included in an expanded business review contained within the directors' report.

In December 2010, the International Accounting Standards Board issued an IFRS Practice Statement *Management Commentary,* which is the international equivalent of the Operating and Financial Review. The IASB stated that management commentary should follow these principles:

(a)   To provide **management's view** of the entity's performance, position and progress;

(b)   To **supplement and complement** information presented in the financial statements;

(c)   To include **forward-looking information**; and

(d)   To include information that possesses the **qualitative characteristics** described in the *Conceptual Framework.*

The Practice Statement says that to meet the objective of management commentary, an entity should include information that is essential to an understanding of the following elements.

Element	User needs
Nature of the business	The knowledge of the business in which an entity is engaged and the external environment in which it operates.
Objectives and strategies	To assess the strategies adopted by the entity and the likelihood that those strategies will be successful in meeting management's stated objectives.
Resources, risks and relationships	A basis for determining the resources available to the entity as well as obligations to transfer resources to others; the ability of the entity to generate long-term sustainable net inflows of resources; and the risks to which those resource-generating activities are exposed, both in the near term and in the long term
Results and prospects	The ability to understand whether an entity has delivered results in line with expectations and, implicitly, how well management has understood the entity's market, executed its strategy and managed the entity's resources, risks and relationships
Performance measures and indicators	The ability to focus on the critical performance measures and indicators that management uses to assess and manage the entity's performance against stated objectives and strategies

5.4 Voluntary disclosure   12/08, 12/11, 6/14

Voluntary disclosure can be defined as any disclosure above the **mandated minimum**. Examples include a chief executive officer's report, a social/environmental report, additional risk or segmental data.

Disclosing information voluntarily, going beyond what is required by law or listing rules can be advantageous for the following reasons.

(a)   **Wider information provision**

Disclosures covering wider areas than those required by law or regulations should give stakeholders a **better idea of the environment** within which the company is operating and how it is responding to that environment. This should enable investors to carry out a more informed analysis of the **strategies** the company is pursuing, **reducing information asymmetry** between directors and shareholders and perhaps attracting investment.

(b)   **Different focus of information**

Voluntary information can be focused on **future strategies and objectives**, giving readers a **different perspective to compulsory information** that tends to be **focused on historical accounting data**.

(c)   **Assurance about management**

Voluntary information provides investors with further yardsticks to **judge the performance of management**, **improving accountability**. Its disclosure demonstrates to shareholders that managers are **actively concerned with all aspects of the company's performance**.

(d)   **Consultation with equity investors and other stakeholders**

The voluntary disclosures a company makes can be determined by consultations with major equity investors such as **institutional shareholders** on what disclosures they would like to see in the accounts. There can also be consultation with other stakeholders if they are influential.

The UK Government has set out principles that are useful for voluntary disclosure in general.

(a)   The process should be **planned** and **transparent**, and communicated to everyone responsible for preparing the information.

(b)   The process should involve **consultation** within the business, and with shareholders and other key groups.

(c)   The process should ensure that **all relevant information** should be taken into account.

(d)   The process should be **comprehensive**, **consistent** and **subject to review**.

Exam focus point

December 2008 Question 1 asked about compulsory and voluntary disclosures, and how voluntary disclosures enhanced accountability. December 2011 Question 1 asked about the significance of disclosure on environmental risk management for shareholders.

Question   Charities and listed companies

Summarise the main differences between listed companies and charities.

Answer

	Listed companies	Charities
Purpose	Maximisation of returns for shareholders	Beneficial purpose for which the organisation is set up and which the law regards as charitable
Requirements	Company law Corporate governance reports Accounting standards	Charity law (although if charity is company limited by guarantee it will need to comply with relevant company legislation as well) Accounting requirements applicable to charities
Stakeholder requirements	Profit maximisation Efficiency Supply of goods and services Fair treatment	Fulfilment of charity's benevolent purposes
Governance	Board of directors Inclusion of non-executive directors	Board of trustees Inclusion of donor and beneficiary representatives Separate executive board possibly

Question   Codes and corporate governance

Discuss how the main measures recommended by the corporate governance codes should contribute towards better corporate governance.

Recommendations of corporate governance codes

Clearly, a company must have senior executives. The problem is how to ensure as far as possible that the actions and decisions of the executives will be for the benefit of shareholders. Measures that have been recommended by various corporate governance codes include the following.

Directors

(a)   A listed company is required by the UK Corporate Governance Code to appoint independent **non-executive directors**. The non-executives are intended to provide a check or balance against the power of the chairman and chief executive.

(b)   The posts of **chairman and CEO** should not be held by the same person, to prevent excessive executive power being held by one individual.

(c)   Non-executive directors should **make up** the **membership** of the remuneration committee of the board, and should determine the remuneration of executive directors. This is partly to prevent the executives deciding their own pay, and rewarding themselves excessively. Another purpose is to try to devise incentive schemes for executives that will motivate them to **achieve results** for the company that will also be in the best interests of the shareholders.

Risk assessment

The requirement in many codes for a risk audit should ensure that the board of directors is **aware** of the **risks** facing the company, and have **systems** in place for managing them. In theory, this should provide some protection against risk for the company's shareholders.

Dialogue with shareholders

The UK Corporate Governance Code encourages **greater dialogue** between a **company** and its **shareholders**. Institutional investor organisations are also encouraging **greater participation by shareholders**, for example in voting.

However, the onus is on shareholders to use this power. In early 2008 there were a number of stories in the UK press about shareholder concerns about excessive levels of directors' remuneration, although these generally did not translate into shareholders voting down the remuneration report, possibly the most effective sanction. They may though have encouraged remuneration committees to impose tougher conditions in future.

Audits

The **audit committee** of the board is seen as having a **major role** to play in promoting dialogue between the external auditors and the board. Corporate governance should be improved if the views of the **external auditors** are given greater consideration, since implementing their feedback should improve control systems.

Chapter Roundup

- The board should be responsible for taking major **policy** and **strategic** decisions.

  Directors should have a **mix of skills** and their **performance** should be assessed regularly.

  Appointments should be conducted by formal procedures administered by a **nomination committee**.

- **Division of responsibilities** at the head of an organisation is most simply achieved by separating the roles of chairman and chief executive.

  Independent non-executive directors have a key role in governance. Their number and status should mean that their views carry significant weight.

- Directors' remuneration should be set by a **remuneration committee** consisting of independent non-executive directors.

  Remuneration should be dependent on **organisation** and **individual performance**.

  Accounts should disclose **remuneration policy** and (in detail) the **packages of individual directors**.

- The board should maintain a **regular dialogue with shareholders**, particularly **institutional shareholders**. **The annual general meeting** is the most significant forum for communication.

  How much organisations consider the interests of other stakeholders will depend on their **legal responsibilities** and the extent to which they view **stakeholders as partners**.

- Annual reports must **convey** a **fair and balanced view** of the organisation. They should state whether the organisation has complied with governance regulations and codes. It is considered best practice to give specific disclosures about the board, internal control reviews, going concern status and relations with stakeholders.

Quick Quiz

1 List the ways in which a director can leave office.

2 What are the main features of the induction programme recommended by the Higgs report?

3 Fill in the blank:

   According to UK guidance boards should have a .... to define their responsibilities.

4 How can an organisation ensure that there is a division of responsibilities at its highest level?

5 What according to the Greenbury report were the key principles in establishing a remuneration policy?

6 The UK Corporate Governance Code recommends that a remuneration committee should be staffed by executive directors.

   True ☐

   False ☐

7 Which of the following is not a recommendation of UK guidance in relation to annual general meetings?

   A Notice of the AGM should be sent to shareholders at least 20 working days before the meeting.

   B To simplify voting, the key proposals made at the AGM should be combined in one resolution.

   C Companies should propose a resolution at the AGM relating to their report and accounts.

   D Institutional shareholders should provide their clients with details of how they've voted at Annual General Meetings.

8 Fill in the blank:

   A .... is a person appointed by a shareholder to vote on behalf of that shareholder at company meetings.

Answers to Quick Quiz

1
- Resignation
- Not offering himself for re-election when his term of office ends
- Failing to be re-elected
- Death
- Dissolution of the company
- Being removed from office
- Prolonged absence meaning that director cannot fulfil duties (may be provided in law or by company constitution)
- Being disqualified (by virtue of the constitution or by the court)
- Agreed departure

2
- Building an understanding of the nature of the company, its business and markets
- Building a link with the company's people
- Building an understanding of the company's main relationships

3   A formal schedule of matters reserved for their decision. (This schedule should include such decisions as approval of mergers and acquisitions, major acquisitions and disposals of assets and investments, capital projects, bank borrowing facilities, major loans and their repayment, foreign currency transactions above a certain limit.)

4
- Splitting the roles of chairman and chief executive
- Appointing a senior independent non-executive director
- Having a strong independent element on the board with a recognised leader

5
- Directors' remuneration should be set by independent members of the board
- Any form of bonus should be related to measurable performance or enhanced shareholder value
- There should be full transparency of directors' remuneration including pension rights in the annual accounts

6   False. The remuneration committee should be staffed by independent non-executive directors.

7   B   The guidance recommends that shareholders should be able to vote separately on each substantially separate issue.

8   Proxy

Now try the question below from the Practice Question Bank.

Number	Level	Marks	Time
Q3	Examination	25	49 mins

Appendix to Chapter 3

1 UK Corporate Governance Code 2012

A Leadership

A1 Role of the board

All listed companies should be led by an **effective board**, responsible for providing **entrepreneurial leadership**, within a **framework of prudent** and **effective controls**, enabling **risk to be assessed** and **managed**. The board is responsible for setting strategic aims, ensuring sufficient resources are available, setting values and standards and ensuring obligations to shareholders. The board should **meet regularly**, with a **formal schedule of matters** reserved for it. The annual report should explain how the board operates, and give details of members and attendance.

A2 Division of responsibilities

A **clear division of responsibilities** should exist so that there is a balance of power, and no one person has unfettered powers of decision. The roles of **chairman** and **chief executive** should not be exercised by one person.

A3 The chairman

The chairman is responsible for leading the board and ensuring its effectiveness. The chairman should establish the board's agenda, and ensure there is **adequate time for discussion**, particularly of strategic matters. The chairman should promote **openness and debate**, help non-executive directors contribute effectively and promote constructive relations between executives and non-executives. The chairman should ensure that the board receives **accurate, timely and clear information** and should ensure communication with shareholders is effective. The chairman should meet the independence criteria for non-executive directors. A chief executive should not go on to become chairman.

A4 Non-executive directors

Non-executive directors should scrutinise management's performance and constructively challenge strategy. They should obtain assurance about the integrity of financial information and that financial controls and risk management systems are **robust** and **defensible**. Other important tasks include **determining executive remuneration** and playing a significant role in decisions about **board changes**. One of the independent non-executives should be appointed as senior independent director, to act as an intermediary with other directors and shareholders. The chairman should hold meetings with the non-executives without the executives being there, and the non-executives should meet without the chairman to appraise the chairman's performance. Directors should ensure that concerns they have that cannot be resolved are formally recorded.

B Effectiveness

B1 Composition of the board

The board and its committees should have a balance of **skills, experience, independence and knowledge** of the company. The board should be of sufficient size to **operate effectively**, but not so large as to be **unwieldy**. The board should have a **balance** of **executive and non-executive directors** so that no individual or small group is dominant. Decisions on committee membership should take into account the need to avoid undue reliance on particular individuals. At least half the board of FTSE 350 companies should be **independent non-executive directors**. Smaller listed companies should have at least **two independent non-executive directors**.

B2 Appointments to the board

There should be a **clear, formal procedure** for appointing new directors. A nomination committee should make recommendations about all new board appointments. The majority of members of this committee should be independent non-executives. Directors should be appointed **on merit**, against objective criteria, and with consideration to the value of diversity, including gender diversity. The annual report should include a section on the board's policy on diversity and its success in achieving those policy objectives. There should be an **orderly succession process** in place.

B3 Commitment

Directors should allocate sufficient time to the company to **discharge their duties effectively**. In particular, the nomination committee should assess the **time commitment expected** of the chairman, and the chairman's other commitments should be disclosed to the board and shareholders. Non-executives' letters of appointment should set out the expected time commitment and non-executives should undertake to have sufficient time to fulfil their responsibilities. Their other significant commitments should be disclosed to the board. A full-time executive director should not take on more than one non-executive directorship of a FTSE 100 company, nor the chairmanship of a FTSE 100 company.

B4 Development

All directors should be properly inducted when they join the board and regularly update their skills and knowledge. The chairman should **agree training and development needs** with each director.

B5 Information and support

The board should be **promptly supplied** with **enough information** to enable it to carry out its duties. Information volunteered by management will sometimes need to be supplemented by information from other sources. The chairman and secretary should ensure good information flows. Directors should be able to obtain independent professional advice and have access to the services of the company secretary. The company secretary is responsible for **advising the chairman** on **all governance matters**. The whole board should be responsible for appointing and removing the company secretary.

B6 Evaluation

There should be a **vigorous annual performance evaluation** of the board as a whole, individual directors (effective contribution and commitment) and board committees. Evaluation of the board of FTSE 350 companies should be externally facilitated at **least once every three years**. The chairman should take action as a result of the review, if necessary proposing new board members or seeking the **resignation of directors**.

B7 Re-election

All directors should submit themselves for **re-election regularly**, and at least once every three years. Directors of FTSE 350 companies should be subject to **annual election by shareholders**.

C Accountability

C1 Financial and business reporting

The board should present a **fair, balanced and understandable assessment** of the **company's position and prospects** in the annual accounts and other reports, such as interim reports and reports to regulators. The board should ensure that narrative sections of the annual report are consistent with the financial statements and the assessment of the company's performance. The directors should explain their responsibility for the accounts, and the auditors should state their reporting responsibilities. The directors should explain the basis on which the company **generates or preserves value** and the **strategy for**

delivering the company's longer-term objectives. The directors should also report on the going concern status of the business.

C2 Risk management and internal control

The board is responsible for determining the **nature and extent of the significant risks** it is willing to take to achieve objectives. Good systems of **risk management and control** should be maintained. The directors should **review effectiveness** annually and report to shareholders that they have done so. The review should cover all controls including financial, operational and compliance controls and risk management.

C3 Audit committee and auditors

There should be **formal and clear arrangements** with the **company's auditors**, and for applying the financial reporting and internal control principles. Companies should have an **audit committee** consisting of independent non-executive directors. One member should have **recent and relevant financial experience**. The committee should **monitor the accounts**, review **internal financial controls** and also other **internal controls and risk management systems** if there is no risk committee. The audit committee should make recommendations for the **appointment and remuneration of the external auditor**, and consider the auditor's **independence and objectivity,** the **effectiveness of the audit process** and whether the external auditor should **provide non-audit services**. FTSE 350 companies should put the external audit contract out to tender at least every ten years. The audit committee should also **review internal audit's work**. If there is no internal audit function, the audit committee should consider annually whether it is needed. The audit committee should also review 'whistleblowing' arrangements for staff who have **concerns about improprieties**. Audit committees should report to shareholders on how they have carried out their responsibilities, including on how they have assessed the effectiveness of the external audit process.

D Directors' remuneration

D1 Level and components of remuneration

Remuneration levels should be sufficient to attract directors of **sufficient calibre** to run the company effectively, but companies should not pay more than is necessary. A proportion of remuneration should be based on **corporate and individual performance**. Comparisons with other companies should be used with caution. When designing performance-related elements of remuneration, the remuneration committee should consider annual bonuses and different kinds of long-term incentive schemes. Targets should be stretching. Levels of remuneration for non-executive directors should reflect **time commitment and responsibilities**, and should not include share options or performance-related options.

Boards' ultimate objectives should be to set **notice periods at one year or less**. The remuneration committee should consider the appropriateness of compensation commitments included in the contracts of service.

D2 Procedure

Companies should establish a formal and clear procedure for **developing policy** on **executive remuneration** and for fixing the remuneration package of individual directors. **Directors should not be involved** in **setting their own remuneration**. A **remuneration committee**, staffed by independent non-executive directors, should make **recommendations** about the framework of executive remuneration, and should determine remuneration packages of executive directors and the chairman. The board or shareholders should determine the remuneration of non-executive directors.

E Relations with shareholders

E1 Dialogue with shareholders

The board should keep up a dialogue with shareholders, particularly **major (institutional) shareholders**. The board should try to understand issues and concerns, and discuss governance and strategy with major shareholders.

E2 Constructive use of the AGM

The AGM should be a **means of communication** with **investors**. Companies should count all proxies and announce proxy votes for and against on all votes on a show of hands, except when a poll is taken. Companies should propose a **separate resolution** on each substantially separate issue, and there should be a resolution covering the **report and accounts**. The chairmen of the audit, nomination and remuneration committees should be available to answer questions at the AGM. Papers should be sent to members at least 20 working days before the AGM.

Compliance with the Code

The UK Corporate Governance Code requires listed companies to include in their accounts:

(a) A narrative statement of how they **applied** the **principles** set out in the UK Corporate Governance Code. This should provide explanations which enable their shareholders to assess how the principles have been applied.

(b) A statement as to whether or not they **complied throughout** the **accounting period** with the provisions set out in the UK Corporate Governance Code. Listed companies that did not comply throughout the accounting period with all the provisions must specify the provisions with which they did not comply, and give **reasons** for **non-compliance**.

Revised guidance for directors on the Combined Code* (Turnbull report)

1 Introduction

The importance of internal control and risk management

The internal control systems have a key role in **managing the risks linked with a company's business objectives, helping to safeguard assets and the shareholders' investment**. The control system also aids the **efficiency and effectiveness of operations**, the **reliability of reporting and compliance with laws** and **regulations**. Effective financial records, including proper accounting records, are an important element of internal control.

A company's environment is constantly evolving and the risks it faces are constantly changing. To maintain an effective system of internal control, the company should regularly carry out a **thorough review of the risks** it faces.

As profits are partly the reward for risk taking in business, the purpose of internal control is to help **manage risk** rather than eliminate it.

Objectives of guidance

The guidance is designed to reflect good business practice by **embedding internal control in a company's business processes**, remaining relevant in the evolving business environment and enabling each company to apply it to its own circumstances. Directors must exercise judgement in determining how the Combined Code has been implemented. The guidance is based on a **risk-based approach**, which should be incorporated within the normal management and governance processes, and not be treated as a separate exercise.

Internal control requirements of the Combined Code*

This guidance aims to provide guidance for the directors on the requirements of the Combined Code relating to:

* Maintaining a **sound system** of internal control
* Conducting an **annual review** of internal control
* **Reporting** on this review in the annual report

2 Maintaining a sound system of internal control

Responsibilities

The board is responsible for the system of internal control, for setting policies and seeking assurance that will enable it to satisfy itself that the system is functioning effectively, in particular in managing risks.

In determining what the system of controls should be, the board should take account of the following.

* The **nature and extent** of risks facing the company
* The **extent and categories** of acceptable risks
* The **likelihood** of the risks materialising
* The company's **ability to reduce** the impact of risks
* The **costs versus the benefits** of internal controls

Management is responsible for implementing board policies on risk and control. Management should **identify and evaluate the risks faced** by the company for board consideration, and **design**, **implement** and **monitor a suitable internal control system**. All employees have some responsibility for internal control as part of their accountability for achieving business objectives. They should have the knowledge, skills, information and authority to operate the system of internal control effectively.

Elements of internal control systems

The control system should **facilitate a company's effective and efficient operation** by enabling it to respond to risks effectively. It should help ensure the quality of reporting by ensuring that the company maintains proper accounting records and processes that generate the necessary information. The system should also help **ensure compliance with laws and regulations**, and internal policies.

Control systems reflect the **control environment and organisational structure**. They include control activities, information and control processes and monitoring the continuing effectiveness of internal control systems. The systems should be **embedded in the company's operations** and form part of its **culture**, be able to **respond quickly to evolving risks** and include procedures for **reporting immediately to management**.

Control systems **reduce** rather than eliminate the possibility of poor judgement in decision-making, human error, control processes being circumvented, management override of controls and unforeseeable circumstances. They provide reasonable but not absolute assurance against risks failing to materialise.

3 Reviewing the effectiveness of internal controls

Reviewing control effectiveness is an essential part of the board's responsibilities. Management is responsible for **monitoring the system of internal control and providing assurance to the board that it has done so**. Board committees may have a significant role in the review process. The board has responsibility for disclosures on internal control in the annual report accounts.

A reliable system of internal control requires **effective monitoring**, but the board cannot just rely on monitoring taking place automatically. The board should regularly **review and receive reports on internal control** and should undertake **an annual assessment for** the purposes of making its report on internal controls.

The reports from management should provide a balanced assessment of the **significant risks and the effectiveness of the internal controls in managing those risks**. Reports should include details of control failings and weaknesses, including their impact and the action taken to rectify them.

When reviewing reports during the year, the board should consider what the risks are and how they have been identified, evaluated and managed. It should **assess the effectiveness of the internal controls**, consider whether any actions are being taken to remedy weaknesses and consider whether more effective monitoring is required.

The board should also carry out an **annual assessment**, considering what has been reported during the year plus any other relevant information. The annual assessment should consider the **changes in the significant risks** and the company's **ability to respond to changes in its environment**. It should also cover the monitoring of risks, the internal control and audit systems, the reports regularly given to the board, the significance of control failings and weaknesses, and the effectiveness of reporting.

4 The board's statement on internal control

The annual report and accounts should include **appropriate high-level information** to aid shareholders' understanding of the main features of the company's risk management and internal control processes. The minimum disclosure should be that a process of risk management exists, it has been in place for the whole period, the board has reviewed it and it accords with the provisions in the Turnbull report. The board should acknowledge its responsibility for internal controls and that the system is designed to manage rather than eliminate the risk of failure. It should disclose details of its review process and what actions have been taken to deal with weaknesses and related internal control aspects.

*The Turnbull guidance was issued before the Combined Code was renamed the UK Corporate Governance Code.

UK Stewardship Code

Seven principles

Institutional investors should:

- Publicly disclose their policy on how they will discharge their stewardship responsibilities
- Have a robust policy on managing conflicts of interest in relation to stewardship which should be publicly disclosed
- Monitor their investee companies
- Establish clear guidelines on when and how they will escalate their stewardship activities
- Be willing to act collectively with other investors where appropriate
- Have a clear policy on voting and disclosure of voting activity
- Report periodically on their stewardship and voting activities

BPP
LEARNING MEDIA

P
A
R
T

B

Internal control and risk

Internal control systems

Topic list	Syllabus reference
1 Purposes of internal control systems	B1, B2
2 Internal control frameworks	B1, B2
3 COSO's framework	B1, B2
4 Evaluating control systems	B1, B2

Introduction

In this chapter we cover the main elements of internal control and risk management frameworks. You will have encountered internal controls in your auditing studies. In this chapter we take an overview of the main frameworks rather than looking at controls in detail.

The UK Turnbull report has provided a lot of useful guidance on internal control, which is referred to in this and other chapters. Turnbull stresses the importance of control systems as means of managing risks. In Section 3 we introduce the very important COSO enterprise risk management framework. Chapters 5 to 8 of this text discuss in detail the elements this framework identifies.

In Section 4 we cover other international control frameworks, which each provide slightly different perspectives.

This is a very important chapter. The examiner has stressed how important a sound system of internal control is.

Study guide

		Intellectual level
B1	**Management control systems in corporate governance**	
(a)	Define and explain internal management control.	2
(b)	Explain and explore the importance of internal control and risk management in corporate governance.	3
(c)	Describe the objectives of internal control systems and how they can help prevent fraud and error.	2
(e)	Identify and assess the importance of elements or components of internal control systems.	3
B2	**Internal control, audit and compliance in corporate governance**	
(e)	Explore and evaluate the effectiveness of internal control systems.	3

Exam guide

You may be asked to provide an appropriate control framework for an organisation or assess a framework that is described in a scenario. Look out in particular for whether the underlying control environment appears to be sound.

1 Purposes of internal control systems

FAST FORWARD

Internal controls should help organisations counter risks, maintain the quality of financial reporting and comply with laws and regulations. They provide **reasonable assurance** that organisations will fulfil their strategic objectives.

Key term

An **internal control** is any action taken by management to enhance the likelihood that established objectives and goals will be achieved. Control is the result of proper planning, organising and directing by management.
(Institute of Internal Auditors)

1.1 Internal management control   12/14

Internal management control can be viewed as management planning, organising and directing performance so that organisational objectives are achieved. Planning and organising includes establishing objectives, determining and obtaining the resources required to fulfil objectives and defining the policies and procedures that will be used in the organisation's operations. Directing means ensuring resources are used efficiently and effectively, and also ensuring that operational tasks are carried out in line with the established procedures and policies.

1.1.1 The process of control

The **cybernetic control model** describes the process of control. A general cybernetic control model has **six key stages**:

Identification of objectives	**Objectives** for the process being controlled must exist, for without an aim or purpose control has no meaning. Objectives are set in response to environmental pressures such as customer demand.
Setting targets	A **target** or **prediction** of the process being controlled is required so that managers can see whether or not objectives have been achieved and whether action will be needed to remedy problems. Targets could include budgets or cost standards.

Measuring achievements/outputs	The **output** of the process must be **measurable**.
Comparing achievements with targets	Managers need to compare the actual outcomes of the process with the plan – this is known as obtaining **feedback**.
Identifying corrective action	It must be possible to **take action** so that failures to meet objectives can be reduced or eliminated.
Implementing corrective action	Action could involve changing objectives, resource inputs, the process or the whole system

1.1.2 Important features of control systems

Fisher has suggested that management control systems can be viewed in terms of the following criteria.

- Flexibility and ease of achievement of targets
- Relative importance of numerical and subjective performance measures
- Relative importance of short- and long-term measures
- Consistency of measures used across the organisation
- Whether management actively intervenes or intervenes by exception
- How automatic control mechanisms are
- Extent of participation below top management
- Extent of reliance on social relationships

1.2 Effectiveness of control systems   12/07

In order for internal controls to function properly, they have to be well directed. Managers and staff will be more able (and willing) to implement controls successfully if it can be demonstrated to them what the objectives of the control systems are. Objectives also provide a yardstick for the board when they come to monitor and assess how controls have been operating.

1.3 Purposes of control systems   12/07

The UK Turnbull report provides a helpful summary of the main purposes of an internal control system.

Turnbull comments that internal control consists of 'the **policies, processes, tasks, behaviours** and other aspects of a company that taken together:

(a) Facilitate its **effective** and **efficient operation** by enabling it to respond appropriately to significant **business, operational, financial, compliance** and other risks to achieving the company's objectives. This includes the **safeguarding of assets** from inappropriate use or from loss and fraud and ensuring that **liabilities** are **identified** and **managed**.

(b) Help ensure the **quality** of **internal** and **external reporting**. This requires the **maintenance** of **proper records and processes** that generate a flow of **timely, relevant and reliable information** from within and outside the organisation.

(c) Help ensure **compliance with applicable laws and regulations**, and also with internal policies with respect to the conduct of businesses.'

1.3.1 Characteristics of internal control systems

The Turnbull report summarises the key characteristics of the internal control systems. They should:

- Be **embedded** in the operations of the company and **form part of its culture**

- Be capable of **responding quickly** to evolving risks within the business

- Include procedures for **reporting immediately to management** significant control failings and weaknesses together with control action being taken

We shall talk more about each of these later in this text.

The Turnbull report goes on to say that a sound system of internal control reduces but does not eliminate the possibilities of losses arising from **poorly judged decisions**, **human error**, **deliberate circumvention of controls**, **management override of controls** and **unforeseeable circumstances**. Systems will provide reasonable (not absolute) assurance that the company will not be hindered in achieving its business objectives and in the orderly and legitimate conduct of its business, but won't provide certain protection against all possible problems.

1.4 Risk

The Turnbull guidance and other guidance on control systems places great emphasis on how control systems deal with risk. In the next few chapters therefore much of our discussion will focus on risk.

Key terms

> **Risk** is a condition in which there exists a quantifiable dispersion in the possible results of any activity.
>
> **Hazard** is the impact if the risk materialises.
>
> **Uncertainty** means that you do not know the possible outcomes and the chances of each outcome occurring.

In other words, risk is the probability, hazard is the consequences, of results deviating from expectations. However, risk is often used as a generic term to cover **hazard as well**.

Question

Risks

What sort of risks might an organisation face?

Answer

Make your own list, specific to the organisations that you are familiar with. Here is a list extracted from an article by Tom Jones, 'Risk Management' (*Administrator*, April 1993). It is illustrative of the range of risks faced and is not exhaustive.

- Fire, flood, storm, impact, explosion, subsidence and other disasters
- Accidents and the use of faulty products
- Error: loss through damage or malfunction caused by mistaken operation of equipment or wrong operation of an industrial programme
- Theft and fraud
- Breaking social or environmental regulations
- Political risks (the appropriation of foreign assets by local governments or of barriers to the repatriation of overseas profit)
- Computers: fraud, viruses and espionage
- Product tamper
- Malicious damage

1.4.1 Types of risk

There are various types of risk that exist in business and in life generally.

Key terms

Fundamental risks are those that affect society in general, or broad groups of people, and are beyond the control of any one individual. For example, there is the risk of atmospheric pollution which can affect the health of a whole community but which may be quite beyond the power of an individual within it to control.

Particular risks are risks over which an individual may have some measure of control. For example, there is a risk attached to smoking and we can mitigate that risk by refraining from smoking.

Speculative risks are those from which either good or harm may result. A business venture, for example, presents a speculative risk because either a profit or loss can result.

Pure risks are those whose only possible outcome is harmful. The risk of loss of data in computer systems caused by fire is a pure risk because no gain can result from it.

Exam focus point

It is important to emphasise that not all risks are pure risks. Plenty of risks have favourable as well as adverse consequences. As we shall see, businesses will take positive as well as negative impacts into account when deciding how risks should be managed.

1.5 Risk and business

A key point to emphasise is that risk **is bound up with doing business**. The basic principle is that 'you have to speculate to accumulate'.

It may **not be possible to eliminate risks** without undermining the whole basis on which the business operates, or without incurring excessive costs and insurance premiums. Therefore in many situations there is likely to be a level of **residual risk** which it is simply not worth eliminating.

There are some benefits to be derived from the management of risk, possibly at the expense of profits, such as:

- Predictability of cash flows
- Limitation of the impact of potentially bankrupting events
- Increased confidence of shareholders and other investors

However, boards should not just focus on managing negative risks but should also seek to **limit uncertainty** and to **manage speculative risks and opportunities** in order to **maximise positive outcomes and hence shareholder value**.

In its **Risk Management Standard**, the Institute of Risk Management linked key value drivers for a business with major risk categories.

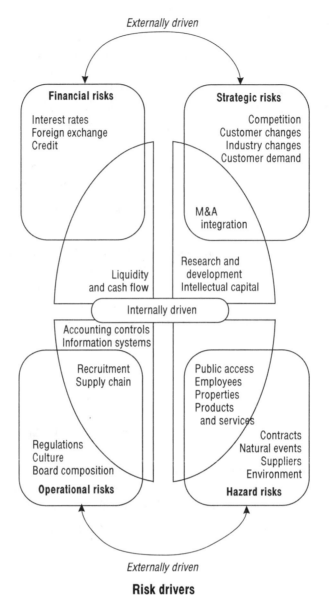

Risk drivers

Source: Institute of Risk Management – A Risk Management Standard

 Case Study

During 2007 a number of UK Government departments suffered security breaches relating to the sensitive personal data they stored. Some criticisms were made of the security of the computer systems; for example, the failure to encrypt information properly.

However, the most serious breaches related to simple errors, which elaborate computer applications could not prevent. The most notorious error related to the loss of personal data of every child benefit claimant (around 25 million). The material was sent between government departments on two disks, using the ordinary postal system, but was delayed en route.

1.6 Risk and corporate governance

One obvious link between risk and corporate governance is the issue of shareholders' concerns, here about the relationship between the level of risks and the returns achieved, being addressed.

A further issue is the link (or lack of) between **directors' remuneration** and risks taken. If remuneration does not link directly with risk levels, but does link with turnover and profits achieved, directors could decide that the company should bear risk levels that are higher than shareholders deem desirable. It has therefore been necessary to find other ways of ensuring that directors pay sufficient attention to risk management and do not take excessive risks. Corporate governance guidelines therefore require directors to:

- **Establish appropriate control mechanisms** for dealing with the risks the organisation faces
- **Monitor risks** themselves by regular review and a wider annual review
- **Disclose their risk management processes** in the accounts

2 Internal control frameworks   12/08, 12/14

FAST FORWARD

The internal control framework includes the **control environment** and **control procedures**. Other important elements are the **risk assessment and response processes**, the **sharing of information** and **monitoring** the environment and operation of the control system.

2.1 Need for control framework

Organisations need to consider the overall framework of controls, since controls are unlikely to be very effective if they are developed sporadically around the organisation and their effectiveness will be very difficult to measure by internal audit and ultimately by senior management.

2.2 Control environment and control procedures

Key terms

The **internal control framework** comprises the **control environment** and **control procedures**. It includes all the policies and procedures (internal controls) adopted by the directors and management of an entity to assist in achieving their objective of ensuring, as far as practicable, the orderly and efficient conduct of its business, including:

- Adherence to internal policies
- The safeguarding of assets
- The prevention and detection of fraud and error
- The accuracy and completeness of the accounting records
- The timely preparation of reliable financial information

Internal controls may be incorporated within computerised accounting systems. However, the internal control system extends beyond those matters which relate directly to the accounting system.

Perhaps the simplest framework for internal control draws a distinction between:

- **Control or internal environment** – the overall context of control, in particular the **culture**, **infrastructure** and **architecture** of control and **attitude** of directors and managers towards control (discussed in Chapter 5)

- **Control procedures** – the detailed controls in place (discussed in Chapter 7)

The Turnbull report also highlights the importance of:

- **Information and communication processes** (covered in Chapter 8)
- Processes for **monitoring** the continuing effectiveness of the system of internal control (covered in Chapter 8)

2.3 Purposes of internal control framework

(a) **Achieving orderly conduct of business**

Internal controls should ensure the organisation's operations are conducted **effectively and efficiently**. In particular they should enable the organisation to respond appropriately to **business, operational, financial, compliance** and other **risks** to achieving its objectives.

(b) **Adherence to internal policies and laws**

Controls should ensure that the organisation and its staff comply with **applicable laws and regulations**, and that staff **comply with internal policies** with respect to the conduct of the business.

(c) **Safeguarding assets**

Controls should ensure that assets are optimally utilised and stop assets being **used inappropriately**. They should prevent the organisation **losing assets** through **theft or poor maintenance**.

(d) **Prevention and detection of fraud**

Controls should include measures designed to prevent fraud, such as **segregation of duties** and **checking references** when staff are recruited. The information that systems provide should **highlight unusual transactions or trends** that may be signs of fraud.

(e) **Accuracy and completeness of accounting records**

Controls should ensure that records and processes are kept that generate a **flow of timely, relevant and reliable information that aids management decision-making**.

(f) **Timely preparation of reliable financial information**

They should ensure that published accounts **give a true and fair view**, and other published information is **reliable** and **meets the requirements** of those stakeholders to whom it is addressed.

2.4 Internal control frameworks and risk

Turnbull states that in order to determine its policies in relation to internal control and decide what constitutes a sound system of internal control, the board should consider:

- The **nature and extent of risks** facing the company
- The **extent and categories of risk** which it regards as acceptable for the company to bear
- The **likelihood of the risks** concerned materialising
- The company's ability to **reduce the incidence and impact on the business** of risks that do materialise
- The **costs of operating particular controls** relative to the benefits obtained in managing the related risks

Turnbull goes on to stress that an organisation's risks are **continually changing**, as its objectives, internal organisation and business environment are continually evolving. New markets and new products bring further risks and also change overall organisation risks. Diversification may reduce risk (the business is not overdependent on a few products) or may increase it (the business is competing in markets in which it is ill equipped to succeed). Therefore the organisation needs to constantly re-evaluate the nature and extent of risks to which it is exposed.

COSO points out that an organisation needs to establish **clear and coherent objectives** in order to be able to tackle risks effectively. The risks that are important are those that are **linked with achievement** of the organisation's objectives. In addition, there should be control mechanisms that identify and adjust for the risks that arise out of changes in economic, industry, regulatory and operating conditions.

2.5 Challenges in developing internal control   6/08, 6/09, 12/11, 12/13

Guidance from the Committee of Sponsoring Organisations of the Treadway Commission (COSO – discussed below) has highlighted a number of potential problems that smaller companies may face when developing internal control. These include:

- **Insufficient staff resources** to maintain segregation of duties

- **Domination of activities by management**, with significant opportunities for management override of controls. This arises from smaller companies having fewer levels of management with wider spans of control and their managers having significant ownership interests or rights

- Inability to recruit directors with the **requisite financial reporting or other expertise**

- Inability to recruit and retain staff with **sufficient knowledge of, and experience in, financial reporting**

- Management having a wide range of responsibilities and thus having **insufficient time** to focus on accounting and financial reporting

- Control over computer information systems with **limited in-house technical expertise**

2.6 Limitations of internal controls   6/08, 6/09, 12/11, 12/12

In addition, an internal control framework in any organisation can only provide the directors with **reasonable assurance** that their objectives are reached, because of **inherent limitations**, including:

- The **costs of control** not **outweighing** their **benefits**; sometimes setting up an elaborate system of controls will be too costly when compared with the financial losses those controls may prevent
- **Poor judgement** in decision-making
- The **potential for human error or fraud**
- **Collusion between employees**
- The **possibility of controls being bypassed** or overridden by management or employees
- Controls being designed to cope with **routine and not non-routine transactions**
- Controls being unable to cope with **unforeseen circumstances**
- Controls depending on the **method of data processing** – they should be **independent** of the method of data processing
- Controls not being **updated** over time

Question   **Problems with controls**

A large college has several sites and employs hundreds of teaching staff. The college has recently discovered a serious fraud involving false billings for part-time teaching.

The fraud involved two members of staff. M is a clerk in the payroll office who is responsible for processing payments to part-time teaching staff. P is the head of the Business Studies department at the N campus. Part-time lecturers are required to complete a monthly claim form which lists the classes taught and the total hours claimed. These forms must be signed by their head of department, who sends all signed forms to M. M checks that the class codes on the claim forms are valid, that hours have been budgeted for those classes and inputs the information into the college's payroll package.

The college has a separate personnel department that is responsible for maintaining all personnel files. Additions to the payroll must be made by a supervisor in the personnel office. The payroll package is programmed to reject any claims for payment to employees whose personnel files are not present in the system.

M had gained access to the personnel department supervisor's office by asking the college security officer for the loan of a pass key because he had forgotten the key to his own office. M knew that the office would be unoccupied that day because the supervisor was attending a wedding. M logged onto the supervisor's computer terminal by guessing her password, which turned out to be the registration number of the supervisor's car. M then added a fictitious part-time employee, who was allocated to the N campus Business Studies department.

P then began making claims on behalf of the fictitious staff member and submitting them to M. M signed off the forms and input them as normal. The claims resulted in a steady series of payments to a bank account that had been opened by P. The proceeds of the fraud were shared equally between M and P.

The fraud was only discovered when the college wrote to every member of staff with a formal invitation to the college's centenary celebration. The letter addressed to the fictitious lecturer was returned as undeliverable and the personnel department became suspicious when they tried to contact this person in order to update his contact details. By then M and P had been claiming for non-existent teaching for three years without detection by external or internal audit.

Required

Evaluate the difficulties in implementing controls that would have prevented and detected this fraud.

Answer

Small amounts

The college employs hundreds of teaching staff on full- and part-time contracts. Payments for one fictitious employee would not be large enough to attract the attention of internal auditors automatically. Even if auditors had checked a random sample of payments each year, given the large population the probability was that the fictitious employee would not be discovered for some time, as indeed happened.

Falsification of records

The records of the employee appeared to be genuine and a routine payment to a lecturer, entered on the payroll supervisor's log-in and signed off by P. There was nothing unusual about these payments that anyone reviewing them could have identified.

Use of payroll supervisor's log-on

The payroll supervisor would normally have been the third person involved with this transaction because of their involvement at the initial stage. However, P was able to bypass the need for the supervisor's involvement by taking advantage of her absence and correctly guessing how to enter the computer on the supervisor's password.

Collusion

Once the fictitious lecturer's details had been entered, the college's systems meant that two people had to be involved for each payment to a lecturer to be made, the head of department and the payroll clerk. The involvement of both in the fraud meant that the segregation of duties between the two staff, that P authorised the payment and M entered it, was lost.

Involvement of senior staff

The system also depended on the authorisation of payments by P. The system would have produced for P a record of the lecturers who had been paid for working in P's department. However, review of this by P would have been worthless, as he would not have reported the fictitious lecturer. The system effectively relied on P's honesty. Many systems are designed on the basis that senior staff act honestly. As P had been appointed to a senior position, there presumably was no indication in his previous record that suggested he could not be trusted.

Exam focus point

Question 1 in June 2008 asked about the problems of applying internal controls to subcontractors.

3 COSO's framework

FAST FORWARD

COSO's enterprise risk management framework provides a coherent framework for organisations to deal with risk, based on the following components.

- Control environment
- Risk assessment
- Control activities
- Information and communications
- Monitoring activities

COCO is an alternative framework that emphasises the importance of the **commitment** of those operating the system.

3.1 Nature of enterprise risk management   6/14

We have seen that internal control systems should be designed to manage risks effectively. There are various frameworks for risk management, but we shall be looking in particular at the framework established by the Committee of Sponsoring Organisations of the Treadway Commission (COSO).

COSO published guidance on internal control, *Internal Control – Integrated Framework*, in 1992. It published wider guidance on Enterprise Risk Management in 2004. In 2006 COSO issued *Internal Control over Financial Reporting – Guidance for Smaller Companies.* This guidance was designed to supplement the guidance in *Internal Control – Integrated Framework*, in the light of the requirement in s 404 of the Sarbanes-Oxley legislation for management of public companies to assess and report on the effectiveness of internal control over financial reporting. An updated version of the framework was issued in 2013 to reflect the increasingly global nature of business activity, the impact of technological advances, the increasing complexity of rules and regulations, and stakeholder concerns over risk management and the prevention of fraud.

Key terms

Enterprise risk management is a process, effected by an entity's board of directors, management and other personnel, applied in strategy setting and across the enterprise, designed to identify potential events that may affect the entity and manage risks to be within its risk appetite, to provide reasonable assurance regarding the achievement of entity objectives.

Internal control is a process effected by an entity's board of directors, management and other personnel designed to provide reasonable assurance regarding the achievement of objectives in the following categories.

- Effectiveness and efficiency of operations
- Reliability of reporting
- Compliance with laws and regulations   COSO

COSO states that enterprise risk management has the following characteristics.

(a)   It is a **process**, a means to an end, which should ideally be intertwined with existing operations and exist for fundamental business reasons.

(b)   It is operated by **people at every level** of the organisation and is not just paperwork. It provides a mechanism for helping people to understand risk, their responsibilities and levels of authority.

(c)   It is applied in **strategy setting,** with management considering the risks in alternative strategies.

(d)   It is applied **across the enterprise**. This means it takes into account activities at all levels of the organisation, from enterprise-level activities such as strategic planning and resource allocation, to business unit activities and business processes. It includes taking an entity-level portfolio view of risk. Each unit manager assesses the risk for their unit. Senior management ultimately consider these unit risks and also **interrelated risks**. Ultimately they will assess whether the overall risk portfolio is consistent with the organisation's risk appetite.

(e) It is designed to **identify events** potentially affecting the entity and manage risk within its **risk appetite**, the amount of risk it is prepared to accept in pursuit of value. The risk appetite should be aligned with the desired return from a strategy.

(f) It provides **reasonable assurance** to an entity's management and board. Assurance can at best be reasonable since risk relates to the uncertain future.

(g) It is geared to the **achievement of objectives** in a number of categories, including **supporting** the **organisation's mission**, making **effective and efficient use** of the **organisation's resources**, ensuring **reporting is reliable**, and **complying** with **applicable laws and regulations**.

Because these characteristics are broadly defined, they can be applied across different types of organisations, industries and sectors. Whatever the organisation, the framework focuses on **achievement of objectives**.

An approach based on **objectives** contrasts with a **procedural approach** based on rules, codes or procedures. A procedural approach aims to eliminate or control risk by requiring conformity with the rules. However, a procedural approach cannot eliminate the possibility of risks arising because of poor management decisions, human error, fraud or unforeseen circumstances arising.

3.2 Framework of enterprise risk management

The COSO framework consists of five interrelated components.

Component	Explanation
Control environment (Chapter 5)	This covers the tone of an organisation, and sets the basis for how risk is viewed and addressed by an organisation's people, including risk management philosophy and risk appetite, integrity and ethical values, and the environment in which they operate. The board's **attitude, participation and operating style** will be a key factor in determining the **strength** of the control environment. An unbalanced board, lacking appropriate technical knowledge and experience, diversity and strong, independent voices is unlikely to set the right tone.
	The example set by board members may be undermined by a failure of management in divisions or business units. Mechanisms to control line management may not be sufficient or may not be operated properly. Line managers may not be aware of their responsibilities or may fail to exercise them properly.
Risk assessment (Chapters 6 and 7)	Risks are analysed considering likelihood and impact as a basis for determining how they should be managed. The analysis process should clearly determine which risks are controllable, and which risks are not controllable.
	The COSO guidance stresses the importance of employing a combination of **qualitative and quantitative risk assessment methodologies**. As well as assessing inherent risk levels, the organisation should also assess **residual risks** left after risk management actions have been taken. Risk assessment needs to be **dynamic**, with managers considering the effect of changes in the internal and external environments that may render controls ineffective.
Control activities (Chapter 7)	Policies and procedures are established and implemented to help ensure the risk responses are effectively carried out. COSO guidance suggests that a **mix of controls** will be appropriate, including prevention and detection and manual and automated controls. COSO also stresses the need for controls to be performed across **all levels of the organisation**, at **different stages within business processes** and over the **technology environment**.

Component	Explanation
Information and communication (Chapter 8)	Relevant information is identified, captured and communicated in a form and timeframe that enable people to carry out their responsibilities. The information provided to management needs to be **relevant and of appropriate quality**. It also must cover all the objectives shown on the top of the cube. Effective communication should be **broad** – flowing up, down and across the entity. There needs to be **communication with staff**. Communication of risk areas that are relevant to what staff do is an important means of strengthening the internal environment by embedding risk awareness in staff's thinking. There should also be effective communication with third parties such as shareholders and regulators.
Monitoring activities (Chapter 8)	Risk control processes are monitored and modifications are made if necessary. Effective monitoring requires **active participation** by the board and senior management, and **strong information systems**, so the data senior managers need is fed to them. COSO has drawn a distinction between **regular review** (ongoing monitoring) and **periodic review** (separate evaluation). However weaknesses are identified, the guidance stresses the importance of **feedback and action**. Weaknesses should be reported, assessed and their root causes corrected.

Diagrammatically all the above may be summarised as follows.

3.3 Benefits of enterprise risk management   6/09

COSO highlights a number of advantages of adopting the process of enterprise risk management.

Alignment of risk appetite and strategy	The framework demonstrates to managers the need to consider risk toleration. They then set objectives aligned with business strategy and develop mechanisms to manage the accompanying risks and to ensure risk management becomes part of the culture of the organisation, embedded into all its processes and activities.
Link growth, risk and return	Risk is part of value creation, and organisations will seek a given level of return for the level of risk tolerated.
Choose best risk response	Enterprise risk management helps the organisation select whether to reduce, eliminate or transfer risk.
Minimise surprises and losses	By identifying potential loss-inducing events, the organisation can reduce the occurrence of unexpected problems.

Identify and manage risks across the organisation	As indicated above, the framework means that managers can understand and aggregate connected risks. It also means that risk management is seen as everyone's responsibility, experience and practice is shared across the business and a common set of tools and techniques is used.
Provide responses to multiple risks	For example risks associated with purchasing, over- and undersupply, prices and dubious supply sources might be reduced by an inventory control system that is integrated with suppliers.
Seize opportunities	By considering events as well as risks, managers can identify opportunities as well as losses.
Rationalise capital	Enterprise risk management allows management to allocate capital better and make a sounder assessment of capital needs.

3.4 Criticisms of enterprise risk management

There have been some criticisms made of COSO's framework:

(a) **Internal focus**

One criticism of the ERM model has been that it starts at the wrong place. It begins with the internal and **not the external environment**. Critics claim that it does not reflect sufficiently the impact of the competitive environment, regulation and external stakeholders on risk appetite and management and culture.

(b) **Risk identification**

The ERM has been criticised for discussing risks primarily in terms of **events**, particularly sudden events with major consequences. Critics claim that the guidance insufficiently emphasises slow changes that can give rise to important risks; for example, changes in internal culture or market sentiment.

(c) **Risk assessment**

The ERM model has been criticised for encouraging an **oversimplified approach to risk assessment**. It has been claimed that the ERM encourages an approach which thinks in terms of a single outcome of a risk materialising. This outcome could be an expected outcome or it could be a worst-case result. Many risks will have a range of possible outcomes if they materialise, for example extreme weather, and risk assessment needs to consider this range.

(d) **Stakeholders**

The guidance fails to discuss the **influence of stakeholders**, although many risks that organisations face are due to a conflict between the organisation's objectives and those of its stakeholders.

3.5 Impacts of enterprise risk management

Although COSO's guidance is non-mandatory, it has been influential because it provides frameworks against which risk management and internal control systems can be assessed and improved. Corporate scandals, arising in companies where risk management and internal control were deficient, and attempts to regulate corporate behaviour as a result of these scandals have resulted in an environment where guidance on best practice in risk management and internal control has been particularly welcome.

3.6 The COCO framework

A slightly different framework is the **criteria of control** or COCO framework developed by the Canadian Institute of Chartered Accountants (CICA).

3.6.1 Purpose

The COCO framework stresses the need for all aspects of activities to be **clearly directed with a sense of purpose**. This includes:

*   Overall objectives, mission and strategy
*   Management of risk and opportunities
*   Policies
*   Plans and performance measures

The corporate purpose should drive control activities and ensure controls achieve objectives.

3.6.2 Commitment

The framework stresses the importance of managers and staff making an **active commitment** to identify themselves with the organisation and its values, including ethical values, authority, responsibility and trust.

3.6.3 Capability

Managers and staff must be equipped with the **resources and competence necessary** to operate the control systems effectively. This includes not just knowledge and resources but also communication processes and co-ordination.

3.6.4 Action

If employees are sure of the purpose, are **committed to do their best** for the organisation and have the ability to deal with problems and opportunities then the actions they take are more likely to be successful.

3.6.5 Monitoring and learning

An essential part of commitment to the organisation is a commitment to its evolution. This includes:

*   Monitoring external environments
*   Monitoring performance
*   Reappraising information systems
*   Challenging assumptions
*   Reassessing the effectiveness of internal controls

Above all each activity should be seen as part of a **learning process** that lifts the organisation to a higher dimension.

Exam focus point

> This emphasises the importance of feedback and continuous improvement in control systems and is something worth looking for in exam scenarios – whether the organisation appears capable of making essential improvements.

4 Evaluating control systems

FAST FORWARD

> A number of factors should be considered when evaluating control systems.

4.1 Principles or rules   6/10

We discussed whether to adopt a principles- or rules-based approach to corporate governance in Chapter 2. This debate is particularly significant for internal controls.

Having rules requiring organisations to implement internal controls should mean that controls are applied consistently by organisations. External stakeholders dealing with these organisations will have the assurance that they should have certain **prescribed controls** in place. However, this does not mean that all organisations will be operating the same controls with the same effectiveness.

A principles-based approach to internal control implementation means that organisations can adopt controls that are most appropriate and cost effective for them, based on their **size and risk profile** and the **sector** in which they operate.

4.2 Assessment of control systems

We shall look in detail at the different elements of risk management and control systems in later chapters, but the following general points apply to review of control systems.

4.2.1 Objectives

The controls in place need to help the company **fulfil key business objectives**, including **conducting its operations efficiently and effectively, safeguarding its assets** and **responding to the significant risks** it faces.

4.2.2 Links with risks

Links between controls and risks faced are particularly important, with the organisation needing a clear framework for dealing effectively with risks. Key elements are the board defining **risk appetite**, which will determine which risks are significant. There need to be reliable systems in place for **identifying and assessing the magnitude of risks**.

4.2.3 Control system compatibility

Guidance on control procedures needs to be supported by other aspects of the control system, and the overall systems need to deliver a consistent message about the importance of controls. **Human resource policies and the company's performance reward systems** should provide incentives for good behaviour and deal with flagrant breaches.

4.2.4 Mix of controls

Detailed controls at the transaction level will not make all that much difference unless there are other controls further up the organisation. There should ideally be a **pyramid of controls** in place, ranging from **corporate controls** at the top of an organisation (for example ethical codes), **management controls** (budgets), **process controls** (authorisation limits) and **transaction controls** (completeness controls). Controls shouldn't just cover the financial accounting areas, but should include **non-financial controls** as well.

4.2.5 Human resource issues

How well control procedures operate will also be determined by the authority and abilities of the individuals who operate the controls. There need to be **clear job descriptions** that identify how much **authority and discretion** individuals have at different levels of the organisation. Controls can be also be undermined if the people who operate them make mistakes. Therefore managers and staff need to have the **requisite knowledge and skills** to be able to operate controls effectively. **Documentation and training** will be required, and individuals' abilities assessed on a continuing basis as part of the **appraisal process**.

4.2.6 Control environment

The control environment (discussed further in the next chapter) matters because the company's **culture** will determine how seriously control procedures are taken. If there is evidence that directors are **overriding controls**, this will undermine them. If staff resent controls, they may be tempted to collude to render controls ineffective.

4.2.7 Review of controls

Directors should demonstrate their **commitment to control by reviewing internal controls**.

4.2.8 Information sources

In order to carry out effective reviews of controls, the board needs to ensure it is receiving sufficient information. There should be a system in place of regular reporting by **subordinates and control functions as well as reports on high-risk activities**. The board also needs to receive confirmation that weaknesses identified in previous reviews have been resolved. Finally there needs to be clear systems of reporting problems to the board.

4.2.9 Feedback and response

A basic principle of control system design is that the **feedback received** should be used as the basis for **taking action** to change the controls or modify the overall control systems. There should be **rapid responses** if serious problems are picked up, for example involvement of senior management in reviewing possible fraud.

4.2.10 Costs and benefits

Rational consideration of whether the costs of operating controls are worth the benefits of **preventing and detecting problems** should be an integral part of the board's review process. Directors may decide not to operate certain controls on the grounds that they are prepared to **accept the risks** of not doing so.

Question	Models

What are the most important features highlighted by risk management models?

Answer

The following strike us as significant. You may well have come up with other points.

- Risk management is a circular, continuous process, feeding on itself with the aim of ensuring continuous improvement.

- The different faces of the COSO model emphasise the need for setting objectives at different levels, and for risk management to be effective in each business unit, division, etc.

- COCO emphasises the need for staff to have the right attitudes, commitment and experience.

- The approaches stress the need for monitoring by the board.

Chapter Roundup

- **Internal controls** should help organisations counter risks, maintain the quality of financial reporting and comply with laws and regulations. They provide **reasonable assurance** that organisations will fulfil their strategic objectives.

- The internal control framework includes the **control environment** and **control procedures**. Other important elements are the **risk assessment and response processes**, the **sharing of information** and **monitoring** the environment and operation of the control system.

- **COSO's enterprise risk management framework** provides a coherent framework for organisations to deal with risk, based on the following components.

  - Control environment
  - Risk assessment
  - Control activities
  - Information and communications
  - Monitoring activities

  COCO is an alternative framework that emphasises the importance of the **commitment** of those operating the system.

- A number of factors should be considered when evaluating control systems.

Quick Quiz

1   What according to Turnbull should a good system of internal control achieve?

2   Lack of flexibility is an important criticism of a rules-based approach to internal control.

   True   ☐

   False   ☐

3   What according to COSO are the key characteristics of enterprise risk management?

4   What are the key stages of the cybernetic control system?

5   Fill in the blank:

   .... risks are risks from which good or harm may result.

6   What are the four components of risk management identified by IFAC?

7   Fill in the blank:

   .... is the impact of a risk materialising.

8   Fill in the blank:

   .... is the overall context of control, the culture, infrastructure and architecture of control, and attitude of directors or managers towards control.

Answers to Quick Quiz

1
- Facilitate effective and efficient operation by enabling it to respond to significant risks
- Help ensure the quality of internal and external reporting
- Help ensure compliance with applicable laws and regulations

2 True

3
- Process
- Operated by people at every level
- Applied in strategy setting
- Applied across the organisation

- Identifies significant events
- Provides reasonable assurance
- Geared to the achievement of objectives

4
- Identification of system objectives
- Setting targets for systems objectives
- Measuring achievements/outputs of the system
- Comparing achievements with targets
- Identifying corrective action
- Implementing corrective action

5 Speculative

6
- Structure
- Resources
- Culture
- Tools and techniques

7 Hazard

8 Control environment

Now try the question below from the Practice Question Bank.

Number	Level	Marks	Time
Q4	Examination	25	49 mins

Risk attitudes and internal environment

Topic list	Syllabus reference
1 Risk and the organisation	D3
2 Impact of risk on stakeholders	C3
3 Internal environment	B1
4 Embedding risk awareness	D2, D3
5 Risk management responsibilities	B1, C1, D1
6 Objective setting	B1

Introduction

In this chapter we examine the internal environment of the organisation and its objective-setting process.

Before we start doing this, we look at the attitudes to risk an organisation and stakeholders have, as these will impact particularly on the internal environment and objective setting. Remember the fundamental point: that a business has to take risks to survive. Without taking risks, it cannot make sufficient profits to satisfy shareholders. However, this leaves open what determines how much risk businesses and other organisations are prepared to tolerate. We examine these issues in the first two sections of this chapter.

Section 3 looks broadly at the control or internal environment within which an organisation operates. We focus on specific aspects of the internal environment in the next two sections. Section 4 deals with how risk awareness becomes part of the environment. Section 5 deals with risk management responsibilities. These are part of the organisational structure that is a key element of the internal environment.

Lastly we look at objective setting by the board. We have already seen in Chapter 3 that the board must organise itself so that it discusses and decides on key issues relating to the business. Section 6 looks further at what the board needs to decide.

Study guide

		Intellectual level
B1	**Management control systems in corporate governance**	
(d)	Identify, explain and evaluate the corporate governance and executive management roles in risk management (in particular the separation between responsibility for ensuring that adequate risk management systems are in place and the application of risk management systems and practices in the organisation).	3
(e)	Identify and assess the importance of elements or components of internal control systems.	3
C1	**Risks and the risk management process**	
(a)	Define and explain risk in the context of corporate governance.	2
(b)	Define and describe management responsibilities in risk management.	2
C3	**Identification, assessment and measurement of risk**	
(a)	Identify, and assess the impact on, the stakeholders involved in business risk.	3
D1	**Targeting and monitoring of risk**	
(a)	Explain and assess the role of a risk manager in identifying and monitoring risk.	3
(b)	Explain and evaluate the role of the risk committee in identifying and monitoring risk.	3
D2	**Methods of controlling and reducing risks**	
(a)	Explain the importance of risk awareness at all levels of an organisation.	2
(b)	Describe and analyse the concept of embedding risk in an organisation's systems and procedures.	3
(c)	Describe and evaluate the concept of embedding risks in an organisation's culture and values.	3
D3	**Risk avoidance, retention and modelling**	
(b)	Explain and evaluate the different attitudes to risk and how these can affect strategy.	3
(c)	Explain and assess the necessity of incurring risk as part of competitively managing a business organisation.	3
(d)	Explain and assess attitudes towards risk and the ways in which risk varies in relation to the size, structure and development of an organisation.	3

Exam guide

The chapter contents could be examined in overview or you may be asked more specific questions about various aspects, such as the responsibilities of senior management.

1 Risk and the organisation

FAST FORWARD

> Management responses to risk are not automatic, but will be determined by their **own attitudes to risk**, which in turn may be influenced by **cultural factors**.

1.1 Risk appetite and attitudes   6/14

Remember we mentioned briefly in Chapter 4 that businesses have to take risks in order to develop. Therefore risk-averse businesses are **not** businesses that are seeking to avoid risks. They are businesses that are seeking to obtain sufficient returns for the risks they take.

Key terms

> **Risk appetite** describes the nature and strength of risks that an organisation is prepared to bear.
> **Risk attitude** is the directors' views on the level of risk that they consider desirable.
> **Risk capacity** describes the nature and strength of risks that an organisation is able to bear.

Different businesses will have different attitudes towards taking risk.

Risk-averse businesses may be willing to **tolerate risks up to a point** provided they receive **acceptable return** or, if risk is 'two-way' or symmetrical, that it has both positive and negative outcomes. Some risks may be an unavoidable consequence of operating in their business sector. However, there will be upper limits to the risks they are prepared to take whatever the level of returns they can earn.

Risk-seeking businesses are likely to focus on maximising returns and may not be worried about the level of risks that have to be taken to maximise returns (indeed their managers may thrive on taking risks).

The range of attitudes to risk can be illustrated as a continuum. The two ends are two possible extremes, whereas real-life organisations are located between the two. At the left-hand extreme are organisations that never accept any risk and whose strategies are designed to ensure that all risks are avoided. On the right-hand side are organisations that actively accept risks and are risk seeking.

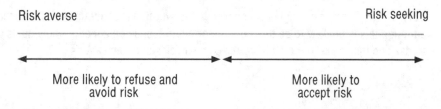

Risk averse   Risk seeking

More likely to refuse and   More likely to
avoid risk   accept risk

Whatever the viewpoint, a business should be concerned with reducing risk where possible and necessary but not eliminating all risks, while managers try to **maximise the returns** that are possible given the levels of risk. Most risks must be managed to some extent, and some should be eliminated as being outside the business. Risk management under this view is an integral part of **strategy**, and involves analysing what the **key value drivers are** in the organisation's activities, and the risks tied up with those value drivers.

For example, a business in a high-tech industry, such as computing, which evolves rapidly within ever-changing markets and technologies, has to accept high risk in its research and development activities, but should it also be speculating on interest and exchange rates within its treasury activities?

Another issue is that organisations that seek to **avoid risks** (for example public sector companies and charities) do not need the elaborate and costly control systems that a risk-seeking company may have. However, businesses such as those that trade in derivatives, volatile share funds or venture capital companies need complex systems in place to monitor and manage risk. The management of risk needs to be a strategic core competence of the business.

Case Study

Since risk and return are linked, one consequence of focusing on achieving or maintaining high profit levels may mean that the organisation bears a large amount of risk. The decision to bear these risk levels may not be conscious, and may go well beyond what is considered desirable by shareholders and other stakeholders.

This is illustrated by the experience of the National Bank of Australia, which announced it had lost hundreds of millions of pounds on foreign exchange trading, resulting in share price instability and the resignation of both the Chairman and Chief Executive. In the end the ultimate loss of A$360 million was 110 times its official foreign exchange trading cap of A$3.25 million.

The bank had become increasingly reliant on speculation and high-risk investment activity to maintain profitability. Traders had breached trading limits on 800 occasions and at one stage had unhedged foreign exchange exposures of more than A$2 billion. These breaches were reported internally, as were unusual patterns in trading (very large daily gains) but senior managers took no action. For three years, the currency options team had been the most profitable team in Australia, and had been rewarded by bonuses greater than their annual salaries. Eventually, however, the team came unstuck, and entered false transactions to hide their losses.

The market, however, was unimpressed by the efforts of the bank to make members of the team scapegoats, and market pressure forced changes at the top of the organisation, a general restructuring and a more prudent attitude to risk. Observers, however, questioned whether this change in attitude would survive the economic pressure that the bank was under in the long term.

1.2 Factors influencing risk appetite

Because risk management is bound up with strategy, how organisations deal with risk will not only be determined by events and the information available about events but also by **management perceptions** of those risks and, as mentioned above, management's **appetite** to take risks. These factors will also influence risk **culture**, the values and practices that influence how an organisation deals with risk in its day-to-day operations.

What therefore influences the **risk appetite** of managers?

1.3 Personal views

Surveys suggest that managers acknowledge the **emotional satisfaction** from successful risk taking, although this is unlikely to be the most important influence on appetite. Individuals vary in their attitudes to risk and this is likely to be transferred to their roles in organisations.

Case Study

Consider a company such as **Virgin**. It has many stable and successful brands, and healthy cash flows and profits. There's little need, you would have thought, to consider risky new ventures.

Yet Virgin has a subsidiary called **Virgin Galactic** to own and operate privately-built spaceships, and to offer 'affordable' sub-orbital **space tourism to everybody** – or everybody willing to pay for the pleasure. The risks are enormous. Developing the project will involve investing very large amounts of money, there is no guarantee that the service is wanted by sufficient numbers of people to make it viable, and the risks of catastrophic accidents are self-evident. In fact a test flight in October 2014 ended in disaster when the rocket broke apart in mid air. The test pilot was killed and the co-pilot was seriously injured.

There is little doubt that Virgin's risk appetite derives directly from the risk appetite of its chief executive, Richard Branson – a self-confessed adrenaline junkie – who also happens to own most parts of the Virgin Group privately, and so faces little pressure from shareholders.

1.4 Response to shareholder demand

Shareholders demand a **level of return** that is consistent with taking a certain level of risk. Managers will respond to these expectations by viewing risk taking as a key part of decision-making.

To some extent it must be true that risk appetite is allied to **need**. If Company A is cash rich in a stable industry with few competitors and satisfied shareholders it has little need to take on any more risky activities. If, a few years later, a significant number of competitors have entered the market and Company A's profits start to be eroded then it will **need** to do something to stop the rot, and it will face demands for change from investors.

Failing to take fresh strategic opportunities may be the most significant risk the business faces. Woolworths in the UK did not fail simply because of the impact of the credit crunch. It had already become **irrelevant** to its customers – people were no longer sure why they should go to Woolworths. The credit crunch simply speeded up the inevitable result of catastrophic strategic wearout. Woolworths had continued to offer the same products to the same customers despite the changing customer and competitor landscape.

1.5 Organisational influences

Organisational influences may be important, and these are not necessarily just a response to shareholder concerns. Organisational attitudes may be influenced by **significant losses** in the past, **changes in regulation and best practice**, or even **changing views** of the benefits that risk management can bring.

Attitudes to risk will also depend on the **size, structure and stage of development** of the organisation.

(a)   **Size of organisation**

A **larger organisation** is likely to require more **formal systems** and will have to take account of **varying risk appetites** and **incidence** among its operations. However, a large organisation will also be able to justify employing risk specialists, either generally or in specific areas of high risk, such as treasury. It is also more likely to be able to **diversify its activities** so that it is not dependent on a few products.

(b)   **Structure**

The risk management systems employed will be dependent on the organisation's management control systems that will in turn depend on the formality of **structure**, the autonomy given to local operations and the degree of centralisation deemed desirable.

(c)   **Attitudes to risk**

Attitudes to risk will change as the **organisation develops** and its **risk profile changes**. For example, attitudes to financial risk and gearing will change as different sources of finance become necessary to fund larger developments.

Unsurprisingly there are particularly onerous responsibilities on trustees of charities. The UK's *Good Governance: A Code for the Voluntary and Community Sector* stresses that trustees must exercise special care when investing the organisation's funds, or borrowing funds for it to use, and must comply with the organisation's governing document and any other legal requirements.

1.6 National influences

There is some evidence that national culture influences attitudes towards risk and uncertainty. Surveys suggest that attitudes to risk vary nationally according to how much people are shielded from the consequences of adverse events.

Risk taking: is it behavioural, genetic, or learned?

Behaviour of individuals

Risky business has never been more popular. Mountain climbing is among the fastest-growing sports. Extreme skiing – in which skiers descend cliff-like runs by dropping from ledge to snow-covered ledge – is drawing ever-wider interest. The adventurer-travel business, which often mixes activities like climbing or river rafting with wildlife safaris, has grown into a **multimillion-dollar** industry.

Under conventional personality theories, **normal individuals** do everything possible to **avoid tension and risk**, and in the not too distant past, students of human behaviour might have explained such activities as an abnormality, a kind of death wish. But in fact researchers are discovering that the psychology of risk involves far more than a simple 'death wish'. Studies now indicate that the inclination to take high risks may be **hard-wired into the brain**, intimately linked to **arousal and pleasure mechanisms**, and may offer such a thrill that it functions like an addiction. The tendency probably affects **one in five** people, mostly young males, and declines with age.

It may **ensure our survival**, even **spur our evolution** as individuals and as a species. Risk taking probably bestowed a crucial evolutionary advantage, inciting the fighting and foraging of the hunter-gatherer.

In mapping out the mechanisms of risk, psychologists hope to do more than explain why people climb mountains. **Risk taking**, which one researcher defines as **'engaging in any activity with an uncertain outcome'**, arises in nearly all walks of life.

Asking someone on a date, accepting a **challenging work assignment**, raising a sensitive issue with a spouse or a friend, **confronting an abusive boss** – these all involve uncertain outcomes, and present some level of risk.

High risk takers

Researchers don't yet know precisely how a risk-taking impulse arises **from within** or what role is played by **environmental factors**, from **upbringing** to the **culture** at large. And, while some level of risk taking is clearly necessary for survival (try crossing a busy street without it!), scientists are divided as to whether, in a modern society, a **'high-risk gene'** is still advantageous.

Some scientists see a willingness to take big risks as **essential for success**, but research has also revealed the **darker side** of risk taking. High-risk takers are easily bored and may suffer low job satisfaction. Their craving for stimulation can make them more likely to abuse drugs, gamble, commit crimes and be **promiscuous**.

Indeed, this peculiar form of dissatisfaction could help explain the explosion of high-risk sports in post-industrial Western nations. In **unstable cultures**, such as those **at war** or **suffering poverty**, people rarely seek out additional thrills. But in rich and safety-obsessed countries, full of guardrails and seat belts, and with personal-injury claims companies swamping TV advertising, **everyday life may have become too safe, predictable and boring** for those programmed for risk taking.

Until recently, researchers were baffled. Psychoanalytic theory and learning theory relied heavily on the notion of **stimulus reduction**, which saw all human motivation geared towards eliminating tension. Behaviours that created tension, such as risk taking, were deemed **dysfunctional**, masking anxieties or feelings of inadequacy.

Yet as far back as the 1950s, research was hinting at alternative explanations. British psychologist Hans J Eysenck developed a scale to measure the personality trait of **extroversion**, now one of the most consistent predictors of risk taking. Other studies revealed that, contrary to Freud, the brain not only **craved arousal** but also somehow regulated that arousal at an optimal level. Researchers have extended these early findings into a host of **theories about risk taking**.

Some scientists concentrate on risk taking primarily as a **cognitive or behavioural** phenomenon, an element of a larger personality dimension which measures individuals' sense of **control over their environment** and their willingness to **seek out challenges**.

A second line of research focuses on risk's **biological** roots. Due to relatively low levels of certain **enzymes and neurotransmitters** the cortical system of a risk taker can handle higher levels of stimulation without overloading and switching to the fight or flight response. Their brains automatically dampen the level of incoming stimuli, leaving them with a kind of excitement deficit. The brains of people who don't like taking risks, by contrast, tend to augment incoming stimuli, and thus desire less excitement.

Even then, enzymes are only part of the risk-taking picture. **Upbringing, personal experience, socioeconomic status and learning** are all crucial in determining how that risk-taking impulse is ultimately expressed. For many climbers their interest in climbing was often **shaped externally**, either through contact with older climbers or by reading about great expeditions. On entering the sport, novices are often immersed in a tight-knit climbing **subculture, with its own lingo, rules of conduct and standards of excellence**.

This **learned** aspect may be the most important element in the formation of the risk-taking personality.

This is much abridged and somewhat adapted from an article in Psychology Today.

Behaviour of organisations

To what extent can these ideas be **applied to organisations**? The case study indicates that the tendency to take risks or not depends on cognitive psychological factors (willingness to take on challenges) and genetic factors (the relative absence of certain chemicals in the brain that suppress the fear that most people feel when confronted with risk). None of this makes much sense when talking about an abstract non-living thing like a company, which exists only on paper and in the eyes of the law.

However, the case study also indicates that upbringing, personal experience, socioeconomic status and learning play a part and that risk takers tend to be immersed in a **subculture** with its own language, rules of conduct and standards of excellence.

Equally, organisations have a history and have unique experiences, and are wealthy or struggling. They set rules of conduct and standards of excellence. Their people possess knowledge and talk in organisational jargon. This is commonly called the organisation's **culture**.

Exam focus point

> In December 2008 Question 1 the differing approaches to a business decision could be distinguished by the risks involved. If you are asked to analyse any business decision, you need to think carefully about the risk implications.

2 Impact of risk on stakeholders

FAST FORWARD

> Organisations' attitudes to risks will be influenced by the **priorities** of their stakeholders and how much **influence** stakeholders have. Stakeholders that have significant influence may try to prevent an organisation bearing certain risks.

2.1 Stakeholders' attitudes to risk

Businesses have to be aware of **stakeholder responses to risk** – the risk that organisations will take actions or events will occur that will generate a response from stakeholders that has an adverse effect on the business.

To assess the importance of stakeholder responses to risk, the organisation needs to determine how much leverage its stakeholders have over it. As we have seen, Mendelow provides a mechanism for classifying stakeholders.

2.2 Shareholders

They can affect the **market price of shares** by selling them or they have the **power to remove management**. It would appear that the key issue for management to determine is whether shareholders:

(a) Prefer a **steady income from dividends** (in which case they will be alert to threats to the profits that generate the dividend income, such as investment in projects that are unlikely to yield profits in the short term)

(b) Are **more concerned with long-term capital gains**, in which case they may be less concerned about a short period of poor performance, and more worried about threats to long-term survival that could diminish or wipe out their investment

2.2.1 Risk tolerances of shareholders

However, the position is complicated by the different risk tolerances of shareholders themselves. Some shareholders will, for the chances of higher level of income, be prepared to **bear greater risks** that their investments will not achieve that level of income. Therefore some argue that because the shares of listed companies can be freely bought and sold on stock exchanges, if a company's risk profile changes, its existing shareholders will sell their shares, but the shares will be bought by new investors who prefer the company's new risk profile. The theory runs that it should not matter to the company who its investors are. However, this makes the assumption that the investments of all shareholders are actively managed and that shareholders seek to reduce their own risks by diversification. This is not necessarily true in practice.

In addition, we have seen that the corporate governance reports have stressed the importance of maintaining links with individual shareholders. It is therefore unlikely that the directors will be indifferent to who the company's shareholders are.

Shareholders' risk tolerance may depend on their views of the organisation's risk management systems, how effective they are and how effective they should be. Shareholder sensitivity to this will increase the pressures on management to ensure that a risk culture is **embedded** within the organisation (covered later in this chapter).

2.3 Debt providers and creditors

Debt providers are most concerned about threats to the amount the organisation owes and can take various actions with potentially serious consequences, such as **denial of credit**, higher interest charges or ultimately putting the company into liquidation.

When an organisation is seeking credit or loan finance, it will obviously consider what action creditors will take if it does default. However, it also needs to consider the ways in which **debt finance providers** can **limit the risks of default** by for example requiring companies to meet **certain financial criteria** or provide security in the form of assets that can't be sold without the creditors' agreement or personal guarantees from directors.

These mechanisms may have a significant impact on the development of an organisation's strategy. There may be a conflict between strategies that are **suitable** from the viewpoint of the business's long-term strategic objectives, but are **unacceptable** to existing providers of finance because of threats to cash flows, or are **not feasible** because finance suppliers will not make finance available for them, or will do so on terms that are unduly restrictive.

2.4 Employees

Employees will be concerned about threats to their **job prospects** (money, promotion, benefits and satisfaction) and ultimately threats to the jobs themselves. If the business fails, the impact on employees will be great. However, if the business performs poorly, the impact on employees may not be so great if their jobs are not threatened.

Employees will also be concerned about threats to their personal **wellbeing**, particularly health and safety issues.

The variety of actions employees can take would appear to indicate the risk is significant. Possible actions include pursuit of their own goals rather than shareholder interests, industrial action, refusal to relocate or resignation.

Risks of adverse reactions from employees will have to be managed in a variety of ways.

- **Risk avoidance** – legislation requires that some risks, principally threats to the person, should be avoided

- **Risk reduction** – limiting employee discontent by good pay, conditions, etc

- **Risk transfer** – for example taking out insurance against key employees leaving

- **Risk acceptance** – accepting that some employees will be unhappy but believing the company will not suffer a significant loss if they leave

2.5 Customers and suppliers

Suppliers can provide (possibly unwillingly) short-term finance. As well as being concerned with the possibility of not being paid, suppliers will be concerned about the risk of making unprofitable sales. Customers will be concerned with **threats to their getting the goods or services** that they have been promised, or not getting the **value** from the **goods or services** that they expect.

The impact of customer-supplier attitudes will partly depend on how much the organisation wants to **build long-term relationships** with them. A desire to build relationships implies involvement of the staff that are responsible for building those relationships in the risk management process. It may also imply a **greater degree of disclosure** about risks that may arise to the long-term partners in order to maintain the relationship of trust.

2.6 The wider community

Governments, regulatory and other bodies will be particularly concerned with risks that the organisation does not act as a good corporate citizen, implementing for example **poor employment or environmental policies**. A number of the variety of actions that can be taken could have serious consequences. Government can impose **tax increases or regulation** or take **legal action**. Pressure groups tactics can include **publicity, direct action, sabotage or pressure on government**.

Although the consequences can be serious, the risks that the wider community are concerned about can be rather less easy to predict than for other stakeholders being governed by varying political pressures. This emphasises the need for careful monitoring as part of the risk management process, of changing attitudes and likely responses to the organisation's actions.

3 Internal environment

The **internal** or **control environment** is influenced by **management's attitude** towards control, the **organisational structure** and the **values** and **abilities** of employees.

3.1 Nature of internal environment   12/14

Key terms

The **internal** or **control environment** is the overall attitude, awareness and actions of directors and management regarding internal controls and their importance in the entity. The internal environment encompasses the management style, and corporate culture and values shared by all employees. It provides the background against which the various other controls are operated.

COSO's guidance stresses that a **strong commitment** at the top of the organisation to sound control **compliance, integrity and ethical values** is essential for a sound control framework to exist. It may be easier in smaller companies for senior managers to reinforce the companies' values and oversee staff, as they are more likely be in close day-to-day contact with staff.

One aspect of a poor control environment would be managers viewing control as an administrative burden, bolted on to existing systems. Instead there needs to be recognition of the business need for, and the benefit from, internal control that is effectively integrated with core processes.

The following factors are reflected in the internal environment.

- The **philosophy** and **operating style** of the directors and management
- The entity's **culture**; whether control is seen as an integral part of the organisational framework, or something that is imposed on the rest of the system
- The entity's **organisational structure** and methods of assigning authority and responsibility (including segregation of duties and supervisory controls)
- The directors' **methods of imposing control**, including the internal audit function, the functions of the board of directors and personnel policies and procedures
- The **integrity, ethical values** and **competence** of directors and staff

The UK Turnbull report highlighted a number of elements of a strong internal environment.

- **Clear strategies** for dealing with the significant risks that have been identified
- The company's **culture, code of conduct, processes and structures, human resource policies** and **performance reward systems** supporting the business objectives and risk management and internal control systems
- Senior management demonstrating through its actions and policies commitment to **competence, integrity** and **fostering a climate of trust** within the company
- **Clear definition** of **authority, responsibility** and **accountability** so that decisions are made and actions are taken by the appropriate people
- **Communication** to employees of what is expected of them and the scope of their freedom to act
- People in the company having the **knowledge, skills** and **tools** to support the achievements of the organisation's objectives and to manage its risks effectively

However, a strong internal environment does not, by itself, ensure the effectiveness of the overall internal control system although it will have a major influence on it.

The internal environment will have a major impact on the establishment of business objectives, the structuring of business activities and dealing with risks.

3.2 Internal environment and financial reporting

Effective control systems and an effective control environment can make a big contribution to the quality of financial reporting. COSO's guidance on internal controls over financial reporting sees **organisational and personnel issues** as having a big impact on the quality of financial reporting. Systems should identify which people or departments are responsible for producing specific information. The lines of reporting for each function and business unit should enable effective reporting. Managers also need to consider carefully whether the **levels of authority and responsibility** staff are given are appropriate. Individuals need to be able to get their jobs done but there is also a need for proper checks. The organisation must also assess the knowledge and skills required that staff involved in financial reporting must have. Staff need to have the **necessary competencies** for the work they are doing, and across the organisation there should be sufficient expertise.

Throughout this section of the text we shall use the example of Mazda, the Japanese car manufacturer, to illustrate how a major international company applies the elements identified in the COSO framework.

Mazda's annual report states that the company does not view compliance as just strictly following legal requirements and regulations. It regards compliance as including conformance with internal rules, the Corporate Ethics code of conduct and social expectations and norms. Mazda aims to instil in employees an understanding of why obedience is required, and the ability to form and carry out faithfully their own standards of behaviour.

4 Embedding risk awareness   12/09, 6/14

FAST FORWARD

Risk awareness should be embedded within an organisation's **processes, environment, culture, structure and systems**. Organisations should **issue a risk policy statement** and **maintain a risk register**.

4.1 The risk environment

How the control environment accommodates risk issues will be decisive in determining whether it is effective. COSO's guidance on the internal environment states that an organisation needs to:

- Establish a **philosophy regarding risk management**
- Recognise that **unexpected events** may occur
- Establish the **entity's risk culture**
- Consider all other aspects of how the **organisation's actions may affect its risk culture**

4.2 Embedding risk awareness and assessment

The Ernst & Young report *Managing Risk Across the Enterprise* emphasises that risk assessment should evolve into a consistent, embedded activity within a company's strategic, business, budget and audit planning process rather than be executed as a significant standalone process. Risk awareness should be taken for granted at all levels of the organisation, and should be the foundation of all control systems. Ernst & Young identifies a number of elements of a **consistent, embedded approach**.

4.2.1 Focus on risk to stakeholder/shareholder value

The Ernst & Young report states that an embedded approach needs to focus not on risks to processes but on **risks to shareholder value**.

'Identifying these risks and ensuring that they are properly managed … and appropriately monitored.'

Share value is driven by looking at risks in two key areas, **future growth opportunities** and **core business operations**.

(a)   **Future growth opportunities**

These are strategies and objectives that the organisation pursues to **increase competitive advantage** and **shareholder value** over time. Ernst & Young argues that risks to realising these opportunities are often overlooked. However, the solution is simple. Since future growth opportunities and supporting actions are described in external reports and internal planning documents, all that is required is to identify the most significant risks preventing achievement of these objectives.

(b)   **Core business operations**

These comprise the assets and processes in the company that **generate or support the largest proportion of profit or revenues**. Organisations should identify the key risks inherent in these processes. They should also identify processes that are significantly risky and place a substantial

portion of capital at risk, but may not generate significant revenues or profits (for example financial derivative trading).

4.2.2 Consistent action-orientated risk assessment criteria

Ernst & Young suggests that the criteria used should **direct and drive monitoring and improvement actions** as well as **focus and accountability**. For this to happen, the report emphasises that as well as considering impact and likelihood, organisations should focus on management response to risk. This will drive the potential improvement or assurance actions.

4.2.3 Common reporting elements and style

Reporting of risks should be **consistent** across processes and functions, fully **support board needs**, be concise and be updated routinely.

4.3 Risk culture   12/07

Key term

> **Culture** is 'the pattern of basic assumptions that a given group has invented, discovered, or developed, in learning to cope with its problems of external adaptation and internal integration, and that have worked well enough to be considered valid and, therefore, to be taught to new members as the correct way to perceive, think and feel in relation to these problems.'   (Schien)

Culture can determine whether new influences and procedures can change things.

Case Study

Learning a culture

Suppose you get a new job that involves operating a machine of some kind. Your induction training taught you that you are expected to spend 15 minutes at the beginning of every production session (morning and afternoon) carrying out routine maintenance on the machine you operate: checking the oil levels, looking out for wear and tear, making sure all the parts are in alignment and properly sharp, and so on.

Of course you will diligently do all this on your first few days, but let's suppose you quickly become aware that the other machine operators around you start productive work long before you do, and are laughing at you for being so cautious.

By Wednesday lunchtime you have received a visit from your manager who wants to know why your daily output is so much lower than that of the other members of the team. You are also concerned about this because along with your basic pay you are paid a small bonus for every job that you finish, and your colleagues seem to produce far more per day than you do.

You explain that you are just doing what you were taught to do in induction but the manager takes you aside and explains that the more experienced operators 'know' when their machines need oiling or adjusting and so on, just from the sound they make and how much they vibrate, and you will soon get to know too. The manager admits that if machines are not properly maintained there is a risk that they will be seriously damaged and production will be lost. But the manager also says that if your machine goes wrong you won't actually be seriously affected anyway. You will get the rest of the day off, on whatever is your average day's pay, while it is being fixed. So, 'between you and your manager', it is actually in your interest to produce as much as you possibly can, and ignore your supposed maintenance responsibilities.

The manager then mentions that a more senior manager has asked the department to fulfil an unusually large order that week, and your lack of productivity may mean that the more senior manager is let down.

By Wednesday afternoon at the latest, you will probably have concluded that your supposed routine maintenance responsibilities are not actually necessary at all and will get on with productive work immediately. Perhaps you will be looking around to see if, when, and why your colleagues get the oil can out, if they ever do, but you will care a lot less about your machine going wrong.

What organisational problems are revealed by the case study above?

Answer

The culture of the machine operations section works against the implementation of procedures that are taught to newcomers. The priority is spending the maximum amount of time doing productive work. The procedures learned during induction are regarded as an impediment to productivity.

However, this does not mean the staff in the machines operations section are necessarily wrong. The procedures laid down are probably inappropriate. The people who actually do the job understand the risks far better than the people who devised the induction training and the people who wrote the procedures manual.

The motivation and rewards system is badly designed. For experienced machine operators the risk is that they will lose a small amount of bonus, but even if they do they get a day off.

For the company the risk is lost production and extra expense on repairing machines that have not been as well maintained as they should have been.

'You' (the new employee) are a problem, though this is harsh. Strictly you should have reported the fact that you were being pressured into doing something that was in breach of official procedures, but this is very hard. Most people tend to try to fit in, at least at first. In any case, who would you report it to?

You may have had additional ideas.

4.4 Types of risk culture

Different writers have identified different types of culture, based on particular aspects of organisation and management.

Case Study

In his evidence to the UK House of Commons Treasury select committee, Paul Moore, former head of Group Regulatory Risk at HBOS, stated:

'There is no doubt that you can have the best governance processes in the world but if they are carried out in a culture of greed, unethical behaviour and indisposition to challenge they will fail.'

4.4.1 Miles and Snow: strategic cultures

Miles and Snow identify three 'superior performing' cultures.

(a)   **Defenders**. Firms with this culture like low risk, secure markets, and tried and trusted solutions. These companies have cultures whose stories and rituals reflect historical continuity and consensus. Decision taking is relatively formalised. (There is a stress on 'doing things right'; that is, efficiency.)

(b)   **Prospectors**. These are organisations where the dominant beliefs are more to do with results (doing the right things; that is, effectiveness), and therefore prospectors often take high risks.

(c)   **Analysers**. These try to balance risk and profits. They use a core of stable products and markets as a source of earnings to move into innovative prospector areas. Analysers follow change, but do not initiate it.

4.4.2 Deal and Kennedy: risk, feedback and reward

Deal and Kennedy (*Corporate Cultures*) consider cultures to be a function of the level of **risks** that **employees** need to take, and how quickly they get **feedback** on whether they got it right or wrong and/or rewards for doing so.

(a)   **Low risk cultures**

    (i)   **Process culture**

        The process culture occurs in organisations where there is low risk and little or no feedback. People become bogged down with how things are done, not with what is to be achieved. These cultures however often produce consistent results, which is ideal in, for example, public services, banking and insurance.

    (ii)   **Work hard, play hard culture**

        This culture is characterised by few risks being taken, all with rapid feedback. This is typical in large organisations, such as retailers which strive for high quality customer service.

(b)   **High risk cultures**

    (i)   **Bet your company culture**

        In the bet your company culture high risk decisions are taken, but it may be years before the results are known. Typically, these might involve development or exploration projects, which take years to come to fruition, such as oil exploration or development of drugs.

    (ii)   **Tough-guy macho culture**

        Feedback is quick and the risks and rewards are high. This often applies to fast-moving financial activities, such as brokerage, but could also apply to the police, athletes competing in team sports, advertising and certain types of construction.

4.5 Changing the culture   12/07,12/09

4.5.1 Importance of control environment

The strength of the control environment will have a very significant impact on how easy or difficult it is to change the control culture. The commitment of top management will be a very significant factor.

4.5.2 Risk awareness and communication

In the first place people cannot be expected to avoid risks if they are not aware that they exist in the first place. Embedding a risk management frame of mind into an organisation's culture requires top-down communications on what the risk philosophy is and what is expected of the organisation's people.

Here is an example of an internal communications programme slightly adapted from an example in the COSO *Framework*.

Internal communications programme

- Management discusses risks and associated risk responses in regular briefings with employees.

- Management regularly communicates entity-wide risks in employee communications such as newsletters and an intranet.

- Enterprise risk management policies, standards and procedures are made readily available to employees along with clear statements requiring compliance.

- Management requires employees to consult with others across the organisation as appropriate when new events are identified.

- Induction sessions for new employees include information and literature on the company's risk management philosophy and enterprise risk management programme.

- Existing employees are required to take workshops and/or refresher courses on the organisation's enterprise risk management initiatives.

- The risk management philosophy is reinforced in regular and ongoing internal communication programmes and through specific communication programmes to reinforce tenets of the company's culture.

The COSO framework also recommends certain organisational measures for spreading ownership of risk management.

(a) Enterprise risk management should be an explicit or implicit part of **everyone's job description**.

(b) Personnel should understand the need to **resist pressure from superiors to participate in improper activities**, and **channels outside normal reporting lines** should be available to permit reporting such circumstances.

4.5.3 Training and involvement

Training is of course essential, especially for new employees and for all when new procedures are introduced. Aside from practical matters like showing employees which buttons to press or how to find out the information they need, training should include an **explanation** of why things are done in the way that they are. If employees are asked to carry out a new type of check but are **not told why**, there is every chance that **they won't bother** to do it, because they don't understand its relevance. It just seems to mean more work for them and slows up the process for everyone.

The people who are expected to own risks and risk management will be more inclined to do so if they are **involved** in the process of identifying risks in the first place and developing responses and controls. This enhances understanding and gives them a stake in risk management.

4.5.4 Performance appraisal and measurement

To influence and alter attitudes, risk issues have to be built into organisations' human resource systems. Staff's **job descriptions** should make clear the extent of their responsibilities for risk management. Their **annual performance objectives** should include objectives relating to risk, and risk management needs to be considered as part of the performance appraisal and reward systems. As we shall see later in the text, this does not necessarily mean **avoiding risks**, as this may be overcautious and prevent the organisation from taking advantage of good opportunities.

4.5.5 Changing risk attitudes

The biggest problems are likely to arise when a risk culture already exists but has become inappropriate and needs to be changed. Some people embrace change and thrive on it, but many resist it. There may be a variety of reasons.

(a) Change involves the **extra effort** of 'unlearning' old knowledge and the learning of new knowledge.

(b) **Self-interest** may be a factor. A new procedure may entail the involvement of another person or department and be seen as an erosion of power.

(c) People may **misunderstand** the nature of the change.

(d) Staff may simply **mistrust** management.

(e) Employees may **not agree** that the change is needed.

Coercion and autocratic methods may be necessary on occasions, especially when time is limited, but in the longer term **resistance must be overcome** if people are ever to accept ownership of risk management. As usual, **communication** and **dialogue** are key to this. Here are some other possible methods.

(a) **Job satisfaction**

   Those driving the change must identify what constitutes job satisfaction for the relevant group in the organisation.

(b) **Learning experiences**

   A change is more likely to be accepted if people have the **opportunity to experience** first hand what it means for them in a 'safe' environment that allows them to make mistakes and to experiment and ask questions to resolve personal concerns. It is often useful to involve people from other parts of the organisation who have already made the transition and can help ease the fears of those who have yet to experience it.

(c) **Key personnel**

   Some individuals are more important than others; for example, individuals with significant **power to disrupt**, individuals with important **technical expertise**, or individuals whose **influence** over other people is significant. These people need to be persuaded to buy in to the change as a first priority.

(d) **Infrastructure**

   Change – especially sudden change – is often hampered because staff do not have adequate tools. For example, it may be **more difficult to obtain the information** needed, or staff may have to override old software controls while programs are being rewritten. These are problems that need to be addressed as soon as possible.

Exam focus point

> Question 2 in December 2007 asked about embedding risk in the culture of an organisation.

Case Study

Writing in *Risk Management* magazine, Gayle Tollifson, chief risk officer at QBE Insurance Company in Australia, emphasises the importance of culture. She comments that in a number of corporate collapses, the tone or culture that boards set for their companies was flawed or ignored. In many instances boards were not aware of problems until too late.

Tollifson emphasises the board's responsibility to ensure that the right culture exists at all levels of an organisation. At the board level selecting a chief executive who embraces the company's cultural values is vital, and board-approved policies and standards must lead the way in risk management practice. Communication is also important. This includes a risk management policy, ensuring the right mechanisms are in place for disclosing issues and that there is a culture of disclosure. This must mean sending a message to staff that the sooner bad news is identified and reported, the sooner the problem can be solved.

As well as embedding risk into the culture, Tollifson explains that companies need to ensure that risk management is an essential part of business operations, considered as part of doing business **every day**. Risk appetite needs to be considered when overall strategy and policy are set. Risk analysis must form a key part of the business planning framework.

Tollifson also stresses that while a risk management team can make a significant contribution to improving risk management, the board must set the culture entrenching risk awareness, disclosure and transparency. The business managers who create risks must also take responsibility for managing them.

4.6 Risk policy statement

Organisations ought to have a statement of risk policy and strategy that is distributed to all managers and staff and that covers the following areas.

- Definitions of risk and risk management
- Objectives of risk policy
- Regulatory requirements
- Benefits of risk management
- How risk management is linked into strategic decision-making and performance
- What areas of risk management (risk avoidance, risk reduction) are particularly important
- Risk classification
- Roles of board, managers, staff and audit and risk committees
- Internal control framework and important controls
- Other tools and techniques
- Assurance reporting
- Role of training
- How to obtain help

4.7 Risk register

Organisations should have formal methods of collecting information on risk and response. A risk register **lists and prioritises the main risks** an organisation faces, and is used as the basis for decision-making on how to deal with risks. The register also details **who is responsible for dealing** with risks and the **actions taken**. The register should show the risk levels **before** and **after** control action is taken, to facilitate a cost-benefit analysis of controls.

Case Study

The Ernst & Young report *Managing Risk Across the Enterprise* recommends a simpler key risk summary report, ideally fitting on a single page and covering:

- Risk type (financial, operations, compliance and strategic)
- Risk description
- Overall ratings (impact, likelihood, control effectiveness)
- Key risk management activities
- Monitoring approach and results
- Gaps, issues and actions
- Risk owner/Accountable party
- Processes, initiatives and objectives affected

Exam focus point

Question 4 in December 2009 illustrated how effective implementation of risk management could be undermined by various aspects of a company's culture.

The **board** has overall responsibility for **risk management** as an essential part of its corporate governance responsibilities. Responsibilities below board level will depend on the extent of delegation to **line managers** and whether there is a **separate risk management function**.

5.1 Responsibilities for risk management

Everyone who works for the organisation has responsibilities for risk management. In this section we shall discuss the responsibilities that directors, operational managers and staff have for managing the risks as part of their duties. The organisation may also employ risk management specialists, who will focus on promoting risk management across the organisation. In larger organisations there will be a separate risk management department. The role of risk specialists is considered in Section 5.2.

5.1.1 The board

As we have seen, the board's role in managing risk is one of its most important. The board is responsible for **determining risk management strategy and monitoring risks** as part of its responsibility for the organisation's overall strategy and its responsibilities to shareholders and other stakeholders. It is also responsible for **setting appropriate policies on internal controls** and **seeking assurance** that the internal control system is **functioning effectively**. It should also communicate the organisation's strategy to employees.

In 2006 COSO demonstrated how elements of its framework could be applied to financial reporting in its report *Internal Control Over Financial Reporting – Guidance for Smaller Public Companies*. The underlying theme of the guidance was that companies should ensure that their control framework was appropriately focused on financial reporting considerations. The recommendations in each area included:

- **Control environment** – the board of directors should have understanding of financial reporting issues. The company should employ individuals with sufficient competence in financial reporting and oversight roles.

- **Risk assessment** – this should be carried out by management, who should specify the objectives of financial reporting and, following on from these, the risks to reliable financial reporting. Fraud risk should be a major concern.

- **Control activities** – appropriate actions should be taken to address risks, including establishing and communicating financial reporting policies and information technology controls.

- **Information and communication** – information should be captured and distributed in an appropriate form and in good time.

- **Monitoring** – the board should evaluate separately whether internal controls over financial reporting are present and functioning.

5.1.2 The chief executive

Ownership of the risk management and internal control system is a vital part of the chief executive's overall responsibility for the company. The chief executive must consider in particular the **risk and control environment**, focusing among other things on how their example promotes a good culture. The chief executive should also **monitor other directors** and senior staff, particularly those whose actions can put the company at significant risk.

5.1.3 Risk committee 12/08

Boards also need to consider whether there should be a separate board committee, with responsibility for monitoring and supervising risk identification and management. If the board doesn't have a separate committee, under the UK Corporate Governance Code the audit committee will be responsible for risk management.

As we have seen, consideration of risk certainly falls within the remit of the audit committee. However, there are a number of arguments in favour of having a separate risk management committee.

(a)   **Staffing**

A risk management committee can be **staffed by executive directors**, whereas an **audit committee** under **corporate governance best practice** should be **staffed by non-executive directors**. However, if there are doubts about the **competence and good faith** of executive management, it will be more appropriate for the committee to be staffed by non-executive directors.

(b)   **Breadth of remit**

As a key role of the audit committee will be to liaise with the external auditors, much of their time could be focused on **financial risks**.

(c)   **Leadership**

A risk management committee can take the lead in **promoting awareness and driving changes in practice**, whereas an audit committee will have a purely monitoring role, checking that a satisfactory risk management policy exists.

(d)   **Investigations**

A risk management committee can carry out **special investigations**, particularly in areas not related to the accounting systems (the audit committee is more likely to investigate the accounting systems, as discussed in Chapter 8).

Companies that are involved in significant financial market risk will often have a risk management committee. The potential for large losses through misuse of derivatives was demonstrated by the Barings bank scandal. A risk management committee can help provide the supervision required. Clearly, though, to be effective, the members will collectively need a high level of financial expertise.

5.1.4 Role and function of risk committee

Evidence of companies that have operated a risk management committee suggests that such a committee will be far more effective if it has clear terms of reference. Morris in *An Accountant's Guide to Risk Management* suggests that written terms of reference might include the following.

- **Approving the organisation's risk management strategy** and **risk management policy**
- **Reviewing reports on key risks** prepared by business operating units, management and the board
- **Monitoring overall exposure** to risk and ensuring it remains within limits set by the board
- **Assessing the effectiveness** of the organisation's **risk management systems**
- **Providing early warning to the board** on emerging risk issues and significant changes in the company's exposure to risks
- In conjunction with the audit committee, **reviewing the company's statement on internal control** with reference to risk management, prior to endorsement by the board

Note that the focus is on supervision and monitoring rather than the committee having responsibility for day-to-day decision-making and implementation of policies.

 Case Study

The UK Walker report recommended that FTSE 100 bank or life assurance companies should establish a risk committee. Reasons for this recommendation included the need to avoid overburdening the audit committee, and to draw a distinction between the largely **backward-looking focus** of the audit committee and the need for **forward-looking focus on determining risk appetite** and from this **monitoring appropriate limits** on exposures and concentrations. The committee should have a majority of non-executive directors. Any executive risk committee should be overseen by the board risk committee.

Walker recommended that the committee should concentrate on the fundamental prudential risks for the institution: leverage, liquidity risk, interest rate and currency risk, credit/counterparty risks and other

market risks. It should advise the board on **current risk exposures** and **future risk strategy**, and the establishment of a **supportive risk culture**.

The committee should regularly review and approve the measures and methodology used to assess risk. A variety of measures should be used. The risk committee should also advise the remuneration committee on risk weightings to be applied to performance objectives incorporated within the incentive structure for executive directors.

Having a separate risk management committee can aid the board in its responsibility for ensuring that **adequate risk management systems** are in place. The application of risk management policies will then be the responsibility of operational managers, and perhaps specialist risk management personnel, as described below.

5.1.5 Internal and external audit   6/15

Risk is integral to the work of internal and external audit, both in terms of influencing **how much work** they do (with more work being done on riskier areas) and also **what work** they actually do. The external auditors will be concerned with risks that impact most on the figures shown in the **financial accounts**. Internal auditors' role is **more flexible**, and their approach will depend on whether they **focus on the controls** that are being operated or on the **overall risk management process**.

5.1.6 Line managers

The UK Turnbull report stresses the role of management in implementing broad policies on risk and control, including **identifying and evaluating risk** and **designing and operating an appropriate system of internal control**. Managers should have an awareness of the risks that fall into their areas of responsibility and possible links with **other areas**. The **performance indicators** they use should help them monitor key business and financial activities and highlight when intervention is required.

Line managers will be involved in communicating risk management policies to staff and will of course 'set a good example'. Line managers are also responsible for **preparing reports** that will be considered by the board and senior managers.

Part of the role of line managers may be to carry out detailed risk management functions. The office manager may deal with fire precautions and the managing director with buying insurances, for example, and each may call in experts to assist with these functions.

In larger organisations, a risk management group of senior operational managers may operate below the board's risk management committee. The risk management group will concentrate on **risk responses** and will also **monitor risk management** to see that the strategies and policies are operating effectively.

5.1.7 Staff

Staff will be responsible for following the **risk management procedures** the organisation has established, and should be alert for any conditions or events that may result in problems. Staff need an understanding of their **accountability** for individual risks and that **risk management** and **risk awareness** are a key part of the organisation's culture. They must be aware of how to **report** any concerns they have, particularly reports of risk, failures of existing control measures, variances in budgets and forecasts.

The UK Turnbull report emphasises the need for employees to take responsibility for risk management and internal control. This requires them to have the necessary **knowledge, skills, information and authority** to operate and monitor the control system. This requires understanding the **company,** its **objectives,** the **industries and markets** in which it operates and the **risks** it faces.

5.2 Risk management personnel

5.2.1 Risk specialists

Because of the variety and size of the risks faced, many organisations employ specialists in risk management or operate a separate risk management department.

Lam (*Enterprise Risk Management*) gives a detailed description of the role of the risk manager. The COSO framework also has a list of responsibilities. Combining these sources we can say that the specialist risk manager is typically responsible for:

(a)   Providing the **overall leadership, vision and direction** for enterprise risk management

(b)   Establishing an **integrated risk management framework** for all aspects of risk across the organisation, integrating enterprise risk management with other business planning and management activities and framing authority and accountability for enterprise risk management in business units

(c)   Promoting an **enterprise risk management competence** throughout the entity, including facilitating development of technical enterprise risk management expertise, helping managers align risk responses with the entity's risk tolerances and developing appropriate controls

(d)   **Developing RM policies**, including the quantification of management's risk appetite through specific risk limits, defining roles and responsibilities, ensuring compliance with codes, regulations and statutes and participating in setting goals for implementation

(e)   **Establishing a common risk management language** that includes common measures around likelihood and impact, and common risk categories; developing the analytical systems and data management capabilities to support the risk management programme

(f)   **Implementing a set of risk indicators and reports** including losses and incidents, key risk exposures, and early warning indicators; facilitating managers' development of reporting protocols, including quantitative and qualitative thresholds, and monitoring the reporting process

(g)   **Dealing with insurance companies**: an important task because of increased premium costs, restrictions in the cover available (will the risks be excluded from cover) and the need for negotiations with insurance companies if claims arise; if insurers require it, demonstrating that the organisation is taking steps actively to manage its risks; arranging financing schemes such as self-insurance or captive insurance

(h)   **Allocating economic capital to business activities** based on risk, and optimising the company's risk portfolio through business activities and risk transfer strategies

(i)   **Reporting to the chief executive on progress** and recommending action as needed. Communicating the company's risk profile to key stakeholders such as the board of directors, regulators, stock analysts, rating agencies and business partners

The risk manager will need to show leadership and persuasive skills to overcome resistance from those who believe that risk management is an attempt to stifle initiative.

The risk manager's contribution will be judged by how much they **increase the value of the organisation**. The specialist knowledge a risk manager has should allow the risk manager to assess **long-term risk** and hazard outcomes and therefore decide what resources should be allocated to combating risk.

Clearly certain strategic risks are likely to have the biggest impact on corporate value. Therefore a risk manager's role may include management of these strategic risks. These may include those having a **fundamental effect on future operations**, such as mergers and acquisitions, or risks that have the potential to cause **large adverse impacts**, such as currency hedging and major investments.

Case Study

The role of the risk manager was highlighted in February 2009 by the evidence given to the UK House of Commons Treasury Select Committee enquiry into the banking system by Paul Moore, the ex-head of Group Regulatory Risk at HBOS. Moore had allegedly been sacked by Sir James Crosby, Chief Executive Officer at HBOS. As a result of Moore making his allegations, Sir James resigned as deputy chairman of London city watchdog, the Financial Services Authority.

Moore stated that in his role he 'felt a bit like being a man in a rowing boat trying to slow down an oil tanker'. He said that he had told the board that its sales culture was out of balance with its systems and controls. The bank was growing too fast, did not accept challenges to policy, and was a serious risk to financial stability and consumer protection. The reason why Moore was ignored and others were afraid to speak up was, he alleged, that the balance of powers was weighted towards executive directors, not just in HBOS but in other banks as well.

'I believe that, had there been highly competent risk and compliance managers in all the banks, carrying rigorous oversight, properly protected and supported by a truly independent non-executive, the external auditor and the FSA, they would have felt comfortable and protected to challenge the practices of the executive without fear for their own positions. If this had been the case, I am also confident that we would not have got into the current crisis.'

Moore was replaced by a Group Risk Director who had never previously been a risk manager. The new head had been a sales manager and was allegedly appointed by the Chief Executive Officer without other board members having much, if any, say in the appointment.

During the time that Paul Moore was head of Group Regulatory Risk, the Financial Services Authority had raised its own concerns about practices at HBOS and had kept a watching brief over the bank. In December 2004 the Authority noted that although the group 'had made good progress in addressing the risks highlighted in February 2004, the group risk functions still needed to enhance their ability to influence the business'. In June 2006 the authority stated that while the group had improved its framework, it still had concerns: 'The growth strategy of the group posed risks to the whole group and these risks must be managed and mitigated.'

At the end of the week in which Paul Moore's evidence was published, Lloyds, which had taken over HBOS, issued a profit warning in relation to HBOS for 2008 for losses of over £10 billion.

5.2.3 Risk management department

Larger companies may have a bigger risk management department whose responsibilities are wider than a single risk manager. The Institute of Risk Management's Risk Management Standard lists the main responsibilities of the risk management department.

- **Setting policy and strategy** for risk management
- **Primary champion of risk management** at a strategic and operational level
- Building a **risk-aware culture** within the organisation including appropriate education
- Establishing **internal risk policy** and structures for business units
- **Designing and reviewing processes** for risk management
- **Co-ordinating the various functional activities** which advise on risk management issues within an organisation
- **Developing risk response processes**, including contingency and business continuity programmes
- **Preparing reports on risks** for the board and stakeholders

Exam focus point

The study guide emphasises the roles of the risk management committee and (specialist) risk management function so you may well be asked to explain what they do.

5.3 Resourcing risk management

Whatever the division of responsibilities for risk management, the organisation needs to think carefully about how risk management is resourced. Sufficient resources will be required to implement and monitor risk management (including the resources required to obtain the necessary information). Management needs to consider not only the **expenditure** required, but also the **human resources** in terms of skills and experience.

6 Objective setting

FAST FORWARD

> The board's **objective-setting process** must encompass various levels of objectives. **Risk appetite** and **risk tolerance** will have a significant impact on objectives.

6.1 Objective setting and corporate governance

Remember we mentioned in Chapter 3 that corporate governance best practice requires boards to draw up a schedule of matters that should be considered by the board itself. This should include the objectives to which the board gives particular attention.

6.2 Mission, corporate objectives and unit objectives

Objectives come in hierarchies, with the objectives lower down in the hierarchy contributing to the objectives higher up. Granger identifies three types of objectives.

- Mission
- Corporate objectives
- Unit objectives

6.2.1 Mission

A mission is a **general objective, visionary, often unwritten, and very open-ended**, without any time limit for achievement. A commercial company in the leisure industry might have a mission of improving the quality of people's lives by providing them with all the leisure activities they want.

6.2.2 Entity (corporate) objectives

Corporate objectives are those which are concerned with the firm as a whole. Objectives should be **explicit**, **quantifiable** and **capable of being achieved**. The corporate objectives outline the expectations of the firm and the strategic planning process is concerned with the means of achieving the objectives. Objectives should relate to the **key factors for business success**, which are typically as follows.

- Profitability (return on investment)
- Market share
- Growth
- Cash flow
- Customer satisfaction
- The quality of the firm's products
- Industrial relations
- Added value

6.2.3 Subsidiary, business unit, division objectives

As well as stressing the importance of setting objectives at the entity level, the COSO model also emphasises the importance of establishing strategy and control at the **division, business unit and subsidiary levels**. They will have strategic objectives, but a lot of their important objectives will be operational objectives.

(a) From the **commercial sector**:

    (i)   Increasing the number of customers by x% (sales department)

    (ii)   Reducing the number of rejects by 50% (production department)

(b) From the **public sector**:

    (i)   To provide cheap subsidised bus travel (a local authority transport department)

    (ii)   To introduce more nursery education (an objective of a borough education department)

6.3 Categories of objectives

As part of its enterprise risk management model, COSO categorises objectives into four categories.

- **Strategic** – high level goals, aligned with and supporting the organisation's mission
- **Operational** – effective and efficient use of resources
- **Reporting** – reliability of reporting
- **Compliance** – compliance with applicable laws and regulations

COSO states that this categorisation allows entities to focus on separate aspects of risk management. The categories have some overlaps, but they address different needs and may be the direct responsibility of different managers.

Case Study

Mazda's CSR Management Strategy Committee convenes twice a year, with members of the Executive Committee in attendance. Its task is to identify CSR implementation policy and high-priority issues from medium to long-term perspectives, and to establish specific issues for each field and area of operations. CSR in Mazda is integral to the company's operations. It includes ensuring customer satisfaction as well as developing environmentally responsible products and participating in local communities.

Mazda's recent strategy has been based on its 'Sustainable Zoom-Zoom' plan, its long-term vision for technology development. The plan stresses Mazda's desire to harmonise driving performance with safety and the environment in building vehicles that 'look inviting to drive, are fun to drive, and make you want to drive them again.'

6.4 Environmental analysis

Environmental analysis should support the board's objective-setting process.

The environment is a source of **uncertainty**. Decision-makers do not have sufficient information about environmental factors. Many things are out of their control. The overall degree of uncertainty may be assessed along two axes: simplicity/complexity and stability/dynamism.

(a) **Simplicity/complexity**

    (i) The **variety of influences** faced by an organisation. The more open an organisation is, the greater the variety of influences. The greater the number of markets the organisation operates in, the greater the number of influences to which it is subject and the greater the exposure to certain risks, for example currency and trading risks.

    (ii) The amount of **knowledge necessary**. Some environments, to be handled successfully, require knowledge. All businesses need to have knowledge of the tax system, for example, but only pharmaceuticals businesses need to know about mandatory testing procedures for new drugs.

    (iii) The **interconnectedness** of environmental influences causes complexity. Importing and exporting companies are sensitive to exchange rates, which themselves are sensitive to interest rates. Interest rates then influence a company's borrowing costs. Scenario-building and modelling are ways of dealing with complexities to develop an understanding of environmental conditions.

(b) **Stability/dynamism**

    (i) An area of the environment is stable if it **remains the same**. Firms which can predict demand face a stable environment.

    (ii) An unstable environment **changes often**. The environment of many fashion goods is unstable, for example.

6.4.1 The changing environment

Changes in the business environment can be driven by various developments, including:

(a) **Globalisation** of business – increased competition and global customers as domestic markets become saturated and companies are able to compete easily anywhere in the world

(b) **Science and technology** developments, especially in communications (the internet) and transport (particularly air travel)

(c) Mergers, acquisitions and strategic **alliances**

(d) Changing **customer values** and behaviour

(e) Increased **scrutiny of business decisions** by government and the public

(f) Increased **liberalisation** of trade, and **deregulation** and co-operation between business and government have eased access to foreign markets

(g) Changes in **business practices** – downsizing, outsourcing and re-engineering

(h) Changes in the **social and business relationships** between companies and their employees, customers and other stakeholders

6.5 Determining strategy

The ERM highlights the need for well-defined objectives and strategies in different parts of an organisation as well as for the organisation as a whole. The organisation needs to consider three levels of strategy.

- **Corporate**: the general direction of the whole organisation
- **Business**: how the organisation or its business units tackle particular markets
- **Operational/functional**: specific strategies for different departments of the business

6.5.1 Corporate strategy

Corporate strategy is concerned with what types of business the organisation is in. It 'denotes the most general level of strategy in an organisation' (Johnson and Scholes).

Aspects of corporate strategy

Characteristic	Comment
Scope of activities	Strategy and strategic management impact on the whole organisation: all parts of the business operation should support and further the strategic plan.
Environment	The organisation counters threats and exploits opportunities in the environment (customers, clients, competitors).
Resources	Strategy involves choices about allocating or obtaining corporate resources now and in the future.
Values	The values of people with power in the organisation influence its strategy.
Timescale	Corporate strategy has a long-term impact.

6.5.2 Business strategy

Business strategy includes such decisions as whether to segment the market and specialise in particularly profitable areas (discussed below), or to compete by offering a wider range of products.

6.5.3 Operational strategy

Operational or functional strategies deal with specialised areas of activity.

Functional area	Comment
Marketing	Devising products and services, pricing, promoting and distributing them, in order to satisfy customer needs at a profit. Marketing and corporate strategies are interrelated
Production	Factory location, manufacturing techniques, outsourcing, and so on
Finance	Ensuring that the firm has enough financial resources to fund its other strategies by identifying sources of finance and using them effectively
Human resources management	Secure personnel of the right skills in the right quantity at the right time, and ensure that they have the right skills and values to promote the firm's overall goals
Information systems	A firm's information systems are very important, as an item of expenditure, as administrative support and as a tool for competitive strength
R&D	New products and techniques

6.6 Areas of strategic decision-making

6.6.1 Markets

One key decision is how the markets within which the business operates are determined.

As well as making broad decisions about the markets in which they will trade, businesses will also determine which segments within those markets they will target.

The total market consists of widely different groups of consumers. However, each group consists of **segments**, people (or organisations) with **common needs and preferences**, who perhaps react to 'market stimuli' in much the same way. Each market segment can become a **target market for an organisation**.

There are many possible **bases for segmentation**.

- Geographical area
- Age
- End use (eg work or leisure)
- Gender
- Level of income
- Occupation
- Education
- Religion
- Ethnicity
- Nationality
- Social class
- Buyer behaviour
- Lifestyle

Clearly the segment decisions will have an impact on the risks that the business faces. Choice of geographical area will influence the level of currency and trading risks. Targeting a market where buyer behaviour is not very stable may involve higher risk levels but also perhaps higher returns.

6.6.2 Business structure

Business structure impacts significantly on the application of the COSO model. The COSO cube demonstrates clearly that the model needs to be applied in each business unit, so how these units are

constituted and the **autonomy** that they are given will have a significant influence on how risk management is carried out.

Divisionalisation is the division of a business into autonomous regions or product businesses, each with its own revenues, expenditures and capital asset purchase programmes, and therefore each with its own profit and loss responsibility and decision-making.

Each division of the organisation might be:

- A subsidiary company under the holding company
- A profit centre or investment centre within a single company
- A strategic business unit (SBU) within the larger company, with its own objectives

The advantages and disadvantages of divisionalisation include the following.

Advantages	Disadvantages
Focuses the attention of management below 'top level' on business performance	In some businesses, it is impossible to identify completely independent products or markets for which separate divisions can be set up.
Reduces the likelihood of unprofitable products and activities being continued	Divisionalisation is only possible at a fairly senior management level, because there is a limit to how much discretion can be used in the division of work. For example, every product needs a manufacturing function and a selling function.
Encourages a greater attention to efficiency, lower costs and higher profits	There may be more resource problems. Many divisions get their resources from head office in competition with other divisions.

6.7 Setting risk appetite and risk tolerance

An organisation needs to have objectives in place and an idea of what strategies can be used to implement those objectives in order for management to identify risks connected with those strategies. However, COSO emphasises that overall risk strategy must be considered when objectives are set and the **risk appetite** (the risks the directors wish to accept) is decided.

Risk tolerance (the risks the organisation bears in relation to particular strategies) needs to be aligned with risk appetite.

Factors directors will take into account include the risks of failure associated with a new product, the need for risky new strategies to expand the company and the level and speed of change in the market or environment.

 Case Study

Paul Moore, in his evidence to the Treasury Select Committee on HBOS, highlighted examples of excessive risk taking.

'There must have been a very high risk if you lend money to people who have no jobs, no provable income and no assets. If you lend that money to buy an asset which is worth the same or even less than the amount of the loan and secure that loan on the value of that asset purchased, and then assume that asset will always continue to rise in value, you must be pretty much close to delusional.'

Enterprise risk management requires the entity to take a **portfolio view** of risk. Management should consider how individual risks **interrelate** and develop an entity perspective from the **business unit** and **entity** levels.

The Turnbull report also provides guidance on what the board should consider when setting objectives:

- The **nature and extent of the risks** facing the company

- The **extent** and **categories of risk** which it regards as acceptable for the company to bear

- The **likelihood** of the **risks materialising**

- The company's ability to **reduce the incidence and impact** on the business of risks that do materialise

- The **costs** of **operating particular controls** relative to the **benefits obtained** in managing the related risks

| Question | | | Risk culture |

Johnson and Scholes have identified various change management strategies that could be used to embed a new risk culture.

Method	Techniques	Benefits	Drawbacks
Education and communication	• Small group briefings • Newsletters • Management development • Training		
Participation and involvement	• Small groups • Delegates and representatives		
Facilitation and support	• One on one counselling • Personal development • Provision of organisational resources		
Negotiation and agreement	• Provision of rewards • Collective bargaining		
Manipulation and co-optation	• Influence staff that are positively disposed • Buy-off informal leaders • Provide biased information		
Explicit and implicit coercion	• Threaten staff with penalties • Create sense of fear • Victimise individuals to send message to the rest		

Required

Complete the table by identifying the benefits and drawbacks of each strategy.

Method	Techniques	Benefits	Drawbacks
Education and communication	• Small group briefings • Newsletters • Management development • Training	Overcomes lack of information	Time consuming Direction of change may be unclear Can't cope with change that opposes vested interests
Participation and involvement	• Small groups • Delegates and representatives	Increases ownership of decisions and change May improve quality of decisions	Time consuming Changes are limited to existing paradigm
Facilitation and support	• One on one counselling • Personal development • Provision of organisational resources	Creates learning Minimises feelings of being left out	No guarantee of valuable outcome Very slow
Negotiation and agreement	• Provision of rewards • Collective bargaining	Retains goodwill Deals with powerful interests	May sacrifice change to need for agreement Agreements may not be adhered to
Manipulation and co-optation	• Influence staff that are positively disposed • Buy-off informal leaders • Provide biased information	Can remove powerful obstacles Creates ambassadors for change Swift	Ethically questionable Becomes like blackmail May eliminate trust
Explicit and implicit coercion	• Threaten staff with penalties • Create sense of fear • Victimise individuals to send message to the rest	Swift Management control direction of change	Ethically questionable May eliminate trust May rebound in future when management are weak

Hopefully you will be able to draw on some of your own experiences when answering this question.

Chapter Roundup

- Management responses to risk are not automatic, but will be determined by their **own attitudes to risk**, which in turn may be influenced by **cultural factors**.

- Organisations' attitudes to risks will be influenced by the **priorities** of their stakeholders and how much **influence** stakeholders have. Stakeholders that have significant influence may try to prevent an organisation bearing certain risks.

- The **internal** or **control environment** is influenced by **management's attitude** towards control, the **organisational structure** and the **values** and **abilities** of employees.

- **Risk awareness** should be embedded within an organisation's **processes, environment, culture, structure and systems**. Organisations should **issue a risk policy statement** and **maintain a risk register**.

- The **board** has overall responsibility for **risk management** as an essential part of its corporate governance responsibilities. Responsibilities below board level will depend on the extent of delegation to **line managers** and whether there is a **separate risk management function**.

- The board's **objective-setting process** must encompass various levels of objectives. **Risk appetite** and **risk tolerance** will have a significant impact on objectives.

Quick Quiz

1 Match the term to the definition.

(a) Risk appetite
(b) Risk capacity
(c) Risk attitude

  (i) The nature and strength of risks that an organisation is able to bear
  (ii) The nature and strength of risks that an organisation is prepared to bear
  (iii) The directors' views on the level of risk that they consider desirable

2 What are the main elements that should be covered by a risk policy statement?

3 Which of the following is not an argument in favour of establishing a risk management committee that is separate from the audit committee?

A The risk management committee can be staffed by executive directors.

B Because they are non-executive directors, members of the audit committee may have insufficient time to consider in sufficient detail all the major risks faced by the company.

C The risk management committee can concentrate on areas where risks are particularly high.

D The role of the audit committee is constrained by corporate governance codes, whereas a risk management committee can have a much wider brief.

4 Shareholders' principal concern is always threats to the level of dividend they receive.

True ☐

False ☐

5 What are the main factors that will be reflected in the organisation's control environment?

6 Fill in the blank:

.... is the pattern of basic assumptions that a given group has invented, discovered or developed in learning to cope with its problems.

7 Name Granger's three types of objectives.

8 What are the main contents of a risk register?

Answers to Quick Quiz

1   (a) (ii) (b) (i) (c) (iii)

2   •   Definitions of risk and risk management
     •   Objectives of risk policy
     •   Regulatory requirements
     •   Benefits of risk management
     •   How risk management is linked to strategic decision-making and performance
     •   What areas of risk management (risk avoidance, risk reduction) are particularly important
     •   Risk classification
     •   Roles of board, managers, staff and audit and risk committees
     •   Internal control framework and important controls
     •   Other tools and techniques
     •   Assurance reporting
     •   Role of training
     •   How to obtain help

3   D   The role of the audit committee can go beyond what is suggested in the corporate governance codes.

4   False. Shareholders may prefer to make a long-term capital gain.

5   •   The philosophy and operating style of the directors and management
     •   The entity's organisational structure and methods of assigning authority and responsibility (including segregation of duties and supervisory controls)
     •   The directors' methods of imposing control, including the internal audit function, the functions of the board of directors and personnel policies and procedures
     •   The integrity, ethical values and competence of directors and staff

6   Culture

7   •   Mission
     •   Corporate objectives
     •   Unit objectives

8   •   List of main risks
     •   Priorities for tackling risks
     •   Who is responsible for dealing with risks
     •   Action taken
     •   Risk levels before and after action taken

Now try the question below from the Practice Question Bank.

Number	Level	Marks	Time
Q5	Examination	25	49 mins

6

Risks

Topic list	Syllabus reference
1 Strategic and operational risks	C2
2 Examples of risks faced by organisations	C2
3 Risk identification	C2, C3

Introduction

We have already mentioned risks when discussing internal controls. In this chapter we look at the risks organisations face. You will have encountered categorisation of risks in your auditing studies – the inherent, control, detection classification. While useful in an external audit context, there are more useful ways of classifying risks faced by organisations, partly because the external auditors are most concerned with risks relating to financial statements, whereas directors have to take a wider perspective.

In Section 1 we draw the important distinction between the strategic risks (integral, long-term risks that the board is likely to be most concerned with) and operational risks (largely the concern of line management). Section 2 lists many of the common business risks. However, it is not comprehensive and you may have to use your imagination to identify other risks.

In Section 3 we look at the processes for identifying risks. This leads on in Chapter 7 to the processes for assessing how serious risks are.

Study guide

		Intellectual level
C2	**Categories of risk**	
(a)	Define and compare (distinguish between) strategic and operational risks.	2
(b)	Define and explain the sources and impacts of common business risks.	2
(c)	Describe and evaluate the nature and importance of business and financial risks.	3
(d)	Recognise and analyse the sector or industry specific nature of many business risks.	2
C3	**Identification, assessment and measurement of risk**	
(h)	Explain and evaluate the concepts of related and covariant risk factors.	3

Exam guide

When trying to identify risks in the exam, consider the scenario and in particular what aspects of the scenario are currently changing – these will point you towards important risks. The most important question, though, when considering what risks could affect an organisation is 'What could go wrong?'

1 Strategic and operational risks   12/08, 12/10, 12/12

FAST FORWARD

Strategic risks are risks that relate to the fundamental decisions that the directors take about the future of the organisation.

Operational risks relate to matters that can go wrong on a day-to-day basis while the organisation is carrying out its business.

There are many different types of risks faced by commercial organisations, particularly those with international activities.

 Case Study

You only need to glance at the business pages of a newspaper on any day you like to find out why risk management is a key issue in today's business world. For example, look at some of the main stories in the UK on the *Daily Telegraph's* business pages on a single day.

(a)   A story about the then likely failure of **MG Rover**. This was in spite of the fact that the four owners of Phoenix Venture Holdings, who bought MG Rover for just £10 in 2000, had made more than £30m for themselves since. They had been heavily criticised for handing themselves a four-way split of a £10m 'IOU' note within months of the deal's completion in 2000. They also set up a £16.5m pension fund for company directors and separately took control of a lucrative car financing business.

(b)   A story about employees of the Bermuda office of the insurer **American International Group (AIG)**, who were caught trying to destroy documents as the company faced ever-expanding enquiries into the conduct of the business.

(c)   A story about how **Glaxo** faces claims in the US courts that its patents for the Aids drug AZT are invalid. The patents are worth around £1.1bn a year to Glaxo which controls 40% of the lucrative Aids drug market.

(d)   A story about clothing retailer **Alexon**, which estimated that £3m would be knocked off its profits as a result of the collapse of **Allders**, the stores where it ran 118 concessions. The story also notes poor sales at the Alexon group's youth fashion chain Bay Trading. 'The company refused to blame the weather'. Robin Piggot, finance director, said: 'We were trimming the value of our garments, making them cheaper and cheaper but less interesting'.

(e)   A story about how shoppers may face shortages of pasta and garlic bread as a result of a fire in a factory at Burton-on-Humber owned by chilled food producer **Geest**.

Here we can observe risks to the wellbeing of companies arising from questionable dealings by directors, questionable actions of employees, the actions of competitors, the problems of customers/partners, the weather, poor product design and fire. And all on a single day!

Exam focus point

Exam questions will cover a range of risks, not just financial risks.

1.1 Strategic risks   6/14

Key terms

> **Strategic risk** is the potential volatility of profits caused by the nature and type of the business operations. **Business risks** are strategic risks that threaten the survival of the whole business.

The most significant risks are focused on the **strategy** the organisation adopts, including concentration of resources, mergers and acquisitions and exit strategies. As we discussed in Chapter 5 the market segments the business chooses will be a significant influence. These will have major impacts on **costs, prices, products and sales**, as well as the **sources of finance** used. Business risks, the most serious risks, are likely to be greatest for those in start-up businesses or cyclical industries. However, perhaps the most notable victim of the credit crunch over the last few years, Lehman Brothers, was not immune to business risks even after 158 years of operating.

Organisations also need to guard against the risk that **business processes and operations** are **not aligned** to **strategic goals**, or are disrupted by events that are not generated by business activities.

Strategic risks can usefully be divided into:

- Threats to profits, the magnitude of which depends on the decisions the organisation makes about the products and services it supplies

- Threats to profits that are not influenced by the products or services the organisation supplies

Risks to products and services include long-term **product** obsolescence. **Changes in technology** also have long-term impacts if they change the production process. The significance of these changes depends on how important technology is in the production processes. Long-term **macroeconomic changes**, for example a worsening of a country's exchange rate, are also a threat.

Non-product threats include risks arising from the long-term **sources of finance** chosen and risks from a collapse in trade because of an **adverse event**, an accident or natural disaster.

1.1.1 Factors influencing strategic risks

Factors that determine the level of strategic risks will include:

- The types of industries/markets within which the business operates
- The state of the economy
- The actions of competitors and the possibility of mergers and acquisitions
- The stage in a product's life cycle, higher risks in the introductory and declining stages
- The dependence on inputs with fluctuating prices, eg wheat, oil
- The level of operating gearing – the proportion of fixed costs to total costs
- The flexibility of production processes to adapt to different specifications or products
- The organisation's research and development capacity and ability to innovate
- The significance of new technology

There may be little management can do about some of these risks; they are inherent in business activity. However, strategies such as **diversification** can contribute substantially to the reduction of many business risks.

1.2 Operational risks

Key term

> **Operational or process risk** is the risk of loss from a failure of internal business and control processes.

Operational risks include:

- Losses from internal control system or audit inadequacies
- Non-compliance with regulations or internal procedures
- Information technology failures
- Human error
- Loss of key-person risk
- Fraud
- Business interruptions

The way operations are organised will influence the level of risks and the ways in which risks are managed. The decisions about structure, such as the level of autonomy to allow divisions discussed in Chapter 5, will be significant here.

1.3 Strategic and operational risks

The main difference between strategic and operational risks is that strategic risks relate to the organisation's **longer-term** place in, and relations with, the **outside environment**. Although some of them relate to internal functions, they are internal functions or aspects of internal functions that have a **key bearing** on the organisation's situation in relation to its environment. Operational risks are what could go wrong on a **day-to-day basis**, and are not generally very relevant to the key strategic decisions that affect a business, although some (for example a major disaster) can have a major impact on the business's future.

You may also think that, as strategic risks relate primarily to the outside environment that is not under the organisation's control, it is more difficult to mitigate these risks than it is to deal with the risks that relate to the internal environment that is under the organisation's control.

Exam focus point

> In fact there have been a number of questions in the P1 exam where serious operational risks, caused by poor internal procedures, have resulted in catastrophes for the organisations described in the questions. Factors contributing to high operational risks have included prioritising profit maximisation/cost minimisation over effective risk management, inadequate testing of the safety of new products and ignoring warning signs of risky conditions.

Many of the risks discussed in Section 2 may be strategic or operational.

(a) For example, the **legal risk of breaching laws in day-to-day activities** (for example an organisation's drivers exceeding the speed limit) would be classed as an **operational risk**. However, the legal risk of stricter health and safety legislation forcing an organisation to make changes to its production processes would be classed as a **strategic risk**, as it is a long-term risk impacting seriously on the way the business produces its goods.

(b) The same is true of information technology risks. The risks of a **system failure resulting in a loss of a day's data** would clearly be an **operational risk**. However, the risks from using **obsolete technology** would be a **strategic risk**, as it would affect the organisation's ability to compete with its rivals.

Exam focus point

> December 2008 Question 1 asked students to discuss strategic and operational risks and explain why a business decision was a source of strategic risk.

2 Examples of risks faced by organisations

> Risks can be **classified** in various ways, including financial, product, legal, IT, operational, fraud and reputation.

2.1 Categories of risk   12/14, 6/15

There are many different types of risks faced by organisations, particularly those with commercial or international activities. The nature of these risks is discussed briefly below.

Exam focus point

> Questions for this paper will undoubtedly cover a range of risks, not just financial risks.

2.1.1 Related and correlated risks   06/13

A major theme running through this section is that many risks are not independent of each other. They may be related because the causes of the risk are the same, or because one type of risk links to another.

One type of risk relationship is risk correlation or co-variance, where two risks **vary together**. Where positive correlation exists, the risks will increase or decrease together. If there is negative correlation, one risk will increase as the other decreases and vice versa. The relationship between the risks is measured by the **correlation coefficient**. A figure close to +1 shows high positive correlation, and a figure close to −1 high negative correlation.

2.2 Entrepreneurial risk

Entrepreneurial risks are the risks that arise from **carrying out business activities**. Entrepreneurial risk has to be incurred if a business is to gain returns. Entrepreneurial risk is forward-looking and opportunistic rather than negative and to be avoided.

Entrepreneurial risk includes the risks of a possible range of returns from a major investment or profits being lessened by competitor's activities. Remember that all businesses apart from monopolies face risks from competitors if they are to carry on business. In addition, it will be necessary to take some risks when doing business to **achieve the level of returns that shareholders demand**.

A number of the risks discussed later in this section are strongly linked to entrepreneurial risks. A manufacturer will have to bear the risks arising from developing new products if it is to develop its business, but obviously has the potential for returns from new products to be positive and much greater than it may have expected. A company involved in hazardous activities, for example one that operates in the extractive industries, will inevitably face high levels of health and safety risks.

2.3 Financial risk   06/13, 6/14

Financial risks include reductions in revenues or profits, or incurring losses. The ultimate financial risk is that the organisation will not be able to continue to function as a going concern.

Financial risks include the risks relating to the **structure of finance** the organisation has, in particular the risks relating to the mix of equity and debt capital, and whether the organisation has an insufficient long-term capital base for the amount of trading it is doing (overtrading). Organisations must also consider the risks of **fraud and misuse** of financial resources. **Longer-term risks** include **currency and interest rate risks**, as well as market risk. **Shorter-term financial risks** include **credit risk** and **liquidity risk**.

2.3.1 Financing risks

There are various risks associated with sources of finance.

- Long-term sources of finance **being unavailable or ceasing to be available**

- Taking on commitments **without proper authorisation**

- Taking on **excessive commitments to paying interest** that the company is unable to fulfil
- Having to **repay multiple sources of debt finance** around the same time
- Being **unable to fulfil other commitments** associated with a loan
- Being stuck with the wrong sort of debt (**floating-rate debt** in a period when **interest rates are rising, fixed-rate debt** in a period when **interest rates are falling**)
- **Excessive use of short-term finance** to support investments that will not yield returns until the long term
- **Ceding of control to providers of finance** (for example banks demanding charges over assets or specifying gearing levels that the company must fulfil)

The **attitudes to risk** of the board and major finance providers will impact significantly on how risky the company's financial structure is.

2.3.2 Liquidity risk

Key term

> **Liquidity risk** is the risk of loss due to a mismatch between cash inflows and outflows.

If a business suddenly finds that it is **unable to cover or renew** its **short-term liabilities** (for example, if the bank suspends its overdraft facilities), there will be a **danger of insolvency** if it cannot convert enough of its current assets into cash quickly. However, current liabilities are often a cheap method of finance (trade payables do not usually carry an interest cost). Businesses may therefore consider that, in the interest of higher profits, it is worth accepting some risk of insolvency by increasing current liabilities, taking the maximum credit possible from suppliers.

If short-term funding is obtained to **cover liquidity problems**, the business may have to pay an **excessively high borrowing rate**. It will then be subject to interest rate risk (discussed below) on borrowing rates and so there is a potentially strong relationship between interest rate risks and liquidity risks.

Liquidity risk can also be extended to cover the risk of gaining a poor liquidity reputation, and therefore having existing sources of finance withdrawn as well. There is also **asset liquidity risk**, failure to realise the expected value on the sale of an asset due to lack of demand for the asset or having to accept a lower price due to the need for quick funds.

2.3.3 Cash flow risks

Cash flow risks relate to the **volatility of a firm's day-to-day operating cash flows**. A key risk is having insufficient cash available because cash inflows have been unexpectedly low, perhaps due to delayed receipts from customers. If for example a firm has had a very large order, and the customer fails to pay promptly, the firm may not be able to delay payment to its supplier in the same way.

2.3.4 Gearing risk

Gearing risks are the risks of financial difficulty through taking on excessive commitments connected with debt. However, the links between gearing and risk are not straightforward. Pecking order theory suggests that managers will prefer to use debt rather than equity finance to finance new investments or expansion, since that sends a signal to finance providers that they are confident about the future success of the company.

2.3.5 Credit risk

Key term

> **Credit risk** is the risk to a company from the failure of its debtors to meet their obligations on time.

The most common type of credit risk is when customers fail to pay for goods that they have been supplied on credit.

A business can also be vulnerable to the credit risks of other firms with which it is heavily connected. A business may suffer losses as a result of a key supplier or partner in a joint venture having difficulty accessing credit to continue trading.

Management of **credit risk** is of particular importance to exporters. You may remember from earlier studies that various arrangements are available to assist in this, such as documentary credits, bills of exchange, export credit insurance, export factoring and forfaiting.

Liquidity risk will often be very strongly correlated to credit risk. If customers delay paying their bills, clearly there is a stronger risk that the business will not have sufficient monies to settle its own liabilities.

2.3.6 Currency risk

Key term

| Currency risk is the possibility of loss or gain due to future changes in exchange rates. |

When a firm trades with an overseas supplier or customer, and the invoice is in the overseas currency, it will expose itself to exchange rate or currency risk. Movement in the foreign exchange rates will create risk in the settlement of the debt – ie the final amount payable/receivable in the home currency will be uncertain at the time of entering into the transaction. Investment in a foreign country or borrowing in a foreign currency will also carry this risk.

There are three types of currency risk.

(a)   **Transaction risk** – arising from exchange rate movements between the time of entering into an international trading transaction and the time of cash settlement

(b)   **Translation risk** – the changes in balance sheet values of foreign assets and liabilities arising from retranslation at different prevailing exchange rates at the end of each year

(c)   **Economic risk** – the effect of exchange rate movements on the international competitiveness of the organisation, eg in terms of relative prices of imports/exports, the cost of foreign labour

Of these three, transaction risk has the greatest immediate impact on day-to-day cash flows of an organisation. There are many ways of reducing or eliminating this risk, for example by the use of **hedging** techniques or **derivatives**. However, derivatives (financial instruments including futures or options) can be used for speculation. If they are, risks will increase.

2.3.7 Interest rate risk

As with foreign exchange rates, future interest rates cannot be easily predicted. If a firm has a significant amount of variable (floating) rate debt, interest rate movements will give rise to uncertainty about the cost of servicing this debt. Conversely, if a company uses a lot of fixed rate debt, it will lose out if interest rates begin to fall. Like currency risks, however, interest rate risks have upsides as well as downsides. A business with floating rate debt will benefit from lower costs if interest rates fall.

There are many arrangements and financial products that a firm's treasury department can use to reduce its exposure to interest rate risk. The treasury department may use **hedging** techniques similar to those used for the management of currency risk.

2.3.8 Finance providers' risk

There are also risks to the organisation if it provides finance for others. If it lends money, there is the **risk of default** on debt payments, and ultimately the risk that the borrower will become insolvent. If it invests in shares, there is a risk that it will receive **low or no dividends**, and share price volatility will mean that it does not receive any **capital gains** on the value of the shares.

However, for this paper and in practice you need to know about non-financial risks as well as financial risks. Remember that performance objective 4 on your PER includes the identification of potential risks.

The global credit crunch

A credit crunch is a crisis caused by banks being too nervous to lend money to customers or to each other. When they do lend, they will charge higher rates of interest to cover their risk.

One of the first obvious high-profile casualties of the recent global credit crisis was New Century Financial – the second largest sub-prime lender in the United States – which filed for Chapter 11 bankruptcy in early 2007. By August 2007, credit turmoil had hit financial markets across the world.

In September 2007 in the UK, Northern Rock applied to the Bank of England for emergency funding after struggling to raise cash. This led to Northern Rock savers rushing to empty their accounts as shares in the bank plummeted. In February 2008 the UK Chancellor of the Exchequer, Alistair Darling, announced that Northern Rock was to be nationalised.

Years of lax lending on the part of the financial institutions inflated a huge debt bubble as people borrowed cheap money and ploughed it into property. Lenders were quite free with their funds – particularly in the US where billions of dollars of 'Ninja' mortgages (no income, no job or assets) were sold to people with weak credit ratings (sub-prime borrowers). The idea was that if these sub-prime borrowers had trouble with repayments, rising house prices would allow them to remortgage their property. This was a good idea when US Central Bank interest rates were low – but such a situation could not last. In June 2004, following an interest rate low of 1%, rates in the US started to climb and house prices fell in response. Borrowers began to default on mortgage payments and the seeds of a global financial crisis were sown.

The global crisis stemmed from the way in which **debt was sold onto investors**. The US banking sector packaged sub-prime home loans into mortgage-backed securities known as **collateralised debt obligations** (CDOs). These were sold onto hedge funds and investment banks that saw them as a good way of generating high returns. However, when borrowers started to default on their loans, the value of these investments plummeted, leading to huge losses by banks on a global scale.

In the UK, many banks had invested large sums of money in sub-prime backed investments and have had to write off billions of pounds in losses. On 22 April 2008, the day after the Bank of England unveiled a £50 billion bailout scheme to aid banks and ease the mortgage market, Royal Bank of Scotland (RBS) admitted that loan losses hit £1.25 billion in just six weeks. In August 2008, RBS reported a pre-tax loss of £691 million (after writing down £5.9 billion on investments hit by the credit crunch) – one of the biggest losses in UK corporate history. At the beginning of 2009, RBS announced that it expected to suffer a loss of up to £28 billion as a result of the credit crunch. On 3 March 2008, it was reported that HSBC was writing off sub-prime loans at the rate of $51 million per day.

2.3.9 Accounts risks

There are various risks associated with the requirements to produce accounts that **fairly reflect financial risks**. The main risk is **loss of reputation or financial penalties** through being found to have produced accounts that are misleading. This doesn't just apply to misreporting financial risks, it also includes **misleading reporting** in other areas, either in accounts or in other reports, for example environmental reporting. The problems companies face if they use financial instruments extensively to manage risks are that there may well be **considerable uncertainty** affecting assets valued at market prices when **little** or **no market currently exists** for those assets.

However, accounts that **fairly account for, and disclose, risks** may also be problematic if investors react badly. This particularly applies if income becomes **increasingly volatile** as a result of using fair value accounting for financial instruments. This may have an **adverse impact on the ability of companies to pay dividends** and on **companies' share price and cost of capital**, if accounts users find it difficult to determine what is causing the volatility. Investors may not be sure if **low market valuations of financial assets are temporary or permanent**.

2.4 Market risk

You may encounter a number of different definitions.

Key term

> **Market risk** is a risk of gain or loss due to movement in the market value of an asset – a stock, a bond, a loan, foreign exchange or a commodity – or a derivative contract linked to these assets. Market risk is often discussed in the context of the stock markets.
>
> **Market risk** is a risk arising from any of the markets in which a company operates, including resource markets (inputs), product markets (outputs) or capital markets (finance).
>
> **Market risk** is the risk that the fair values or cash flow of a financial instrument will fluctuate due to market prices. Market risk reflects interest rate risk, currency risk and other price risks. (IFRS 7)

Market risk is connected to interest rate or foreign exchange rate movements when derivatives are used to hedge these risks. Market risk can be analysed into various other risks that cover **movements in the reference asset**, the **risk of small price movements** that change the **value of the holder's position**. Market risks also include the risks of losses relating to a change in the **maturity structure** of an asset, the **passage of time** or **market volatility**. Market risk can also apply to making a major investment, for example a recently floated company, where the market price has not yet reached a 'true level', or if there are other uncertainties about the price, for example lack of information.

Market risk is a good example of a speculative risk. Businesses can benefit from favourable price movements as well as lose from adverse changes. These considerations are very relevant when considering the work of the **treasury department**.

One important decision when running a treasury department is whether to restrict market activities to **hedging** market risks arising from other activities, such as exchange risks from trading abroad, or whether to **speculate** on the markets with a view to earning profits from speculation. A hedging approach is not itself a risk-free activity and a business could make large losses through poor decision-making. However, speculating on the markets would naturally be expected to carry greater risk of loss and risk incurring losses of much greater magnitude than hedging activities.

Market risks may also arise because other risks have crystallised. Poor weather, for example, may push up the price of raw materials as they become scarcer or more difficult to transport. As well as suffering higher prices, a business may also suffer delays in supply for the same reasons.

Case Study

In September 2011, Kweku Adoboli, a trader at the Swiss bank UBS, was arrested after allegedly having lost the bank £1.5 billion. The frauds that Kweku Adoboli was charged with allegedly took place between October 2008 and September 2011 and allegedly involved reporting fictitious hedges against legitimate derivative transactions. Mr Adoboli worked for UBS's global synthetic equities division, buying and selling exchange traded funds which track different types of stocks or commodities such as precious metals. Mr Adoboli was convicted in November 2012 on charges of fraud.

In September 2011, UBS announced plans to scale back its investment banking activities to reduce its risks. Its chief executive, Oswald Gruebel, resigned. In November 2010 Mr Gruebel reportedly justified the bank's decision at that time to increase its risk appetite with these words: 'Risk is our business. I can assure you, as long as I'm here, as long as my colleagues are here, we do know about risk. (If things go wrong) you won't hear us saying we didn't know it.'

A subsequent investigation by UBS revealed a failure of key controls in two areas:

- Failure to obtain bilateral confirmation with counterparties of certain trades within the bank's equities business

- Failure by those involved in inter-desk reconciliation processes to ensure transactions were valid and accurately recorded in the bank's records. Cancellations of, or amendments to, internal trades that should have been supervisor-reviewed were not checked

There was also evidence that compliance systems did detect some unauthorised or unexplained activity, but this was not adequately investigated.

2.5 Product risk

Product risks will include the risks of financial loss due to producing a poor quality product. These include the need to **compensate dissatisfied customers**, possible **loss of sales** if the product has to be withdrawn from the market or because of loss of reputation (see below) and the need for **expenditure on improved quality control procedures**. However, product risks also include the risks involved in developing a new product, and the risks cover the range of outcomes from the products being a great success to a total failure.

Case Study

Toyota responded to concerns over the safety of its cars by recalling millions of models worldwide during 2009 and 2010. Sales of a number of models were suspended in the US. Although the actions by Toyota aimed to resolve risks to health and safety, the company may have been less effective in mitigating the risks to its reputation. Commentators highlighted an initial reluctance to admit the problem and poor communication of what it intended to do to regain control of the situation. The impact threatened car sales and share price, with investors reluctant to hold Toyota shares because of the level of uncertainty involved.

2.5.1 Legal risks

(a) Determination of minimum **technical standards** that the goods must meet, eg noise levels, contents.

(b) **Standardisation measures** such as packaging sizes

(c) **Pricing regulations**, including credit (eg some countries require importers to deposit payment in advance and may require the price to be no lower than those of domestic competitors.

(d) **Restrictions on promotional messages**, methods and media

(e) **Product liability**; different countries have different rules regarding product liability (ie the manufacturer's/retailer's responsibility for defects in the product sold and/or injury caused) – US juries are notoriously generous in this respect

(f) **Acceptance of international trademark, copyright and patent conventions**; not all countries recognise such international conventions

Businesses that fail to comply with the law run the risk of **legal penalties** and accompanying **bad publicity**. Companies may also be forced into legal action to counter claims of allegedly bad practice that is not actually illegal.

The issues of legal standards and costs have very significant implications for companies that trade internationally. Companies that meet a strict set of standards in one country may face accusations of **hypocrisy** if their practices are laxer elsewhere. Ultimately higher costs of compliance, as well as costs of labour, may mean that companies **relocate** to countries where costs and regulatory burdens are lower.

Bear in mind that organisations may also face legal risks from lack of legislation (or lack of enforcement of legislation) designed to protect them.

Case Study

The Welsh company Performance Practitioners devised a new product, the Sales Activator, for the global sales development market. This product needed to be protected from imitators, particularly as it gave access to new markets overseas.

Performance Practitioners found that it was essential to obtain expert advice. The company decided on a portfolio of measures. Copyright protection was free, but a weak form of protection in many environments. The company also registered the Sales Activator as a trademark and communicated its intellectual property rights at every opportunity.

However, Performance Practitioners had to risk not being able to take effective action to protect its rights if it wanted to operate in some markets. In some countries it can take months for an intellectual property case to come to court. Performance Practitioners also had to consider the need to limit costs because of its desire to invest in the rest of its business. Therefore some options, like global patent protection, were too expensive. Nevertheless, the company needed enough funds to police its rights. The ability to protect intellectual property is diminished if a company cannot afford to take offenders to court.

2.5.2 Products and cultural differences

National culture may have a **significant impact** on the **demand for products**. For example, consumers in some countries prefer front-loading washing machines and others prefer top-loading washing machines. In some countries the lack of electricity will restrict the demand for electronic items.

Products also have **symbolic and psychological aspects** as well as physical attributes. As a result, entry into a market with a different set of cultural, religious, economic, social and political assumptions may cause extreme consumer reactions.

Some products are extremely sensitive to the **environmental differences**, which bring about the need for adaptation. Others are not at all sensitive to these differences, in which case standardisation is possible.

Environmentally sensitive	Environmentally insensitive
Adaptation necessary	Standardisation possible
• Fashion clothes • Convenience foods	• Industrial and agricultural products • World market products, eg jeans

 Question

Managing risk

How might you attempt to manage the risk that you would lose money developing an entirely new product that turned out to be unsuccessful?

Answer

Conduct market research, even if it is only possible to describe the concept of the new product to potential customers. Perhaps only develop product ideas that derive from customers. (Though there is a risk that they might not be good ideas, and you may miss the opportunity to develop ideas that would appeal to customers, if only they were asked.) Do not commit to major expenditure (for example a new factory, large inventories of raw materials) without creating and market testing a prototype.

You may have had other ideas. The key is to gather as much information as possible.

2.6 Legal and political risks

2.6.1 Legal risks

Breaches of legislation, regulations or codes of conduct can have very serious consequences for organisations. Risks include **financial or other penalties** (including ultimately closedown), having to **spend money and resources** in fighting litigation and **loss of reputation**. Key areas include health and safety, environmental legislation, trade descriptions, consumer protection, data protection and employment issues. Legal risks may therefore be strongly correlated with other risks if a business is potentially affected by legislation that relates to those other risks, for example health and safety or environmental legislation.

Governance codes are a particularly important example of best practice, and organisations must consider the risks of breaching provisions relating to integrity and objectivity, and also control over the organisation.

2.6.2 Political risks

Political risk is the risk that political action will affect the position and value of an organisation. It is connected with **country risk**, the risk associated with undertaking transactions with, or holding assets in, a particular country.

Political risk is another example of a risk that may have upsides or downsides. Political changes may occur that are favourable to businesses, for example the election of a government that is committed to outsourcing to the private sector activities previously carried on in the state sector.

Political risks may also be strongly linked to serious reputation risks. We discuss below how reputation risks are dependent on the level of other risks. With political risks, the relationship may work in the other direction. If a company suffers a collapse in its reputation as a result of a public outcry, this may force politicians to take action against it.

Case Study

In the UK the outcry over the *News of the World* phone hacking scandal in 2011 resulted in the UK Government setting up two public enquiries and UK Prime Minister David Cameron stating that the existing regulatory body, the Press Complaints Commission, should be replaced.

2.7 Technological risks   12/13

2.7.1 Strategic risks and opportunities

The technological risks discussed below are mainly operational risks with negative consequences. However, investment in technology can have a considerable upside, as well as carrying major risks if the technology fails to work properly. Investment in IT can produce dramatic changes in individual businesses and whole industries. The right strategy may provide a possible source of competitive advantage or new channels for distributing and collecting information and conducting transactions. There are likely to be strong positive correlation between technology risks and product development risk levels, as the success of many products will depend on getting the technology right.

However, the wrong strategy may result in adverse consequences. Directors may decide, for example, that a new system is justified for strategic reasons and force through a system that is impractical for operational purposes, ignoring the valid objections of staff who have to use the system. If in the end the system has to be abandoned, the write-off costs can be large and the damage to operational efficiency significant.

Often though, strategic and operational technological risks may be linked. A management environment where strategic opportunities for the use of information technology are neglected may also be one where operational controls are lax. Management may simply be paying insufficient attention to information technology and systems.

2.7.2 Physical damage risks

Fire is the **most serious hazard** to computer systems. Destruction of data can be even more costly than the destruction of hardware. **Water** is also a serious hazard. In some areas flooding is a natural risk, for example in many towns and cities near rivers or coasts. Basements are therefore generally not regarded as appropriate sites for large computer installations. Wind, rain and storms can all cause substantial **damage to buildings**. **Lightning and electrical storms** can play havoc with power supplies, causing power failures coupled with power surges as services are restored.

Organisations may also be exposed to physical threats through the actions of humans. **Political terrorism** is the main risk, but there are also threats from individuals with **grudges**. Staff are a physical threat to computer installations, whether by spilling a cup of coffee over a desk covered with papers, or tripping and falling, doing some damage to themselves and to an item of office equipment.

2.7.3 Data and systems integrity risks

The **risks** include **human error**, such as entering incorrect transactions, failing to correct errors, processing the wrong files and failing to follow prescribed security procedures. Possible **technical errors** include malfunctioning hardware or software and supporting equipment such as communication equipment, normal and emergency power supplies and air conditioning units.

Other threats include commercial espionage, malicious damage and industrial action.

These risks may be particularly significant because of the nature of computer operations. The **processing** capabilities of a computer are **extensive**, and enormous quantities of data are processed without human intervention, and so without humans necessarily knowing what is going on.

2.7.4 Fraud risk

Computer fraud usually involves the theft of funds by **dishonest use** of a computer system. **Input fraud** is where data input is falsified. Good examples are putting a **non-existent employee** on the salary file or a non-existent supplier on the purchases file. With **processing fraud** a programmer or someone who has broken into this part of the system may **alter a program**. **Output fraud** involves **documents** being **stolen or tampered with** and control totals being altered. Cheques are the most likely document to be stolen, but other documents may be stolen to hide a fraud.

Over the last few years there have been rapid developments in all aspects of computer technology and these have increased the opportunities that are available to commit a fraud. The most important of the recent developments is **increased computer literacy**. The use of public communication systems has increased the ability of people outside the organisation to break into the computer system. These 'hackers' could not have operated when access was only possible on site. A consequence of increased use of computers is often a **reduction** in the number of **internal checks** carried out for any transaction.

2.7.5 Internet risk

Establishing organisational links to the internet brings numerous security dangers.

- Corruptions such as **viruses** on a single computer can spread through the network to all of the organisation's computers.

- If the organisation is linked to an external network, **hackers** may be able to get into the organisation's internal network, either to steal data or to cause damage.

- Employees may **download inaccurate information** or imperfect or **virus-ridden software** from an external network.

BPP
LEARNING MEDIA

Part B Internal control and risk | **6: Risks**   201

- Information transmitted from one part of an organisation to another may be **intercepted**. Data can be 'encrypted' (scrambled) in an attempt to make it unintelligible to hackers.

- The **communications link itself may break down or distort data**.

2.7.6 Denial of service attack

A fairly new threat relating to internet websites and related systems is the 'Denial of Service (DoS)' attack. A denial of service attack is characterised by an attempt by attackers to prevent legitimate users of a service from using that service. Examples include attempts to:

- 'Flood' or bombard a site or network, thereby preventing legitimate network traffic (major sites such as Amazon.com and Yahoo! have been targeted in this way)

- Disrupt connections between two machines, thereby preventing access to a service

- Prevent a particular individual from accessing a service

2.8 Health and safety risk   12/11

Health and safety risks include loss of employees' time because of injury and the risks of having to pay compensation or legal costs because of breaches. Health and safety risks can arise from:

- **Lack of health and safety policy** – due to increased legislation in this area this is becoming less likely

- **Lack of emergency procedures** – again less likely

- **Failure to deal with hazards** – often due to a failure to implement policies such as inspection of electrical equipment, labelling of hazards and training

- **Poor employee welfare** – not just threats to health such as poor working conditions or excessive exposure to computer monitors, but also risks to quality from tired staff making mistakes

- Generally **poor health and safety culture**

Question	Health and safety

Can you think of some signs of a poor health and safety culture in an organisation?

Answer

Glynis Morris in the book *An Accountant's Guide to Risk Management* lists a number of signs.

- Trailing wires and overloaded electricity sockets
- Poor lighting
- Poor ventilation
- Uneven floor surfaces
- Sharp edges
- Cupboards and drawers that are regularly left open
- Poorly stacked shelves or other poor storage arrangements
- Excessive noise and dust levels
- Poor furniture design, workstation or office layout

Morris points out that all these problems can be solved with thought.

2.9 Environmental risk

Environmental risk is a loss or liability arising from the effects of the natural environment on the organisation or a loss or liability arising out of the environmental effects of the organisation's operations.

The risk is possibly greatest with business activities such as agriculture and farming, the chemical industry and transportation generally. These industries have the greatest direct impact on the environment and so face the most significant risks. However, other factors may be significant. A business located in a **sensitive area**, such as near a river, may face increased risks of causing pollution. A key element of environmental risk is likely to be waste management, particularly if waste materials are toxic.

However, as we shall see in Chapter 11, there may be upsides associated with environmental risks and the way they are managed. Businesses may run the risks of incurring unexpectedly high costs if they deal effectively with these risks, but there may also be substantial gains in terms of reputation and how key stakeholders act towards them.

2.10 Fraud risk

All businesses run the risk of loss through the fraudulent activities of employees, including management.

Case Study

Bankers in Zambia may be accused of fraud because the country's police do not have enough resources to catch the real fraudsters. The Bankers' Association of Zambia chairman, Xavier Chibiya, stated that bank staff who processed fraudulent transactions could be arrested. They could lose their jobs or be sent to jail. Bank staff needed to be particularly wary around the Christmas period: 'Fraudsters normally act during December when the experienced bankers have gone on break and the experts have also gone on break.'

The following is a list of possible fraud risks; you will see that a number of the signs listed are examples of poor corporate governance procedures, such as overdomination by one person or pressure on the accounting or internal audit departments.

Fraud and error	
Previous experience or incidents which call into question the integrity or competence of management	Management dominated by one person (or a small group) and no effective oversight board or committee
	Complex corporate structure where complexity does not seem to be warranted
	High turnover rate of key accounting and financial personnel
	Personnel (key or otherwise) not taking holidays
	Personnel lifestyles that appear to be beyond their known income
	Significant and prolonged understaffing of the accounting department
	Poor relations between executive management and internal auditors
	Lack of attention given to, or review of, key internal accounting data such as cost estimates
	Frequent changes of legal advisors or auditors
	History of legal and regulatory violations

Fraud and error	
Particular financial reporting pressures within an entity	Industry volatility
	Inadequate working capital due to declining profits or too rapid expansion
	Deteriorating quality of earnings, for example increased risk taking with respect to credit sales, changes in business practice or selection of accounting policy alternatives that improve income
	The entity needs a rising profit trend to support the market price of its shares due to a contemplated public offering, a takeover or other reason
	Significant investment in an industry or product line noted for rapid change
	Pressure on accounting personnel to complete financial statements in an unreasonably short period of time
	Dominant owner-management
	Performance-based remuneration
Weaknesses in the design and operation of the accounting and internal controls system	A weak control environment within the entity
	Systems that, in their design, are inadequate to give reasonable assurance of preventing or detecting error or fraud
	Inadequate segregation of responsibilities in relation to functions involving the handling, recording or controlling of the entity's assets
	Poor security of assets
	Lack of access controls over IT systems
	Indications that internal financial information is unreliable
	Evidence that internal controls have been overridden by management
	Ineffective monitoring of the system which allows control overrides, breakdown or weakness to continue without proper corrective action
	Continuing failure to correct major weakness in internal control where such corrections are practicable and cost effective
Unusual transactions or trends	Unusual transactions, especially near the year end, that have a significant effect on earnings
	Complex transactions or accounting treatments
	Unusual transactions with related parties
	Payments for services (for example to lawyers, consultants or agents) that appear excessive in relation to the services provided
	Large cash transactions
	Transactions dealt with outside the normal systems
	Investments in products that appear too good to be true, for example low-risk, high-return products
	Large changes in significant revenues or expenses

Fraud and error	
Problems in obtaining sufficient appropriate audit evidence	Inadequate records, for example incomplete files, excessive adjustments to accounting records, transactions not recorded in accordance with normal procedures and out-of-balance control accounts
	Inadequate documentation of transactions, such as lack of proper authorisation, unavailable supporting documents and alteration to documents (any of these documentation problems assume greater significance when they relate to large or unusual transactions)
	An excessive number of differences between accounting records and third party confirmations, conflicting audit evidence and unexplainable changes in operating ratios
	Evasive, delayed or unreasonable responses by management to audit enquiries
	Inappropriate attitude of management to the conduct of the audit, eg time pressure, scope limitation and other constraints
Some factors unique to an information systems environment which relate to the conditions and events described above	Inability to extract information from computer files due to lack of, or non-current, documentation of record contents or programs
	Large numbers of program changes that are not documented, approved and tested
	Inadequate overall balancing of computer transactions and databases to the financial accounts

Question

Procurement fraud

Give examples of indicators of fraud in the tendering process.

Answer

(a) **Suppliers**

Examples include **disqualification of suitable suppliers**, a very **short list of alternatives** and **continual use** of the **same suppliers** or a single source. The organisation should also be alert for any signs of personal relationships between staff and suppliers.

(b) **Contract terms**

Possible signs here include **contract specifications** that do not make commercial sense and contracts that include special but unnecessary specifications that only one supplier can meet.

(c) **Bid and awarding process**

Signs of doubtful practice include **unclear evaluation criteria**, **acceptance of late bids** and **changes in the contract specification** after some bids have been made. Suspicions might be aroused if reasons for awarding the contract are unclear or the contract is awarded to a supplier with a **poor performance record** or who appears to **lack the resources** to carry out the contract.

(d) **After the contract is awarded**

Changes to the contract after it has been awarded should be considered carefully, along with a large number of **subsequent changes in contract specifications** or **liability limits**.

This is perhaps one of the risk areas over which the company can exert the greatest control, through a coherent corporate strategy set out in a **fraud policy statement** and the setting up of strict **internal controls**.

A report by UK accountants BDO in July 2010 highlighted the alarming statistic that fraud losses in the UK for the first six months of 2010 were almost the same as for the whole of 2008. The average value of a single fraud had increased to almost £6m. BDO commented that in the past there had been much procurement fraud, with fraudulent employees working with outside accomplices to defraud employers through bogus or inflated invoices for goods and services. More common recently, however, was revenue dilution fraud, where management commits fraud by either setting up companies within companies or diverting lucrative contracts to accomplices.

2.11 Probity risk

Key term

> **Probity risk** is the risk of unethical behaviour by one or more participants in a particular process.

Being the victims of bribery or corruption or being pressurised into it are obvious examples of probity risk.

However, assumptions about how different cultures view corruption can also be dangerous. *Accountancy* magazine ran a series about the major cultural issues involved in dealing with particular countries. Its article on Greece suggested that 'unorthodox' methods might be required to be successful there.

'The concept of a bribe is one that is well understood in Greece.'

Unsurprisingly the magazine received a number of complaints about this article.

Probity risk is also commonly discussed in the context of procurement, the process of acquiring property or services. Guidance issued by the Australian Government's Department of Finance and Administration Financial Management Group comments that:

'Procurement must be conducted with probity in mind to enable purchasers and suppliers to deal with each other on the basis of mutual trust and respect. Adopting an ethical, transparent approach enables business to be conducted fairly, reasonably and with integrity. Ethical behaviour also enables procurement to be conducted in a manner that allows all participating suppliers to compete as equally as possible. The procurement process rules must be clear, open, well understood and applied equally to all parties to the process.'

In this context probity risk would not only be the risk that the 'wrong' supplier was chosen as a result of improper behaviour, but it relates to other issues as well, for example **failing to treat private information** given by another party as **confidential**. It would also relate to the **risks of lack of trust** making business **dealings between certain parties** impossible, or time and **cost having to be spent resolving disputes arising** from the process. Probity risk is clearly linked with reputation risk, discussed below.

There may be a strong relationship between probity risk and political risk. Companies may operate in certain countries where illicit payments can facilitate favourable political action on their behalf. However, they may face severe legal and reputation consequences if they are found to have been involved in corruption. We discuss this further in Chapter 10.

2.12 Knowledge management risk

Knowledge management risk concerns the effective management and control of knowledge resources. Threats might include unauthorised use or abuse of intellectual property, area or system power failures, competitor's technology or loss of key staff.

2.13 Property risk

Property risks are the risks from **damage**, **destruction** or **taking of property**. Perils to property include fire, windstorms, water leakage and vandalism.

If the organisation suffers damage, it may be liable for repairs or ultimately the building of an entirely new property. There may also be a risk of **loss of rent**. If a building is accidentally damaged or destroyed, and the tenant is not responsible for the payment of rent during the period the property cannot be occupied, the landlord will lose the rent.

If there is damage to the property, the organisation could suffer from having to **suspend or reduce** its **operations**.

There is also the risk of loss of value of property. This may be linked to changes in other risks. For example, perceptions that there is a risk of interest rates rising may depress property prices. A fall in the value of property may in turn have an adverse effect on certain financial risks. A business may find it more difficult to obtain finance on favourable terms if the value of the main security it can offer, its property, is falling.

2.14 Trading risk

Both domestic and international traders will face trading risks, although those faced by the latter will generally be greater due to the increased distances and times involved. The types of trading risk include the following.

2.14.1 Physical risk

Physical risk is the risk of goods being **lost** or **stolen in transit**, or **the documents** accompanying the goods **going astray**.

2.14.2 Trade risk

Trade risk is the risk of the customer refusing to accept the goods on delivery (due to substandard/inappropriate goods), or the cancellation of the order in transit.

2.14.3 Liquidity risk   12/10

Liquidity risk is the inability to finance the organisation's trading activities. It is generally regarded as a lack of short-term financing needs and a mismatch between short-term assets and liabilities.

2.15 Disruption risk

Obviously one of the most important disruptions is a failure of information technology, but operations may be delayed or prevented for other reasons as well. These include employee error, product problems, health and safety issues, losses of employees or suppliers, problems in obtaining supplies or delivering products because of environmental reasons such as bad weather or legal action.

2.16 Cost and resource wastage risk

Important operational risks for most organisations are incurring excessive costs (through poor procurement procedures, lack of control over expenditure) or waste of employees' time and resources (employees being unproductive or their efforts being misapplied).

2.17 Organisational risk

Organisational risks relate to the behaviour of groups or individuals within the organisation. These are particularly important to organisations that are going through **significant change**, as failure by people or teams to adapt may jeopardise change.

2.18 Reputation risk

Key term

> **Reputation risk** is a loss of reputation caused as a result of the adverse consequences of another risk.

Of all the major risks, reputation risk is the risk that is most strongly correlated to other risks, since its level partly depends on the **likelihood** that other risks materialise.

The other main determinant of the level of reputation risk is how shareholders and other stakeholders react to the other risks crystallising. The loss of reputation may have serious consequences, depending on the strength of stakeholders' reaction and the influence they have on what happens to the organisation.

The loss of reputation will be usually perceived by external stakeholders, and may have serious consequences, depending on the **strength of the organisation's relationship** with them.

So what are likely to be the most significant risks to a business's reputation?

2.18.1 Poor customer service

This risk is likely to arise because of the failure to understand **why** the customers buy from the business, how they view the business and what they expect from the business in terms of product quality, speed of delivery and value for money. Early indications of potential reputation risks include **increasing levels** of returns and customer complaints followed inevitably by loss of business.

2.18.2 Failure to innovate

We have discussed this under strategic risks.

2.18.3 Poor ethics

We shall consider ethics in detail in Part E of this text. We discussed in Chapter 1 the consequences of a poor reputation, principally an unwillingness of stakeholders to engage with the organisation resulting in falling demand, supply and staffing problems and weakening share price as investors lose confidence.

Environmental and social issues may also pose a greater threat to reputation because there is increasing emphasis on them in corporate governance best practice. The 2009 update of the King report in South Africa emphasised sustainability as the primary moral and economic imperative of the 21st century, and it is also a concept rooted in the South African constitution.

 Case Study

Anti-tax avoidance protests caused disruption in 2010 to several of the leading stores in the UK on the Saturday before Christmas, one of the busiest shopping days of the year. The protests resulted in store closures for some time in London and a number of other towns and cities. A significant feature of the protests was that demonstrations were started by people acting autonomously (ie they were not arranged through existing organisations) and were organised using social networking sites.

2.18.4 Poor corporate governance

Poor corporate governance may also be a source of reputation risk. An example is a lack of board diversity, with the board having an exclusively male membership. The most serious consequences of this may be to demotivate female employees and alienate female customers.

Exam focus point

> Since the risks you'll be considering for organisations will often be serious, the threat to organisations' reputation, and probably therefore the financial consequences, will also be serious.

2.19 Industry-specific risks

Key term

> **Industry-specific risks** are the risks of unexpected changes to a business's cash flows from events or changing circumstances in the industry or sector in which the business operates.

Unexpected changes can arise for example due to new technology, a change in the law or a rise or fall in the price of a key commodity.

Case Study

In its 2011 annual report, GlaxoSmithKline – one of the world's largest pharmaceutical companies – identified a number of key risks that may have a significant impact on business performance and ultimately the value of shareholders' investment in the company.

'There are risks and uncertainties relevant to the Group's business, financial condition and results of operations that may affect the Group's performance and ability to achieve its objectives. The factors below are among those that the Group believes could cause its actual results to differ materially from expected and historical results.

- Risk that R&D will not deliver commercially successful new products
- Failure to obtain effective intellectual property protection for products
- Expiry of intellectual property rights protection
- Risk of competition from generic manufacturers
- Risk of potential changes in intellectual property laws and regulations
- Risk of substantial adverse outcome of litigation and government investigations
- Product liability (such as claims for pain and suffering allegedly caused by drugs and vaccines)
- Anti-trust litigation
- Sales and marketing regulation
- Pricing controls (government intervention in setting prices can affect margins)
- Regulatory controls (which can affect the length of time a product takes to reach the market, if at all)
- Risk of interruption of product supply (including product recalls and interruptions to production)
- Taxation (including changes in tax laws)
- Strategic risks relating to sales in emerging markets, such as vulnerability to global financial crisis or limited resources to spend on healthcare
- Risks that restructuring would not deliver the required cost savings
- Bribery and corruption claims resulting in legal sanctions
- Risk of concentration of sales to wholesalers (which results in a concentration of credit risk that could potentially have a material and adverse effect on the Group's financial results)
- Global political and economic conditions, affecting consumer markets, distributors and suppliers
- Environmental liabilities
- Accounting standards (that could lead to changes in recognition of income and expenses, thus adversely affecting reported financial results)
- Failure to protect electronic information and assets

- Being unable to complete alliances and acquisitions on satisfactory terms, and entering alliances and acquisitions which turn out to have unpredicted liabilities or fail to realise the expected benefits

- Human resources (failure to continue to recruit and retain the right people could have a significant adverse effect on the Group)

Question

Try listing as many significant risk areas that you think might be of relevance to major international banks. Try to list at least ten risks.

Answer

There isn't a 'correct' answer to this question, but shown below are the top 18 risks mentioned by senior bankers in a survey of risks in the banking industry, and published by the Centre for the Study of Financial Innovation in March 2005 (*Banana Skins* 2005). This list is not comprehensive, and you might have thought of others.

- Too much regulation
- Credit risk
- Corporate governance
- Complex financial instruments
- Hedge funds
- Fraud
- Currencies
- High dependence on technology
- Risk management techniques

- Macroeconomic trends
- Insurance sector problems
- Interest rates
- Money laundering
- Commodities
- Emerging markets
- Grasp of new technology
- Legal risk
- Equity markets

A notable extra was environmental risk which, while positioned low in the overall ranking (28th), was seen to be gaining strongly because of fears about the impact of pollution claims and climate change on bank assets and earnings.

Exam focus point

In the exam you may be given a scenario of a specific business and asked to identify the risks. Some of the most significant risks for that business may be industry-specific risks. You may therefore have to use some imagination to identify risks, but don't be too worried about this sort of question. The sector the business operates in is likely to be fairly mainstream, and the risks therefore will not be too obscure.

3 Risk identification

Risk identification involves looking at the specific events and conditions that could result in risks materialising.

This section will help you fulfil performance objective 4 of your PER. One of the competencies for objective 3 is the requirement to evaluate activities in your area and identify potential risks.

3.1 Event (risk) identification

Event (risk) identification is part of the COSO framework.

No one can manage a risk without first being aware that it exists. Some knowledge of perils and what items they can affect and how is helpful to improve awareness of whether **familiar risks** (potential sources and causes of loss) are present, and the extent to which they could harm a particular person or organisation. Managers should also keep an eye open for **unfamiliar risks** which may be present.

Actively identifying the risks before they materialise makes it easier to think of methods that can be used to manage them.

Risk identification is a **continuous process**, so that new risks and changes affecting existing risks may be identified quickly and dealt with appropriately, before they can cause unacceptable losses.

Businesses also need to ensure that risks are identified:

- At an **organisational level**, particularly key risks affecting strategy such as risks relating to competition

- At a divisional **level**, for example supply shortages

- At a **day-to-day operational level**, for example the risks of machine breakdown delaying production

Case Study

Mazda collects quality information about defects from its dealers.

Mazda's risk analysis highlighted the threat of widespread influenza to the company's operations. When a new strain of influenza began to spread in 2009, Mazda announced measures to prevent infection and procedures to follow in the case of exposure.

3.2 Risks and opportunities

COSO emphasises that risk identification needs to differentiate negative-impact risks from opportunities, which may have positive consequences and a major impact on strategy. Management should channel opportunities back to strategy setting.

3.3 Risk conditions

Means of identifying conditions leading to risks (potential sources of loss) include:

(a)   **Physical inspection**, which will show up risks such as poor housekeeping (for example rubbish left on floors, for people to slip on and to sustain fires)

(b)   **Enquiries**, from which the frequency and extent of product quality controls and checks on new employees' references, for example, can be ascertained

(c)   **Checking** a copy of every letter and memo issued in the organisation for early indications of major changes and new projects

(d)   **Brainstorming** with representatives of different departments

(e)   **Checklists** ensuring risk areas are not missed

(f)   **Benchmarking** against other sections within the organisation or external experiences

3.4 Specific events

As well as underlying conditions, specific events can lead to the crystallisation of risks that could impact on implementation of strategy or achievement of objectives. Event analysis includes identification of:

(a)   **External events**. These could be economic changes, political developments or technological advances.

(b)   **Internal events**. These could be equipment problems, human error or difficulties with products.

(c) **Leading event indicators**. By monitoring data correlated to events, organisations identify the existence of conditions that could give rise to an event, for example customers who have balances outstanding beyond a certain length of time being very likely to default on those balances.

(d) **Trends and root causes**. Once these have been identified, management may find that assessment and treatment of causes is a more effective solution than acting on individual events once they occur.

(e) **Escalation triggers**, certain events happening or levels being reached that require immediate action. It will be important to identify and respond to signs of danger as soon as they arise. For example, quick responses to product failure may be vital in ensuring that lost sales and threats to reputation are minimised.

(f) **Event interdependencies**, identifying how one event can trigger another and how events can occur concurrently. For example, a decision to defer investment in an improved distribution system might mean that downtime increases and operating costs go up.

Once events have been identified, they can be **classified** horizontally across the whole organisation and vertically within operating units. By doing this, management can gain a better understanding of the interrelationships between events, gaining enhanced information as a basis for risk assessment.

3.5 Acceptable risks

In common with other aspects of risk assessment and management, risk identification procedures will have costs and require time and resources. Risk identification may therefore be influenced not by a desire to identify all risks, but rather by a focus on **identifying unacceptable risks**. We shall discuss later in this Text why organisations may accept some risks, and try to follow the ALARP principle (as low as reasonably practicable) when dealing with others.

Case Study

Early warnings in the supply chain

When Edscha, a German manufacturer of sun roofs, door hinges and other car parts, filed for insolvency last month, it presented BMW with a crisis. The luxury carmaker was about to introduce its new Z4 convertible – and Edscha supplied its roof. 'We had no choice to go to another supplier, as that would have taken six months and we don't have that. We had to help Edscha and try and stabilise it,' BMW says. Today, Edscha is still trading, thanks to the support offered by its leading clients. Nevertheless, BMW remains so worried about disruption to its supply chain that it has increased staff numbers in its risk monitoring department looking only at components-makers.

Richard Milne, *Financial Times*, 24 March 2009

Risk management techniques can be applied in any type of organisation, although they are more commonly associated with large companies. If you were involved in the management of a school for children between the ages of 11-16/18, what might be some of the risks that you would need to consider and adopt a policy for managing?

Answer

In no particular order a list of risks to be assessed might include:

- The risk of failing to attract sufficient numbers of students
- The risk of poor examination results
- The risk of inadequate numbers of students going on to higher education
- The risk of focusing too much on academic subjects, and ignoring broader aspects of education
- Physical security: risks to students, teachers and school property
- The risk of theft of individuals' property
- Inability to recruit sufficient teachers
- Not having enough money to spend on essential or desirable items
- The risk of an adverse report from school inspectors

Chapter Roundup

- **Strategic risks** are risks that relate to the fundamental decisions that the directors take about the future of the organisation.

  Operational risks relate to matters that can go wrong on a day-to-day basis while the organisation is carrying out its business.

- Risks can be **classified** in various ways, including financial, product, legal, IT, operational, fraud and reputation.

- **Risk identification** involves looking at the specific events and conditions that could result in risks materialising.

Quick Quiz

1   Which of the following would not normally be classified as a strategic risk?

   A   The risk that a new product will fail to find a large enough market

   B   The risk of competitors moving their production to a different country and being able to cut costs and halve sale prices as a result

   C   The risk that a senior manager with lots of experience will be recruited by a competitor

   D   The risk of resource depletion meaning that new sources of raw materials will have to be found

2   List three business risks that are associated with the internet.

3   What are the main signs of fraud identified by SAS 110?

4   The level of reputation risk depends significantly on the level of other risks.

   True   ☐

   False   ☐

5   What does event analysis aim to identify?

6   What is a leading event indicator?

   A   An event which requires immediate action
   B   Conditions that could give rise to an event and a risk crystallising
   C   One event triggering another
   D   The root cause of an event

7   Fill in the blank:

   …… risk is the risk of unethical behaviour by one or more participants in a particular process.

8   Give three examples of items that could be subject to market risk.

Answers to Quick Quiz

1   C   The risk that a senior manager with lots of experience will be recruited by a competitor would normally be classified as an operational risk.

2   Any three of:

- Hackers accessing the internal network
- Staff downloading viruses
- Staff downloading inaccurate information
- Information being intercepted
- The communication link breaking down or distorting data

3
- Previous experience or incidents that call into question the integrity or competence of management
- Particular financial reporting pressures within an entity
- Weaknesses in the design and operation of the accounting and internal control systems
- Unusual transactions or trends
- Problems in obtaining sufficient audit evidence
- Information systems factors

4   True, although the threat to reputation also depends on how likely it is that the organisation will suffer bad publicity if risks in other areas materialise.

5
- External events
- Internal events
- Escalation triggers
- Leading event indicators
- Trends and root causes
- Event interdependencies

6   B   Conditions that could give rise to an event and a risk crystallising

7   Probity

8   Any three of:

- Stock/shares
- Bond
- Loan
- Foreign exchange
- Commodity

Now try the question below from the Practice Question Bank.

Number	Level	Marks	Time
Q6	Examination	20	39 mins

LEARNING MEDIA

Risk assessment and response

Topic list	Syllabus reference
1 Risk assessment	C1, C3
2 Risk response strategies	D2, D3
3 Financial risk management	D2, D3
4 Control activities	B1, B2, B3
5 Control activities and risk management	B1, B2
6 Costs and benefits of control activities	B1, B2

Introduction

In this chapter we look at how directors and managers assess and respond to risk, and the control procedures they use.

In Section 1 we discuss a framework for assessing risks. You may encounter other slightly different frameworks but they all involve the same activities. However, you need to understand that risk assessment has its limitations. Risks are not always easy to categorise and can arise from all kinds of familiar and unfamiliar sources. Both the probability of the risk materialising and the consequences can be difficult to quantify. Risk assessments also need to be amended over time as risks change.

Section 2 covers the various ways in which risk can be dealt with, and is one of the most important sections in this Text.

The remainder of this chapter deals with control procedures. Section 2 contains a reminder of what you will have studied for F8. For P1, though, you particularly need to have a view of control activities as part of overall control systems. Hence we briefly consider internal controls in the context of risk management. We also look at wider cost-benefit considerations. Is it worth implementing internal controls for the benefits they will bring?

Study guide

		Intellectual level
B1	**Management control systems in corporate governance**	
(a)	Define and explain internal management control.	2
(b)	Explain and explore the importance of internal control and risk management in corporate governance.	3
(e)	Identify and assess the importance of elements or components of internal control systems.	3
B2	**Internal control, audit and compliance in corporate governance**	
(e)	Explore and evaluate the effectiveness of internal control systems.	3
B3	**Internal control and reporting**	
(c)	Explain and assess how internal controls underpin and provide information for accurate financial reporting.	3
C1	**Risk and the risk management process**	
(c)	Explain the dynamic nature of risk assessment.	2
(d)	Explain the importance and nature of management responses to changing risk assessments.	2
(e)	Explain risk appetite and how this affects risk policy.	2
C3	**Identification, assessment and measurement of risk**	
(b)	Explain and analyse the concepts of assessing the severity and probability of risk events.	2
(f)	Explain and assess the ALARP (as low as reasonably practicable) principle in risk assessment and how this relates to severity and probability.	3
(g)	Evaluate the difficulties of risk perception including the concepts of objective and subjective risk perception.	3
(h)	Explain and evaluate the concepts of related and correlated risk factors.	3
D2	**Methods of controlling and reducing risks**	
(d)	Explain and analyse the concepts of spreading and diversifying risk and when this would be appropriate.	2
(e)	Identify and assess how business organisations use policies and techniques to mitigate various types of business and financial risks.	3
D3	**Risk avoidance, retention and modelling**	
(a)	Explain, and assess the importance of, risk transference, avoidance, reduction and acceptance.	2

Exam guide

You may well be asked when different methods of dealing with risk might be appropriate.

1 Risk assessment

FAST FORWARD

Risk assessment involves **analysing, profiling** and **consolidating risks**.

1.1 Assessing the effects of risks

It is not always simple to forecast the financial effects of a risk materialising, as it is not until **after** the event has occurred that all the costs – the extra expenses, inconveniences and loss of time – can be seen.

Case Study

If your car is stolen, for example, and found converted to a heap of scrap metal, in addition to the cost of replacing it you can expect to pay for some quite **unexpected items**.

(a)   Fares home, and to and from work until you have a replacement

(b)   Telephone calls to the police, your family, your employer, and others affected

(c)   Movement and disposal of the wrecked car

(d)   Increased grocery bills from having to use corner shops instead of a distant supermarket

(e)   Notifications to the licensing authority that you are no longer the owner

(f)   Work you must turn down because you have no car

(g)   Lease charges on the new car because you have insufficient funds to buy one

(h)   Your time (which is difficult to value)

These are all hazards.

1.1.1 Risk assessment and dynamics

As well as deciding how to assess risks, organisations also need to decide how often assessment should take place. This will depend on how **dynamic** the environment is within which they operate, and how changes in that environment could result in **significant and sudden changes** in risks, which will in turn mean that the ways they are managed will change. Maybe the methods used to mitigate risks will alter, perhaps the priorities given to dealing with particular risks will change.

In some environments, risks will change very little, but in others risks will change a great deal and change quickly. The continuum below shows the two extremes and the variable state between them. On the left no risks ever change. On the right all risks are changing all the time. The two extremes don't exist in reality but situations close to them do exist.

Static   Dynamic

Increasing environmental
change and turbulence

Some changes in the environment will arise from the **strategic decisions** businesses make, for example launching a new product, penetrating a new market or significantly changing their financial structure. Here the need for accurate risk assessment to support the strategic decisions may seem obvious, but there will also be changes in risk assessment once the strategy is launched to monitor the risks resulting from the new strategy.

Other significant changes to risks may arise from the **decisions taken by other participants** in the industry in which the business operates, in particular decisions by competitors, suppliers and customers.

In other instances businesses may face changes in risks that they do not themselves influence, but are a result of external forces acting on their environment. Factors that may result in significant rapid changes in risks may include the following.

- **Technology.** Sectors where developments in new technology can quickly and significantly benefit innovators.

- **Supply.** Businesses may be dependent on sources of raw materials that are increasingly uncertain.

- **Social.** Businesses selling goods in markets where fashion is a significant influence on consumer demand.

- **Economic.** Sellers of non-essential goods or services to consumers being particularly vulnerable to adverse swings in the business cycle or even short-term losses of confidence caused by stock market volatility, such as was seen worldwide during the summer of 2011.

- **Political.** Businesses operating in unstable political environments or facing major changes in legislation.

Internal risks may alter quickly too. If for example the business is dependent on a few staff, loss of these staff may significantly increase the risk of errors occurring or loss of business to competitors if these staff join rivals.

1.1.2 Risk quantification

Risks that require more analysis can be quantified in various ways, which you have covered in previous exams.

IMPORTANT!

> The examiner has stated that they are introducing the possibility of bringing in some simple arithmetic calculations from the June 2011 exam.
>
> 'Students should not expect complicated calculations but should be prepared to manipulate numerical data and accordingly, a calculator may be helpful in future P1 exams.'
>
> The examiner has clarified that they would not introduce any new techniques that haven't been covered in previous papers, particularly F9. However, as well as requiring calculations, they might require students to assess quantitative information in a general sense in scenarios, such as an extract of a financial report, selected financial ratios or trends to assess risk and other aspects relating to financial gearing, operating gearing and liquidity.

Organisations can calculate **possible results or losses** and **probabilities** and add on **distributions** or **confidence limits**. They can ascertain certain key figures.

- **Average or expected result or loss** (discussed below)
- **Frequency of losses**
- **Chances of losses**
- **Largest predictable loss**

1.1.3 Risk rating

A simple risk rating may be based on a probability, for example the risk has a 60% chance of materialising. Impacts can be measured using objective amounts or rated, perhaps on a scale of 1-100.

Exam focus point

> Simple ratings were used in June 2010 Question 1, which was about the risks associated with a nuclear power station.
>
> The reasonableness of the ratings was one issue, particularly as the assessments had been made by an anti-nuclear group. A second issue was an issue that may well recur in the P1 exam; what to do when the impact of a risk materialising is potentially catastrophic but the probability of it happening is low.

1.1.4 Sensitivity analysis

Sensitivity analysis was covered in F9 in the context of capital investment.

The basic approach of sensitivity analysis is to calculate under **alternative assumptions** how sensitive the outcome is to changing conditions. An indication is thus provided of those variables to which the calculation is most sensitive (**critical variables**) and the **extent** to which those variables **may change** before the decision based on the results of that calculation changes (generally the point at which the project moves from a positive to negative outcome or vice versa).

Management should review critical variables to assess whether or not there is a strong possibility of events occurring which will lead to a different decision. Management should also pay particular attention to controlling those variables to which the calculation is particularly sensitive, once the decision has been made.

Sensitivity analysis has a number of weaknesses.

(a)   **Changes** in each key variable need to be **isolated**. However, management is more interested in the combination of the effects of changes in two or more key variables.

(b)   Looking at factors in isolation is unrealistic since they are often **interdependent**. The same risks may influence a number of variables in the calculation.

(c)   Sensitivity analysis does not examine the **probability** that any particular variation in costs or revenues might occur. The probability of a loss will be a key factor in management decision-making.

(d)   In itself sensitivity analysis does not provide a decision rule. Managers' **risk appetite** will influence whether the variation required to change a positive outcome is considered too small to take the risk of a negative outcome.

1.1.5 Expected values

You will remember that expected values are a means of calculating the average outcome. Where probabilities are assigned to different outcomes, the decision can be evaluated on the basis of weighting the different outcomes.

If a decision-maker is faced with a number of alternative decisions, each with a range of possible outcomes, a simple decision rule would be to choose the **one which gives the highest expected value**.

However, this decision rule has two significant problems. Firstly the expected value may not be a **possible actual outcome** or anything near an actual outcome.

Secondly the decision rule does not take into account the **range of possible outcomes**. Managers may reject a project with a high expected value if they believe that the probability of that project making a loss is too great or the maximum possible loss is too large. Expected values take no account of the **risk versus return** considerations.

Therefore, when expected values are used in practice, it is often as part of a two-stage process that takes risk into account as well.

Step 1   Calculate an expected value.

Step 2   Measure risk, for example in the following ways.

(a)   By identifying the worst possible outcome and its probability

(b)   By calculating the probability that the project will fail to achieve a positive result

(c)   By calculating the standard deviation of the result

(d)   By identifying the most likely possible outcome (remembering that the expected value may not be a possible outcome)

In the exam you may be given data about different investments where the data available gives contrary indications. For example, one investment may have a higher expected value, but also a higher chance of making a loss than the other investments, or a much bigger loss in its worst-case scenario. If you are analysing the situation, remember that you cannot just go by the numbers but must also bring in other information in the scenario, such as risk appetite of management, attitude to risk of shareholders, and potential threat to the business if the worst possible outcome occurs.

1.1.6 Accounting ratios

You covered the use of accounting ratios to analyse financial statements in F7. Accounting ratios that are likely to be significant in this paper are as follows.

$$\text{Debt ratio} = \frac{\text{Total debt}}{\text{Total assets}} \times 100\%$$

Although 50% is a helpful benchmark, many companies operate with a higher debt ratio. As with other ratios, the trend over time is as important as actual figures.

Stakeholder reaction to the debt ratio will be important. If the debt ratio appears heavy, finance providers may be unwilling to advance further funds. Shareholders may be unhappy with an excessive interest burden that threatens dividends and the value (perhaps the existence) of their long-term investment in the company.

$$\text{Gearing} = \frac{\text{Interest bearing debt}}{\text{Shareholders' equity} + \text{interest bearing debt}} \times 100\%$$

Again a gearing ratio of more than 50% can be used as a benchmark, but many companies are more highly geared than that. However, there is likely to be a point when a high geared company has difficulty borrowing more unless it can also boost its shareholders' capital, either with retained profits or by a new share issue. This emphasises the significance of **shareholder reaction**. Shareholders may not wish to have their dividends threatened by an excessive interest burden, but likewise they may be unwilling to see dividends fall as the company attempts to build up its equity base. They may also be unwilling (or unable) to provide extra equity funding.

$$\text{Interest cover} = \frac{\text{Profit before interest and tax}}{\text{Interest charges}}$$

The interest cover ratio shows whether a company is making enough profits before interest and tax to pay its interest costs comfortably, or whether its interest costs are so high that a fall in PBIT would have a significant effect on profits available for ordinary shareholders.

An interest cover of three times or less is generally considered as worryingly low.

$$\text{Cash flow ratio} = \frac{\text{Net cash inflow}}{\text{Total debts}}$$

A low figure for the cash flow ratio may not be a particular concern if the majority of debt is due to be repaid a long time ahead. Shareholders and finance providers will be more concerned about the company's ability to meet its shorter-term loans, and the risks that could threaten the cash inflows required to repay amounts owed.

$$\text{Current ratio} = \frac{\text{Current assets}}{\text{Current liabilities}}$$

The current ratio is a key indicator of liquidity, the amount of cash available to a company to settle its debts quickly.

A company should have enough current assets that give a promise of 'cash to come' to meet its current liabilities. Although a **ratio in excess of 1 may be expected**, in many industries businesses operate without problems with ratios below 1.

$$\text{Quick ratio} = \frac{\text{Current assets less inventory}}{\text{Current liabilities}}$$

The quick ratio reflects the fact that some companies may not be able to convert inventory into cash quickly. Inventory is not a very liquid asset and so can distort the current ratio if that is used to assess liquidity. The **quick ratio**, or **acid test ratio**, should ideally be **at least 1** for companies with a slow inventory turnover. For companies with a fast inventory turnover, a quick ratio can be comfortably less than 1 without suggesting that the company could be in cash flow trouble.

As well as calculating these ratios, you should consider whether there are other obvious signs of risk in the figures you have been given.

- **Changes in revenues.** A business may not have the infrastructure to cope with rapid increases in demand. A fall in revenues may indicate longer-term threats to existence.

- **Changes in costs.** A large increase in costs may indicate the business is becoming unprofitable or is not being controlled well. A fall in costs could indicate better control. However, it could alternatively indicate that the business is providing less value to customers or is cutting down on expenditure in risky areas, such as health and safety.

- **Increases in receivables or inventories.** Increases may indicate poor control and a risk of not realising these assets. Decreased revenue and increased inventory together may be a strong indicator of commercial problems.

- **Increase in short-term creditors.** This could imply a risky dependence on finance that has to be repaid soon.

- **Loan finance that has to be repaid in the next 12-24 months.** Here the key risk is whether the business has the cash to make the repayment without a serious impact on its operations.

1.2 Likelihood/Consequences matrix   6/09, 6/11

This stage involves using the results of a risk analysis to group risks into risk families. One way of doing this is a likelihood/consequences matrix.

Consequences (Impacts or hazard)

	Low	High
Low	**Accept**	**Transfer**
	Loss of suppliers of small-scale and unimportant inputs	Loss of key customers Failure of computer systems
	Reduce	**Avoid**
High	Loss of lower-level staff	Loss of senior or specialist staff Loss of sales to competitor Loss of sales due to macroeconomic factors

Likelihood (risk probability)

This diagram maps two continuums on which risks are plotted. The **nearer the risk is** towards the **bottom right-hand corner** (the high-high corner), the **more important** and the **more strategic** the risk will be. The position of risks can vary over time as environmental conditions vary. The diagram is very similar to Mendelow's stakeholder map covered in Chapter 1, and in that map as well the position of stakeholders can move over time.

This profile can then be used to set priorities for risk mitigation.

The diagram also includes the four basic risk management strategies which we shall discuss below.

Case Study

CIMA's *Guide to risk management* provides a list of factors that can help determine in which section of the quadrant the risk is located.

- The importance of the strategic objective to which the risk relates
- The type of risk and whether it represents an opportunity or a threat
- The direct and indirect impact of the risk
- The likelihood of the risk
- The cost of different responses to the risk
- The organisation's environment
- Constraints within the organisation
- The organisation's ability to respond to events

1.2.1 Objective and subjective risk perception   12/11

CIMA's list highlights a significant problem with the matrix, the issue of **measurability**. The matrix rests on the assumption that both hazard and risk can be quantified or at least ranked. In some instances the assessment can be made with a high degree of certainty, maybe even scientific accuracy. In these circumstances the risks can be **objectively assessed**.

In other instances however quantitative accuracy is not possible and the risks have to be **subjectively assessed**. How accurate these judgements are will depend on the knowledge and skills of the person making the judgement, the information available and the factors that may influence the risk levels. Some risks may depend on so many factors that only a subjective assessment is possible. However, judgements may be biased by the possible **consequences** of the risks, with the likelihood of potentially high impact risks being overrated.

An example of a risk, the likelihood of which can be objectively measured, is the next outcome of tossing a coin. A risk, the impact of which can be objectively measured, is the number of shareholders affected by a loss of company value. A risk with a subjective likelihood is the risk of an accident occurring, and a risk with a subjective impact is the possible financial loss from a spillage from a factory.

Case Study

The 2009 Turner report highlighted faulty measurement techniques as a reason why many UK financial institutions underestimated their risk position. The required capital for their trading activities was excessively light. Turner also highlighted the rapid growth of off-balance sheet vehicles that were highly leveraged but were not included in standard risk measures. However, the crisis demonstrated the economic risks of these vehicles, with liquidity commitments and reputational concerns requiring banks to take the assets back onto their balance sheets, increasing measured leverage significantly.

Turner also saw the complexity of the techniques as being a problem in itself. 'The very complexity of the mathematics used to measure and manage risk made it increasingly difficult for top management and boards to assess and exercise judgements over risks being taken. Mathematical sophistication ended up not containing risk, but providing false assurance that other *prima facie* indicators of increasing risk (eg rapid credit extension and balance sheet growth) could be safely ignored.'

1.3 Risk consolidation

Risk that has been analysed and quantified at the divisional or subsidiary level needs to be aggregated to the corporate level and grouped into categories (categorisation). This aggregation will be required as part of the overall review of risk that the board needs to undertake which we shall look at in more detail in later chapters.

Case Study

A CIMA research paper on *Reporting and Managing Risk* explained that RBS was another business that appeared to have strong risk management systems in many ways, but still ran into problems. Its risk management function was well staffed and internal audit checked the application of controls. The board defined overall risk appetite, and named senior managers were responsible for overseeing high-level risks. The chief risk officer prior to 2007 appeared to have a good understanding that his role included enforcement and promotion of good practice. The system for defining and categorising risk was logical and the risk register was continually updated.

However, in 2007 there were two changes of chief risk officer in quick succession. As the risk management committees operated below board level, the extent of their influence on the board, particularly the dominant chief executive, was limited. Some of the models used may have underestimated exposure to credit risks. There appears to have been too much trust placed in the calculations of some of the complex models, and not enough judgement exercised on their results. Above all, the stage of risk consolidation was not applied properly and so risks that applied across the business were not adequately managed. Divisional managers took risks that appeared to be appropriately managed at a divisional level, but were not well managed at a group level.

1.3.1 Related and correlated risks

One significant part of the risk consolidation process may be to analyse risks that are not independent of each other.

Correlation of risks is also important when considering the costs and benefits of risk management. Major expenditure on controls may reduce risks, but it could increase financial risks such as running short of funds or not being able to make profitable investments.

Exam focus point

> The examiner may well draw your attention to related risks, but watch out for them anyway in exam scenarios.

1.3.2 Relationship between business and financial risk

Business risk is borne by both the firm's equity holders and providers of debt, as it is the risk associated with investing in the firm in whatever capacity. The only way that either party can get rid of the business risk is to withdraw its investment in the firm.

Financial risk, on the other hand, is borne entirely by equity holders. This is due to the fact that payment to debt holders (ie interest) takes precedence over dividends to shareholders. The more debt there is in the firm's capital structure, the greater the financial risk to equity holders, as the increased interest burden coming out of earnings reduces the likelihood that there will be sufficient funds remaining from which to pay a dividend. Debt holders however know there is a legal obligation on the firm to meet their interest commitments.

Mazda conducts tests for every conceivable impact possible on the road.

Mazda also conducts environmental risk assessments to minimise risks and prevent pollution and other incidents. Its assessments are based on environmental monitoring that tracks levels of air and water pollution.

1.4 Importance of accurate risk assessment 6/10

As we shall see in the next section, the assessment of risks will determine the risk mitigation or risk management strategy employed. There are therefore a number of risks associated with incorrect risk assessment, and these are likely to be higher the more subjective the risk assessment is.

(a) If the assessment process **underestimates** the importance of the risks, risk management procedures may be inadequate. The risks may then materialise and the company may not only have to bear the losses arising from the risks crystallising but also suffer opportunity cost for expenditure on risk management that turns out to be ineffective.

(b) If the importance of risks is **exaggerated** by the risk assessment process, then excessive measures may be taken to manage these risks. These may involve **unnecessary costs and inefficient resource allocation**, and mean that the business is unable to take advantage of profitable opportunities.

In addition, a number of stakeholders may be concerned with the adequacy of the risk assessment process. If they are dissatisfied, this may impact on the company.

(a) **Governments and legislators** require risk assessment in a number of areas. The EU requires companies to carry out risk assessment in health and safety, product liability and finance.

(b) **Insurance companies** require active assessment and management of risks.

(c) Companies often want to pass legal responsibilities to their **suppliers** and also look for evidence of active risk management by their suppliers.

(d) **Public expectations** that companies will take steps to identify and manage risks such as pollution and fraud have risen.

Accurate risk assessment has two aspects:

(a) Making sure the assessment covers all **relevant risks**; the process should not be limited only to those risks that the organisation can control

(b) Ensuring the **severity and frequency of risks** are fairly **assessed**

It involves gathering information from as many sources as possible on a regular basis, and circulating that information.

COSO's guidance for smaller companies on controls over financial reporting stresses the need for risk assessment to focus on risks linked with key financial reporting objectives. The organisation should identify 'trigger events' that could lead to reassessment of risks. To do this, finance personnel need to be aware of what is going on within the organisation and to meet with executive management to identify new initiatives, commitments and activities affecting financial reporting risks.

The guidance discusses fraud in some detail. It is concerned not only with the impact of fraud on financial statements but also with whether financial reporting issues could motivate individuals to commit fraud. Meeting or not meeting financial reporting targets may have a significant impact on job prospects and the business needs to be aware of the impact of this on motivation.

Being able to demonstrate that you have made sound assessments of risks where you work is an important part of fulfilling performance objective 4 of your PER.

2 Risk response strategies

2.1 Dealing with risk   12/07, 12/08, 6/11, 6/15

> Methods for dealing with risk include **risk avoidance**, **risk reduction**, **risk acceptance** and **risk transference**.

In the rest of the chapter we shall consider **risk portfolio management**, the various ways in which organisations can try to mitigate risks or indeed consider whether it will be worthwhile for them to accept risks.

Risk management strategies can be linked into the likelihood/consequences matrix, discussed earlier.

Consequences (hazard)

	Low	*High*
Low	**Accept** Risks are not significant. Keep under view, but costs of dealing with risks unlikely to be worth the benefits.	**Transfer** Insure risk or implement contingency plans. Reduction of severity of risk will minimise insurance premiums.
High	**Reduce** Take some action, eg self-insurance to deal with frequency of losses.	**Avoid** Take immediate action to reduce severity and frequency of losses, eg charging higher prices to customers or ultimately abandoning activities.

Likelihood (vertical axis label)

Exam focus point

> This diagram is worth committing to memory as the examiner sees this as a vital framework. The mnemonic is TARA (Transfer, Avoid, Reduce, Accept).

2.1.1 Controllable and uncontrollable

How controllable risks are considered to be is likely to be an important influence on management strategies. Risks that are largely uncontrollable may not be tackled effectively by risk reduction measures, so the choice may be between accepting the risk and avoiding the activity that causes the risk.

2.1.2 Stop and go

When deciding on the best risk management strategy, organisations will be mindful of the returns they can make. Boards should consider the factors that determine **shareholder valuations** of the company, the **risks** associated with these and the ways in which shareholders would like **risks to be managed**.

They will not only consider the potential losses through inadequate management of risk, but also the potential loss in possible revenues caused by an overcautious risk management strategy.

Two types of error are Stop and Go errors.

(a)   **Stop errors**

Stop errors are where activities are abandoned as too high-risk that would have produced returns that were higher than the costs incurred. The error was to stop the activity rather than go ahead with it.

(b) **Go errors**

Go errors are where activities are pursued and risks are retained, the risks crystallise and costs are incurred that are greater than expected revenues. The error was to go ahead with the activity rather than to abandon it or drop it.

Boards therefore should not just focus on preventing negative risks from materialising but should also **manage speculative risks and opportunities** in order to **maximise positive outcomes and therefore shareholder value**.

2.1.3 Risk appetite

Decisions on risk management will not only depend on assessment of possible returns but, as we have seen, on **managers' appetite** for taking risks. Some types of organisation, for example charities or public sector, will seek to **avoid certain risks**. Other organisations may seek to **reduce the same risks**. This will mean that the organisations avoiding the risks will not incur the potentially substantial costs of risk reduction.

2.1.4 The ALARP principle   12/11

In many businesses the focus will be on **reducing most of the significant risks** rather than eliminating them. This raises the issue of the extent to which managers will seek to reduce risks. The general principle is that the **higher** the level of risk, the **less acceptable** it is.

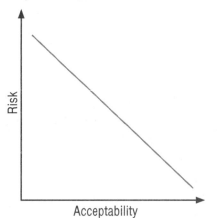

However, many risks cannot be avoided. Many businesses undertake **hazardous activities** where there is a risk of injury or loss of life (for example on an oil rig, factory or farm). These risks cannot be avoided completely but instead have to be **reduced to an acceptable level** by incurring the costs of risk mitigation – installing protective shielding, issuing safety equipment like hats or protective glasses. The level of risk mitigation is a trade off between cost and the assessment derived from the risk's likelihood and impact.

Businesses will also of course need to comply with the law. However, some legislation or guidance recognises that precautions need to be practicable, for example the UK Health and Safety Executive's guidance which acknowledges that measures are not required if the sacrifice involved in those measures is grossly disproportionate to the risks.

Judgement will be involved in deciding what **level of risk** is **as low as reasonably practicable** (ALARP). It may be that new control systems could reduce risks further, but they are judged to be far too expensive. The level of risk considered as low as reasonably practicable may well be a compromise.

Exam focus point

ALARP will often be a very important issue when risk management is examined.

2.1.5 Impact of dynamic environment

We discussed in Chapter 5 the factors that can result in changes in the environment within which the business operates.

As indicated above, businesses facing more dynamic environments are likely to have to carry out **frequent risk assessments** of risks that can change suddenly and significantly. It will be important for the results of the assessments to be reported quickly to management. Reporting of high-impact likelihood risks may occur daily; other risks may be reported monthly or quarterly.

Managers will of course need to respond to these assessments and devote enough time to delivering effective risk management strategies. Businesses' response to **higher-level strategic risks** will depend on the speed of management decision-making; that is, how quickly the board can change strategies in the light of altered circumstances. Having an appropriate combination of short- and long-term strategies may also be important. For example, shortages in raw materials may have to be met in the short term by contingency planning and use of other supply sources. In the longer term the business may redefine production processes, to reduce or eliminate dependence on the vulnerable resource.

Changes in risks may mean that **policies** for dealing with specific risks also need to **change**. For example a business may decide to avoid moving production facilities to an otherwise convenient location if that location is liable to frequent flooding. Improved flood defences may reduce the likelihood and consequences associated with the risk, and the business may therefore move there while taking steps to reduce risks (contingency plans) and transfer risks (the reduced risks may mean that insurance will be available).

Alternatively if a risk is still judged to be located in the risk reduction sector of the quadrant, but has moved towards the centre as likelihood and consequences increase, greater resources may be needed to manage that risk and resources therefore have to be moved away from managing other risks.

Overall, businesses operating in environments where risks are complex and likely to change suddenly are more likely to have to **invest in complex risk assessment and management systems**. A key feature of these systems will be **flexibility**. The Turnbull report highlighted the need for systems to be capable of responding quickly to evolving risks in the business arising from internal and external changes.

2.1.6 Residual risk

Key term

> **Residual risk** is the risk remaining after actions have been taken to manage risks.

The level of residual risk indicates how far the business believes that risks can be reduced. As part of their regular review of risks, managers should compare residual risks with gross risks, the assessment of risks before the application of controls or management responses. This comparison will show how effective responses to risk have been.

Case Study

The impact of the oil spill in the Gulf of Mexico on BP was a significant news story in much of 2010. On 3 August 2010 the US Government stated that the oil spill in the Gulf of Mexico was officially the biggest leak ever, with an estimated 4.9 million barrels of oil leaked before the well was capped in July 2010. The consequences of the spill included the departure of BP's chief executive, Tony Hayward. BP created a compensation fund of $20bn and had paid out a further $8bn in the clean-up campaign by the end of 2010.

The results of BP's own internal investigation were published in September 2010. It blamed a 'sequence of failures involving a number of different parties'; that is, BP and two other companies working on the well, although both of the other companies criticised this report. Problems highlighted by the BP report included 'a complex and interlinked series of mechanical failures, human judgements, engineering design, operational implementation and team interfaces.'

Critics have pointed to other operational problems BP has had, from the explosion at its Texas City refinery to the temporary shutdown at Prudhoe Bay. CNN news quoted an employee who had worked at both locations as saying that no one should be surprised by the 2010 disaster: 'The mantra was "Can we cut costs by 10%."' Transocean, one of the other companies criticised in BP's September 2010 report,

also blamed BP for cost cutting. Transocean was quoted by Associated Press as commenting: 'In both its design and construction BP made a series of cost-saving decisions that increased risk – in some cases severely.'

The US Commission that reported on BP in January 2011 found that BP did not have adequate controls in place, and that its failures were systemic and likely to recur. The report apportioned blame between the various companies involved, although it emphasised that BP had overall responsibility. The report highlighted failures of management of decision-making processes, lack of communication and training and failure to integrate the cultures and procedures of the different companies involved in the drilling.

The report drew attention to the failure of BP's engineering team to conduct a formal, disciplined analysis of the risk factors on the prospects for a successful cement job and also the failure to address risks created by late changes to well design and procedures. The report highlighted the flawed design for the cement used to seal the bottom of the well, that the test of the seal was judged successful despite identifying problems and the workers' failure to recognise the first signs of the impending blowout. The commission found that decisions were taken to choose less costly alternative procedures. These were not subject to strict scrutiny that required rigorous analysis and proof that they were as safe as the more expensive regular procedures.

The report also blamed inadequate government oversight and regulation, with the agency responsible lacking staff who were able to provide effective oversight. Many aspects of control over drilling operations were left to the oil industry to decide. There were no industry requirements for the test that was misinterpreted, nor for testing the cement that was essential for well stability. When BP contacted the agency to ask for a permit to set the plug so deep in the well, the agency made the same mistake as BP, focusing on the engineering review of the well design and paying far less attention to the decisions regarding procedures during the drilling of the well.

However, on the basis of what BP has published, its risk management approach did not appear to differ greatly from other oil companies and from many other large organisations across the globe. For example BP had sophisticated risk assessment processes in place. In 2007 it completed 50 major accident risk assessments. BP's monitoring procedures included the work carried out by the safety, ethics and environment assurance committee. The committee's work encompassed all non-financial risks. BP's systems also received external backing. Accreditations BP held included ISO 14001 at major operating sites, reporting to GRI A+ standard and assurance by Ernst & Young to AA100AS principles of inclusivity, materiality and responsiveness.

It's possible that BP relied on generally accepted risk management practices which may have become less effective over time.

2.2 Avoidance of risk

Organisations will often consider whether risk can be avoided and if so whether avoidance is desirable. That is, will the possible savings from losses avoided be greater than the advantages that can be gained by not taking any measures, and running the risk?

An extreme form of business risk avoidance is **termination of operations**, for example operations in politically volatile countries where the risks of loss (including loss of life) are considered to be too great or the costs of security are considered to be too high.

2.3 Reduction of risk   6/15

Often risks can be avoided in part, or reduced, but not avoided altogether. This is true of many business risks, where the risks of launching a new product can be reduced by market research, advertising, and so on.

| ✎ | Question | Supplier risk reduction |

What measures could you take to reduce the risk that suppliers do not deliver supplies of the required quality or do not deliver on time?

Measures might include:

- Getting references from the suppliers' other customers
- Setting standards for quality and delivery time and monitoring suppliers' delivery performance against those standards (eventually eliminating those who are consistently unreliable)
- Developing good relationships with suppliers
- Ensuring that suppliers have all the information they need
- Insisting that suppliers are ISO 9001 certified
- Regularly scanning the market for new suppliers

You may have had other ideas. The point is that 'risk reduction' techniques are simply a matter of good management. If you mentioned methods such as imposing penalties for poor performance or incentives for good performance that's fine, but such approaches are really risk **sharing**.

2.3.1 Policies and techniques

One important distinction in risk reduction is between risk management policies and techniques. This distinction refers to the way risk management operates at different levels in an organisation.

(a)   **Risk policies** are agreed at very senior levels of the organisation, by the board, risk committee or risk manager. They may be directed at particular risks.

(b)   **Risk mitigation techniques** will be the means of implementing the policies, applied at various levels in the organisation by operational managers and staff, guided by the risk management function.

Other risk reduction measures include contingency planning and loss control.

2.3.2 Contingency planning

Contingency planning involves identifying the **post-loss needs** of the business, **drawing up plans** in advance and **reviewing them regularly** to take account of changes in the business. The process has three basic constituents.

Information	How, for example, do you turn off the sprinklers once the fire is extinguished? All the information that will need to be available during and after the event should be gathered in advance. This will include names and addresses of staff, details of suppliers of machinery, waste disposal firms, and so on. The information should be kept up to date and circulated so that it will be readily available to anyone who might need it.
Responsibilities	The plan should lay down what is to be done by whom. Duties should be delegated as appropriate. Deputies should be nominated to take account of holidays and sickness. Those who hold responsibilities should be aware of what they are, how they have changed, who will help them, and so on.
Practice	Unless the plan has been tested there is no guarantee that it will work. A full-scale test may not always be possible. Simulations, however, should be as realistic as possible and should be taken seriously by all involved. The results of any testing should be monitored so that amendments can be made to the plan as necessary.

Although the response to the threat of the millennium bug in the year 2000 is now often dismissed as something of an over the top embarrassment, it does appear to have changed attitudes towards business continuity planning for low likelihood-high consequences risks. It meant that organisations now think more broadly about the possibility of threats like sabotage and consider how their business interacts with customers and suppliers. The year 2000 threat also meant that organisations updated technology and systems applications to more current technology and introduced uninterrupted power supply.

2.3.3 Loss control

Control of losses also requires careful advance planning. There are two main aspects to good loss control: the physical and the psychological.

(a)   There are **many physical devices** that can be installed to minimise losses when harmful events actually occur. Sprinklers, fire extinguishers, escape stairways, burglar alarms and machine guards are obvious examples.

   However, it is **not enough** to **install such devices**. They will need to be **inspected** and **maintained** regularly, and back-up measures will be needed for times when they are inoperational. Their adequacy and appropriateness in the light of changes to the business also needs to be kept under constant review.

(b)   The key psychological factors are **awareness** and **commitment**. Every person in the business should be made aware that losses are possible and that they can be controlled. Commitment to loss control can be achieved by making individual managers accountable for the losses under their control. Staff should be encouraged to draw attention to any aspects of their job that make losses possible.

2.3.4 Diversification of risks   12/12

Risk diversification is designed to **spread risk and return**. Risk diversification involves creating a **portfolio of different risks** based on a number of events, some of which will turn out well and others will turn out badly. The average outcome will be neutral. What an organisation has to do is to avoid having all its risks **positively correlated**, which means that everything will turn out **extremely well** or **extremely badly**. Ideally returns from different businesses should be negatively correlated as far as possible.

Diversification can be used to manage risks in a variety of ways:

• Having a **mix of higher and lower risk investments, products, markets and geographical locations**; the exact mix will depend on **risk appetite**

• Having a **mix** of equity and debt finance, of short- and long-term debt, and of fixed- and variable-interest debt

• Having a **diversified structure**, for example separate divisions or subsidiaries

• Expanding through the supply chain by **forward or backward integration**

However, except where restrictions apply to direct investment, investors can probably reduce investment risk more efficiently than companies, as they may have a wider range of investment opportunities.

Diversification may also be difficult for companies to achieve for a number of reasons:

• Their product portfolio may be **skewed** towards products which are positively correlated. Many successful businesses achieve good results by specialising. Other businesses, if they diversify, do so into related areas.

• The assets the business owns can only be used to **produce specific products**.

- The business may **lack the resources to adjust its portfolio**.

- Diversification may **increase risks** in certain ways. For example, businesses may lack the internal expertise to compete in too many diverse markets and managing a portfolio of unrelated operations may be very difficult.

2.3.5 Diversification and CAPM

The capital asset pricing model (CAPM), which you covered in Paper F9, provides helpful insights into, and methods of quantifying, business diversification.

(a)   CAPM draws the distinction between **market** or **systematic risks** that cannot be diversified away and **non-systematic** or **unsystematic risks** that can be reduced by diversification.

(b)   It highlights how to **eliminate unsystematic risk** by holding a balanced portfolio of investments and gives an indication of the extent of the portfolio required to eliminate unsystematic risk.

(c)   It provides a means of **linking the systematic risk of a portfolio** or an individual investment with the **return required** and therefore helps the business decide the extent of risks it is able to tolerate.

Exam focus point

> In the exam you may need to explain briefly the use of CAPM as a business tool. However, you will not be required to carry out any calculations using CAPM.

2.3.6 International diversification

Many risks bear particularly heavily on companies that trade or invest extensively overseas. A business can reduce its exposure to risks internationally by **diversification** of its trading interests or portfolio of investments. **International portfolio diversification** can be very effective for the following reasons.

(a)   Different countries are often at **different stages of the trade cycle** at any one time.

(b)   **Monetary, fiscal and exchange rate policies** differ internationally.

(c)   Different countries have **different endowments of natural resources** and different industrial bases.

(d)   Potentially **risky political events** are likely to be localised within particular national or regional boundaries.

(e)   Securities markets in different countries differ considerably in the **combination of risk and return** that they offer.

However, there are a number of factors that may limit the potential for international diversification:

(a)   **Legal restrictions** exist in some markets, limiting ownership of securities by foreign investors (discussed below under political risk).

(b)   **Foreign exchange regulations** may prohibit international investment or make it more expensive.

(c)   **Double taxation** of income from foreign investment may deter investors.

(d)   There are likely to be higher **information and transaction costs** associated with investing in foreign securities.

(e)   Some types of investor may have a parochial **home bias** for domestic investment.

2.4 Acceptance of risks

Risk acceptance is where the organisation bears the risk itself and, if an unfavourable outcome occurs, it will suffer the full loss. Risk retention is inevitable to some extent. However good the organisation's risk identification and assessment processes are, there will always be some unexpected risk. Other reasons for risk retention are that the risk is considered to be **insignificant** or the cost of avoiding the risk is considered to be too great, set against the potential loss that could be incurred.

The decision of whether to retain or transfer risks depends first on whether there is anyone to transfer a risk to. The answer is more likely to be 'no' for an individual than for an organisation because:

(a)   Individuals have **more small risks** than do organisations and the administrative costs of transferring and carrying them can make the exercise impracticable for the insurer

(b)   The individual has **smaller resources** to find a carrier

As a last resort organisations usually have customers to pass their risks or losses to, up to a point, and individuals do not.

2.4.1 Self-insurance

An option sometimes associated with accepting risks is **self-insurance**. In contrast to non-insurance, which is effectively gritting one's teeth and hoping for the best, self-insurance is putting aside funds of whatever size, in a lump or at intervals, in a reserve dedicated to defraying the expenses involved should a particular sort of loss happen.

A **more sophisticated method of self-insurance** is setting up a **captive**.

2.4.2 Captive insurance

Key terms

A **captive**, or **captive insurer**, is an insurance company wholly owned by a commercial organisation, and usually dedicated solely to the underwriting of its parent company's risks. Its primary purpose, therefore, is to be a vehicle for transfer of the parent company's risks.

An organisation with a risk that it cannot carry, which cannot find one or more insurers to take the bulk of that risk from it, may form a **captive insurer** to carry that risk. The captive insurer has all the parent's experience of the risk to call on, so its premiums will not be unnecessarily large, and its policy terms will be reasonable.

Question   Definite variables

Arunshire Council is the local government authority responsible for the running of public services in a district. The Council is responsible for the maintenance of the entire public infrastructure in its area of responsibility, including the roads and sewerage systems. The Council also manages education and care for vulnerable residents such as the elderly and infirm.

Employment law requires that every employer, including Arunshire Council, must maintain a register of all workplace injuries sustained by employees. There is no precise definition of a reportable injury, but Council guidelines indicate that anything that requires a dressing, such as a bandage or sticking plaster, must be reported as minor injuries. Injuries are classified as 'serious' if they require the victim to be absent from work for more than three days and 'severe' if they require admission to hospital or involve a fatality.

The latest injury statistics show that there were 130 injuries during the year ended 31 December 20X0, of which 25 were serious injuries and four were severe. The Council's Operations Director is satisfied with these figures because the number of injuries is no worse than in previous years. He holds the view that such figures are to be expected given the diverse range of jobs, many of which are risky, throughout the Council. The Chief Executive of the Council does not share these views: they think that the Council should try to prevent all injuries by eliminating accidents in the workplace.

Required

(a)   Discuss the Director of Operations' view that it is impossible to prevent all workplace injuries.

(b)   Discuss the Chief Executive's view that it is unacceptable for Arunshire Council to tolerate any workplace injuries.

Answer

(a) **Points in favour of view**

Human error

Even if Arunshire has strong risk management systems in place, they may still be undermined by human error. An isolated lapse in concentration could result in an accident.

Credible policies

In order to minimise or eliminate risks, more onerous health and safety procedures may be introduced, including investigation of the factors that have led to injuries. However, staff may not take these procedures seriously if they feel they are impractical. Staff failing to operate onerous procedures properly may result in greater risk than staff operating less strict procedures effectively.

Points against view

Complacency

The director's view appears to be complacent. The current injury statistics seem to be high. There is scope for reducing injuries towards zero, even if Arunshire can never prevent all injuries.

Reduction measures

Practical measures can be taken to reduce injuries. Health and safety training can be improved. Arunshire can introduce requirements for staff performing certain tasks, for example lifting heavy objects.

Negligence claims

The Director's toleration of an 'acceptable' level of injuries may leave the council vulnerable to legal claims. Staff who have been injured could use the Director's statements as evidence of a negligent attitude by senior management towards employee safety.

(b) **Points for**

Consequences of breaches

A strong argument in favour of zero tolerance is the consequences of accidents, possibly serious injury or death. Although a lapse may only have resulted in a minor injury on one occasion, the same lapse another time could have much more severe consequences.

Duty of council

However health and safety law is drafted, the Council has a clear moral duty to ensure its employees' safety.

Safety culture

Aiming towards eliminating injuries can help promote a strong culture of safety. If staff understand that there is no such thing as an acceptable level of injuries, they are unlikely to become complacent and will take steps to reduce the level of accidents further.

Points against

Employee involvement in hazardous activities

The extent of the Council's responsibilities make it inevitable that some staff will have to be involved in hazardous activities. This will mean that there will always be a risk of injuries occurring, even if it can be reduced to very small levels.

Costs

Some risk prevention procedures, for example requiring staff to wear cumbersome clothing, may be impractical. The costs and time taken to investigate minor problems may be excessive.

2.5 Transfer of risk

Alternatively, risks can be transferred – to other internal departments or externally to suppliers, customers or insurers. Risk transfer can even be to the state.

Decisions to transfer should not be made without careful checking to ensure that as many influencing factors as possible have been included in the assessment. A decision not to rectify the design of a product, because rectification could be as expensive as paying out on claims from disgruntled customers, is in fact a decision to transfer the risk to the customers without their knowledge. The decision may not take into account the possibility of courts awarding exemplary damages to someone injured by the product, to discourage people from taking similar decisions in the future.

Internal risk transfer can also cause problems if it is away from departments with more 'clout' (eg sales) and towards departments such as finance who may be presumed to downplay risks excessively.

2.5.1 Hold harmless agreements

Indemnity or **hold harmless agreements** can be useful. They:

- **Reduce the price of goods** for a party who takes on extra responsibility
- **Preserve good trading relations** by avoiding arguments
- **Preserve good public relations** if efficiently and sympathetically operated

2.5.2 Limitation of liability

Some contracts, in which one party accepts strict liability up to a set limit, or liability which is wider than the law would normally impose, follow very ancient customs. Examples are contracts for carriage of passengers or goods by air or sea.

2.5.3 Legal and other restrictions on transferring risks

The first restriction is that a supplier or customer may **refuse** to enter a contract unless your organisation agrees to take a particular risk. This depends on the trading relationship between the firms concerned, and not a little on economics. How many suppliers could supply the item or service in question, for example, and how great is your need for the item?

2.5.4 Risk sharing

Risks can be partly held and partly transferred to someone else. An example is an insurance policy, where the insurer pays any losses incurred by the policyholder above a set amount.

Risk-sharing arrangements can be very significant in business strategy. For example in a **joint venture** arrangement each participant's risk can be limited to what it is prepared to bear.

Case Study

The Swiss Cheese model is used to show the continual variability of the risks organisations face and how control systems interact to counter risks – and on occasions fail to interact, leading to accidents happening and losses being incurred.

The psychologist Paul Reason, the creator of this model, hypothesised that most accidents are due to one or more of the four levels of failure.

- Organisational influences
- Unsafe supervision
- Preconditions for unsafe acts
- Unsafe acts

The first three elements in the list can be classified as 'latent failures', contributory factors that may have lain dormant for some time. Unsafe acts can be classified as active errors, human actions in the form of careless behaviour or errors.

Organisations can have control systems in place to counter all of these, but they can be seen as a series of slices of Swiss cheese. Slices of Swiss cheese have holes in them, and seeing control systems in these terms emphasises the weaknesses inherent in them. Reason went on to say that the holes in the systems are continually varying in size and position. Systems failure occurs and accidents happen when the holes in each system align.

Reason points out, that viewed this way, the focus shifts away from blaming a person to focusing on organisational and institutional responsibility. In the field of healthcare, on which Reason concentrated, blaming the person leads to a failure to realise that the same set of circumstances could lead to similar errors, regardless of the people involved. Ultimately it thwarts the development of safer healthcare institutions.

'Active failures are like mosquitoes. They can be swatted one by one but they still keep coming. The best remedies are to create more effective defences and to drain the swamps in which they breed, the swamps (being) the ever-present latent conditions.'

Reason emphasised the importance of a sound reporting culture in a system of risk management. 'Without a detailed analysis of mishaps, incidents, near misses and free lessons, we have no way of uncovering recurrent error traps or of knowing where the edge is until we fall over it.'

2.6 Communication of risk

Communicating to shareholders and other stakeholders particularly those risks that cannot be avoided is an important aspect of risk management. Of course, the stock market may react badly to this news. If risks are to be successfully communicated, the messages need to be consistent and the organisation has to be trusted by the recipients.

The Institute of Risk Management's Risk Management Standard suggests that **formal reporting** of risk management should address:

- **Control methods** – particularly management responsibilities for risk management
- **Processes used to identify risks** and how they are addressed by the risk management systems
- **Primary control systems** in place to manage significant risks
- **Monitoring and review** systems

We consider reporting in the context of directors' review of risk and internal control in Chapter 8.

 Case Study

Mazda has a basic risk management policy and more detailed risk management regulations in place. Responsibility for risk management is split between departments in charge of business areas and departments that carry out business on a company-wide basis.

In addition to measures to protect its manufacturing sites and other important facilities against fire and earthquakes, Mazda has concluded natural disaster insurance contracts and taken other steps to minimize the financial risk of such events.

Exam focus point

Question 2 in December 2007 required students to select the most appropriate strategies for managing a selection of risks. Importantly it asked students to give reasons for their chosen strategies. Thus students had some flexibility in choosing a strategy, provided they could justify sensibly what they had selected.

3 Financial risk management

Diversification limits financial risk by taking on a portfolio of different risks constructed so that, should they all crystallise, the outcome will be **neutral**.

Hedging is the main method used to control **interest rate and exchange rate risks**.

3.1 Importance of financial risk management

Sound management of financial risks has a number of benefits. These were highlighted in the Management Accounting Guideline *Financial Risk Management for Management Accountants* by Margaret Woods and Kevin Dowd.

- Better reputation
- Reduction in earnings volatility meaning that published information is more reliable
- More stable earnings reducing average tax liabilities
- Protection of cash flows
- Reduction of cost of capital
- More opportunities to invest because of improved credit rating and more secure access to capital
- Stronger position in merger and acquisition negotiations
- Better managed supply chain and more secure customer base

3.2 Role of the treasury function

The Association of Corporate Treasurers' definition of **treasury management** is 'the corporate handling of all financial matters, the generation of external and internal funds for business, the management of currencies and cash flows, and the complex strategies, policies and procedures of corporate finance'.

Larger companies have specialist treasury departments to handle financial risks.

3.3 Risk diversification

As mentioned above, diversification can be used to manage financial risks in a variety of ways.

3.4 Risk hedging

Key term

> **Hedging** means taking an action that will **offset** an **exposure to a risk** by incurring a **new risk** in the **opposite direction**.

Hedging is perhaps most important in the area of currency or interest rate risk management. You covered the main instruments used to hedge these risks in F9 and we shall recap on them briefly. Generally speaking, they involve an organisation making a commitment to offset the risk of a transaction that will take place in the future.

3.4.1 Advantages of hedging

Hedging can lead to a **smoother flow of cash** and **lower risks of bankruptcy** and can result in a fall in the company's cost of capital.

3.4.2 Disadvantages of hedging

From the shareholders' viewpoint hedging will not affect their position if they hold a well-diversified portfolio. There will be possibly **significant transaction costs** from purchasing hedging products including brokerage fees and transaction costs. Because of lack of expertise, **senior management** may be **unable to monitor hedging activities effectively**. There may also be **tax and accounting complications**, particularly arising from IASs 32 and 39 and IFRSs 7 and 9.

3.5 Methods of hedging

The business can take advantage of its own circumstances to **hedge naturally**. Some of its risk exposures may cancel out. **Internal netting**, the management of multiple internal exposures across a range of currencies so that receipts and payments cancel out, is a form of natural hedging.

3.5.1 Forward contracts

A forward contract is a **commitment to undertaking a future transaction at a set time and at a set price**. For example a forward exchange contract is a binding contract between a bank and its customers for a specified quantity of a stated foreign currency at a rate of exchange fixed at the time the contract is made. The performance of the contract will take place at a future time specified when the contract is made.

Traders will therefore know in advance how much of their local currency they will receive or pay in exchange for the foreign currency that they have to sell or buy arising from the future transaction.

However, they cannot take advantage of any favourable currency movements.

3.5.2 Futures

A future represents a **commitment** to an **additional transaction** in the future that limits the risk of existing commitments. For example currency futures are standardised contracts to buy or sell a fixed amount of currency at a fixed rate at a fixed future date. Because futures are traded on an exchange they can be bought or sold as required, and a business using futures to hedge transactions can close out (dispose of their interest in the futures) before the contract is settled.

If a trader is going to make a foreign currency payment in the future, it can hedge the risk of adverse exchange rate movements increasing the payment by buying foreign currency futures now and selling them at the date the payment is settled. If foreign exchange rates move adversely, the impact of this movement should be mitigated by a profit on the futures.

3.5.3 Options

An option represents a commitment by a seller to undertake a future transaction, where the buyer has the **option of not undertaking the transaction**. With options the risks are **transferred** to the seller (writer) of the option.

For example an interest rate option will grant the buyer the right, but not the obligation, to deal at an agreed interest rate at a future maturity date. When the option expires the buyer must decide whether or not to exercise the right.

Clearly, a buyer of an option to borrow will not wish to exercise it if the market interest rate is now below that specified in the option agreement. Conversely, an option to lend will not be worth exercising if market rates have risen above the rate specified in the option by the time the option has expired.

Options are most useful when there is **uncertainty about price movements**, and a reasonable chance that prices could move adversely or favourably. An option protects against adverse movements, and allows the buyer to take advantage of favourable movements. An option also allows the buyer the chance to avoid exercising the option if the **transaction being hedged does not take place**.

However, the cost of the option (the premium) which has to be settled when the option is purchased may be expensive.

3.5.4 Swaps

A swap is a formal arrangement where two parties agree to **exchange payments on different terms**, for example in different currencies or one at a fixed rate and the other at a floating rate. It can be a method of exploiting the different terms available to the two parties in different markets. It can also be a means of hedging financial risks. For example, a borrower borrowing at floating interest rates and worried about significant upward movements can swap the floating rate commitment for a commitment to borrow at a fixed rate.

BPP LEARNING MEDIA

3.6 Hedging and speculation

As well as hedging, some types of derivative are used for speculation. The speculator is hoping to make a profit by prejudging how the price of the underlying asset will move. Indeed there would be no market for hedging unless counterparties were prepared to be involved in speculation. Because the derivatives market is **highly leveraged**, the speculator can, for a small deposit, invest in derivatives, where the movements in price are **proportionally much greater** than those of the underlying commodity. As a result the profit or loss per pound invested is much greater than speculating on the underlying commodity. Hence Warren Buffett and others view them as a potential time bomb.

Case Study

The hedging activities of the banking sector in general were put under the media spotlight in May 2012 when J.P. Morgan announced that a trading desk in London had lost more than $2bn. J.P. Morgan had had a reputation for being one of the better managed and cautious banks. However, the chief executive, Jamie Dimon, blamed 'errors, sloppiness and bad judgement' for the losses.

Initial reports suggested the transactions were not unauthorised or carried out by a rogue trader, but were the result of a change in hedging strategy. This change made the strategy more complex and more risky, when hedge funds took advantage of the volatility stemming from J.P. Morgan's trades. According to an executive at the bank, Dimon wasn't immediately told about the shift in strategy and didn't know the magnitude of the losses until after the company reported earnings on 13 April. However, Dimon had reportedly previously encouraged the trading desk to make bigger and riskier speculative trades.

It was reported that the desk had taken positions so large that even J.P. Morgan, the largest and most profitable US bank, couldn't unwind them at all easily.

Dimon had called previous news coverage in April 2012 about the positions that the bank was taking as a 'complete tempest in a teacup'. Days before the announcement of the loss he had led bank chief executives in a meeting to lobby the American Federal Reserve to soften proposed banking reforms.

J.P. Morgan's share price fell by 9% on the day the losses were announced. The share price of other banks also suffered.

3.7 Other risk management methods

3.7.1 Internal strategies

Internal strategies for managing financing and credit risks include working capital management and maintaining reserves of easily liquidated assets. Specific techniques that businesses use include:

- **Vetting** prospective partners to assess credit limits
- **Position limits**, ceilings on limits granted to counterparties
- **Monitoring** credit risk exposure
- **Credit triggers**, terminating an arrangement if one party's credit level becomes critical
- **Credit enhancement**, settling outstanding debts periodically
- **Matching** so that receipts in a currency are equalised as near as possible by payments in the same currency and likewise assets and liabilities

3.7.2 Risk sharing

FAST FORWARD

There are various instruments that businesses can purchase in order to share credit risks. These include:

- **Credit guarantees** – the purchase from a third party of a guarantee of payment
- **Credit default swaps** – a swap in which one payment is conditional on a specific event such as a default
- **Total return swaps** – one part is the total return on a credit-related reference asset
- **Credit-linked notes** – a security that includes an embedded credit default swap

However, credit derivatives are not a means of eliminating risk. Risks include **counterparty default** and **basis risk**, the risk that derivative prices don't move in the same direction or to the same extent as the underlying asset.

3.7.3 Risk transfer

Credit insurance can be used for a **specific transaction** or **all of the business**.

An alternative method of transferring risk is **securitisation**. This is the conversion of financial or physical assets into tradable financial instruments. This creates the potential to increase the scale of business operations by converting relatively illiquid assets into liquid ones.

An operational method of transferring the foreign currency risk on a future transaction is for exporters to **invoice** their customers in the **exporters' domestic currency**, and for importers to arrange with suppliers to be invoiced in their domestic currency.

4 Control activities

FAST FORWARD

Controls can be classified in various ways including **corporate**, **management**, **business process** and **transaction**, **administrative** and **accounting**, **prevent**, **detect** and **correct**, **discretionary** and **non-discretionary**, **voluntary** and **mandated**.

The mnemonic **SPAMSOAP** can be used to remember the main types of control.

Key term

> **Control activities** are those policies and procedures that help ensure that management directives are carried out. Control activities are a component of internal control.   (UK Financial Reporting Council)

4.1 COSO guidance

COSO's guidance in *Internal Control – Integrated Framework* stresses that control activities are a means to an end and are effected by people. The guidance states:

'It is not merely about policy manuals, systems and forms but people at every level of an organisation that impact internal control.'

Because the human element is so important, it follows that many of the reasons why controls fail is because of problems with managers and staff operating controls. These include failing to operate controls because they are not taken seriously or due to mistakes, collusion between staff or management telling staff to override controls. The COSO guidance therefore stresses the importance of **segregation of duties**, to reduce the possibility of a single person being able to act fraudulently and to increase the possibility of errors being found.

4.1.1 Controls over financial reporting

COSO's 2006 guidance concentrates on the needs of smaller companies, because of the challenges they face in implementing Sarbanes-Oxley effectively. The guidance highlights the need for focusing on key financial reporting objectives. This should help managers carry out effective risk assessments and mean they only implement appropriate controls, rather than implementing 'standard' controls that are not useful for the business.

4.2 Classification of control procedures

You may find internal controls classified in different ways, and these are considered below.

4.2.1 Corporate, management, business process and transaction controls

This classification is based on the idea of a pyramid of controls from corporate controls at the top of the organisation, to transaction controls over the day-to-day operations.

- **Corporate controls** include general policy statements, the established core culture and values and overall monitoring procedures such as the audit committee.

- **Management controls** encompass planning and performance monitoring, the system of accountabilities to superiors and risk evaluation.

- **Business process controls** include authorisation limits, validation of input, and reconciliation of different sources of information.

- **Transaction controls** include complying with prescribed procedures and accuracy and completeness checks.

4.2.2 Administrative controls and accounting controls

Administrative controls are concerned with achieving the objectives of the organisation and with implementing policies. The controls relate to the following aspects of control systems.

- Establishing a suitable organisation structure
- The division of managerial authority
- Reporting responsibilities
- Channels of communication

Accounting controls aim to provide accurate accounting records and to achieve accountability. They apply to the following.

- The recording of transactions
- Establishing responsibilities for records, transactions and assets

4.2.3 Prevent, detect and correct controls   6/11

Prevent controls are controls that are designed to prevent errors from happening in the first place. Examples of **prevent controls** are as follows.

- Effective development and design procedures which should ensure that for example safety features are built into new products, enough time is spent testing for susceptibility to key risks and a project and product is not being signed off until all the weaknesses identified during testing have been addressed

- Checking invoices from suppliers against goods-received notes before paying the invoices

- Regular checking of delivery notes against invoices, to ensure that all deliveries have been invoiced

- Signing of goods-received notes, credit notes, overtime records and so forth, to confirm that goods have actually been received, credit notes properly issued, overtime actually authorised and worked, and so on

How can prevent controls be used to measure performance and efficiency?

Answer

In the above examples the system outputs could include information, say, about the time lag between delivery of goods and invoicing:

(a)   As a measure of the **efficiency of the invoicing section**

(b)   As an **indicator of the speed and effectiveness** of **communications** between the despatch department and the invoicing department

(c)   As **relevant background information** in assessing the effectiveness of cash management

You should be able to think of plenty of other examples. Credit notes reflect customer dissatisfaction, for example. How quickly are they issued?

Detect controls are controls that are designed to detect errors once they have occurred. Examples of detect controls in an accounting system are bank reconciliations and regular checks of physical inventory against book records of inventory.

Correct controls are controls that are designed to minimise or negate the effect of errors. An example of a correct control would be back-up of computer input at the end of each day, or the storing of additional copies of software at a remote location.

Direct controls direct activities or staff towards a desired outcome. Examples include operational manuals or training in dealing with customers.

4.2.4 Discretionary and non-discretionary controls

Discretionary controls are controls that, as their name suggests, are subject to human discretion. For example, a control that goods are not dispatched to a customer with an overdue account may be discretionary (the customer may have a good previous payment record or be too important to risk antagonising).

Non-discretionary controls are provided automatically by the system and cannot be bypassed, ignored or overridden. For example, checking the signature on a purchase order is discretionary, whereas inputting a PIN number when using a cash dispensing machine is a non-discretionary control.

4.2.5 Voluntary and mandated controls

Voluntary controls are chosen by the organisation to support the management of the business. Authorisation controls, certain key transactions requiring approval by a senior manager, are voluntary controls.

Mandated controls are required by law and imposed by external authorities. A financial services organisation may be subject to the control that only people authorised by the financial services regulatory body may give investment advice.

4.2.6 General and application controls

These controls are used to reduce the risks associated with the computer environment. **General controls** are controls that relate to the environment in which the application system is operated. **Application controls** are controls that prevent, detect and correct errors and irregularities as transactions flow through the business system.

4.2.7 Financial and non-financial controls

Financial controls focus on the key transaction areas, with the emphasis being on the **safeguarding of assets** and the **maintenance of proper accounting records** and **reliable financial information**. Financial controls need to ensure that:

- Assets and transactions are recorded **completely** in the accounting records

- Entries are posted **correctly** to the accounting records, for example to the correct accounts

- **Cut-off** is applied correctly, so that transactions are recorded in the correct year

- The accounting system **can provide** the necessary data to prepare the annual report and accounts – relating to how the data within the accounting system is **organised** as well as the completeness and accuracy of the data

- The accounting system **does provide the data as required** – that the system is organised to supply on time and in a usable format the data that underpins the accounts and the other content of the annual report

Non-financial controls tend to concentrate on wider performance issues. **Quantitative non-financial controls** include numeric techniques, such as **performance indicators**, the **balanced scorecard** and **activity-based management**. **Qualitative non-financial controls** include many topics we have already discussed, such as organisational structures, rules and guidelines, strategic plans and human resource policies.

You need a good understanding of what controls are designed to achieve, to be able to implement them effectively. Demonstrating your role in the implementation of internal controls will help you fulfil performance objective 4 of your PER.

Case Study

Over the last 20 years the Basel Committee on Banking Supervision has made important recommendations affecting risk management and internal control operated by banks. The committee's recommendations include recommendations about the minimum capital banks should hold and also how credit, operational and market risk should be measured and managed.

The Committee highlights the need for boards to treat the analysis of a bank's current and future capital requirements in relation to its strategic objectives as a vital element of the strategic planning process. Control systems should relate risk to the bank's required capital levels. The board or senior management should understand and approve control systems such as credit rating systems. Banks should use value at risk models that capture general market risks and specific risk exposures of portfolios.

The Committee stresses the importance of banks having an operational risk management function that develops strategies, codifies policies and procedures for the whole organisation and designs and implements assessment methodology and risk reporting systems. It is particularly important for banks to establish and maintain adequate systems and controls sufficient to give management and supervisors the confidence that their valuation estimates are prudent and reliable.

Banks' risk assessment system (including the internal validation processes) must be subject to regular review by external auditors and/or supervisors. The regular review of the overall risk management process should cover:

- The adequacy of the documentation of the risk management system and process
- The organisation of the risk control unit
- The integration of market risk measures into daily risk management
- The approval process for risk pricing models and valuation systems
- The validation of any significant change in the risk measurement process
- The scope of market risks captured by the risk measurement model
- The integrity of the management information system
- The accuracy and completeness of position data
- The verification of the consistency, timeliness and reliability of data sources
- The accuracy and appropriateness of volatility and correlation assumptions

- The accuracy of valuation and risk calculations
- The verification of the model's accuracy through frequent testing and review of results

Further details about the reports of the Basel committee are on the website of the Bank for International Settlements: www.bis.org/list/bcbs/index.htm

Exam focus point

Remember the importance of the control system looking well beyond financial controls and including quantitative performance indicators and a variety of non-financial controls.

4.3 Types of procedure

International Standard on Auditing 315 *Identifying and assessing the risks of material misstatement through understanding the entity and its environment* provides examples of specific procedures (control activities).

- Authorisation
- Performance reviews
- Information processing
- Physical controls
- Segregation of duties
- IT general controls
- IT application controls

The following mnemonic, SPAMSOAP, is useful for classifying the different types of control activities.

Segregation of duties
Physical
Authorisation and approval
Management
Supervision
Organisation
Arithmetical and accounting
Personnel

At Professional level, you should be thinking in particular about higher-level 'management' controls. Using the above mnemonic, we can give examples of higher-level internal controls.

(a)   **Segregation of duties**. For example, the chairman/chief executive roles should be split.

(b)   **Physical**. These are measures to secure the custody of assets, eg only authorised personnel are allowed to move funds on to the money market.

(c)   **Authorisation and approval**. All transactions should require authorisation or approval by an appropriate responsible person. Limits for the authorisations should be specified, eg a remuneration committee is staffed by non-executive directors to decide directors' pay.

(d)   **Management**. Management should provide control through analysis and review of accounts, eg variance analysis and provision of internal audit services.

(e)   **Supervision** of the recording and operations of day-to-day transactions. This ensures that all individuals are aware that their work will be checked, reducing the risk of falsification or errors, eg budgets, managers' review, exception or variance reports.

(f)   **Organisation**: identify reporting lines, levels of authority and responsibility. This ensures that everyone is aware of their control (and other) responsibilities, especially in ensuring adherence to management policies, eg avoid staff reporting to more than one manager. Procedures manuals will be helpful here.

(g)   **Arithmetical and accounting**. This involves checking the correct and accurate recording and processing of transactions, eg reconciliations, trial balances.

(h) **Personnel**. Attention should be given to selection, training and qualifications of personnel, as well as personal qualities. The quality of any system is dependent on the competence and integrity of those who carry out control operations, eg use only qualified staff as internal auditors.

Case Study

In June 2007 Mazda established a dedicated section for the promotion of internal controls. In particular it worked with related departments and affiliates to help them respond to reporting requirements on internal control.

4.4 Controls over financial reporting

In particular robust controls need to be in place to ensure the quality of financial reporting. COSO's guidance stresses that disciplined policies and procedures need to cover all aspects of the recording process. Examples include journal entries being authorised, supported by adequate documentation and reviewed by a senior manager.

Some controls will operate across the organisation, but additional controls will be needed for **high-risk areas**, such as **accounting estimates** or **areas where frauds** could occur. The organisation also needs to ensure that software used for financial reporting activities has appropriate controls inbuilt.

A logical division of duties is particularly important in mitigating risks to the integrity of financial reporting. This can be reinforced, for example, by IT controls restricting access to data and programs. Where segregation of duties is not practical and access to accounting records cannot be limited, then it is more important for managers to monitor records closely. This may include regular review of transaction reports, reviews of selected transactions, periodic asset counts and checks on reconciliations.

Other particularly important controls to ensure the accuracy of information include:

* **Full documentation** of assets, liabilities and transactions
* **Matching of source documents** and accounting records
* **Confirmation** of information by suppliers, customers and banks
* **Reconciliation of information** from different source documents and other sources
* **Completeness checks** over **documents and accounting entries**
* **Reperformance** of accounting calculations

Case Study

A survey into companies that disclosed control weaknesses when reporting under the Sarbanes-Oxley legislation revealed that poor internal control was often related to an insufficient commitment of resources to accounting controls. The most common areas of weakness included:

* Account-specific weaknesses, particularly in the accounts receivable and payable and inventory accounts, with inaccurate adjustments to inventory and failure to track inventory transactions; other problems were reported in complex accounts, for example income taxes and derivatives

* Training – inadequate qualified staff and resourcing, lack of expertise in complex accounts and financial reporting

* Period-end issues and accounting policies, including lack of controls over application of accounting principles and no compliance checking for SEC filings

- Revenue recognition problems such as lack of formal detail in contracts or 'channel-stuffing' (shipping excess products which were subsequently returned)

- Lack of segregation of duties

- Problems with accounts reconciliation and lack of compliance with procedures for monitoring and adjusting balances

Rather worryingly, a 2010 audit report on the US Securities and Exchange Commission found material weaknesses that resulted in the conclusion that the Commission had not maintained effective internal control over financial reporting. The Commission had struggled to maintain financial control since it first prepared financial statements in 2004, but by 2010 still had weaknesses in the areas of information security, the financial reporting process, budgetary resources, deposits, information systems, penalties and required supplementary information.

5 Control activities and risk management

FAST FORWARD
An organisation's internal controls should be designed to counter the **risks** that are a consequence of the objectives it pursues.

5.1 Links between controls and risks

COSO's guidance states that risk assessment should determine where controls are most needed, helping the organisation focus on the risks that have the greatest impact on achievement of its operational objectives.

The UK Turnbull report also stresses the links between internal controls and risk very strongly.

Question
Responses to risk

A new employee in the marketing department has asked you about the business objective of meeting or exceeding sales targets.

Required

(a)   What is the main risk associated with the business objective to meet or exceed sales targets?

(b)   How can management reduce the likelihood of occurrence and impact of the risk?

(c)   What controls should be associated with reducing the likelihood of occurrence and impact of the risk?

Answer

This question is based on an example in the COSO guidance.

(a)   One very important risk would be having insufficient knowledge of customers' needs.

(b)   Managers can compile buying histories of existing customers and undertake market research into new customers.

(c)   Controls might include checking the progress of the development of customer histories against the timetable for those histories and taking steps to ensure that the data is accurate.

COSO also suggests that the links between risks and controls may be complex. Some controls, for example calculation of staff turnover, may indicate how successful management has been in responding to several risks, for example competitor recruiting and lack of effectiveness of staff training and development programmes. On the other hand, some risks may require a significant number of internal controls to deal with them.

6 Costs and benefits of control activities   6/08, 6/09, 12/14

Sometimes the benefits of controls will be outweighed by their costs, and organisations should compare them. However, it is difficult to put a monetary value on many **benefits** and **costs** of controls, and also the potential losses if controls are not in place.

6.1 Benefits of internal controls

The benefits of internal control, even well-directed ones, are not limitless. Controls can provide reasonable, not absolute, assurance that the organisation is progressing towards its objectives, safeguarding its assets and complying with laws and regulations. Internal controls cannot guarantee success, as there are plenty of **environmental factors** (economic indicators, competitor actions) beyond the organisation's control.

In addition, we have seen that there are various inherent limitations in control systems, including faulty decision-making and breakdowns occurring because of human error. The control system may also be vulnerable to **employee collusion** and **management override** of controls **undermining** the **control systems**.

However, the benefits of internal control are not always measurable in financial terms. They may include improvements in **efficiency and effectiveness**. There may also be indirect benefits, such as improved control systems resulting in external audit being able to place more reliance on the organisation's systems, hence needing to do less work and (hopefully) charging a lower audit fee.

6.2 Costs of internal controls

As well as realising the limitations of the benefits of controls, it is also important to realise their costs. Some costs are obvious; for example, the salary of a night security officer to keep watch over the premises. There are also **opportunity costs** through, for example, increased manager time being spent on review rather than dealing with customers.

More general costs include reduced **flexibility**, **responsiveness** and **creativity** within the organisation.

One common complaint is that the controls stifle initiative, although this is not always well founded, particularly if the initiative involves too casual an approach to risk management.

6.3 Benefits vs costs

The principle that the costs of controls need to be compared with benefits is reasonable. The internal controls may not be felt to be worth the **reduction in risk** that they achieve.

However, the comparison of benefits and costs may be difficult in practice.

- It can be difficult to **estimate the potential monetary loss or gain** that could occur as a result of exposure to risk if no measures are taken to combat the risk.

- It can be difficult to assess by how much the **possible loss or gain** is affected by a control measure, particularly if the benefit of control is to reduce, but not eliminate the risk (something which will be true for many controls).

- As we have seen, many benefits of controls are **non-monetary**, for example improvements in employee attitudes or the reputation of the organisation.

- Certain drawbacks of controls are also difficult to factor into decisions, including adherence to controls meaning an **inability to cope with the unexpected** and controls giving the **illusion** that **all risks are being reduced**.

Remembering costs versus benefits arguments should help you keep your answer in perspective. A common complaint of examiners of papers where internal controls are tested is that the controls many students suggest are too elaborate and therefore not appropriate for the organisations described in the questions.

Question

Which SPAMSOAP controls are you most likely to be discussing in this paper?

Answer

Management is obviously particularly important, not least showing that there is a clear distinction between management and **supervision**. Other very important controls are those linked to the control environment, **organisation** and **personnel**. We have seen in Chapter 3 that **authorisation and approval** at board level are extremely important, with the board having certain decisions reserved for itself. **Physical** controls over major assets might also be important if there is a significant risk of loss.

Segregation of duties may be most significant in the context of splitting the role of chairman and chief executive. You may see questions where a lack of segregation has led to losses. **Arithmetic and accounting** controls may appear to be of least importance. However, they may be significant insofar as they guarantee the quality of the information provided to management for decision-making. We shall look at issues related to this information in the next chapter.

Chapter Roundup

- **Risk assessment** involves **analysing, profiling** and **consolidating risks**.

- Methods for dealing with risk include **risk avoidance, risk reduction, risk acceptance** and **risk transference**.

- **Diversification** limits financial risk by taking on a portfolio of different risks constructed so that, should they all crystallise, the outcome will be **neutral**.

  Hedging is the main method used to control **interest rate and exchange rate risks**.

- Controls can be classified in various ways including **corporate, management, business process** and **transaction, administrative** and **accounting, prevent, detect** and **correct, discretionary** and **non-discretionary, voluntary** and **mandated**.

  The mnemonic **SPAMSOAP** can be used to remember the main types of control.

- An organisation's internal controls should be designed to counter the **risks** that are a consequence of the objectives it pursues.

- Sometimes the benefits of controls will be outweighed by their costs, and organisations should compare them. However, it is difficult to put a monetary value on many **benefits** and **costs** of controls, and also the potential losses if controls are not in place.

1   Give five examples of factors that will determine the chances of a risk materialising and the consequences of it materialising.

2   What key indicators should risk quantification provide?

3   Complete the likelihood-consequences matrix in relation to methods of dealing with risk.

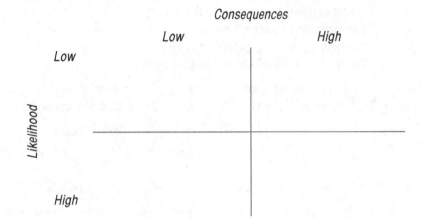

4   Fill in the blank:

.... is taking an action that will offset an exposure to a risk by incurring a new risk in the opposite direction.

5   Match the control and control type:

(a)   Checking of delivery notes against invoices
(b)   Back-up of computer input
(c)   Bank reconciliation

(i)   Prevent
(ii)   Detect
(iii) Correct

6   Fill in the blank:

A .... control is required by law and imposed by external authorities.

7   Which of the following is an example of a business process control?

A   Audit committee   C   Authorisation limits
B   Reporting process to superiors   D   Completeness of input check

8   When deciding whether the benefits of controls justify the costs, organisations should always focus on the financial benefits and costs.

True   ☐

False ☐

1   Any five from:

- The importance of the strategic objective to which the risk relates
- The type of risk and whether it represents an opportunity or a threat
- The direct and indirect impact of the risk
- The likelihood of the risk
- The cost of different responses to the risk
- The organisation's environment
- Constraints within the organisation
- The organisation's ability to respond to events

2
- Average or expected result
- The frequency of losses
- The chances of loss
- The largest predictable loss

3

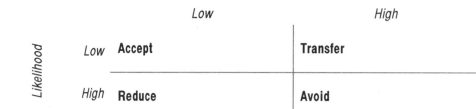

	Consequences	
	Low	High
Low	Accept	Transfer
High	Reduce	Avoid

Likelihood

4   Risk hedging

5   (a)(i), (b)(iii), (c)(ii)

6   Mandated

7   C   A   Audit committee is a corporate control
            B   Reporting process to superiors is a management control
            C   Authorisation limit is a business process control
            D   Completeness of input check is a transaction control

8   False. Organisations might also consider the improvements in efficiency and effectiveness that internal controls can bring, and these can't necessarily be measured in financial terms. Likewise there may be opportunity losses in terms of management time being spent on operating controls which can't be measured financially.

Now try the question below from the Practice Question Bank.

Number	Level	Marks	Time
Q7	Examination	25	49 mins

8

Information, communication and monitoring

Topic list	Syllabus reference
1 Information requirements of directors	B4
2 Communication with employees	D2
3 Monitoring	B1, D2
4 Role of management in monitoring	B1, D2
5 Internal audit	B2
6 Audit committee	A4, B2, D1
7 Board monitoring and reporting	B3, C3

Introduction

This chapter looks at the last two areas covered in the COSO enterprise risk management model: information, communication and monitoring.

Communication is at the heart of the chapter. We begin by looking at the qualities that the information received by directors needs to have in order to enable directors to discharge their duties effectively and in particular manage risk. However, the board and management will only receive quality information if there are strong communication procedures. Two-way communication is important; the directors need to consider not only what they are looking to receive but also what should be communicated to staff. Directors must communicate desired behaviour effectively.

In the remainder of the chapter, we examine the monitoring procedures that need to be carried out in an organisation. Monitoring will involve both ongoing monitoring and separate evaluation exercises.

Internal audit will have responsibility for carrying out much of the detailed separate evaluation work, and we look at its role in Section 5. To carry out effective reviews, internal auditors have to maintain their independence, so we examine the independence issues that could undermine their work. The audit committee monitors the work of internal audit and we examine its role in Section 6.

In the last section we cover in detail board monitoring of risk and internal control that we have mentioned in earlier chapters. One objective of this review is to produce a report communicating to shareholders how the organisation has been addressing the major risks it faces. The board has to try to obtain strong assurance that the internal control systems are working well, as internal control failures can cause strategic failure and loss of capital value.

Study guide

		Intellectual level
A4	**Board committees**	
(b)	Explain and evaluate the role and purpose of the following committees in effective corporate governance: remuneration committee, nominations committee, risk committee, audit committee.	3
B1	**Management control systems in corporate governance**	
(a)	Define and explain internal management control.	2
(d)	Identify, explain and evaluate the corporate governance and executive management roles in risk management (in particular the separation between responsibility for ensuring adequate risk systems are in place and the application of risk management procedures and practices in the organisation).	3
B2	**Internal control, audit and compliance in corporate governance**	
(a)	Describe the function and importance of internal audit.	1
(b)	Explain, and discuss the importance of, auditor independence in all client audit situations (including internal audit).	3
(c)	Explain, and assess the nature and sources of risks, to auditor independence. Assess the hazard of auditor capture.	3
(d)	Explain and evaluate the importance of compliance and the role of the internal audit function in internal control.	3
(f)	Describe and analyse the work of the audit committee in overseeing the internal audit function.	2
(g)	Explain, and explore the importance and characteristics of, the audit committee's relationship with external auditors.	2
B3	**Internal control and reporting**	
(a)	Describe and assess the need to report on internal controls to shareholders.	3
(b)	Describe the content of a report on internal control and audit.	2
B4	**Management information in audit and internal control**	
(a)	Explain and assess the need for adequate information flows to management for the purposes of the management of internal control and risk.	3
(b)	Evaluate the qualities and characteristics of information required in internal control and risk management and monitoring.	3
C3	**Identification, assessment and measurement of risk**	
(c)	Describe and evaluate a framework for board-level consideration of risk.	3
(d)	Describe the process and importance of (externally) reporting on internal control and risk.	2
(e)	Explain the sources, and assess the importance of, accurate information for risk management.	3
D1	**Targeting and monitoring of risk**	
(c)	Describe and assess the role of internal or external risk auditing in monitoring risk.	3
D2	**Methods of controlling and reducing risk**	
(a)	Explain the importance of risk awareness at all levels in an organisation.	2

Exam guide

In scenarios, look out for information on communication links. Poor communication is often an important sign of a weak control system. Board review and reporting are key elements in the control system and you'll need to know what an effective board review involves. The role of risk audits, the independence of internal audit and the role of the audit committee are also popular exam issues.

1 Information requirements of directors 12/09, 12/14

FAST FORWARD

Directors need **information** from a **large variety of sources** to be able to supervise and review the operation of the internal control systems. Information sources should include normal reporting procedures, but staff should also have channels available to report problems or doubtful practices of others.

1.1 Types of information

1.1.1 Strategic information

Strategic information is used to **plan** the **objectives** of the **organisation**, and to **assess** whether the objectives are being met in practice. Such information includes overall profitability, the profitability of different segments of the business, future market prospects, the availability and cost of raising new funds, total cash needs, total manning levels and capital equipment needs.

Strategic information is:

- Derived from both **internal and external** sources
- **Summarised** at a high level
- Relevant to the **long term**
- Concerned with the **whole organisation**
- Often prepared on an **'ad hoc'** basis
- Both **quantitative and qualitative**
- Often **uncertain**, as the future cannot be accurately predicted

1.1.2 Tactical information

Tactical information is used to decide **how the resources of the business should be employed**, and to **monitor** how they are being and have been employed. Such information includes productivity measurements (output per hour), budgetary control reports, variance analysis reports, cash flow forecasts, staffing levels and short-term purchasing requirements.

Tactical information is:

- Primarily **generated internally** (but may have a limited external component)
- **Summarised at a lower level**
- Relevant to the **short and medium term**
- Concerned with **activities or departments**
- Prepared **routinely and regularly**
- Based on **quantitative** measures

1.1.3 Operational information

Operational information is used to ensure that **specific operational tasks** are planned and carried out as intended.

Operational information is:

- Derived from **internal** sources such as transaction recording methods
- **Detailed**, being the processing of raw data (for example transaction reports listing all transactions in a period)
- Relevant to the **immediate term**
- **Task-specific**
- Prepared very **frequently**
- Largely **quantitative**

1.2 The qualities of good information   12/12

The COSO guidance stresses the importance of the board and management having good quality information. 'Good' information is information that adds to the understanding of a situation. The qualities of good information are outlined in the following table.

Quality		Example
A	ccurate	Figures should add up, the degree of rounding should be appropriate, there should be no typos, items should be allocated to the correct category, and assumptions should be stated for uncertain information.
C	omplete	Information should include everything that it needs to include, for example external data if relevant, comparative information and qualitative information as well as quantitative. Sometimes managers or strategic planners will need to build on the available information to produce a forecast using assumptions or extrapolations.
C	ost-beneficial	It should not cost more to obtain the information than the benefit derived from having it. Providers of information should be given efficient means of collecting and analysing it. Users should not waste time working out what it means.
U	ser-targeted	The needs of the user should be borne in mind; for instance, senior managers need strategic summaries, and junior managers need detail.
R	elevant	Information that is not needed for a decision should be omitted, no matter how 'interesting' it may be.
A	uthoritative	The source of the information should be a reliable one. However, subjective information (eg expert opinions) may be required in addition to objective facts.
T	imely	The information should be available when it is needed. It should also cover relevant time periods and the future as well as the past.
E	asy to use	Information should be clearly presented, not excessively long, and sent using the right medium and communication channel (email, telephone, hard-copy report).

1.3 Needs of directors

We have emphasised above that board and senior manager involvement is a critical element of internal control systems and the control environment.

They will need:

- **Financial information** – important for internal purposes and to fulfil legal requirements for true and fair external reporting
- **Non-financial information** such as quality reports, customer complaints, human resource data
- **External information** about competitors, suppliers, impact of future economic and social trends

There are various ways in which management can obtain the information they need to play the necessary active part in control systems.

Managers also need to take into account the needs of internal and external auditors for accurate and precise information.

You need to appreciate what information managers require and why they require it to fulfil performance objective 4 of the PER.

Exam focus point

Question 1 in December 2009 asked about the qualities of information and why the board needed to have information relating to key operational risks and controls.

1.4 Information sources

The information directors need to be able to monitor controls effectively comes from a wide variety of sources. Directors can obtain information partly through their own efforts. However, if information systems are to work effectively, it is vital that they identify particular people or departments who are responsible for providing particular information. Controls must be built into the systems to ensure that those **responsible provide that data**. This is particularly important in the context of the information that supports the contents of the financial statements and is used by internal and external audit and the audit committee.

1.4.1 The directors' own efforts

Directors will receive reports from the audit committee and risk committee. Management **walking about** and regular visits by the directors to operations may yield valuable insights and should help the directors understand the context in which controls are currently operating.

1.4.2 Reports from subordinates

There should be systems in place for all staff with supervisory responsibilities to report on a regular basis to senior managers, and senior managers in turn to report regularly to directors. The COSO guidelines comment:

> 'Among the most critical communications channels is that between top management and the board of directors. Management must keep the board up to date on performance, developments, risk and the functioning of enterprise risk management and other relevant events or issues. The better the communications, the more effective the board will be in carrying out its oversight responsibilities, in acting as a sounding board on critical issues and in providing advice, counsel and direction. By the same token the board should communicate to management what information it needs and provide feedback and direction.'

However, COSO's guidance also emphasises the need for the board to use information sources other than sub-board management, including internal and external auditors and regulators. There should be channels for stakeholders who have information about the effectiveness of internal controls to communicate with the company.

1.4.3 Lines of communication

Very importantly directors must ensure that staff have lines of communication that can be used to **address concerns**. There should be normal communication channels through which most concerns are addressed, but there should also be alternative channels for reporting if normal communication channels are ineffective. These include communication channels for staff to report, or **whistleblow**, particularly serious problems and perhaps active seeking of feedback through **staff attitude surveys**.

As well as channels existing, it is also important that staff believe that directors and managers want to know about problems and will deal with them effectively. Staff must believe that there will be **no reprisals** for **reporting relevant information**.

As part of its initiative to enhance internal control, Mazda carries out educational and awareness-raising activities throughout the company and its affiliates. These include circulating case studies of compliance and risk management problems at other companies, and the solutions used to deal with them.

Mazda is particularly concerned with information security. Employees are trained on the management of confidential information when they join and subsequently go on refresher courses.

When employees are unsure of how to proceed with integrity, Mazda encourages them to consult with other employees. Mazda's global hotline accepts reports of ethical violations in complete confidentiality.

1.4.4 Reports from control functions

Organisational functions that have a key role to play in internal control systems must report on a regular basis to the board and senior management. One example is the need for a close relationship between **internal audit** and the **audit committee**. The **human resources function** should also report regularly to the board about personnel practices in operational units. Poor human resource management can often be an indicator of future problems with controls, since it may create dissatisfied staff or staff who believe that laxness will be tolerated.

1.4.5 Reports on activities

The board should receive regular reports on **certain activities**. A good example is major developments in computerised systems. As well as board approval before the start of key stages of the development process, the board needs to be informed of progress and any problems during the course of the project, so that any difficulties with potentially serious consequences can be rapidly addressed.

1.4.6 Reports on resolution of deficiencies

Similarly, the board should obtain evidence to confirm that control deficiencies that have previously **been identified** have been **resolved**. When it has been agreed that action should be taken to deal with problems, this should include a **timescale** for action and also **reporting** that the actions have been implemented.

1.4.7 Results of checks

The board should receive confirmation as a matter of course that the necessary **checks** on the operation of the controls have been **carried out** satisfactorily and that the results have been clearly reported. This includes gaining assurance that the **right sort** of check has been **performed**. For example, **random checks** may be required on high risk areas, such as unauthorised access to computer systems. Sufficient **independent** evidence from external or internal audit should be obtained to reinforce the evidence supplied by operational units.

1.4.8 Exception reporting

Exception reports highlighting variances in **budgeting systems**, **performance measures**, **quality targets** and **planning systems** are an important part of the information that management receives. Organisations should have a system of exception reporting that will trigger action if potential risks have been identified.

You will remember from your management accounting studies that adverse variances are often an important sign of problems, and indicate a need to tighten internal control.

Managers may consider the following issues when deciding whether to investigate further.

(a)   **Materiality. Small variations in a single period** are bound to occur and **are unlikely to be significant**. Obtaining an 'explanation' is likely to be time consuming and irritating for the manager concerned. The explanation will often be 'chance', which is not particularly helpful.

(b) **Controllability**. Controllability must also influence the decision whether to investigate further. If there is a general worldwide price increase in the price of an important raw material there is **nothing that can be done internally** to control the effect of this.

(c) **Variance trend**. If, say, an efficiency **variance** is £1,000 adverse in month 1, the obvious conclusion is that the process is **out of control** and that corrective action must be taken. This may be correct, but what if the same variance is £1,000 adverse every month? The **trend** indicates that the process is **in control** and the standard has been wrongly set.

(d) **Cost**. The likely cost of an investigation needs to be weighed against the cost to the organisation of allowing the variance to continue in future periods.

(e) **Interrelationship of variances**. Quite possibly, individual variances should not be looked at in isolation. One variance might be interrelated with another, and much of it might have occurred only because the other, interrelated, variance occurred too.

1.4.9 Feedback from customers

Customer responses, particularly complaints, are important evidence for the board to consider, particularly as regards how controls ensure the **quality of output**.

Case Study

For governmental organisations, monitoring the quality of service is particularly important. The UK's *Good Governance Standard for Public Services* points out that users of public services, unlike consumers in the private sector, have little or no option to go elsewhere for services or to withdraw payment. The governing body of a public service therefore needs to decide how to measure quality of service, and be able to measure it effectively and regularly. It should ensure it has processes in place to hear the views of users and non-users from all backgrounds and communities about their needs, and the views of service users from all backgrounds about the suitability and quality of services.

1.5 Making best use of information

1.5.1 Comparison of different sources of information

The pictures gleaned from different sources must be compared and discrepancies followed up and addressed. Not only does the board need to have a **true picture** of what is happening but discrepancies might highlight problems with existing sources of information that need to be addressed. In particular, if random or special checks identify problems that should have been picked up and reported through regular channels, then the **adequacy** of these channels needs to be considered carefully.

1.5.2 Feedback to others

Directors need to ensure that as well as their obtaining the information needed in order to review internal control systems, **relevant information on controls** is also **passed to all those** within the organisation who need it directly. For example sales staff who obtain customer feedback on product shortcomings need to be aware of the channels for communicating with staff responsible for product quality and also staff responsible for product design.

1.5.3 Review procedures

As well as investigating and resolving problems with the information they receive, the board ought to undertake a **regular review** of the information sources that they need. They should, as we will see in Section 3, review in general the whole system of supervision to assess its adequacy and also to assess whether any layers of supervision or review can be reduced.

COSO's guidance on controls over financial reporting emphasises that information systems must capture the data for financial transactions and events that underlie financial statements. This information will be used for adjusting entries, estimates and reasonableness checks. Managers responsible for financial reporting need to discuss with operational staff information used to manage and control day-to-day operations and how this information relates to accounting and financial reporting.

1.6 Failures in information provision

As with other controls, a failure to take provision of information and communication seriously can have adverse consequences. For example, management may not insist on a business unit providing the required information if that business unit appears to be performing well. Also, if there is a system of reporting by exception, what is important enough to be reported will be left to the judgement of operational managers who may be disinclined to report problems. Senior management may then not learn about potential problems in time.

Exam focus point

A key question to ask when analysing control systems is how strong the feedback mechanisms appear to be and whether they are appropriate for the organisation.

2 Communication with employees

FAST FORWARD

Procedures improving staff abilities and attitudes should be built into the control framework. **Communication** of control and risk management issues and strong **human resource procedures** reinforce the control systems.

2.1 Importance of human element

It is very easy to design a control system that appears good on paper but is unworkable because it is **not geared** to the **user's practicality and usefulness.** A detailed technical manual covering information technology controls may be of little use if staff lack sufficient knowledge of information technology. Controls may not work very well if staff lack motivation or the basic skills for the job in the first place. On the other hand, if good staff are taken on, they may well develop the necessary controls as part of their day-to-day work.

2.2 Important human resource issues

The UK Turnbull report stresses that all employees have some responsibility for internal control and need to have the **necessary skills**, **knowledge** and **understanding** in particular of the risks the organisation faces.

2.3 Improving staff awareness and attitudes

Turnbull stresses that it is important that all staff understand that risk management is an **integral, embedded part** of the **organisation's operations**. Elaborate risk management innovations may not be the best way to improve performance. It may be better to build **warning mechanisms** into existing information systems rather than develop separate risk reporting systems.

Turnbull suggests that it is vital to communicate policies in the following areas in particular.

- Customer relations
- Service levels for both internal and outsourced activities
- Health, safety and environmental protection
- Security of assets and business continuity
- Expenditure
- Accounting, financial and other reporting

The briefing suggests that the following steps can be taken.

- **Initial guidance** from the chief executive

- **Dissemination of the risk management policy** and codes of conduct as well as of key business objectives and internal control

- **Workshops** on risk management and internal control

- A **greater proportion of the training budget** being spent on internal control

- Involvement of staff in **identifying and responding** to change and in operating warning mechanisms

- **Clear channels of communication** for reporting breaches and other improprieties

2.4 Training staff

An interactive training event, with participants identifying for themselves the most significant risks and key controls, is likely to be most valuable.

Training days can be particularly useful in emphasising to staff the importance of different types of control (preventative, detective etc) and also the need for some controls to assist staff development, but others to enforce sanctions particularly in cases of dishonesty or negligence.

 Case Study

Here is an example of an internal communications programme slightly adapted from an example in the COSO *Framework*.

Internal communications programme

- Management discusses risks and associated risk responses in regular briefings with employees.

- Management regularly communicates entity-wide risks in employee communications such as newsletters and an intranet.

- Enterprise risk management policies, standards and procedures are made readily available to employees along with clear statements requiring compliance.

- Management requires employees to consult with others across the organisation as appropriate when new events are identified.

- Induction sessions for new employees include information and literature on the company's risk management philosophy and enterprise risk management programme.

- Existing employees are required to take workshops and/or refresher courses on the organisation's enterprise risk management initiatives.

- The risk management philosophy is reinforced in regular and ongoing internal communication programmes and through specific communication programmes to reinforce tenets of the company's culture.

2.5 Problems of communication

Large companies, particularly those operating in several jurisdictions, may face particular problems when communicating with and training staff through local cultural and ethical filters. We shall discuss the influence of the country in which individuals work on their ethical attitudes in the next chapter.

3 Monitoring

FAST FORWARD

To be effective, monitoring by management needs to be **ongoing** and involve **separate evaluation** of systems. Deficiencies need to be communicated to all the appropriate people.

Key term

Monitoring ensures that internal control continues to operate effectively. This process involves assessment by appropriate personnel of the design and operation of control on a suitable timely basis, and the taking of necessary actions. It applies to all activities within an organisation and sometimes to outside contractors as well.

Monitoring (means) that the entirety of enterprise risk management is monitored and modifications made as necessary. Monitoring is accomplished through ongoing management activities, separate evaluations or both. (COSO)

In 2009 COSO published guidance on monitoring internal control systems.

3.1 Aims of monitoring   6/10

Monitoring should help ensure that internal controls continue to operate effectively and that systems produce accurate and reliable information. It involves the assessment of the design and operation of controls, and involves both ongoing monitoring and separate evaluations. If deficiencies are found, they should be **reported, assessed** and their **root causes corrected**.

Correction of root causes may address why staff have made errors. In this case correction processes may include training, discipline or control redesign. It may involve implementing better controls when controls have been found to be inadequate. The aim of correcting **root causes** distinguishes monitoring procedures from control procedures. Control procedures seek **only** to **correct errors**.

The COSO guidance highlights two fundamental principles.

(a)   **Ongoing monitoring** and **separate evaluation** enable management to determine whether internal controls continue to function over time.

   (i)   **Ongoing monitoring** includes routine review of reconciliations and system action applications. It may be particularly effective in smaller companies, since their managers will have high-level first-hand knowledge of the company's activities. Their close involvement in operations should help them identify variances and inaccuracies.

   (ii)   **Separate evaluation** is generally carried out by the audit committee and internal audit, and also includes annual reviews of control procedures. Separate evaluation is likely to be more difficult if a company does not have an internal audit department, as review of control effectiveness within a business unit by a manager responsible for that unit will lack objectivity.

(b)   Internal control deficiencies should be **identified and communicated** to those responsible for taking corrective action, management and the board.

The COSO guidance emphasises that monitoring should relate to **all control objectives**, not just financial reporting objectives. It should evaluate the internal control system's ability to manage or mitigate meaningful risks to organisational objectives.

If the operation of controls is not measured and monitored by management, their effectiveness may deteriorate over time as circumstances change. Different controls will need more monitoring over time as an organisation's strategy develops, and the tolerances allowed by those controls will also need to change.

3.2 Role of information

As discussed in earlier sections of this chapter, effective information-gathering processes are an essential part of monitoring. The information provided needs to be **suitable** and **sufficient**. The COSO document highlights two types of information.

Direct	Clearly substantiates the operation of controls, obtained by observing and testing controls in operation. These techniques provide most effective evidence of control operation, as they occur frequently, are integrated with operations and provide direct information about control operation.
Indirect	Other relevant information about operation of controls, including operating statistics, key risk and performance indicators. Seeking indirect information means identifying anomalies that indicate controls might fail to operate effectively. Indirect information will be more useful in stable situations, where risk assessment processes are effective.

3.3 Effective and efficient monitoring

Ineffective monitoring results in control breakdowns and material impacts on the organisation's ability to achieve its objectives. **Inefficient** monitoring leads to a lack of focus on the areas of greatest need. Three elements influence the effectiveness and efficiency of monitoring:

- **Establishing a foundation for monitoring** that includes a proper tone at the top, an effective organisational structure, a starting point or baseline of non-effective internal control

- **Designing and executing monitoring procedures** based on prioritising risks and identifying persuasive information about the operation of key controls that mitigate the significant risks

- **Assessing and reporting results**, which includes evaluating the severity of any identified deficiencies, prioritising findings, reporting to the correct level and following up on corrective action

3.4 Control environment

To be effective, the control environment elements that have to be in place are:

- **Emphasis at the top of the organisation** about the importance of internal control

- An organisational structure that places people with **appropriate skills and authority**, **objectivity and competence** in monitoring roles

3.4.1 Prioritising effective monitoring procedures

The COSO guidance stresses that the business's overall risk assessment process will also influence the scope of monitoring. Key factors will include the **size and complexity of the organisation**, the **nature of the organisation's operations**, the **purpose for which monitoring is being conducted** and the **relative importance of the underlying controls**. COSO provides helpful guidance on how organisations may vary their approach to monitoring.

Control importance	Risks controls address	Possible monitoring approach
Highest	High likelihood, high significance	Ongoing monitoring using direct and indirect information, periodic separate evaluation of direct information
Moderate in short term	Low likelihood, high significance	Ongoing monitoring using indirect information, periodic separate evaluation of direct information

Control importance	Risks controls address	Possible monitoring approach
Moderate in long term	High likelihood, low significance	Ongoing monitoring using direct and indirect information, less frequent separate evaluation of direct information
Lowest	Low likelihood, low significance	Relatively infrequent separate evaluations

To ensure monitoring has an appropriate risk-based focus, the organisation should establish a structure that firstly ensures that internal control is effective in a given area and focuses monitoring attention on areas of change. This structure will have the following elements.

Control baseline	A reasonable basis for believing internal controls operate effectively
Change identification process	Identifying changes in processes or risks that indicate controls should have changed; monitoring should focus on the ability of the risk assessment procedures to identify changes in processes or risks that should result in changes in controls and should also assess whether indicators of change in control design and operation are effective
Change management process	Verifying that the internal control systems have managed changes in controls effectively
Control reconfirmation	Reconfirming control operation through separate evaluation

3.4.2 Communication structure for monitoring   12/12

The results of monitoring need to be reported to the right people and corrective action taken. Deficiencies in internal controls should be reported to the person **responsible for the control's operation** and **to at least one level higher**. The deficiencies need to be assessed in the same terms as risks, the **likelihood** that a control will fail to detect or prevent a risk's occurrence and the **significance** of the potential impact of the risk.

Where control deficiencies are potentially significant, additional monitoring procedures may be needed during the correction period to protect against errors.

COSO's guidance on controls over financial reporting stresses that **effective communication of financial reporting deficiencies** is essential. Deficiencies should not only be reported to management responsible but also to at least one level above. This should help ensure that effective action is taken to deal with problems.

Management should also develop a list of signs of **control deficiencies** that seriously threaten the reliability of financial reporting. If these are identified, they must be reported to senior management and the board. They include illegal or improper acts, significant loss of assets or evidence of previous improper external financial reporting.

3.5 Scale of monitoring

The **size of the organisation** and the **complexity of its operations and controls** will be key determinants.

Case Study

The practical example given in the COSO guidance is a distinction between the purchase function in a large and small company. A company that has 20 people processing invoices, one of whom is not properly trained, may be able to operate for some time without material error. Senior management would not therefore be concerned. A company with only one person processing invoices cannot afford that person to be inadequately trained. Senior management monitoring on a day-to-day basis may be required.

3.6 Monitoring procedures

Monitoring procedures may include:

- **Periodic evaluation and testing of controls** by internal audit

- **Continuous monitoring programs** built into information systems

- Analysis of, and appropriate follow-up on, **operating reports** or metrics that might identify anomalies indicative of a control failure

- **Supervisory reviews of controls**, such as reconciliation reviews as a normal part of processing

- **Self-assessment** by the board and management regarding the tone they set in the organisation and the effectiveness of their oversight functions

- **Audit committee enquiries** of internal and external auditors

- **Quality assurance reviews** of the internal audit department

3.6.1 Formality of monitoring

Increased formality will be required in larger organisations, where managers' knowledge of day-to-day operational control activities is less. If the results of monitoring are being reported outside the organisation, monitoring will also need to be more formal. In particular the organisation will need to be able to provide evidence that supports the reports made.

Increased formality may include:

- Processes to **document and retain monitoring information**

- Policies and processes regarding **aggregation, evaluation and reporting of deficiencies** to the board, or to the audit and risk committees.

Case Study

Mazda has separated the execution and management functions through the introduction of the executive officer system. These measures are intended to enhance management efficiency by helping the Board of Directors function more effectively as a supervisory body, enhancing the effectiveness of the Board's deliberations and speeding up decision-making by delegation of authority to executive officers.

Mazda's board of corporate auditors, the majority of whom are external auditors, is responsible for auditing business execution by the directors. The Global Auditing Department contributes to sound and efficient management by checking management's targets, policies and plans, as well as compliance with laws and regulations.

As well as its board of directors, Mazda has established an executive committee to discuss policies and matters of importance. Mazda's management advisory committee, consisting of the directors and leading external professionals from a diverse range of backgrounds, reviews the soundness and transparency of Mazda's management practices.

4 Role of management in monitoring

FAST FORWARD

Management is responsible for the **implementation of effective monitoring procedures**. The board is responsible for **ensuring a system of effective monitoring** is in place, and for **monitoring management's activities**.

4.1 Distinction between role of management and role of board

The UK Turnbull report draws a distinction between the role of senior (operational) management and the role of the board.

4.1.1 Role of management

Turnbull emphasises that monitoring forms part of management's role to **implement board policies** on risk and control. Ongoing monitoring is an essential element of a sound system of internal control.

4.1.2 Role of board

Turnbull emphasises that the board cannot just rely on the management monitoring processes to discharge its responsibilities. It should **regularly receive and review reports on internal control** to ensure that management has implemented an effective monitoring system. It should also carry out an annual assessment that forms the basis of its report on internal controls.

Although the board need not understand the details of every management procedure, it should focus on controls performed directly by senior management, and controls designed to prevent or detect senior management override.

We shall examine the board's role further in Section 7 of this chapter.

4.2 Qualities of management

COSO stresses the need for **competence** and **objectivity** in management monitoring.

4.2.1 Competence

This relates to managers' knowledge of how controls operates and what constitutes an effective weakness. Managers must be able to identify the **root causes** and to do this they must have knowledge of the underlying control and the risks the control is designed to mitigate.

4.2.2 Objectivity

Different reviewers provide different levels of objectivity. **Self-review**, review of one's own work, is obviously the least objective. **Review by peers or superiors** is more objective. **Review by impartial evaluators** is the most objective. Impartial evaluators may include internal auditors, people from other departments or external parties. However, because impartial evaluators are distant from the operation of controls, they tend to carry out separate evaluations rather than be involved in ongoing monitoring.

5 Internal audit

> The role of internal audit will **vary** according to the **organisation's objectives** but is likely to include review of **internal control systems, risk management, legal compliance** and **value for money**.

Key term

> **Internal audit** is an independent appraisal function established within an organisation to examine and evaluate its activities as a service to the organisation. The objective of internal audit is to assist members of the organisation in the effective discharge of their responsibilities. To this end, internal audit furnishes them with analyses, appraisals, recommendations, counsel and information concerning the activities reviewed.
> (UK Institute of Internal Auditors)
>
> **Internal audit** is an appraisal or monitoring activity established by management and directors for the review of the accounting and internal control systems as a service to the entity. It functions by, among other things, examining, evaluating and reporting to management and the directors on the adequacy and effectiveness of components of the accounting and internal control systems.
> (UK Financial Reporting Council)

You covered the work of internal audit in Paper F8. This section summarises briefly the **role** of internal audit. It concentrates on the main issues for this exam, the **independence** of internal audit and its significance as part of the control and risk management systems.

5.1 The need for internal audit   12/08

The Turnbull report in the UK stated that listed companies without an internal audit function should **annually review** the need to have one, and listed companies with an internal audit function should annually review its **scope, authority** and **resources**.

Turnbull states that the need for internal audit will depend on:

Scale, diversity and complexity of the company's operations	The more complex the operations, the more that can go wrong. Also, the greater the need for an independent internal audit department to look at the system as a whole, to see if risk management and internal controls are appropriately focused. In addition, where there is close scrutiny of the company's operations by regulators with the power to remove the company's licence to operate, the case for internal audit is much stronger.
Number of employees	Number of employees is generally used as a proxy for size. Investors would expect that the larger the company, the more formal the systems of internal control, including a separate internal audit department. A larger company may have complex reporting lines and it may have less shared culture between different locations.
Cost-benefit considerations	As with other controls, the costs of internal audit (salary, management time lost dealing with internal audit) should not outweigh the benefits. The benefits however may be difficult to quantify (how do you quantify the errors that internal audit has prevented).
Changes in organisational structure	A simplification of the organisational structure may often lead to a slimming down of the internal audit department. However, a slimming down should really mean the opposite. The removal of the checks and balances implied by a bureaucratic structure would seem to increase the need for an effective internal audit function.
Changes in key risks	If the business is developing in new areas, an internal audit assessment of how effectively it is handling consequent changes in risk can be very significant.
Problems with internal control systems	Internal audit assessment would help to determine how serious these problems are and what can be done to resolve them.
Increased number of unexplained or unacceptable events	This applies not just to events that cause problems with the accounting records but also to problems that delay production or result in inferior-quality goods or services. The costs of internal audit may need to be weighed against the possibilities of lost sales.

Although there may be alternative means of carrying out the routine work of internal audit, those carrying out the work may be involved in operations and hence lack **objectivity**.

It seems likely that once the task of reviewing internal control and risk management systems becomes complex, a skilled and objective internal audit team will be needed to give the audit committee the evidence it needs about how systems are working.

 Case Study

The PwC report *Internal Audit 2012* suggests ten imperatives for a high-performance internal audit function in the future.

- **Strategic stature within the organisation**. The chief audit executive should ensure that priorities align with the wishes of the audit committee and management and should be a trusted adviser to key stakeholders.

- **Development and update of strategic plan aligned with objectives and stakeholder expectations**. The plan should indicate how internal audit will develop and be organised to deliver service, and suggest specific goals or strategic initiatives to bridge capability gaps.

- **Communication with key stakeholders**. In particular there should be regular dialogue with the audit committee chairman and external auditors.

- **Align HR strategies with enterprise and stakeholder needs**. This means internal audit ensuring that skills gaps relating to new and emerging skills are bridged.

- **Focus continually on enterprise risks**. As well as testing controls, internal auditors ought to focus on the risks themselves, keeping management informed about risk exposures and conducting an annual enterprise-wide risk assessment, which feeds into the audit plan. Risk assessments need to be transparent, aligned with business units and involve external audit as well as internal management.

- **Integrated approach to IT audit**. There should be an annual IT risk assessment, which addresses risks within business processes and seeks to enhance IT audit capabilities. The IT audit plan needs to be aligned with organisational IT strategies and objectives.

- **Use of technology to improve efficiency, effectiveness and quality**. This includes automating tracking and reporting, testing populations automatically and using technology to conduct real-time reviews.

- **Development of knowledge management plan**. The aim of this plan should be to make internal audit knowledge and expertise available to other internal auditors and business unit and enterprise management.

- **Commitment to continuous quality assurance**. There should be a quality improvement programme and external assessment of performance and benchmarking.

- **Link performance measures to strategic goals**. This means in particular using a balanced scorecard approach to track performance to the strategic plan.

5.2 Objectives of internal audit 6/10

The role of the internal auditor has expanded in recent years as internal auditors seek to monitor all aspects (not just accounting) of organisations, and add value to their employers. The work of the internal auditor is still prescribed by management, but it may cover the following broad areas.

(a) **Review of the accounting and internal control systems**. The establishment of adequate accounting and internal control systems is a responsibility of management and the directors. Internal audit is often assigned specific responsibility for the following tasks.

    (i)   Reviewing the design of the systems

    (ii)   Monitoring the effectiveness of the operation of the systems by risk assessment and detailed testing

    (iii)   Recommending cost-effective improvements

    Review will cover both financial and non-financial controls.

(b) **Examination of financial and operating information**. This may include review of the means used to identify, measure, classify and report such information and specific enquiry into individual items including detailed testing of transactions, balances and procedures.

(c) **Review of the economy, efficiency and effectiveness** of operations. In the public sector especially this helps to determine whether or not value for money has been achieved.

(d) **Review of compliance**. This should be carried out in relation to laws, regulations and other external requirements, with internal policies and directives, and with other requirements including appropriate authorisation of transactions.

(e) **Review of the safeguarding of assets**. Are valuable, portable items such as computers or cash secured, is authorisation needed for dealing in investments?

(f) **Review of the implementation of corporate objectives**. This includes review of the effectiveness of planning, the relevance of standards and policies, the organisation's corporate governance procedures and the operation of specific procedures such as communication of information.

(g) **Identification of significant business** and financial **risks**. This involves **monitoring** the **organisation's overall risk management policy** to ensure it operates effectively, and **monitoring** the **risk management strategies** to ensure they continue to operate effectively.

(h) **Special investigations**. These can be carried out in particular areas, for example suspected fraud.

It is inevitable that internal audit will focus on **operational controls**. In some companies, however, the problem may be a failure of strategic level controls, due to management override of controls or poor strategic decision-making. However, internal audit's role in relation to strategic controls will be limited, as most checking procedures have been followed at board level. The board must ultimately be responsible for the operation of strategic controls.

Exam focus point

You may need to apply your knowledge of what internal audit does to argue in favour of a particular organisation establishing an internal audit function.

5.3 Risk auditing   6/14

Risk-based audits are a development of systems audits. Auditors will be concerned to see that managers have put in place **risk assessment processes that are capable of identifying risks on a timely basis**, and have **designed robust risk management processes and internal control systems**. Auditors will attempt to confirm that these risk management processes and controls **operate to mitigate risks** and ensure that management **receives accurate information** about risks, particularly high consequences-likelihood risks, risks outside the organisation's risk appetite or risks that have materialised due to serious deficiencies in internal control. Risk audits are not compulsory for all organisations, although in some regulated industries (banking and financial services) a form of ongoing risk assessment and audit is compulsory in most jurisdictions.

Internal audit's work will be influenced by **business objectives**, the risks that may **prevent** the organisation **achieving its objectives** and the organisation's attitude towards risk (that is, its degree of risk acceptance or risk aversion).

The main stages of the risk audit are:

(a) **Identification of risks**

Risk auditors need to identify **what risks** are relevant to the work they will be required to do.

(b) **Assessment of risks**

The auditors need to obtain evidence of the probability of those **risks crystallising** and their **likely impact**. Where the risk management framework is insufficient, auditors will have to rely on their own **risk assessment** and **recommend an appropriate framework**. Where an adequate framework for risk management and control is embedded in operations, auditors will aim to use **management assessment of risks** and concentrate on **auditing the risk management processes**.

(c) **Review of management and controls**

The auditors will assess the **operation and effectiveness** of the **risk management processes** and the **internal controls** in operation to **limit risks**. A comprehensive risk audit will extend to the risk management and control **culture**.

(d)   **Reporting**

Reporting will mostly be to the board, or to the audit or risk committee. The report will concentrate on the extent of the **key risks**, the **quality of existing assessment procedures** and the **effectiveness of controls**.

5.3.1 Internal or external risk auditing? 12/09, 6/14

If internal auditors carry out the audit, they should be familiar with the organisation, its systems and procedures, its culture and the regulations that affect it. The internal auditors should be able to carry out a well-targeted audit and report in a way that is appropriate and helpful for the organisation.

However, internal auditors may suffer from the disadvantages of **lack of independence and over-familiarity**. An internal audit may be undermined by internal politics and divisions. An external auditor can provide an unbiased, fresh view. A risk audit carried out by external auditors should give a higher degree of confidence to external stakeholders. It is also possible that external auditors' knowledge of best practice and current developments may be more up to date. The external auditor may have a better awareness of certain risks than internal auditors do.

Exam focus point

If you are asked in the exam about the areas where internal audit should focus, you should consider the concerns outlined in the scenario. For example, in a highly regulated business where compliance failures are a significant business risk, internal audit is likely to focus on compliance work.

Case Study

COSO stresses the role of internal auditors in adding value.

- Reviewing critical control systems and risk management processes
- Performing an effectiveness review of management's risk assessment and internal controls
- Providing advice in the design and improvement of control systems and risk mitigation strategies
- Challenging the basis of management's risk assessments and evaluating the adequacy and effectiveness of risk treatment strategies
- Providing advice on enterprise risk management
- Defining risk tolerances

5.4 Independence of internal audit

Auditors should be independent of the activities audited.

Although an internal audit department is part of an organisation, it should be **independent** of the **line management** whose sphere of authority it may audit.

5.4.1 Audit process

A lack of independence can mean that audits cannot be carried out to the extent and effectiveness desired. Internal auditors may not be able to examine all the areas they'd like to, or determine how the areas selected will be audited. They may feel inhibited from carrying out certain procedures for fear of upsetting powerful or vocal managers or staff.

In addition, internal audit will be **trusted more by managers and staff**, and therefore are more likely to have **sensitive information disclosed to them**, if they are felt to be independent.

5.4.2 Value of recommendations

Internal audit's recommendations will only be valuable if they are **influenced solely by what they find**, and not biased by other factors. Factors that can distort the judgements which internal audit make include a willingness to take sides, motives of personal advantage or a desire to use the audit to confirm their own previous judgements (for example a dislike of certain individuals).

5.4.3 Increased costs of internal audit

Clearly if internal audit produce recommendations that are flawed because they reflect the auditors' lack of independence, the **costs of their salaries** will be wasted. In addition, costs will ratchet up if management uses internal audit's recommendations as the basis for decisions about risk management. Risks unnecessarily highlighted by internal audit may be **over-managed**, incurring excessive costs. Risks that are not highlighted by internal audit when they should have been may materialise, causing significant losses for the organisation.

5.4.4 Confidence in recommendations

Line managers will be less willing to implement internal audit recommendations if they believe that internal audit is biased against them.

 Case Study

Spencer Pickett in the *Internal Auditing Handbook* suggests that the concept of independence involves a number of key qualities.

Objectivity	Judgements made in a state of detachment from the situation or decision
Impartiality	Not taking sides, in particular not being influenced by office politics in determining the work carried out and the reports given
Unbiased views	Avoiding the perception that internal audit is out to 'hit' certain individuals or departments
Valid opinion	The audit opinion should be based on all relevant factors, rather than being one that pleases everyone
No spying for management	Again internal audit should serve the whole organisation. Managers who want their staff targeted might be trying to cover up their own inadequacies
No no-go areas	Being kept away from certain areas will fatally undermine the usefulness of internal audit and mean that aggressive (incompetent?) managers are not checked
Sensitive areas audited	Internal audit must have the abilities and skills to audit complex areas effectively
Senior management audited	Internal audit must cover the management process and not just audit the detailed operational areas
No backing off	Audit objectives must be pursued fully in a professional manner and auditors must not allow aggressive managers to deflect them from doing necessary work and issuing valid opinions

5.5 Threats to independence

5.5.1 Involvement in systems design

If internal audit has been involved in the design of systems, it is very doubtful that they can audit what they have recommended.

5.5.2 Overfamiliarity

As a result of working for the same organisation, and being involved with the same issues, internal auditors may develop close professional or personal relationships with the managers and staff they are auditing. This may well make it very difficult to achieve independence. This particularly applies to staff who come into internal audit from operational departments. There may also be the risk of self-review – that they review work that they have previously done for operational departments.

As we shall see in Chapter 9, an organisation's culture and informal networks of staff can have a big influence on individuals' attitudes to ethics.

5.5.3 Reporting relationships

The principle that internal audit should be **independent** of the **line management** whose sphere of authority it audits ideally should extend to internal audit being **independent of the finance director**.

The reason for this is best seen by thinking about what could happen if the internal audit department reported some kind of irregularity to a finance director without realising that the finance director was actually involved. The director would take the report and decide that it was all very interesting, but not worth pursuing. A very different line might be taken by another, independent director!

Exam focus point

> You may encounter other threats in the exam, possibly linked to the factors described in the case example above. However, the point about whether internal audit should report to the finance director may come up regularly in this exam.

5.6 Dealing with threats to independence

Independence of internal auditors can be achieved by the following.

- The department should report to the **board** or to a special **audit committee** and not to the finance director (discussed further later in this chapter).

- Management should ensure staff recruited to internal audit internally **do not conduct audits** on departments in which they have worked.

- Where internal audit staff have also been involved in **designing** or **implementing new systems**, they should not **conduct post-implementation audits**.

- Internal auditors should have **appropriate scope** in carrying out their responsibilities, and unrestricted access to records, assets and personnel.

- **Rotation of staff** over specific departmental audits should be implemented.

5.6.1 Review and consultancy

Consultancy projects (one-off projects designed to address ad-hoc issues) are playing an **increasing role** in the work of **internal audit**. Taking on these projects enables internal auditors to extend their skills and the organisation to draw on the knowledge of internal auditors. However, there are dangers in becoming too involved in consultancy projects.

(a) Internal audit staff may be diverted to consultancy projects, and the regular audit reviews may be **inadequately resourced**.

(b) By taking on consultancy projects and suggesting **solutions**, internal audit could be getting too involved in **operational concerns**. There is a serious potential lack of independence if internal audit has to review solutions that **internal audit** staff have provided.

(c) Management is relying on internal audit to **solve problems** instead of having operational staff and managers solve or preferably prevent them.

Certain steps therefore need to be taken in order to avoid these problems.

(a) The **terms of reference** of the internal audit department (the main responsibilities) should draw a clear distinction between **regular audit services** and **consultancy work**.

(b) **Enough resources** for **regular work** should be **guaranteed**. Consultancy work should be separately resourced and additional resources obtained if necessary.

(c) If managers are concerned about **improving controls**, reviewing these improvements can legitimately be included in the work of internal audit.

(d) **Regular audit reviews** and **consultancy projects** can be undertaken by different staff.

(e) If consultancy work **identifies serious control deficiencies**, these must be incorporated into **internal audit reviews** as **high risk areas**.

5.7 Recruiting internal auditors

The decision about where to recruit internal auditors from will partly depend on the skills available internally and externally. Clearly an internal recruit has **familiarity** with the organisation that an external recruit would lack. However, there are a number of arguments in favour of recruiting externally.

5.7.1 Other experience

An external recruit can bring in **fresh perspectives** gained from working elsewhere. They can use their experience of other organisations' problems to **identify likely risk areas** and **recommend practical solutions and best practice from elsewhere**.

5.7.2 Independence of operational departments

An internal recruit is likely to have built up **relationships and loyalties** with people whom they have already worked, perhaps owing people favours. Equally they could have **grievances or have come into conflict with** other staff. These could **compromise their independence** when they come to audit their departments.

5.7.3 Prejudices and biases

An internal recruit is likely to have **absorbed the perspectives and biases** of the organisation, and thus be more inclined to treat certain individuals or departments strictly, while giving others the benefit of the doubt when it may not be warranted.

Exam focus point

A question issued by the examiner asked students to argue in favour of appointing an internal auditor from outside the company.

5.8 Differences between internal and external audit

The following table highlights the differences between internal and external audit.

	Internal audit	External audit
Purpose	Internal audit is an activity designed to **add value** to and improve an **organisation's operations**. Its work can cover any aspect of an organisation's business or operations, and is not just concerned with issues affecting the **truth and fairness of the financial statements**. Internal audit will mean different things in different organisations.	External audit is an exercise to enable auditors to **express an opinion on the financial statements**.

	Internal audit	External audit
Reporting to	Internal audit reports to the **board of directors**, or others charged with governance, such as the audit committee.	The external auditors report to the **shareholders**, or members, of a company on the stewardship of the directors.
Relating to	Internal audit's work relates to the **operations of the organisation**.	External audit's work relates to the **financial statements**. They are concerned with the financial records that underlie these.
Relationship with the company	Internal auditors are very often **employees of the organisation**, although sometimes the internal audit function is outsourced.	External auditors are **independent of the company and its management**. They are appointed by the shareholders.

The table shows that although some of the procedures that internal audit undertake are very similar to those undertaken by the external auditors, the whole **basis** and **reasoning** of their work is fundamentally **different**.

The **difference** in **objectives** is particularly important. Every definition of internal audit suggests that it has a **much wider scope** than external audit, which has the objective of considering whether the accounts give a true and fair view of the organisation's financial position.

5.9 Quality control and internal auditing

Whatever the criteria used to judge effectiveness, quality control procedures will be required to monitor the professional standards of internal audit. Internal audit departments should establish and monitor quality control policies and procedures designed to ensure that **all audits** are **conducted** in **accordance** with **internal standards**. They should communicate those policies and procedures to their personnel in a manner designed to provide reasonable assurance that the policies and procedures are understood and implemented.

Quality control policies will vary depending on factors such as the following.

- The size and nature of the department
- Geographic dispersion
- Organisation
- Cost-benefit considerations

Policies and procedures and related documentation will therefore vary from company to company.

The Institute of Internal Auditors has suggested that a formal system of quality assurance should be implemented in the internal audit department. This should cover the department's compliance with appropriate standards, encompassing quality, independence, scope of work, performance of audit work and management of the internal audit department.

5.10 Annual review of internal audit

The board or audit committee (discussed in Section 6) should conduct an annual review of the internal auditors' work. The reviews should include the following areas.

5.10.1 Scope of work

The review will be particularly concerned with the work done to test:

- The **adequacy, effectiveness** and **value for money** of internal control
- **Risk assessment** and **management processes**
- **Compliance with laws, regulations** and **policies**
- **Safeguarding** of assets
- **Reliability** of information
- **Value for money**
- **Attainment** of organisation's **objectives** and **goals**

It should be possible to see from the plans submitted by internal audit to the audit committee that internal audit's work forwards the organisation's aims and that internal audit is **responsive** to organisational change.

5.10.2 Authority

The review should cover the formal **terms of reference** and assess whether they are adequate.

It should consider whether there are senior personnel in the organisation who can ensure that the scope of internal audit's work is **sufficiently broad** and that there is **adequate consideration** of **audit reports** and **appropriate action** taken as a result of audit findings and recommendations.

5.10.3 Independence

The review should consider carefully whether there are **adequate safeguards** in place to ensure the independence of internal audit. These include reporting by the head of internal audit to the audit committee, **dismissal of the head of internal audit** being the responsibility of the board or audit committee, internal auditors not assuming operational responsibilities and internal auditors being excluded from systems, design, installation and operation work.

5.10.4 Resources of internal audit

Again the review should consider the documentation provided by internal audit and confirm that resourcing plans indicate that there will be **sufficient resources** to review all areas. This should be assessed in terms of not just the hours set aside but also physical resources such as computers and also of course the necessary **knowledge**, **skills and experience**.

Exam focus point	The annual review of internal audit is a likely subject of a part-question in the exam.

6 Audit committee   12/08, 06/13, 6/15

6.1 Role and function of audit committee

> **FAST FORWARD**
>
> An audit committee of **independent non-executive directors** should **liaise with external audit, supervise internal audit** and **review the annual accounts and internal controls**.

Exam focus point	Audit committees are very significant because of their responsibilities for supervision and overall review. In particular they should have a close interest in the work of internal audit and internal audit should have unrestricted access to the audit committee.

Audit committees are now compulsory for companies trading on the New York Stock Exchange.

In order to be effective, the audit committee has to be well staffed. The UK Smith report recommends that the **audit committee** should consist entirely of **independent non-executive directors** (excluding the chairman), and should include at least one member with **significant and recent financial experience**. The Singapore code suggests that at least two members should have accounting or related financial management expertise.

The Cadbury report summed up the benefits that an audit committee can bring to an organisation:

'If they operate effectively, audit committees can bring significant benefits. In particular, they have the potential to:

(a) Improve the quality of financial reporting, by reviewing the financial statements on behalf of the Board

(b) Create a climate of discipline and control which will reduce the opportunity for fraud

(c) Enable the non-executive directors to contribute an independent judgement and play a positive role

There are, however, some possible drawbacks with an audit committee:

(a)   Since the findings of audit committees are rarely made public, it is not always clear **what they do or how effective** they have been in doing it.

(b)   The audit committee's approach may act as a **drag** on the drive and entrepreneurial flair of the company's senior executives.

(c)   The Cadbury report warned that the effectiveness of the audit committee may be compromised if it acts as a **'barrier'** between the external auditors and the main (executive) board.

(d)   The Cadbury committee also suggested that the audit committee may be compromised if it allows the main board to '**abdicate its responsibilities** in the audit area', as this will weaken the board's responsibility for reviewing and approving the financial statements.

(e)   The audit committee may function less effectively if it falls under the influence of a **dominant board member**, particularly if that board member is the only committee member with significant financial knowledge and experience.

The main duties of the audit committee are likely to be as follows.

6.2 Review of financial statements and systems

The committee should review both the **quarterly/interim** (if published) and **annual accounts**. This should involve assessment of the judgements made about the overall appearance and presentation of the accounts, key accounting policies and major areas of judgement.

As well as reviewing the accounts, the committee's review should cover the financial reporting and budgetary systems and controls. This involves considering **performance indicators** and **information systems** that allow **monitoring** of the **most significant business and financial risks**, and the progress towards financial objectives. The systems should also highlight developments that may require action (for example large variances), and communicate these to the right people. The audit committee also needs to consider carefully the control systems that **underpin accurate financial reporting** by ensuring that information is correct and complete. This will mean considering the personnel and organisational structure issues discussed in Chapter 5, the controls in place to guarantee information is correct or detect errors discussed in Chapter 7, and the responsibilities for providing information discussed earlier in this chapter.

6.3 Review of internal control   6/11, 12/14

The audit committee should play a significant role in reviewing internal control.

(a)   Committee members can use their own experience to **monitor** continually the **adequacy** of **internal control systems in mitigating risks**, focusing particularly on the control environment, management's attitude towards controls and overall management controls.

(b)   The audit committee's review should cover **legal compliance** and **ethics**, for example listing rules or environmental legislation. Committee members should check that there are systems in place to promote compliance. They should review reports on the operation of **codes of conduct** and investigate violations.

(c)   The audit committee must actively **monitor the effectiveness of control over financial reporting** and needs to demonstrate **professional scepticism** when doing so.

(d)   The committee should also address the risk of **fraud**, ensuring that employees are aware of risks and that there are mechanisms in place for staff to report fraud, and fraud to be investigated.

(e)   Each year the committee should be responsible for **reviewing the company's statement on internal controls** prior to its approval by the board.

(f)   The committee should consider the **recommendations of the auditors** in the management letter and management's response. Because the committee's role is ongoing, it can also ensure that recommendations are publicised and see that actions are taken as appropriate.

(g)   The committee may play a **more active supervisory role**, for example reviewing major transactions for reasonableness.

6.4 Review of risk management

The audit committee can play an important part in the review of risk recommended by the Turnbull report. This includes confirming that there is a **formal policy** in place for **risk management** and that the policy is backed and regularly monitored by the board. The committee should also **review** the **arrangements**, including training, for ensuring that managers and staff are aware of their responsibilities. Committee members should use their own knowledge of the business to confirm that risk management is updated to **reflect current positions and strategy**. The extent of their work may depend on whether there is a separate **risk management committee** (see Chapter 5).

6.5 Liaison with external auditors

The audit committee's tasks here will include:

(a)   Being responsible for the **appointment or removal of the external auditors** as well as fixing their remuneration.

(b)   Considering whether there are **any other threats to external auditor independence**. In particular the committee should consider **non-audit services** provided by the external auditors, paying particular attention to whether there may be a **conflict of interest**.

(c)   **Discussing the scope of the external audit** prior to the start of the audit. This should include consideration of whether external audit's coverage of all areas and locations of the business is fair, and how much external audit will rely on the work of internal audit.

(d)   Acting as a **forum for liaison** between the external auditors, the internal auditors and the finance director.

(e)   **Helping the external auditors to obtain the information** they require and in resolving any problems they may encounter.

(f)   **Making themselves available** to the external auditors for consultation, with or without the presence of the company's management.

(g)   Dealing with any **serious reservations** which the external auditors may express either about the accounts, the records or the quality of the company's management.

6.6 Oversight of internal audit

The audit committee needs to oversee the work of internal audit and ensure its work **supports the company's strategic objectives** and the **compliance** needs of the company.

6.6.1 Reporting relationship

Internal audit normally reports to the audit committee for the following reasons.

(a) **Independence**

The fact that internal audit is reporting to a committee of independent non-executive directors itself **helps guarantee internal audit's independence**. As they are not involved in day-to-day management, committee members will have no self-interest in diverting internal audit's attention away from their area of the business. The audit committee should be able to take steps to ensure that internal audit remains **independent** and that its work is not compromised by pressure from operational management. This particularly applies if internal audit needs to review higher-level strategic matters which are likely to be the responsibility of very senior management.

(b) **Strategic oversight**

Having internal audit report to the audit committee makes clear the responsibility the committee has for **determining the strategy** adopted by internal audit. The committee should help internal audit fulfil some of the objectives discussed in the *Internal Audit 2012* report covered above to deliver services and specific goals, including being responsive to the views and needs of different stakeholders. The committee also needs to take decisions about the level of **resources** available to internal audit and where these resources should be employed. This is a subsidiary part of its general responsibility to look at whether internal controls are **effective**, internal audit being a control just like any other.

(c) **Authority**

We discussed earlier the need for internal audit to have whatever **access** is necessary to people and documents and that there should be no no-go areas. The backing of the audit committee should reinforce the authority that internal audit has to enforce its demands.

(d) **Role of audit committee**

Internal audit provides the evidence that **informs the reviews** of financial statements, internal control and risk management that the audit committee undertakes.

(e) **Monitoring of internal audit**

Monitoring the role of internal audit forms part of the audit committee's involvement in the overall monitoring process carried out by the board, discussed earlier in this chapter. The annual review of internal audit, discussed in Section 5, will be a key part of this monitoring process.

(f) **Ensuring action taken**

The audit committee should provide a forum for internal audit's conclusions to be **considered fairly**. It can also follow up the reports of internal audit by obtaining evidence of whether its recommendations have been implemented. It has the **authority** to hold managers accountable if they have failed to take action.

6.6.2 Annual review of internal audit

The review should cover the formal **terms of reference** and assess whether they are adequate.

It should also cover the following aspects of internal audit.

- **Standards** including **objectivity**, **technical knowledge** and **professional standards**
- **Scope** including how much emphasis is given to different types of review
- **Resources** – is the number of staff hours enough and are the technical and personal skills of the staff collectively sufficient for the work they are required to do?
- **Reporting arrangements**
- **Work plan**, especially review of controls and coverage of high risk areas
- **Liaison** with external auditors
- **Results**

The head of internal audit should have **direct access** to the audit committee.

6.7 Investigations

The committee will also be involved in implementing and reviewing the results of **one-off investigations**. UK guidance recommends that audit committees should be given specific authority to investigate matters of concern, and in doing so have access to sufficient resources, appropriate information and external professional help.

7 Board monitoring and reporting

Boards should **review risks** and the **effectiveness of internal controls regularly**.

Boards should carry out an **annual review** that looks more widely at risks faced and control systems and also at how these issues should be reported.

7.1 Significance of board review

We have mentioned throughout the last few chapters the importance of manager review of internal controls and the results of internal audit work obviously play a major part in this review. In the last section of this chapter we shall look in more detail at management's review of internal controls, since it is effectively the last stage of the audit process.

7.2 Review of internal controls

The UK **Turnbull committee** suggests that review of internal controls should be an **integral part** of the **company's operations**. The board, or board committees, should actively consider reports on control issues from others operating internal controls.

In order to be able to carry out an effective review, boards should regularly receive and review reports and information on internal control, concentrating on:

(a)   What the **risks** are and strategies for **identifying**, **evaluating** and **managing** them

(b)   The **effectiveness** of the management and internal control systems in the management of risk, in particular how risks are **monitored** and **how** any **deficiencies** have been dealt with

(c)   Whether **actions** are being taken to **reduce** the risks found

(d)   Whether the results indicate that **internal control** should be **monitored more extensively**

Question   Internal control review

(a)   What sort of information would help the board carry out an effective review of internal control?
(b)   What sort of employee attitudes would help or hinder an effective review of internal control?

Answer

(a)   **The UK's Institute of Internal Auditors suggests that the board needs to consider the following information in order to carry out an effective review**.

   (i)   The organisation's **Code of Business Conduct** (if it has one – see Chapter 10)

   (ii)   Confirmation that line managers are **clear as to their objectives**

   (iii)   The overall results of a **control self-assessment** process by line management or staff

   (iv)   **Letters of representation** ('comfort letters') on internal control from line management (confirmations about the operation of systems or specific transactions)

   (v)   A **report** from the audit committee on the **key procedures** which are designed to provide effective internal control

(vi) **Reports from internal audit** on audits performed

(vii) The audit committee's **assessment** of the **effectiveness of internal audit**

(viii) Reports on **special reviews** commissioned by the audit committee from internal audit or others

(ix) Internal audit's **overall summary opinion on internal control**

(x) The **external auditors' report on deficiencies** in the accounting and internal control systems and other matters, including errors, identified during the audit

(xi) **Intelligence** gathered by board members during the year

(xii) A **report on avoidable losses** by the finance director

(xiii) A **report on any material developments** since the balance sheet date and up to the present

(xiv) The board's proposed wording of **the internal control report** for publication

(b) The following employee attitudes will be relevant.

Response to management behaviour

Employees may take controls with the **same degree of seriousness** that management does. They will take into account how strictly controls are applied by senior managers, whether senior managers override controls, and whether follow-up action is taken by management if control deficiencies are identified.

Realism of controls

If employees see **controls as unrealistic** because for example there is insufficient time to operate them, they may not take management review of controls seriously.

Employee collusion

If employees do collude, the evidence available to management may be **undermined**. Collusion may not necessarily be hiding fraud. It could be a shared intention to thwart what is seen as unnecessary bureaucracy. The fact for example that there are two signatures on a document does not necessarily mean that it has been checked properly.

Focus on certain controls

If a **lot of emphasis is placed on certain controls**, reports on which the annual review is based will stress the operation of those controls and provide less detail of other controls that are also significant.

Prioritisation

Many employees may feel that controls are bureaucracy and as such interfere with more important day-to-day work. This may mean for example that controls are **not operated when they should be** but some time later, and so the evidence the annual review is relying on may not be as strong as it appears.

Reliance on memory

Some controls may be dependent on **knowledge held in the mind of employees**. The employees concerned may be happy about this because it reinforces their position, but it can lead to a lack of clarity about whether controls have operated, and also inconsistency and misunderstanding when controls depend on the attitudes of the person operating them.

In an appendix Turnbull provides more detailed guidance on what should be assessed as part of the regular review of internal controls:

Risk assessment	• Does the organisation have clear objectives and have they been communicated to provide direction to employees (examples include performance targets)? • Are significant risks identified and assessed on an ongoing basis? • Do managers and employees have a clear understanding of what risks are acceptable?
Control environment and control activities	• Does the board have a risk management policy and strategies for dealing with significant risks? • Do the company's culture, code of conduct, human resource policies and performance reward systems support the business objectives and risk management and control systems? • Does senior management demonstrate commitment to competence, integrity and fostering a climate of trust? • Are authority, responsibility and accountability clearly defined? • Are decisions and actions of different parts of the company appropriately co-ordinated? • Does the company communicate to its employees what is expected of them and the scope of their freedom to act? • Do company employees have the knowledge, skills and tools necessary to support the company's objectives and manage risks effectively? • How are processes and controls adjusted to reflect new or changing risks or operational deficiencies?
Information and communication	• Do managers receive timely, relevant and reliable reports on progress against business objectives and risks to provide the information needed for decision-making and review processes? • Are information needs and systems reassessed as objectives and related risks change or reporting deficiencies are identified? • Do reporting procedures communicate a balanced and understandable account of the company's position and prospects? • Are there communication channels for individuals to report suspected breaches of law or regulations or other improprieties?
Monitoring	• Are there ongoing embedded processes for monitoring the effective application of the policies, processes and activities relating to internal control and risk management? • Do these processes monitor the company's ability to re-evaluate risks and adjust controls effectively in response to changes in objectives, business and environment? • Are there effective follow-up procedures to ensure action is taken in response to changes in risk and control assessments? • Are there specific arrangements for management monitoring and reporting to the board matters of particular importance (including fraud or illegal acts)?

7.3 Annual review of controls

In addition, when directors are considering annually the disclosures they are required to make about internal controls, the Turnbull report states they should conduct an **annual review** of internal control. This should be wider ranging than the regular review. In particular, it should cover:

(a) The **changes** since the last **assessment** in **risks** faced, and the company's **ability** to **respond** to **changes** in its business environment

(b) The **scope** and **quality** of management's monitoring of risk and internal control and of the work of internal audit, or consideration of the need for internal audit if the company does not have it

(c) The **extent** and **frequency** of reports to the board

(d) **Significant controls**, **failings** and **deficiencies** with material impacts on the accounts

(e) The **effectiveness** of the **public reporting** processes

7.4 Internal risk reporting

Risk reporting needs to cover all stages of the risk management system and be carried out on a **systematic**, **regular basis**. The system also needs to ensure that significant changes in the risk profile are notified quickly to **senior management**. Reporting of high impact-likelihood risks may occur daily; other risks may be reported **monthly or quarterly**. The **risk register** is a key document in risk reporting, not only in terms of identifying risks but also in allocating responsibility for **managing, monitoring and reporting**.

Reports should show the **risk levels before controls are implemented** and the **residual risk** after controls are taken into account.

Reporting also needs to include comparisons of actual risks against predicted risks and **feedback** on the **action taken** to manage and reduce risks that the system has identified.

- Have the actions taken **fulfilled their objectives**?
- What **further action** is needed?
- Have the **costs of taking action justified the benefits**?

If risks have not been managed effectively at lower levels of the organisation, senior management may need to take a **more active role**.

As it will not be worthwhile to eliminate all risks, the reporting system needs to highlight **residual risks**, the **remaining exposure to risk** after appropriate management action has been taken.

7.5 External reporting on risk management and internal controls
6/08, 12/10

Stricter requirements on external reporting have been introduced over the last ten years because of the contribution of internal control failures to corporate scandals. The requirements have tried to address the concerns of shareholders and other stakeholders that management has exercised proper control.

Per the UK Turnbull report, the board should disclose in the accounts as a minimum the existence of a **process** for **managing risks**, how the board has **reviewed** the **effectiveness** of the process and that the **process accords** with the **Turnbull guidance**. The board should also include:

(a) An **acknowledgement** that they are **responsible** for the **company's system of internal control** and **reviewing its effectiveness**

(b) An **explanation** that such a system is designed to **manage** rather than eliminate the **risk of failure** to **achieve business objectives**, and can only provide **reasonable** and not absolute **assurance** against material misstatement or **loss**

(c) A **summary** of the process that the **directors** (or a board committee) have **used to review the effectiveness** of the system of internal control and consider the need for an internal audit function if the company does not have one; there should also be disclosure of the process the board has used to deal with **material internal control aspects** of **any significant problems** disclosed in the annual accounts

(d)   **Information** about those **deficiencies** in internal control that have resulted in material losses, contingencies or uncertainties which require disclosure in the financial statements or the auditor's report on the financial statements

The information provided must be meaningful, taking an overall, high-level view. It must also be reliable. The work of the internal audit and audit committee can help ensure reliability.

Exam focus point

> Although the Turnbull report was issued in the UK, it can be regarded as setting out best practice on board review and reporting for most jurisdictions.

Case Study

Diageo, the global premium drinks business, disclosed risks under the following headings in its 2011 accounts.

- Competition reducing market share and margins
- Not deriving expected benefits from strategy of focusing on premium drinks or its cost-saving and restructuring programmes
- Not deriving expected benefits from systems change programmes and disruption caused by systems failures
- Regulatory decisions and changes resulting in increased costs and liabilities, or limitation of business activities
- Having to fight litigation directed at the beverage industry or other litigation
- Contamination, counterfeiting or other circumstances affecting brand support
- Decreased demand due to changes in consumer preferences and tastes, or declining economy
- Decreased demand due to decline in social acceptability of products
- Adverse effect on business due to unfavourable local economic conditions or political or other developments
- Poorer results due to increased costs or shortages of labour
- Increases in the cost of raw materials or energy
- Poorer results due to disruption to production facilities, business service centres or information systems or change programmes not delivering intended benefits
- Adverse impact on business or operations of climate change or regulatory market measures to address climate change
- Adverse impact on production costs and capacity of water scarcity or poor quality
- Poorer results due to movements in value of pension funds, fluctuations in exchange rates and fluctuations in interest rates
- Disruption to operations caused by failure to renegotiate distribution, supply, manufacturing or licensing arrangements
- Inability to protect intellectual property rights
- Inability to enforce judgements of US courts against directors based outside the US

Diageo's corporate governance statement includes a general statement on risks and internal controls. It stresses that the business is aiming to avoid or reduce risks that can cause loss, reputational damage or business failure. Nevertheless the company aims to control business cost effectively and exploit profitable business opportunities in a disciplined way. Each year risk is assessed as an integral part of strategic planning by:

- All significant business units
- The Diageo executive committee

These assessments are reviewed by relevant executives and the audit and risk committees. The committees gain assurance from:

- Summary information in relation to the management of identified risks
- Detailed review of the management of selected key risks
- The work of the audit and risk function

Risk assessment also covers major business decisions and initiatives and significant operational risks such as health and safety, product quality and environmental risk management.

There is also specific detail on how such treasury risks as currency, interest rate, liquidity, credit and commodity price risks are being managed.

7.5.1 Sarbanes-Oxley requirements

The requirements relating to companies that are under the Sarbanes-Oxley regime are rather stricter than under the UK regime.

The most significant difference is that in the UK directors should say that they have assessed the effectiveness of internal controls **in general**, whereas Sarbanes-Oxley requires the directors to say specifically in the accounts whether or not **internal controls over financial reporting** are **effective**. The directors cannot conclude that controls are effective if there are **material deficiencies** in controls, severe deficiencies that result in a more than remote likelihood that material misstatements in the financial statements won't be prevented or detected.

Under Sarbanes-Oxley disclosures should include a **statement of management responsibility**, details of the **framework** used, disclosure of **material deficiencies** and also a **statement by the external auditors** on management's assessment of the effectiveness of internal control.

How much value reports give has been debated, particularly in America where some believe that the Sarbanes-Oxley legislation is too onerous. If reporting is compulsory, companies cannot apply a cost-benefit analysis to determine whether it is justified. It would certainly appear to be more beneficial for a larger company with elaborate control systems, where most of the shares are held by external shareholders.

7.6 Factors affecting extent of reporting

Companies may have a number of reasons for internal control reporting beyond **legal compliance**. Internal control reporting is an important way for directors to **demonstrate their accountability for managing the company**. Detailed reporting can be a part of **policy**, to provide shareholders and other finance suppliers with assurance that controls are operating effectively to limit their risks.

Depending on how much leeway companies have on how they report on risk and control, the following factors may influence what they say.

7.6.1 Other accounts disclosures

The risk and control report should **link in with other disclosures** in the accounts about business developments. UK 2008 regulations require disclosure in the directors' report of likely future developments in the business of the company, including changes in risk exposure. The UK Corporate Governance Code 2010 included a requirement for companies to explain their business model.

7.6.2 Interests of users

The directors must also take account of the views of shareholders, who will be interested in learning about the risks that could have most impact on the **value of their investment**, and how these risks are being controlled. These would include **principal strategic and financial risks**, and also **operational risks** that could have severe financial consequences. The views of other principal **stakeholders** will also be important.

7.6.3 Risks materialising or changing over the year

Disclosure of risks that have **significantly changed** will be important, as will how control systems have developed to meet these changes.

7.6.4 Reputation risks

Risks that could cause a significant decline in the organisation's reputation may well be risks about which the board wishes to reassure stakeholders. Disclosures may focus on threats to reputation that may have a large impact on the business, particularly **product safety**.

7.6.5 Limitations on risk disclosures

The board may be less willing to disclose some risks on the grounds of **commercial confidentiality**. Directors may also fear that **disclosures about certain risks** will be **misinterpreted** by readers of the accounts. However, they may also be motivated to include matters covered in the reports of competitors or those identified as **best practice** to demonstrate how they are managing the risks that are common in this industry.

7.7 Compulsory external reporting   12/10

The factors listed above will be significant if reporting is regarded as voluntary or, at most, best practice. There are a number of arguments in favour of compulsory reporting.

(a)   **Improved confidence of shareholders**. Shareholders wish to be sure that boards are managing risk responsibly and that risk levels are not excessive. Compulsory reporting also helps to **reinforce confidence in the quality of information**.

(b)   **Stimulus to directors**. Directors will know that they cannot avoid being held to account if controls are poor, as investors will be able to read the report and seek more information on areas where controls are weak.

(c)   As well as providing information to ordinary shareholders, compulsory reporting can provide valuable information for **stakeholders with power** to hold directors accountable, particularly market regulators and institutional investors.

(d)   It should remove the possibility of companies with poor controls being able to **hide them** and keep investors satisfied by good results.

Question	Turnbull

In the last few chapters we have mentioned the Turnbull guidance on a number of occasions.

What do you think are the most important qualities that the Turnbull guidance has? (You may wish to refer back to the summary of the guidance at the end of Chapter 3.)

Key features of the Turnbull guidance include the following.

(a)   It is **forward looking**.

(b)   It does **not seek** to **eliminate risk**. It is constructive in its approach to opportunity management, as well as concerned with 'disaster prevention'. To succeed, companies are not required to take fewer risks than others but they do need a good understanding of what risks they can handle.

(c)   It **unifies all business units** of a company into an integrated risk review.

(d)   It is **strategic**, and driven by business objectives, particularly the need for the company to adapt to its changing business environment.

(e)   It should be **durable**, evolving as the business and its environment changes.

(f)   In order to create shareholder value, a company needs to **manage the risks** it faces and communicate to the capital markets how it is carrying out this task. This helps shareholders make informed decisions – remember shareholders are prepared to tolerate risk provided they receive an acceptable level of return. It will also provide more confidence in the company and therefore lower the required return of shareholders and lenders.

Chapter Roundup

- Directors need **information** from a **large variety of sources** to be able to supervise and review the operation of the internal control systems. Information sources should include normal reporting procedures, but staff should also have channels available to report problems or doubtful practices of others.

- Procedures improving staff abilities and attitudes should be built into the control framework. **Communication** of control and risk management issues and strong **human resource procedures** reinforce the control systems.

- To be effective, monitoring by management needs to be **ongoing** and to involve **separate evaluation** of systems. Deficiencies need to be communicated to all the appropriate people.

- Management is responsible for the **implementation of effective monitoring procedures**. The board is responsible for **ensuring a system of effective monitoring** is in place, and for **monitoring management's activities**.

- The role of internal audit will **vary** according to the **organisation's objectives** but is likely to include **review of internal control systems, risk management, legal compliance** and **value for money**.

- An audit committee of **independent non-executive directors** should liaise with **external audit, supervise internal audit**, and **review the annual accounts and internal controls**.

- Boards should **review risks** and the **effectiveness of internal controls regularly**.

  Boards should carry out an **annual review** that looks more widely at risks faced and control systems, and also how these issues should be reported.

1 Fill in the blank:

.... ensures that internal control continues to operate effectively. This process involves assessment by appropriate personnel of the design and operation of control on a suitable timely basis, and the taking of necessary actions. It applies to all activities within an organisation and sometimes to outside contractors as well.

2 Complete the mnemonic in respect of the qualities of good information.

A

C

C

U

R

A

T

E

3 What are the main elements of internal audit's review of the accounting and control systems?

4 Which of the following is not a measure designed to enhance the independence of internal audit?

A Internal audit should have unrestricted access to records, assets and personnel.

B Internal audit should report ultimately to the finance director.

C Internal auditors should not audit systems that they have designed.

D The terms of reference of the internal audit department should draw a clear distinction between regular audit services and consultancy work.

5 List the main responsibilities of audit committees.

6 Audit committees are generally staffed by executive directors.

True ☐

False ☐

7 According to the Turnbull report, what should be the main elements of the board's regular review of internal controls?

8 And what should be the main elements of the board's annual review of internal controls?

Answers to Quick Quiz

1   Monitoring

2   **A**ccurate

    Complete

    Cost-beneficial

    User-targeted

    Relevant

    Authoritative

    Timely

    Easy to use

3
   - Reviewing the design of systems
   - Monitoring the operation of systems by risk assessment and detailed testing
   - Recommending cost-effective improvements

4   B   Internal audit should ultimately report to the audit committee.

5
   - Review of financial statements and systems
   - Liaison with external auditors
   - Review of internal audit
   - Review of internal control
   - Review of risk management
   - Investigations

6   False   Non-executive directors should staff the audit committee to enhance its function as an independent monitor, and a forum to which internal and external audit can address their concerns.

7
   - What the risks are and strategies for identifying, evaluating and managing them
   - The effectiveness of the management and internal control systems
   - Whether actions are being taken to reduce the risks found
   - Whether the results indicate that internal control should be monitored more extensively

8
   - The changes since the last assessment in risks faced and the company's ability to respond to changes in its business environment
   - The scope and quality of management's monitoring of risk and internal control, and of the work of internal audit
   - The extent and frequency of reports to the board
   - Significant controls, failings and deficiencies having material impacts on the accounts
   - The effectiveness of the public reporting processes

Now try the question below from the Practice Question Bank.

Number	Level	Marks	Time
Q8	Examination	25	49 mins

BPP
LEARNING MEDIA

Professional values and ethics

Personal ethics

9

Introduction

This chapter begins the detailed coverage of ethics, which is a core topic not only in this paper but generally in ACCA's professional exams. ACCA has introduced an online ethics module as part of its training and this section of the syllabus develops ethical themes covered in the online module. Remember when working through this chapter that **personal ethics** are emphasised by ACCA as well as business ethics.

We start by examining certain important ethical theories and in doing so highlight a couple of key issues; whether there are objective, universal standards and to what extent ethics should be concerned with the consequences of actions. We then look at what may influence approaches to ethics. In particular Kohlberg's framework of ethical maturity is very important.

In the last two sections of the chapter we concentrate on how ethical problems should be approached in practice and also the way to tackle exam questions that cover ethical scenarios. We focus on the AAA and Tucker models that are highlighted in the study guide.

Study guide

		Intellectual level
E1	**Ethical theories**	
(a)	Explain and distinguish between the ethical theories of relativism and absolutism.	2
(b)	Explain, in an accounting and governance context, Kohlberg's stages of human moral development.	3
(c)	Describe and distinguish between deontological and teleological/consequentialist approaches to ethics.	2
(d)	Apply commonly used ethical decision-making models in accounting and professional contexts: American Accounting Association model; Tucker's 5 question model.	2
E2	**Different approaches to ethics and corporate social responsibility**	
(c)	Describe and analyse the variables determining the cultural context of ethics and corporate social responsibility (CSR).	2
E6	**Ethical characteristics of professionalism**	
(a)	Explain and analyse the content and nature of ethical decision-making using content from Kohlberg's framework as appropriate.	2
(b)	Explain and analyse issues related to the application of ethical behaviour in a professional context.	2

Exam guide

The Pilot Paper asked for a straightforward description of certain approaches to ethics. Other questions may be more complex, requiring consideration of influences on a person's or organisation's ethical position. A typical question might ask you to interpret people's actions or attitudes in light of the ethical theories or suggest how one of the theories might affect behaviour.

You may also be asked to apply the ethical theories and models to a business decision. The examiner has emphasised the importance of 'the ethics parts of the study guide and the ethical reasoning capabilities in particular. Well-prepared candidates should not only be aware of the ethical theories but also be able to use them and apply them. It will not be sufficient to merely define. An ability to adapt and apply is also essential.' Questions may require you to use a particular ethical framework, or choose an appropriate ethical framework to construct an ethical case.

1 Ethical theories   6/15

FAST FORWARD

A key debate in ethical theory is whether ethics can be determined by **objective**, **universal principles**. How important the **consequences of actions** should be in determining an ethical position is also a significant issue.

1.1 An introduction to ethics

In this chapter you will encounter various philosophical, academic terms. We have to use this terminology, as the examiner will use it in questions. However, provided that you focus on certain basic issues, you will be able to negotiate this chapter successfully.

1.1.1 Do ethics change over time and place?

One viewpoint is that ethics do vary between time and place. Slavery for example is now regarded as wrong, whereas in Roman times slavery was acceptable. The view that ethics vary between different ages and different communities is known as **ethical relativism** and is discussed in Section 1.3.

The opposing view is that ethics are unchanging over time and place. Some courses of action are always right, others are always wrong. A simple example would be saying that it is always wrong to steal. The view that there are certain unchanging ethical rules is known as **ethical absolutism** and is discussed in Section 1.4.

1.1.2 Should you consider the consequences of your actions when making ethical decisions?

One view is that society is best served by everyone following certain ethical rules, and obeying them no matter what the results are. The argument is that people will undermine society if they disobey the ethical rules, even if they do so with the intention of avoiding adverse consequences. This viewpoint, known as **deontological ethics**, was developed by Kant.

The opposing viewpoint is that you cannot divorce an action from its consequences, and when taking ethical decisions you must take account of what the consequences will be. This viewpoint is known as **teleological ethics**. If you take this viewpoint, it implies that you have to define the best possible consequences. The different variations of the teleological viewpoint try to do this.

1.1.3 What thought processes do people use when making ethical decisions?

What the theories are aiming to do is to complete the following sentence.

> 'You should act ethically because ... '

In Section 2 we shall look at the work of Kohlberg who supplied various examples of thought processes, depending on the degree of ethical development of the individual.

- People who are less ethically developed may think: 'You should act ethically because you'll be punished if you don't.'

- People who have more advanced ethical development may think: 'You should act ethically because your country's laws say you should.'

- People at the highest level of ethical development may think: 'You should act ethically because it's always right to do so, no matter what the consequences and costs are to you personally.'

Question — Ethical issues

Briefly explain the main ethical issues that are involved in the following situations.

(a) Dealing with a repressive authoritarian government abroad
(b) An aggressive advertising campaign
(c) Employee redundancies
(d) Payments or gifts to officials who have the power to help or hinder the payees' operations

Answer

(a) Dealing with unpleasantly authoritarian governments can be supported on the grounds that it **contributes to economic growth and prosperity** and all the benefits they bring to society in both countries concerned. This is a consequentialist argument. It can also be opposed on consequentialist grounds as **contributing to the continuation of the regime**, and on deontological grounds as **fundamentally repugnant**.

(b)   Honesty in advertising is an important problem. Many products are promoted exclusively on image. Deliberately creating the impression that purchasing a particular product will enhance the happiness, success and sex appeal of the buyer can be attacked as **dishonest**. It can be defended on the grounds that the supplier is actually **selling a fantasy or dream** rather than a physical article.

(c)   Dealings with employees are coloured by the **opposing views of corporate responsibility and individual rights**. The idea of a job as property to be defended has now disappeared from labour relations in many countries, but corporate decisions that lead to redundancies are still deplored. This is because of the obvious **impact of sudden unemployment on aspirations and living standards**, even when the employment market is buoyant. Nevertheless, businesses have to consider the cost of employing labour as well as its productive capacity.

(d)   The main problems with payments or gifts to officials are making distinction between those that should never be made, and those that can be made in certain cultural circumstances.

  (i)   **Extortion**. Foreign officials have been known to threaten companies with the complete closure of their local operations unless suitable payments are made.

  (ii)   **Bribery**. This is payment for services to which a company is not legally entitled. There are some fine distinctions to be drawn. For example, some managers regard political contributions as bribery.

  (iii)   **Grease money**. Multinational companies are sometimes unable to obtain services to which they are legally entitled because of deliberate stalling by local officials. Cash payments to the right people may then be enough to oil the machinery of bureaucracy.

  (iv)   **Gifts**. In some cultures (such as Japan) gifts are regarded as an essential part of civilised negotiation, even in circumstances where to Western eyes they might appear ethically dubious. Managers operating in such a culture may feel at liberty to adopt the local customs.

1.2 Role of ethical theory

Ethics is concerned with right and wrong and how conduct should be judged to be good or bad. It is about how we should live our lives and, in particular, how we should **behave towards other people**. It is therefore relevant to all forms of human activity.

Business life is a fruitful source of ethical dilemmas because its whole purpose is **material gain**, the making of profit. Success in business requires a constant, avid search for potential advantage over others and businesspeople are under pressure to do whatever yields such advantage.

It is important to understand that, if ethics is applicable to corporate behaviour at all, it must therefore be a fundamental aspect of **mission**, since everything the organisation does flows from that. Managers responsible for strategic decision-making cannot avoid responsibility for their organisation's ethical standing. They should consciously apply ethical rules to all their decisions in order to filter out potentially undesirable developments. The question is, however, which ethical rules should be obeyed; those that always apply or those that hold only in certain circumstances?

Ethical assumptions underpin all business activity as well as guiding behaviour. The continued existence of capitalism makes certain assumptions about the 'good life' and the desirability of private gain, for example. As we shall see in Chapter 10, accountancy is allegedly not a value-neutral profession. It establishes and follows rules for the protection of shareholder wealth and the reporting of the performance of capital investment. Accordingly accounting, especially in the private sector, can be seen as a servant of capital, making the implicit assumptions about morality that capitalism does.

Key term

> **Relativism** is the view that a **wide variety of acceptable ethical beliefs and practices** exist. The ethics that are most appropriate in a given situation will depend on the conditions at that time.

The relativist approach suggests that all moral statements are essentially subjective and arise from the culture, belief or emotion of the speaker.

Non-cognitivism recognises the differences that exist between the rules of behaviour prevailing in different cultures. The view that right and wrong are culturally determined is called **ethical relativism** or **moral relativism**. Ethical rules will differ in different periods within the same society, and will differ between different societies. Acceptance of ethical relativism implies that a society should not impose moral imperatives strictly, since it accepts that different ethical and belief systems are acceptable.

This is clearly a matter of significance in the context of international business. Managers encountering cultural norms of behaviour that differ significantly from their own may be puzzled to know what rules to follow.

Question   Morality

What can be said about the morality of a society that allows abortion within certain time limits in certain circumstances, or which allows immigration if immigrants fulfil certain requirements (will benefit the local economy)?

Answer

The suggested treatment of these issues suggests that the society is a non-cognitivist, ethically relative society. Banning abortion would be one sign of an ethically absolute society.

1.3.1 Strengths of relativism

(a)   Relativism highlights how ethical positions depend on **what people observe** and biases due to the limits of their perception.

(b)   Relativism also highlights differences in **cultural beliefs**. For example, all cultures may say that it is wrong to kill innocents, but different cultures may have different beliefs about who innocents actually are.

(c)   The philosopher Bernard Crick argued that differing absolutist beliefs result in **moral conflict** between people. (Relativist) ethics should act to resolve such conflicts.

(d)   In the global economy, where companies conduct businesses in many different countries and cultures, adopting a relativist approach presumes **more flexibility** and therefore greater success.

1.3.2 Criticisms of relativism

(a)   Put simply, strong relativism is based on a **fundamental contradiction**. The statement that 'All statements are relative' is itself an absolute, non-relative statement. However, it is possible to argue that some universal truths (certain laws of physics) exist, but deny other supposedly objective truths.

(b)   A common criticism of relativism, particularly by religious leaders, is that it leads to a **philosophy of 'anything goes'**, denying the existence of morality and permitting activities that are harmful to others.

(c) Alternatively some critics have argued for the existence of **natural moral laws** (discussed below). These are not necessarily religious laws. The atheist scientist Richard Dawkins has argued in favour of natural laws.

(d) Ideas such as **objectivity and final truth** do have value – consider for example the ethical principle that we shall discuss later for accountants to be objective.

(e) If it's valid to say that everyone's differing opinions are **right**, then it's equally valid to say that **everyone's differing opinions are wrong**.

1.4 Ethical absolutism and cognitivism   6/08, 12/10

Key term

> **Absolutism** is the view that there is an unchanging set of ethical principles that will apply in all situations, at all times and in all societies.

Absolutist approaches to ethics are built on the principle that **objective, universally applicable moral truths** exist and can be known. There is a set of moral rules that are always true. There are various methods of establishing these.

(a) **Religions** are based on the concept of universally applicable principles.

(b) **Law** can be a source of reference for establishing principles. However, ethics and law are not the same thing. Law must be free from ambiguity. Unlike law, though, ethics can quite reasonably be an arena for debate, about both the principles involved and their application in specific rules.

(c) **Natural law** approaches to ethics are based on the idea that a set of objective or 'natural' moral rules exists and we can come to know what they are. In terms of business ethics, the natural law approach deals mostly with **rights and duties**. Where there is a right, there is also a duty to respect that right. For those concerned with business ethics there are undeniable implications for behaviour towards individuals. Unfortunately, the implications about duties can only be as clear as the rights themselves and there are wide areas in which disagreement about rights persists.

(d) **Deontological approaches** (see below).

Many absolutists would accept that some ethical truths may differ between different cultures. However, they would also believe in certain basic truths that should be common to all cultures (for example 'thou shall not kill').

1.4.1 Strengths of absolutism

(a) Fundamentally the statement that **absolute truth does not exist** is **flawed**. If it does not exist, then the statement that it does not exist cannot be true.

(b) Absolutism lays down certain unambiguous rules that people are able to follow, knowing that their **actions are right**.

1.4.2 Criticisms of absolutism

(a) Absolutist ethics takes **no account of evolving norms** within society and the development of 'advances' in morality; for example, development of the belief that slavery is wrong.

(b) From **what source** should absolutist ethics be derived? Should it be religion, universal laws, human nature? Whatever source is used, it is then possibly subject to human interpretation with the result that different views may exist on the same issue and there will never be universal agreement.

(c) What happens when **two absolutist positions** appear **incompatible**? For example, is it permissible to tell a lie in order to save an innocent life?

(d) A theory can be **true according to a relative framework** as well as true according to an absolute framework. What differs is the nature of the framework and not the truth of the statement.

December 2010 Question 1 asked students to consider an ethical dilemma from both the absolutist and relativist perspectives.

1.5 Deontological ethics   12/08

Deontology is concerned with the application of absolute, universal ethical principles in order to arrive at rules of conduct, the word deontology being derived from the Greek for 'duty'.

Deontology lays down **criteria** by which actions may be judged in advance; the outcomes of the actions are not relevant. The definitive treatment of deontological ethics is found in the work of the 18th century German philosopher, Immanuel Kant.

Kant's approach to ethics is based on the idea that facts themselves are neutral. They are what is. They do not give us any indication of what should be. If we make moral judgements about facts, the criteria by which we judge are separate from the facts themselves. Kant suggested that the criteria come from within ourselves and are based on a **sense of what is right**, an intuitive awareness of the nature of good.

Kant spoke of motivation to act in terms of 'imperatives'.

A **hypothetical imperative** lays down a course of action to achieve a certain result. For instance, if I wish to watch a play in a theatre I must purchase a ticket.

A **categorical imperative**, however, defines a course of action in terms of acting in accordance with **moral duty** without reference to outcomes, desire or motive. For Kant, moral conduct is defined by categorical imperatives. We must act in certain ways because it is right to do so – right conduct is an **end in itself**.

Kant arrived at three formulations of the categorical imperative. These were published at different times, and do overlap. The term maxim means an expression of a general rule of conduct.

(a)   **Principle of Consistency**

'So act that the maxim of your will could hold as a principle establishing universal law.'

This is close to the common sense maxim called the golden rule found in many religious teachings, for example the bible:

'In everything do to others what you would have them do to you, for this sums up the Law and the Prophets.' (Matthew 7:12)

The difference between Kant's views and the golden rule is that under the golden rule, one could inflict harm on others if one was happy for the same harm to be inflicted on oneself. However, Kant would argue that certain actions were universally right or wrong irrespective of the personal, societal or cultural conditions.

Kant went on to suggest that this imperative meant that we have a duty not to act by maxims that result in logical contradictions. Theft of property for example implies that it is permissible to steal, but also implies the existence of property. However, if theft is allowed there can be no property, a logical contradiction. Kant also argued that we should act only by maxims that we believe should be universal maxims. Thus if we only helped others when there was advantage for ourselves, no one would ever give help to others.

(b)   **Principle of Human Dignity**

'Do not treat people simply as means to an end but as an end in themselves.'

The point of this rule is that it distinguishes between **people** and **objects**. We use objects as means to achieve an end. A chair is for sitting on, for instance. People are different.

We regard people differently from the way we regard objects, since they have unique intellects, feelings, motivations, and so on of their own. Treating them as objects denies their rationality and therefore rational action.

Note, however, that this does not preclude us from using people as means to an end as long as we, at the same time, recognise their right to be treated as distinct beings. Clearly, organisations and even society itself could not function if we could not make use of other people's services.

(c) **Principle of Autonomy**

'So act as though you were through your maxims a law-making member of the kingdom of ends.'

Autonomous human beings are not subject to any particular interest and are therefore only subject to the laws which they make for themselves. However, they must regard those laws as binding on others, or they would not be universal and would not be laws at all.

1.5.1 Criticisms of Kant

(a) **Contradictions**

Critics have pointed out a dualism in Kant's views. He sees humans as part of nature whose actions can be explained in terms of natural causes. Yet Kant also argues that human beings are **capable of self-determination** with full freedom of action and in particular an ability to act in accordance with the principles of duty. Man is therefore capable in effect of rising above nature, which appears to conflict with the view that man is a natural animal.

(b) **Consequences**

It is argued that you cannot take actions in a vacuum and must have regard for their **consequences**. The Swiss philosopher Benjamin Constant put forward the 'enquiring murderer' argument. If you agree with Kant and hold that Truth telling must be universal, then one must, if asked, tell a known murderer the location of his prey. Kant's response was that lying to a murderer denied the murderer's rationality, and hence denied the possibility of there being free rational action at all. In addition, Kant pointed out that we cannot always know what the consequences of our actions would be.

(c) **Self-reform**

Kierkegaard argued that, whatever their expectations of others, **people failed to apply Kant's duties** to themselves, either by not exercising laws morally or not punishing themselves if they morally transgressed.

1.6 Teleological or consequentialist ethics: utilitarianism   12/08

There are two versions of consequentialist ethics:

- Utilitarianism – what is best for the greatest number
- Egoism – what is best for me

The teleological approach to ethics is to make moral judgements about courses of action by reference to their **outcomes or consequences**. Right or wrong becomes a question of **benefit or harm** rather than observance of universal principles.

Key term

> **Utilitarianism** can be summed up in the **'greatest good'** principle – 'greatest happiness of the greatest number'.

This says that when deciding on a course of action we should choose the one that is likely to result in the greatest good for the greatest number of people. It therefore contrasts sharply with any absolute or universal notion of morality. The 'right' or 'wrong' can **vary between situations and over time** according to the greatest happiness of the greatest number.

Utilitarianism underlies the assumption that the **operation of the free market** produces the **best possible consequences**. Free markets, it is argued, create wealth, leading to higher tax revenue, and this can pay for greater social welfare expenditures.

Exam focus point

> The Pilot Paper asked for the consequentialist and deontological approaches to ethics to be contrasted.

1.6.1 Problems with utilitarianism

There is an immediate problem here, which is how we are to define what is good for people. Bentham, a philosopher who wrote on utilitarianism, considered that **happiness** was the measure of good and that actions should therefore be judged in terms of their potential for promoting happiness or relieving unhappiness. Others have suggested that longer lists of harmful and beneficial things should be applied.

The utilitarian approach may also be questioned for its potential effect on minorities. A situation in which a large majority achieved great happiness at the expense of creating misery among a small minority would satisfy the 'greatest good' principle. It could not, however, be regarded as ethically desirable.

However, utilitarianism can be a useful guide to conduct. It has been used to derive wide-ranging rules and can be applied to help us make judgements about individual, unique problems.

Exam focus point

Absolutism and deontology come from a similar basis, and so do relativism and teleology. However, absolutism and relativism are **assumptions**, whereas deontology and teleology are ethical **theories**.

If a question asks about the deontology or teleology theories, this will involve more than just discussing the assumptions underpinning them.

 Case Study

A connected problem lies in outcomes that may in fact be beneficial but are not recognised as such. The **structural adjustment programmes** provided by the International Monetary Fund (IMF) are a case in point. They are designed to align a country's economic incentives so that, by improving trade and public finances, they meet an objective, such as debt repayment. The IMF might argue, therefore, that the pain and dislocation suffered are short-term difficulties for long-term wellbeing. Critics of IMF structural adjustment programmes might suggest the opposite; that they are designed to remove money from the very poorest. The rights of the poor are more important than those of bondholders and to insist on repayment is unethical.

Exam focus point

December 2008 Question 4 required discussion of an ethical dilemma from deontological and teleological (consequentialist) ethical perspectives.

1.7 Teleological or consequentialist ethics: egoism

Key term

Egoism states that an act is ethically justified if decision-makers freely decide to pursue their own short-term desires or long-term interests. The subject to all ethical decisions is the self.

Adam Smith argued that an egoistic pursuit of individual self-interest produced a desired outcome for society through **free competition and perfect information** operating in the marketplace. Producers of goods for example have to offer value for money, since competition means that customers will buy from competitors if they don't. Egoism can also link in with enlightened self-interest, such as a business investing in good facilities for its workforce to keep them content and hence maintain their loyalty.

1.7.1 Criticisms of egoism

One criticism of pure egoism is that it makes short-term selfish desires equivalent to longer-term, more beneficial interests. A modified view would give most validity to exercising those short-term desires that were in long-term interests. A more serious criticism has been that the markets do not function perfectly, and that some participants can benefit themselves at the expense of others and also the wider environment – hence the debate on sustainability which we shall consider in Chapter 11. Most fundamentally egoism is argued to be the **ethics of the thief** as well as the short-termist.

1.8 Pluralism

Pluralism accepts that different views may exist on morality, but suggests a consensus may be able to be reached in certain situations. A pluralist viewpoint is helpful in business situations where a range of perspectives have to be understood in order to establish a **course of action**. It emphasises the importance of morality as a **social phenomenon**. Some rules and arrangements need to be established for us to live together and we therefore need a good understanding of the different moralities that we will encounter.

However, a consensus may not always be possible, and this is a key message of this section of the text. Irreconcilable ethical disputes tend to arise when absolutists argue with relativists, or if you have a deontological viewpoint opposed to a teleological viewpoint. For example during the recent debate in the UK about embryology, deontological arguments on the sanctity of life were opposed to teleological arguments about the scientific benefits of experimentation on embryos.

2 Influences on ethics

FAST FORWARD

Ethical decision-making is influenced by **individual and situational factors**.

Individual factors include **age and gender**, **beliefs, education and employment**, how much **control** individuals believe they have over their own situation and their **personal integrity**.

Kohlberg's framework relates to individuals' degree of **ethical maturity**; the extent to which they can take their own ethical decisions.

Situational factors include **the systems of reward**, **authority** and **bureaucracy**, **work roles**, **organisational factors**, and the **national and cultural contexts**.

2.1 The cultural context of ethics and corporate social responsibility
12/14, 6/15

Models of ethical decision-making divide the cultural factors that influence decision-making into two categories.

*   **Individual** – the characteristics of the individual making the decision
*   **Situational** – the features of the context which determine whether the individual will make an ethical or unethical decision

The problem with identifying these factors is that it is difficult to break them down individually since many of them are interdependent. In addition, evidence on the importance of **individual factors** seems to come mainly from the **US**, whereas information on **situational factors** seems mainly to come from **Europe**. This arguably reflects an American focus on individual economic participants, whereas European attention is more focused on the design of economic institutions and how they function morally and promote moral behaviour in others.

2.2 Individual influences

2.2.1 Age and gender

Although some evidence suggests that the ways in which men and women respond to ethical dilemmas may differ, empirical studies do not clearly show whether men or women can be considered as more ethical. Similarly, although different age groups have been influenced by different experiences, again empirical evidence does not suggest that certain age groups are more moral than others.

2.2.2 National and cultural beliefs

By contrast, national and cultural beliefs seem to have a significant effect on ethical beliefs, shaping what individuals regard as acceptable business issues. Hofstede has indicated that significant differences lie in the following four areas.

(a) **Individualism/collectivism** – the extent to which the culture emphasises the autonomous individual as opposed to group and community goals

(b) **Power distance** – how much acceptance there is in the society of the unequal distribution of power, and the perceived gap between juniors and seniors in a society or social structure (eg children/parents, students/teachers, citizens/legislators)

Hickson and Pugh describe power distance as 'how removed subordinates feel from superiors in a social meaning of the word distance. In a high power distance culture, inequality is accepted … in a low power distance culture inequalities and overt status symbols are minimised and subordinates expect to be consulted and to share decisions with approachable managers'.

(c) **Uncertainty avoidance** – individuals' preferences for certainties, rules and absolute truths

(d) **Masculinity/femininity** – or the extent to which money and possessions are valued against people and relationships

These factors may influence how an individual tackles an ethical problem, alone (in an individualist culture) or in consultation (in a collectivist situation). Other influences might be on how individuals respond to ethically questionable directives from their superiors. In power distance cultures, where hierarchy is respected, commands are less likely to be questioned (I was only obeying orders). Globalisation may weaken the influence of national factors, although there is often a close connection between the local culture and a particular geographical region.

2.2.3 Education and employment

By contrast, globalisation might be expected to strengthen the influence of education and employment. There do appear to be some differences in ethical decision-making between those with different educational and professional experiences.

2.2.4 Psychological factors

Psychological factors are concerned with the ways in which people think and therefore **decide what is the morally right or wrong course of action**. Discussion has centred on **cognitive moral development** and **locus of control**.

2.2.5 Locus of control

The locus of control is **how much influence individuals believe** they have over the course of their own lives. Individuals with a high internal locus believe that they can shape their own lives significantly, whereas those with external locus believe that their lives will be shaped by circumstances or luck. This distinction suggests that those with an internal locus will take more responsibility for their actions and are more likely to consider the moral consequences of what they do. However, research does not clearly indicate whether this is true in practice. As we saw in Chapter 5, this may also link into attitudes towards risk and what can be done to deal with risk.

2.2.6 Personal integrity

Integrity can be defined as adhering to moral principles or values. Its ethical consequences are potentially very significant, for example in deciding whether to **whistleblow** on questionable practice at work despite pressure from colleagues or superiors or negative consequences of doing so. However, evidence of its importance is limited because strangely it has not been included in many ethical decision models.

2.2.7 Moral imagination

Moral imagination is the level of awareness individuals have about the variety of moral consequences of what they do and how creatively they reflect on ethical dilemmas. The consequences of having a wide moral imagination could be an ability to see beyond the conventional organisational responses to moral difficulties and formulate different solutions. Again there is little research on this subject, but differing levels of moral imagination would seem to be a plausible reason why individuals with the same work background view moral problems in different ways.

2.3 Kohlberg's cognitive moral development   12/07, 6/09, 6/11, 6/14

Kohlberg's cognitive moral development theories relate to the thought processes people go through when making ethical decisions.

Kohlberg explains the ethical development of individuals in terms of development through three levels of moral development with two stages within each level. Although these levels are meant to relate to an individual's experience, in fact all three levels can be related to ethical behaviour. They show the **reasoning process** of individuals. It is possible that individuals at different levels will make the same moral decisions, but they will do so as a result of different reasoning processes. Kohlberg emphasises **how** the decision is reached, not **what** is decided.

Level 1 Pre-conventional (rewards/punishment/self-interest)

The decisions individuals make on ethical matters will have nothing to do with the ethical issues involved, but instead will depend on the personal advantage or disadvantage to the individual.

Stage 1 Punishment-obedience orientation

Individuals will see ethical decisions in terms of the rewards and punishments that will result.

- How will I be rewarded if I do this?
- What punishment will I suffer if I do this?

Stage 2 Instrumental-relativist orientation

Individuals will see ethical decisions in the more complex terms of acting in their own best interests. They will see the decision in terms of the deals they can make and whether these deals are fair for them. For example, it can mean helping others when others appear overworked, but in return expecting others to help them when the situation is reversed.

Level 2 Conventional

Stage 3 Good boy-nice girl orientation

This stage can be defined as individuals learning to live up to what is **expected** of them by their **immediate circle** (friends, workmates or even close competitors). This can work both ways in a business context. An individual might feel pressurised into staying out for a long lunch because everybody else in his team does. On the other hand, individuals may feel they have to be at work by a certain time because everybody else is, even if it is earlier than their prescribed hours.

Stage 4 Law and order orientation

Individuals are seen as operating on a higher stage within this level if they operate in line with the rules laid down by society or what society believes to be socially or culturally acceptable. This implies looking at what society in general wants, rather than just the opinion of those around them. It certainly means **complying with the law** but it doesn't just mean that. Directors may for example decide to offer better terms to overseas workers because of the activities of pressure groups campaigning against 'sweatshop labour'. Many business managers appear to think with Level 2 reasoning, as do many accountants. Arguably Stage 4 reasoning underlies most behaviour by accountants, as they comply with financial reporting and corporate governance requirements.

Level 3 Post-conventional

The most advanced level relates to individual development towards making their **own ethical decisions** in terms of what they believe to be right, not just acquiescing in what others believe to be right.

Stage 5 Social contract orientation

On the lower stage what individuals believe to be right is in terms of the **basic values** of their society, including ideas of mutual self-interest and the welfare of others. This differs from Stage 4 in that individuals act **according to their own interpretation** of what the basic values are, rather than being influenced by the rules of society or the interpretations of others in society.

Stage 6 Universal ethical principle

On the higher stage, individuals base their decisions on **wider universal ethical principles**, such as justice, equity or rights, and Kant's framework. It also means respecting the demands of individuals' consciences. Business decisions made on these grounds could be disclosure on grounds of right to know that isn't compelled by law, or stopping purchasing from suppliers who test products on animals, on the grounds that animals' rights to be free from suffering should be respected. We must stress here that using Stage 6 reasoning may involve a personal cost, since it may mean failing to comply with existing social norms and regulations as they are seen as unethical.

2.3.1 Criticisms of Kohlberg

Kohlberg argued that the higher the stage, the more ethical a decision was. However, Kohlberg's work has been criticised for:

(a) **Biased sample**

Critics have claimed that Kohlberg's sample is too **narrowly founded** on the typical abstract principles of American males such as fairness, impartiality, rights and maintenance of rules. Carol Gilligan, one of Kohlberg's former students(!), argued that women tend to use an ethic of care with a focus on empathy, harmony and interdependent relationships.

(b) **Own values**

Kohlberg has also been criticised for basing the **framework on his own value judgements**. Critics argue that the framework values rights and justice above other bases of morality, such as basing actions on social consequences or the need to achieve a peaceful settlement of conflict or problems.

(c) **Influences on acceptability**

Kohlberg's argument that the **acceptability of a solution** depends on the method of reasoning has been questioned. The stage of moral development reached here would also appear to be significant.

(d) **Method of reasoning**

Critics have also questioned the assumption that moral action is **primarily decided by formal reasoning**. Social intuitionists argue that people make moral judgements in real life without necessarily considering concerns such as fairness, law, human rights and abstract values. The judgements they make to solve a problem in real life may be different to those if given the same problem as a theoretical problem.

(e) **Assuming individual development**

This is perhaps the most serious criticism of Kohlberg, that individuals do not necessarily progress during their lives, and even if they do progress, it may only be in certain situations. They may use different methods of moral reasoning inside and outside the workplace.

Kohlberg's framework is emphasised significantly in the syllabus, and you therefore will need to consider it when dealing with various ethical situations. For example, does the organisation's ethical framework allow people to make up their own minds on ethics, or does it assume (or promote) a lower level of ethical awareness?

You may also need to identify the Kohlberg level that someone is at, given that they are behaving in a certain way; suggest the most appropriate level at which someone should operate; and produce arguments for and against operating at certain levels.

Question
Kohlberg's framework

Lowfloat Airlines has been under pressure from its institutional shareholders to cut costs and boost margins. Its Board issued an internal memo to all budget holders with a demand to 'seek all possible cost reductions'. The memo is strongly worded and, among other things, encourages budget holders 'to push back the boundaries, innovate, and to think the unthinkable'.

Traditionally a major area of cost had been aeroplane maintenance. Aircraft are constructed largely from aluminium, which is notoriously difficult to weld. In order to overcome this problem the manufacturers of aircraft resorted to the use of aluminium composite rivets to hold the super-structure together. However, due to the molecular properties of the aluminium used, and the extremes of temperature that planes are exposed to in-flight, these rivets fatigue very quickly. Failure to replace rivets has been attributed as the cause of many of the crashes suffered by Russian airlines in the past few years.

Many aviation authorities lay down strict rules on the replacement of aircraft rivets because the reliability of the aircraft is severely compromised if rivets remain on the aircraft beyond a set number of flying hours. The rivets are very expensive due to the price of the raw materials and the fact that they must be stored in freezers prior to fitting to maintain the integrity of the composite. As such, all rivets produced by aerospace manufacturers are colour-coded in line with an international agreement so that once a rivet is past its replacement date it can be easily identified and replaced during maintenance checks.

In order to cut costs senior managers in the Engineering department are recommending that maintenance staff paint over the heads of rivets that are approaching the end of their recommended life. It is the view of the maintenance managers that rules governing rivet use are too strict and that it is perfectly safe to extend their use by two to three years.

At the board meeting the following opinions were expressed.

(a)   We should find out whether and how our competitors are cutting maintenance.

(b)   We shouldn't trade human lives off against shareholder value.

(c)   Passengers travel with us on the assumption that we're providing a safe form of transport.

(d)   We should weigh up the penalties we might suffer if we're discovered against the very high costs of our current maintenance schedule.

(e)   We have an obligation to meet the aircraft industries' regulations.

(f)   We should find out the chances of being grounded if the aviation regulators discover what we've done.

Required

Identify the levels and stages of moral development from Kohlberg's framework that are demonstrated by the six contributions made at the meeting.

Pre-conventional

Stage 1

(f)   The decision is seen solely in terms of how Lowfloat will be punished if its deception is discovered.

Stage 2

(d)   This shows a more sophisticated view of economic self-interest with the costs of different options being weighed up.

Conventional

Stage 3

(a)   This argument is based on Lowfloat doing what its peers are doing. Peers can include competitors, so the director is arguing that Lowfloat should behave in a way that is normal for the industry.

Stage 4

(e)   This argument grounds ethical compliance as obeying aircraft industry regulations. It differs from Stage 3 in that it sees decisions in terms of best practice as defined by regulation; what Lowfloat and its competitors should be doing rather than what they are doing.

Post-conventional

Stage 5

(c)   This is based on the underlying ideas of how society operates and what is expected of business. Passengers, when paying Lowfloat, have the expectation that Lowfloat will be able to convey them safely. If they do not have that expectation of airlines, then the whole business model would be undermined.

Stage 6

(b)   This is based on the absolute ethical view that it is always wrong to give economic considerations priority over human safety. Lowfloat should spend whatever it takes to ensure that passengers are conveyed safely.

2.4 Situational influences

The reason for considering situational influences on moral decision-making is that individuals appear to have 'multiple ethical selves' – they make different decisions in different circumstances. These circumstances might include **issue-related factors** (the nature of the issue and how it is viewed in the organisation) and **context-related factors** (the expectations and demands that will be placed on people working in an organisation).

2.5 Issue-related factors

2.5.1 Moral intensity

Thomas Jones proposed a list of six criteria that decision-makers will use to decide how ethically significant an issue was, and therefore what they should do.

- **Magnitude of consequences** – the harms or the benefits that will result

- **Social consequences** – the degree of general agreement about the problem

- **Probability of effect** – the probability of the harms or benefits actually happening

- **Temporal immediacy** – the speed with which the consequences are likely to occur; if they are likely to take years, the moral intensity may be lower

- **Proximity** – the feelings of nearness that the decision-maker has for those who will suffer the impacts of the ethical decision

- **Concentration of effect** – whether some people will suffer greatly or many people will suffer lightly

Research suggests that moral intensity is significant but has to be seen in the context of how an issue is perceived in an organisation.

2.5.2 Moral framing

Moral framing sets the context for how issues are **perceived** in organisations. Language is very important. Using words such as fairness and honesty is likely to trigger moral thinking. However, evidence suggests that many managers are reluctant to frame issues in moral terms, seeing it as promoting disharmony, distorting decision-making and suggesting that they are not practical. Instead, issues are more likely to be discussed in terms of **rational corporate self-interest**.

2.6 Context-related factors

2.6.1 Systems of reward

Reward mechanisms have obvious potential consequences for ethical behaviour. This works both ways. Basing awards on sales values achieved may encourage questionable selling practices. Failing to reward ethical behaviour (or worse still, penalising whistleblowers or other staff who act ethically) will not encourage an ethical culture.

Sadly a majority of studies in this area seem to indicate that there is a significant link between the rewarding of unethical behaviour and its continuation.

2.6.2 Authority

There are various ways in which managers may encourage ethical behaviour, for example by **direct instructions** to subordinates and by setting subordinates **targets** that are so challenging that they can only be achieved through taking unethical shortcuts. Failing to act can be as bad as acting, for example failing to prevent bullying. Studies suggest that many employees perceive their managers as lacking ethical integrity.

2.6.3 Bureaucracy

Key term

> **Bureaucracy** is a system characterised by detailed rules and procedures, impersonal hierarchical relations and a fixed division of tasks.

Bureaucracy underpins the authority and reward system, and may have a number of impacts on individual's reactions to ethical decision-making.

- **Suppression of moral autonomy** – individual ethical beliefs tend to be overridden by the rules and roles of the bureaucracy

- **Instrumental morality** – seeing morality in terms of following procedures rather than focusing on the moral substance of the goals themselves

- **Distancing** individuals from the consequences of what they do

- **Denial of moral status** – that ultimately individuals are resources for carrying out the organisation's will rather than autonomous moral beings

2.6.4 Work roles

Education and experience build up expectations of how people in particular roles will act. Strong evidence suggests that the expectations staff have about the roles that they adopt in work will override the individual ethics that may influence their decisions in other contexts.

2.6.5 Organisational field

Key term

> An **organisational field** is a community of organisations with a common 'meaning system' and whose participants interact more frequently with one another than those outside the field.

Organisations within an organisation field tend to share a common business environment, such as a common system of training or regulation. This means that they tend to cohere round common norms and values.

Within an organisational field a **recipe** is a common set of assumptions about organisational purposes and how to manage organisations. If the recipe is followed, it means that organisations within the organisational field can provide consistent standards for consumers, for example. However, it can also mean that managers within the field cannot appreciate the lessons that could be learned from organisations outside the field, and therefore transition outside the field may be difficult.

 Case Study

An example would be a private sector manager joining a public service organisation and having to get used to different traditions and mechanisms; for example, having to build consensus into the decision-making process.

The result of being in an organisational field can be a desire to achieve **legitimacy** – meeting the **expectations** that those in the same organisational field have in terms of the assumptions, behaviour and strategies that will be pursued.

2.6.6 Organisational culture

Key term

> **Organisational culture** is the 'basic assumptions and beliefs that are shared by members of an organisation, that operate unconsciously and define in a basic taken-for-granted fashion an organisation's view of itself and its environment.'
> (Handy)

Organisational culture relates to ways of acting, talking, thinking and evaluating. It can include shared:

- **Values** that often have 'official' status being connected to the organisation's mission statement but which can be vague (acting in the interests of the community)

- **Beliefs** that are more specific than assumptions but represent aspects of an organisation that are talked about, for example using 'ethical suppliers'

- **Behaviours**, the ways in which people within the organisation and the organisation itself operate, including work routines and symbolic gestures

- **Taken for granted assumptions**, which are at the core of the organisation's culture which people find difficult to explain but are central to the organisation; the **paradigm** represents the common assumptions and collective experience that an organisation must have to function meaningfully

Organisational culture may be different to (may conflict with) the official rules of the bureaucracy. Unsurprisingly it has been identified as a key element in decisions of what is morally right or wrong, as employees become conditioned by it into particular attitudes to ethical decision-making.

In addition to the main organisational culture, there may also be **distinct subcultures** that are often dependent on the way the organisation is structured, for example function or division subcultures.

2.6.7 National and cultural context

In an organisational context, this is the **nation** in which the ethical decision is made rather than the nationality of the decision-maker. If someone spends a certain length of time working in another country, their views of ethical issues may be shaped by the norms of that other country, for example on sexual harassment. Globalisation may complicate the position on this.

Case Study

In May 2009 revelations about the size and nature of MPs' expense claims rocked politics in the UK. The controversy could be viewed from several ethical viewpoints. The controversy certainly illustrated most of Kohlberg's stages of reasoning.

Pre-conventional Stage 2. The idea of deals in MPs' own interests was illustrated by one argument used to defend the system. The argument was that a generous expenses system had been introduced to compensate MPs for the failure to grant them politically unpopular salary rises. Labour MP Harry Cohen stated that the former Conservative minister John Moore had told MPs 'Go out boys and spend it' when he introduced a big uprating of the allowance in the 1980s to head off a pay revolt by backbench Tories.

Conventional Stage 3. Some MPs and their supporters claimed that they were being unfairly singled out: 'He has only done what everyone else has done, so I don't blame him for that.'

Conventional Stage 4. The argument used by many MPs was that their claims were within the rules that Parliament had approved, and were granted by the UK Parliament's Fees Office. This for example was the argument used by Labour politician John Prescott to justify expenditure on the fitting of mock Tudor beams to the front of his constituency home in Hull. 'Every expense was within the rules of the House of Commons on claiming expenses at the time.'

Post-conventional Stage 5. An argument used by many critics was that, in a time of recession, MPs should not be using taxpayers' money to fund large expense claims. 'He has claimed the maximum amount and I find that morally shocking. The constituency he represents is extremely deprived in parts.'

Post-conventional Stage 6. Some critics went further, arguing that MPs enjoyed a position of trust. They should not abuse this by claiming for categories of expenses that were not entirely necessary to carry out their duties. 'It's not a question of what the rules were. If he and others cannot and did not see what they were doing as morally wrong, then it's time to move aside.'

3 Practical situations

FAST FORWARD

Exam questions will often be founded on what should be done if breaches of laws, regulations or ethical guidelines occur. **Close relationships** between the parties or other **conflicts of interest** will often be a complication.

3.1 Examination questions

Examination questions will expect you to be able to apply your understanding of ethical issues to practical problems arising in organisations. Later in this chapter we are going to see how to deal with such questions, but first we are going to take the bare bones of a situation and see how it might be built up into the kind of scenario you will have to face.

3.2 The problem

The exam may present you with a scenario, typically containing an array of detail of which much is potentially relevant. The problem, however, will be one or other of two basic types.

(a) **A wishes B to do C which is in breach of D**

where A = a situation, person, group of people, institution or the like
B = you/an accountant, the person with the ethical dilemma
C = acting, or refraining from acting, in a certain way
D = an ethical principle, quite possibly one of ACCA's fundamental principles

(b) Alternatively, the problem may be that A has done C, B has become aware of it and D requires some kind of response from B.

3.3 Example: the problem

An accountant joined a manufacturing company as its Finance Director. The company had acquired land on which it built industrial units. The Finance Director discovered that, before they had started at the company, one of the units had been sold and the selling price was significantly larger than the amount which appeared in the company's records. The difference had been siphoned off to another company – one in which their boss, the Managing Director, was a major shareholder. Furthermore, the Managing Director had kept their relationship with the second company a secret from the rest of the board.

The Finance Director confronted the Managing Director and asked them to reveal their position to the board. However, the Managing Director refused to disclose their position to anyone else. The secret profits on the sale of the unit had been used, they said, to reward the people who had secured the sale. Without their help, they added, the company would be in a worse position financially.

The Finance Director then told the Managing Director that unless they reported to the board they would have to inform the board members themselves. The Managing Director still refused. The Finance Director disclosed the full position to the board.

The problem is of the **second basic type**. **B** is of course the easiest party to identify. Here it is the **Finance Director**. A is clear, as well; it is the **Managing Director**. C is the **MD's breach of their directorial duties** regarding related party transactions not to obtain any personal advantage from their position of director without the consent of the company for whatever gain or profit they have obtained. **D** is the **principle that requires B not to be a party to an illegal act**. (Note that we distinguish between ethical and legal obligations. B has legal obligations as a director of the company. They have ethical obligations not to ignore their legal obligations. In **this** case the two amount to the same thing.)

3.4 Relationships

You may have a feeling that the resolution of the problem described above is just too easy, and you would be right. This is because A, B, C and D are either people, or else situations involving people, who stand in certain relationships to each other.

- A may be B's boss, B's subordinate, B's equal in the organisational hierarchy, B's husband, B's friend.

- B may be new to the organisation, or well established and waiting for promotion, or ignorant of some knowledge relevant to the situation that A possesses or that the people affected by C possess.

- C or D, as already indicated, may involve some person(s) with whom B or A have a relationship – for example the action may be to misrepresent something to a senior manager who controls the fate of B or A (or both) in the organisation.

Identify the relationships in the scenario above. What are the possible problems arising from these relationships?

Answer

The MD is the Finance Director's boss. They are also a member of the board and longer established as such than B, the Finance Director.

In outline, the problems arising are that **by acting ethically the Finance Director will alienate the MD.** Even if the problem were to be resolved the episode would sour all future dealings between these two parties. Also, **the board may not be sympathetic to the accusations of a newcomer**. The Finance Director may find that they are ignored or even dismissed.

Relationships should never be permitted to affect ethical judgement. If you knew that your best friend at work had committed a major fraud, for example, **integrity** would demand that **as a last resort** you would have to bring it to the attention of somebody in authority. But note that this is only as a last resort. Try to imagine what you would do in practice in this situation.

Surely your **first course** would be to try to **persuade your friend** that what they had done was wrong, and that they themselves had an ethical responsibility to own up. Your **second option**, if this failed, might be to try to get **somebody** (perhaps somebody outside the organisation) that you knew could **exert pressure** on your friend to persuade them to own up.

There is obviously a limit to how far you can take this. The important point is that just because you are dealing with a situation that involves ethical issues, this **does not mean that all the normal principles of good human relations and good management have to be suspended**. In fact this is the time when such business principles are most important.

3.5 Consequences

Actions have consequences and the consequences are quite likely to have their own ethical implications (remember the teleological approach we covered earlier in this chapter).

In the example given above, we can identify the following further issues.

(a)   The MD's secret transaction appears to have been made in order to secure the sale of an asset, the proceeds of which are helping to prop up the company financially. Disclosure of the truth behind the sale may mean that the company is pursued for compensation by the buyer of the site. The **survival of the company** as a whole may be jeopardised.

(b)   If the truth behind the transaction becomes public knowledge this could be highly damaging for the company's **reputation**, even if it can show that only one person was involved.

(c)   The board may simply rubber stamp the MD's actions and so the Finance Director may still find that they are expected to be party to dishonesty. (This assumes that the **company as a whole is amoral** in its approach to ethical issues. In fact the MD's refusal to disclose the matter to the board suggests otherwise.)

In the last case we are back to square one. In the first two cases, the Finance Director has to consider the ethicality or otherwise of taking action that could lead to the collapse of the company, extensive redundancies, unpaid creditors and shareholders, and so on.

3.6 Actions

In spite of the difficulties, your aim will usually be to reach a satisfactory resolution to the problem. **The actions that you recommend** will often include the following.

(a) **Informal discussions** with the parties involved

(b) **Further investigation** to establish the full facts of the matter. What extra information is needed?

(c) The **tightening up of controls or the introduction of new ones**, if the situation arose due to laxity in this area; this will often be the case and the principles of professional competence and due care and of technical standards will usually be relevant

(d) **Attention to organisational matters** such as changes in the management structure, improving communication channels, attempting to change attitudes

Question   Cunning plan

Your finance director has asked you to join a team planning a takeover of one of your company's suppliers. An old schoolfriend works as an accountant for the company concerned, the finance director knows this, and has asked you to try and find out 'anything that might help the takeover succeed, but it must remain secret'.

Answer

There are three issues here. Firstly you have a **conflict of interest** as the finance director wants you to keep the takeover a secret, but you probably feel that you should tell your friend what is happening as it may affect their job.

Second, the finance director is asking you to deceive your friend. Deception is unprofessional behaviour and will break your ethical guidelines. Therefore the situation is presenting you with **two conflicting demands**. It is worth remembering that no employer should ask you to break your ethical rules.

Finally, the request to break your own ethical guidelines constitutes **unprofessional behaviour** by the finance director. You should consider reporting them to the relevant body.

Exam focus point

In an internal company role, ethical problems could be in the following forms.

- Conflict of duties to different staff superiors

- Discovering an illegal act or fraud perpetrated by the company (ie its directors)

- Discovering a fraud or illegal act perpetrated by another employee

- Pressure from superiors to take certain viewpoints, for example towards budgets (pessimistic/ optimistic etc) or not to report unfavourable findings

4 Frameworks for dealing with ethical situations

4.1 Dealing with questions   6/10, 6/14

FAST FORWARD

In a situation involving ethical issues, there are **practical steps** that should be taken.

- Analysis of the situation
- Identifying the ethical issues
- Considering the alternative options
- Stating the best course of action based on the steps above
- Justifying your recommendations

The **AAA** and **Tucker** models can be used to resolve ethical dilemmas.

An article in a student magazine contained the following advice for candidates who wish to achieve good marks in ethics questions. (The emphasis is BPP's.)

'The precise question requirements will vary, but in general marks will be awarded for:

- **Analysis of the situation**

- **A recognition of ethical issues**

- **Explanation if appropriate of relevant part of ethical guidelines**, and **interpretation** of its relevance to the question

- Making clear, logical and appropriate **recommendations** for action. Making inconsistent recommendations does not impress examiners

- **Justifying recommendations** in practical business terms and in ethical terms

As with all scenario-based questions there is likely to be **more than one acceptable answer**, and marks will depend on how well the case is argued, rather than for getting the "right" answer.'

As well as helping you deal with ethical situations in the P1 exam, this section will also help you demonstrate the competencies you need to fulfil performance objective 1 of the PER. In particular it will help you deal with situations where your professional ethics, values and judgements are challenged.

4.1.1 Weaknesses in answers

Possibly the most **common fault** in students' answers to questions on ethics is that they include large **amounts of unanalysed detail copied out from the question scenarios** in their answers. This earns no marks.

Other things to avoid doing include:

Paraphrasing the question	This doesn't add anything.
Regurgitating the Ethical Guidelines	As in other areas of the exam, you won't get any credit unless you apply relevant knowledge.
Failing to make a decision or failing to recommend action if asked	The examiner may ask you to consider different viewpoints, but if you are asked to advise or recommend you must do so.
Justifying your decision merely by saying 'This should be done because it's ethical'	That won't convince the marker. Stronger justification will be necessary.

4.2 Justifying your decision

The article quoted above says that **marks will be awarded for 'justifying recommendations in practical business terms and in ethical terms'**. A good example is set out below.

> 'Perhaps the first thing to do is to **report** the whole matter, **in confidence** and **informally**, to the chief internal auditor with suggestions that a **tactful investigation** is undertaken to **verify as many of the facts** as possible. The fact that the sales manager has already been tackled (informally) about the matter may be a positive advantage as **he/she may be recruited** to assist in the investigation. It could however be a problem as the information needed for further **investigation** may have already been removed. **Tact** is crucial as handling the matter the wrong way could adversely influence the whole situation. An understanding of who participants are and how they are implicated can be used positively to bring about change with the **minimum of disruption**.'

4.3 Ethics models

In the exam you may be asked to consider an ethical decision and how you do so is left up to you. In other instances you may be asked to use a specific model. Two models highlighted by the examiner are:

- American Accounting Association model
- Tucker's 5 question model

You can also use these models if the choice is left up to you.

4.4 American Accounting Association (AAA) model   12/09

The AAA model was set out in a report by Langenderfer and Rockness in 1990. They recommended a seven-step model:

Step	Question	Approach to use in answers
1	**What are the facts of the case?**	The aim is to show clearly what is at issue. A brief summary should suffice, maybe just one sentence.
2	**What are the ethical issues in the case?**	These should be based on the facts.
3	**What are the norms, principles and values related to the case?**	This means placing the decision in its social, ethical and professional behaviour context, including considering professional codes of ethics or social expectations of the profession. Use the terminology of the ethical guidelines, for example fairness, bias and influence when discussing objectivity. Don't be afraid to use the term justice if that's most appropriate.
4	**What are the alternative courses of action?**	State each course without making reference at this stage to the norms, principles and values. To generate ideas, consider the issue from the points of view of the 'guilty' party and the organisation.
5	**What is the best course of action that is consistent with the norms, principles and values identified in Step 3?**	Combine Steps 3 and 4 to see which options accord with the norms and which don't.
6	**What are the consequences of each possible course of action?**	This is to ensure that each of the outcomes are unambiguous.
7	**What is the decision?**	This is based on the analysis in Steps 1-6.

Question

Cadge is a clothing manufacturer based in Europe that supplies various large retail groups. Over the last two years it has suffered falls in profits due to the loss of a couple of large contracts and a general fall in demand for its clothes. Industry opinion is that Cadge has failed to innovate sufficiently in its clothing designs.

A few days ago an unknown factory owner based outside Europe contacted Cadge's Design Director out of the blue. He introduced himself only as 'Mr Sim', and offered to sell – for what appeared to be a reasonable sum of money – the new up and coming season's designs belonging to one of Cadge's key competitors who was using Sim's factories to manufacture its goods. If these designs could be purchased by Cadge and launched onto the market before the competition could launch theirs, Cadge's profitability for the coming year could significantly increase.

Required

Analyse, using the American Accounting Association model, the decision of whether to accept Mr Sim's offer.

Answer

What are the facts of the case?

The facts are that the company has been offered some designs that appear to have been stolen.

What are the ethical issues in the case?

The ethical issue is whether to gain a business advantage by using designs that belong to someone else.

What are the norms, principles and values related to the case?

Accepting the offer is likely to be illegal in Cadge's home country or illegal under international design protection laws. Even if the action could be justified as legal, it would demonstrate a lack of honesty and integrity if Cadge used designs that belonged to someone else whom it had not paid.

What are the alternative courses of action?

1   Reject Mr Sim's offer.
2   Accept Mr Sim's offer, pay Mr Sim money and use the designs.

What is the best course of action that is consistent with the norms, principles and values identified in Step 3?

The best course of action is Option 1, as accepting the designs would be dishonest. The directors would need to decide whether to have no further dealings with Mr Sim, or to whistleblow on him to the competitors.

What are the consequences of each possible course of action?

1   Cadge will not be able to gain a competitive advantage.

2   Cadge may be able to gain a temporary advantage, but the consequences if the transaction is discovered could be severe. Cadge's customers are likely to view this activity unfavourably and this could jeopardise existing contracts. The board may come under pressure from other shareholders who find this behaviour unacceptable.

What is the decision?

The ethical decision in Option 1, to refuse Mr Sim's offer.

4.5 Tucker's 5 question model   12/08, 12/12

Tucker's model can also be used to determine the most ethical outcome in a particular situation, generally an ethical problem for business. It focuses on five key questions. Is the decision:

- Profitable
- Legal
- Fair
- Right
- Sustainable

Not all of Tucker's criteria will be relevant in every situation. In addition, there are complications with each of the criteria.

Is the decision:	
Profitable?	Compared with what? Use of profitability as criteria also implies the Tucker model may be more useful for business decisions than for individuals' moral dilemmas
Legal?	This obviously depends on the jurisdiction(s) involved
Fair?	In whose perspective? Need to consider who stakeholders are and the impact of the decision on them
Right?	This depends on the ethical position; in particular the distinction between deontological and teleological approaches of whether account should be taken of the consequences of the transaction is significant
Sustainable?	Is the decision environmentally sound or sustainable in other ways?

Exam focus point

December 2008 Question 1 included a good illustration of how an ethical decision could be analysed using Tucker's model.

 Question   Tucker's 5 question model

Refuse Recycling (RR) is a large recycling company, which collects waste and recycles a large variety of products. Its most profitable product for recycling is glass, although it also collects other materials including plastics. Most of the plastics it collects are under local government contracts for domestic waste collection and recycling. Because RR lacks facilities and expertise in the recycling of plastics, the plastic waste it collects is sorted by item/type and transported long distances to specialised plastic recycling plants operated by other recycling companies.

For some time now the board of RR has been concerned about reduced margins. As a result of a study initiated by the finance director, the company has established that the collection and recycling of plastics is proving unprofitable. Transportation costs have been extremely high, as many recycling operators have not been accepting plastics collected by RR in the hope that this would make the contracts less profitable for RR. They believed this would increase their own chances of winning future tenders.

The chairman of RR recently called a board meeting to examine the terms of the company's existing contracts with local governments for domestic waste collection and recycling. At this meeting the finance director stated that, though he felt strongly about the value of recycling to society as a whole, he also felt that RR simply should not continue to perform unprofitable activities if there was 'a way out'.

On examining the contracts the board discovered that several specified an overall percentage of material collected that must be recycled of 70% (others specified 80%). Based on the volumes of paper, glass, metal and plastics collected over the past year, the board decided that in some locations RR could meet a contractual obligation of 70% without recycling any plastics at all. Plastic collected under these '70% contracts' could simply be dumped at landfill sites, with significant savings from reduced sorting and

transport costs. Some board members had reservations about implementing this policy, but were swayed by the strength of the finance director's reasoning.

The dumping of plastics is about to start. Although the board of RR feels the company's actions do not breach the terms of their contracts, it was decided that the vehicles involved in the dumping process would not carry the RR name.

Required

Analyse the board's decision to dump plastics at landfill sites, using Tucker's 5 question model.

Answer

Using Tucker's five question model, we have to ask, is the decision:

Profitable

The main justification for the decision is to **increase short-term profitability** and if the finance director's figures are correct, that aim has been achieved. However, the effect on long-term profitability may be very different if what RR has done becomes public. A recycling company, even one operating in a commercial environment, must be seen as **caring about the environment** if it is to attract and retain customers. Some local government customers may try to cancel existing contracts on the grounds that RR is not abiding by the spirit of these contracts. In any case local government agencies are likely to be unwilling to renew contracts and RR may be unable to win other new contracts.

Legal

Clearly RR is using **legal landfill sites**. Assuming the board has interpreted the contracts correctly, the company has not breached the strict legal terms of the contract even if it has possibly breached the spirit. Transporting the waste in unmarked vans may be questionable legally though.

Fair

If the view is taken that the customers are vital stakeholders, then what RR is doing is unfair to them, as they may have made **claims** about the support they are giving to recycling which are unintentionally misleading. Any loss of reputation that local authorities suffer in the fallout that follows discovery of what RR has done may be particularly serious, as it may impact on re-election chances of local councillors. The only mitigation for RR under this heading is that the problem has arisen because of other recycling operators refusing to take RR's waste. They too appear to be putting their commercial interests ahead of the objective of supporting recycling.

Right

The fact that the waste is being **transported in unmarked vans** is effectively an admission by the board that what they are doing is indefensible on moral grounds. Any mitigation may be based on other criteria, that RR is acting within the law and doing its best for its shareholders, but it is nearly impossible to defend the actions on these grounds.

Sustainable

This is potentially the easiest criterion of them all, as what RR is doing appears to be going against environmental best practice. Apart from anything else, RR's ability to continue doing this depends on the **availability of landfill sites**. In some countries they are running out. The only environmental justification is that by using the landfill sites, RR is cutting down the miles plastics are transported, and is reducing its carbon footprint to that extent.

Exam focus point

> If you are asked to apply either the AAA model or Tucker's model, but struggle to apply certain stages of either model, say so in your answer. The examiner wants you to identify the weaknesses in any model you are asked to use.

How would different people operating at each of Kohlberg's levels of ethical reasoning view Tucker's criteria? (Kohlberg's three levels are pre-conventional, conventional and post-conventional.)

Answer

Here are some suggestions, although this is not a definitive answer.

	Pre-conventional	**Conventional**	**Post-conventional**
Profitable	A very important criteria, as the pre-conventional level is based on the idea of rewards for self.	Profitability may be seen as quite important depending on the local ethos – very important if the decision-maker works in a major financial centre for example. Decision-makers will also be influenced by any local requirements in company law to seek profit maximisation.	Surprisingly perhaps this could be a very important criterion. Equally it could have no importance if the decision-maker believes it goes against other concepts. Those holding the pristine capitalist viewpoint (discussed further in Chapter 11) would argue that companies have a moral duty to make profits to reward the shareholders whose finance underwrites their existence. Use of monies for other purposes is effectively theft of shareholders' funds under this stance.
Legal	The pre-conventional level will be more concerned with the consequences of breaking the law than its content.	At the higher conventional level this will be seen as all-important. At the lower level it may depend on the views of local society, some societies having a more relaxed view to certain laws than others.	Strangely, obedience to the law may not be seen as so significant at this level. This is because post-conventional viewpoint may see the law as inadequately defining ethics and thus decision-makers need to go beyond it. Alternatively some laws may be seen as immoral (for example, requiring the decision-maker to swear allegiance to a cause with which they disagree).
Fair	The concept of fairness is likely to be interpreted as confined to fairness to the decision-maker alone.	Fairness may be significant if it means fairness to others in society whose approval is sought, or fairness is a concept enshrined in law.	Fairness may well be a key ethical concept, but fairness to whom may be a difficult issue, dependent on who are seen as legitimate stakeholders.

	Pre-conventional	Conventional	Post-conventional
Right	The consequences of being caught doing wrong are more likely to be an issue than whether the decision is actually right.	The decision-maker will see what is right as significant, but they will see right as defined by others in their local society or right as enshrined in law. The decision-maker may not be able to supply their own definition of what is right.	Right will always be important for post-conventional decision-makers. Remember though the distinction between the two levels at this stage. Right may be as defined by the decision-maker's society's ethics or it may be outside society's ethics.
Sustainable	Again the consequences for the decision-maker rather than anyone else will be paramount.	This depends on how sustainability is viewed in the decision-maker's local environment, or the importance given to it in law. The campaigns conducted by many organisations internally to improve sustainability awareness are perhaps an acknowledgement that many of their employees are taking decisions at this level. Thus the organisations are trying to change the ethos to make employees behave in a more socially responsible way.	Sustainability may well be a key ethical concept for post-conventional decision-makers, although what sustainability means exactly may cause problems (discussed further in Chapter 11).

Chapter Roundup

- A key debate in ethical theory is whether ethics can be determined by **objective**, **universal principles**. How important the **consequences of actions** should be in determining an ethical position is also a significant issue.

- Ethical decision-making is influenced by **individual and situational factors**.

  Individual factors include **age and gender**, **beliefs**, **education and employment**, how much **control** individuals believe they have over their own situation and their **personal integrity**.

  Kohlberg's framework relates to individuals' degree of **ethical maturity**, the extent to which they can take their own ethical decisions.

  Situational factors include **the systems of reward**, **authority** and **bureaucracy**, **work roles**, **organisational factors**, and the **national and cultural contexts**.

- Exam questions will often be founded on what should be done if breaches of laws, regulations or ethical guidelines occur. **Close relationships** between the parties or other **conflicts of interest** will often be a complication.

- In a situation involving ethical issues, there are **practical steps** that should be taken.

  - Analysis of the situation
  - Identifying the ethical issues
  - Considering the alternative options
  - Stating the best course of action based on the steps above
  - Justifying your recommendations

  The **AAA** and **Tucker** models can be used to analyse ethical dilemmas.

Quick Quiz

1   Which view of ethics states that right and wrong are culturally determined?

   A   Ethical relativism   C   Teleological
   B   Cognitivism   D   Deontological

2   Fill in the blank:

   The .... approach to ethics is to make moral judgements about courses of action by reference to their outcomes or consequences.

3   In what areas of national and cultural beliefs has Hofstede identified significant differences?

4   At which stage of the Kohlberg model do individuals make their own ethical decisions in terms of what they believe to be right, not just acquiescing in what others believe to be right?

   A   Pre-conventional   C   Post-conventional
   B   Conventional

5   Fill in the blank:

   The .... is the amount of influence individuals believe they have over the course of their own lives.

6   What are the six criteria that Jones suggests will be used to determine how significant an ethical issue is?

7   What are the seven stages of the AAA model?

8   What are the five questions in the Tucker model?

1   A   Ethical relativism

2   Teleological or consequentialist

3
- Individualism vs collectivism
- Acceptance of unequal distribution of power and status
- How much individuals wish to avoid uncertainties
- Masculinity vs femininity, money and possessions vs people and relationships

4   C   Post-conventional

5   Locus of control

6
- Magnitude of consequences
- Social consequences
- Probability of effect
- Temporal immediacy
- Proximity
- Concentration of effect

7
- What are the facts of the case?
- What are the ethical issues in the case?
- What are the norms, principles and values related to the case?
- What are the alternative courses of action?
- What is the best course of action that is consistent with the norms, principles and values identified in Step 3?
- What are the consequences of each possible course of action?
- What is the decision?

8   Is the decision:

- Profitable
- Legal
- Fair
- Right
- Sustainable

Now try the question below from the Practice Question Bank.

Number	Level	Marks	Time
Q9	Examination	25	49 mins

10

Professional ethics

Topic list	Syllabus reference
1 Corporate codes of ethics	E4
2 Professional codes of ethics	B2, E4, E6
3 Independence and conflicts of interest	B2, E5, E6
4 Problems facing accountants in business	B2, E4, E5, E6
5 Bribery and corruption	E5
6 The accountancy profession and the public interest	E3

Introduction

In this chapter we examine how organisations and professional bodies encourage ethical behaviour. In Section 1 we look at corporate codes, covering their contents and impact.

In Section 2 we discuss the main features of professional codes. As with governance codes, a key issue is whether the guidance should be based on principles or on detailed rules. Section 3 examines independence issues that affect accountants in practice. You will have covered these before, but we recap them as they are emphasised in the study guide.

In Section 4 we look in detail at the role of accountants in business and the ethical problems that they face and focus on bribery and corruption in Section 5.

Lastly we go beyond the concepts of ethical codes to discuss the wider context of serving the public interest. Defining an acceptable position for the profession has proved very difficult, partly because of the varying definition of public interest, and how much weight to give the interests of different stakeholders.

Study guide

		Intellectual level
B2	**Internal control, audit and compliance in corporate governance**	
(b)	Explain and discuss the importance of auditor independence in all client-auditor situations (including internal audit).	3
(c)	Explain and assess the nature and sources of risks to auditor independence. Assess the hazard of auditor capture.	3
E3	**Professions and the public interest**	
(a)	Explain and explore the nature of a profession and professionalism.	2
(b)	Describe and assess what is meant by the public interest.	2
(c)	Describe the role of, and assess the influence of, accounting as a profession in the organisational context.	3
(d)	Analyse the role of accounting as a profession in society.	2
(e)	Recognise accounting's role as a value-laden profession capable of influencing the distribution of power and wealth in society.	3
(f)	Describe and critically evaluate issues surrounding accounting and acting against the public interest.	3
E4	**Professional practice and codes of ethics**	
(a)	Describe and explore the areas of behaviour covered by corporate codes of ethics.	3
(b)	Describe and assess the content of, and principles behind, professional codes of ethics.	3
(c)	Describe and assess the codes of ethics relevant to accounting professionals such as the IESBA (IFAC) or professional body codes.	3
E5	**Conflicts of interest and the consequences of unethical behaviour**	
(a)	Describe and evaluate issues associated with conflicts of interest and ethical conflict resolution.	3
(b)	Explain and evaluate the nature of impacts of ethical threats and safeguards.	3
(c)	Explain and explore how threats to independence can affect ethical behaviour.	3
(d)	Explain and explore 'bribery' and 'corruption' in the context of corporate governance, and assess how these can undermine confidence and trust.	3
(e)	Describe and assess best practice measures for reducing and combating bribery and corruption, and the barriers to implementing such measures.	3
E6	**Ethical characteristics of professionalism**	
(b)	Explain and analyse issues related to the application of ethical behaviour in a professional context.	2
(c)	Describe and discuss rules-based and principles-based approaches to resolving ethical dilemmas encountered in professional accounting.	2

Exam guide

You may gain a few marks for describing basic ethical threats, but the main focus in questions on ethics will be on practical situations. In these situations the ethical issues, or at any rate the solutions, will not be clear-cut. Although resignation or withdrawing from an audit or assurance engagement may be the last resort that has to be adopted in certain circumstances, it will **not** always be the solution.

Although we have quoted from IESBA and ACCA guidance as obvious examples of best practice, the examiner has emphasised that these are not the only sources of ethical guidance. Using examples from other, relevant codes will also gain you credit.

You should also expect to see some discussion questions on the neutrality (or otherwise) of the accountancy profession and whether its activities unduly support certain interests in society.

1 Corporate codes of ethics

FAST FORWARD

Organisations have responded to pressure to be seen to act ethically by publishing **ethical codes**, setting out their **values and responsibilities** towards stakeholders.

1.1 Corporate codes and corporate culture

Exam focus point

An examination question may include an extract from a set of corporate guidelines on which you will be expected to comment. Even if you are not given specific information about a company's ethical policy, though, remember that all organisations have ethical standards. There will be something in the information that you are given that will give some indication of the ethical values held by the people or departments involved.

You may also be asked to criticise or evaluate a code of ethics, to interpret actions in a case scenario in the light of a code or to argue the pros and cons of adopting corporate codes of ethics.

Question   Code of ethics

Here are some extracts from an article that appeared in the UK *Financial Times*.

> 'Each company needs its own type of code: to reflect the national culture, the sector culture, and the exact nature of its own structure.
>
> The nature of the codes is changing. NatWest's code, for example, tries to do much more than simply set out a list of virtues. Its programme involves not only the production of a code, but a dedicated effort to teach ethics, and a system by which the code can be audited and monitored.
>
> For example, it has installed a 'hot-line' and its operation is monitored by internal auditors. The board of NatWest wanted it to be confidential – within the confines of legal and regulatory requirements – and the anonymity of 'whistle-blowers' has been strictly maintained.
>
> The code contains relevant and straightforward advice. For example: "In recognising that we are a competitive business, we believe in fair and open competition and, therefore, obtaining information about competitors by deception is unacceptable. Similarly, making disparaging comments about competitors invariably invites disrespect from customers and should be avoided." Or: "Employment with NatWest must never be used in an attempt to influence public officials or customers for personal gain or benefit."
>
> Jonathan Bye, manager of public policy at NatWest, said the bank is continually looking at ways of refreshing the code and measuring its effectiveness.'

How would you suggest that the effectiveness of a company's policy on ethics could be measured?

Some ideas that you might think through are:

- Training effectiveness measures
- How breaches of the code are dealt with
- Activity in the ethics office
- Public perceptions of the company

Try to flesh them out and think of some other ideas. The extract above should suggest some.

1.2 Company code of ethics   12/08, 12/11

An **ethical code** typically contains a **series of statements setting out the organisation's values and explaining how it sees its responsibilities towards stakeholders**.

Codes of corporate ethics normally have the following features.

- They **focus on regulating individual employee behaviour**.
- They are **formal documents**.
- They **cover specific areas** such as gifts, anti-competitive behaviour, and so on.
- Employees may be **asked to sign** that they will comply.
- They may be **developed from third-party codes** (eg regulators) or use third parties for monitoring.
- They tend to **mix moral with technical imperatives**.
- Sometimes they do **little more than describe current practices**.
- They can be used to **shift responsibility** (from senior managers to operational staff).

1.2.1 Purposes of code of ethics   6/14

(a) **Establishment of organisation's values**

Ethical codes form part of the organisation's **underlying environment**. They develop and promote values that are linked to the organisation's mission statement.

(b) **Promotion of stakeholder responsibilities**

Codes also demonstrate whom the organisation regards as **important stakeholders**. They show what action should be taken to maintain good **stakeholder relationships** (such as keeping them fully informed). They can show external stakeholders that they are dealing with people who **do business fairly**. Drafting parts of the code to comply with customer wishes demonstrates that businesses are **responsive to customers**.

(c) **Control of individuals' behaviour**

By **promoting or prohibiting certain actions**, ethical codes form part of the human resources mechanisms by which employee behaviour is controlled. All staff should be aware of the importance of the ethical code and it should be referred to when employee actions are questioned.

(d) **Promotion of business objectives**

Codes can be an important element in a company's strategic positioning. Taking a **strong stance on responsibility and ethics** and earning a good ethical reputation can enhance appeal to consumers in the same way as producing the right products of good quality can.

(e) **Conveying values to stakeholders**

The code is a **communications device**, not only acting to communicate between partners and staff, but also increasing the transparency of the organisation's dealings with its stakeholders.

1.2.2 Example of code of ethics

Typical statements in a corporate code

- The company conducts all its business on **ethical principles** and expects staff to do likewise.

- **Employees** are seen as the most important component of the company and are expected to work on a basis of trust, respect, honesty, fairness, decency and equality. The company will only employ people who follow its ethical ideals.

- **Customers** should be treated courteously and politely at all times, and the company should always respond promptly to customer needs by listening, understanding and then performing to the customer requirements.

- The company is dedicated to complying **with legal or regulatory standards** of the industry, and employees are expected to do likewise.

- The company's relationship with **suppliers and subcontractors** must be based on mutual respect. The company therefore has responsibilities including ensuring fairness and truthfulness in all its dealings with suppliers including pricing and licensing, fostering long-term stability in the supplier relationship, paying suppliers on time and in accordance with agreed terms of trade and preferring suppliers and subcontractors whose employment practices respect human dignity.

- The company has a responsibility to: foster open markets for trade and investment, promote **competitive behaviour** that is socially and environmentally beneficial and demonstrates mutual respect among competitors, and refrain from either seeking or participating in questionable payments or favours to secure competitive advantages.

- A business should protect and, where possible, improve **the environment**, promote sustainable development and prevent the wasteful use of natural resources.

- The company has a responsibility in **the community** to: respect human rights and democratic institutions, and promote them wherever practicable, recognise government's legitimate obligation to the society at large and support public policies and practices that promote human development through harmonious relations between business and other segments of society, collaborate with those forces in the community dedicated to raising standards of health, education, workplace safety and economic wellbeing, respect the integrity of local cultures, and be a good corporate citizen through charitable donations, educational and cultural contributions and employee participation in community and civic affairs.

Question   Employee behaviour

How can an organisation influence employee behaviour towards ethical issues?

Answer

Here are some suggestions.

- Recruitment and selection policies and procedures
- Induction and training
- Objectives and reward schemes
- Ethical codes
- Threat of ethical audit

1.3 The impact of codes of conduct

A code of conduct can set out the company's expectations, and in principle a code such as that outlined above addresses many of the problems that the organisations may experience. However, **merely issuing a code is not enough**.

BPP
LEARNING MEDIA

(a) The **commitment of senior management** to the code needs to be real, and it needs to be very clearly communicated to all staff. Staff need to be persuaded that expectations really have changed.

(b) Measures need to be taken to **discourage previous behaviours** that conflict with the code.

(c) **Staff need to understand** that it is in the **organisation's best interests** to change behaviour and become committed to the same ideals.

(d) Some employees – including very able ones – may find it very difficult to buy into a code that they **perceive may limit their own earnings** and/or restrict their freedom to do their job.

(e) In addition to a general statement of ethical conduct, **more detailed statements** (codes of practice) will be needed to set out formal procedures that must be followed.

Case Study

The co-operative bank www.goodwithmoney.co.uk pursues ethical policies through its banking and insurance divisions. Both are founded on the assumption that investors have no say in, and do not know how, other banks invest their money. The co-operative bank on the other hand consults its customers.

The banking division's ethical policy has two sides to it. It seeks to encourage certain businesses or organisations, or certain business practices. For example, it supports charities, credit unions and community finance initiatives. It also supports businesses involved in recycling, renewable energy and sustainable natural products. On the other hand, it will not invest in businesses or practices that operate in areas of concern to customers. These include currency speculation, tobacco product manufacture, irresponsible marketing practices in developing countries, unsustainable harvesting of natural resources and animal testing of cosmetic or household products.

Co-operative Insurance's ethical engagement policy is based on using its influence as a corporate shareholder to change companies from the inside. It has asked companies to seek modifications to the working conditions of Chinese factory workers and encouraged oil and energy companies to pursue biofuels with long-term potential for sustainable production. It focuses in particular on corporate governance practices such as directors' pay, board appointments and treatment of employees.

1.4 Problems with codes of conduct

1.4.1 Inflexibility

Inflexible rules may not be practical. One example would be a **prohibition on accepting gifts from customers**. A simple prohibition that would be quite acceptable in a Western context would not work in other cultures, where non-acceptance might be seen as insulting.

1.4.2 Clarity

It is difficult to achieve **completely unambiguous wording**.

1.4.3 Irrelevancy

Surveys suggest that ethical codes are often perceived as irrelevant for the following reasons.

(a) They fail to say anything about the sort of **ethical problems that employees encounter**.

(b) Other people in the organisation **pay no attention** to them.

(c) They are **inconsistent with the prevailing organisational culture**.

(d) Senior managers' behaviour is **not seen as promoting ethical codes**. Senior managers rarely blatantly fail to comply; rather they appear out of touch on ethics because they are too busy or unwilling to take responsibility.

One area explored by a question issued by the examiner was the justification for issuing a code of ethics. The viewpoints were roughly that a normative code is justified because being ethical is desirable in itself versus an instrumental code is justified if it gives strategic advantage and doesn't cost too much.

1.5 Identity and values guidance

Corporate ethical codes are often **rather legalistic documents**, consisting largely of prohibitions on specific undesirable actions such as the acceptance of gifts from suppliers. More general guidance with an emphasis on principles may be more appropriate.

Identity and values programmes describe corporate values without specifying in detail what they mean. Rather than highlighting compliance with negatives they **promote positive values** about the company and form part of its culture. (Compliance programmes are about limiting legal and public relations disasters.) Even so, they need to be integrated with a company's values and leadership.

1.6 Other measures

To be effective, ethical guidance needs to be accompanied by **positive attempts to foster guiding values, aspirations and patterns of thinking that support ethically sound behaviour** – in short a **change of culture**.

Increasingly organisations are responding to this challenge by devising **ethics training programmes** for the entire workforce, instituting comprehensive **procedures for reporting and investigating ethical concerns** within the company, or even setting up an **ethics office** or department to supervise the new measures.

Case Study

'The view from the trenches'

Badaracco and Webb (1995) carried out in-depth interviews with 30 recent Harvard MBA graduates. They found that unethical behaviour appeared to be widespread in the middle layers of business organisations.

> '… in many cases, young managers received explicit instructions from their middle-manager bosses or felt strong organisational pressures to do things that they believed were sleazy, unethical, or sometimes illegal.'

However, these young managers categorised only a few of their superiors as fundamentally unethical. Most were basically decent, but were themselves pushed into requiring unethical behaviour by four strong organisational pressures.

(a)   Performance outcomes are what really count.
(b)   Loyalty is very important.
(c)   Don't break the law.
(d)   '… don't over-invest in ethical behaviour'.

The outcome of these pressures was a firm impression that ethical conduct was a handicap and a willingness to evade ethical imperatives an advantage in career progression.

You may need to discuss corporate ethical behaviour as part of a wider discussion on the control environment. There is a good example of this sort of question in the Pilot Paper.

2 Professional codes of ethics

Professional codes of ethics apply to the **individual behaviour** of professionals and are often based on principles, supplemented by guidance on **threats and safeguards**.

2.1 Contents of professional codes

The International Ethics Standards Board for Accountants (IESBA) *Code of Ethics for Professional Accountants* is a good illustration of how codes not just for accountants but for other professionals are constructed.

(a) The Code begins by stating that it reflects the acceptance by the accountancy profession of the responsibility to act in the **public interest**.

(b) The detailed guidance begins with establishment of **fundamental principles of ethics**.

(c) The guide then supplies a **conceptual framework** that requires accountants to identify, evaluate and address **threats to compliance**, applying **safeguards** to eliminate the threats or to reduce them to an acceptable level.

Exam focus point

Depressingly the examiner reported that in the December 2008 exam some students confused corporate and professional ethical codes.

2.1.1 Advantages of professional codes

(a) Codes represent a clear statement that **professionals** are expected to act in the public interest, and act as a **benchmark** against which behaviour can be judged. They should thus enhance public confidence in the professions.

(b) Codes emphasise the importance of professionals **considering ethical issues actively** and seeking to comply, rather than only being concerned with avoiding what is forbidden.

(c) ACCA and IESBA codes state that they can be **applied internationally**. Local differences are not significant.

(d) Codes can include detailed guidance, which should **assist ethical decision-making**.

(e) Codes can include **explicit prohibitions** if necessary.

(f) Codes prescribe **minimum standards of behaviour** that are expected.

2.1.2 Disadvantages of professional codes

(a) Professional codes, with their **identification of many different situations**, can lose focus on key issues.

(b) Evidence suggests that some treat codes as a set of rules to be **complied with and 'box-ticked'**.

(c) **International codes** such as the IESBA code cannot fully capture **regional variations in beliefs and practice**.

(d) The value of international codes may be limited by their not being legally enforceable around the world (although ACCA can **enforce sanctions** against members for serious breaches).

(e) **Illustrative examples** can be interpreted mistakenly as rules to follow in similar circumstances.

(f) Giving a lot of illustrative examples in codes may give the impression that ethical considerations are **primarily important** only when accountants are facing decisions illustrated in the codes. They may **downplay the importance of acting ethically** when facing decisions that are not clearly covered in the codes.

2.2 Contents of professional codes

IESBA suggests that the sheer variety of threats to compliance with the fundamental principles mean that no guidance can cover every situation where there is a potential threat.

2.2.1 Advantages of principles-based guidance

IESBA suggests that requiring use of a principles-based conceptual framework rather than a set of specific rules is in the public interest for the following reasons.

(a)   It places the onus on the professional to **consider actively** relevant issues in a given situation, rather than just agreeing action with a checklist of forbidden items. It also requires him to **demonstrate** that a responsible conclusion has been reached about ethical issues.

(b)   It **prevents professionals from interpreting legalistic requirements narrowly** to get around the ethical requirements. There is an extent to which rules engender deception, whereas principles encourage compliance.

(c)   It **allows for variations** that are found in every **individual situation**. Each situation is likely to be different.

(d)   It can accommodate a **rapidly changing environment**, such as the one in which auditors are.

(e)   It can include **examples** to illustrate how the principles are applied.

2.2.2 Disadvantages of principles-based guidance

(a)   As ethical codes cannot include all circumstances and dilemmas, accountants need a very good understanding of the **underlying principles**.

(b)   A principles-based code can be difficult to enforce legally, unless the breach of the code is blatant. Most are therefore **voluntary** and perhaps therefore less effective.

Exam focus point

> A question in the Pilot Paper asked whether the benefits of codes of ethics outweighed the costs of producing them.

2.3 Accountancy ethical codes

ACCA publishes guidance for its members, the *Code of Ethics and Conduct*. IESBA publishes a *Code of Ethics for Professional Accountants*. Both are based on the same fundamental principles.

You need this knowledge not only to answer questions in the exam, but also to fulfil part of performance objective 1 of the PER, the competency to inform clients about the ethical standards that apply to professional activities.

2.4 Fundamental principles   6/10

These principles are designed to ensure that the accountant fulfils the public interest and meets the expectations of society.

Fundamental principles	
Professional competence and due care	Members have a continuing duty to maintain **professional knowledge and skill** at a level required to ensure that a client or employer receives competent professional service based on current developments in practice, legislation and techniques. Members should act diligently and in accordance with applicable technical and professional standards when providing professional services.
Integrity	Members should be **straightforward** and **honest** in all business and professional relationships.
Professional behaviour	Members should comply with relevant laws and regulations and should avoid any action that discredits the profession.

Fundamental principles	
Confidentiality	Members should respect the **confidentiality of information** acquired as a result of professional and business relationships and should not disclose any such information to third parties without proper or specific authority or unless there is a legal or professional right or duty to disclose. Confidential information acquired as a result of professional and business relationships should not be used for the personal advantage of members or third parties.
Objectivity	Members should not allow **bias**, **conflicts of interest** or **undue influence** of others to override professional or business judgements.

2.5 Ethical threats to compliance with the fundamental principles for accountants in practice   6/11, 6/14

Both IESBA and ACCA identify certain ethical threats to compliance with the fundamental principles.

Threat	Definition	Examples
Self-interest	Financial or other interests of a professional accountant or of an immediate family member inappropriately influence judgement or behaviour	Having a financial interest in a client
Self-review	Evaluation of a judgement by the accountant who made the judgement, or a member of the same organisation	Auditing financial statements prepared by the firm
Advocacy	Accountant promoting a position or opinion to the point where objectivity may be compromised	Advocating the client's case in a lawsuit
Familiarity	A close relationship resulting in excessive trust in, or sympathy for, others	Audit team member having family at the client
Intimidation	Accountant not acting objectively because of actual or perceived pressures	Threats of replacement due to disagreement

As we shall see in the next section, these threats are particularly relevant in the context of threats to independence.

2.6 Ethical safeguards for accountants in practice   6/14

There are two general categories of ethical safeguard identified in the IESBA and ACCA guidance.

- Safeguards created by the profession, legislation or regulation
- Safeguards within the assurance client/the firm's own systems and procedures

2.6.1 Examples of ethical safeguards created by the profession, legislation or regulation

- Educational training and experience requirements for entry into the profession
- Continuing professional development requirements
- Corporate governance regulations
- Professional standards
- Professional or regulatory monitoring and disciplinary procedures

The International Federation of Accountants (IFAC) issues ethical standards (via IESBA), quality control standards and auditing standards that work together to ensure independence is safeguarded and quality audits are carried out.

2.6.2 Examples of ethical safeguards in the firm's own systems and procedures

If ACCA members work for an accountancy practice, the firm should have the following safeguards in place in relation to the firm.

- The firm's leadership stressing **compliance with fundamental principles**
- Leadership of the firm establishing the expectation that **employees will act in the public interest**
- **Quality control policies and procedures**
- Documented policies on **identification and evaluation of threats** and **identification and application of safeguards**
- Documented policies covering **independence threats and safeguards** in relation to assurance engagements
- Documented internal procedures requiring **compliance with fundamental principles**
- Policies and procedures enabling **identification of interests and relationships between the firm's team** and **clients**
- Policies and procedures to **manage reliance on revenue from a single client**
- Using **different teams for non-assurance work**
- Prohibiting individuals who are not team members from **influencing the outcome of the engagement**
- **Timely communication of policies and procedures** and appropriate training and education
- Designating a senior manager to be **responsible for overseeing quality control**
- Advising staff of **independence requirements** in relation to specific clients
- **Disciplinary measures**
- **Promotion of communication** by staff to senior management of any ethical compliance issue that concerns them

There should also be safeguards relating to specific assignments:

- Involving an additional professional accountant to review the work done or otherwise advise as necessary
- Consulting an independent third party, such as a committee of independent directors, a professional regulatory body or another professional accountant
- Rotating senior personnel
- Discussing ethical issues with those in charge of client governance
- Disclosing to those charged with governance the nature of services provided and extent of fees charged
- Involving another firm to perform or re-perform part of the engagement
- Rotating senior assurance team personnel

2.7 Ethical threats to compliance with the fundamental principles for accountants in business

Threat	Examples
Self-interest	Financial interests, loans and guarantees, incentive compensation arrangements, personal use of corporate assets, external commercial pressures, acceptance of a gift
Self-review	Business decisions being subject to review and justification by the same accountant responsible for making those decisions or preparing the data supporting them

Threat	Examples
Advocacy	Furthering the employer's cause aggressively without regard to reasonableness of statements made (furthering legitimate goals of employer organisation would not generally create an advocacy threat)
Familiarity	Long association of a business contact
Intimidation	Threats of dismissal from employment, influence of a dominant personality

2.8 Ethical safeguards for accountants in business

The safeguards created by the profession, legislation or regulation also apply to accountants in business.

2.8.1 Ethical safeguards in the workplace for accountants in business

- The employer's oversight systems
- The employer's ethics and conduct programmes
- Recruitment procedures
- Strong internal controls
- Appropriate disciplinary processes
- Leadership that stresses ethics
- Policies and procedures that promote and monitor employee performance
- Timely communication of the employer's policies and procedures to all employees
- Training and education of employees
- Whistleblowing provisions
- Consultation with another professional accountant

In other words, a strong control environment.

However, if these safeguards are ineffective, the professional accountant may have to seek legal advice or resign.

2.9 Ethical conflict resolution

The IESBA Code states that firms should have established policies to resolve conflict and should follow those established policies.

Professional accountants should consider:

- The facts
- The ethical issues involved
- Related fundamental principles
- Established internal (firm) procedures
- Alternative courses of action, considering the consequences of each

2.10 Ethical codes and Kohlberg's guidance

One key aim of a principles-based ethical code is in effect to move subjects to **levels of reasoning** as defined in Kohlberg's framework. The principles are meant to provide ideals towards which ethical decisions should aspire. The emphasis in the code that the examples given are not a comprehensive list of every situation that could be affected by the code indicates the expectation that the code is aiming beyond giving examples of common situations in which individuals follow set behaviour. It is aiming to encourage individuals to make their own ethical judgements.

2.11 Responsibilities to employer and responsibilities as a professional
6/08

Clearly there is a lot of overlap between an accountant's employment and professional responsibilities. The professional body and (hopefully) the employer would expect the accountant to act with **integrity** and **probity**. Both would require the accountant to act with **diligence and due care**.

However, there may be conflict in the following areas.

(a) **Confidentiality**

Confidentiality may be a major issue. An employer will wish for the employee to respect confidentiality about all sensitive matters both during and after the period of employment. Confidentiality is a professional duty too. However, the accountants may, in the **public interest**, have to report an errant employer to the relevant authorities.

(b) **Interests served**

The employer may wish the accountant to put shareholder and commercial interests above all others. However, the accountant may believe that a duty is owed to a **wider stakeholder group**.

(c) **Organisational vs professional norms**

Accountants may be said to owe a general duty to '**fit in**', be part of a team and behave in ways that are in accordance with the **organisational culture** of their employer. However, as members of a professional accounting body, accountants owe a duty to act in accordance with the **norms** of that body, including its stress on **professional behaviour**. These may not be in line with the employer's culture.

(d) **Requirement for obedience**

The employer may require **obedience** to its wishes even if it appears to conflict with the accountants' professional duties.

Exam focus point

Situations where professional and employer responsibilities conflict are likely to occur frequently in this exam. Question 4 in the Pilot Paper is an example.

3 Independence and conflicts of interest 6/08, 6/09, 12/12, 12/14

FAST FORWARD

Threats to independence of accountants in practice include **self-interest**, **self-review**, **advocacy**, **familiarity** and **intimidation**.

Accountants in practice may face **conflicts of interest** between their own and clients' interests, or between the interests of different clients.

3.1 Independence

We have looked at independence guidelines relating to internal auditors in Chapter 8. You will have encountered the guidance relating to external auditors in your earlier studies, but we cover the main threats here. Both IESBA and ACCA list examples of threats to independence and applicable safeguards.

Exam focus point

Remember it is important that you can apply the spirit of the guidance to a given situation in this exam rather than just learning and regurgitating the guidance. June 2009 Question 2 is a good example of an application question, where students had to assess the ethical threats implied by what an accountant said.

Independence is most important for accountants acting as auditors and assurance providers for the following reasons.

(a) **Reliability of financial information**

Corporate governance reports have highlighted **reliability of financial information** as a key aspect of corporate governance. Shareholders and other stakeholders need a trustworthy record of **directors' stewardship** to be able to take decisions about the company. Assurance provided by independent auditors is a key quality control on the reliability of information.

(b) **Credibility of financial information**

An unqualified report by independent external auditors on the accounts should give them more **credibility**, enhancing the appeal of the company to investors. It should represent the views of independent experts, who are not motivated by personal interests to give a favourable opinion on the annual report.

(c) **Value for money of audit work**

Audit fees should be set on the basis of charging for the work **necessary to gain sufficient audit assurance**. A lack of independence here seems to mean important audit work may not be done, and the shareholders are not receiving value for the audit fees.

(d) **Threats to professional standards**

A lack of independence may lead to a failure to **fulfil professional requirements** to obtain enough evidence to form the basis of an audit opinion, here to obtain details of a questionable material item. Failure by auditors to do this **undermines the credibility of the accountancy profession** and the standards it enforces.

Most of the guidance also applies to accountants providing assurance services as well as audit.

There are **two general types** of assurance engagement.

(a) An **assertion-based** engagement where the accountant declares that a given premise (assertion) is either correct or not

(b) A **direct reporting** engagement where the accountant reports on issues that have come to their attention during their evaluation

3.2 Self-interest threat   6/11

The ACCA *Code of Ethics and Conduct* highlights a great number of areas in which a self-interest threat to independence might arise.

3.2.1 Financial interests

> **Financial interests** exist where an audit firm has a financial interest in a client's affairs; for example, the audit firm owns shares in the client, or is a trustee of a trust that holds shares in the client.

A financial interest in a client constitutes a substantial self-interest threat. According to both ACCA and IESBA, **the parties listed below are not allowed to own a direct financial interest or an indirect material financial interest in a client**.

- The **assurance firm**
- **Partners in the same office** as the engagement partner (and their immediate families)
- A **member of the assurance team**
- An **immediate family member of a member of the assurance team**

The following safeguards will therefore be relevant.

- Disposing of the interest
- Removing the individual from the team if required
- Keeping the client's audit committee informed of the situation
- Using an independent partner to review work carried out if necessary

3.2.2 Close business relationships

Examples of when a firm and client have an inappropriately close business relationship include:

- Having a **material financial interest** in a joint venture with the assurance client

- **Arrangements to combine one or more services or products** of the firm with one or more services or products of the assurance client and to market the package with reference to both parties

- **Distribution or marketing arrangements** under which the firm acts as distributor or marketer of the assurance client's products or services or vice versa

Again, it will be necessary to judge the materiality of the interest and therefore its significance. However, unless the interest is clearly insignificant, an **assurance provider should not participate** in such a venture with a client. Appropriate safeguards are therefore to end the assurance provision or to terminate the (other) business relationship.

3.2.3 Employment with client

It is possible that staff might transfer between a firm and a client, or that negotiations or interviews to facilitate such movement might take place. Both situations are a threat to independence.

- An audit staff member might be **motivated by a desire to impress a future possible employer** (objectivity is therefore affected).

- A former partner turned Finance Director has **too much knowledge of the audit firm's systems** and procedures.

The extent of the threat to independence depends on various factors, such as the **role** the individual has taken up at the client, the **extent of their influence** on the audit previously, the length of time that has passed between the individual's connection with the audit and the new role at the client.

Various safeguards might be considered:

- Considering **modifying the assurance plan**

- Ensuring the audit is assigned to someone of **sufficient experience** compared with the individual who has left

- Involving an **additional professional accountant** not involved with the engagement to review the work done

- Carrying out a **quality control review** of the engagement

In respect of audit clients, ethical guidance states that a partner should not **accept a key management position** at an audit client until **at least two years** have elapsed since the conclusion of the audit they were involved with. An individual who has moved from the firm to a client should **not be entitled to any benefits or payments** from the firm unless these are made in accordance with predetermined arrangements. A firm should have procedures setting out that an individual involved in serious employment negotiations with an audit client should **notify the firm** and that this person would then be removed from the engagement.

3.2.4 Partner on client board

A partner or employee of an audit/assurance firm should **not serve on the board** of an assurance client. It may be acceptable for a partner or an employee of an assurance firm to perform the role of company secretary for an assurance client, if the role is essentially administrative. (However, don't forget the increased emphasis on the role of the company secretary in governance reports, aiming to enhance the secretary's role to go beyond routine administrative tasks.)

3.2.5 Family and personal relationships   6/08, 6/10

Family or close personal relationships between assurance firm and client staff could seriously threaten independence. Each situation has to be evaluated individually. Factors to consider are:

- The individual's responsibilities on the assurance engagement
- The closeness of the relationship
- The role of the other party at the assurance client

When an immediate family member of a member of the assurance team is a **director, an officer or an employee of the assurance client** in a position to exert direct and significant influence over the assurance engagement, the individual should be removed from the assurance team.

The audit firm should also consider whether there is any threat to independence if an employee who is not a member of the assurance team has a **close family or personal relationship** with a director, an officer or an employee of an assurance client.

A firm should have **quality control policies and procedures** under which staff should disclose if a close family member employed by the client is promoted within the client.

Exam focus point	June 2010 Question 4 demonstrated how close personal relationships can make an ethical problem even more difficult.

3.2.6 Gifts and hospitality

Unless the value of the gift/hospitality is clearly insignificant, a firm or a member of an assurance team should not accept it, as it clearly threatens objectivity. In addition, there may be an intimidation threat if there is a suggestion that the receipt of the gift will be made public.

3.2.7 Loans and guarantees

The advice on loans and guarantees falls into two categories.

- The client is a bank or other similar institution
- Other situations

If a **lending institution client** lends an **immaterial amount to** an audit firm or a member of the assurance team on normal commercial terms, there is no threat to independence. If the loan were material it would be necessary to apply safeguards to bring the risk to an acceptable level. A suitable safeguard is likely to be an **independent review** (by a partner from another office in the firm).

Loans to members of the assurance team from a bank or other lending institution client are likely to be **material to the individual** but, provided that they are on normal commercial terms, these do not constitute a threat to independence.

However, an audit firm or individual on the assurance engagement should not enter into any loan or guarantee arrangement with a client that is not a bank or similar institution.

3.2.8 Overdue fees

In a situation where there are overdue fees, the auditor runs the risk of, in effect, making a loan to a client, whereupon the guidance above becomes relevant.

Audit firms should guard against fees building up and being significant by **discussing the issues with the audit committee or others involved in governance** and, if necessary, the possibility of resigning if overdue fees are not paid.

3.2.9 Percentage or contingent fees

> **Contingent fees** are fees calculated on a predetermined basis relating to the outcome or result of a transaction or the result of the work performed.

Ethical guidelines state that a firm should not enter into any fee arrangement for an assurance engagement under which the amount of the fee is contingent on the result of the assurance work or on items that are the subject matter of the assurance engagement. It would also usually be inappropriate to accept a contingent fee for non-assurance work from an assurance client.

3.2.10 High percentage of fees

A firm should be alert to the situation arising where the **total fees generated by an assurance client** represent a **large proportion of a firm's total fees**. Factors such as the **structure of the firm** and the length of time it has been trading will be relevant in determining whether there is a threat to independence. It is also necessary to be aware of situations where the fees generated by an assurance client are a large proportion of the revenue of an individual partner.

Safeguards in these situations might include:

- Discussing the issues with the audit committee
- Taking steps to reduce the dependency on the client
- Obtaining external/internal quality control reviews
- Consulting a third party such as ACCA

Ethical guidance states that the public may perceive that a member's objectivity is likely to be in jeopardy where the fees for audit and recurring work paid by one client or group of connected clients **exceed 15%** of the firm's total fees. Where the entity is listed or public interest, this figure should be 10%.

It will be difficult for new firms establishing themselves to keep within these limits and firms in this situation should make use of the safeguards outlined.

3.2.11 Lowballing

When a firm quotes a significantly lower fee level for an assurance service than would have been charged by the predecessor firm, there is a significant self-interest threat. If the firm's tender is successful, the firm must apply safeguards, such as:

- **Maintaining records** such that the firm is able to demonstrate that appropriate staff and time are spent on the engagement
- **Complying with all applicable assurance standards**, guidelines and quality control procedures

3.2.12 Recruitment

Recruiting senior management for an assurance client, particularly those able to affect the subject matter of an assurance engagement, creates a self-interest threat for the assurance firm.

Assurance providers must not make management decisions for the client. Their involvement could be limited to reviewing a shortlist of candidates, provided that the client has drawn up the criteria by which they are to be selected.

3.3 Self-review threat

The key area in which there is likely to be a self-review threat is where an assurance firm provides services other than assurance services to an assurance client (providing multiple services). There is a great deal of guidance in the ACCA and IESBA rules about various other services accountancy firms might provide to their clients, and these are dealt with below.

The distinction between listed companies, or public limited companies, and private companies is perceived to be an important issue in the question of providing other services to clients.

Key term

> **Public interest companies** are those that for some reason (size, nature, product) are in the 'public eye'. Auditors should treat these as if they are listed companies.

In the United States the Sarbanes-Oxley rules concerning auditor independence for **listed** companies state that an accountant is not independent if they provide certain non-audit services to an audit client. The relevant services are:

- Bookkeeping
- Financial information systems design and implementation
- Appraisal or valuation services or fairness opinions
- Actuarial services
- Internal audit services
- Management functions
- Human resources
- Broker-dealer services
- Legal services

Exam focus point

> In exam questions, bear in mind the nature of the entity being audited. Is it a small owner-managed business where the auditor is in effect an all-round business adviser and accountant, or is it a listed company where the above rule is relevant?

3.3.1 Recent service with an assurance client

Ethical guidance focuses on individuals who have been a **director or officer of the client**, or an employee in a position to exert **direct and significant influence** over the subject matter information of the assurance engagement in the period under review or the previous two years to the assurance team.

If an individual had been closely involved with the client prior to the time limits set out above, the assurance firm should consider the threat to independence arising and apply appropriate safeguards, such as:

- Obtaining a quality control review of the individual's work on the assignment
- Discussing the issue with the audit committee

3.3.2 General services

For assurance clients, accountants are not allowed to:

- Authorise, execute or consummate a transaction
- Determine which recommendations should be implemented
- Report in a management capacity to those charged with governance

Having custody of an assurance client's assets, supervising client employees in the performance of their normal duties and preparing source documents on behalf of the client also pose significant self-review threats which should be addressed by safeguards. These could be:

- Ensuring that non assurance team staff are used for these roles
- Involving an independent professional accountant to advise
- Putting in place quality control policies on what staff are and are not allowed to do for clients
- Making appropriate disclosures to those charged with governance
- Resigning from the assurance engagement

3.3.3 Preparing accounting records and financial statements

There is clearly a significant risk of a self-review threat if a firm prepares **accounting records and financial statements** and then audits them. On the other hand, auditors routinely assist management with the preparation of financial statements and give advice about accounting treatments and journal entries.

Therefore, assurance firms must analyse the risks arising and put safeguards in place to ensure that the risk is at an acceptable level. Safeguards include:

- **Using staff members other than assurance team members** to carry out work
- **Obtaining client approval for work** undertaken

The rules are more stringent when the client is listed or public interest. Firms should not prepare accounts or financial statements for listed or public interest clients unless an emergency arises.

For any client, assurance firms are also not allowed to:

- Determine or change journal entries without client approval
- Authorise or approve transactions
- Prepare source documents

3.3.4 Valuation services

Key term

> A **valuation** comprises the making of assumptions with regard to future developments, the application of certain methodologies and techniques, and the combination of both in order to compute a certain value, or range of values, for an asset, a liability or for a business as a whole.

If an audit firm performs a valuation which will be included in financial statements audited by the firm, a self-review threat arises.

Audit firms should not carry out valuations on matters that will be material to the financial statements.

If the valuation is for an immaterial matter, the audit firm should **apply safeguards** to ensure that the risk is reduced to an acceptable level. Matters to consider when applying safeguards are the extent of the audit client's knowledge of the relevant matters in making the valuation and the degree of judgement involved, how much use is made of established methodologies and the degree of uncertainty in the valuation. Safeguards include:

- Second partner review
- Confirming that the client understands the valuation and the assumptions used
- Ensuring the client acknowledges responsibility for the valuation
- Using separate personnel for the valuation and the audit

3.3.5 Taxation services

The **provision of taxation services** is generally not seen to impair independence.

3.3.6 Internal audit services

A firm may provide internal audit services to an audit client in most jurisdictions, but not in America under Sarbanes-Oxley. However, it should ensure that the client **acknowledges its responsibility** for **establishing, maintaining and monitoring the system** of internal controls. It may be appropriate to use safeguards, such as ensuring that an employee of the client is designated as responsible for internal audit activities and that the board or audit committee approve all the work that internal audit does.

3.3.7 Corporate finance

Certain aspects of corporate finance will create self-review threats that cannot be reduced to an acceptable level by safeguards. Therefore, assurance firms are **not allowed to promote, deal in or underwrite** an assurance client's shares. They are also not allowed to commit an assurance client to the terms of a transaction or consummate a transaction on the client's behalf.

Other corporate finance services, such as assisting a client in defining corporate strategies, assisting in identifying possible sources of capital and providing structuring advice, may be acceptable in jurisdictions other than the US provided that safeguards are in place, such as using different teams of staff and ensuring that no management decisions are taken on behalf of the client.

3.3.8 Other services

The audit firm might sell a variety of other services to audit clients, such as:

- IT services
- Temporary staff cover
- Litigation support
- Legal services

The assurance firm should consider whether there are any barriers to independence. Examples include the firm being asked to design internal control IT systems, which it would then review as part of its audit, or the firm being asked to provide an accountant to cover the chief accountant's maternity leave. The firm should consider whether the threat to independence could be reduced by appropriate safeguards. Again the rules in America are stricter than elsewhere.

3.4 Advocacy threat

An advocacy threat arises in certain situations where the assurance firm is in a position of **taking the client's part** in a dispute or somehow **acting as their advocate**. The most obvious instances of this would be when a firm offered legal services to a client and, say, defended them in a legal case or provided evidence on their behalf as an expert witness. An advocacy threat might also arise if the firm carried out corporate finance work for the client; for example, if the audit firm was involved in advice on debt reconstruction and negotiated with the bank on the client's behalf.

As with the other threats above, the firm has to appraise the risk and apply safeguards as necessary. Relevant safeguards might be using **different departments** in the firm to carry out the work and making disclosures to the audit committee. Remember, the ultimate option is always to withdraw from an engagement if the risk to independence is too high.

3.5 Familiarity threat 6/08

A familiarity or association threat is where independence is jeopardised by the audit firm and its staff becoming overfamiliar with the client and its staff. There is a substantial risk of loss of professional scepticism in such circumstances.

We have already discussed some examples of when this risk arises, because very often a familiarity threat arises in conjunction with a self-interest threat.

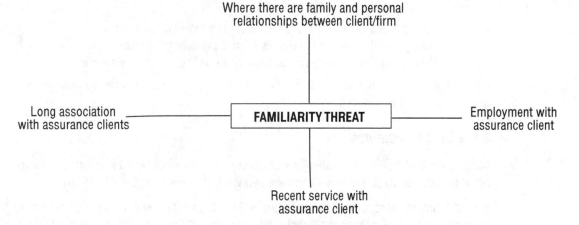

3.5.1 Long association of senior personnel with assurance clients

Senior members of staff at an audit firm having a long association with a client is a significant threat to independence. All firms should therefore monitor the relationship between staff and established clients and use safeguards to independence, such as **rotating senior staff off the assurance team**, involving **second partners** to carry out reviews and obtaining independent (but internal) quality control reviews.

3.6 Intimidation threat

An intimidation threat arises when members of the assurance team have reason to be intimidated by client staff.

These are also examples of self-interest threats, largely because intimidation may only arise significantly when the assurance firm has something to lose.

3.6.1 Actual and threatened litigation

The most obvious example of an intimidation threat is when the client threatens to sue, or indeed sues, the assurance firm for work that has been done previously. The firm is then faced with the **risk of losing the client, bad publicity** and the **possibility that they will be found to have been negligent**, which will lead to further problems. This could lead to the firm being under pressure to produce an unqualified audit report when they have been qualified in the past, for example.

Generally, assurance firms should seek to avoid such situations arising. If they do arise, factors to consider are:

- The materiality of the litigation
- The nature of the assurance engagement
- Whether the litigation relates to a prior assurance engagement

The following safeguards could be considered.

- Disclosing to the audit committee the nature and extent of the litigation
- Removing specific affected individuals from the engagement team
- Involving an additional professional accountant on the team to review work

However, if the litigation is at all serious, it may be necessary to **resign from the engagement**, as the threat to independence is so great.

3.6.2 Second opinions

Another way that auditors can suffer an intimidation threat is when the audit client is unhappy with a proposed audit opinion, and seeks a **second opinion** from a different firm of auditors.

In such a circumstance, the second audit firm will not be able to give a formal audit opinion on the financial statements – only an appointed auditor can do that. However, the problem is that if a different firm of auditors indicates to someone else's client that a different opinion might be acceptable, the appointed auditors may feel under pressure to change their opinion. In effect, a self-interest threat arises, as the existing auditor may feel that they will lose next year's audit if they do not change this year's opinion.

There is nothing to stop a company director talking to a second firm of auditors about treatments of matters in the financial statements. However, the firm being asked for a second opinion should be very careful, because it is very possible that the opinion they form could be incorrect anyway if the director has not given them all the relevant information. For that reason, firms giving a second opinion should ensure that they **seek permission** to communicate with the existing auditor and they are appraised of all the facts. If permission is not given, the second auditors should decline to comment on the audit opinion.

Given that second opinions can cause independence issues for the existing auditors, audit firms should generally take great care if asked to provide one anyway.

3.7 Conflicts of interest

Audit firms should take reasonable steps to identify circumstances that could pose a conflict of interest. This is because a conflict of interest could result in the ethical code being breached (for example, if it results in a self-interest threat arising).

Case Study

IIn his blog, business ethics guru Chris MacDonald points out that there is nothing inherently unethical about being in a conflict of interest – it may well be something that happens through no fault of an individual's, for example one client of a lawyer deciding to sue another. What is most often at stake in conflicts of interest is the integrity of the decision-making process. The approach to dealing with a conflict should be to recognise it, disclose it and take appropriate action (often to withdraw from involvement in the decision-making process).

3.7.1 Conflicts between members' and clients' interests

A conflict between members' and clients' interests might arise if members compete directly with a client, or have a joint venture or similar with a company that is in competition with the client.

The rules state that members and firms should not accept or continue engagements in which there are, or are likely to be, significant conflicts of interest between members, firms and clients.

3.7.2 Conflicts between the interests of different clients

Assurance firms can have clients who are in competition with each other. However, the firm should ensure that it is **not the subject of a dispute** between the clients. It must also manage its work so that the interests of one client do not adversely affect the other client. Where acceptance or continuance of an engagement would, even with safeguards, **materially prejudice** the interests of any client, the appointment should not be accepted or continued.

Auditors often give their clients business advice unrelated to audit. In such a position, they may well become involved when clients are involved in issues such as share issues and takeovers. Neither situation is inherently wrong for an auditor to be in. With regard to **share issues**, audit firms should not underwrite an issue of shares to the public of a client they audit. In a **takeover situation**, if the auditors are involved in the audits of both predator and target company, they must take care. They should not:

- Be the principal advisers to either party
- Issue reports assessing the accounts of either party other than their audit report

If they find that they possess material confidential information, they should contact the appropriate body or regulator.

3.7.3 Managing conflicts between clients' interests

When considering whether to accept a client or when there is a change in a client's circumstances, assurance firms should take reasonable steps to ascertain whether there is a **conflict of interest** or if there is likely to be one in the future. Relationships that ended two or more years earlier are unlikely to create a conflict. Disclosure is the most important safeguard in connection of conflicts between clients' interests. Safeguards would usually include:

- **Notifying the client** of the interest/activities that may **cause a conflict of interest** and obtaining their consent to act in the circumstances, or

- **Notifying all known relevant parties** that the member is **acting for two or more parties** in respect of a matter where their respective interests are in conflict, and obtaining their consent so to act, or

- Notifying the client that the member **does not act exclusively for any one client** in the provision of proposed services, and obtaining their consent so to act

Other safeguards

- Using separate engagement teams
- Procedures to prevent access of information (such as special passwords)
- Clear guidelines for the respective teams on issues of security and confidentiality
- The use of confidentiality agreements signed by the partners and staff
- Regular review of the safeguards by an independent partner
- Advising one or both of the clients to obtain additional independent advice

3.7.4 Individuals' conflicts of interest

Individuals within a firm may also face their own conflicts of interest. These may include conflicts between loyalty and responsibilities to their bosses and to staff who work for them. There may also be conflicts between individuals' desire to maintain or improve their own position in the firm and a wish to be certain that their ethical stance is correct, for example how far to follow up an audit query.

A December 2009 question covered a conflict that a junior partner had between their loyalty to a trainee who had raised well-founded concerns about a client and their loyalty to a senior partner who had dismissed the issue.

Case Study

In September 2011, the accountancy press reported that a draft European Union green paper would, if implemented, force accountancy firms to take very significant steps to deal with the problems of independence outlined in this section. The most radical proposal was that firms should be forced to specialise in either audit or non-audit services. The proposed rules would prohibit audit firms offering consultancy and advisory services even to non-audit clients. The list of consultancy and advisory services prohibited was similar to the list in the Sarbanes-Oxley legislation, but the draft went further than Sarbanes-Oxley in prohibiting the provision of these services to non-audit clients.

The draft also reportedly proposed mandatory rotation of audit firms to enhance professional scepticism and remove the pressure on partners not to lose longstanding clients. The report stressed a need to remove comfortable relationships between auditors and clients as a means of establishing market confidence.

Other suggestions included compulsory joint audits for public interest entities (double the scrutiny), audit quality reviews and expanded audit reports.

The proposals were scaled back to some extent later in 2011, with the proposals for mandatory joint audits being dropped.

4 Problems facing accountants in business

FAST FORWARD

The accountant in business may face a variety of difficulties, including conflicts between **professional and employment obligations**, pressure to **prepare misleading information**, and whether the accountant has **sufficient expertise, financial interests** or **inducements**.

4.1 Conflicts between professional and employment obligations

Ethical guidance stresses that a professional accountant should normally support the **legitimate and ethical obligations** established by the employer. However, they may be pressurised to act in ways that threaten compliance with the fundamental principles. These include:

- Acting contrary to law, regulation, technical or professional standards
- Aiding unethical or illegal earnings management strategies
- Misleading auditors or regulators
- Issuing or being associated with a report that misrepresents the facts

If the accountant faces these problems they should obtain advice from the employer, the ACCA or lawyers, or use the formal procedures within the organisation.

4.2 Preparation and reporting of information

As well as complying with financial reporting standards, the professional accountant in business should aim to prepare information that **clearly describes the nature of the business transactions**, **classifies and records information in a timely and proper manner** and **represents the facts accurately**. If the accountant faces pressure to produce misleading information, they should consult with superiors. The accountant should not be associated with misleading information, and may need to seek legal advice or report to the appropriate authorities.

4.3 Acting with sufficient expertise

Guidance stresses that the professional accountant should only undertake tasks for which they have **sufficient specific training or experience**. Certain pressures may threaten the ability of the professional accountant to perform duties with appropriate competence and due care.

- Lack of time
- Lack of information
- Insufficient training, experience or education
- Inadequate resources

Whether this is a significant threat will depend on the other people the accountant is working with, their seniority and the level of supervision over their work. If the problem is serious, the accountant should take steps to remedy the situation, including obtaining training, ensuring time is available and consulting. Refusal to perform duties is the last resort.

4.4 Financial interests

Ethical guidance highlights financial interests as a self-interest threat to objectivity and confidentiality. In particular the temptation to **manipulate price-sensitive information** in order to gain financially is stressed. Financial interests may include shares, profit-related bonuses or share options.

This threat can be countered by the individual consulting with superiors and **disclosing all relevant information**. Having a remuneration committee composed of **independent non-executive directors** determining the remuneration packages of executive directors can help resolve the problems at senior level.

4.5 Inducements   6/11

Ethical guidance highlights the possibility that accountants may be offered inducements to influence actions or decisions, encourage illegal behaviour or obtain confidential information. We cover bribery and corruption in more detail below.

5 Bribery and corruption

FAST FORWARD

The involvement of directors and others responsible for corporate governance in bribery and corruption can **undermine the relationships of trust** on which corporate governance is based.

5.1 Impact of bribery and corruption

Key terms

Bribery is the offering, giving, receiving or soliciting of any item of value to influence the actions of an official or other person in charge of a public or legal duty. (Black's Law Dictionary).
Corruption can be defined as deviation from honest behaviour.

The purpose of bribery is to influence the conduct of the recipient. A bribe may not be money or a tangible gift. It can be granting a privilege to the recipient. A bribe need not be paid to be effective. Sometimes a promise or undertaking may be sufficient to influence decision-making and conduct. As well as the payer and the recipient of the bribe, others may be complicit if they know about the bribe and fail to report it, if they ignore signs that bribery is taking place or if they hold a position of responsibility and fail to take action to prevent bribery. Legislation such as the Bribery Act 2011 in the UK therefore makes commercial organisations liable if their employees pay bribes, unless they take adequate procedures to prevent bribery.

Bribery is an example of corruption. Other forms of corruption include the following.

- **Abuse of a system** – using a system for improper purposes

- **Bid rigging** – promising a contract in advance to one party, although other parties have been invited to bid for the contract

- **Cartel** – a secret agreement by supposedly competing producers to fix prices, quantity or market share

- **Influence peddling** – using personal influence in government or connections with persons in authority to obtain favours or preferential treatment for another, usually in return for payment

5.2 Why bribery and corruption are problems

5.2.1 Lack of honesty and good faith

Corruption means that someone in a position of authority or responsibility, including corporate governance responsibility, will no longer be **acting impartially** and in accordance with a position of trust. Bribery encourages others to **violate a duty of service**. It can also undermine behaviour in other ways. If staff are aware that bribery goes on within their organisation, even if they are not involved in it themselves, then this may undermine attempts by the organisation to **impose standards of behaviour**. It may also result in an **overall lack of trust** in what the organisation is doing.

5.2.2 Conflicts of interest

Those taking bribes will face a conflict between their **legitimate duties and responsibilities** (for example to shareholders), and any **personal gains** they may make through unethical activities. The personal gains may not be directly in the forms of money or gifts. Involvement by directors in bid rigging, for example, may generate higher profits for their company, which in turn may enhance their performance bonuses.

Further conflicts of interest may also arise if anyone who has participated in corruption is threatened with **public exposure**. The actions they take to ensure public exposure does not occur may also not be in the interests of their organisation, or those whose interests they should be representing.

5.2.3 International risk management

UK Government guidance on the 2011 UK Bribery Act acknowledges that commercial organisations in some parts of the world and in some sectors may come under pressure to pay 'facilitation payments' to foreign officials to promote their business ends. However, the number of places where businesses need to pay bribes to conduct business legitimately is debatable. If businesses had effective procedures for assessing and managing risks, then they should probably decide to avoid these places anyway.

5.2.4 Economic issues

Bribery and corruption results in a **misallocation of resources**. Contracts do not go to the most efficient producer but the producer that pays the highest bribes. Costs of doing business will increase. Bribery and corruption therefore threaten the basis on which markets are established and the operation of those markets. Participation in economic activity may be less likely if it is felt that bribery or market rigging make it unlikely that an acceptable return will be achieved for the risks taken. Alternatively, if one company is believed to be thriving by offering bribes, other companies may then follow its example and those being bribed may come to expect illicit payments as a matter of course.

5.2.5 Reputation

Those who do business with the organisation, for example suppliers or customers, may cease to do so if they have **no confidence in its honesty**. Honest staff may decide to leave if they feel that they cannot trust their employer.

We shall discuss professionalism and professional reputation in the next section. If accountants are found guilty of bribery, this can have an adverse impact not only on their employer but also on the **reputation** of the **profession** as a whole, giving the impression of dishonesty and lack of objectivity.

Case Study

In April 2012 *The New York Times* published details of an alleged bribery scandal at retail giant Wal-Mart. The paper alleged that executives in Wal-Mart's Mexican subsidiary had given payoffs to local officials in return for help getting permits to build new Wal-Mart stores in Mexico. Top executives in Mexico had known about these payments but had concealed them from Wal-Mart's main board.

In 2005 the main board was tipped off by a former executive in Mexico. An internal investigation allegedly revealed $24 million in suspected bribery payments. However, the original investigation team was accused of being too aggressive and was dropped from the case. Responsibility for the investigation was transferred to one of the Mexican executives alleged to have authorised bribes. This executive exonerated their fellow executives and Wal-Mart's main board accepted this. Although a report was made at the time to the US Justice Department, Wal-Mart played down the significance of the allegations. Executives in Mexico were not disciplined – one was promoted to vice chairman.

At the time of the investigation in 2005 Wal-Mart was facing pressure on its share price. The company's Mexican operations were its biggest success, highlighted to investors as a model of future growth. *The New York Times* said that there was evidence that main board directors were well aware of the devastating consequences the allegations could have if made public.

This was not the first time that there had been issues over corruption in Mexico. An investigation in 2003 revealed that Wal-Mart de Mexico had systematically increased sales by helping high-volume customers evade sales taxes. Executives had failed to enforce anti-corruption policies and ignored warnings from internal auditors. The company ultimately paid back taxes of $34.3 million.

Wal-Mart's shares fell by nearly 9% in the days after *The New York Times* published its allegations. The fall at Wal-Mart also dragged down the whole Dow Jones Industrial Average. Wal-Mart faced the possibility of massive legal liabilities under the US's Foreign Corrupt Practices Act. One of Wal-Mart's institutional investors began action against executives and board members, and sought changes in the company's corporate governance. A group of New York City pension funds said they would vote against re-electing five Wal-Mart directors. One of Wal-Mart's managers started an online petition urging the company to undertake a thorough and independent investigation. The manager claimed that most of the signatories were current and former employees fed up with the philosophy of expansion at all costs.

Even only a few days after the story broke, there was evidence that Wal-Mart's strategic ambitions may have been damaged by scandals. Its attempts to open stores in new areas and other dealings appeared to be coming under increased scrutiny. It had recently been focusing on bigger cities where there was more bureaucracy to overcome than in suburban and rural areas. The bribery scandal appeared to have made it more difficult for Wal-Mart to proceed with its expansion plans.

5.3 Measures to combat bribery and corruption

Many of the measures we have already discussed will be relevant to combating bribery.

Recent legislation in certain countries has put pressure on businesses to introduce sufficient controls. As mentioned above, under the UK Bribery Act, for example, if an employee or associate of a commercial organisation bribes another person, the organisation will be liable if it cannot show that it had adequate procedures in place to prevent bribes being paid. Under previous legislation, a company was only likely to be guilty if senior management was involved. Now, however, it must demonstrate that its anti-corruption procedures are sufficient to stop any employees, agents or other third parties acting on the company's behalf from committing bribery.

Guidance published in 2011 by the UK Ministry of Justice on the Bribery Act suggests that what is seen as adequate will depend on the bribery risks faced by the organisation, and the nature, size and complexity of the business. The UK guidance is based on six principles:

- **Proportionate procedures**. Measures taken should be proportional to risks and nature, size and complexity.

- **Top-level commitment**. Top-level management should be committed to preventing bribery and promoting a culture where bribery is viewed as unacceptable.

- **Risk assessment**. Organisations should assess the nature and extent of their exposure to bribery internally and externally. Some activities, for example extraction, and some markets, for example countries where there is no anti-bribery legislation, may be at higher risk.

- **Due diligence**. The organisation should carry out due diligence procedures in relation to those who perform services for it, or on its behalf.

- **Communication**. Bribery prevention policies and procedures should be embedded and understood throughout the organisation through communication and training.

- **Monitoring and review**. The organisation should monitor and review anti-bribery procedures and improve them as required. The guidance emphasises that risks are dynamic, and procedures may need to change if risks alter.

5.3.1 Establishing culture

The UK guidance highlights the need for board commitment to fight corruption. Directors may seek to establish a commitment against corruption by a formal statement, setting out a **zero tolerance policy** and spelling out the consequences for employees or managers who transgress. The statement should include an assertion of the benefits of avoidance of corrupt activity (for example maintaining reputation, and customer and business partner confidence). The commitment of the management team should be reinforced by the **involvement of senior management** in the development and implementation of bribery prevention procedures.

As with other areas, **communication** of the organisation's procedures and policies, and **training** in their application, will be very important in helping to establish the culture. Training should include general training on the threat of bribery on induction, and also specific training for those involved in higher risk activities such as purchasing and contracting.

However, while establishing the right culture is an important part of taking effective action to combat corruption, a culture that is ambiguous or not enforced may adversely affect the success of other measures. This may occur if managers and staff feel that they are receiving mixed messages. They may believe that they are expected to do what it takes to earn sufficient returns in environments where ethical temptations exist, or that ethically dubious conduct will be ignored or implicitly accepted.

5.3.2 Code of conduct

A code of conduct is perhaps the most important element of communication that the UK guidelines stress. As well being central to communication with employees, a publicly communicated code also reassures those doing business with the organisation and can act as a deterrent to misconduct.

We have already seen in this chapter the example code of conduct that includes provisions about dealing truthfully with suppliers and refraining from seeking or participating in questionable behaviour to secure competitive advantage. Businesses may decide to issue a separate anti-bribery code. However, there may also be the same issues with an anti-bribery code as a general ethical code, that for example staff do not feel it is relevant to them. This reinforces the need for effective training of staff.

5.3.3 Risk assessment

Identification of circumstances where bribery may be a problem must be built into business risk assessments. Sensitive areas could include the activities of intermediaries or agents or staff within the organisation responsible for hospitality or promotional expenditure. Note that the UK guidance stresses that risks may change over time (for example as the business enters new markets) and so may need to be reassessed. A poor internal control environment may also be a factor that contributes significantly to increased risk.

 Case Study

The guidance published in 2011 by the UK Ministry of Justice highlighted five areas where the risk of bribery and corruption may be high.

- **Country.** Countries with high levels of corruption, that lack anti-bribery legislation and which fail to promote transparent procurement and investment policies are at high risk.

- **Sectoral.** Higher-risk sectors include the extractive and large-scale infrastructure sectors.

- **Transaction.** Risky transactions include charitable and political contributions, licences and permits, and transactions relating to public procurement.

- **Business opportunity.** Potentially risky projects include high-value projects, projects involving many contractors or intermediaries, and projects not apparently undertaken at market price or which lack a clear business objective.

- **Business partnership risk.** Risky situations could include the use of intermediaries in transactions with foreign public officials, involvement with consortia or joint venture partners and relationships with politically exposed persons.

The guidance also highlights various internal failings that could add to risk.

- Deficiencies in employee training, skills and knowledge

- Bonus culture that rewards excessive risk taking

- Lack of clarity in the organisation's policies on, and procedures for, hospitality and promotional expenditure and political or charitable contributions

- Lack of clear financial controls

- Lack of clear anti-bribery message from top-level management

5.3.4 Conduct of business

As the UK guidance states, a strong tone at the top and the ethical code may be undermined by a lack of detailed guidance on the implementation of anti-bribery procedures.

Areas where detailed guidance may be required include the extent of **due diligence procedures** on potential business partners or intermediaries – highlighted as a key area in the UK guidance above. The guidance points out that due diligence is both risk assessment and a means of mitigating risks.

Due diligence procedures may be carried out at different levels. They may be at a low level, for example, when contracting for the provision of information services, but at a higher level when a business is obliged to use a local agent in another country or is selecting an intermediary when establishing business abroad. Procedures may include questioning, investigations or general investigation. Appraisal and monitoring should continue once the relationship has been established.

Other important areas will include:

- The need for **contractual terms** with consultants and intermediaries to reflect internal rules and to emphasise zero tolerance of bribery

- Policies on **hospitality and promotional expenditure and charitable and political donations**
- **Procurement and tendering** guidelines
- Differentiation between **properly payable fees** (for example inspection certificates) and **facilitation payments** (often bribes)
- **Recruitment and human resource procedures** to mitigate the risks of employees in business-sensitive areas becoming involved in bribery

However detailed the procedures, they will not be able to give absolute assurance that corrupt activities will not take place. Staff may **misinterpret the requirements**, or may encounter ethically dubious situations not covered by the guidance. They may assume that conduct not forbidden by the guidance is legitimate.

There is also the issue that detailed guidance is meant to ensure compliance with the law. In many countries the law is not entirely clear. The US Chamber of Commerce, for example, has criticised American law for prohibiting bribery in some circumstances but not others, although critics have claimed that the evidence supporting this claim is thin.

5.3.5 Reporting of transactions and whistleblowing

Ethical guidance points out that threats to compliance may appear to arise not only from the accountant **making or accepting the inducement** but also from the offer **having been made in the first place**. It recommends that directors or senior managers be **informed**, and disclosure may have to be made to third parties. An organisation's guidance should make it clear that managers and staff should seek guidance about, and disclose, any activities that are questionable. Guidance on whistleblowing procedures should also make clear that they extend to reporting suspicions of bribery and corruption. Staff should have the opportunity to make suggestions for improvement of bribery prevention procedures.

5.3.6 Monitoring

As part of their regular monitoring of risk management, the board should receive reports on compliance with internal procedures, such as due diligence on agents and details about questionable behaviour that has been discovered. The UK guidance makes it clear that monitoring the systems designed to prevent bribery is an important element of the board's overall monitoring of internal control systems and consideration of whether systems need to be improved as the risk environment changes. Events that may result in changes to systems include changes of government, reports of bribery or other negative press coverage.

Case Study

A survey by consulting firm Proviti and the law firm Covington & Burling identified five common control weaknesses in firms that had faced legal action under the US Foreign Corrupt Practices Act (FCPA).

1. Inadequate contract pricing review

Controls could not determine whether contract prices were inflated to conceal kickbacks. They could not identify when illicit commissions were disguised as legitimate business expenses and unwarranted additional fees were added to contract prices. Firms needed to introduce competitive bidding and insist on invoices showing sufficient detail.

2. Inadequate due diligence and verification of foreign business representatives

Failings included inadequate risk assessments, a lack of written contracts containing FCPA compliance terms and using representatives with a previous history of dubious payments.

3. Ineffective accounts-payable payments and review

Weaknesses included making inappropriate payments that were disguised as legal fees, lack of back-up for payments and paying for services that were not included in contracts.

4. Ineffective financial account reconciliation and review

Documentation failed to describe transactions so that reviewers could identify problems. Issues included inflated revenues, recording of entries that were false or placed in the wrong account and payment of false invoices.

5. Ineffective commission payment review and authority

Commissions were not verified and as a result bribery payments to foreign government officials were not identified. Commissions were also paid for duties that were not assigned by the contract, misleading information was presented to internal auditors and commission payments were inflated to include bribes. There needed to be careful review of commissions, including reviewing contracts to see if agents were entitled to a commission and the amount of the commission, and determining whether the work met the contract. Payments should be made to the contract counter-party and not a third party. Checks should be carried out to make sure that the payments were not made to an offshore account.

6 The accountancy profession and the public interest

FAST FORWARD

Professionalism means **avoiding actions** that bring **discredit on the accountancy profession**.

Acting in the public interest means acting for the welfare of society at large.

Various commentators have argued that the **figures** accountants produce are **not neutral**, but incorporate value judgements and are in accordance with the wishes of certain viewpoints in society.

6.1 Professions and professionalism   6/10

6.1.1 Profession

The theory and skills are acquired by a structured training process, validated by examination and maintained through continuing professional education.

Values underpin the professional's actions. For example, the medical profession is underpinned by the principle of the sanctity of life. The common code of values and conduct should be independently administered by a governing body.

The skills and values **enhance the weight of a professional's judgement**. They are what the professional holds themselves out to have by virtue of calling themselves an accountant (for example) and belonging to a professional institute.

In return for accepting a duty to society, members of a profession are allowed privileges, for example being able to practise certain activities or to use a title.

Key term

A **profession** is based on a body of theory and skills, adherence to a common code of values and conduct, and acceptance of a duty to society as a whole.

6.1.2 Professionalism and professional behaviour

IESBA's code of ethics defines professionalism in terms of **professional behaviour**. Professional behaviour imposes an obligation on professional accountants to act in the **public interest**. They should **comply with relevant laws and regulations** and **avoid any action** that may **bring discredit to the**

profession. Professional behaviour is one of the fundamental principles that we discussed earlier this chapter, and professional behaviour in a wider sense would include compliance with the other four ethical principles.

Professionalism can also be seen as a state of mind, a concern to take action in the **public interest** and sometimes to lead public opinion, for example in developing guidance on reporting.

In marketing themselves and their work, professional accountants should not bring the profession into disrepute. They should avoid making exaggerated claims for their own services, qualifications and experience and should not refer to others disparagingly. Accountants may also have other professional responsibilities depending on the roles they hold, for example responsibilities as company directors.

An ACCA survey in 2005 produced a wider definition of professionalism. The survey suggested that the most important competencies for modern professionals were:

- Maintaining confidentiality and upholding ethical standards
- Preparing financial information
- Complying with legal and regulatory requirements
- Interpreting financial statements
- Communicating effectively
- Preparing financial statements
- Problem solving and managerial skills

Professionalism is also important when dealing with professional colleagues, particularly if the individual is a senior member of the organisation. As leaders, senior accountants should aim to work well with other team members, and deal appropriately with concerns they raise about the work they are doing. They should also look to set an example to junior staff.

6.2 The public interest   6/09, 6/14

Key term

> The **public interest** is considered to be the collective wellbeing of the community of people and institutions the professional accountant serves, including clients, lenders, governments, employers, employees, investors, the business and financial community and others who rely on the work of professional accountants. (IESBA)

IESBA comments that an accountant's responsibility is not exclusively to satisfy the needs of an **individual client or employer**. It extends to society, and often consists of supplying information that society needs.

One fundamental problem with the debate about accountants acting in the public interest is the lack in most jurisdictions of a robust definition of what the public interest is that is backed by enforcement mechanisms. Within UK law for example there is no statutory definition of the public interest. As one critic, Lovell, comments: 'Its malleability possibly explains both its longevity and its unreliability in a court of law.'

Critics of the view that accountants act in the public interest have focused on the alleged closeness between accountants' definition of the public interest and the profession's own self-interest. Critics have claimed that accountants' insistence on self-regulation indicates where their priorities lie. Some believe that the accountancy profession has always been vulnerable to this charge. Lee's history of the accountancy profession in the 19th century comments: 'The most obvious feature of early UK professionalisation is the pursuit by accountants and their institutions of economic self-interest in the name of a public interest'.

Exam focus point

> Question 2 in June 2009 asked about accountants' relationship with the public interest.

6.3 Influence of the accountancy profession on organisations

That the influence of the accountancy profession is potentially huge can be established simply by considering all the different involvements that accountants have.

- Financial accounting
- Audit
- Management accounting
- Consulting
- Tax
- Public sector accounting

Accountants' advice will also be crucial in situations of change, where accountants are advising on the financial and information systems aspects of new developments.

Case Study

Accountants dominate senior business positions in many countries. The variety of involvements that accountants have within each area of their expertise is also very large. The Institute of Chartered Accountants in England and Wales' recruitment literature highlights for example the role of tax accountants.

'Some professionals will advise on policy for our tax system, others will write the tax law. Someone else will administer the collection of taxes for the Government. Others will act for businesses of all types who have to pay these taxes. Marketing, IT, media and publishing all need tax specialists.'

Accountants therefore have a significant impact, a significant footprint, on the organisations for which they work. Is this always for the best?

Case Study

In the book *Ethical Issues in Accounting* a chapter by Alan Lovell points out that accountants will be responsible for managing public sector organisations in as cost effective a way as possible, which may not necessarily be compatible with the service objectives of those organisations nor the codes of other professional staff who work within those organisations.

Lovell utilises Kohlberg's view of ethical hierarchy to explain how accountants effectively view other professionals. The accounting system in effect assumes that, as the other professionals do not trust the system or those who operate it, this illustrates that they have a low level of moral reasoning and therefore justifies a strict performance management system, together with anti-whistleblowing codes designed to deter employees from revealing shortcomings in patient care.

However, the ethical codes to which doctors and nurses adhere are founded on the idea that they are their patients' advocates and this implies that they need to use a much higher level of moral reasoning.

6.4 The accountancy profession in society

At one level the numbers included within accounts can have a number of impacts.

(a) **Mechanistic issues** are where the accounts are used to judge the performance of a company or its directors in line with a regulation or contract. Examples are company borrowing limits which are frequently defined as a multiple of share capital and reserves and directors' bonus schemes that are based on some proportion of reported profits.

(b)   **Judgemental issues** are where the figures in the accounts influence the judgement of their users. The accounts may influence not just the view of investors, but governments seeking to assess what a reasonable tax burden would be and employees determining their wage claims.

6.5 Accountancy as a value-laden profession

Critics of the accountancy profession claim that the work done and the conclusions drawn by accountants are determined by a set of beliefs and values that imply a particular view of how power and wealth should be distributed in society. Accountants, it is claimed, believe that precedence should be given to the interests of suppliers of financial capital.

Many accountants would argue in response that the numbers in accounts support no cause and it is for others to draw conclusions on the figures produced. If pressed they might argue that they are following the requirements of laws or of their clients. However, the laws may be ethically suspect and the following the requirements of clients argument does not support ideas of accountants' independence or, worse, leads to the suspicion that accountants are pursuing ethically dubious courses.

Even if the ends are not explicitly ethically suspect, much accounting literature does assume that accountants are producing information for individuals or corporations seeking to **maximise their personal wealth**. If this has a moral justification, it is based on the ideas of **liberal economic democracy**. These ideas are that individuals should be free to **exercise their economic choices** and are equally able to do so. No group in society dominates either economically or politically. The result of the individual pursuit of economic benefit is economic efficiency, maximum profits and economic growth, and everyone within society being better off.

6.5.1 Criticisms of liberal economic democracy

Critics have claimed that the model of liberal economic democracy is far from reality and has various flaws. By providing the information that supports the present systems, accountants are complicit in perpetuating its flaws.

(a)   **Lack of equality**

One significant criticism is that individuals are not equal economically and are evidently **not able to make economic choices** that will benefit themselves. The argument that people make a rational economic choice to be homeless is clearly wrong. Accountants are therefore accused of supporting those who can make economic choices and by doing so perpetuate social inequality, ensure that wealth continues to be distributed among the already wealthy, and suppress minorities and the disenfranchised and powerless.

(b)   **Role of institutions**

A related criticism is that individuals do not exercise the real power but institutions – principally the **Government and corporations**. Indeed, critics point to many instances of governments acting to protect the interests of shareholders and the information rights of the financial community against less well-off groups in society.

Marxist arguments take this viewpoint to its furthest conclusion, arguing that power is held by **capital**, that capital and labour are inevitably in conflict and that the state acts to protect capital and suppress labour. Accountants too are complicit in this.

(c)   **Failure to increase social welfare**

The argument that the pursuit of individual self-interest leads to maximum social welfare appears tenuous. Even if wealth is maximised, there is **no guarantee** that all aspects of **social welfare** will be **maximised**. Indeed, some aspects of social welfare, such as quality of life or health, would not seem to have an obvious link with maximising income. In addition, maximisation of wealth does not imply that wealth will be fairly distributed. Critics have claimed that economic growth has been at the expense of a widening gap between rich and poor, both within developed countries and between developed and developing countries.

(d)   **Environmental problems**

Critics such as the 'deep ecologists' (discussed in Chapter 11) have claimed that the pursuit of growth has been at the expense of **environmental degradation** and that society needs to change its priorities. By aiding the promotion of economic growth, accountants are complicit in supporting activity that harms the environment.

(e)   **Ethical viewpoint**

Some critics have gone back to ethical theories outlined earlier and have claimed that accountants are complicit in a version of **utilitarianism** with the economic ends justifying the means rather than another (preferable) ethical position.

Exam focus point

The examiner has stressed that students must be able to discuss whether accountants' role is that of the servant of capital.

6.6 Criticisms of the accountancy profession

Inevitably perhaps it has been the critics of the accountancy profession who have been most vocal in highlighting the influence of accounting in resource allocation, seeking to demonstrate its complicity in wealth distribution and its role as the agent of capital.

6.6.1 Accountants in management accounting

In his book *The Social and Organisational Context of Management Accounting* Puxty argued that the 'received wisdom' of management accounting cannot legitimately be taken for granted.

Case Study

Puxty highlighted behavioural studies of budgeting that use the phrase 'dysfunctional behaviour', meaning behaviour that is harmful to the **organisation**. But why should this be so? Is it not 'dysfunctional' from the point of view of the **manager** that they are expected to suffer the misery of having their actions constrained by budget targets? There are many other examples: what, for instance, is 'favourable' about a favourable labour rate variance, from the point of view of the workforce?

Puxty went on to show that traditional management accounting is rooted in modes of thought that are only considered to be 'common sense' for the time being. 'Common sense' he asserted, is determined by the **beliefs** and **values** of the society in which it supposedly applies. It is not common to all eras (it is relativist).

In particular, the ideas that considerations of society (of which businesses are a part and a microcosm) should take the individual as their starting point and that individuals have rights to liberty and property are fundamental to accounting, yet they only originated with philosophers like Hobbes and Locke in the 17th century.

Puxty also argues that Foucault's ideas about the way in which **regimes of power** have grown and been sustained through **disciplinary mechanisms** and the **institution of norms** for human behaviour are very relevant to the role of the accountancy profession.

Case Study

Other studies along similar lines to Puxty have attempted to show how the origins of accounting reside in the exercise of social power and how accounting is 'implicated in the creation of structures of surveillance and power that permit modern management to function at a distance from the work process itself.'

One study considers the development of standard costing and budgeting in the 1920s as simply one part of a general widening of the apparatus of power at this time.

'The practices that developed were intended to make the person ... more amenable to being managed and controlled'.

This should be seen in the context of other drives current at the time, such as the wide advocacy of eugenics (the sterilisation of the 'unfit' to improve the country's breeding stock) and an interest in 'mental hygiene' to be promoted by means of such methods as IQ testing.

Macintosh in *Management Accounting and Control Systems* (1994) looks at Foucault's ideas about the general principles of discipline and control that became widespread in the Western world from about 1700 onwards.

(a) The **enclosure principle**, in essence keeping people in confined spaces (at the desk, at their workstation)

(b) The **efficient body principle**, which disciplines individuals' time when they are in their confined spaces

(c) The **correct comportment principle**, disciplining behaviour through surveillance, through the imposition of norms of behaviour, and through examination

Macintosh has little difficulty in drawing parallels with management accounting – responsibility accounting, standard costing practices and performance measurement systems among the examples chosen.

6.6.2 Accountants and financial accounting

Unsurprisingly accountants have been criticised in similar terms for the picture published financial accounts give and the support they provide to capital markets. Prem Sikka argues that many accountants:

'... believe that mobilising accounting and auditing practices in support of markets and financial capital (held by shareholders) is ethically acceptable but mobilising accounting to give visibility to poverty and institutionalised exploitation is somehow unethical ... Accounting and auditing practices remain preoccupied with prioritising capital over labour (in the statement of profit or loss) and the property rights (in the statement of financial position). Most accounting books have little to say about social justice or the rights of employees.'

For example, Professor Sikka and others proposed expanding the level of disclosures in accounts in the early 1990s to include disclosures of low pay. This proposal was made at a time when the Labour party was pressing for the introduction of the minimum wage.

Sikka and others have emphasised the idea that accountancy decisions inevitably have **political consequences** and that it is difficult to see how accountants could hold positions that are not influenced by wider values. However, one criticism of their view is that accountants are not free to determine their own stance, and that instead they are constrained by politicians' attitudes expressed in legislation.

6.6.3 Accountants and taxation advice

Prem Sikka and others have also criticised accountants for being complicit in their clients' paying less than their 'fair' share of tax. In some cases accountants have been found guilty of helping clients evade tax and duly punished. However some critics seem to suggest that accountants should not be involved in helping their clients legally avoid tax. Again, however, the question arises as to whether accountants should base their advice on the law, or on some sort of notion as to what a fair tax liability is.

6.7 Acting against the public interest

Criticism of the accountancy profession has extended to the rules that it follows. Critics have argued that the rules:

(a) Are **too passive**, allowing too great a variety of accounting treatments, and failing to impose meaningful responsibilities on auditors such as an explicit responsibility to detect and report fraud

(b) **Emphasise the wrong principles**, giving priority to client confidentiality over disclosure in the wider public interest, and teaching accountants to follow rules rather than question them

(c) Allow auditors to **establish a long-term, cosy relationship** with clients by the failure to require compulsory rotation of auditors and allowing auditors to provide non-audit services, rather than forcing auditors to maintain a distance

(d) Allow the creation of **too small a number of large firms** who dominate the audit of major listed companies and therefore can effectively set the agenda as regards scope of audit work (although arguably it is only large firms that can audit the very biggest companies)

Arguably these views depend to some extent on hindsight, the implication being that, as auditors and governance structures have failed to identify corporate malpractice, there must be something wrong with the rulebook that is being followed.

However, we've seen how the fallout from the Enron case influenced the development of the stricter Sarbanes-Oxley rules in the United States. Partly this was due to Enron appearing in a number of ways to 'tick the right boxes'. It had a good number of non-executive directors on its board with a strong range of experience, for example.

Exam focus point

> The examiner has emphasised that students will need to show that they can act as the moral conscience of the organisation. They see the granting of professional status to accountants and other experts as a privilege, given on the understanding that it is used in the interests of society and clients.

Question
Stakeholders

Think about all the major activities that you are involved in if you work as an accountant. Who are the stakeholders involved? Who do you treat as the most important stakeholders? And why?

Answer

Answers will vary depending on your responsibilities. If for example you're involved in audit and answered the clients because they pay our bills, who do you mean when you say the client – the directors or shareholders? If you work in tax planning, by reducing your client's tax bill, are you contributing to society as a whole losing out through diminished tax revenues?

Chapter Roundup

- Organisations have responded to pressures to be seen to act ethically by publishing **ethical codes**, setting out their **values and responsibilities** towards stakeholders.

- Professional codes of ethics apply to the **individual behaviour** of professionals and are often based on principles, supplemented by guidance on **threats and safeguards**.

- Threats to independence of accountants in practice include **self-interest**, **self-review**, **advocacy**, **familiarity** and **intimidation**.

    Accountants in practice may face **conflicts of interest** between their own and clients' interests, or between the interests of different clients.

- The accountant in business may face a variety of difficulties, including conflicts between **professional and employment obligations, pressure to prepare misleading information and whether the accountant has sufficient expertise, financial interests** or **inducements**.

- The involvement of directors and others responsible for corporate governance in bribery and corruption can **undermine the relationships of trust** on which corporate governance is based.

- Professionalism means **avoiding actions** that bring **discredit on the accountancy profession**.

    Acting in the public interest means acting for the welfare of society at large.

    Various commentators have argued that the **figures** accountants produce are **not neutral** but incorporate value judgements and are in accordance with the wishes of certain viewpoints in society.

Quick Quiz

1   What does an organisation's ethical code usually contain?

2   What are the key elements of IESBA's Code of Ethics?

3   Which of the following is not an advantage of a principles-based ethical code?

    A   It prevents narrow, legalistic interpretations.
    B   It can accommodate a rapidly changing environment.
    C   The illustrative examples provided can be followed in all similar situations.
    D   It prescribes minimum expected standards of behaviour.

4   Fill in the blank:

    .... means that members should be straightforward and honest in all business and professional relationships.

5   According to the IESBA Code of Ethics, what should professional accountants consider when attempting to resolve ethical issues?

6   Give four examples of a familiarity threat.

7   A firm that is sued by a client must resign from engagement with that client.

    True   ☐

    False ☐

8   Fill in the blank:

    .... is the collective wellbeing of the community of people and interests that the accountant serves.

Answers to Quick Quiz

1   A statement of the organisation's values and an explanation of its responsibilities towards its stakeholders

2
- An acceptance by the accountancy profession of the responsibility to act in the public interest
- Fundamental principles of ethics
- Conceptual framework, requiring accountants to address threats to compliance and apply safeguards

3   C   Although the examples may be good guides for conduct in many instances, circumstances will vary, so they should not be seen as totally prescriptive.

4   Integrity

5
- The facts
- The ethical issues involved
- Related fundamental principles
- Established internal procedures
- Alternative courses of action, considering the consequences of each

6
- Family and personal relationships between the client and the firm
- Long association with assurance client
- Employment with assurance client
- Recent service with assurance client

7   False. Not necessarily. Other safeguards can be used (disclosure to the audit committee, removing certain individuals from the team, involving an additional professional accountant on the team to review work). However, resignation may be required in the end.

8   The public interest

Now try the question below from the Practice Question Bank.

Number	Level	Marks	Time
Q10	Examination	20	39 mins

Corporate
social responsibility

Introduction

In this last chapter we focus on the ethical and corporate social responsibilities organisations have. These can be seen as following on from the ideas in the last section of Chapter 10. The idea is that the public interest means businesses should follow stricter ethical practices than legislation, regulations or governance codes require. In Section 1 we pick up on the social responsibility ideas that we discussed first in Chapter 2 and focus on the specific concept of corporate citizenship. In Section 2 we look at how ideas of ethics and social responsibility are combined. The Gray, Owen and Adams viewpoints have been highlighted by the examiner as particularly important, and tie in with the issue of which **stakeholders** are important to the organisation.

In Sections 3 to 6 we examine the impact organisations have on the environment. The concept of sustainability, discussed in Section 4, is particularly important, as it relates to whether the impact the organisation makes on the environment can be limited to what the environment can bear. We also consider aspects of reporting, managing and auditing the environmental effects of organisations' activities, including integrated reporting.

Study guide

		Intellectual level
A7	**Corporate governance and corporate social responsibility**	
(d)	Explain the concept of the organisation as a corporate citizen of society with rights and responsibilities.	3
E2	**Different approaches to ethics and social responsibility**	
(a)	Describe and evaluate the Gray, Owen and Adams seven positions on social responsibility.	2
(b)	Describe and evaluate other constructions of the corporate and personal ethical stance.	2
(c)	Describe and analyse the variables determining the cultural context of ethics and corporate social responsibility.	2
(d)	Explain and evaluate the concepts of 'CSR strategy' and 'strategic CSR'.	2
E7	**Integrated reporting and sustainability issues in the conduct of business**	
(a)	Explain and assess the concept of integrated reporting and evaluate the issues concerning accounting for sustainability, including the alternative definitions of capital.	3
(b)	Describe and assess the social and environmental impacts that economic activity can have (in terms of social and environmental footprints and environmental reporting).	3
(c)	Describe the main features of internal management systems for underpinning environmental and sustainability accounting such as EMAS and ISO 14000.	1
(d)	Explain and assess the typical content elements and guiding principles of an integrated report, and discuss the usefulness of this information to stakeholders.	3
(e)	Explain the nature of social and environmental audit and evaluate the contribution it can make to the assurance of integrated reports.	3

Exam guide

You may see a whole optional question on the issues covered in this chapter as it covers various aspects of organisations' activities and control systems. Alternatively, as in Pilot Paper Question 1, some of the themes may be brought in as part of a wider question.

1 Corporate citizenship

FAST FORWARD

Corporate citizenship has been used to describe how an organisation's values are shaped and the impact concepts of responsibility have on business decision-making.

1.1 Corporate social responsibility

We examined the concept of corporate social responsibility (CSR) in Chapter 2, mainly in the context of corporate governance. Remember the four levels of corporate social responsibility identified by Carroll:

Economic	To shareholders wanting dividends/capital gains, to employees wanting fair employment, to customers wanting good quality products
Legal	Obeying the law is a requirement in all societies, though legal compliance imposes greater burdens in some societies rather than others
Ethical	Acting in a fair and just way
Philanthropic	Voluntary contributions to society

Carroll's viewpoint can be matched with the various stages of a business's development. At the start it is concerned with economic survival. As it grows larger, other issues become important and society's expectations of it become greater.

In recent years corporations have recognised more and more the importance of CSR and have developed strategies to demonstrate its implementation. Such strategies are commonly defined under the following headings.

Environmental

A focus on sustainability, for example by using renewable energy sources, recycling, using green technology, minimising waste and pollution

Social

Engagement with local communities, for example by supporting local charities and social events, employing local people, investing in the local economy

Ethical

Adopting ethical business practices, for example by paying living wages, avoiding the exploitation of child labour, respecting health and safety, eliminating fraud and corruption

Some commentators have criticised the CSR approach, claiming that large corporations engage in this exercise for cynical or insincere motives; in other words, they are employing 'strategic CSR' in order to enhance their image and their brand value. Indeed some business activities are considered beyond the reach of CSR altogether, for example arms manufacturers and tobacco firms. Others, notably Milton Freidman, argue that corporations have no responsibility to society, only to their shareholders, and that their sole purpose is to make profits on behalf of those shareholders.

 Case Study

Even businesses acting philanthropically may receive criticism from stakeholders if for example their customers disagree with the causes they are supporting. TOMS shoes faced criticism from its more socially progressive customers when it became linked to the right-wing group Focus on the Family.

As ethics writer Chris MacDonald pointed out, people who wished corporations to adopt social causes should perhaps be careful what they wished for. There was no guarantee companies would not give to causes that some of their customers found to be abhorrent.

Chris MacDonald highlighted a case of a reverse situation – a charity having problems with a corporate donor with a poor reputation. The St Patrick Center, a Catholic charity providing assistance to homeless people, cancelled a fundraising dinner at a Hooters restaurant after complaints that the collaboration was contrary to the Christian faith. Hooters' restaurants employ waitresses wearing provocative clothing and have attracted accusations that they exploit women.

Macdonald points out that charities have to draw a line somewhere, as their ability to raise funds depends on their reputation and the goodwill of donors. Whether drawing of the line is a matter of ethics or prudence is arguable, however. Many large corporate donors have ethical questions over some of their activities, but can charities refuse all their donations?

> **Corporate citizenship** is the business strategy that shapes the values underpinning a company's mission and the choices made each day by its executives, managers and employees as they engage with society. Three core principles define the essence of corporate citizenship, and every company should apply them in a manner appropriate to its distinct needs: minimizing harm, maximizing benefit, and being accountable and responsive to stakeholders. (Boston Center for Corporate Citizenship)

Much of the debate in recent years about **corporate social responsibility** has been framed in terms of corporate citizenship, partly because of unease about using words like ethics and responsibility in the context of business decisions. Discussion of corporate citizenship also often has political undertones, with corporations acting instead of governments that cannot – or will not – act to deal effectively with problems. Commentators have also pointed to liberalisation, deregulation and privatisation placing more power in the hands of corporations and less in the hands of the state.

The general concepts of rights and responsibilities are fundamental to the debate on citizenship.

1.2.1 Rights

The rights that a corporate citizen has include **being able to take actions that are lawful and to enjoy the protection of the law**. The rights of a company include the right to **exist as a separate legal entity** and **carry on a lawful business**. Society will grant it protection under the law and will also permit it to develop and expand.

1.2.2 Responsibilities

Responsibilities are the **duties owed to society** by the citizen as a consequence of the citizen belonging to the society and enjoying rights within it. In order to enjoy the protection, the individual or organisation has to **comply with the laws** that affect it and **act in accordance with society's behavioural norms**.

1.3 Perspectives on corporate citizenship

Matten *et al* have suggested that there are three perspectives or corporate citizenship.

1.3.1 Limited view

The business's philanthropy consists of limited projects undertaken in the business's self-interest. The main stakeholder groups that the corporation engages with are local communities and employees.

1.3.2 Equivalent view

This is based on a wider concept of **corporate social responsibility** based on stakeholder theory. The corporation responds to the demands of society and focuses on balancing the interests of different stakeholders. Acting according to the business's self-interest is not the most important priority.

1.3.3 Extended view

This view is based round a partly voluntary, partly imposed view of **active social and political** citizenship. Corporations must promote citizens' rights, particularly as governments have failed to provide some of the safeguards necessary for their society's citizens and corporations are the most powerful institutions in society.

Under the extended view, organisations will promote:

- **Social rights** of citizens by provision of, for example, decent working conditions
- **Civil rights**, by intervening to promote citizens' individual rights themselves or to pressurise governments to promote citizens' rights
- **Political rights** by allowing individuals to promote their causes by using corporate power

Again the focus is on a wide range of stakeholders, with a combination of self-interest promoting corporate power (and responding to political campaigns aimed at corporations) and wider responsibility towards society.

Case Study

Companies have devised a number of different definitions of corporate citizenship.

Abbott Laboratories

Global citizenship reflects how a company advances its business objectives, engages its stakeholders, implements its policies, applies its social investment and philanthropy, and exercises its influence to make productive contributions to society.

At Abbott, global citizenship also means thoughtfully balancing financial, environmental and social responsibilities with providing quality health care worldwide. Our programs include public education, environment, health and safety, and access to health care. These efforts reflect an engagement and partnership with stakeholders in the pursuit of sustainable solutions to challenges facing the global community.

AT&T

For AT&T, corporate citizenship means caring about the communities it is involved with, keeping the environment healthy, making AT&T a safe and rewarding place to work and behaving ethically in all its business dealings.

Coca-Cola

Responsible corporate citizenship is at the heart of The Coca-Cola Promise, which is based on four core values – in the marketplace, the workplace, the environment and the community.

- **Marketplace**. We will adhere to the highest ethical standards, knowing that the quality of our products, the integrity of our brands and the dedication of our people build trust and strengthen relationships. We will serve the people who enjoy our brands through innovation, superb customer service, and respect for the unique customs and cultures in the communities where we do business.

- **Workplace**. We will treat each other with dignity, fairness and respect. We will foster an inclusive environment that encourages all employees to develop and perform to their fullest potential, consistent with a commitment to human rights in our workplace. The Coca-Cola workplace will be a place where everyone's ideas and contributions are valued, and where responsibility and accountability are encouraged and rewarded.

- **Environment**. We will conduct our business in ways that protect and preserve the environment. We will integrate principles of environmental stewardship and sustainable development into our business decisions and processes.

- **Community**. We will contribute our time, expertise and resources to help develop sustainable communities in partnership with local leaders. We will seek to improve the quality of life through locally relevant initiatives wherever we do business.

DHL

DHL takes its definition of Corporate Citizenship from the World Economic Forum: Corporate citizenship is about the contribution a company makes to society through its core business activities, its social investment and philanthropy programmes, and its engagement in public policy.

Texas Instruments

Beyond the bottom line, the worth of a corporation is reflected in its impact in the community. At TI, our philosophy is simple and dates back to our founding fathers. Giving back to the communities where we operate makes them better places to live and work, in turn making them better places to do business. TI takes its commitment seriously and actively participates in community involvement in three ways – philanthropy, civic leadership and public policy and grass roots efforts.

1.4 Impact of the concept of corporate citizenship

Looking at the definitions, it seems that the only one that adds a **fresh perspective** to the concept of the company in society is the extended view, since it emphasises the **political role of the corporation** and therefore the importance of its **accountability**. It also provides perspectives on the organisation as a **global participant**, having to cope with different concepts of citizenship worldwide.

Exam focus point

In the exam you may have to bring these ideas in when discussing the role of institutional shareholders.

1.5 Critiques of corporate citizenship

Corporate citizenship and corporate social responsibility have been attacked for introducing concepts that are counter to good order in the free market. The underlying idea of these criticisms is that economic self-interest and allocative efficiency ensure **maximum economic growth** and therefore **maximum social welfare**.

On the other hand, other critics of corporate citizenship argue that it often tends to be restricted to what should be disclosed in the accounts that organisations themselves prepare, and that the range of concerns and stakeholders to which organisations are accountable is limited. More fundamentally, critics claim that its supporters operate and therefore acquiesce in the free market and take attention away from the need for **fundamental structural change** in economies.

Nevertheless supporters argue that corporate citizenship and corporate social responsibility reporting can be extended to illuminate **inequalities in distribution** in society and **limitations of traditional accounting methods**. Reporting has a major role in making organisations more visible and transparent.

 Case Study

Scottish Power's corporate social responsibility programme has been developed from multi-stakeholder consultation. The stakeholders emphasised the need for the company to prioritise its most significant social and environmental impacts. This consultation identified 12 impacts, and Scottish Power's corporate social responsibility report detailed what had been done to address these.

(a) **Provision of energy**

Scottish Power was involved in a competition to develop carbon capture and storage. It spent £456 million in refurbishing its electrical network and committed £20 million in investment to its hydroelectric plant.

(b) **Health and safety**

The Lost-Time Accident rate fell for the fifth successive year. Its children's safety education programme won two major awards.

(c) **Customer experience**

Scottish Power achieved the highest satisfaction rating for online energy service in the market and was ranked the second UK gas supplier. Its customer base increased by 4%.

(d) **Climate change and emission to air**

Scottish Power's Green Energy Trust awarded £232,809 to 20 small renewable energy projects. It entered a contract to supply all Debenhams' properties with electricity generated from green sources and met 57% of its carbon emission reduction programme through its customer energy efficiency programme.

(e) **Waste and resource usage**

Scottish Power increased its investment in oil containment and received a Queen's Award in the Sustainable Development category.

(f) **Biodiversity**

The company took steps to allow the public to watch wildfowl. A cable pipeline was drilled below the Dovey Estuary to avoid disturbance to a Site of Special Scientific Interest.

(g) **Sites, siting and infrastructure**

Scottish Power completed connections to more renewable energy sources and implemented a programme to keep parts of its network underground in Snowdonia.

(h) **Employee experience**

The company launched two new employee share plans. Staff participated in community development programmes that provided training for young people.

(i) **Customers with special circumstances**

Scottish Power contributed £1 million to the Scottish Power Energy People Trust. It launched a new social tariff that combined low prices with energy efficiency advice and measures to take vulnerable customers out of fuel poverty.

(j) **Community**

Over 58,000 primary schoolchildren benefited from Powerwise, Scottish Power's classroom safety education programme.

(k) **Procurement**

Scottish Power developed a group-wide responsible procurement policy and spent £74 million on customer energy efficiency measures.

(l) **Economic**

Scottish Power provided employability training to 68 Skillseekers during the year.

2 Organisations' ethical and social responsibility stances

12/14, 6/15

FAST FORWARD

An organisation's ethical stance relates to how it **views its responsibilities** to shareholders, stakeholders, society and the environment.

2.1 The ethical stance

12/11

Key term

An organisation's **ethical stance** is defined by Johnson and Scholes as the extent to which it will exceed its minimum obligation to stakeholders.

Crane and Matten and Johnson and Scholes have identified a number of key assumptions (in the form of questions) on which ethical and social responsibility stances are based.

Who is responsible for ethical conduct in business?	Is it the individual, or is control exercised socially, by governments?
Who is the key actor in business ethics?	Is it the corporation, or is it the Government or other collective bodies such as trade unions?
What are the key guidelines for ethical behaviour?	Again does it rest with the corporation in the form of corporate codes of ethics, or is the key guidance a legal framework negotiated with, or imposed on, business?
What are the key issues in business ethics?	Are they single-decision issues involving misconduct and immorality, or are they social issues surrounding the framework of business?

To whom are businesses responsible?	Should the focus be on enhancing shareholder value or on multiple stakeholders?
How should performance be measured?	Should it be measured by bottom line financial results or by pluralistic measures?
How should an ethical stance be incorporated into business activity?	Should an ethical stance be seen primarily in terms of compliance with law/corporate governance codes, or should it be actively incorporated into an organisation's mission and strategy?
How important is reputation?	Does it make any difference to financial results? Should organisations strive to have a good reputation even if doing so makes no demonstrable difference to their bottom line profits?

Johnson and Scholes illustrate the range of possible ethical stances for organisations and individuals by giving four illustrations.

- Short-term shareholder interest
- Long-term shareholder interest
- Multiple stakeholder obligations
- Shaper of society

2.1.1 Short-term shareholder interest

An organisation or individual might limit its ethical stance to taking responsibility for **short-term shareholder interest** on the grounds that it is for **government** alone to impose wider constraints on corporate governance. This approach may not look much beyond the current financial year. This minimalist approach would accept a duty of obedience to the demands of the law, but would not undertake to comply with any less substantial rules of conduct. This stance can be justified on the grounds that going beyond it can **challenge government authority**. This is an important consideration for organisations operating in developing countries.

2.1.2 Long-term shareholder interest

The longer view will look years rather than months ahead and consider the legitimacy of a claim in terms of its effect on long-term shareholder value. There are two reasons for taking a wider view of ethical responsibilities when considering the **longer-term interest of shareholders**.

(a) **Corporate image** may be enhanced by an assumption of wider responsibilities. The cost of undertaking such responsibilities may be justified as essentially promotional expenditure.

(b) The responsible exercise of corporate power may prevent a build-up of social and political **pressure for legal regulation**. Freedom of action may be preserved and the burden of regulation lightened by acceptance of ethical responsibilities.

2.1.3 Multiple stakeholder obligations

An organisation or individual might accept the **legitimacy of the expectations and/or claims of stakeholders other than shareholders** and build those expectations into its stated purposes. This would be because, without appropriate relationships with groups such as suppliers, employers and customers, the organisation would not be able to function.

The **legal rights** of stakeholders other than shareholders have to be respected. These are extensive in the UK, including wide-ranging **employment law** and **consumer protection law**, as well as the more basic legislation relating to such matters as contract and property. Where **moral entitlements** are concerned, organisations need to be practical. They should take care to establish just what expectations they are prepared to treat as **obligations**, bearing in mind their general ethical stance and degree of concern about bad publicity.

Acceptance of obligations to stakeholders implies that **measurement of the performance** must give due weight to these extra imperatives.

2.1.4 Shaper of society

It is difficult enough for a commercial organisation to accept wide responsibility to stakeholders. The role of **shaper of society** is even more demanding and largely the concern of public sector organisations and charities, though some well-funded private organisations or very powerful and wealthy individuals might act in this way. The legitimacy of this approach for organisations depends on the framework of **corporate governance** and **accountability**. Where organisations are clearly set up for such a role, either by government or by private sponsors, they may pursue it. However, they must also satisfy whatever requirements for financial viability are established for them.

Case Study

Traidcraft aims to fight poverty through a wide range of trade-related activities. The company's structure is that of a trading company and a development charity working together, pioneering the development of fair trade by:

- Building lasting relationships with small-scale producers in developing countries
- Supporting people to trade out of poverty
- Working to bring about trade justice and fair business practices
- Striving to be transparent and accountable

In poorer countries Traidcraft supports traders by providing business training, information and help in winning sales. In the UK Traidcraft works to encourage businesses to apply corporate social responsibility and provide social accounts. It aims to persuade UK businesses to change their practices so that they have a positive impact on their suppliers.

Traidcraft's policy unit exists to campaign for changes in the rules of trade and work with business and institutions to deliver poverty-alleviating policies. The organisation has recently campaigned against European partnership agreements – agreements between European countries and their former colonies – on the grounds that these are forcing the colonies' economies to liberalise too fast. This will result in farmers and industries having to compete openly with EU corporations before they are ready, and resulting in their losing markets and going out of business.

2.2 Social responsibility stances   12/07, 6/09, 6/11, 12/11

Gray, Owen and Adams in their book *Accounting and Accountability* identify seven viewpoints of social responsibility.

Pristine capitalists	**The private property system** is the best system; companies exist to **maximise profits** and **seek economic efficiency**. Businesses therefore have **no moral responsibilities** beyond their obligations to shareholders and creditors. Pursuing the objectives of stakeholders other than shareholders, and thus reducing shareholder wealth, is theft from shareholders. Shareholders have risked their money to become legal owners, and therefore they should determine objectives and strategies.
Expedients	Economic systems do generate some **excesses**, therefore businesses have to accept some (limited) **social legislation and moral requirements** if such behaviour is in **the business's economic interests**.

Proponents of the social contract	Organisations should behave in a way that is broadly in conformance with the ethical norms in society because there is effectively a **contract or agreement** between the **organisations** in power and those who are **affected by the exercise of this power**. A business effectively enjoys a licence to operate. However, this licence will only continue to be granted by society if the business's actions deserve it. A business may therefore have to deliver benefits (or avoid causing harm) to society in general. It may also be responsible for delivering benefits to the specific groups from whom it derives its power (such as customers or employees).
Social ecologists	Businesses leave a social and environmental footprint. In particular, problems exist with the human environment that large organisations have created and need to eradicate. Economic processes that result in **resource exhaustion, waste and pollution** must be **modified**. Organisations must adopt socially responsible positions accordingly. This may involve going beyond what is required or regarded as desirable by society.
Socialists	Socialists see the business framework as one class (capitalists) manipulating and oppressing another class (workers and the socially oppressed). Business therefore acts to **concentrate wealth** in society. Business decision-making should no longer be determined by the requirements of capitalism and materialism but should **promote equality**. Policies to enhance corporate social responsibility will fail if they continue to take place in the existing framework. Business should be conducted in a fundamentally different way, to redress the imbalances in society and provide benefits to many stakeholders, not just finance providers.
Radical feminists	Economic and social systems privilege masculine qualities such as aggression, conflict and competition over **feminine values such as co-operation and reflection**. Developing corporate social responsibility in the existing masculine framework won't work. A fundamental readjustment is required in the culture and structure of society with potentially far-reaching implications for accountability relationships. Society needs to emphasise qualities traditionally seen as feminine, such as equality, dialogue, compassion and fairness.
Deep ecologists	Human beings have **no greater right to resources or life** than other species and do not have the rights to subjugate social and environmental systems. Economic systems that trade off threats to the existence of species against economic objectives are **immoral**. Arguably businesses cannot be trusted to maintain something as important as the environment. Existing economic systems are beyond repair as they are based on the wrong values, privileging humans over non-humans. A full recognition of all stakeholders would mean that business had to be conducted in a completely different way. This viewpoint is connected with ideas on sustainability which are covered below.

Question

Gray, Owen and Adams 1

Which of the seven Gray, Owen and Adams viewpoints do the following statements appear to illustrate?

Our corporate responsibility stance will appeal to our customers and ethical shareholders.	
The building of the new shopping centre shouldn't disrupt the lives and livelihood of the local community.	
Companies should continuously strive to reduce their environmental footprint.	
The problem with stakeholder analysis such as Mendelow's matrix is that it consistently prioritises those who provide finance over those who produce.	

Companies can never do enough to reduce their environmental footprint.	
Isn't there room for the small shop as well as the supermarket?	
The business of business is business.	

Answer

Bear in mind that it would be helpful to have knowledge of the motivation of the individuals making these statements.

Our corporate responsibility stance will appeal to our customers and ethical shareholders.	**Expedient**: a very pragmatic and perhaps very common view
The building of the new shopping centre shouldn't disrupt the lives and livelihood of the local community.	**Social contract**: the idea that business developments should take account of the impact on the local community
Companies should continuously strive to reduce their environmental footprints.	**Social ecologist**: the difference between this view and that of the deep ecologist is the implication that this reduction should take place within the existing framework
The problem with stakeholder analysis such as Mendelow's matrix is that it consistently prioritises those who provide finance over those who produce.	**Socialist**: the idea that superiority of the capital providers or capitalists is inherently wrong
Companies can never do enough to reduce their environmental footprint.	**Deep ecologist**: the implication being that business activity as currently pursued is inherently unsustainable
Isn't there room for the small shop as well as the supermarket?	**Radical feminist**: the key concept is that there is room for peaceful coexistence in the business world, rather than one type of business trying to drive another type out of business
The business of business is business.	**Pristine capitalist**: a good one-line summary of this viewpoint

2.3 Using the Gray, Owen and Adams corporate responsibility positions

The examiner may ask you to discuss situations using Gray, Owen and Adams' positions, for example asking you how different positions would rank stakeholder concerns about a business development.

Step 1 Analysing the scenario

You need to look out in the scenario for key information that is relevant to each position, such as:

Pristine capitalists	The financial implications of the decision, and the extent to which each stakeholder can influence the level of profits made
Expedients	Society's current views on social responsibility, also what the impact on profits will be of not being seen as socially responsible (the significance of reputation risk and strategic positioning)
Proponents of the social contract	Impact on the community as a whole, groups of different stakeholders within the community, the position of local or national government, importance of relationships with the local community
Social ecologists	Impact (footprint) on the environment, the problems caused by the business
Socialists	Indications that the owners are benefiting at the expense of the employees

Radical feminists	Adverse impact of competition or aggressive behaviour by businesses, signs feminine values are being exploited for profit
Deep ecologists	Adverse impact on any aspect of the natural environment, signs of the natural world being exploited for profit, suggestions that economic objectives are being compared with environmental objectives

Step 2 Constructing your answer

Your answer will need to focus on factors that are relevant to each position.

Pristine capitalists	Concentrate on how shareholders' wealth can be maximised. Other stakeholders will only be important if they threaten shareholder wealth
Expedients	Demonstrate how business will gain advantages for itself if it responds to corporate responsibility concerns. Show how business should cope with trading off economic values with social responsibilities
Proponents of the social contract	Bring out society's norms and beliefs and the need for business to act in accordance with them. Show how the business can serve interests of different groups in society and, if necessary, reconcile competing interests
Social ecologists	Concentrate on how the business should solve the human and environmental problems its activities cause and the changes necessary in business, economic and accounting practice
Socialists	Focus on ways workers are being treated unfairly. Suggest methods of remedying inequalities including political and organisational change
Radical feminists	Highlight problems with pursuit of economic advantage and conflict, ways competition is unfairly promoted over co-operation/nurturing/family, or ways that feminine qualities (non-confrontation, co-operation) are being exploited for profit
Deep ecologists	Concentrate on showing how business activities inevitably impact on the natural environment and that they wrongly prioritise human needs over other needs

The question below is an example of a possible scenario.

Question

Gray, Owen and Adams 2

Leavis is a firm of recruitment consultants, operating in the capital city of its home country. At its most recent board meeting, the Human Resources Director reported some worrying trends. Leavis has recently suffered a significant number of losses of experienced staff, in particular female staff. It has been suggested that they had been asked to take on work at times when they had never had to work in the past, such as during antisocial hours, sometimes in conflict with their employment contracts. Some had taken on the extra work in fear of losing their jobs.

Furthermore, a number of skilled female employees are complaining they are being paid lower rates than their male colleagues who are doing the same work. The Human Resources Director has stated that this is due to extra responsibilities taken on by many of the male employees, but this is leading to friction between staff, increased absenteeism, falling productivity and, more worryingly, falling quality of work.

The Chief Executive has also joined in the debate, as Leavis is aiming to defend its title of 'Consultant of the Year' (won primarily due to its high quality service from start to finish), and he and the Director of Quality Management wish to win again in view of the substantial bonuses they received for doing so last year.

The country in which Leavis operates implemented the provisions of the European Union's social chapter a number of years ago.

Required

Compare and contrast how Gray, Owen and Adams' 'pristine capitalist', 'socialist' and 'radical feminist' positions would affect responses to stakeholder concerns about this situation.

Answer

Pristine capitalists

The pristine capitalist's viewpoint would view the workers **solely in economic terms**. The view would be that workers are paid to fulfil the company's economic objectives. If they cannot do this, they should no longer work for the company. Pristine capitalists would deplore employment and sexual discrimination legislation that enforced on companies the non-economic objective of providing **flexibility for certain workers**. However, if the economic costs of disobeying the legislation were greater than the business costs that could be cut, they would recommend compliance.

Socialists

The socialist viewpoint would be that the company's ability to force these conditions on its employees **reflected its superior economic power**. Legislation could help to mitigate the adverse effects on employees, but it would be inadequate if it was implemented within the current framework of business decision-making. Instead decision-making processes would need to be changed so that **all the workers in the company** had the rights to approve their working conditions, rather than having the conditions imposed on them by shareholders acting through management.

Radical feminists

Like the socialists, radical feminists would see as inadequate legislation within the existing framework acting to mitigate the impact of aggressive labour practices. The problem over the hours could be resolved by **dialogue between management and employees**, and managers **seeking to treat employees fairly**. However they would differ from the socialists in taking the focus away from economic activity. They would argue that pursuit of aggressive competitive goals should not be given automatic priority over other life activities, particularly those that enhanced family nurturing, contemplation and spirituality. Excessive hours at work could lead to insufficient time being given to those activities that are essential for human wellbeing.

Exam focus point

> The examiner regards questions that require students to argue from a specific Gray, Owen and Adams position as a good test of application and has frequently set questions on this area.

3 Social and environmental effects of economic activity
6/10

FAST FORWARD

> There is increasing concern about businesses' relationship with the natural environment. Businesses may suffer **significant costs** and a **loss of reputation** if problems arise.

3.1 Significance of environmental effects

Is there a problem and how serious is it?

The World Wildlife Fund warned in a report published in October 2006 that current global consumption levels could result in a large-scale ecosystem collapse by the middle of the 21st century. It warned that if demand continued at the current rate, two planets' worth of resources would be needed to meet the consumption demand by 2050. The loss in biodiversity is the result of resources being consumed faster than the planet can replace them.

The report based its findings on two measures.

Living Planet Index – assessing the health of the planet's ecosystems by tracking the population of over 1,000 vertebrate species. It found that species had declined by about 30% since 1970.

The Ecological Footprint – measuring the amount of biologically productive land and water to meet the demand for food, timber and shelter and absorb the pollution from economic activity. The report found that the global footprint exceeded the world's biocapacity by 25% in 2003, which meant that the earth could no longer meet what was being demanded of it.

Most seriously of all, there is the issue of whether business activities have contributed to climate change.

Intergovernmental Panel

The Intergovernmental Panel on Climate Change reported in February 2007. The report emphasised that global atmospheric concentrations of carbon dioxide, methane and nitrous oxide have increased markedly as a result of human activities since 1750 and now exceed pre-industrial values. The main causes are fossil-fuel usage (the most significant cause), land-use change and agriculture.

The report stated that evidence of warming of the climate system is unequivocal, as is seen from observations of increases in global average air and ocean temperatures, widespread melting of snow and ice, and rising global average sea level. Numerous changes in climate are long term. These are most likely to be due to increases in greenhouse gas concentrations.

For the next two decades a warming of about 0.2°C is projected based on projected levels of greenhouse gas emissions. Continued greenhouse gas emissions at or above current rates would cause further warming and induce many climate changes in the 21st century that will be larger than those observed in the 20th century. These include increases in heatwaves, spells of heavy rain and intensity of tropical cyclones.

Stern report

A few months before the Intergovernmental panel report was published, a UK report was published on the costs of climate change. The report's author was Sir Nicholas Stern, former chief economist at the World Bank, and adviser to the former UK Chancellor of the Exchequer Gordon Brown who commissioned the report. The report warned of a global recession that could cut between 5% and 20% from the world's wealth later this century, unless the world invests now in the technologies needed to create a global low-carbon economy.

The effects would be on a scale similar to those associated with the two World Wars and the 1930s depression. They include huge disruption to African economies as drought hits food production, up to a billion people losing water supplies, hundreds of millions losing their homes to sea level rises and potentially big increases in damage from hurricanes.

Stern called for a global investment of about 1% per year of global GDP over the next 50 years to combat these threats. His findings contradicted past claims from economists that the world would do better adapting to climate change rather than trying to halt it. In response to the report, Gordon Brown called for industrialised countries to cut their carbon dioxide emissions by at least 30% by 2020 and by at least 60% by 2050.

World Wildlife Fund

The World Wildlife Fund's Climate Savers programme encourages companies to reduce carbon dioxide emissions by:

- Increasing the energy efficiency of buildings and factories

- Taking advantage of recent advances in combined heat and power to increase energy efficiency and lower energy costs

- Purchasing power generated from renewable energy sources

- Integrating next-generation efficiency measures into the design of new buildings, factories and products

- Integrating energy and environmental efficiency into building, product and process design

- Optimising existing manufacturing processes

- Educating employees, customer base and supply chain to help take advantage of best practices for greenhouse gas mitigation

Examples of companies who have joined the programme include:

- Johnson & Johnson, 30% of whose total US energy use is from green power sources such as wind power, on-site solar, low-impact hydro, renewable energy sources

- IBM, whose energy-saving methods include installing motion detectors for lighting in bathrooms and copier rooms, rebalancing heating and lighting systems and resizing high purity water pumping systems in semi-conductor manufacturing lines

- Polaroid, which is upgrading and replacing compressors, chillers, boilers, hot water systems, lighting systems and motors, purchasing green power and switching to cleaner forms of fuel for on-site operations; Polaroid's Facilities organisation now requires each employee to identify energy-saving projects as part of their performance evaluation

- Nike, which offsets the majority of its business travel carbon dioxide emissions through partnerships with air carriers, rental car companies, government energy departments and the retail market

- Lafarge, the cement manufacturer which uses industrial by-products such as fly-ash from coal-fired power plants and slag from the steel industry as substitutes for raw materials that consume significant energy to produce; Lafarge has also shifted some of its fuel use to waste fossil fuels (industrial waste, tyres, oils, plastic and solvents) and waste biomass (rice husks, coffee shells, animal meal)

The WWF points out the following benefits of joining Climate Savers.

- **Knowledge increase**, providing an opportunity to develop relationships with other stakeholders, business colleagues and technology experts

- **Visibility** through publicity in the WWF's literature and press reports

- **Cost advantages**, greater efficiency leading to reduction in energy costs

Climate change will be one of the most topical areas of your syllabus, so we would advise you to read and keep copies of stories on how businesses are responding to climate change.

Clearly there are concerns which need to be closely examined. Note, however, that organisations can also have **positive impacts**, for example improving the energy efficiency of their buildings.

3.2 Impact on environment of economic activities

Key term

Environmental footprint is the impact that a business's activities have on the environment including its resource consumption and pollution emissions. It concerns the environmental consequences of a business's inputs and outputs.

At an individual firm or business level, environmental impact can be measured in terms of environmental costs in various areas. Much business activity takes place at some cost to the environment. A 1998 IFAC report identified several examples of impacts on the environment.

- Depletion of natural resources
- Noise and aesthetic impacts
- Residual air and water emissions
- Long-term waste disposal (exacerbated by excessive product packaging)
- Uncompensated health effects
- Change in the local quality of life (through for example the impact of tourism)

With some of these impacts, however, a business may be contributing negatively to the environment but positively in other ways. An increase in tourism will provide jobs and other economic benefits to the community, but could lead to adverse effects on the environment as the roads become more crowded or because of infrastructure improvements.

Ways of assessing the impact of inputs include the **measurement of key environmental resources** used, such as energy, water, inventories and land. Measurement of the impact of outputs includes the proportion of product **recyclability**, **tonnes of carbon or other gases produced by company activities**, **waste or pollution**. A business may also be concerned with the **efficiency of its processes**, maybe carrying out a mass balance or yield calculation.

3.2.1 Direct and indirect impacts

Measures of impact can apply directly and narrowly to the organisation, or they can be applied more broadly to the indirect, associated impacts that it has. For a manufacturer, indirect measures could report on the forward and backward supply chains which it uses from sourcing its raw materials to bringing its products to market. A bank could include the environmental consequences of the activities it finances through its business loans. However, reporting of indirect measures is rare, as the other parties are primarily responsible for reporting the direct impacts that they have. Clearly also it would be particularly difficult for a bank to track the impacts of all its business borrowers.

Case Study

In May 2008 Marks & Spencer (M&S) introduced a 5p charge for its single-use food carrier bags in all its UK stores. M&S aims to:

- Encourage customers to reduce their bag usage by changing from single-use carrier bags to reusable bags

- Raise monies for the charity Groundwork to invest in creating or improving greener living spaces (parks, play areas and gardens).

In 2012/13 M&S used 274 million single-use carrier bags, a reduction of 58% since 2006/07 (657 million bags).

3.3 Impact on organisation of environmental costs

In addition, the IFAC report listed a large number of costs that the business might suffer internally.

Direct or indirect environmental costs

- Waste management
- Remediation costs or expenses
- Compliance costs
- Permit fees
- Environmental training
- Environmentally driven research and development
- Environmentally related maintenance
- Legal costs and fines
- Environmental assurance bonds
- Environmental certification and labelling
- Natural resource inputs
- Recordkeeping and reporting

Contingent or intangible environmental costs

- Uncertain future remediation or compensation costs
- Risk posed by future regulatory changes
- Product quality
- Employee health and safety
- Environmental knowledge assets
- Sustainability of raw material inputs
- Risk of impaired assets
- Public/customer perception

Exam focus point

A Pilot Paper question asked for a definition of environmental footprint.

Clearly, failing to take sufficient account of environmental impact can have a significant impact on the business's accounts as well as the outside world.

Exam focus point

You may be asked about the main impacts on the environment that a particular organisation's activities are likely to have. You will need to use a little imagination, but hopefully the ideas we suggest in this chapter will help you come up with suggestions.

3.4 Social impacts of activities   12/12

Key term

Social footprint is the impact of an organisation on human, social and constructed capitals (Anthro capitals). (The Center for Sustainable Organizations)

Partly because of the publicity generated by reports like the recent WWF report, there is now significant focus on the environmental impact of businesses' activities. However, corporate social responsibility does not start and end with the environment. Organisations need to consider other aspects of corporate social responsibilities.

The definition of social footprint formulated by the Center for Sustainable Organizations is measured in terms of impacts that arise from organisational activities.

'Sustainability entails the **maintenance and/or production of vital capitals** as required to ensure human (and non-human) well-being.'

The definition concentrates on anthro capital which is created by people and can be produced at will – more can always be created. It is thus different from natural capital which humanity cannot reproduce. The focus is on providing enough resources to maintain levels of social capital.

The Center provides more details about the categories of capital given in the definition. The different types of capital are all used to take effective action and ensure their own wellbeing.

Capitals	
Human	Personal health, knowledge, skills, experience, human rights, ethical entitlements. Relied on by individuals
Social	Social networks and mutually held knowledge. Relied on by collectives
Constructed	Material things such as tools, technologies, roads, utilities and infrastructures

Again, business strategies may have **positive and negative consequences** for social sustainability. A business that outsources production to a low-cost economy abroad may create new jobs and provide training and development opportunities for the employees in that country. However, it may also be accused of exploiting those employees by paying them an insufficient wage. In addition, the jobs that may be lost in the business's home country will have adverse social consequences such as increased unemployment and the need for benefits to support the unemployed.

3.4.1 Stakeholder expectations

Pressure on organisations to widen the scope of their corporate public accountability comes from **increasing expectations of stakeholders** and knowledge about the **consequences of ignoring such pressures**.

Stakeholders in this respect include communities (particularly where operations are based), customers (product safety issues), suppliers and supply chain participants and competitors. Issues such as plant closures, pollution, job creation, sourcing, etc can have powerful **social effects** for good or ill on these stakeholders.

Case Study

These are a few examples in which consumers have been successful in applying pressure to seek changes in business practices.

(a)   Consumers began boycotting Shell filling stations in large numbers, leading the company to reverse its policy on a controversial environmental subject concerning the disposal of an oil drilling platform.

(b)   Pressure was applied to change the Nestlé company's practice of exploiting the market for processed milk in developing countries.

Similar campaigns have targeted Nike (alleged exploitation of overseas garment-trade workers) and McDonalds (alleged contribution to obesity and related illnesses).

3.4.2 Reputation risk

We have discussed the importance of **loss of corporate reputation** in earlier chapters. Increasingly a business must have the reputation of being a **responsible business** that enhances long-term shareholder value by addressing the needs of its **stakeholders** – employees, customers, suppliers, the community and the environment.

Case Study

In April 2008 Greenpeace protestors dressed as orangutans stormed a number of sites owned by Unilever in Europe. The protest was against the damage to Indonesian tropical rainforests by the production of palm oil, used in many Unilever products. As well as damaging the forests, the process of deforestation has resulted in large emissions of carbon dioxide and also threatened local wildlife (including orangutans).

Soon after the protest, Unilever announced that it would be drawing all the palm oil it purchased from sustainable sources by 2015. However, Greenpeace wanted Unilever to take tougher action, by ceasing to buy from suppliers who were breaking the law. Enquiries by Unilever embarrassingly revealed that all its Indonesian suppliers were flouting Indonesian law or sustainability standards.

Case Study

Reputation can be affected adversely even if the company has good intentions. An example was Monsanto believing that investment in genetically modified (GM) products would be seen as helping farmers in developing countries by increasing yields. However, they failed to take on board the fact that these farmers usually save seed from one crop to sow the following season. This would not be possible with GM crops.

Bad publicity portrayed Monsanto as exploiting, rather than helping, developing countries. In addition, inadequately addressed environmental concerns about the effect of GM crops on nature led to:

- A consumer boycott of GM products
- Trial crops being destroyed
- A tumbling share price

The final straw was the news that Monsanto's UK staff canteen was GM free!

Case Study

Mining companies in Canada are carrying out social risk assessment for major projects, assessing how the local social, economic and cultural conditions may affect the project. These assessments reflect the impact that mining projects often have on environmentally and socially sensitive areas such as wildlife habitats, biodiversity points and indigenous communities. Linked issues may include poverty, conflict, political instability and human rights violations. Failure to take account of these issues may result in serious opposition, cultural conflict, delays in granting of mining rights and rejections of mining licences.

Social risk assessments aim to engage stakeholders and understand their concerns as well as assessing key social and political issues. They feed through into strategic and operational plans as well as community investment, stakeholder engagement and communication plans.

Exam focus point

June 2010 Question 1 asked students to discuss the social and environmental impacts of a nuclear power station.

3.5 Corporate social responsibility and risk management

The Deloitte (2008) guide *The Risk Intelligent Approach to Corporate Responsibility and Sustainability* suggests that sustainability can be approached from a perspective of risk management, seeing corporate responsibility issues as providing opportunities as well as dangers. This should in turn mean that the organisation's approach to these issues is aligned and integrated with strategic initiatives in other parts of the business.

Deloitte recommends a nine-stage approach.

1 Understanding the present	This includes assessing regulatory trends, benchmarking against competitor activity, finding out what is important to stakeholders, understanding all the CSR activity currently happening in the organisation
2 Envisioning the future	Assessing the legacy the organisation wishes to leave. This will mean integrating CSR activities with business strategies, for example a publishing company sending its employees to libraries and schools, or donating books
3 Planning the journey	CSR issues should be prioritised using a gap analysis between current and future states, and the organisation and its competitors. Assess opportunities for action, risks of inaction and not achieving objectives
4 Planning and building	The human resource element is vital, including example set and oversight by senior management. CSR achievements should be built into performance reviews and remuneration. Assess availability of grants and tax concessions for green behaviour. Also consider broadening stakeholder base and organisation's ethical culture
5 Execution	Develop in controlled fashion, enhancing governance procedures related to implementation
6 Review and revision	Develop metrics to measure activities. Use hard data rather than impressions, though stakeholder feedback is important
7 Reporting and communicating	A CSR development programme may mean reporting on CSR needs to be revamped. The organisation could report in accordance with various external reporting standards or produce customised report
8 Assuring internally	Adapt measures used initially to assess CSR development to monitor how the organisation is doing. Use internal resources such as internal audit, legal, health and safety and human resources to assist in development
9 Assuring externally	When CSR reaches a certain level, seek verification from outside the organisation of assertions in CSR report

3.6 Corporate Social Responsibility   6/15

The primary purpose of a business organisation is to make profits, thereby increasing the wealth of its owners, the shareholders. Businesses do not, however, exist in splendid isolation; they are dependent on the society in which they operate, and they should therefore contribute to that society. Businesses make use at least in part of the infrastructure of the country or countries in which they operate, for example roads, utilities and other social goods paid for through taxation. For this reason it can be seen as only fair that businesses are aware of their social responsibility, and their ethical reputation can depend on the extent to which they take this responsibility seriously.

3.7 CSR Strategy

A business that has a strategy in place to demonstrate its corporate social responsibility will have a deliberate plan with specific activities identified. Examples of CSR activities might include:

- Making donations to charity
- Contributing to the activities on non-governmental organisations (NGOs)
- Supporting local good causes
- Including stakeholders in key decisions
- Managing the social and environmental impacts of the business

Having a strategy means making choices, providing funding for the CSR initiatives chosen, and monitoring the outcomes.

3.8 Strategic CSR

It could be argued that CSR activities should reflect the ethos of the business, which leads to the concept of strategic CSR. When CSR activities become strategic, they are concerned with the long-term success of the business, and should therefore be beneficial to the business as well as to society.

Examples of strategic CSR initiatives might include:

- A pharmaceutical company funding the training of medical staff, in the hope that when qualified they will source drugs from that company.

- A bank providing free internet training for senior customers, who might then be disposed to buying financial products.

- Encouraging employees to nominate and get involved in good causes, in order to develop loyalty to the company.

Sponsoring sports teams in return for advertising space on shirts, other merchandise, and at the ground.

The decision as to whether CSR should be strategic is an ethical one. From a pristine capitalist point of view all CSR activities should be strategic, since all of a company's money should be used to benefit shareholders. On the other hand a deep green perspective would argue that, because businesses take from society, they should give something back.

One difference between 'CSR strategy' and 'strategic CSR' is the extent to which an organisation will promote the support given to a CSR cause, making it more likely that strategic CSR will be more visible. Consequently, the ethical viewpoint most likely to support this could be that of the expedient (promoting strategic CSR in a way that benefits the organisation).

Exam focus point

In the June 2015 exam there was a question on CSR Strategy and Strategic CSR. The examining team has produced a technical article on this area.

4 Sustainability   6/08, 12/10, 12/13

Sustainability means limiting use of resources to what can be replenished.

The **Global Reporting Initiative** provides a framework for a **sustainability report**.

Full cost accounting is a method of accounting for all relevant costs including externalities.

4.1 Defining sustainability

Key terms

In relation to the development of the world's resources, **sustainability** has been defined as ensuring that development meets the needs of the present without compromising the ability of future generations to meet their own needs.

For organisations, sustainability involves developing strategies so that the organisation only uses resources (inputs) at a rate that allows them to be replenished (in order to ensure that they will continue to be available). At the same time emissions of waste (outputs) are confined to levels that do not exceed the capacity of the environment to absorb them.

Sustainable development is development that is '... not a fixed state of harmony, but rather a process of change in which the exploitation of resources, the direction of investments, the orientation of technological development and institutional change are made consistent with future as well as present needs'.   (Brundtland report)

Sustainability in this context does **not** mean the ability of the business to continue as a going concern.

4.1.1 The Brundtland report

The United Nations convened the World Commission on Environment and Development, which became known as the Brundtland committee after its chairman, in the 1980s. The committee reported in 1987. Its brief was to propose long-term environmental strategies for achieving sustainable development by the year 2000 and to recommend ways the international community could co-operate in dealing with those concerns.

The report's definition of sustainability, quoted in the Key terms box above, has become a standard definition. When defining sustainability the committee emphasised two key concepts.

- The concept of needs, in particular the **essential needs of the world's poor**
- The **limitations** imposed by the **state of technology and social organisations** on the environment's ability to meet present and future needs

4.1.2 Recommendations of the Brundtland report

The commission emphasised that sustainable development could successfully be pursued. However, it would only be possible if development policies paid attention to such considerations as **changes in access to resources** and the **distribution of costs and benefits**. Population expansion can also increase the pressure on resources. Therefore sustainable development could only be pursued if **demographic developments** are **consistent** with **changing productive potential**.

At the time the report was issued, the basic needs of many in society were not being met, and this increased the risk of **ecological crises**. If for example a drop in prices left farmers feeling vulnerable, then they could overexploit natural resources to maintain incomes. This risk was enhanced further by much of the world's population living beyond the world's ecological means, for example in their pattern of energy use. Sustainable development therefore required the promotion of values that encouraged ecologically possible consumption.

Above all, sustainable development must not endanger the natural systems that support life on earth, the atmosphere, water, soil and living beings. The report summed up sustainable development as requiring:

- A **political system** securing effective citizen participation in decision-making
- An **economic system** able to generate surpluses and technical knowledge on a self-reliant and sustained basis
- A **social system** providing solutions for the tensions arising from disharmonious developments
- A **production system** respecting the obligation to preserve the ecological base for development
- A **technological system** searching continuously for new solutions
- An **international system** fostering sustainable patterns of trade and finance
- An **administrative system** that is flexible and has the capacity for self-correction

4.1.3 Extension of sustainability

Although it's possible to come up with a general definition of sustainability that's uncontroversial but vague, problems arise when you try to extend that definition. Key issues include whether sustainability just implies **natural sustainability**, or whether **social and economic sustainability** are important as well. Particularly if social and economic sustainability are acknowledged, there is also the issue that sustainability may vary over time and between groups.

One approach to sustainability is known as the **triple bottom line** (or 'TBL', '3BL', or 'People, Planet, Profit') approach.

- **People** means balancing up the interests of different stakeholders and not automatically prioritising shareholder needs.
- **Planet** means ensuring that the business's activities are environmentally sustainable.
- **Profit** is the accounting measure of the returns of the business.

Dow Jones Sustainability Index

The Dow Jones Sustainability Index is one of a number of global indexes that have been developed to **assess corporate sustainability**. The creators of the index argue that corporate sustainability is attractive to investors, because it aims to **increase long-term shareholder value by gearing strategies and management to harness the potential for sustainability products and services while also reducing and avoiding sustainability costs and risks**. Companies included in the index as sustainability leaders are expected to show superior performance and favourable risk and return profiles.

The index is designed to provide **quantification** of sustainability strategies and management of sustainability opportunities, risks and costs. A corporate sustainability assessment is carried out, and companies are ranked and selected for the index if they are among the **sustainability leaders** in their field. The assessment uses the following criteria.

Dimension	Criteria
Economic	Corporate governance
	Codes of conduct/Compliance
	Risk and crisis management
	Customer relationship management
	Innovation management
	Industry specific criteria
Environment	Environmental management system
	Climate strategy
	Product stewardship
	Biodiversity
	Industry specific criteria
Social	Human capital development
	Talent attraction and retention
	Occupational health and safety
	Stakeholder engagement
	Social reporting
	Industry specific criteria

Once the initial assessment has taken place, companies' performance is monitored and they are removed from the index if their performance is judged unsatisfactory. A key aspect of this monitoring is seeing how the company copes with **crisis situations** that carry a serious **reputation risk**.

Supersector leaders in the Dow Jones index in 2011 include Pearson, the leader in the media sector. Principal areas in which Pearson reports its environmental and sustainability performance include:

Property management	Pearson has targets to reduce energy use and is investing in renewable energy at some of its sites.
Business travel	Ways in which Pearson is trying to reduce air travel include upgrading videoconferencing facilities.
Climate neutrality	Initiatives include a carbon management programme focusing on energy efficiency in buildings, use of renewable energy sources and establishing partnerships that deliver carbon offsets.

Supply chain	Pearson has introduced various initiatives to improve resource efficiency, such as using the whole tree rather than part of the tree, reducing the base weight of papers used and custom publishing. Environmental responsibility is included in contracts between Pearson and its suppliers. Pearson collects environmental data on the papers it purchases. It holds training sessions for production teams around the world and discusses its approach to paper purchasing with various stakeholders. Pearson has also sought accreditation from the Forest Stewardship Council.
Employee engagement	Green messages are a regular part of Pearson's internal communications. It uses green teams – volunteers working to improve environmental practice. An intranet site offers ideas for carbon reductions, links to local green groups and performance reports. Pearson's books, magazines and newspapers cover climate change.

FTSE4Good Index

The FTSE4Good index aims to appeal to investors who are looking to:

- Invest in companies that demonstrate good standards in corporate social responsibility

- Minimise the social and environmental risks within their portfolios

- Capitalise on the benefits of good corporate responsibility (eg eco-efficiencies, improved brand image)

- Encourage companies to be more responsible

To be included in the index, companies need to demonstrate that they are working towards:

- Environmental management
- Climate change mitigation and adaption
- Countering bribery
- Upholding human and labour rights
- Supply chain labour rights

There are a few sector exclusions from the index.

- Tobacco producers
- Companies involved in nuclear weapons manufacture
- Companies manufacturing whole weapons systems

Exam focus point

If a question asks about sustainability, make sure you appreciate the limits of what you are being asked. June 2008 Question 1 required students to discuss **environmental** sustainability, and no marks were awarded for discussion of other kinds of sustainability.

4.2 Aspects of sustainability

4.2.1 Sustainable for whom

Issues here include the **species to be sustained other than mankind** and the **level of world population** that should be sustained, natural resources, pollution absorption and the needs of developing countries.

We examined the deep ecologist viewpoint earlier in this chapter, that man has 'had his chance' and that socioeconomic considerations are irrelevant to sustainability. They are intrusions on the natural world. Other views are that population pressures and social and economic disparities inevitably have to be addressed as well if sustainability for other species is to be maintained. However, what then happens if there is conflict between social and ecological sustainability?

4.2.2 Sustainable in what way

The ecological focus would be on preserving the ability of the environment to **function as naturally as possible**, continue to support all life forms on the planet and maintain its evolutionary potential.

Extending the definition to **social sustainability** poses various problems. Social sustainability has been defined as including personal growth and development, maintaining physical and mental health, equity, infrastructure and involvement in decision-making. However, to what extent are these human **needs** and to what extent are they human **wants** (which may not be necessary)? There is also the issue of the extent to which social sustainability means preserving the existing institutions and customary behaviour of society, or whether these need to change (see the discussion on strong sustainability below).

Economic sustainability is even more controversial. Critics claim that it defines wellbeing in terms of production of goods and services. Social and ecological sustainability are only seen as important in providing a framework for a system to operate that supports production.

Another significant issue here is whether the developing world should be encouraged to reach and sustain the **same level of economic development** as the Western economies. One argument is that without economic growth the investment necessary for ecological sustainability will not be available. However, encouraging all world economies to reach the levels of economic growth that may have caused environmental degradation may lead to more, not less, rapid resource depletion.

Case Study

Various studies have shown that we would need two or more worlds that each had the same level of natural resources that this world has to sustain this world, if all countries enjoyed the same rate of consumption per head as the developed countries.

4.2.3 Sustainable for how long

A key issue here is **generational equity**, ensuring that future generations are able to enjoy the same environmental conditions, and in social terms per capita welfare is maintained or increased.

However, with raw materials having finite levels, any use of these resources ultimately cannot be sustained. In other areas the question of **how long** things can be sustained is bound up with the **level** at which they will be sustained. Perspectives on how to maintain a sustainable society indefinitely may also have to change in the light of changing climatic and ecological conditions, some of which are independent of whatever mankind does.

4.2.4 Sustainable at what cost

Again the deep ecologist view is that threats to the existence of other species are unacceptable, and that a system that rewards ecologically unsustainable behaviour is flawed and needs to be changed.

Those who hold other views must address the **issue of non-renewable resources** and whether some **ecological capital is irreplaceable**. Should the emphasis therefore be on preservation, or is substitution of other resources or capital possible? Alternatively would it be possible to compensate future generations for the resources and capital this generation exhausts?

4.2.5 Sustainable by whom

Ideally by the whole world, but meaningful global international agreements look unlikely at present. Sustainability must therefore be on an individual basis by nations, individuals – and businesses.

4.3 Strong and weak sustainability

One distinction that is often drawn in the sustainability debate is the distinction between strong and weak sustainability. These two approaches to the idea of sustainability relate to their supporters' views of the extent, causes and solutions.

4.3.1 Weak sustainability

Supporters of this view are concerned to **prevent the kind of catastrophe** that would threaten society. They believe that the focus should be on **sustaining the human species** and the natural environment can be regarded as a resource. However, the human race needs to have **better mastery of the natural environment**. This can be achieved by incremental change driven by market forces and legal regulation and requiring **economic development** to drive the technological changes necessary. Weak sustainability argues that it is possible to substitute natural and capital-made stocks that have been reduced with other items. Sustainability can be achieved within the next 30-50 years.

The weak sustainability viewpoint tends to dominate discussion within the Western economic sphere. However, critics suggest that it is based on hope rather than evidence, and is ultimately underpinned by a desire to maintain existing economic and social systems.

4.3.2 Strong sustainability

Supporters of strong sustainability argue that far more fundamental changes are needed in society. The viewpoint is linked with other critiques of our society that we have seen in earlier chapters such as the feminist or anti-capitalist agenda. Supporters stress the **need for harmony** with the natural world. It is important to sustain all species, not just the human race. They see a requirement for **fundamental change**, including a change in how man perceives economic growth (and whether it is pursued at all). They suggest that we have little or no idea at present of what sustainability would be, and the **timespan** for achieving it is likely to be very long, perhaps over a century.

Supporters of strong sustainability argue man-made capital stocks cannot be substituted for natural stocks. Use of natural capital stocks will inevitably affect future generations' abilities to meet their own needs.

Supporters of strong sustainability stress the need for participation and democracy in achieving sustainable growth. However, this course faces opposition from political and business leaders who are benefiting from the current system.

4.4 Businesses and sustainability

Key term

> **Externality** is the difference between the market and social costs, or benefits, of an activity. An externality is a cost or benefit that the market fails to take into account.

How can individual businesses help to promote sustainability, bearing in mind that competitors have other priorities? One important way is to develop environmental reporting systems that provide information about the external environmental effects – the **externalities** – of their activities. This data can then be used in decision-making processes, both of government and of other organisations, by **internalising** the costs of environmental effects. In addition, better costing of externalities will **influence the price mechanism** and therefore the economic decisions that are taken.

4.5 External social and environmental reporting

As well as developing a system of internal reporting on social and environmental issues, a business may also provide social and environmental data in its external reports. This can be seen as an aspect of a business being a corporate citizen that receives benefits from, and therefore owes duties back to, society. Accountability as a corporate citizen can partly be demonstrated by not just reporting items that can be easily measured and are required by laws, regulations or accounting standards. Large companies are finding the pressure to report difficult to resist.

4.6 Media of reporting

Environmental reporting is done in a number of different media, including annual reports, standalone reports, company websites, advertising or promotional media. Recently, larger companies in particular have produced a separate report on social and environmental issues, although many companies still include the information within their annual reports. Titles used for separate reports have included Sustainability report, Citizenship report, Corporate responsibility report and Environment, Social and Governance report.

4.7 Contents of environmental reports   6/13

Reports generally include **narrative and numerical information** about environmental impact. Narrative information includes objectives, explanations and reasons why targets have or have not been achieved. Reports can also address concerns of specific internal or external stakeholders. Useful numerical measures can include pollution amounts, resources consumed or land use.

 Case Study

BT's Social and Environmental Report for the year ended 31 March 2011 complies with the Global Reporting Initiative Guidelines (discussed below). To give an overview of the company's social and environmental performance, the report selects 12 non-financial key performance indicators.

(a)   Customer service – 3% increase in service quality

(b)   Employee engagement index (measure of success of BT's relationship with employees) – a small rise to 3.61 out of 5

(c)   Diversity – BT maintains a top 10 placement in 4 out of 5 major diversity benchmarks

(d)   Health and safety lost time injury rate – up from 0.209 cases per 100,000 working hours to 0.225 cases per 100,000 working hours

(e)   Health and safety sickness and absence rate – down from 2.46% calendar days lost due to sickness/absence to 2.41% calendar days lost

(f)   Supplier relationship success – 86% satisfaction

(g)   Ethical trading (a measure of the application of BT's supply chain human rights standard) – 70 risk assessments with 100% follow-up

(h)   Community effectiveness (such as charity partnerships and support for learning and skills and helping people get online) – rated at 98%

(i)   Investment in community improvements – 1.9% of pre-tax profits

(j)   Global warming CO_2 emissions – fell from 653,000 to 628,000 tonnes

(k)   Waste to landfill and recycling (a measure of use of resources) – reduction of 69%

(l)   Ethical performance – a small increase to 4.16 out of 5 in a measure designed to assess employee awareness and training, compliance with the company's ethical code and behaviour with integrity

4.8 Advantages of external social and environmental reporting

(a)   **Transparency and accountability**

Social and environmental reporting can be seen as fulfilling the key governance principle of transparency, and the requirement of various governance codes for the board to provide a **balanced and understandable assessment of the company's position**. This includes negative impacts such as environmental impacts. Environmental reporting can **strengthen accountability to shareholders** by providing shareholders with important information about how their agents, the directors, are running the company. Because environmental reports include details about use of resources and pollution over time, companies are also **demonstrating their accountability to future generations**.

(b) **Impact on internal control systems**

The need to **specify the impact on the environment in external reports** means that environmental reporting must be adequately integrated into internal control systems. Companies need to establish internal measurement systems that collect and process the data required to support environmental reports. As well as spurring reductions in environmental impact, the information that these systems generate can be used to develop an understanding of how to **reduce cost and waste** and improve internal efficiency.

(c) **Addressing investor concerns about risk**

Investors and other stakeholders are becoming more interested in the level of environmental disclosures, seeing them as very important **disclosures** in the context of **risk management and strategic decision-making**. This can lead to investors seeing companies as lower risk, as more risks are known about and reported, hence companies' cost of capital falling.

(d) **Improved reputation**

An increasing number of companies see voluntary environmental reporting as a means of demonstrating their commitment to good practice and hence **enhancing their reputation for ethical and competent behaviour**, leading to **marketing opportunities** as green companies. In particular, companies that have a high environmental impact, such as oil or gas companies, often provide the most information about their impacts.

(e) **Damage limitation**

When a company is involved in a well-publicised incident or commits a serious environmental error, it can result in stakeholders having doubts about the **legitimacy** of its activities. This can mean that threats to its licence to operate arise or its relationships with society are damaged. Environmental reporting can be used to address these concerns by **providing reassurance** that the company has learnt lessons from its experiences.

4.9 The Global Reporting Initiative (GRI)

Companies can adopt whatever approach they choose when reporting voluntarily on environmental impacts. However, two developments designed to provide guidance on supplying more social and environmental information are the **Global Reporting Initiative (GRI)** and the development of **full cost accounting**.

The Global Reporting Initiative, as its name suggests, is a reporting framework and arose from the need to **address the failure of the current governance structures to respond to changes in the global economy**.

The GRI aims to develop **transparency**, **accountability**, **reporting** and **sustainable development**. Its vision is that reporting on economic, environmental and social importance should become as routine and comparable as financial reporting.

Case Study

The forum SustainAbility's Tomorrow's Value rating examines how well companies manage their most pressing social and environmental issues. The Tomorrow's Value Rating of the 15 largest companies in Silicon Valley in America found that many of them were developing innovative practices, but were doing less well in day-to-day matters. They showed commitment to industry initiatives such as the Global e-Sustainability Initiative. They also showed greater concern about how their products, services and initiatives tie into the goal of generating positive change in society, for example investing in social media to create more interactive stakeholder engagement. However, day-to-day practices are weaker, with reporting lacking detail of areas of concern to stakeholders, including employee development, community investment, labour standards, economic contributions and supplier development.

4.9.1 GRI Guidelines

The GRI published revised guidelines in 2006.

The main section of the Guidelines (Report contents) sets out the framework of a sustainability report. It consists of five sections:

(a) **Strategy and analysis.** Description of the reporting organisation's strategy with regard to sustainability, including a statement from the CEO. In addition, there should be a description of key impacts, risks and opportunities. This section should focus firstly on key impacts on sustainability and associated challenges and opportunities, and how the organisation has addressed the challenges and opportunities. It should secondly focus on the impact of sustainability risks, trends and opportunities on the long-term prospects and financial performance of the organisation.

(b) **Organisational profile.** This should provide an overview of the reporting organisation's structure, operations, markets served and scale.

(c) **Report parameters.** Details of the time and content of the report, including the process for defining the report content and identifying the stakeholders that the organisation expects to use the report. Details should also be given of the policy and current practice for seeking external assurance for the report.

(d) **Governance, commitments and engagement structure and management systems.** Description of governance structure and practice, and statements of mission and codes of conduct relevant to economic, environmental and social performance. The report should give a description of charters, principles or initiatives to which the organisation subscribes or which the organisation endorses. The report should also list the stakeholder groups with which it engages and detail its approaches to stakeholder engagement.

(e) **Performance indicators.** These divide measures of the impact or effect of the reporting organisation into integrated indicators.

4.9.2 Indicators in the GRI framework

GRI structures performance indicators according to a hierarchy of category and aspect.

Category	Aspect
Environmental	Materials Water Biodiversity Emissions, effluents and waste Products and services Compliance Transport Overall
Human rights	Investment and procurement practices Non-discrimination Freedom of association and collective bargaining Child labour Forced and compulsory labour Security practices Indigenous rights Scale of assessment Remediation of grievances

Category	Aspect
Labour practices and decent work	Employment Labour/management relations Occupational health and safety Training and education Diversity and equal opportunity Equal remuneration for women and men
Society	Local community Corruption Role in public policy Anti-competitive behaviour Compliance
Product responsibility	Customer health and safety Product and service labelling Marketing communications Customer privacy Compliance
Economic	Economic performance Market presence Indirect economic impacts

4.10 Integrated reporting   12/14, 6/15

The King report of 2009 required South African companies to integrate reporting on sustainability issues with reporting on financial results and operations. The report stressed the need to demonstrate positive and negative impacts, and the need to report on goals and strategies as well as economic, social and environmental issues.

In December 2013 the International Integrated Reporting Council (IIRC) published *The International Integrated Reporting Framework*.

The aim of integrated reporting is to **demonstrate the linkage between strategy, governance and financial performance** and the **social, environmental and economic context within which the business operates**. By making these connections, businesses should be able to take more sustainable decisions, helping to ensure the effective allocation of scarce resources. Investors and other stakeholders should better understand how an organisation is really performing. In particular, they should make a meaningful assessment of the long-term viability of the organisation's business model and its strategy.

Integrated reporting should also achieve the simplification of accounts, with excessive detail being removed and critical information being highlighted.

4.10.1 Capitals

Integrated reporting is designed to make visible the capitals (resources and relationships) on which the organisation depends, how the organisation uses those capitals and its impact on them.

Financial	Funds available for use in production obtained through financing or generated through operations
Manufactured	Manufactured physical objects used in production or service provision: • Buildings • Equipment • Infrastructure

Human	Skills, experience and motivation to innovate:
	• Alignment and support for organisation's governance framework and ethical values
	• Ability to understand and implement organisation's strategies
	• Loyalties and motivations for improvements
Intellectual	Knowledge-based intangibles providing competitive advantage:
	• Patents, copyrights, software, rights and licences
	• Tacit knowledge, systems and protocols
Natural	Input to goods and services and what activities impact:
	• Water, land, minerals and forests
	• Biodiversity and ecosystem health
Social and relationship	Institutions and relationships within each community stakeholder group and network to enhance wellbeing:
	• Common values and behaviour
	• Key relationships
	• Brand and reputation
	• Social licence to operate

4.10.2 Guiding principles

A number of guiding principles underpin the content and presentation of an integrated report.

Strategic focus and future orientation	Insights into strategy, and how it relates to organisation's ability to create value in the short, medium and long term, and how it affects the capitals
Connectivity of information	A holistic view of the combination, interrelatedness and dependencies between the factors that affect the ability to create value over time
Stakeholder relationships	The nature and quality of relationships with key stakeholders and how their legitimate needs and interests are taken into account
Materiality, conciseness, reliability and completeness	Provision of important and reliable information including all material items, both positive and negative, in a concise manner
Consistency and comparability	Consistent over time and comparable with other organisations

4.10.3 Content elements

The content elements follow on from the guiding principles.

- Organisational overview and external environment
- Governance
- Business model

- Risks and opportunities
- Strategy and resource allocation
- Performance
- Outlook
- Basis of presentation

4.10.4 Benefits of integrated reporting

The following are potential benefits of integrated reporting.

(a) **Stakeholder needs**

The information will be more in line with **investor and other stakeholder requirements**, leading to a higher level of trust from, and engagement with, stakeholders. Investors will have better information to assess ability to generate cash flows and risk opportunities. The connections made in reporting will enable investors to assess better the combined impact of the diverse factors affecting the business. This should result in better investment decisions and more effective capital allocation.

(b) **Decision-making**

Having the information will enable better resource allocation decisions, enhanced risk management and better identification of opportunities.

(c) **Reputation**

Greater transparency should result in a decrease in reputation risk and lower cost of, and better access to, capital.

(d) **Harmonisation**

Integrated reporting provides a platform for standard-setters and decision-makers to harmonise reporting.

(e) **Stewardship**

Because of its emphasis on resources and relationships and a longer timeframe, organisations are better placed to act, and be more accountable, as stewards of common resources.

(f) **Stakeholder relationships**

The emphasis on stakeholder engagement should lead to greater consultation with stakeholder groups and dealing with their concerns.

4.10.5 Challenges to integrated reporting

There are a number of challenges to the development of integrated reporting.

(a) **Local regulation**

Regulations that vary between jurisdictions currently affect components of integrated reporting and progress towards integrated reporting will happen at different speeds in different countries.

(b) **Directors' duties**

Directors' duties also vary between jurisdictions. Integrated reporting will be influenced by the users of accounts whom the directors are required to address.

(c) **Directors' liability**

Concerns about liability will need to be addressed, as directors will be reporting on the future and on evolving issues.

(d) **Confidentiality**

Organisations will need to balance the benefits of integrated reporting with the desire to avoid disclosing competitive information.

(e)   **Incentives**

Integrated reporting needs to assist in overcoming focus on short-term rewards.

5 Environmental management systems   12/11

Question   Environmental control systems

How do the main elements of control systems for environmental management systems differ from control systems in other areas?

Answer

As we shall see in this section, they don't. Environmental management systems are a good illustration of how control systems work in practice.

5.1 EMAS

The European Union's Eco-Management and Audit Scheme (EMAS) was adopted in 1993 as a voluntary scheme. Its emphasis is on **targets and improvements**, **on-site inspections** and requirements for **disclosure and verification**. The insistence on targets means that organisations that subscribe to it cannot just rely on monitoring. They have to **improve their environmental performance**.

The **disclosure and verification requirements** are seen as essential, as companies need to know that their performance will be subject to public scrutiny based on data that has been reliably audited, to become 'good little goldfish' (Elkington). Disclosure means that companies have to address the very real difficulties and conflicts of interest that arise in weighing up the need to maximise profits against the need to comply with disclosure requirements. However, many businesses were opposed to the requirement of EMAS and lobbying meant that compliance was introduced as voluntary rather than compulsory as was originally intended.

EMAS's adoption has been rather more extensive in Germany than elsewhere in the European Union. However, many companies that had felt that the requirements of EMAS were excessive eventually had to respond to pressures regarding their environmental performance and adopt a recognised standard (ISO 14000).

5.1.1 Requirements for EMAS registration

- An environmental policy containing commitments to comply with legislation and achieve continuous environmental performance improvement

- An on-site environmental review

- An environmental management system that is based on the environmental review and the company's environmental policy

- Environmental audits at sites at least every three years

- Audit results to form the basis of setting environmental objectives and the revision of the environmental policy to achieve those objectives

- A public environmental statement validated by accredited environmental verifiers containing detailed disclosures about policy, management systems and performance in such areas as pollution, waste, raw material usage, energy, water and noise

5.2 ISO 14000

ISO 14000 was first published in 1996 and based on earlier quality management standards. It provides a general framework on which a number of specific standards have been based (the ISO family of standards). ISO 14001 prescribes that an environmental management system must comprise:

- An environmental policy statement
- An assessment of environmental aspects and legal and voluntary obligations
- A management system
- Internal audits and reports to senior management
- A public declaration that ISO 14001 is being complied with

Critics of ISO 14000 claim that its emphasis on management systems rather than performance is misplaced, and that it is much less effective because it does not include EMAS's rigorous verification and disclosure requirements.

5.3 Environmental policy statement

The policy statement should be the basis for future action. It therefore needs to be based on **reliable data** and allow for the development of **specific targets**.

Organisations may wish to develop their own in-house policy statement or adopt one of the public charters such as the **CERES principles** (see below) or the **ICC's Charter for Sustained Development**. An in-house charter can be tailored to the organisation's needs and be compatible with the mission statement in other areas. However, it may be viewed by outsiders as too general and bland, and also may not be internationally comparable. Adopting internationally recognised standards means adherence to standards that have been **determined objectively**, and assisting stakeholders by enabling comparison with other organisations that have adopted the same standards.

Case Study

The Coalition for Environmentally Responsible Economics, CERES, created the CERES principles in 1989. The principles are a code of environmental conduct to be publicly endorsed by companies as an environmental mission statement or ethic.

- **Protection of the biosphere** – aiming to eliminate the release of any substance that may cause environmental damage, safeguarding habitats and protecting biodiversity

- **Sustainable use of natural resources** – making sustainable use of renewable natural resources and conserving non-renewable natural resources through efficient use and careful planning

- **Reduction and disposal of waste** – elimination of waste where possible through source reduction and recycling, and disposal where necessary of waste through safe and responsible methods

- **Energy conservation** – conserving energy, improving energy efficiency of internal operations, goods and services and making every effort to use environmentally safe and sustainable energy sources

- **Reduction in environmental and health and safety risks** through safe technologies, facilities and operating procedures, and being prepared for emergencies

- **Safe products and services** – elimination where possible of products and services that cause environmental damage or health and safety hazards, together with informing customers of environmental impacts

- **Environmental restoration** – correcting conditions caused by the organisation that have resulted in damage to the environment and aiming to redress injuries

- **Informing the public** of conditions that might endanger health and safety and the environment, regular dialogue with nearby communities and not taking any action against whistleblowing employees who report dangerous incidents or conditions

- **Management commitment** – environmental commitment being a factor in the selection of directors, board kept informed about environmental issues and acknowledgement of board responsibility for environmental issues

- **Audits and reports** – annual self-evaluation of progress in implementing principles, support for the timely creation of generally accepted environmental audit principles – and annual endorsement of the CERES principles

5.4 Management roles

Whatever the standards adopted, they must be promoted by a member of the senior management team for the standards to be **effective**, and the **audit committee** is likely to be involved in monitoring and reporting on environmental compliance. Depending on the size of the organisation and its impact on the external environment, an **environmental manager** or an **environmental management department** may be employed.

5.5 Assessment of environmental aspects and obligations

Many companies have been forced to act on environmental issues because of shocks such as environmental disasters or attention from pressure groups. To reduce the chances of these happening, organisations must not only monitor their internal performance but also include within their monitoring of the external situation an assessment of the impact of environmental issues. It will be particularly important to monitor:

- Emerging environmental issues
- Likely changes in legislation
- Changes in industry best practice
- Attitudes of suppliers, customers, media and the general public
- Activities of environmental enforcement agencies
- Activities of environmental pressure groups

5.6 Management systems

In *Accounting for the Environment* Gray and Bebbington listed the functions that environmental management systems should cover.

Environmental review and policy development	A first review of environmental impacts of materials, issues and products and of business issues arising, also the development of a tailored in-house policy or measures to ensure adherence to external standards
Objectives and target development	As with all business objectives and targets, it is preferable that those set be unambiguous and achievable. Initiatives such as the WWF initiative described above encourage quantified targets within a specified time period eg reducing carbon dioxide emissions by X% within a specified time period

Life-cycle assessment	This aims to identify all interactions between a product and its environment during its lifetime, including energy and material usage and environmental releases.
	• Raw materials used have to be traced back to the biosphere and the company recognise impact on habitat, gas balance, the energy used in the extraction and transportation and the energy used to produce the means of extraction
	• For intermediate stages, emissions, discharges and co-products
	• At the consumer purchase stage, the impact of manufacture and disposal of packaging, transport to shops and ultimately impacts of consumers using and disposing of the product
Establishment and maintenance of environmental management systems	Key features of environmental management systems (as with other management systems) including information systems, budgeting, forecasting and management accounting systems, structure of responsibilities, establishment of an environmentally friendly culture, considering impact on human resource issues such as education and performance appraisal
Regulatory compliance	Making sure that current legal requirements are being fulfilled and keeping up to date with practical implications of likely changes in legislation
Environmental impact assessment	A regular review of interactions with the environment, the degree of impact and an environmental SWOT analysis, also the impact of forthcoming major investments
Eco-label applications	Eco-labelling allows organisations to identify publicly products and services that meet the highest environmental standards. To be awarded an eco-label requires the product to be the result of a reliable quality management system
Waste minimisation	Whether waste can be minimised (or, better still, eliminated), possibility of recycling or selling waste
Pollution prevention programmes	Deciding what to target
Research, development and investment in cleaner technologies	How to bring desirable features into product development, bearing in mind product development may take several years, and opinion and legal requirements may change during that period. Desirable features may include minimum resource usage, waste, emissions, packaging and transport, recycling, disassembly and longer product life
Environmental performance and issues reporting	Consideration of the benefits and costs of reporting, how to report and what to include (policies, plans, financial data, activities undertaken, sustainability)

5.7 Environmental reporting

Predictably the main arguments in favour of environmental reporting are similar to those for reporting on other aspects of internal control, including following the principles of **transparency** and **openness, disclosing matters of concern** to investors and other stakeholders and generally presenting a **balanced and understandable assessment** of the **company's position and prospects**.

5.8 Advantages of environmental management systems

Operating an environmental management system can have the following benefits.

(a) **Control of impacts**

Operating a system should result in a **structured approach** to controlling impacts and ensuring compliance with laws and regulations.

(b)   **Limiting costs and resource usage**

The system should ensure **reduced costs** in such areas as waste management and resource inputs, as resources are used more efficiently.

(c)   **Reputation**

Commitment to a system should **demonstrate to stakeholders the organisation's commitment** to environmental responsibility. It can result in reduced pressure from active stakeholders, such as government, regulators or pressure groups.

Exam focus point

Question 1 in December 2011 asked about reporting on environmental risk management systems.

6 Social and environmental audits

Social and environmental audits are designed to ascertain whether the organisation is complying with codes of best practice or internal guidelines, and is fulfilling the wider requirements of being a good corporate citizen.

6.1 Social audits

The process of checking whether an organisation has achieved set targets may fall within a social audit that a company carries out. Social audits may cover sustainable use of resources, health and safety compliance, labour conditions (no exploitation of labour) and equal opportunities.

General social audits will involve:

- Establishing whether the organisation has a **rationale** for engaging in socially responsible activity, such as community support or enlightened treatment of employees
- Identifying that all current environment programmes are **congruent** with the mission of the company
- **Assessing objectives and priorities** related to these programmes
- **Evaluating company involvement** in such programmes past, present and future

Whether or not a social audit is used depends on the degree to which social responsibility is part of the **corporate philosophy**. A cultural awareness must be achieved within an organisation in order to implement social policy, which requires board and staff support.

6.1.1 Specific social audits

Specific social audits may cover the consequences of a major decision; for example, costs such as unemployment costs and indirect redundancies of shutting a major manufacturing plant.

6.1.2 External social audits

Another type of social audit is an audit carried out by an external body with or without the organisation's co-operation. These types of audit might for example cover **involvement in controversial areas** such as animal testing, aggressive marketing, low-wage employment overseas and investment in countries governed by oppressive regimes. More positive areas that could be covered include industrial democracy, equal opportunities, community involvement and disclosure of information.

Key term

> An **environmental audit** is a systematic, documented, periodic and objective evaluation of how well an entity and its management and equipment are performing, with the aim of helping to safeguard the environment by facilitating management control of environmental practices and assessing compliance with entity policies and external regulations.
>
> Environmental auditing is also used for auditing the **truth and fairness** of an environmental report rather than the organisation itself. The same is true of social auditing.

An environmental audit might be undertaken as part of obtaining or maintaining the BSI's ISO 14001 standard.

It may also be undertaken as a result of various pressures:

- As environmental issues are a **source of risk** due to unforeseen liabilities or reputation damage, an environmental audit may be organised as part of the **risk audit**.

- Potential **stakeholders** (customers, employees) may decide whether to engage with the organisation on the basis of its environmental records.

- Potential **investors** may be influenced by **social and environmental factors** when making investment decisions.

In practice environmental audits may cover a number of different areas, and some of the examples below may go beyond what you have encountered in your earlier auditing studies. The scope of the audit must be determined and this will depend on each individual organisation. Often the audit will be a general review of the organisation's environmental policy. On other occasions the audit will focus on specific aspects of environmental performance (waste disposal, emissions, water management, energy consumption) or particular locations, activities or processes.

There are other specific aspects of the approach to environmental auditing which are worth mentioning.

(a) **Environmental Impact Assessments (EIAs)**

These are required, under an EU directive, for all major projects which require planning permission and have a material effect on the environment. The EIA process can be incorporated into any environmental auditing strategy.

(b) **Environmental surveys**

These are a good way of starting the audit process, by looking at the organisation as a whole in environmental terms. This helps to identify areas for further development, problems, potential hazards and so forth.

(c) **Environmental SWOT analysis**

A 'strengths, weaknesses, opportunities, threats' analysis is useful as the environmental audit strategy is being developed. This can only be done later in the process, when the organisation has been examined in much more detail.

(d) **Environmental Quality Management (EQM)**

This is seen as part of TQM (Total Quality Management) and it should be built into an environmental management system. Such a strategy has been adopted by companies such as IBM, Dow Chemicals and by the Rhone-Poulenc Environmental Index which has indices for levels of water, air and other waste products.

(e) **Eco-audit**

The European Commission has adopted a proposal for a regulation for a voluntary community environmental auditing scheme, known as the eco-audit scheme. The scheme aims to promote improvements in company environmental performance and to provide the public with information about these improvements. Once registered, a company will have to comply with certain ongoing obligations involving disclosure and audit.

(f) **Eco-labelling**

Developed in Germany, this voluntary scheme will indicate those EU products which meet the highest environmental standards, probably as the result of an EQM system. It is suggested that eco-audit **must** come before an eco-label can be given.

(g) **BS 7750 Environmental Management Systems**

BS 7750 also ties in with eco-audits and eco-labelling and with the quality BSI standard BS 5750. Achieving BS 7750 is likely to be a first step in the eco-audit process.

(h) **Supplier audits**

They ensure that goods and services bought in by an organisation meet the standards applied by that organisation.

6.2.1 Environmental audit stages

There are three main stages in most environmental audits.

(a) **Establishing the metrics**

The greater the variety of metrics, the more information provided. However, measuring against a number of metrics could result in a **costly audit**.

(b) **Measuring planned or desirable performance against actual performance**

This is an important aspect of a system, as we discussed in Chapter 4. Some metrics will be objective; for example, the level of carbon emissions or plastic bag issues can be measured. However other aspects, for example public perceptions, cannot be measured objectively and may therefore be difficult to measure precisely.

(c) **Reporting the results of the audit**

Important decisions will include the form that the report should take and how widely it should be distributed, in particular whether the organisation's annual report should include a report by the auditors.

6.2.2 Auditor concerns

(a) Board and management having **good understanding** of the environmental impact and related legislation of the organisation's activities in areas such as buildings, transport, products, packaging and waste

(b) Adoption and communication of adequate policies and procedures to ensure **compliance with relevant standards and laws**

(c) Adoption of **appropriate environmental information systems**

(d) Adoption and **review of progress** against quantifiable targets

(e) Assessment of whether **progress** is being made **economically and efficiently**

(f) Implementation of **previous recommendations** of improvements to processes or systems

(g) **True, fair and complete reporting** of environmental activities

6.2.3 Auditing environmental policy

Auditing the appropriateness of, and compliance with, the organisation's environmental policy will be at the heart of internal environmental audits.

(a)   Review evidence of the **organisation's environmental interactions.**

(b)   Obtain a copy of the **organisation's environmental policy and targets** and assess whether the policy is likely to achieve objectives:

    (i)   Meet legal requirements
    (ii)   Meet environmental standards
    (iii)   Satisfy key customers/suppliers' criteria

(c)   Test **implementation and adherence to the targets** set out in the policy by:

    (i)   Discussion
    (ii)   Observation
    (iii)   'Walk-though tests' where possible

(d)   Report on the **level of compliance or variance**.

The targets measured in the audit may include:

- Measures of emissions (pollution, waste and greenhouse gases)
- Consumption (energy, water and non-renewable food stocks)

Often a target will be set for reduction in aspects of the organisation's environmental footprint, possibly the footprint attributable to each unit of output.

The value of the audit may be questioned, as for most companies an environmental audit is not compulsory, there are no mandatory audit standards and no compulsory auditable activities. Unless one of the international frameworks such as ISO 14000 is used, stakeholders may question how rigorous the process has been. Also in some instances the audit will be for internal use only, although an audit report may be part of external environmental reporting.

Question   Social and environmental reporting

What are the key elements in ensuring effective social and environmental reporting?

Answer

The answer brings together several themes that we have discussed in earlier chapters.

(a)   Shareholders and other stakeholders should have **input** into the process.

(b)   Use of external benchmarks and external, independent verifiers to report on the quality of the information provided **enhances credibility**.

(c)   The information reported must be supported by effective **control and information systems**.

(d)   Information must be **clear, complete and unbiased**, fairly reporting on negative aspects as well as positive.

(e)   Information reported must be seen by the organisation as feedback that forms the basis of **continuous improvement** in these areas.

Question   Ways of doing business

Dale Vince, founder and managing director of Ecotricity (described as the UK's first green electricity company) was asked by *The Guardian* newspaper to comment on the UK television series, The Apprentice. In particular he was asked about the aggressive competition between the contestants, who were vying to be employed by business magnate Lord Sugar.

Vince said successful businesses can incorporate idealism, fairness and a concern for the environment. 'I believe in sustainable relationships where everybody is willing to do business again. They like each other because they haven't been screwed to the floor.'

Do you agree with Vince's comments? What are your reasons for your views on them?

Answer

Your answer should have demonstrated where you stand, for example, in the Gray, Owen and Adams spectrum. Hopefully you will have been inspired by the ideas we have discussed in this chapter. A key feature of Vince's argument which hopefully you picked up on was that sustainability is not just about environmental issues – it influences a business's whole way of operating. It is therefore an integral part of the internal environment.

Chapter Roundup

- **Corporate citizenship** has been used to describe how an organisation's values are shaped and the impact that concepts of responsibility have on business decision-making.

- An organisation's ethical stance relates to how it **views its responsibilities** to shareholders, stakeholders, society and the environment.

- There is increasing concern about businesses' relationship with the natural environment. Businesses may suffer **significant costs** and a **loss of reputation** if problems arise.

- **Sustainability** means limiting use of resources to what can be replenished.

  The **Global Reporting Initiative** provides a framework for a **sustainability report**.

  Full cost accounting is a method of accounting for all relevant costs including externalities.

- **ISO statements** provide a framework for an **environmental management system** including a policy statement, assessment, functions and reporting.

- **Social and environmental audits** are designed to ascertain whether the organisation is complying with codes of best practice or internal guidelines, and is fulfilling the wider requirements of being a good corporate citizen.

1   Fill in the blank:

.... is the business strategy that shapes the values underpinning a company's mission and the choices made each day by its executives, managers and employees as they engage with society.

2   Match the position on social responsibility with the viewpoint held.

(a)   Pristine capitalist
(b)   Expedient
(c)   Social contract proponent
(d)   Social ecologist
(e)   Socialist
(f)   Radical feminist
(g)   Deep ecologist

(i)   Economic systems that trade off threats to the existence of species with economic imperatives are flawed.

(ii)   Businesses have to accept some social legislation and moral requirements if they are to be able to generate profits.

(iii)   Companies exist to make profits and seek economic efficiency.

(iv)   The economic framework should change from being one that promotes materialism to one that promotes equality.

(v)   Economic processes that result in resource exhaustion, waste and pollution must be modified.

(vi)   Economic systems emphasise aggression, conflict and competition rather than co-operation and reflection.

(vii)   An organisation's survival and prosperity is based on delivery of benefits to society in general.

3   Fill in the blank:

.... is the impact that a business's activities have on the environment including its resource environment and pollution emissions.

4   What is sustainability in relation to a company's activities?

5   Give three examples of the environmental indicators mentioned in the Global Reporting Initiative.

6   Fill in the blank:

.... is a system that allows current accounting and economic numbers to incorporate all potential/actual costs and benefits into the accounting equation, including environmental and social externalities.

7   What are the main elements of an environmental management system per ISO 14001?

8   By what criteria is an auditor likely to test an organisation's environmental policy?

Answers to Quick Quiz

1 Corporate citizenship

2 (a) (iii) (b) (ii) (c) (vii) (d) (v) (e) (iv) (f) (vi) (g) (i)

3 Environmental footprint

4 Sustainability involves developing strategies so that the company only uses resources at a rate that allows them to be replenished (in order to ensure that they will continue to be available). At the same time the company's emissions of waste are confined to levels that do not exceed the capacity of the environment to absorb them.

5 Three from:

- Materials
- Energy
- Water
- Biodiversity
- Emissions, effluents and waste
- Suppliers
- Products and services
- Compliance
- Transport
- Overall

6 Full cost accounting

7
- An environmental policy
- An assessment of environmental aspects and legal and voluntary obligations
- A management system
- Internal audits and reports to senior management
- A public declaration that ISO 14001 is being complied with

8
- Meet legal requirements
- Meet environmental standards
- Satisfy key customers'/suppliers' criteria

Now try the question below from the Practice Question Bank.

Number	Level	Marks	Time
Q11	Examination	25	49 mins

Practice question and answer bank

1 Bonus schemes
49 mins

It has been suggested that optimal bonus schemes for profit centre managers promise significant rewards for the achievement of challenging targets in areas they can influence. These schemes balance short-term pressure with incentives to maintain a long-term focus and protect managers from the distorting effects of uncontrollable factors.

It has also been suggested that many bonus schemes have additional features with different motivational effects.

The following are possible features of bonus schemes.

- Limiting the range of performance within which rewards are linked to results, in particular ignoring losses and limiting maximum payments
- Linking incentive payments wholly or partly to the profit of the organisation as a whole

Required

(a) (i) Explain why bonus schemes might include these features.

(ii) Discuss the benefits and drawbacks of incorporating these features into bonus schemes.

(16 marks)

Bonus schemes are normally designed to motivate full-time employees who have no other employment and are wholly dependent on the organisation for their income. Part-time employees and short-term employees might not be included.

(b) Describe and advise on the possible features of bonus schemes which are designed to motivate non-executive directors who are part time, remunerated by fees under contracts for a fixed number of years and required by corporate governance codes to maintain independence. **(9 marks)**

(Total = 25 marks)

2 Cedric Coffee
49 mins

Cedric Coffee is a company that operates a chain of coffee shops. It is based in Europe and has been expanding over the last few years. Its managing director considers it to have reached its maximum growth potential in its own country and should expand into other European countries. It will need substantial finance to do this and is planning to obtain a listing on its local stock exchange.

The country in which Cedric Coffee is based is not part of the European Union and has not developed its own governance code. International investors who invest on the local stock exchange and whom the board of Cedric Coffee is hoping to attract tend to favour companies who follow national guidance from major countries such as Sarbanes-Oxley, or international codes such as the Organisation for Economic Co-operation and Development principles of corporate governance and the International Corporate Governance Network report on corporate governance. Cedric Coffee's managing director wants to have a greater understanding of the reasons that have led to the development of the corporate governance codes and wants to see comparisons between different international guidance.

The managing director also believes that Cedric Coffee's competitive position may be enhanced by adopting a corporate social responsibility code.

Required

Prepare a memorandum for the managing director of Cedric Coffee that:

(a) Discusses the main issues that led to the development of international corporate governance codes. **(7 marks)**

(b) Contrasts the requirements of the Sarbanes-Oxley legislation with the Organisation for Economic Co-operation and Development principles of corporate governance and the International Corporate Governance Network report on corporate governance. **(13 marks)**

(c) Discusses the case for Cedric Coffee developing a corporate social responsibility policy. **(5 marks)**

(Total = 25 marks)

3 Peter Postgate
49 mins

You have recently received a phone call from an uncle of a friend of yours, Peter Postgate. He is the managing director of a manufacturing firm that has been expanding over the last few years. Its success has been noticed in the press, and as a result he has been asked to become a non-executive director of a listed company based near to his own company's headquarters.

Peter Postgate's company does not have any non-executive directors on its board and he is somewhat uncertain about their role. In particular he has been told that the distinction between independent and non-independent non-executive directors is important, but does not understand what it means and why it is significant. He recalls reading somewhere in a newspaper that non-executive directors are meant to 'keep the peace' between the executive directors and the shareholders. He doesn't understand why there should be a conflict and is worried about what he'll have to do.

Peter Postgate has also been asked whether he wants to be paid partly in shares or share options, in line with the way executive directors are paid in the listed company.

Required

Write a letter to Peter Postgate:

(a) Explaining the distinction between independent and non-independent non-executive directors.

(5 marks)

(b) Assessing the main areas for a potential conflict of interest between the shareholders of a listed company and its executive directors, and explaining how the use of non-executive directors should help to deal with this problem.
(13 marks)

(c) Discussing the issues connected with paying NEDs in shares or share options of the company.
(7 marks)

(Total = 25 marks)

4 PKG High School
49 mins

PKG High School has 900 pupils, 40 teachers, 10 support staff and a budget of $3 million per annum, 85% of which represents salary and salary-related costs. PKG's local authority allocates government funding for education to schools based on the number of pupils. It ensures that the government-approved curriculum is taught in all schools in its area with the aim of achieving government targets. All schools, including PKG, are subject to an independent financial audit as well as a scrutiny of their education provision by the local authority, and reports of both are presented to the school governing body.

The number of pupils determines the approximate number of teachers, based on class sizes of approximately 30 pupils. The salary costs for teachers are determined nationally and pay scales mean that more experienced teachers receive higher salaries. In addition, some teachers receive school-specific responsibility allowances.

PKG is managed on a day-to-day basis by the headteacher. The governance of each school is carried out by a governing body comprising the headteacher, elected representatives of parents of pupils, and members appointed by the local authority. The principles of good corporate governance apply to school governing bodies which are accountable to parents and the local authority for the performance of the school.

The governing body holds the headteacher accountable for day-to-day school management, but on certain matters such as building maintenance the headteacher will seek expert advice from the local authority.

The governing body meets quarterly and has as its main responsibilities budgetary management, appointment of staff and education standards. The main control mechanisms exercised by the governing body include scrutiny of a year-to-date financial report, a quarterly non-financial performance report, teacher recruitment and approval of all purchases over $1,000. The headteacher has expenditure authority below this level.

The financial report (which is updated monthly) is presented to each meeting of the governing body. It shows the local authority's budget allocation to the school for the year, the expenditure incurred for each month and the year to date, and any unspent balances. Although there is no external financial reporting requirement for the school, the local authority will not allow any school to overspend its budget allocation in any financial year.

PKG's budget allocation is only just sufficient to provide adequate educational facilities. Additional funds are always required for teaching resources, building maintenance, and to upgrade computer equipment. The only flexibility the school has in budget management is to limit responsibility allowances and delay teacher recruitment. This increases pupil-contact time for individual teachers, however, and forces teachers to undertake preparation, marking and administration after school hours.

Note. A local authority (or council) carries out services for the local community and levies local taxes (or council tax) to fund most of its operations.

Required

(a)   Explain why the review and audit of control systems is important for the governing body of a school such as PKG.   **(5 marks)**

(b)   Evaluate the effectiveness of the governing body's control over PKG High School and recommend ways in which it might be improved.   **(20 marks)**

(Total = 25 marks)

5 Widmerpool   49 mins

You are a partner in an accountancy practice. One of your clients, Widmerpool, has expanded significantly over the last few years and is likely to seek a listing in a couple of years' time. You have been contacted by the Chief Executive, Mr Kenneth, for advice on areas relating to the control and risk management systems.

Up until recently, the main board has dealt with all significant issues relating to the company. In view of the current plans to seek a listing, Widmerpool has recently appointed three non-executive directors, and has used them to staff the audit committee that has just been established. Mr Kenneth is also wondering whether to set up a separate risk committee. Ideally he would like the audit committee's brief to be restricted to the accounting systems. There have recently been various incidents that appear to indicate problems with the ways Widmerpool's employees deal with risk.

In one incident a worker was trapped in a machine. A fellow worker tried to help and both were seriously injured. A subsequent investigation found that safety instructions appeared to be adequate and there was sufficient safety equipment available. However, staff had not been using the right equipment, appeared ignorant of safety issues and seemed unwilling or unable to comply with instructions.

In another instance one of Widmerpool's most significant suppliers, Stringham, with whom Widmerpool has been trying to develop much closer relations, supplied Widmerpool with confidential information concerning its operations. Two of Widmerpool's managers discussed these details in a local restaurant, but left the documentation relating to Stringham behind when they left the restaurant. Another customer removed this information and offered to sell it to one of Stringham's main competitors. The competitor declined the offer, and reported the situation to the police and Stringham. As a result Stringham has decided to terminate its relationship with Widmerpool. Widmerpool's organisational handbook stresses the need to keep sensitive business information confidential, but does not provide detailed guidance.

Widmerpool recently carried out a staff satisfaction survey. One of the comments made was that as the company has grown bigger, the board has become more distant from operations and seems primarily concerned with ensuring that profits increase each year. As a result, staff have become laxer in following internal procedures, as they believe that they are being judged solely on whether their department fulfils its financial targets.

Required

(a) Explain why Widmerpool's internal guidance and control procedures have failed to ensure that Widmerpool's employees deal carefully with business risks. **(8 marks)**

(b) Explain the ways in which the board of directors can, by their own example, promote a better risk culture than has recently been apparent at Widmerpool. **(8 marks)**

(c) Evaluate the case for Widmerpool establishing a separate risk committee, staffed by non-executive directors. **(9 marks)**

(Total = 25 marks)

6 Pacific Group   39 mins

Pacific Group Ltd (PG) is a publisher of a monthly magazine 'Sea Discovery'. Approximately 70% of the magazine's revenue is derived from advertising, the remainder being subscription income.

Individual advertisements, which may be quarter, half or whole page, are priced at £750, £1,250 and £2,000 respectively. Discounts of 10% to 25% are given for repeat advertisements and to major advertising customers.

PG's management has identified the following risks relating to its advertising revenues.

(a) Loss of revenue through failure to invest in developments which keep the presentation of advertisements up to date with competitor publications (such as 'The Deep').

(b) Due to unsuitable credit limits being set, business is accepted from a small proportion of advertising customers who are uncreditworthy.

(c) Published advertisements may not be invoiced due to incomplete data transfer between the editorial and invoicing departments.

(d) Individual advertisements are not charged for at approved rates – either in error or due to arrangements with the advertisers. In particular, the editorial department does not notify the invoicing department of reciprocal advertisement arrangements, whereby advertising customers provide PG with other forms of advertising (such as website banners).

(e) Individual advertisers refuse to pay for the inaccurate production of their advertisement.

(f) Cash received at a front desk, which is significant, may not be passed to cashiers, or be misappropriated.

(g) The risk of error arising from unauthorised access to the editorial and invoicing systems.

(h) The risk that the editorial and invoicing systems are not available.

(i) The computerised transfer of accounting information from the invoicing system to the nominal ledger may be incomplete or inaccurate.

(j) The risk that PG may be sued for advertisements which do not meet the British Standards Authority's 'Code of Advertising'.

Risks are to be screened out as 'non-applicable' if they meet **any** of the following criteria.

(1) The effect of the risk can be quantified and is less than £5,000.
(2) The risk is mitigated by an effective risk strategy eg insurance.
(3) The risk is likely to be low or its effect insignificant.

Those risks not screened out, called 'applicable risks', will require further consideration and are to be actively managed.

Required

For each of the above risks identified by management, evaluate, with a reason, whether it should be considered an 'applicable risk'. **(20 marks)**

7 Azure Airline

Azure, a limited liability company, was incorporated in Sepiana on 1 April 20X6. In May, the company exercised an exclusive right granted by the government of Pewta to provide twice weekly direct flights between Lyme, the capital of Pewta, and Darke, the capital of Sepiana. The introduction of this service has been well advertised as 'efficient and timely' in national newspapers. The journey time between Sepiana and Pewta is expected to be significantly reduced, so encouraging tourism and business development opportunities in Sepiana.

Azure operates a refurbished 35 year old aircraft which is leased from an international airline and registered with the Pewtan Aviation Administration (the PAA). The PAA requires that engines be overhauled every two years, putting the aircraft out of commission for several weeks.

The aircraft is configured to carry 15 first class, 50 business class and 76 economy class passengers. The aircraft has a generous hold capacity for Sepiana's numerous horticultural products (eg of cocoa, tea and fruit) and general cargo.

The six-hour journey offers an in-flight movie, a meal, hot and cold drinks and tax-free shopping. All meals are prepared in Lyme under a contract with an airport catering company. Passengers are invited to complete a 'satisfaction' questionnaire which is included with the in-flight entertainment and shopping guide. Responses received show that passengers are generally least satisfied with the quality of the food – especially on the Darke to Lyme flight.

Azure employs ten full-time cabin crew attendants who are trained in air stewardship including passenger safety in the event of accident and illness. Flight personnel (the captain and co-pilots) are provided under a contract with the international airline from which the aircraft is leased. At the end of each flight the captain completes a timesheet detailing the crew and actual flight time.

Ticket sales are made by Azure and travel agents in Sepiana and Pewta. On a number of occasions Economy seating has been overbooked. Customers who have been affected by this have been accommodated in business class, as there is much less demand for this, and even less for first class. Ticket prices for each class depend on many factors, for example, whether the tickets are refundable/non-refundable, exchangeable/non-exchangeable, single or return, midweek or weekend.

Azure's insurance cover includes passenger liability, freight/baggage and compensation insurance. Premiums for passenger liability insurance are determined on the basis of passenger miles flown.

Required

(a) Explain the business risks facing Azure. **(12 marks)**

(b) Recommend how the risks identified in (a) could be managed and maintained at an acceptable level by Azure. **(13 marks)**

Note. You should assume it is 5 December 20X6. **(Total = 25 marks)**

8 LMN

LMN is a charity that provides low-cost housing for people on low incomes. The Government has privatised much of the home building, maintenance and management in this sector. The sector is heavily regulated and receives some government money but there are significant funds borrowed from banks to invest in new housing developments, on the security of future rent receipts. Government agencies subsidise much of the rental cost for low-income residents.

The board and senior management have identified the major risks to LMN as: having insufficient housing stock of a suitable type to meet the needs of local people on low incomes; making poor property investment decisions; having dissatisfied tenants due to inadequate property maintenance; failing to comply with the requirements of the regulator; having a poor credit rating with lenders; poor cost control; incurring bad debts for rental; and having vacant properties that are not earning income. LMN has produced a risk register as part of its risk management process. For each of more than 200 individual risks, the risk register identifies a description of the risk and the (high, medium or low) likelihood of the risk eventuating and the (high, medium or low) consequences for the organisation if the risk does eventuate.

The management of LMN is carried out by professionally qualified housing executives with wide experience in property development, housing management and maintenance, and financial management. The board of LMN is composed of volunteers with wide experience and an interest in social welfare. The board is representative of the community, tenants and the local authority, any of whom may be shareholders (shareholdings are nominal and the company pays no dividends). The local authority has overall responsibility for housing and social welfare in the area. The audit committee of the board of LMN, which has responsibility for risk management as well as internal control, wants to move towards a system of internal controls that are more closely related to risks identified in the risk register.

Required

For an organisation like LMN:

(a)   Discuss the purposes and importance of risk management and its relationship with the internal control system.   **(8 marks)**

(b)   Explain the importance of a management review of controls for the audit committee.   **(5 marks)**

(c)   Discuss the principles of good corporate governance as they apply to the Board's role:

  (i)   In conducting a review of internal controls; and
  (ii)   Reporting on compliance.   **(12 marks)**

Illustrate your answer with examples from the scenario.

(Total = 25 marks)

9 Pogles   49 mins

Pogles is a clothing manufacturer, based in an EU member state, with an international market for its designs. The company's regular monthly board meeting will take place in a couple of days' time. It seems likely that most of the meeting will be taken up with discussing two issues.

Factory closure

The chief executive of Pogles has received an offer from a property developer for one of its factories in its home country. The proposal is to buy the freehold and to demolish the factory to build office units. The developer is offering €3 million for the site which presently employs 150 staff. The developer wishes to exchange contracts as soon as possible, but would not take possession of the site for another year. The chief executive believes that accepting the offer makes strategic and financial sense for Pogles. The developer is quite happy for the offer to be made public once contracts have been exchanged.

It will be possible to relocate all but one of the current manufacturing contracts currently being undertaken by this factory to Pogles' remaining factories in other countries over time, without undue delay. However, the one exception is by far the largest contract Pogles currently has. The customer has imposed tight time limits on this contract and will terminate it if its requirements are not met. Production on this contract must continue uninterrupted for the next six months at this factory if the customer's requirements are to be met.

The policy of Pogles is to offer either jobs elsewhere in the group or redundancy packages of 30% of current salary to staff who are affected by a factory closure. The redundancy packages are rather more generous than the statutory minimum in Pogles' home country. However, only 20% of staff, mostly at managerial level, are likely to receive offers to transfer to other parts of the group. There are no similar jobs available locally.

The chief executive is concerned that rumours may possibly soon start circulating about the offer and staff may start demanding assurances from management that their jobs are safe. The chief executive fears that if staff knew or feared that the factory will close, there would be a fall-off in output and quality, and possibly industrial action. These would seriously jeopardise Pogles' ability to fulfil the large contract.

Treatment of staff

One of the company's directors has recently returned from visiting a factory located in another European Union member state. Over the last few years this factory has performed better than any other in comparison with cost budgets, and has been particularly good at keeping its labour costs under control. However, on his return from his visit, the director reported some worrying facts to the chief executive.

The factory had suffered a significant number of losses of experienced part-time female staff. Although none had been dismissed, other employees still working at the factory made serious accusations that some had been 'forced' to resign by the actions of the factory manager. Among other accusations, it was suggested that they had been pressurised to take on work outside their contractual hours, or at times when they had never in the past had to work, such as during school holidays, weekends or on late shifts.

Some had taken on the extra work in fear of losing their jobs and in the knowledge that other clothing factories locally had closed down in recent months. However, many of the other staff had found the new working arrangements impossible to fit in with their domestic situations and had reluctantly handed in their notice. To replace the staff who had left, the factory manager recruited full-time staff on flexible contracts, which required them to accept shift changes provided two weeks' notice was given to them.

Required

(a)   Analyse whether to disclose the decision to close the factory to the staff working in the factory, using the American Accounting Association ethics model.   **(15 marks)**

(b)   Analyse whether the factory manager's treatment of his staff is ethical using Tucker's 5 question criteria.   **(10 marks)**

(Total = 25 marks)

10 Zos   39 mins

Zos is a chain of coffee shops that operates 75 shops in its home country. A number of ethical problems have recently arisen at Zos, and an emergency meeting of its board has been convened to discuss their implications.

Thefts from stores

Three employees in one shop have been dismissed for thefts of both produce and cash. These thefts were only identified because one of the employees was foolish enough to steal, and then sell, the bags of coffee beans on the premises of the Zos coffee shop in which they worked. A customer reported the incident to the chief executive of Zos and an investigation of the shop revealed that two other employees had also been involved in the theft.

Drug dealing

One of the coffee shop managers was reported by a customer, and subsequently arrested, for selling illegal Class A substances in their Zos coffee shop and allowing drugs to be taken on the site. Police investigations showed that this had been taking place for at least ten months.

Fair trade

A routine advertising campaign promoting Zos stated, '*Zos is aiming to have all its coffee supplied by Fair Trade suppliers*'. However, a former Zos Head Office employee recently stated in the national press that only around 60% of Zos coffee was procured from Fair Trade suppliers. An investigation revealed that the figure was in fact around 80% but the percentage bought from Fair Trade suppliers had fallen by 5% over the past year.

Zos's Chief Executive is very concerned about all these issues. They feel that they demonstrate that Zos has a poor ethical culture and could seriously damage the company's reputation. They wish to introduce measures to improve Zos's ethical culture and to use the company's recently appointed internal auditors to ensure that the measures are effective.

Required

(a)   Recommend the control mechanisms that should be implemented to reduce the problems
        associated with the ethical risks.   **(12 marks)**

(b)   Discuss the extent of the responsibilities of internal audit for ensuring that the ethical problems do
        not recur.   **(8 marks)**

                                                                          (Total = 20 marks)

11 Loxwood   49 mins

You are the chief internal auditor of Loxwood, a company that manufactures pleasure boats. The board is
currently considering improving the company's corporate responsibility profile, particularly in relation to
environmental issues. You have been asked to conduct an environmental audit to this end. You have also
been asked for your views on a new idea that Loxwood's development department has been considering.
The directors are keen for you to indicate the range of opinions that they may need to consider in deciding
whether to market this idea.

New idea

Recently the incidence of sea lion collisions with pleasure boats has been increasing off the local coast.
Loxwood's development department has recently come up with the idea of a sonic sea lion repellent, a
sonic device emitting a sound frequency that would be extremely distressing for sea lions. In theory this
sound would be sufficient to keep the sea lions at a safe distance from the boat.

Required

(a)   Explain how you would test for employee awareness, and how you would involve all employees in
        the initiative.   **(6 marks)**

(b)   Discuss the reasons why companies wish to disclose environmental information in their financial
        statements. Discuss whether the content of such disclosure should be at the company's discretion.
                                                                                    (10 marks)

(c)   Compare and contrast Gray, Owen and Adams' 'expedient', 'social contractarian' and 'deep
        ecologist' positions and explain how these positions could determine attitudes to the development
        of the sonic sea lion repellent.   **(9 marks)**

                                                                          (Total = 25 marks)

1 Bonus schemes

> **Top tips.** The biggest dangers in (a) are failing to read the question carefully and the temptation to overrun on the time allowed for the solution, given the marks available. Bonus schemes are a recurring feature of this exam and most candidates should be able to write about them both from theoretical and personal knowledge without too much difficulty.
>
> (b) requires much more thought – think about the key issue of independence for NEDs. As long as the features you suggest do not compromise independence or suggest awarding too generous bonuses you will be earning marks.

(a)   **Limiting the range of performance within which rewards are linked to results**

Many schemes do indeed limit the range of performance within which rewards are linked to results, in particular ignoring losses and limiting maximum payments.

Ignoring losses

Unless the organisation in question was operating in an extremely stable and predictable environment, it would be unacceptable to the vast majority of managers to be asked to participate in a remuneration system that might require them to reimburse their employer in the event of losses being incurred. In general, managers want to receive their standard salary. They do not want the threat of some of it being taken away if their organisation reports losses. If the organisation were to **impose penalties for poor performance**, managers may well **manipulate their targets to ensure that they did not suffer financially**.

Benefits and drawbacks of ignoring losses

If **losses are excluded** from the range of performance, **full participation** in the scheme is likely as no financial penalty (or negative bonus) can be imposed on a manager if levels of performance are particularly poor. Salaries will be viewed as fair payment for duties performed, with any bonus being regarded as a genuine reward for effort.

Managers may **take unnecessary risks**, however, as they are under no financial risk themselves, and **poor levels of performance may be deliberately further depressed** to ensure easier future targets.

Capping maximum payments

Reasons for capping maximum payments include a desire by risk-averse managers to **limit the organisation's maximum liability** and the **prevention of payments which shareholders might regard as excessive**.

Benefits and drawbacks of capping maximum payments

Capping maximum payments should ensure that managers **concentrate on improvements which will be sustainable year on year**. The financial incentive provided should be large enough to motivate without being excessive.

Managers might feel **no incentive to improve performance beyond the cut-off level**, however, and they could be forced into **holding back for future periods profit-generating or cost-cutting strategies and ideas** once the maximum limit has been reached. A limit on maximum payments could also cause managers to feel **disempowered**, the message being sent out by the bonus system indicating that no matter how good their performance, the most they would receive is £X.

Linking incentive payments to the profits of the organisation as a whole

This is a **popular feature** in many bonus schemes for a number of **reasons**.

(i)   Profit is a **widely understood measure**, and the maximisation of organisational profit is generally accepted to be congruent with the goals of shareholders.

(ii) As **profit reporting forms** part of most organisations' **standard reporting procedures**, little additional work is required for profit to be used as the standard measure of performance (compared with more elaborate performance reward mechanisms which can generate substantial data collection costs).

(iii) It also provides a **basis for participation** in bonus schemes by service centre staff such as those of internal audit and IT departments, for whom the use of other measures can be much more problematic.

(iv) The profit reported by many profit centres will be **significantly affected** by **head office policies** on, for example, salary levels or stock valuation, and so overall organisational profit may be more objective.

(v) Rather than arguing over scarce resources, the use of organisational profit may persuade **profit centre managers** to **work together** to further the aims of the organisation as a whole.

(vi) As agents of the organisation's shareholders, **managers' rewards should be closely linked to the rewards of shareholders**.

Benefits of linking payments to organisational profits

(i) Inter-profit centre/-divisional **conflicts should be minimised**, with all parts of the organisation concentrating on group results.

(ii) Management attention should be focused on the need to **cut unnecessary expenditure**.

(iii) Management will **not be diverted from performing their regular duties** to agree on more elaborate performance-reward systems.

Drawbacks of linking payments to organisational profits

(i) If the proportion of the bonus that is linked to overall organisational performance is significant and other profit centres do not perform well, managers will get a **reduced bonus** payment or even no payment at all. Managers who consistently perform well and achieve their individual targets are likely to become demotivated if they receive no bonus because of poor levels of performance in other parts of the organisation.

(ii) Managers could feel that their **area of responsibility** is **too small** to have a substantial impact on group profits and may become demotivated.

(iii) Managers may **cut short-term, discretionary costs** in order to achieve current profit targets at the **expense of future profits**.

(b) **Bonus schemes for non-executive directors (NEDs)**

The design of bonus schemes for NEDs is **problematic**. If the bonus is **too small** the NEDs may **not be motivated** to do anything more than the minimum required to collect their fees. If the bonus is **too generous** they may **stop acting in the best interests of shareholders for fear of incurring the displeasure of the executive directors** and thereby jeopardising their bonus payments.

A bonus scheme for NEDs will therefore need to include the following **features**.

(i) It should ensure that **high quality and motivated NEDs** are recruited, thereby ensuring that shareholders will benefit from the appointment of the NEDs.

(ii) The bonus should be paid either **in cash or in the companies' shares**.

(iii) The bonus scheme could be **linked to the long-term performance of the company**, rather than simply to the financial performance of the current period. A **balanced range of performance measures** such as increase in market share or stock market valuation in relation to competitors over a certain period of time (depending on the NEDs' length of contract) and so on should **encourage NEDs to take a broader view of corporate governance**.

(iv)   It is important that **good corporate governance is seen to be maintained**. Shareholders'
        prior approval of any bonus scheme should be obtained to avoid any impression that NEDs'
        bonuses are being offered as a *quid pro quo* for the executive directors' remuneration.

(v)   Any bonus scheme should be designed to provide an incentive for the NED to **achieve
        specific objectives** or complete specific tasks outside their normal duties as a NED.

        Bonuses are justified for such tasks as carrying out competitor reviews or designing staff
        remuneration schemes, which will enhance the NED's understanding of the business
        without compromising their independence.

(vi)   Any **goal-orientated bonuses** should **be paid immediately following the work to which
        they relate**. Rolling up of bonus payments may silence any criticism from the NED as the
        payment date approaches.

2 Cedric Coffee

Top tips. (a) emphasises that pressures to improve financial reporting and auditing practices have not
been the only influences on corporate governance development. There has been emphasis as well on
various aspects of directors' conduct that would be considered unacceptable even if there were no
problems with the financial statements and audit. Don't forget the role of globalisation, as this has led to
the development of international codes.

(b) illustrates how you should approach a comparison question. Your answer should be a point by point
comparison rather than the first half of the answer dealing with the Sarbanes-Oxley Act, the second half
with the OECD/ICGN principles. Although the answer does include some detail on the requirements, it also
brings out the comparison by exploring what the legislation and guidelines aimed to achieve.

Note in (c) the links between corporate responsibility and stakeholder interests.

Memo

To: Managing Director, Cedric Coffee
From: Consultant
Date: 30 May 20X8
Subject: Corporate governance and corporate social responsibility

You asked me to provide you with guidance on why corporate governance codes have developed, points
of comparison between different international governance codes and the advantages of developing a
corporate social responsibility code.

(a)   Several different issues triggered moves towards systematised corporate governance.

       Global investment

       The trend towards global investment has meant that large investment institutions in the US in
       particular, but also in other countries such as the UK, have been seeking to invest large amounts of
       capital in companies in other countries. US investors, expecting **similar treatment** from foreign
       companies that they received from US companies, expressed concern about the inadequacy of
       corporate governance in many countries. Many of their concerns focused on the **lack of
       shareholder rights**, or the disregard for minority shareholder rights shown by major shareholders
       or the boards of foreign companies.

       The move towards systematised corporate governance still has a long way to go in many countries.
       However, in issuing its principles of corporate governance, the OECD recognised that the demands
       and expectations of global investors would have to be met if the trend towards global investment
       (and efficient capital allocation) is to continue.

       Financial reporting and auditing

       There were serious concerns about the standards of financial reporting. In the late 1980s, there
       were a number of well-publicised corporate failures, which were unexpected because the financial

statements of those companies had not given any indication of their financial problems. This also raised questions about the **quality of external auditing** and the **effectiveness of professional auditing standards**.

Executive directors

There were also concerns that many large companies were being run for the benefit of their executive directors and senior managers, and not in the interests of shareholders. For example, there were concerns that acquisitions were sometimes made to **increase the size of a company** and the power of its chief executive, rather than as a means of adding shareholder value. These concerns raised the question of the conflict of interest between the directors and shareholders.

A particular concern was the **powerful position of individuals** holding the positions of both chairman and chief executive officer in their company, and the lack of 'balance' in boards.

Directors' remuneration

Directors' remuneration also became an issue. There is a widely held view that executive directors are paid **excessive amounts**, in terms of basic salary, 'perks' and incentives. Some directors appeared to receive high rewards even when the company **performed badly** or no differently from the 'average' of other companies. Although investment institutions did not object to high pay for talented executives, they believed that incentive schemes were often badly conceived, and that executives were being rewarded for performance that was not necessarily linked to the benefits provided to shareholders, for example in terms of a higher share price.

Insider dealings

Although convictions for insider dealing have been rare, there was a suspicion that some directors might be **using their inside knowledge** about their company to make a personal gain by dealing in shares in the company. For example, directors might sell a large number of shares just ahead of a profits warning by their company, or buy shares just ahead of a public announcement that might be expected to boost the share price.

Risks and controls

Again poor controls have been a symptom of poor corporate governance with, for example, **inadequate management control of individuals** such as Nick Leeson at Barings. In addition, the development of risk management frameworks, such as the COSO guidance, has impacted on regulations.

Internationalisation

More investors, in particular institutional investors, have begun to **invest outside their home countries**. In order to limit the risks of their investments, they seek to promote a common **international governance framework**.

(b) **Purpose**

The main purpose of the Sarbanes-Oxley Act was to **tackle various problems** that had been brought to light by Enron and other corporate scandals. These included poor internal controls, misleading financial statements and ineffectiveness of non-executive directors and auditor monitoring of companies. They relate to the situation in **America**, although foreign companies with a listing on the US stock market have to comply as well.

The OECD principles have been designed to establish an credible international framework that **promotes global investment**. Investors who are investing in different countries can have confidence in the corporate governance of companies that adopt the OECD principles or regimes that base their own governance codes on the OECD. The ICGN report is designed to enhance the OECD principles by providing practical guidance for boards wishing to **enhance their reputation** for **good corporate governance** and to establish better dialogue with their investors.

Board roles

Sarbanes-Oxley aims to reinforce the **monitoring role of the board and the responsibility of the**

board for producing true and fair financial statements. It lays stress on the role of the audit committee, which is compulsory for all listed companies. The audit committee should oversee the role of external auditors and establish mechanisms for dealing with complaints. Board responsibility is enforced by the chief executive officer and the chief financial officer being required to certify the financial statements, and having to forfeit their bonuses if the financial statements subsequently have to be restated.

The OECD/ICGN guidelines provide rather more general guidance on the role and responsibilities of the board. They aim to promote **board effectiveness**. The OECD principles do this by stressing the board's **overall role in strategic development**, that board members should exercise **care and good faith** as well as **independent judgement**, and assigning non-executive directors to appropriate roles. The ICGN code gives some specific guidelines on how to achieve the OECD guidelines. These include listing **strategic matters** that would normally be considered by the board, recommending that certain **board committees** (nomination, remuneration and audit) be established, suggesting that the **chairman and chief executive** should be **different people** and stating that **scrutiny of director performance** would be enhanced by yearly appraisal and regular re-election.

Accounts

A major aim of the Sarbanes-Oxley legislation is to tighten up accounting rules that were perceived as too lax, allowing Enron to produce accounts that may have complied with existing standards but were misleading. Hence the Act targets the kinds of **off-balance sheet arrangements** that Enron employed. Sarbanes-Oxley also seeks to **promote effective internal controls** by requiring disclosure of management responsibility for control system maintenance, and an audited **assessment of the effectiveness of the internal control structure and the procedures for financial reporting**.

The OECD/ICGN guidelines contain **various recommendations for disclosure** based on good practice in major jurisdictions. The disclosures reflect the important areas highlighted in the guidelines including governance structures and policies, and relationships with shareholders and stakeholders. They aim to **promote disclosure** that aids investors by recommending the provision of analysis or advice that is relevant to investors. The guidelines also stress the importance of the company **excelling in the returns it achieves** in comparison with its equity-sector peer group.

Audit

Sarbanes-Oxley responded to concerns about external auditing practice by stiffening the requirements relating to auditor independence. The **enhanced role of the audit committee** was part of this, but the Act also includes **provisions limiting the non-audit services** auditors can provide and **requiring the regular rotation of lead audit partners**. The Act also includes a number of provisions relating to the **conduct of audits** and **audit firm procedures**, including retention of working papers and quality control requirements, and the requirement for auditors to review internal control systems.

The OECD/ICGN guidelines place less stress than Sarbanes-Oxley on the role of the auditor, although they do stress the importance of the auditor providing **external and objective assurance** and audit committee-auditor links. The issue of non-audit services affecting **independence is raised**, the guidance noting the various methods different regimes have used to deal with this potential problem.

Shareholders

Sarbanes-Oxley does not contain significant provisions enhancing the role of shareholders. The OECD and ICGN guidelines do contain provisions promoting shareholder interests, in line with their key objective of enhancing investor confidence. The OECD principles stress the importance of **treating all shareholders equitably** and **eliminating cross-border impediments to shareholding**. The ICGN report seeks to reinforce these general aims with some specific guidance on how **shareholder voting rights** can be **protected** and also **promoting the role of institutional**

shareholders, with the idea that their active involvement can encourage better corporate governance.

Stakeholders and ethics

The provisions relating to ethics in Sarbanes-Oxley were mainly inspired by the examples of unacceptable behaviour at Enron. They are designed to reduce the chances of **poor ethical behaviour occurring** and **remaining undetected**. Hence companies are required to state whether they have **adopted a code of conduct for senior financial officers** and the **contents** of that code. The Act also contains strong provisions protecting the position of auditors, employees and lawyers who **whistleblow** on unethical behaviour.

The OECD/ICGN guidance also stresses the importance of companies establishing an ethical code and protecting whistleblowers. However, these requirements are set in the rather wider context of encouraging companies to act in an **economically, socially and environmentally friendly manner** and the board promoting a **culture of integrity**. The guidance also emphasises the **importance of successful and productive relationships** with stakeholders, particularly employees, and suggests various methods of enhancing employee participation.

Enforcement

Sarbanes-Oxley has passed into US law and thus companies listed on the US Stock Exchange **have to comply** with its provisions. The OECD/ICGN principles have no legislative power. However, countries are using the OECD principles as a basis for developing or judging their own regimes.

(c)   **Benefits of a CSR policy**

Marketing advantage

CSR offers marketing advantages and is a differentiator, appealing to certain types of customer. It produces a **'feel good' factor**.

Publicity

CSR neutralises poor publicity from **high interest, low power stakeholders** such as pressure groups. For example using Fair Trade suppliers would mean that Cedric Coffee cannot be criticised for exploiting coffee growers. In other words, CSR can provide some assistance in **managing reputation risk**.

Staff turnover

If CSR extends to the management of employees, and Cedric Coffee is known as a good employer, the **costs of staff turnover** might be **contained**. High staff turnover means high recruitment costs, high training costs and, perhaps, an adverse impact on customer service. However, a high level of staff turnover is perhaps inevitable in a business such as this.

Impact on other stakeholders

CSR makes a **good impression on other stakeholders** eg the Government or local community. CSR can influence a company's reputation. Being known to be a good corporate citizen may help the company if it has business dealings with other significant stakeholders.

Drawbacks of a CSR policy

Failure to maximise shareholder value

Managers in charge of corporations are responsible to the owners of the business. CSR may be a distraction from **maximising shareholder wealth**. If Cedric Coffee has a statutory duty to maximise shareholder wealth, the scope of CSR may be restricted.

Costs of compliance

There may be costs in complying. This could include **direct costs** (eg paying premium prices or higher salaries) and **indirect costs**, such as management time.

3 Peter Postgate

Anystreet
Anytown
1 May 20X8

Mr P Postgate
Anyroad
Anytown

Dear Mr Postgate

I enjoyed our conversation the other day and am pleased to provide the further guidance and information you requested about non-executive directors.

(a)   **Independent NEDs**

The definition of independent NEDs in corporate governance guidance is quite strict. An independent NED is a person who **has no connection with the company** other than as a NED. Because they are independent, a NED should be able to give an independent opinion on the affairs of the company without influence from any other director or shareholder.

Non-independent NEDs

A NED is not independent if they are representing the interests of **specific shareholders**. If a director is on the board to represent the interests of a **major shareholder**, then they will not be regarded as independent, because the views given by the director will be seen as influenced by the best interests of that shareholder. The same applies to directors who could be seen as **representing other stakeholders**. If the company appointed as a NED a director of one of its suppliers, then that director would be seen as representing that supplier. NEDs with **close personal relationships** to executive directors would also not be independent. This would mean, for example, that a former chief executive of the company who was given a non-executive role after retirement would not be independent.

(b)   **Conflicts of interest**

A potential conflict of interest can occur when the **executive directors** of a company take decisions that would not be in the **interests of the company's shareholders**. Although there are several areas where a conflict of interest could arise, the most difficult areas are **remuneration of the directors and senior managers**, **financial reporting** and **nominations of new board members**.

Remuneration

If executive directors **decide their own remuneration**, they could pay themselves as much as possible, without having to hold themselves to account or justify their high pay. If executive directors are allowed to **devise incentive schemes** for themselves, these may be linked to achieving performance targets that are **not necessarily in the shareholders'** interests. For example rewarding directors with a bonus for achieving profit growth is of no value to shareholders if the result is **higher business risk and a lower share price**.

Remuneration committee

Corporate governance in many countries, such as the UK Corporate Governance Code, calls for a **remuneration committee of the board** to be established to decide on directors' pay, including incentive schemes. The committee's members should **all be independent non-executive directors**.

The remuneration committee should have delegated responsibility for **setting remuneration packages for all executive directors and the chairman**, including pension rights and any compensation payments. The committee should also **recommend and monitor the level and structure of remuneration** for senior management. The NEDs should be able to devise **fair remuneration packages**, which include an incentive element where the performance targets align the **objectives of the executive directors** with those of the **shareholders**.

Financial reporting

A second problem area is financial reporting. The executive directors might be tempted to **distort the financial results of the company** in order to present them in a way that reflects better on themselves and their achievements.

Audit committee

The board should establish an **audit committee**, consisting of non-executive directors, whose task should be to consider issues relating to **financial reporting and financial control systems**. This committee should be responsible for liaising regularly with the external and internal auditors. The board should satisfy itself that at least one member of the audit committee has **recent and relevant financial experience**.

Nominations to the board

A third potential area for conflict is nominations of new board members. A powerful chairman or chief executive could be tempted to **appoint their supporters or 'yes' men** to the board, and so strengthen their position on the board.

Nomination committee

The UK Corporate Governance Code recommends that the board should establish a **nomination committee** of the board, manned by NEDs. The committee should oversee recruitment, keep the balance of the board under review and consider longer-term succession planning.

Other areas

Other areas of potential conflict of interest include the board's decisions on making acquisitions or in preparing defences against a takeover bid. In each of these areas NEDs should be able to provide a **counterbalance** to self-interested views of executive directors.

(c)   **Share payments**

In many companies, NEDs receive a **fixed cash payment** for their services, without any incentives.

However, some companies pay their NEDs in shares. They would argue that the more equity the NEDs hold, the more likely they will be to look at issues from the **point of view of the shareholders**.

A NED holding shares could however be more concerned with **short-term movements in the share price** and the opportunity of making a short-term profit from selling their shares than the long-term interests of the company and its other shareholders. However, a suitable precaution against this could be to obtain the agreement of a NED not to sell their shares until after leaving the board.

Share options

The view that NEDs should be rewarded with **share options** to align their interests with other shareholders is more contentious. However, it has been widely practised in the UK and is even more common in the US.

The argument against rewarding NEDs with share options is that it could **align the interests of the NEDs more closely with the executive directors**, who also hold share options. NEDs should give independent advice, and it can be argued that it is not appropriate to incentivise them in the same way as the executives.

The UK Corporate Governance Code points out that holding share options could be relevant to the determination of a **non-executive director's independence**. It states that remuneration for non-executive directors should not include share options. If, exceptionally, options are granted, **shareholder approval** should be sought in advance. Any share acquired by exercise of the options should be held until at least one year after the non-executive director leaves the board.

I hope this letter has been helpful. Please do get in touch if you want to discuss anything further.

Yours sincerely

A N Accountant

4 PKG High School

Top tips. This is a tough question at this stage but it should get you thinking about the controls all organisations should have.

In (a) the stakeholders are different to those of a company, but they still need the assurance provided by an objective review. Benchmarking is likely to be a particularly important aspect of the audit, given that the governing body is responsible for educational standards.

It is very easy in (b) to stray from the subject and talk too generally about controls – the question asks you to evaluate (often as here concentrating on the deficiencies), and recommend what the governing body should be doing. Our answer is based around the structure of:

- How the governing body is constituted and how it operates
- The data it gets (financial/non-financial, internal-external)
- The decisions it takes and the monitoring it carries out

This is a useful way of analysing how any governing body works.

You may have felt that the question could have given more detail about what the governing body is doing and the information it receives. It is valid to assume that if you're not told anything about key aspects of governance such as a committee system, then they aren't being operated when they should be.

It's also easy in (b) to fail to consider whether financial and other resources are being used to maximum efficiency. Spending limits often mean that expenditure is made to the limits set down, with little consideration of whether value for money has been obtained.

(a) **Independent and objective assurance**

Having an external review carried out should provide an **unbiased view** of how the school is performing. In particular this provides **reassurance to stakeholders such as parents and the local authority** that the school is providing education of sufficient quality and expenditure is being properly controlled.

Aid to monitoring

Like the board of directors in a listed company, the governors are responsible for establishing and maintaining a sound system of internal control and risk management. The review should provide **feedback** to the headteacher and governing body to enable them to set priorities for systems improvements, based on the areas of **greatest risk**. It should also highlight where the headteacher and governors should **focus their own monitoring activity**.

Expert opinion

The external reviewers can make recommendations based on their **knowledge of best practice in other schools**. This can provide the school with **benchmarks** that it can incorporate into financial and non-financial performance indicators.

(b)   (i)   **Structure and workings of governing body**

Membership

The governing body includes representatives of the key stakeholder group of parents and the local authority.

However, it may be a **more effective monitor** if it includes representation from key internal stakeholders. Certainly it should include staff representatives and might include pupil representatives as well.

Committee system

Having the full governing body consider all relevant items at every meeting may not be the most efficient way of operating, and it may mean that some **key risk areas receive insufficient attention**.

Although committees may be difficult to staff, a **committee system** with each committee concentrating on certain key aspects of running the school may be the best way to conduct decision-making, with committees reporting into the main governing body. Certainly it may provide a good mechanism for parent representatives to use their particular expertise.

(1)   **Audit committee**

An **audit committee**, including members with financial expertise, could be responsible for detailed scrutiny of expenditure and liaising with auditors. Its remit could also cover **compliance with legislation** and the **operation of internal controls**. This would leave the main governing body to concentrate on the split of expenditure and the overall review of control systems.

(2)   **Staff recruitment committee**

Because of the significance of staffing the board should establish a separate recruitment committee. The committee should be involved in specific recruitment decisions, and should also proactively consider **staffing needs**. For example, are there **sufficient experienced members** of staff and does the staff body as a whole have an **appropriate range of skills** in key areas such as IT? The committee must consider how **staffing headcount needs** can be **reconciled with planned staff expenditure**.

The committee should also consider the **balance between teachers and other support staff**, whether support staff, with specific skills, need to be recruited or whether their numbers could be reduced and more teachers recruited. It should also be involved in **internal promotion decisions** and consider the effectiveness of the **system of responsibility allowances**.

Induction of governing body members

There appear to be **no induction procedures** for new governing body members that would enhance their knowledge of what the school does and the requirements the governing body has to meet.

Certainly parent governors will need this understanding if they are to be **effective governors** (hopefully the local authority will have selected suitably qualified and knowledgeable members).

(ii) **Information received by governing body**

Financial information

It is unclear whether the financial information is sufficiently detailed. The governing body needs to ensure that it receives **sufficient information about expenditure,** particularly because of the wide discretion the headteacher has and the lack of **segregation of duties**.

Expenditure should be **classified** into **different categories** depending on its materiality and the ways it is controlled. The information should include what **has been spent**, **expenditure commitments** and **phasing of expenditure during the year;** not all expenditure will be made in even amounts over the year. The governing body also needs to ensure that the **reliability** of the monthly financial report is reviewed because of its importance for decision-making. As the external auditors may not spend time on this, this review should perhaps be carried out by members of the audit committee.

Financial variances

Although the governors receive information about variances from budgeted expenditure, there is nothing mentioned about how they are, as they should be, informed of action planned if an overspend appears likely.

They should have input into what should be done.

Non-financial information

There appears to be a lack of non-financial information that the governors need in order to **ensure that educational standards** are being **maintained**. An **annual inspection by the local education authority** would not be frequent enough.

Governors should be supplied with the results of internal methods of assessing the effectiveness of teaching such as **termly exams** and **internal quality reviews** of teaching programmes. Since staffing is both a major element of expenditure and vital in ensuring standards, governors should be receiving details about staff such as **results of appraisals** and **staff development programmes**. Having parent, staff and pupil representatives on the governing body will help measure the **satisfaction levels** of these key stakeholder groups; the governors ought to consider other methods such as regular staff and parent surveys.

External information

No mention of whether the governing body is receiving the external information which it will need for longer-term decision-making.

The governing body should be receiving details of population trends in the area and the impact of changes in schools provision. It should also be considering specific information about other schools in the area that it can use for **benchmarking purposes**, such as pupil numbers, disposition of staff, facilities and exam results.

(iii) **Actions taken by governing body**

Strategic decision-making

The governing body's time horizon appears to be limited to a year, and it does not appear to be considering longer-term issues; there seems to be **no strategic plan**.

Better information should help it **modify** its strategy in response to local issues such as changes in pupil numbers, the opening of new schools, particularly specialist schools or government-promoted schools (such as UK academies) and changes in educational practice (such as increased use of information technology).

Flexibility of decision-making

The governing body needs to consider whether its decision-making is too constricted; the governors may have the flexibility to take decisions that ensure **better use of resources** and **better risk management**.

For example it may consider whether class sizes can be increased in the lower age ranges to allow smaller class sizes and greater preparation time for more advanced teaching. It should also consider whether to include a **contingency fund** for urgent items of additional expenditure on staff, buildings and IT.

Review of small items of expenditure

The governing body does not appear to take any interest in expenditure under $1,000. There may be scope for the headteacher to abuse this by **spreading significant expenditure** out so that individual items are below $1,000, but the total sum is quite substantial.

The governors should **review all expenditure** below $1,000 even if they don't approve it in advance. There may be scope for raising the limit on certain types of expenditure, so that the governing body does not spend time considering what is essentially non-discretionary expenditure.

Communication

The governing body needs to consider how its **work should be communicated**; there is **no evidence** of how this is happening at present.

Clearly the headteacher will have prime responsibility for communicating and what the governing body publishes should be consistent with what the headteacher is saying. However, **communication of what the governing body is doing** and the **issues it is considering** should prove to staff, pupils and current and prospective parents that the school is **well run**. It should also aid **future recruitment** onto the governing body.

5 Widmerpool

Top tips. (a) is a good example of why you need to read scenarios carefully and highlight all relevant data. Every point our answer makes is supported by relevant information from the scenario.

You need to read the requirement to (b) quite carefully. The key words are 'by their own example' so that your discussion should be confined to what the board should be doing (and seen to be doing).

In (c) remember that the requirement evaluate means that you should consider the strength of the arguments for and against. The risk committee need not be staffed by non-executive directors, although in many instances it would be (this would be consistent with the audit committee which we'll look at in Chapter 8).

(a) **Lack of detail in guidance**

The problems over the suppliers' data may indicate that some of the organisational guidance is written too much in terms of **general principles**, without enough examples of detailed application. It would appear that the guidance needs to spell out that confidential information should not be removed from the office, and staff should not talk about business matters outside work.

Lack of awareness of risks

The accident with the machine indicates that **staff did not understand the risks** involved, despite the health and safety documentation. This could be because they failed to read the documentation or they read it but failed to understand it. This also suggests that **training**, on the job or in formal courses, was **non-existent or ineffective**.

Poor culture

The problems over Stringham's information and the difficulties over the machine indicate that a **culture of carelessness** is prevalent at Widmerpool. Managers, in positions of responsibility, should naturally be careful with confidential information. The comments in the staff survey also seem to suggest the culture is poor, that the board is seen as **not caring** about internal controls and procedures.

Lack of enforcement

The staff comments underline what happened over the machine, that the company's internal procedures are not being **enforced by managers**. The survey comments suggest that, while the board is receiving sufficient financial information about the profitability of operations, it is not getting the non-financial data it needs to obtain assurance that **control systems are operating effectively**.

(b) **Personal example**

The board's **day-to-day behaviour** can help set the right tone in Widmerpool. This includes being seen to comply fully with health and safety requirements, for example wearing the right clothing in the factory. More importantly perhaps, it means avoiding the sort of careless behaviour of which the managers were guilty, taking confidential information outside the workplace.

Adherence to code

The board needs to order all staff to **demonstrate full commitment** to Widmerpool's control procedures. Directors and staff should acknowledge in writing their responsibilities, including adherence to internal codes. Directors should reinforce this by communicating, through internal newsletters, what is expected of staff.

Participation in training

Directors should **fully and enthusiastically participate in training** in areas such as health and safety. Excusing themselves on the grounds that they are 'too busy' significantly increases the risk that staff will not take the training seriously.

Internal meetings

Directors should set up a **system of meetings to discuss risk and compliance issues**. They should meet with senior managers, the senior managers should meet with the staff who work for them, and so on.

Taking disciplinary action

If necessary, the directors should show that poor behaviour will not be tolerated by being **personally involved in disciplinary action against staff**.

(c) **Benefits of risk committee**

Independent viewpoint

If the risk committee consists of non-executive directors, they can take a **detached view of Widmerpool's risk exposure**, using their own experience from other organisations. Delegation of duties from the main board to the committee will allow the executive directors to concentrate more on matters connected with obtaining a listing.

Determining acceptable exposure

Widmerpool has expanded significantly over the last few years, and it is likely that the company's risk profile has also changed significantly. The committee needs to press the board to **consider regularly what constitutes acceptable levels of risk**, bearing in mind the likelihood of the risks materialising and the board's ability to reduce the incidence and impact on the business.

Monitoring acceptable exposure

Once the board has **defined acceptable risk levels**, the committee should **monitor whether Widmerpool is remaining within those levels**, and whether **earnings are sufficient** given the levels of risks that are being borne.

Reviewing reports

There should be a regular system of reports to the risk committee covering areas known to be of **high risk**, as well as **one-off reports** covering conditions and events likely to arise in the near future. This should facilitate the monitoring of risk.

Monitoring risk management systems

The committee should consider whether the risk management systems are operating effectively. For Widmerpool this will mean obtaining evidence that procedures are being followed, through **evidence from internal audit** and **reports by line managers**. The committee will also ascertain whether measures taken to correct problems in risk management have been **effective**. For example it will find out whether all staff have **received the health and safety training that they need**, and seek to obtain evidence that the training has **resulted in safer working practices**.

Sign of board action

Setting up a risk committee would demonstrate to managers and staff that the board was **taking risk management seriously**. The risk committee could also be a **point of contact** if staff had concerns, for example about safety procedures not being followed.

Drawbacks of risk committee

Over-commitment of non-executive directors

Non-executive directors already have to attend full board meetings and audit committee meetings. The board will have to set up a **nomination committee**, consisting of non-executive directors, if Widmerpool achieves a **listing**. Non-executive directors may not have enough time to fulfil all their responsibilities. One result may be that the risk committee does not meet frequently enough to monitor risks effectively.

Confusion with responsibilities of audit committee

If different directors staffed the risk committee and the audit committee, there could be confusion over the **responsibilities** of each. **Clear terms of reference** will be required to determine, for example, the laws and regulations for which each committee is responsible for monitoring compliance.

Need for active involvement in strategy

The members of the risk committee need to be clear of Widmerpool's **strategies** in all major areas, as they should be concentrating on the risks arising out of those strategies.

6 Pacific Group

> **Top tips.** This question might seem overwhelming, but bear in mind that the examiner has done the hard part already. The risks have been identified, you simply have to assess how serious they are. Make sure that you read the question properly and understand the criteria that the examiner gives you to judge whether risks are applicable or not, then apply those criteria to each risk in the question. If you are not sure, decide whether you can say more in support of classifying it as applicable or non-applicable. You gain marks for your explanations.

Applicable risks

(a) **Failure to invest in new developments**

Applicable risk

The majority of PG's income comes from advertising revenue and therefore it is crucial that they keep up to the cutting edge of advertising developments, particularly when their competitors do. This could have a substantial adverse financial impact if advertisers decide to cut advertising in PG in favour of more up to date advertising techniques in competitor publications such as The Deep.

(b) **Unsuitable credit limits**

Non-applicable risk

As credit limits (albeit unsuitable) are set, and the majority of customers are likely to be creditworthy, the effect of a small number of advertisers being uncreditworthy is not likely to be substantial.

(c) **Incomplete data transfer (editorial – invoicing departments)**

Applicable risk

It is crucial to cash flow and business operations that published adverts are invoiced. Only two full page adverts and a half page advert would have to be omitted from invoicing before the effect of this risk would be greater than £5,000. If the system is failing to transfer data, there is no reason to assume that the problem should be limited to so few adverts.

(d) **Rates charged**

Applicable risk

As seen above, given the prices of adverts, a problem with a small number of adverts can have a significant (>£5,000) impact. So, for example, if two full page and three half page adverts were given a 50% discount and the same number were given 'free' for reciprocal advertising, this could have a significant financial impact.

(e) **Individual errors**

Non-applicable risk

PG is likely to have reasonable controls over production to ensure that errors in production such as typos and colour problems are likely to be isolated and no individual advertisement has a significant financial effect on PG.

(f) **Cash misappropriation**

Applicable risk

Cash received at front desk is significant and there appear to be no controls to ensure that it is secure and passed on to cashiers. This is a big risk to PG, as they may simply lose a large amount of income this way. Again, it only requires payment for three full page adverts to be misappropriated to have a significant impact.

(g) **Errors due to unauthorised access**

Non-applicable risk

It is likely that PG has basic computer system controls making this risk a low risk.

(h) **Availability of systems**

Applicable risk

This risk is applicable because if PG does not have contingency plans against systems failure, and many companies with computerised systems do not, then the financial and operational risk of delay in invoicing and processing advertising orders could be significant in terms of customer dissatisfaction and delayed payments.

(i) **Incomplete transfer of information to nominal ledgers**

Non-applicable risk

This is potentially significant to the reported results of the company but should not affect their operational or financial strength.

(j)   **Risk of litigation for inappropriate advertising**

Applicable risk

As PG carries a large amount of advertising in its publication this risk is significant. Although PG is likely to have insurance for the financial impact of such litigation, the cost in terms of loss of reputation and/or customers could be significant.

7 Azure Airline

> **Top tips.** When asked to identify, you should aim to be brief and not copy out chunks of the scenario. Instead concentrate on explaining the risks well. In (a) you would probably need to identify and explain half a dozen risks to gain full marks. The answer below contains more than this for illustration. Most of the risks identified below are signalled in the question. However, it is acceptable to use your general knowledge to identify a risk not signposted in the question, such as the fact that the price of fuel can escalate, and Azure needs fuel to operate. You can easily spend too much time on competition risk and on (a) in general, though. It's easy to overrun on this part and lose the chance of gaining marks elsewhere.
>
> In (b) you are asked for controls for the risks, and you must think widely about how the risks could be managed. For example, think about the lease contract. It must have contingencies and protections for Azure's operation in it. It's also important to make realistic suggestions. For example, saying that the company should buy a new plane or employ its own captain and co-pilot would be irrelevant, as it is only operating two days a week.

(a)   **Business risks**

(i)   **Leasing of equipment and specialist staff**

As Azure leases its equipment and the most specialised of its staff from another airline, there is a risk that its **equipment and/or pilots** could be **withdrawn** leaving it unable to operate.

(ii)   **Conditions of exclusive right**

The PAA requires Azure's aircraft engines be overhauled biannually. There is a risk that Azure will be **unable to meet this condition**, if the **lessor company does not agree** to regular overhaul, or if it will be **too expensive** for Azure to meet this requirement. It could then lose the right to operate, or its exclusivity, opening it up to competition. There may be other conditions which Azure has to meet, such as the two weekly flights being a minimum.

(iii)   **Necessary service suspension**

As Azure is required to overhaul its engines every two years, there will be a significant period every two years where Azure will either have to **incur the cost of leasing** other planes (assuming this is possible) or will have to **suspend services**. The cost of leasing other planes might be prohibitively expensive or the disruption to service might mean that conditions relating to the right to operate might not be met. As Azure only has one plane, service would also be interrupted if there was an emergency relating to the plane, such as fire or a crash.

(iv)   **Age of aircraft**

The aircraft being leased is old. This raises **operational risks** (it may not always be able to fly due to necessary maintenance), **finance risks** (it may require regular repair) and **compliance risks** (it may not meet environmental or safety standards, now or in the future).

(v)   **High proportion of expensive seats**

The plane leased by Azure has a **high proportion of empty expensive seats** and therefore **insufficient (overbooked) cheaper seats**. Although Azure can appease customers by upgrading them, this means the airline is operating well below capacity.

(vi)   **Cargo**

The flight route results in the airline carrying a large amount of horticultural produce. This raises various risks. Azure might be liable to passengers if their **cargo deteriorates in transit**. The airline might be **liable for any breaches of law** by its passengers (for example, if prohibited items are transferred into Pewta or Sepiana. Many countries prohibit the importation of animals or meat products or plants).

(vii)   **On-board services**

Customers are currently **dissatisfied with the food provision** on the flight and there is a risk that food prepared in Lyme may become **less appealing** and even dangerous when served on a Darke to Lyme flight (when it has been prepared a substantial time earlier, given a six hour flight, at least an hour's turn around time, and time for getting to the airline in the first place). If the food makes customers ill, Azure might be faced with compensation claims.

(viii) **Pricing**

There is a **complex system of pricing** and a large number of sales agents, and Azure is at risk of **operating at a sales value less than required** to cover costs (for example, if too many of the cheapest tickets are sold).

(ix)   **Safety**

The airline industry has **stringent safety conditions** and Azure may face **customer boycotts** or difficulty in recruiting staff if safety requirements are not met, as well as the threat of not being allowed to fly.

(x)   **Fuel**

The aircraft **cannot fly without fuel**, which can be a scarce or high-cost resource. If fuel prices escalate due to world conditions, the company might not be able to meet the costs of operating.

(b)   **Managing risks**

(i)   **Leasing of equipment and specialist staff**

Azure must ensure that the **terms of the contract** with the international airline ensure that aircraft and staff **cannot be withdrawn** without reasonable notice, and, that in the event of withdrawal, substitutes will be provided.

(ii)   **Conditions of exclusive rights**

Azure must ensure that all staff are **aware of any conditions** and the **importance of meeting them**. However, this risk must simply be accepted. as there is little Azure can do about conditions imposed on them by the governing body of their industry.

(iii)   **Necessary service suspension**

Azure must have **contingency plans for service suspension**, such as ensuring its contract with the international airline ensures alternative aircraft will be made available in the event of maintenance or damage to the aircraft, or by making arrangements to lease from a different airline in the event of emergency. As a minimum, Azure must ensure that the airline it leases from would give it **financial compensation** in the event of aircraft or staff not being available, so that Azure's customers could be compensated.

(iv)   **Age of aircraft**

Azure should have plans in place to be able to **lease/afford newer planes** if required to by law. Again, this could be written into its contract with the airline. Azure should **manage cash flow and borrowing facilities** so as to be able to afford ongoing maintenance when required.

(v) **High proportion of expensive seats**

Azure should negotiate a **reconfiguration of the plane** with the **lessor** so that business and first class seating could be reduced and more economy seats made available. If this is not possible with the current lessor, Azure should **investigate leasing differently configured planes** from a different company. If it is not feasible to adjust the plane seating, Azure should consider **its pricing and on-board facilities policies** to make business and first class seats more attractive to customers. As the seats are not being sold anyway, it is probable that a reduction in prices would increase overall revenue.

(vi) **Cargo**

Azure should **publish a cargo policy** to ensure that customers are aware of their legal obligations. They should ensure that staff are **sufficiently trained** to discuss the contents of baggage with customers and are aware what items Azure should not carry. They should insure against lost and damaged cargo.

(vii) **On-board services**

Azure should consider **entering into a contract with a company in Darke** to **provide food** for the Darke to Lyme journey. Obviously they must not breach any existing contract with the Lyme company and so in the meantime should review the type of food provided. For example, it might be safer to only offer cold food like sandwiches and cakes until a Darke contract can be set up. Even if a new contract is set up, it might still be best to offer cold food, as there is less chance of health problems arising as a result of serving cold food rather than hot food.

(viii) **Pricing**

As discussed above, Azure should **review the pricing policy**. It should also **establish limits on how many of certain types of tickets** (non-refundable/single etc) can be issued for one flight and it should institute a **centralised system** to ensure that each agent is aware when limits have been reached. As the agents must be linked to a similar system already (to be aware of whether tickets are available for sale) this should not be too difficult to achieve.

(ix) **Safety**

The company should appoint a member of staff to be **specifically responsible for safety operations** (such as training, updating for legal requirements, educating passengers) and should ensure that staff are regularly appraised about safety issues.

(x) **Fuel**

The company could take out **hedging contracts** against the cost of fuel. Other than this, there is little it can do about this matter, and it is another risk that has to be accepted.

8 LMN

Top tips. This question illustrates that questions won't always be about companies.

In (a) the link between controls and risk management is highlighted in the question details. The discussion in the first part of (a) should be assisted by examples from the scenario, and in the risks-controls you need to include some examples of appropriate controls for LMN. Your answer needs to differentiate clearly, as ours has done by using headers, between purposes and importance to maximise your marks.

It's necessary to read (b) quite carefully to see what the question wants – an assessment of how much a review by the professional managers contributes to the work of the audit committee, and therefore why the review should be carried out. You should start off by defining what the work of the audit committee is, then consider how much managers' review contributes compared with other sources of information that they can use.

In (c) again you can't be too theoretical. Any discussion of principles has to be related to how they impact on the audit committee and board's reviews. Selected examples from the scenario information are also needed here to boost the discussion. If you can remember that the board needs to carry out a regular and annual review and the main elements you would have scored well in (c) and gone a long way towards passing this question.

(a) **Purposes of risk management**

Alignment of risk appetite and strategy

LMN's board should consider what **risks** it is prepared to **tolerate** in the light of the organisation's strategy. Risk management comprises the systems and processes for dealing with the risks that the board is prepared to tolerate in order for LMN to fulfil its **strategic objectives**, including its **social goals**.

Develop a consistent framework for dealing with risk

A coherent risk management framework can help LMN **compare risks with obvious financial consequences** (poor cost control, loss of income due to bad debts) with risks whose financial consequences are less obvious (dissatisfied tenants). It also should provide guidelines that can be applied by staff operating across all areas of LMN's activities.

Develop risk response strategies

The risk management process should **identify and evaluate risks** (for example by the high-medium-low method described) and therefore provide the information necessary for management to decide what the best **response to risk** should be – acceptance, control, avoidance or transfer.

Importance of risk management

Improve financial position

The risk management framework can provide a means of judging the **costs of treating the risks** measured against the **benefits**. It can also help LMN's directors judge whether to take advantage of opportunities, for example property investment.

Minimise surprises and losses

By **identifying risks in the risk register**, the risk management process should reduce the occurrence of unexpected shocks. For example, identifying **property maintenance** as a risk issue should encourage a programme of regular maintenance designed to deal with the risks associated with the types and ages of property.

Maintain reputation

As LMN is a charity, its reputation as a **good corporate citizen** is very important. Risk management should help it avoid risks to its reputation such as **poor treatment of tenants** or **failing to comply with regulatory requirements**.

Risk management and the internal control system

Internal control is action taken by management to achieve organisational objectives and goals. Internal control is thus bound up with the organisation's strategies, and is therefore also bound up with risk management that is dependent on the organisation's strategies. Internal control is made up of two elements.

(i) **Control environment**, the framework within which controls operate and within which attitudes towards risk are an important element. **Communication** between directors and employees is a key element of the control environment.

(ii) **Internal controls**, which should be operated when their **benefits outweigh costs**; controls focused on dealing with the most significant risks will have obvious benefits. Given the risks LMN faces, key controls will include **debtor management**, **maintenance inspections and** logs, **financial appraisal of new investments** and **tenant satisfaction questionnaires**, as well as **accounting**, **compliance** and **cost limitation** controls.

(b) **Audit committee's role in internal control**

Under corporate governance guidelines audit committees are responsible for creating a **climate of discipline and control**. To do this, they have to obtain assurance that internal control is working **effectively** and providing an **adequate response** to the **risks** faced; in particular for LMN, controls over expenditure.

Importance of management review

The management review provides the audit committee with evidence of whether the control systems appear to be **effectively managing the most significant risks**. It also gives the audit committee an indication of the **scope and quality** of management's monitoring of risk and internal control; whether it appears to be **adequate** given the risks faced. In the circumstances of LMN, the board of volunteers will wish to gain assurance that the **professional managers** are carrying out their duties effectively and are worth the salaries LMN is paying them. The review should provide **feedback** on weaknesses and should lead to improvements in the control systems.

Other sources of evidence

However, management's review of internal control is only one source of evidence that the audit committee should use to gain assurance. LMN's committee should also receive **reports from staff** undertaking important and high-risk activities, such as property investment, and **from control functions**, such as human resources or internal audit (if any). Feedback from external sources such as **external audit** or **regulatory visits** will also provide information.

(c) (i) **Review of internal controls**

The UK's Turnbull committee emphasises the importance of a regular review and an annual review of internal control as part of an organisation's strategy for **minimising risk**, **ensuring adherence to strategic objectives**, **fulfilling responsibilities to stakeholders** and **establishing accountability at its senior levels**.

Regular review

Regular review is an essential part of the strategy for minimising risks. The audit committee is likely to have responsibility for this review, and as best practice recommends at least **three audit committee meetings a year**; this is therefore how often the review should take place. Its findings should be communicated to the board.

The review should cover the following areas.

(1) **Risk evaluation**

Whether LMN is **identifying** and **evaluating all key risks**, financial and non-financial. This is a very significant task given the variety of risks faced and also the need to devote limited resources to the most important risks.

(2) **Risk responses**

Whether responses and management of risks are appropriate.

(3) **Effectiveness of internal controls**

The effectiveness of internal controls in countering the risks. The board should consider to what extent controls could be expected to reduce the incidence of risks, any evidence that controls have not been operating effectively and how weaknesses are being resolved. The board would consider such evidence as incidence of bad debts, records of property occupation and complaints from tenants.

Annual review

The annual review of internal control should be more wide ranging, taking into account the **strategic objectives of the charity** and undertaken by the **whole board** rather than just the audit committee. It should examine controls and risk management systems in all major areas.

(1) **Changes in risks**

The **changes** since the last assessment **in risks faced**, and the charity's ability to **respond to changes in its environment**. For example, the board would consider any changes in LMN's credit ratings andlonger-term trends such as changes in the incidence of low-income earners.

(2) **Monitoring**

The **scope and quality of management's monitoring of risk and control**, also whether internal audit is required. In particular the review should consider whether the **scope and frequency of the regular review** should be increased.

(3) **Reports**

The review should consider the **extent and frequency of reports** to the board; whether reports on high incidence, high likelihood risks should be made more regularly.

(4) **Impact on accounts**

Significant controls, failings and weaknesses that may materially impact on the financial statements, for example problems over its property portfolio management should be looked at.

(ii) **Disclosures in the annual report**

The report on compliance is a key part of the annual report by which LMN demonstrates its **compliance with regulations** and how it has **fulfilled the differing requirements of its stakeholders**, including tenants, donors, banks and local government.

Responsibility

The board should also **acknowledge its accountability** for LMN's system of control and **reviewing its effectiveness**.

Risk management

The Turnbull report recommends that as a minimum the board should disclose what has been done to **manage risk** and how the board has **reviewed the effectiveness of the risk management process**. The board should explain the limits of the process (it aims at risk management rather than risk elimination) and disclose any **material problems** or **weaknesses** that have been found. It should communicate **risks, objectives, targets** and **measures to counter risks**.

9 Pogles

Top tips. In (a) two sentences is about the right length for the summary of the facts. It is legitimate in this exam to raise the issue of whether the factory should be closed at all – the examiner expects you not to prioritise automatically the interests of shareholders over other stakeholders. Key wording in the scenario was that it was not certain that rumours would start circulating, and so you needed to consider separately what the directors should do if they weren't pressurised to tell the truth and what they should do if they were.

In (b) it's possible to extend the concept of sustainability as we have done. Note that the concept of right can be seen as meaning what is profitable – this is the pristine capitalist view we shall discuss in Chapter 11. However, you do need to consider other definitions of right as well.

It would be possible (and a good exercise for you to attempt) to apply Tucker to the situation in (a) and the AAA model to the situation in (b).

(a)   **What are the facts**

Pogles has **received an offer** for one of its factories and it appears to be in the interests of shareholders that the board should accept the offer. However, if staff learn of the acceptance of the offer, they are likely to take industrial action and jeopardise Pogles' biggest contract.

What are the ethical issues

The first issue is whether the factory should be closed at all. The staff in the factory are clearly adding value. They are after all working on Pogles' biggest contract. One viewpoint is that staff are key stakeholders, and the decision to close the factory wrongly prioritises shareholder interests over staff interests.

If the board decides the factory should be sold:

- Whether to disclose the sale of the factory to the staff in the absence of any pressure to do so

- If rumours start circulating and staff ask whether the factory will be closing, whether to tell staff the truth or deny the rumours

What are the norms, principles and values that relate to the case

In most jurisdictions, companies have a general duty to act in the **interests of their shareholders**. Closing the factory would be in line with this responsibility. Pogles would be acknowledging it had **some responsibility towards its employees** by giving them a generous pay-off package.

If the offer was accepted, and the board did not come under pressure to disclose it, the situation is finely balanced. The board would generally be regarded as having a right to keep **some information confidential for commercial reasons**. The question is whether the need of staff to have this information as soon as possible so that they can start making **alternative employment arrangements overrides the board's right to keep the information confidential**. It could also be argued that failing to tell staff is itself a distortion of the truth.

If staff do start asking questions, the ethical issue then becomes not only whether the board can keep the information confidential but also whether to do so it has the **right to give staff incorrect information**.

What are the alternative courses of action

One course would be to decline the developer's offer.

If the offer is accepted and the board does not come under any pressure to disclose the information, it could nevertheless:

- Tell staff as soon as the deal is finalised
- Or wait six months and tell staff once the work on the large contract is finished

If the board comes under pressure from staff because rumours are circulating, it can either:

- Maintain that the rumours are misguided or state that an offer has been received but rejected
- Tell staff the truth

What is the best course of action that is consistent with the norms, principles and values that relate to the case

The best course of action would appear to **sell the site and tell staff the truth** only when the board is **pressurised to do so**. This would certainly be in shareholders' best interests, as the factory sale would go ahead and the board would be making every effort not to jeopardise the large contract. However, if the board is pressed on the issue, it would seem most ethical for the truth to be told then.

What are the consequences of each course of action

If the developer's offer is declined, and it becomes public knowledge that it has been declined, the board **may come under pressure from shareholders** for failing to take decisions in their best interests.

Assuming no pressure is applied, telling the employees now is most likely to jeopardise the large contract. The board may be able to **mitigate the unrest** by providing more generous redundancy packages, giving assistance in job hunting and possibly giving staff a **consultation period** to come up with an alternative business plan.

Not telling employees until after the contract is completed would mean that **production was not disrupted**. However, although staff in other factories may not wish to take industrial action, there may be a loss of trust in senior management and hence worsening industrial relations.

Telling staff the truth when pressure is applied would also jeopardise the contract, but is less likely to do so the later in the **six months the disclosure is made**. Again the board may be able to mitigate the unrest, although the factory's staff may be less inclined to co-operate if they are angry that the board has kept the news from them.

Denying the news until after the contract is completed may lead to **legal repercussions** and certainly a loss of trust in the board by other employees.

What is the decision

The recommendation is that the board **accept the offer** and to **tell the employees immediately**. If it is in shareholders' interest for the factory to be closed, then loss of the contract would be a necessary cost. The board would appear to be acting in good faith and doing its best to mitigate the hardship faced by its employees.

(b)   **Profitable**

At present the decision appears to be profitable. The factory is performing well against budget and the **changes in the employment terms** offered to new staff should mean the factory is more flexible in meeting customer demands. However, if the factory manager's treatment of staff is challenged successfully in the courts, Pogles may have to pay fines and compensation.

Legal

It certainly seems that **some of the factory manager's actions** could be held to contravene the law, particularly as Pogles is located in an EU State. EU law does not look kindly on employers who are **unwilling to allow their staff to work part time** as long as this is reasonably practicable for their business, as always seems to have been the case for Pogles. Pogles will also probably have contravened local employment laws if the **allegations of bullying are held to be justified**.

Fair

From the point of view of the **longstanding employees**, the treatment is clearly unfair, if they are viewed as significant stakeholders because of the **commitment** they have **shown to Pogles over the years**. The factory managers' actions are also not fair to the new employees in the sense that they are working under different terms to longstanding employees. However, arguably they are being given employment opportunities that they are willing to take up, so the terms do not appear to be a significant issue for them.

Right

If right is judged solely in terms of maximising profits, then the manager's treatment of staff can be justified. However, most societies would regard **bullying in the workplace** as wrong. The board would need to consider the threat to Pogles' reputation if the behaviour became public knowledge.

Sustainable

If the idea of sustainability is confined to the natural environment, then this criterion is not relevant. It can however be extended. If labour is treated in the same way as a **natural resource**, then the factory manager's exploitation of the labour market may have its limits. Eventually they may find that people are not prepared to be employed on those terms. If the concept of sustainability is extended to **social sustainability**, then the factory manager's treatment of staff is not sustainable in the sense that they are ignoring their need for **decent working conditions** that do not cause them stress.

10 Zos

> **Top tips.** The answer to (a) illustrates that ethical non-compliance can be prevented by a number of aspects of the control environment and strong controls over human resources and information reporting and review.
>
> The point at the start of (b) is very important – that internal auditors have no statutory responsibilities and it's up to the directors to define what they should be. Assuming they are responsible for investigating ethical non-compliance, the answer looks at the direct and indirect links between audit work and ethical compliance, and also considers different ways auditors can approach the audit. However, the point in the last paragraph is also vital – internal auditors should not be responsible for **implementing** procedures to prevent **non-compliance**.

(a) **Board example**

The board should make clear when communicating with staff that they are committed to ethical behaviour and they expect staff to be committed as well. Appointing a board member as **ethics champion** emphasises board commitment as well as being a contact point for whistleblowing (discussed further below).

Code of conduct

A code of conduct could be used to **remind staff of Zos's objectives** of being an ethical business. Staff should be required to commit to the code when they join Zos. This would strengthen the basis for disciplinary action if they transgress.

Communication with employees

The board needs to ensure that specific **ethical objectives** are **communicated unambiguously** to staff. With Zos, although coffee was ideally meant to be sourced 100% from Fair Trade suppliers, it has been impossible recently to attain this target. There may therefore have been confusion, and local managers may have regarded it as acceptable to source from non Fair Trade suppliers if there were significant cost advantages in doing so.

Central policies

One way of preventing problems with the use of non Fair Trade suppliers would be to insist that shops only used suppliers on a **centrally approved list**. Alternatively, a **central purchasing function** could be responsible for making purchases for all shops.

Recruitment

One way of reducing the risk of dishonest acts by staff is to ensure that staff who are recruited do not have records of bad behaviour. References should be **required and confirmed for all staff**.

Appraisal

Staff should also be **regularly appraised** and the results of appraisals **communicated to senior management**. If appraisals indicate staff unhappiness, this may suggest that problems are more likely to occur.

Disciplinary procedures

There should be clear disciplinary sanctions against staff who are found guilty of dishonesty or unethical behaviour, including **dismissal from employment**. If necessary, staff accused of dishonesty should be suspended until the accusation is resolved.

Manager rotation

Staff may not have reported problems because of misplaced loyalty to, or fear of, management or colleagues. One way of preventing this would be to **rotate managers between shops on a regular basis**, to prevent a situation where managers allow problems to persist over a long time.

Whistleblowing

Both the drug dealing and the coffee beans sales were reported by customers and not staff. This suggests a lack of channels for staff to **report problems confidentially**, and therefore the board needs to make clear who staff should contact if they have concerns.

Monitoring procedures

Lastly the board should review evidence available from **information systems and internal audit work** and investigate signs of problems. The shops where there were ethical problems may have been underperforming in other areas.

(b) ### Extent of responsibilities

The **extent of internal auditors' responsibilities** are **defined by the board**. They can be given wide-ranging duties in relation to fraud, unlike external auditors whose responsibilities are concentrated on frauds that have a material impact on the financial statements.

Specific tests

Audit tests could be used as a matter of course to pick up certain problems. Here for example **reviewing shop purchase records** and checking whether suppliers used were, or could have been, Fair Trade would have identified that problem.

Consideration of other evidence

Internal audit should be alert for evidence that does not directly indicate fraud, but indicates the **general possibility of problems** at the shops. These include accounting results that are very much better or worse than other shops and high staff turnover. Inadequate records or unwillingness to respond to auditor enquiries should also put the auditors on alert. These are signs that the shop may be high risk and thus require greater audit work.

Recommendations for improvements

Internal audit will be responsible for making recommendations to management for improvements in systems that could prevent problems occurring, or make it easier for management to detect them. These include **shortcomings in human resource procedures**, such as failure to check references properly. They could also include improvements in the **reports** provided by the information systems. Internal audit feedback could be a very useful source of information when changes in the information systems are being considered.

Audit approach

Conducting audits solely by **preannounced visits** may limit the assurance the audit gives, since staff at the shops may behave while the auditors are there and cover their tracks beforehand. **Surprise visits** may identify issues such as **shortages of cash or inventory**.

Lack of evidence

However, internal audit can only reasonably be expected to detect frauds that impact in some way on the **business's systems**. It appears that the drug dealing manager took care to ensure that they covered their tracks, and did not leave any information for the internal auditors to detect. Internal auditors can also only be expected to work within their **own areas of expertise**. They are not trained members of the Police Drug Squad.

Prevention of problems

Internal audit should always have a **monitoring and detection role**. To preserve internal audit independence, it should not be responsible for implementing systems that prevent problems occurring. If these are fully effective, then there will be nothing for internal audit to detect.

11 Loxwood

Top tips. In (a) observation is likely to be the most useful audit technique, although if staff are being observed, they may behave differently. You may have come up with other means for informing staff.

(b) is good revision of issues that we have discussed throughout this text; the impact of stakeholder views and voluntary principles-based disclosure versus compulsory rules-based disclosure.

Interestingly in (c) taking the expedient view may lead to Loxwood being more cautious about developing the product than if it took the social contractarian view, if the local community was strongly in favour of action being taken about the sea lions.

(a) **Testing for employee awareness**

Employee awareness could be measured by **observation, questionnaire and interview**. In a large organisation a sampling approach could be taken. Observation could be largely unobtrusive and might provide a useful control on the results of interview, since some staff might make exaggerated claims about their environmental awareness.

Involvement of employees

The techniques of **internal marketing** could be used to involve employees. Internal marketing is the use of marketing techniques that are normally associated with communications flowing out from the organisation, for internal purposes. It is a concept associated with change management and therefore may be appropriate here.

A concerted campaign could be created. This could include messages in salary advices, posters, presentations, the **formation of discussion groups**, and the creation of a **suggestion scheme** specifically aimed at environmental issues. If there are any existing empowerment schemes, such as quality circles, it may be possible to introduce an environmental dimension into them.

(b) **Stakeholder interest**

Public interest in corporate social responsibility is steadily increasing. Although financial statements are primarily intended for investors and their advisers, there is growing recognition that companies actually have **a number of different stakeholders**. These include **customers, employees and the general public,** all of whom are **potentially interested** in the way in which a company's operations affect the natural environment and the wider community. These stakeholders can have a **considerable effect on a company's performance**. As a result many companies now deliberately attempt to build a **reputation for social and environmental responsibility**. Therefore the disclosure of environmental and social information is essential.

Regulatory and professional interest

Another factor is **growing interest by governments and professional bodies**. Although there are **no IFRSs** that specifically require environmental and social reporting, it may be required by **company legislation**. There are now a number of **awards for environmental and social reports** and high quality disclosure in financial statements. These provide further encouragement to disclose information.

Performance impact

There is also growing recognition that **corporate social responsibility is actually an important part of an entity's overall performance**. Responsible practice in areas such as reduction of damage to the environment and recruitment **increases shareholder value**. Companies that act responsibly and make social and environmental disclosures are **perceived as better investments** than those that do not.

Compulsory or voluntary disclosure

At present companies are normally able to disclose **as much or as little information as they wish in whatever manner that they wish**. This causes a number of **problems**. Companies tend to disclose information **selectively** and it is difficult for users of the financial statements to **compare the performance of different companies**. However, there are **good arguments** for continuing to allow companies a certain amount of freedom to determine the information that they disclose. If detailed rules are imposed, **companies are likely to adopt a 'checklist' approach** and will **present information in a very general and standardised way**, so that it is of very little use to stakeholders.

(c) **Expedients**

The expedient's view would be that Loxwood should primarily pursue **profit maximisation**. However, the board has to realise that Loxwood's activities generate, or are seen as generating, **some excesses**. The board therefore needs to accept CSR legislation and moral requirements, if it is broadly in line with Loxwood's **economic interests**.

The board has decided that having a more enlightened corporate social responsibility position is in line with Loxwood's interests. It may therefore be cautious about developing the sea lion repellent further, even if it is a **profitable opportunity**. Doing so may undermine **Loxwood's CSR policy**, and cause Loxwood more problems than if it did **not have its current focus on CSR**. Loxwood could be accused of hypocrisy, which could carry a serious **reputation risk**.

Social contractarian

The social contractarian would see Loxwood's duty as to **deliver benefits to the local community** from which it derives its power. Loxwood effectively has an agreement with the local community as it uses labour from it, and sells boats that impact on the local environment. It therefore should act in accordance with the ethical norms of the community.

However, this viewpoint may not be a very helpful guide for Loxwood, if the local community's view is split. Local boat owners may be very happy for the company to **develop its sea lion repellent** and reduce the risks of their boats being damaged. Other members of the community may think it unethical for Loxwood to develop a product that causes animals distress.

Deep ecologist

The deep ecologist position would be that human interests, either **as individuals or collectively as a community**, should not be prioritised over the interests of other species.

Even if the community felt that its pleasure was disrupted by having to be careful around sea lions, this is not relevant to the decision. The view of the deep ecologists would be that the device should not be developed because of the **pain caused to the sea lions**. The fact that the sea lions would suffer distress must be regarded as more important than the leisure activities of the community.

Index

Tollifson, Gayle, 172
Tough-guy macho culture, 170
Toyota, 198
Trade risk, 207
Trade unions, 30
Trading risks, 207
Traidcraft, 371
Training, 171
Transaction controls, 242
Transaction costs theory, 18
Transaction risk, 195
Translation risk, 195
Transparency, 6, 60, 61, 64
Treasury function, 238
Trinity Mirror, 116
Tucker's 5 question model, 317
Turnbull committee, 279
Turnbull report, 58, 139, 247, 277
Turner report, 224

UBS, 197
UK Corporate Governance Code, 58
UK Higgs, 104
UK Smith, 275
Uncertainty, 140
Uncertainty avoidance, 303
Unit objectives, 179
Unit trusts, 36
Unitary boards, 106

Unknown stakeholders, 24
Unprofessional behaviour, 313
Unrecognised stakeholders, 23
Unsystematic risk, 233
Utilitarianism, 300

Valuation, 341
Valuation services, 341
Value-laden profession, 356
Values, 309
Variance trend, 259
Virgin, 160
Virgin Galactic, 160
Viruses, 201
Voluntary and mandated controls, 243
Voluntary disclosure, 122
Voluntary stakeholders, 24

Wal-Mart, 349
Water, 201
Weak sustainability, 388
Whistleblowing, 67, 352
Wide stakeholders, 23
William Hill, 116
Work hard, play hard culture, 170
Work roles, 308
World Wildlife Fund, 377

BPP
LEARNING MEDIA

Review Form – Paper P1 Governance, Risk and Ethics (02/16)

Please help us to ensure that the ACCA learning materials we produce remain as accurate and user-friendly as possible. We cannot promise to answer every submission we receive, but we do promise that it will be read and taken into account when we update this Study Text.

Name: _____   Address: _____

_____

_____

How have you used this Study Text?
(Tick one box only)

☐ Home study (book only)

☐ On a course: college _____

☐ With 'correspondence' package

☐ Other _____

Why did you decide to purchase this Study Text? *(Tick one box only)*

☐ Have used BPP Study Texts in the past

☐ Recommendation by friend/colleague

☐ Recommendation by a lecturer at college

☐ Saw information on BPP website

☐ Saw advertising

☐ Other _____

During the past six months do you recall seeing/receiving any of the following?
(Tick as many boxes as are relevant)

☐ Our advertisement in ACCA *Student Accountant*

☐ Our advertisement in *PQ*

☐ Our brochure with a letter through the post

☐ Our website www.bpp.com

Which (if any) aspects of our advertising do you find useful?
(Tick as many boxes as are relevant)

☐ Prices and publication dates of new editions

☐ Information on Study Text content

☐ Facility to order books off-the-page

☐ None of the above

Which BPP products have you used?

Study Text	☑	Home Study	☐
Kit	☐	i-Pass	☐
Passcards	☐		

Your ratings, comments and suggestions would be appreciated on the following areas.

	Very useful	Useful	Not useful
Introductory section	☐	☐	☐
Chapter introductions	☐	☐	☐
Key terms	☐	☐	☐
Quality of explanations	☐	☐	☐
Case studies and other examples	☐	☐	☐
Exam focus points	☐	☐	☐
Questions and answers in each chapter	☐	☐	☐
Fast forwards and chapter roundups	☐	☐	☐
Quick quizzes	☐	☐	☐
Question Bank	☐	☐	☐
Answer Bank	☐	☐	☐
Index	☐	☐	☐

Overall opinion of this Study Text	Excellent ☐	Good ☐	Adeqate ☐	Poor ☐

Do you intend to continue using BPP products?   Yes ☐   No ☐

On the reverse of this page is space for you to write your comments about our Study Text. We welcome your feedback.

The author of this edition can be emailed at: accaqueries@bpp.com

Please return this form to: Head of ACCA and FIA Programmes, BPP Learning Media Ltd, FREEPOST, London, W12 8AA

TELL US WHAT YOU THINK

Please note any further comments and suggestions/errors below. For example, was the text accurate, readable, concise, user-friendly and comprehensive?